Lecture Notes in Computer Science 1445
Edited by G. Goos, J. Hartmanis and J. van Leeuwen

Springer
Berlin
Heidelberg
New York
Barcelona
Budapest
Hong Kong
London
Milan
Paris
Singapore
Tokyo

Eric Jul (Ed.)

ECOOP'98 – Object-Oriented Programming

12th European Conference
Brussels, Belgium, July 20-24, 1998
Proceedings

Series Editors

Gerhard Goos, Karlsruhe University, Germany
Juris Hartmanis, Cornell University, NY, USA
Jan van Leeuwen, Utrecht University, The Netherlands

Volume Editor

Eric Jul
University of Copenhagen, Department of Computer Science
Universitetsparken 1, DK-2100 Copenhagen, Denmark
E-mail: eric@diku.dk

Cataloging-in-Publication data applied for

Die Deutsche Bibliothek - CIP-Einheitsaufnahme

Object oriented programming : 12th European conference ; proceedings / ECOOP '98, Brussels, Belgium, July 20 - 24, 1998 / Eric Jul (ed.). - Berlin ; Heidelberg ; New York ; Barcelona ; Budapest ; Hong Kong ; London ; Milan ; Paris ; Singapore ; Tokyo : Springer, 1998
(Lecture notes in computer science ; Vol. 1445)
ISBN 3-540-64737-6

CR Subject Classification (1991): D.1-3, H.2,F.3, C.2, K.4.3, K.6

ISSN 0302-9743
ISBN 3-540-64737-6 Springer-Verlag Berlin Heidelberg New York

Typesetting: Camera-ready by author
SPIN 10638091 06/3142 – 5 4 3 2 1 0 Printed on acid-free paper

Preface

For the twelfth time, the European Conference on Object-Oriented Programming, ECOOP, provides a gathering place for researchers and practitioners in the field of object technology. Despite numerous other conferences on object-related topics, ECOOP has established itself as the premier object technology conference. One reason is the composition of the conference week and the high quality of the presented material. The first two days of the conference are devoted to a comprehensive tutorial program running in parallel with a very selective workshop program. The remaining three days are devoted to the technical program and organized as a single track where about two dozen high quality technical papers are presented and discussed intermixed with panels and invited talks. The size of the conference and the choice of sites typically leads to a very cozy and informative atmosphere that fosters significant scientific exchange and learning.

This volume constitutes the proceedings of the Twelfth ECOOP held in Brussels, Belgium in July 1998. Previous ECOOP conferences were held in Paris (France), Oslo (Norway), Nottingham (England), Ottawa (Canada, jointly with OOPSLA), Geneva (Switzerland), Utrecht (the Netherlands), Kaiserslautern (Germany), Bologna (Italy), Århus (Denmark), Linz (Austria), and Jyväskylä (Finland).

The ECOOP'98 technical programme consists of 24 technical papers (selected from 124 submissions), two invited speakers, and two panels. The programme committee, consisting of 29 distinguished researchers in object orientation, met at the University of Copenhagen in Denmark on January 29 and 30. All papers were reviewed by between three and six members of the programme committee. The accepted papers cover a number of different topics both practical, such as garbage collection, and more theoretical, such as type theory. It is our hope that you will find the resulting mix interesting and enlightening.

I would like to express my appreciation to the authors of submitted papers, the programme committee members, the external referees, the invited speakers and panel members, and the many others who have contributed to the ECOOP'98 technical programme. We hope that the resulting technical programme is another solid step towards advancing object-oriented software technology, just as previous ECOOPs have been.

Finally, I would like to thank the numerous people in AITO and at VUB who are responsible for organizing ECOOP'98.

Ultimately, the success of any conference is measured by the number of attendees who actually feel that they spent their time well—a feeling that we all can share by active participation in the conference. Have fun!

May, 1998

Eric Jul
ECOOP'98 Programme Chair

Organization

ECOOP'98 is organized by the Programming Technology Lab of the Vrije Universiteit Brussel, under the auspices of AITO (Association Internationale pour les Technologies Objets), and in cooperation with ACM SIGPLAN (Association for Computing Machinery, Special Interest Group for Programming Languages).

Executive Commitee

Conference Chair:	Luc Steels (Vrije Universiteit Brussel, B)
Programme Chair:	Eric Jul (Aalborg University & University of Copenhagen, DK)
Organizing Chair:	Theo D'Hondt (Vrije Universiteit Brussel, B)

Programme Commitee

Mehmet Aksit (University of Twente, NL)
Jean-Pierre Briot (Laboratoire d'Informatique de Paris 6, F)
Frank Buschmann (Siemens AG, D)
Vinny Cahill (Trinity College, IRL)
Luca Cardelli (Microsoft Research Ltd., UK)
Craig Chambers (University of Washington, USA)
Derek Coleman (King's College London, UK)
Charles Consel (University of Rennes, F)
Peter Dickman (University of Glasgow, UK)
Bjorn Freeman-Benson (Object Technology International, CDN)
Erich Gamma (Object Technology International, CH)
Rachid Guerraoui (Swiss Federal Institute of Technology, CH)
Norman C. Hutchinson (University of British Columbia, CDN)
Yutaka Ishikawa (Real World Computing Partnership, J)
Gerti Kappel (Johannes Kepler University, A)
Jørgen Lindskov Knudsen (Aarhus University, DK)
Sacha Krakowiak (Université Joseph Fourier, F)
Bent Bruun Kristensen (Odense University, DK)
Karl J. Lieberherr (Northeastern University, USA)
Ole Lehrmann Madsen (University of Aarhus, DK)
Boris Magnusson (Lund Institute of Technology, S)
Satoshi Matsuoka (Tokyo Institute of Technology, J)
Paola Mello (University of Ferrara, I)
Ana Moreira (Universidade Nova de Lisboa, P)
Ron Morrison (University of St Andrews, UK)
Oscar Nierstrasz (Universitaet Bern, CH)
Jens Palsberg (Purdue University, USA)
Dag I.K. Sjöberg (University of Oslo, N)
Jan Vitek (University of Geneva, CH)

Organizing Committee

Tutorial Chair: Viviane Jonckers (Vrije Universiteit Brussel, B)
Workshop Chair: Serge Demeyer (IAM-SCG, CH)
Panel Chair: Ghislain Hoffman (University of Ghent, B)
Demonstration Chair: Eric Steegmans (University of Leuven, B)
Poster Chair: Patrick Steyaert (Vrije Universiteit Brussel, B)
Exhibition Chair: Eddy Vandijck (Vrije Universiteit Brussel, B)

Organizing Team at Vrije Universiteit, B

Carine Lucas (Conference Manager), Koen De Hondt, Jan De Laet, Kris De Volder, Wolfgang De Meuter, Wim Lybaert, Kim Mens, Tom Mens, Tom Tourwé, Werner Van Belle, Mark Willems, and Roel Wuyts

Organizing Team at the University of Twente, NL

Richard van de Stadt (Electronic Submission & Reviewing System)

Organizing Team at the University of Copenhagen, DK

Morten Frank (Proceedings Organizer)

Cooperating Associations

Aito (Association Internationale pour les Technologies Objects)
http://iamwww.unibe.ch/ECOOP/AITO/

ACM SIGPLAN (Association for Computing Machinery, Special Interest Group for Programming Languages)
http://www.acm.org/sigplan/

Sponsoring Companies

EDS: Main Sponsor
http://www.eds.com/

IBM: Host for the Conference Banquet
http://ibm.com/

Sabena: Official Carrier for ECOOP'98
http://www.sabena.be/

Referees

Franz Achermann
Constantin Arapis
Costas Arapis
Jean-Paul Bahsoun
Dharini Balasubramaniam
Lodewijk Bergmans
Didier Bert
Walter Binder
Pim van den Broek
Ciaran Bryce
Lars Kirkegaard Bækdal
Luis Caires
Shigeru Chiba
Henrik B. Christensen
Michael Christensen
A. Ciampolini
Robert Clark
Antonio Corradi
Laurent Dami
Enrico Denti
Anne Doucet
Stephane Ducasse
Roland Ducournau
Erik Ernst
Marc Evers
Andrew Gordon
Zahia Guessoum
Pedro Guerreiro
Michel Habib
Görel Hedin
Roger Henriksson
Martin Hitz
Marianne Huchard
Bernard Huet
Eydun Eli Jacobsen
Eric Jacopin
Bo N. Jørgensen
Graham Kirby
Dimitri Konstantas
Evelina Lamma
Philippe Laublet
Julia Lawall
Letizia Leonardi
Markus Lumpe
Munenori Maeda
Margarida Mamede
Renaud Marlet
Marco Meijers
Mira Mezini
Hanspeter Moessenboeck
Gilles Muller
Dave Munro
Palle Nowack
Werner Obermair
Andrea Omicini
Doug Orleans
Francois Pachet
Ulrik Pagh Schultz
Guenter Pilz
Christian Queinnec
Sigi Reich
Werner Retschitzegger
Tamar Richner
Fabrizio Riguzzi
Michel Riveill
Xavier Rousset de Pina
Elmer Sandvad
Ichiro Sato
Jean-Guy Schneider
Wieland Schwinger
Cesare Stefanelli
Markus Stumptner
Mario Suedholt
Bedir Tekinerdogan
Scott Thibault
Sander Tichelaar
Mads Torgersen
Vasco Vasconcelos
Andre Weinand
Mikal Ziane

Contents

Invited Talk 1

Modelling Ideas and Experiences

Design Patterns and Frameworks

Language Problems and Solutions

Distributed Memory Systems

Reuse, Adaption and Hardware Support

Invited Talk 2

Reflection

Extensible Objects and Types

Mixins, Inheritance and Type Analysis Complexity

Mobile Objects and Mobile Agents: The Future of Distributed Computing?[1]

Danny B. Lange

General Magic, Inc.
Sunnyvale, California, U.S.A
danny@acm.org, http://www.acm.org/~danny

Abstract. This paper will lead you into the world of mobile agents, an emerging technology that makes it very much easier to design, implement, and maintain distributed systems. You will find that mobile agents reduce the network traffic, provide an effective means of overcoming network latency, and perhaps most importantly, through their ability to operate asynchronously and autonomously of the process that created them, helps you to construct more robust and fault-tolerant. Read on and let us introduce you to software agents - the mobile as well as the stationary ones. We will explain all the benefits of mobile agents and demonstrate the impact they have on the design of distributed systems before concluding this paper with a brief overview of some contemporary mobile agent systems.

1 What's a Software Agent?

So what is a software agent? Well, what actually constitutes an agent, and how it differs from a normal program, has been heavily debated for several years now. While this debate is by no means over, we more and more often see agents loosely defined as *programs that assist people and act on their behalf.* This is what we prefer to call the "end-user perspective" of software agents.

Definition of an Agent (End-User Perspective)

An agent is a program that assists people and acts on their behalf. Agents function by allowing people to delegate work to them.

While this definition is basically correct, it does not really get under the hood. Agents come in myriad different types and in many settings. They can be found in computer operating systems, networks, databases, and so on. What properties do these agents share that constitute the essence of being an *agent*?

---

[1] This paper is based on a chapter of a book by Lange and Oshima entitled *Programming and Deploying Java™ Mobile Agents with Aglets™*, Addison-Wesley, 1998. (ISBN: 0-201-32582-9).

This is not the place to examine the characteristics of the numerous agent systems made available to the public by many research labs. But if you looked at all these systems, you would find that a property shared by all agents is that fact that they live in some environment. They have the ability to interact with their execution environment, and to act asynchronously and autonomously upon it. No one is required either to deliver information to the agent or to consume any of its output. The agent simply acts continuously in pursuit of its own goals.

In contrast to software objects of object-oriented programming, agents are active entities that work according to the so-called *Hollywood Principle*: "*Don't call us, we'll call you!*"

Definition of an Agent (System Perspective)

An agent is a software object that

- is situated within an execution environment;
- possesses the following mandatory properties:
    - Reactive - senses changes in the environment and acts accordingly to those changes;
    - Autonomous - has control over its own actions;
    - Goal driven - is pro-active;
    - Temporally continuous - is continuously executing;
- and may possess any of the following orthogonal properties:
    - Communicative - able to communicate with other agents;
    - Mobile - can travel from one host to another;
    - Learning - adapts in accordance with previous experience;
    - Believable - appears believable to the end-user.

2 What's a Mobile Agent?

Mobility is an orthogonal property of agents. That is, all agents do not necessarily *have* to be mobile. An agent can just sit there and communicate with the surroundings by conventional means. These include various forms of remote procedure calling and messaging. We call agents that do not or cannot move *stationary agents.*

Definition of a Stationary Agent

A stationary agent executes only on the system where it begins execution. If it needs information that is not on that system, or needs to interact with an agent on a different system, it typically uses a communication mechanism such as remote procedure calling (RPC).

In contrast, a *mobile* agent is not bound to the system where it begins execution. The mobile agent is free to travel among the hosts in the network. Created in one execution environment, it can transport its state and code with it to another execution environment in the network, where it resumes execution.

By the term "state," we typically understand the agent attribute values that help it determine what to do when it resumes execution at its destination. By the term "code," we understand, in an object-oriented context, the class code necessary for the agent to execute.

Definition of a Mobile Agent

A mobile agent is not bound to the system where it begins execution. It has the unique ability to transport itself from one system in a network to another. The ability to travel, allows a mobile agent to move to a system that contains an object with which the agent wants to interact, and then to take advantage of being in the same host or network as the object.

3 Seven Good Reasons for Using Mobile Agents

Although mobile agent technology sounds exciting, our interest in mobile agents should not be motivated by the technology *per se*, but rather by the benefits they provide for the creation of distributed systems. So here are seven good reasons for you to start using mobile agents.

They reduce the network load. Distributed systems often rely on communications protocols that involve multiple interactions to accomplish a given task. This is especially true when security measures are enabled. The result is a lot of network traffic. Mobile agents allow you to package a conversation and dispatch it to a destination host where the interactions can take place locally, see Figure 1. Mobile agents are also useful when it comes to reducing the flow of raw data in the network. When very large volumes of data are stored at remote hosts, these data should be processed in the locality of the data, rather that transferred over the network. The motto is simple: move the computations to the data rather than the data to the computations.

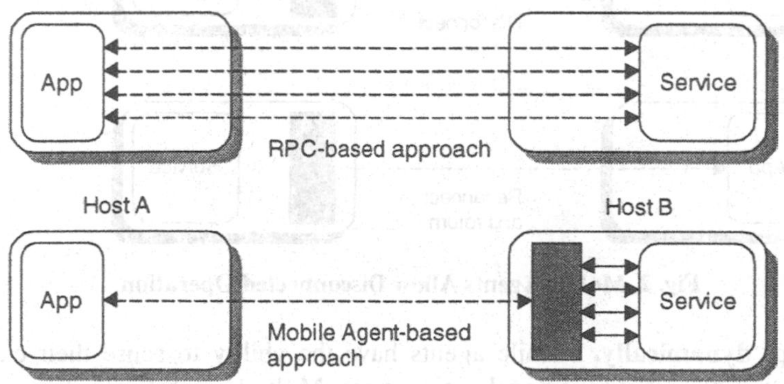

Fig. 1. Mobile Agents Reduce Network Load

They overcoming network latency. Critical real-time systems such as robots in manufacturing processes need to respond to changes in their environments in real time. Controlling such systems through a factory network of a substantial size involves significant latencies. For critical real-time systems, such latencies are not acceptable. Mobile agents offer a solution, since they can be dispatched from a central controller to act locally and directly execute the controller's directions.

They encapsulate protocols. When data are exchanged in a distributed system, each host owns the code that implements the protocols needed to properly code outgoing data and interpret incoming data, respectively. However, as protocols evolve to accommodate new efficiency or security requirements, it is a cumbersome if not impossible task to upgrade protocol code properly. The result is often that protocols become a legacy problem. Mobile agents, on the other hand, are able to move to remote hosts in order to establish "channels" based on proprietary protocols.

They execute asynchronously and autonomously. Often mobile devices have to rely on expensive or fragile network connections. That is, tasks that require a continuously open connection between a mobile device and a fixed network will most likely not be economically or technically feasible. Tasks can be embedded into mobile agents, which can then be dispatched into the network. After being dispatched, the mobile agents become independent of the creating process and can operate asynchronously and autonomously, see Figure 2. The mobile device can reconnect at some later time to collect the agent.

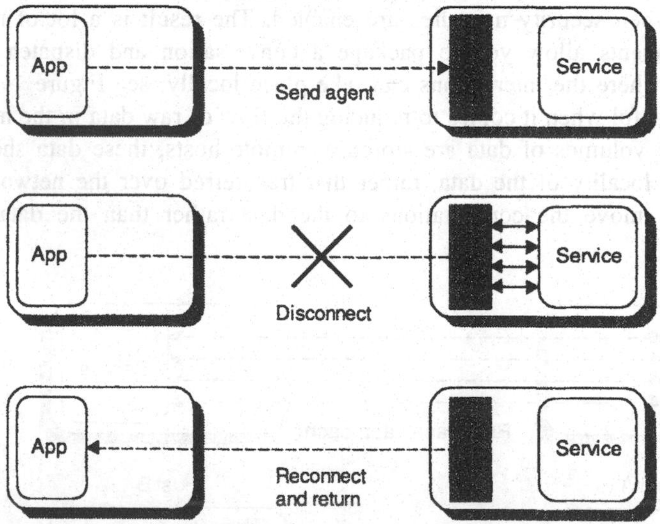

Fig. 2. Mobile Agents Allow Disconnected Operation

They adapt dynamically. Mobile agents have the ability to sense their execution environment and react autonomously to changes. Multiple mobile agents possess the unique ability to distribute themselves among the hosts in the network in such a way as to maintain the optimal configuration for solving a particular problem.

They are naturally heterogeneous. Network computing is fundamentally heterogeneous, often from both hardware and software perspectives. As mobile agents are generally computer- and transport-layer-independent, and dependent only on their execution environment, they provide optimal conditions for seamless system integration.

They are robust and fault-tolerant. The ability of mobile agents to react dynamically to unfavorable situations and events makes it easier to build robust and fault-tolerant distributed systems. If a host is being shut down, all agents executing on that machine will be warned and given time to dispatch and continue their operation on another host in the network.

4 Network Computing Paradigms

Our experience shows us that mobile agents provide a very powerful uniform paradigm for network computing. Mobile agents can revolutionize your design and development of distributed systems. To put this claim into perspective, we will provide a brief overview and comparison of three programming paradigms for distributed computing: *client-server*, *code-on-demand*, and *mobile agents*. Note that we put more emphasize on how the paradigm is perceived by the developer than on the underlying hardware-software architecture.

Client-Server Paradigm. In the client-server paradigm, see Figure 3, a server advertises a set of services that provide access to some *resources* (e.g., databases). The code that implements these services is hosted locally by the server. We say that the server holds the *know-how*. Finally, it is the server itself that executes the service, and thus has the *processor* capability. If the client is interested in accessing some resource hosted by the server, it will simply use one or more of the services provided by the server. Note that the client needs some "intelligence" to decide which of the services it should use. The server has it all, the know-how, resources, and processor. So far, most distributed systems have been based on this paradigm. We see it supported by a wide range of technologies such as remote procedure calling, object request brokers (CORBA), and Java remote method invocation (RMI).

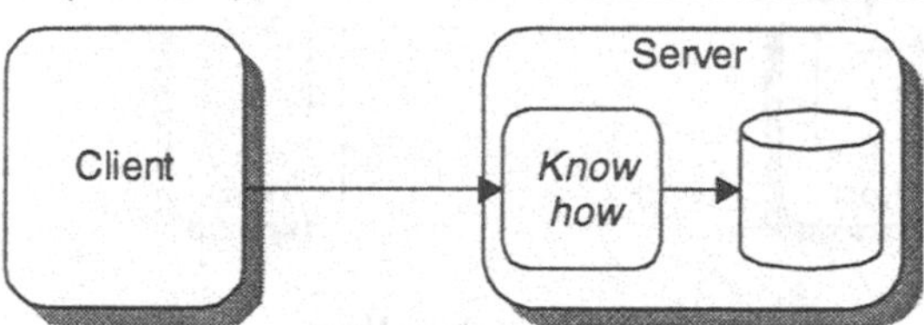

Fig. 3. Client-server Paradigm

Code-on-Demand Paradigm. Accordingly to the code-on-demand paradigm, see Figure 4, you first get the know-how when you need it. Say one host (A) initially is unable to execute its task due to a lack of code (know-how). Fortunately, another host (B) in the network provides the needed code. Once the code is received by A, the computation is carried out in A. Host A holds the processor capability as well as the local resources. Unlike in the client-server paradigm, A does not need knowledge about the remote host, since *all* the necessary code will be downloaded. We say that one host (A) has the resources and processor, and another host (B) has the know-how. Java applets and servlets are excellent practical examples of this paradigm. Applets get downloaded in Web browsers and execute locally, while servlets get uploaded to remote Web servers and execute there.

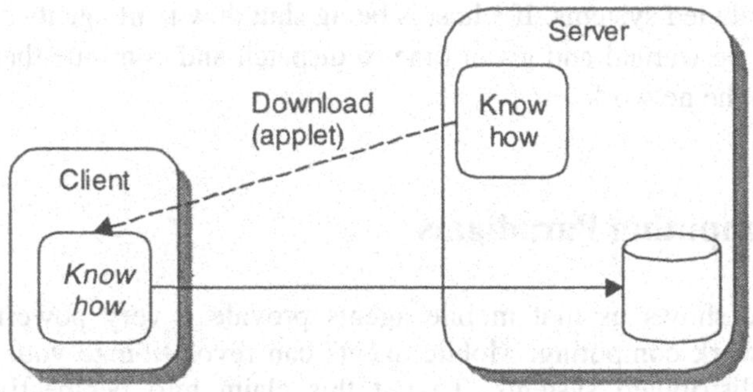

Fig. 4. Code-on-demand Paradigm

Mobile Agent Paradigm. A key characteristic of the mobile agent paradigm, see Figure 5, is that any host in the network is allowed a high degree of flexibility to possess any mixture of know-how, resources, and processors. Its processing capabilities can be combined with local resources. Know-how (in the form of mobile agents) is not tied to a single host but available throughout the network.

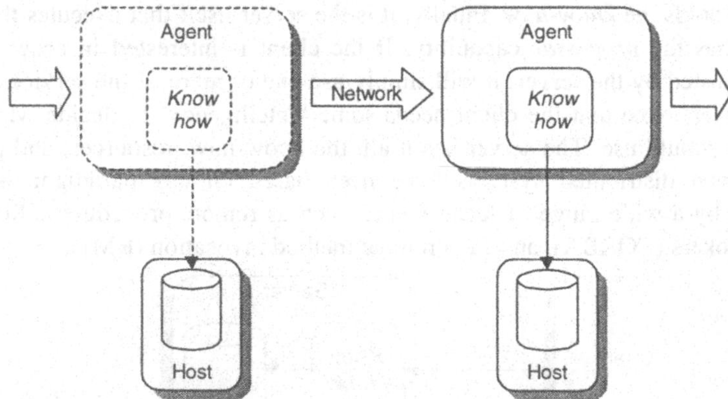

Fig. 5. Mobile Agent Paradigm

If you compare these three paradigms, you will see the chronological trend toward greater flexibility. The client and the server have merged and become a *host*. The applet and the servlet, while serving as client and server extenders, respectively, have been combined and improved with the emergence of mobile agents.

5 Mobile Agent Applications

We will now take a closer look at some applications that benefit particular from the mobile agent paradigm. Please note that this is by no means intended to be an exhaustive list.

Electronic commerce. Mobile agents are well suited for electronic commerce. A commercial transaction may require real-time access to remote resources such as stock quotes and perhaps even agent-to-agent negotiation. Different agents will have different goals, and will implement and exercise different strategies to accomplish these goals. We envision agents that embody the intentions of their creators, and act and negotiate on their behalf. Mobile agent technology is a very appealing solution to this kind of problem.

Personal assistance. The mobile agent's ability to execute on remote hosts makes it suitable as a "assistant" capable of performing tasks in the network on behalf of its creator. The remote assistant will operate independently of its limited network connectivity, and the creator can feel free to turn his or her computer off. To schedule a meeting with several other people, a user could send a mobile agent to interact with the representative agents of each of the people invited to the meeting. The agents could negotiate and establish a meeting time.

Secure brokering. An interesting application of mobile agents is in collaborations where not all the collaborators are trusted. In this case, the involved parties could let their mobile agents meet on a mutually agreed secure host, where collaboration can take place without the risk of the host taking the side of one of the visiting agents.

Distributed information retrieval. Information retrieval is an often-used example of a mobile agent application. Instead of moving large amounts of data to the search engine so that it can create search indexes, you dispatch agents to remote information sources, where they locally create search indexes that can later be shipped back to the origin. Mobile agents are also able to perform extended searches that are not constrained by the hours during which the creator's computer is operational.

Telecommunication networks services. Support and management of advanced telecommunication services are characterized by dynamic network reconfiguration and user customization. The physical size of these networks and the strict requirements under which they operate call for mobile agent technology to form the "glue" that keeps such systems flexible yet effective.

Workflow applications and groupware. It is in the nature of workflow to support the flow of information between co-workers. The mobile agent is particular useful here since, in addition to mobility, it provides a degree of autonomy to the workflow item. Individual workflow items fully embody the information and behavior needed for them to move through the organization independent of any particular application.

Monitoring and notification. This is one of the "classical" mobile agent applications that highlight the asynchronous nature of mobile agents. An agent is able to monitor a given information source without being dependent on the location from which it originates. Agents can be dispatched to wait for certain kinds of information to become available. It is often important that monitoring agents have life spans that exceed or are independent of the computing processes that create them.

Information dissemination. Mobile agents embody the so-called Internet "push" model. Agents are able to disseminate information such as news and automatic software updates for vendors. The agents will bring the new software components as well as the installation procedures directly to the customer's personal computer and will autonomously update and manage the software on the computer.

Parallel processing. Given that mobile agents can create a cascade of clones in the network, one potential use of mobile agent technology is to administer parallel processing tasks. If a computation requires so much processor power as to that it must be distributed among multiple processors, an infrastructure of mobile agent hosts could be a plausible way to get the processes out there.

6 Contemporary Mobile Agent Systems

So what kind of mobile agent systems are available for you? Fortunately, Java has generated a flood of experimental mobile agent systems. Numerous systems are currently under development, and most of them are available for evaluation on the Web.

The field is developing so dynamically and so fast that any attempt to map the agent systems will be outdated before this book goes to press. We will, however, mention a few interesting Java-based mobile agent systems: Aglets, Odyssey, Concordia, and Voyager.

Aglets. This system, created by the authors of this book, mirror the applet model in Java. The goal was to bring the flavor of mobility to the applet. The term *aglet* is indeed a portmanteau word combining *agent* and *applet.* We attempted to make Aglets an exercise in "clean design," and it is our hope that applet programmers will appreciate the many ways in which the aglet model reflects the applet model.

Odyssey. General Magic Inc. invented the mobile agent and created the first commercial mobile agent system called Telescript. Being based on a proprietary language and network architecture, Telescript had a short life. In response to the popularity of the Internet and later the steamrollering success of the Java language, General Magic decided to re-implement the mobile agent paradigm in its Java-based Odyssey. This system effectively implements the Telescript concepts in the shape of

Java classes. The result is a Java class library that enables developers to create their own mobile agent applications.

Concordia. Mitsubishi's Concordia is a framework for the development and management of mobile agent applications which extend to any system supporting Java. Concordia consists of multiple components, all written in Java, which are combined together to provide a complete environment for distributed applications. A Concordia system, at its simplest, is made up of a standard Java VM, a Server, and a set of agents.

Voyager. ObjectSpace's Voyager is a platform for agent-enhanced distributed computing in Java. While Voyager provides an extensive set of object messaging capabilities it also allows object to move as agents in the network. You can say that Voyager combines the properties of a Java-based object request broker with those of a mobile agent system. In this way Voyager allows Java programmers to create network applications using both traditional and agent-enhanced distributed programming techniques.

We would like to note that the Java-based mobile agent systems have a lot in common. Beside the programming language they all rely on standard versions of the Java virtual machine and Java's object serialization mechanism. A common server-based architecture permeates all the systems. Agent transport mechanisms and the support for interaction (messaging) varies a lot.

Although a majority of the contemporary mobile agent systems are based on the Java language system, you will also be able to find other languages in use. Most significant languages are Tcl and Python.

Agent Tcl. This is a mobile agent system whose agents can be written in Tcl. Dartmouth College's Agent Tcl has extensive navigation and communication services, security mechanisms, and debugging and tracking tools. The main component of Agent Tcl is a server that runs on each machine and that allows the entire execution state including local variables and instruction pointer to move. When an agent wants to migrate to a new machine, it calls a single function, *agent_jump*, which automatically captures the complete state of the agent and sends this state information to the server on the destination machine. The destination server starts up a Tcl execution, loads the state information into this execution environment, and restarts the agent from the exact point at which it left off.

Ara. Tcl-based Ara from University of Kaiserslautern is a platform for the portable and secure execution of mobile agents in heterogeneous networks. The research project is primarily concerned with system support for general mobile agents regarding secure and portable execution, and much less with application-level features of agents, such as agent cooperation patterns, intelligent behavior, and user modeling.

TACOMA. The TACOMA project focuses on operating system support for agents and how agents can be used to solve problems traditionally addressed by operating systems. The TACOMA system is based on UNIX and TCP. The system supports agents written in C, Tcl/Tk, Perl, Python, and Scheme (Elk). The system itself is implemented in C.

Common for a number of the Tcl-based projects is that they anticipate a move toward support for multiple language which essentially means added support for Java.

We recommend the following Web sites for more information on the specific agent systems and projects:

- Aglets at `www.trl.ibm.co.jp/aglets`.
- Odyssey at `www.genmagic.com/agents`.
- Concordia at `www.meitca.com/HSL/Projects/Concordia`.
- Voyager at `www.objectspace.com/voyager`.
- Agent Tcl at `www.cs.dartmouth.edu/~agent`.
- Ara at `www.uni-kl.de/AG-Nehmer/Ara`.
- TACOMA at `www.cs.uit.no/DOS/Tacoma`.

7 Mobile Agent Standardization: MASIF

Let us conclude this paper with a brief overview of ongoing standardization efforts in the mobile agent field.

Clearly, the above mentioned systems differ widely in architecture and implementation, thereby impeding interoperability and rapid deployment of mobile agent technology in the marketplace. To promote interoperability, some aspects of mobile agent technology must be standardized. The companies Crystaliz, General Magic Inc., GMD Fokus, IBM Corporation, and the Open Group have jointly developed a proposal for a *Mobile Agent System Interoperability Facility* (MASIF) and brought it to the attention of the Object Management Group (OMG).

MASIF addresses the interfaces between agent systems, not between agent applications and agent systems. Even though the former seems to be more relevant for application developers, it is the latter that allows mobile agents to travel across multiple hosts in an open environment. MASIF is clearly not about language interoperability. Language interoperability for mobile objects is very difficult and MASIF is limited to interoperability between agent systems written in the same language, but potentially by different vendors. Furthermore, MASIF does not attempt to standardize local agent operations such as agent interpretation, serialization, or execution. You can that say MASIF defines the interfaces at the agent system level rather than at the agent level.

MASIF standardizes the following four areas:

– **Agent Management.** There is interest in the mobile agent community to standardize agent management. It is clearly desirable that a system administrator who manages agent systems of different types can use the same standard operations. It should be possible to create an agent given a class name for the agent, suspend an agent's execution, resume its execution, or terminate it in a standard way.

- **Agent Transfer.** It is desirable that agent applications can spawn agents that can freely move among agent systems of different types, resulting in a common infrastructure.

- **Agent and Agent System Names.** In addition to standardizing operations for interoperability between agent systems, the syntax and semantics of various parameters must be standardized too. Specifically, agent name, and agent system name should be standardized. This allows agent systems and agents to identify each other, as well as applications to identify agents and agent systems.

- **Agent System Type and Location Syntax.** The location syntax must be standardized so that an agent can access agent system type information from a desired destination agent system. The agent transfer can only happen if the destination agent system type can support the agent. Location syntax also needs to be standardized so that agent systems can locate each other.

8 Summary

With agent *mobility* being the focus of this paper we defined a mobile agent as an agent that is not bound to the system where it begins execution. It has the unique ability to transport itself from one system in a network to another. The ability to travel, allows a mobile agent to move to a system that contains an object with which the agent wants to interact, and then to take advantage of being in the same host or network as the object. We gave you seven good reasons for you to start using mobile agents: they reduce the network load, they overcoming network latency, they encapsulate protocols, they execute asynchronously and autonomously, they adapt dynamically, they are naturally heterogeneous, and they are robust and fault-tolerant.

Among some of the application domains that benefits from mobile agent technology are: electronic commerce, personal assistance, secure brokering, distributed information retrieval, telecommunication networks services, workflow applications and groupware, monitoring and notification, information dissemination, and parallel processing.

Several Java-based mobile agent systems exist: Aglets, Odyssey, Concordia, Voyager, and many more. Although these Java-based mobile agent systems have a lot in common they do not interoperate. To promote interoperability, some aspects of mobile agent technology has been standardized by OMG's MASIF. It will be interesting to see what impact increased standardization activities will have on the mobile agent field.

References

1. Lange, D.B. and Oshima, M.: Programming and Deploying Java™ Mobile Agents with Aglets™, Addison-Wesley, 1998.
2. Aridor, Y. and Lange, D.B.: Agent Design Patterns: Elements of Agent Application Design, In Proceedings of the Second International Conference on Autonomous Agents (Agents '98), ACM Press, 1998, pp. 108-115.
3. Karjoth, G., Lange, D.B., and Oshima, M.: A Security Model for Aglets, IEEE Internet Computing 1, 4, 1997, pp. 68-77.
4. The Object Management Group: The Mobile Agent System Interoperability Facility, OMG TC Document orbos/97-10-05, The Object Management Group, Framingham, MA., 1997.
5. White, J.: Mobile Agents, In Software Agents, Bradshaw, J. Ed., MIT Press, 1997.

The M.A.D. Experience:

Multiperspective Application Development in evolutionary prototyping

Michael Christensen, Andy Crabtree, Christian Heide Damm, Klaus Marius Hansen, Ole Lehrmann Madsen, Pernille Marqvardsen, Preben Mogensen, Elmer Sandvad, Lennert Sloth, Michael Thomsen

Department of Computer Science, University of Aarhus, Building 540, Ny Munkegade, DK-8000 Aarhus C, Denmark.

{toby, andyc, damm, marius, olm, pernille, preben, ess, les, miksen}@daimi.aau.dk

Abstract. This paper describes experience obtained through a joint project between a university research group and a shipping company in developing a prototype for a global customer service system. The research group had no previous knowledge of the complex business of shipping, but succeeded in developing a prototype that more than fulfilled the expectations of the shipping company. A major reason for the success of the project is due to an experimental and multiperspective approach to designing for practice. Some of the lessons to be learned for object-orientation are (1) analysis is more than finding nouns and verbs, (2) design is more than filling in details in the object-oriented analysis model, and (3) implementation is more than translating design models into code. Implications for system development in general and object-orientation in particular consist in the preliminary respecification of the classical working order: analysis – design – implementation.

Keywords: Large-scale system development, multiperspective application development, cooperative design, ethnography, object-orientation, rapid prototyping, evolutionary prototyping, OO-tools, experience report.

1 Introduction

In late January 1997 a globally distributed shipping company contacted CIT, proposing a joint project for the purpose of developing a prototype of a Global Customer Service System (GCSS). The initial concept of GCSS emerged from within the company as a means of supporting the global implementation of business process improvements (BPI). A month later a team was assembled that had never worked together before and had no knowledge of shipping whatsoever. A project description was made and ten weeks and 5 major iterations later, the prototype was appraised and approved by the company's highest executive body. Work is still on-going. This experience report tries to describe central success criteria and lessons learnt to date.

Partners in the project (known as the Dragon Project) were the company (which cannot be named for commercial reasons) and the DEVISE research group.

The project was funded by The Danish National Centre for IT-research (CIT, `http://www.cit.dk`). The company is a large world-wide provider of containerised transport solutions, employing some two and a half thousand people in over 250 offices in some 70 countries on six continents. Having a superior customer service in an increasingly competitive market as its key value, the company has and is investing substantially in IT support for proposed business solutions.

The DEVISE group was originally founded with the research goal of increasing productivity and quality in the development of large, complex systems, and now incorporates a large number of diverse competencies. Participants in the Dragon Project include, from the university: one project coordinator, one participatory designer, three full-time and three half-time object-oriented developers, one ethnographer and for a part of the project, one usability expert. Participants from the business include senior management, business representatives from the major continental regions, administrative staff, customer service personnel and members from a private consultancy company.

Although the essence of shipping in our context might be described as the actual transport of cargo in containers, our concern is with the provision and delivery of customer services, which the transport of containers relies upon. Work here includes the handling of interactions with customers in formulating prices for transport (quoting), in booking containers, in arranging inland haulage, in documenting ownership of cargo, in notifying the consignee of cargo's arrival, and so on.

From this all too brief description, the job of design might sound like a relatively straightforward task but for many reasons the challenge that GCSS has to meet is anything but simple. Currently, no global system or formal practice exists, yet GCSS should support coordination between globally distributed sites as well as support a customer service that, while streamlined (i.e. operating with less resources), is both effective and efficient and at the same time respects local needs in the various regions. Thus, the main design issue in many respects was to develop a prototype supporting these needs. Important issues in addressing these needs consisted in:

- Developing an approach for obtaining detailed knowledge of shipping in a short period of time; this knowledge had to be developed during the project due to the very short project period.
- Similarly, the initial requirements and formal specifications for the prototype from the business were vague and had to be developed during the project.
- The architecture of the prototype / system had to be flexible and allow for local customisations.

In order to satisfy these issues we thought it necessary to form a development group consisting of people with diverse but nevertheless complementary qualifications, who would be able to utilise their own specialities and at the same time be able to work together in an extremely focused group. The focus being to develop a prototype to support customer service. The roles of the different team members may, somewhat simplistically, be described as follows:

- The ethnographer: focus on current practice within customer service and related areas.
- The participatory designer: focus on the design of future practice and technological support with users.
- The OO developers: develop the object model, and implementation.

In what follows we describe the contributions to the project from the perspectives of ethnography, cooperative design and object-orientation. Having explicated what we take to be the approach's main strength, namely its experimental and multiperspective character in designing for practice, the paper concludes by stating lessons that we take to be of value with particular regard to object-orientation. In so much as object-orientation played a major role as a technology for developing a model of shipping and for implementing the prototype, then a number of lessons for object-orientation were learned. Perhaps the most important ones are:

1. *Analysis is more than finding nouns and verbs.* We will argue that it is often necessary and useful to base analysis on much more powerful means than currently advocated, such as ethnographic analyses of the social organisation of work.
2. *Design is more than filling in details in the OO analysis model.* Here we will argue that often techniques from participatory or cooperative design are necessary and useful in formulating concrete design-solutions and relating them to practice.
3. *Implementation is more than translating design models into code.* Our experience shows that it is important to start implementation early in the design. The initial design model will always be changed during implementation and the feedback from initial implementation should appear early in the project so as to facilitate further development.

The above lessons are of course not relevant for all kinds of projects but for a project as the one described in this paper we think they are relevant. Perhaps most important are the implications our work has for structured techniques of object-oriented analysis, design and implementation. Specifically, towards the inadequacies of formal development methods in accomplishing rapid prototyping.

2 M.A.D – system development using a common frame of reference

The Dragon development team came from backgrounds ranging from ethnography to cooperative design to object-oriented development. These competencies should not be treated in strict separation but rather, in the ways in which they interact and complement one another and in this way achieve a synergetic effect.

A guiding principle in this multiperspective approach was (indeed is) an orientation to a common frame of reference: everyday business practice in customer service. In this paper, we use an example – a real world 'instance' of working practice, namely "rerouting" - that was employed by all the perspectives at work to show how design was practically achieved. In so much as the instance was oriented to by each perspective, we use it to illuminate the *character* of each perspective. Furthermore, in so much as the instance was employed by each perspective, then we use it to illuminate the *ways* in which the perspectives *interrelated* in practice and, reciprocally, while preserving individual achievements, to display the *organisation of work* from which GCSS emerged as a design product.

The instance of rerouting was only one of many used during development. Furthermore, the competencies or perspectives did not treat the instances sequentially but rather, treated them in parallel or at different times thereby mutually informing one another and the prototype as work progressed.

In order to display the organisation of multiperspective application development in rapid, evolutionary prototyping, we now turn to a description of how the three main perspectives, that is the ethnographic perspective, the cooperative design perspective and the object-oriented perspective, approached development and coordinated their activities into a coherent 'process' from which a concrete product (more than) satisfying the requirements of a large geographically distributed organisation emerged. After this account we will outline some of the major lessons learnt.

3 The ethnographic perspective

Whether operating within the context of rapid prototyping or not, the ethnographic perspective places an emphasis on securing a real world reference to work and organisation, informing the design of cooperative systems (Heath et al., 92; COMIC 2.2, 93; Blomberg et al., 94). Working on the presupposition that systems design is work design (in contrast to model building for example[1]), it might otherwise be said that ethnography seeks to base design on an 'understanding of praxis' in which the system is to be *put to work*. The intention is to predicate design on enacted practice thus supporting the development of systems that resonate or 'fit' with the activities in which they are to be embedded, thereby circumventing a major cause of systems

[1] This is not to abnegate modelling but rather, to remind designers of the relevance of modelling – it is not an end in itself but a means to an end, namely the (re)organisation of human activities.

failure (Grudin, 89; Shmidt et al., 93; Hughes et al., 94). The notion of understanding praxis is 'bracketed' in that it is selective – ethnography orients to praxis in a certain or particular way.

From ethnography's point of view, work is seen to be socially organised with organisation itself emerging as a local production out of the *routine accomplishment and coordination of tasks* experienced by practitioners (and generally understood) as the working division of labour (Anderson et al., 89). Ethnography's task is to make the working division of labour visible and available to designers in the concrete details of its accomplishment – i.e. in terms of work's real time organisation in contrast to idealised form (Rouncefield et al., 94). This is achieved through direct observation and naturalistic description of working practice portrayed from the point of view of parties to the work (Crabtree et al., 97). The notion of 'social organisation' refers to the conventional ways in which activities are accomplished and coordinated by *any and every* competent member engaged in the work. The notion of 'convention' refers, conjointly, to members' reoccurring actions and interactions, the artefacts used and the practical reasoning employed in doing the work. Work's social organisation is discovered through 'mapping the grammar' of the domain by empirical instance[2].

Simply and briefly put, the notion of 'mapping grammar' refers to *ordinary language* which is seen to embody 'language-games' (Wittgenstein, 68). Language-games are distinct practices - computer science, sociology, customer service in shipping for example are *unique* ways of talking and thus of *acting* in the world – each of which consists in a unique family of concepts ('quoting', 'export handling', 'documentation', 'rerouting' in customer service for example). In so much as language-game concepts *are* activities and in so much as they are *intersubjectively* employed ~ enacted by a unique *collectivity* of people (customer service staff for example), then to describe the actual *performative* details of their use is to describe the *social* organisation of the named activity. The activity of description is called 'mapping', the concepts mapped the 'grammar' of the language-game, the description itself the 'instance'. Empirical examples or 'real world' instances of language-game concepts-in-use not only preserve the social organisation of work in describing that organisation *in its own terms* but in so doing *make visible* what the work is 'really all about'[3] (Hughes et al., 92).

3.1 The Bremerhaven Instance (1)

Mapping grammar, a practical example: Customer service work in the container shipping business consists in the activities of 'quoting', 'export handling', 'alloca-

---

[2] The notion of 'mapping grammar' is explicated in *Talking Work: language-games, organisations and computer supported cooperative work* (Crabtree, forthcoming).

[3] It should be said that in so far as ethnography does preserve the real world character of work then it does so through an attention to concepts-in-use, to 'rerouting' as a contingent but nevertheless routine human achievement in, of and as work in contrast to 'rerouting' as an abstract information process (Garfinkel et al., 70; Hughes et.al, 96). This is not to rule abstraction out of play but to ground abstraction in formal properties of enacted (in contrast to idealised) praxis

tion', 'documentation' and 'inbound handling'. These concepts or categories delineate the working division of labour. One important feature of allocation work is to 'reroute' freight in response to contingencies. Rerouting occasions collaboration between equipment management, export and import handling, and documentation[4] and is itself occasioned for various reasons: bad weather, customer requirements, running off schedule etc. Rerouting consists in 'reallocating' containers to a substitute vessel or vessels - there may be several 'legs' and different vessels on any particular container's journey. The substitute vessel may be located in a different port to either the load or leg port. More: the destination port of rerouted cargo from a particular vessel may well be different. Thus, the activity of rerouting is all about arranging appropriate transport for cargo going to multiple destinations from some contingent point either to the destinations direct or, failing that, to a point from which cargo can be delivered to its respective destination ports. Real world instances of rerouting's accomplishment – actual *responses* to a vessel being delayed – revealed that route alterations occasioned not only changing the first leg of a journey but also the first half of the second leg for instance, or, indeed several legs on a journey. Furthermore, these changes were discovered to be subject to criteria of rerouting, specifically of time and cost: independent local carrier was specified wherever possible if time allowed, rail failing local carrier, truck failing rail; local carrier is more cost effective than rail, rail more cost effective than truck although time pressures may necessitate everything being moved by truck. It also transpired that rerouted cargo must be grouped: in some locations refrigerated containers, used for perishable products in particular, cannot be moved to transhipment points by rail for example (due to concerns of supervision – the temperature of refrigerated containers must be monitored at regular intervals), freight for this or that destination must be identified and the criteria applied. Furthermore, as a result of 'hard-wiring' working processes into the existing system, rerouting had to be accomplished individually – groups of freight could not be selected and assigned to alternate vessels except in the simplest of cases: 'roll over', i.e. temporal rescheduling to the next available vessel.

3.2 Analysing the instance

Mapping the socially organised details of activities accomplishment by empirical instance not only allows us to understand praxis in the context of the working division of labour[5] but in so doing, to identify *practical problems of work* and their *situated methods of solution*. Taken together, the practical problems of work and members' intersubjective or shared methods of solving those problems, and of solving them routinely, day-in-day-out in the face of any and all contingencies, show us just 'what

[4] Space prevents a detailed description of the work involved here but in practice (i.e. design) these details were central to the formulation of design-solutions.

[5] Which enables us to get 'hands on' the actual ways in which activities of work are *coordinated* and thus identify what is essential to successful work-oriented design – if activities cannot be coordinated, work simply cannot be achieved and we can add another systems failure to the list.

the work is really all about' and make *concrete possibilities* for support through design *visible and available to* design. Thus, the 'instance' circumscribes a **problem-space** for design. More: in illuminating the socially organised ways in which staff routinely go about solving practical problems of work, the instance circumscribes a **solution-space** for design.

The outcome of analysing the rerouting instance for example, a collaborative task performed by members from each of the perspectives at work, was the development of a flexible 'tree structure' supporting local decision-making and the coordination of a complex task by actively displaying all destinations for cargo on a delayed vessel and through the application of which one can specify any number of leg changes and different modes of transport for any group of selected containers, updating all members of the specified group in one go.

3.3 The limits of ethnography

Clearly there is a great deal more to observing praxis than meets the unaccustomed eye. In securing a real world reference preserving the context of work the ethnographic perspective provides concrete topics and resources for design. In so much as system design is work design, ethnography thus supports the development of systems that resonate or 'fit' with the activities of work in which they are embedded thereby supporting the local production of organisation in innovative social and technical ways (Kensing et al., 97). Virtues aside, ethnography is not without its limitations: it is one thing to identify a **problem-solution space**, another to identify design-solutions – a very practical problem resolved in practice through prototyping.

4 The cooperative design perspective

Cooperative design (also known as participatory design), as developed in Scandinavia over the last decades, stresses the importance of creative involvement of potential users (end-users, managers, affected parties, etc.) in design processes (Bjerknes et al.,87; Greenbaum et al., 91). It does so both from a "moral" perspective – users are the ones who have to live with the consequences of design – and from a practical perspective – they are competent practitioners understanding the practical problems of work, a capacity which enables them to assess and / or come up with alternatives to design. From this perspective, design is seen to be a cooperative activity involving not only end users but also other groups with very different but indispensable competencies. A primary means to the end of designing successful products is, accordingly, to bring these competencies together. This is often achieved in workshop like settings through the appliance of the different perspectives and competencies on a common and concrete issue, e.g. descriptions of current work, scenarios for future possibilities, mock-ups, and prototypes. The underlying assumptions and claims as well as a number of tools and techniques for the practical employment of cooperative design may be found in (Greenbaum et al., 91; Grønbæk, 91; Grønbæk et al., 93; Grønbæk et al., In Press; Mogensen, 94)

Closely related to the cooperative design activities, a number of usability studies were conducted. In this context 'usability' is attempting to transcend a history of work "with one user in a lab thinking aloud" and move evaluation into the workplace itself. In this respect, it is a deliberate attempt to move away from a conception of users as human factors to a conception of users as human actors, and from the notion of finding 'problems' to a notion of the user as an active participant in design (Bannon, 91; Bødker, 91; Wiklund, 94). Despite struggling with an in-built cognitive bias (Grudin, 89; Bannon et al., 93; Twidale et al., 94) particular workplace studies supplemented with more traditional one-to-one lab type evaluations focusing on human computer interaction (HCI), provided detailed information relating to specific usage of the prototype and thus supplemented cooperative design activities.

Cooperative design has, by and large and up until now, been carried out in situations where the potential users constituted groups of manageable proportions. One of the major challenges for cooperative design in the Dragon Project is to resolve problems of scale: the organisation is distributed across more than 250 offices in 70 countries around the world and users may be found on many different levels in the organisation. How does one work with such dispersed groups? How does one find representative users? How does one deal with all the different (and frequently conflicting) perspectives and interests among not only different levels in the managerial hierarchy, but also culturally and regionally dispersed groups?

The strategy employed so far can be characterised as a mix of two approaches. On the one hand we have worked in various specific areas, regarding geographical locations, specific work domains, and corresponding functionality (e.g. rerouting, initially with the Aarhus site as primary point of reference). Embedding design in actual practice has helped to ensure in-depth knowledge regarding the issues being designed for at the given time. On the other hand, and at the same time, we have tried to maintain and elaborate "the big picture", both regarding the functionality GCSS eventually will provide as well as the regional aspects in order to prepare for, or at least not counteract, later developments. Both strategies have been approached in parallel and, naturally, both approaches have influenced one another.

To date, most of the concrete design activities involving developers and users have been carried out in four ways:

- Presentations of the prototype with subsequent comment / discussion sessions (all in all 100+ users from over 20 countries).
- Workshops (1-3 days) elaborating the details of current problems, current stage of the prototype, and various alternatives (all in all 25 users from around 10 different countries).
- Continuous workshops analysing and designing aspects in various versions of the prototype (6 users from 4 countries).
- A series of usability studies (8) with the business representatives attached to the project and with customer service staff in the local office in Aarhus (one to two users at a time).

An example of how the first two types of interaction have worked is a recent visit to Singapore: Four developers and the two business representatives working with us in Aarhus arrived in Singapore on Thursday. Friday morning we presented the prototype and its intended use to some 20 people from various positions in the Singapore office for around 3 hours. In the afternoon we all joined various people doing their usual work in the office. Saturday morning, we had a workshop with four people centred on export handling. Saturday afternoon, we discussed lessons learned so far and decided on changes to be implemented immediately, issues for redesign when we came home, issues that were out of scope, and features that would be 'nice to have'. Monday, we split up. The ethnographer focused on issues where we needed more information (allocation and pricing), observing work-in-progress and interviewing people in the office. The cooperative designer and three users discussed and elaborated details regarding booking in a 'hands on' session with the prototype. The two OO developers started to implement changes prompted by the presentation and observations of work which were agreed upon on Saturday. Tuesday morning, we presented the changes in the prototype for around 10 people and went into detail regarding the next issue on the agenda, allocation and documentation (including pricing). Tuesday afternoon, we went to Malaysia. Wednesday morning, we presented the prototype in the Malaysian office ...

4.1 The Bremerhaven Instance (2)

An example of the continuous work 'back home' between developers and users is the Bremerhaven example. When rerouting came on to the agenda, company personnel gave us a brief introduction to the problem. The ethnographer went to the office in Aarhus and collected a series of examples or instances of actual reroutings dealt with at the office. The cooperative designer started to come up with ideas for supporting rerouting based on existing knowledge and experience. The next morning was spent in a continuous 'ping-pong' between various suggestions for supporting rerouting and the instances of actual reroutings coming out of the ethnography. After three to four iterations, an understanding of the problem as well as a first suggestion for the design emerged. Both were presented to and discussed with business representatives in the afternoon. Shown in Figure 1 is an account of the emergent understanding of the problem as well as the first design-solution (in real time, the example and the design was constantly produced and reproduced on paper sketches and white-boards).

You have 200 bookings out of Aarhus, going to Rotterdam via a local carrier. 100 of these bookings are transhipped on the intercontinental, *OC1*, headed for the Americas; another 100 are transhipped on to another intercontinental, *OC2*, headed for Asia.
Problem: the local carrier does not call Aarhus this week, we have to reroute or reschedule the 200 bookings.

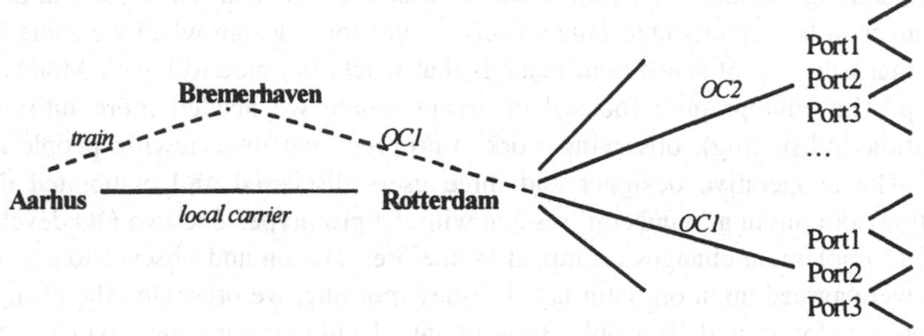

Solution: *OC1* calls Bremerhaven the day before it calls Rotterdam, so we can send all the containers to Bremerhaven by train, get them on the *OC1* a day before planned - everything is "back to normal". *OC2* does not serve Bremerhaven, we have to reschedule both for another local carrier and *OC2*.

Figure 1. The Bremerhaven instance

In considering how this is achieved in practice, it became apparent that affected cargoes' *destination* were different, spreading out globally like the branches on a tree. The suggested design was to represent all affected bookings in a tree structure with alternating ports and carriers. When the user, for example, clicks on *OC1* (see the above sketch) in the tree structure, it means that the user is now operating on all bookings out of Aarhus, transhipped in Rotterdam, and going out on *OC1*. Having selected the intercontinental carrier *OC1*, all further transhipment ports and final destinations may be seen. From here it is now possible to do rerouting via Bremerhaven for any particular group of bookings

Naturally, the above instance does not capture all possible problems in rerouting, neither does the design represent the final solution. The point is that the above understanding presented, in a very compact and understandable form, a good starting point and served as a powerful tool in further development where both the design solutions and the 'Bremerhaven instance' were refined and elaborated. As a paradigm case in point, the Bremerhaven instance was:

- Used and reproduced within the development group as common point of reference for design. The example states problems and solutions from current practice in respect to a specific design problem (designing for the rerouting and rescheduling of multiple bookings). Whenever we encountered problems in the implementation, the instance worked as a common resource: whatever the specific design ideas and problems were, the quality criteria was always whether we could support the instance, not, for example, whether we fulfilled some predefined requirements.

- Used and reproduced in a large number of presentations and workshops between people from the development team and users from various locations and levels. It is an integral part of the prototype: on the one hand it explains a problem the prototype is trying to resolve, on the other hand, discussing ways of solving the problem triggers new understanding of the problem and possible methods of solution. Roughly a week after the first formulation of the instance, it was confronted with staff from a large 'import' port. As was pointed out, the design works very well for rerouting in out-bound, it does not work when you are sitting in in-bound, because here the focus is on what is coming towards you. The instance was expanded with that example, and in the design we catered for the option of having either the receipt or the delivery port as the 'root' in the tree structure.
- Used and reproduced in the usability studies where, embodied in scenarios, it provided the starting point and context for assessing the prototype. In testing the prototype, the instance as well as the design was further elaborated. Up until testing for example, we provided for either an 'outbound' or an 'inbound' view of the tree-structure. What came out of thc usability studies in this respect was the idea that we actually needed both at the same time, facilitating an overview of both what was 'coming in' and what was 'going out'.

5 The object-oriented perspective

The OO perspective applied in this project is based on the Scandinavian tradition (Madsen et al., 93) where the focus is on modelling as opposed to technical concepts like encapsulation and inheritance. The first OO language, Simula was originally designed as a means for writing simulation programs and when writing simulation programs, it is useful to have a language with good modelling capabilities. The modelling approach has been very explicit in the design of BETA (which was the language used in the implementation of the prototype). One of the main advantages of object-orientation is that it provides an integrating perspective on analysis, design and implementation, but in order to fully realise this potential, there should be a proper balance and integration between modelling and implementation capabilities of the languages (Madsen, 96).

The application being developed (in this case the prototype) is considered as a physical model of a perspective on the problem domain. Selected phenomena and concepts in the application domain are synthesised into the model and represented as classes, objects, properties of objects and relations between objects. This model is a very explicit part of the application and it can be regarded as a view on the application expressed in problem domain-specific terms. The latest version of the model is always the one in the application.

Below we discuss the concept of modelling, how the model was produced, the evolution of the model, the architecture in which the model is embodied, and the crucial role of tools in responding to amendment and change.

5.1 The concept of modelling

Working within our OO-perspective, system development is based on an understanding of the concepts used within the settings that the system will eventually support. The setting we refer to as the *referent system* and the process of translating referent system specific concepts to concepts within the computer system we refer to as *modelling*. The result of the modelling process we refer to as the *model system* or just the model (Madsen et al., 93, pp.289, Knudsen et al., 94, pp.52). Using the model within a referent system context we denote *interpretation*. This can, for example, be discussion of business concepts with business users while referring to the model system. Below we discuss how modelling was actually achieved.

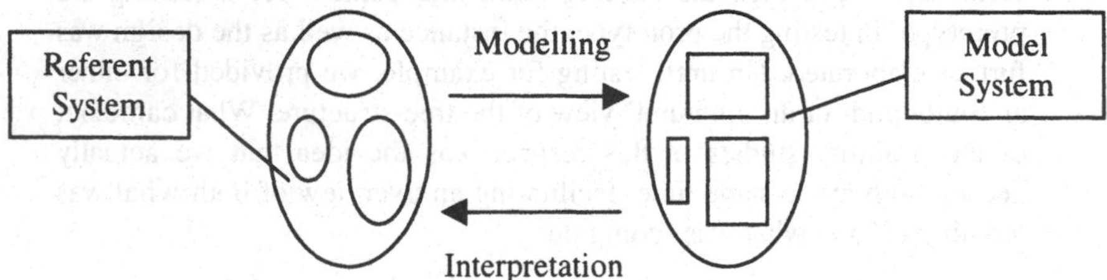

Figure 2. Customer service practice (referent system) in relation to the GCSS prototype (model system)

5.2 The production of the model

The activity of modelling was started right from the beginning of the project. Modelling has been an intentionally integrated part of each of the rapid prototyping cycles, in a sense on the same terms as the user interface and the architecture. The length of these cycles - the actual time spent on each – precludes a sharp distinction between the activities of analysis, design and implementation[6]. Working in an interdisciplinary context, our experiences extend existing notions of analysis, design and implementation. As such, a number of various resources and artefacts were used in producing the model. These included sessions with business representatives,

[6] A distinction which, as (Madsen et al., 93, pp 316) remind us, is highly questionable: 'In practice it is very difficult to do analysis without doing some design, and similarly doing design without doing some implementation.' Our experiences concur.

descriptions of the database of the current system, Yourdon diagrams of current and future business processes and, of the utmost importance, our own collaborative studies of *current practice*. The Yourdon diagrams, which came about as an output from the BPI analysis, exemplify the way in which the above resources and artefacts informed the development of the model, being used, much as use case diagrams may be used, as *'sensitising'* devices providing for the initial identification of objects. It should be stressed that the Yourdons were in no way used as requirements specifications (as such diagrams do not display actual practice in sufficient detail), rather it was a matter of using whatever resources were available to get an understanding of the problem domain.

Modelling proceeded in iterative phases: focussing on a particular area of business in collaboration with the business representatives attached to the project, the participatory designer and ethnographer; identifying important phenomena and concepts; analysing structure, and synthesising into a new iteration of the model. In the following example we exemplify and explain how modelling was achieved.

Modelling, a practical example - identifying concepts in the quote process*:* By a combination of review constraints, formal business process descriptions stemming from the BPI and the need to start the modelling process with an accessible instance of business, the quote process was treated first. A particular discussion about the quote process with a business representative allowed us to identify important concepts and phenomena embodied *within* the quote process, such as 'corridor', 'routing', 'container', 'rate' and 'customer'. This session, as other sessions including other participants as mentioned above, was recorded in the form of a *blackboard snapshot* showing the concepts, some properties of the concepts, examples of values of properties along with textual and pictorial annotations clarifying or explaining referent system specific concepts. Figure 3 displays the features of the snapshot from the discussion with the business representative regarding the quote process.

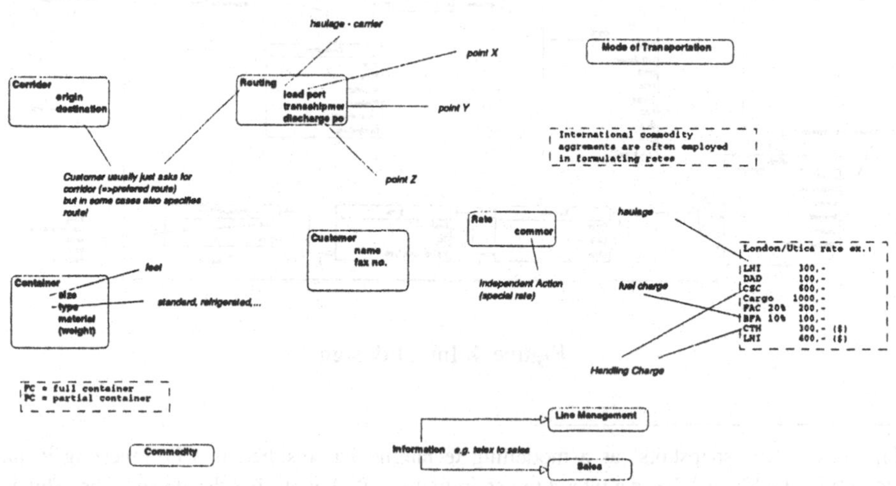

Figure 3. A blackboard snapshot

Blackboard snapshots produced through preliminary analysis of descriptions of working practice and the artefacts used were of considerable value and practical utility in creating the model. They provided rich detail and a firm basis upon which we were able to build a first model of the quote process. Furthermore, they worked as an important means of communication between the respective competencies at work.

Having created an initial model (see Figure 4), the model was then *interpreted* in the context of the referent system. The reason for this was to discuss the model with relevant members of the development team (including business representatives) in order to assess the state of the model and gain additional information as to the substance as well as the structure of the quote process. Other parts of the referent system were then analysed in the same way and synthesised with the parts of the model already elaborated[7].

Furthermore, the model was used for triggering *business* discussion. In this context the business representatives were able to see *referent system concepts instead of model system concepts;* comments on, for example, multiplicity's in associations, were put forward in the context and linguistic terms of business instead of in object-oriented terminology. In the context of formal reviews, in which participants from the

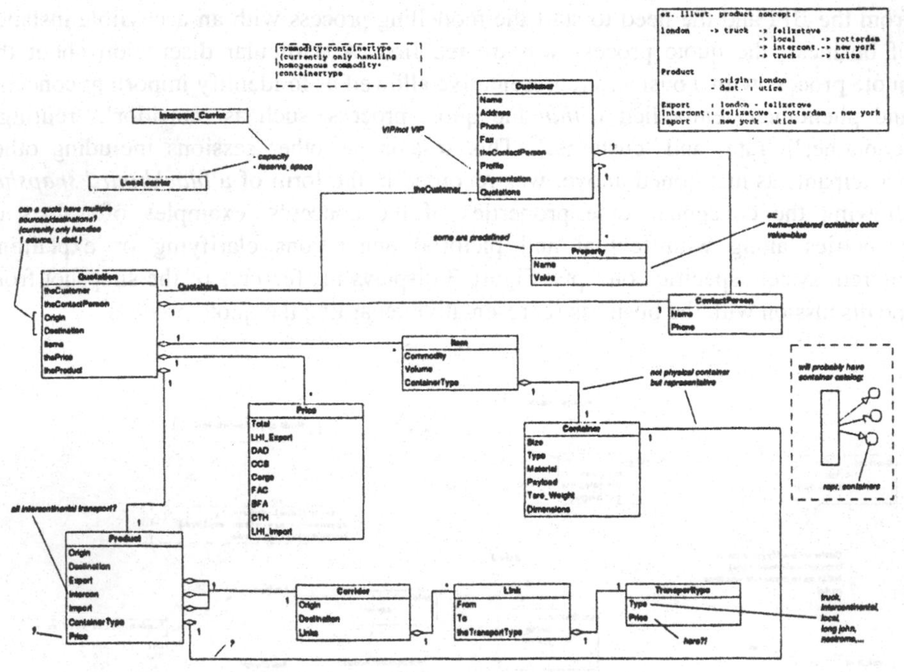

Figure 4. Initial design

---

[7] The success of 'snapshots' as a modelling technique has resulted in CIT investing in an electronic blackboard that we intend to use in future initial analysis / design sessions. This is just a first step in developing some supportive tools to support initial analysis / design.

business (including the consultants) had been involved in the BPI project and thus had an abstract perception of the business, the model triggered business discussions regarding *future practice*. It should be said that the model was not intelligible in all settings. In other contexts, participants who had not been part the BPI and who did not therefore have some knowledge of formal methodologies of design, had a hard time grasping the whole intent of discussing such a model.

As can be seen in Figure 4, the model exhibits technical simplicity: almost no implementation-specific attributes or classes have been added and only limited subset of UML's class diagram notation (Rational, 98), has been used namely inheritance, association and aggregation. In keeping the model "clean" it is kept interpretable and by using a formal notation the model is also executable in the sense that it is a living thing inside the actual prototype.

5.3 The evolution of the model

The model was by no means finished before coding started. It evolved along two dimensions: horizontally and vertically. Horizontally the model was gradually extended to cope with new areas in the referent system in the manner described above, with the first iteration of the prototype focusing on quoting, then booking and so on. In proceeding in this manner, both the model and the prototype were mutually elaborated. This was also the case vertically. The first iterations of a class or collection of related classes were focused on data and the relationships between the classes. In the following iterations the focus moved to high level functionality (the business functions), which introduced methods to the classes. Development of new business functions occasioned many amendments to the relevant parts of the model. Amendments primarily consisted in the addition of attributes and methods, modification of existing attributes and adjustments in class relationships.

Amendment to the model tended to be at a rather detailed level and our experience shows both that the model does not have to be complete either horizontally or vertically before coding can start, and that one does not need to spend too much time on the details in the design model before coding as they will be changed during implementation. The problem of when to start coding is not a question of validating the model but rather, in our experience, one of putting up and satisfying practical development requirements such as meeting deadlines for formal reviews. It should also be said that a major development requirement from our point of view is to have a running prototype even of minimal design to confront practice with and, in reaction, thereby elaborate modelling issues. Given this, our experience also shows that a model cannot be effectively created in isolation from implementation. As the model evolves together with the prototype in an evolutionary process, it becomes more and more stable with respect to the parts of the referent system so far covered. The Bremerhaven instance illustrates this.

5.4 The Bremerhaven Instance (3)

The problem of rerouting as elaborated through the perspectives and interaction of ethnography and participatory design and as visualised in the notion of a tree structure, emerged as a design issue relatively late in the process. Rerouting was on the agenda for the last review of the first phase of the project. At that time the basic functionality of the prototype had been developed to the point where the model supported a diverse set of business concepts including the concept of booking and related concepts such as products, schedules, allocation etc. The problem of rerouting is all about changing a bulk of bookings, a high-level operation that involves manipulation of multiple sets of bookings and related concepts. In so much as we already had the basic building blocks available, the development of the rerouting functionality was developed with only minor changes to the model. The basic structure did not need to be reconstructed. Radical reconstruction of the model was unnecessary because it was constructed on a natural understanding of the business concepts at work. Having said that, in dealing with the issue of rerouting, a new concept was introduced. The notion of rerouting being akin to a tree with an elaborate network of branches was not discovered among existing business concepts, but emerged out of a joint analysis of the work from the ethnographic and participatory design perspectives. Our approach to modelling allows new concepts to be introduced easily thus allowing the model to develop in an evolutionary manner.

The Bremerhaven instance is also a good example of how instances were used as a communication media between in this case the cooperative designer and the OO developers. Discussions between the cooperative designer and the cooperative developers regarding rerouting were centered around the Bremerhaven instance. The rerouting functionality is rather complex and it is difficult to get it right the first time. When problems arose during implementation the instance was used as a guideance for what at least should work in order to illustrate the basic idea. I.e. the Bremerhaven instance was used as a mediator in the design / implementation cycles as well as a minimal test case.

5.5 Prototype architecture

Working on the assumption that vertical, evolutionary prototyping needs to be performed within some well-defined architecture of the prototype, architecture was designed before actual programming on the prototype began, i.e. within two to three weeks. In this architecture the object model played a central role as being the *common frame of concepts* structuring the code in a referent system specific way. As we mentioned earlier, dealing with the concept of rerouting did not occasion any major reconstruction of the model, however, it did impact upon the architecture. Implementing rerouting in the prototype was problematic in that we did not know if the functionality required was already there, ready to reuse, or if abstractions of existing functionality were required. Through analysing the Bremerhaven instance we anticipated that major parts of the existing routing functionality could be reused. As it turned out however, the existing architecture did not provide the proper abstractions.

Constraints of time meant that the first design / implementation employed 'copy-paste reuse' of existing routing functionality. This was not construed as a problem in itself because, working in an evolutionary manner, we had the opportunity to design a new architecture in the next iteration cycle. As such, after the first major iteration of the prototype, we designed and implemented a component architecture (see Figure 5). This enabled us to implement rerouting using the cleaner abstractions afforded by the new architecture. These still, of course, need further iteration and as work continues more and more aspects of the Bremerhaven and other instances of work are brought into discussion. Change is now less problematic however, as the current architecture allows us to deal with the complex issues emerging from prototyping sessions: during the trip to Asia, for example, the power of component architecture was experienced as it was actually possible to add major components to the system "on the fly". The component architecture is the first step in the direction of an architecture with COM objects, (Microsoft, 95).

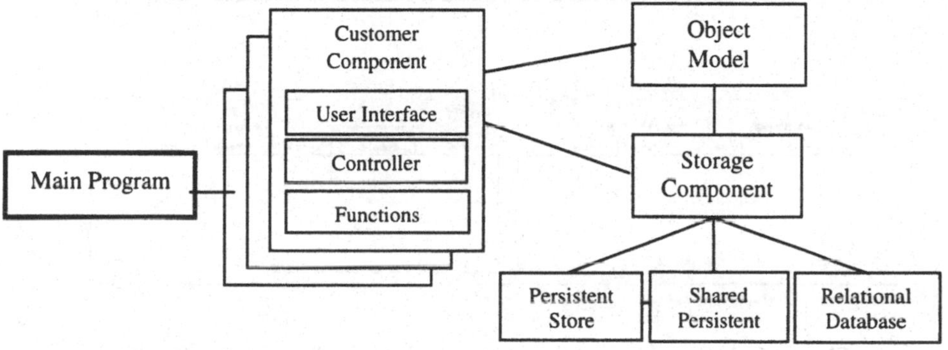

Figure 5. Current architecture of the prototype

5.6 The user interface of the prototype

In the user interface of the prototype we are combining an object-oriented user interface (in so much as part of the model is visualised in the user interface) with an activity-oriented user interface. The screen dump in Figure 6 shows this: business processes are displayed in a sequence of *process buttons* using a simple colour scheme for showing work's state of completion but not enforcing the accomplishment of work in a sequential manner, whereas the *tabbed controls* visualise the actual objects - customer, quote, transport - that are being worked on. Most upper tabs correspond to important domains in the model, whereas the sub-tabs visualise aggregated or referenced concepts.

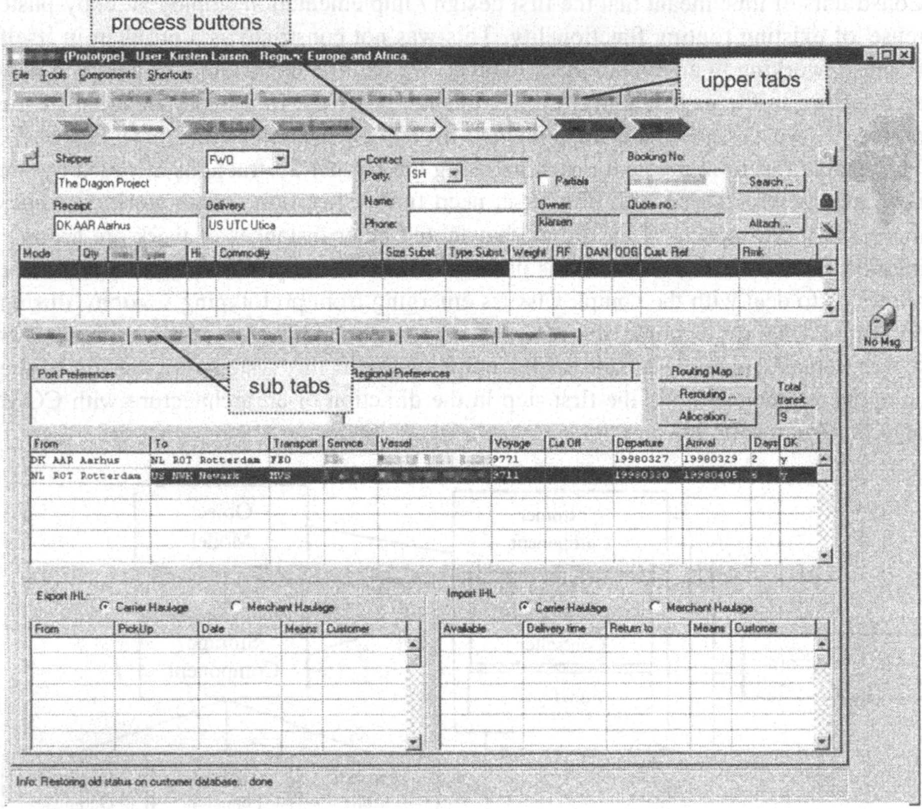

Figure 6. An overview of the main principles in the user interface of the prototype. (Image blurred for confidentiality)

6 Usage of tools

Within the context of any perspective the use of and support by tools is important. Working with evolutionary prototyping of architecture, functionality, user interface and model, tools supporting many iterations over a short period of time are a necessity. In the Dragon Project the main software engineering tools used are a CASE tool, a GUI builder, a code editor, a persistent store and a concurrent engineering tool.

The first four tools are part of the Mjølner System (Knudsen et al. 94, Ch. 2;`http://www.mjolner.com`) and the fifth tool used was concurrent versioning system (CVS, 98). The programming language used is BETA (Madsen et al., 93).

6.1 CASE tool

The CASE tool was used to draw the model using UML notation and to automatically generate the corresponding BETA code. In the beginning the CASE tool was also used to create the unstructured blackboard snapshots that later were used as input for the construction of the model. As diagrams of the model were created or modified, code was generated incrementally. Although code was thus available at any time, the early versions of the model were only used in the form of UML diagrams, as the emphasis was on communication and discussion.

The model can be changed via the diagrams or via the textual code. As emphasis moved to code and redesign cycles, model changes were mostly made in the code editor (see below) – only structural changes requiring overview of the model were made in the CASE tool. When the main emphasis is on coding, it is often more convenient to do the changes in the textual representation, especially when the changes are at a detailed level. Using the reengineering capability, the UML diagram was recreated from time to time and posters of it were made for discussion as mentioned earlier The reverse engineering capability is not based on having any additional information besides the BETA code, e.g. comments or other kinds of annotations, which means that the code editor – or in fact *any* editor – could be used to manipulate the model in its code representation.

6.2 GUI builder

The GUI builder is used to create the user interface in a direct manipulation graphical editor. Like the model the user interface can be changed via the graphical representation or via the textual code. The user interface was created from the start with the graphical editor, but was initially used for discussions only, although code is generated automatically. Changes regarding the physical appearance of the user interface, i.e. what type of UI controls used, and their concrete layout, were typically made in the graphical editor and changes regarding the basic functionality of the user interface and the interface to the model and functionality layer were typically made in the code editor. Due to reverse engineering and incrementality it is easy to alternate between using the two tools.

The user interface was often used as means for organising and/or coordinating activities between the cooperative designer and the OO developers. The initial user interface design was, by and large, made by the cooperative designer and it was then further elaborated by the OO developers in collaboration with the cooperative designer. Again due to reverse engineering it was possible for the cooperative designer to make changes to the user interface throughout the process, even very late in a prototype cycle.

The GUI builder generates code for a platform independent framework. This framework, which also had great importance to the development of the prototype, had to be extended during development in order to support platform specific UI controls. The new UI controls were manually inserted in the code, but they could coexist with the automatically generated UI controls without affecting the reverse engineering process.

One problem or annoyance was that a large amount of time was spent on coding a strict programming interface to the user interface to achieve independence between the user interface, the model and functionality layer. The separation, however, showed to provide advantages in stability of interface and those advantages are considered to outweigh the difficulties. Furthermore, preliminary investigations show that much of this work can actually be automated (Damm et al., 97).

6.3 Code Editor

All of the tools mentioned above integrate with a structure editor. The editor knows the grammar for the BETA language allowing it to incrementally "catch" syntax errors and provide facilities for syntactic and semantic browsing of code.

Furthermore, the editor offers an abstract representation of the code, where any part of the code can be hidden. As became evident when a new developer was introduced to the system (and its architecture) relatively late in the process, this presentation of code and the semantic browsing facilities helped in gaining a quick understanding of the architecture of the relatively large prototype. Also, the abstract presentation of code and the editing operations at that level were helpful in restructuring even large pieces of code (Knudsen et al., 94, chapter 23).

6.4 Persistence

Another major player on the stage of tools was the persistent store that supports orthogonal and transparent persistence. In this way any object can be stored and given a *persistent root* all reachable objects will be made persistent transparently. This meant that only a little time had to be used on persistence issues in the first versions of the prototype. Persistent stores generated from data from existing databases simulated interfaces to legacy systems, and data non-existing in legacy systems was added. A point has been made of identifying those chunks that are within the object model to prepare for current work on interfacing to actual legacy systems. In the current version of the prototype the focus has turned to multi-user functionality in a client / server architecture and a storage component has been developed. The storage component (see Figure 4) constitutes a transparent interface to three different storage media: the initial single-user persistent store, a shared persistent store (Brandt, 93,94; Wiederhold, 97), and a relational database (for a selected part of the data).

6.5 Concurrent engineering tool

Although preliminary implementation was worked out on separate pieces of code the need for use of the versioning system CVS very quickly emerged. As implementation progressed it became evident that its presence was absolutely crucial: It facilitated seven developers concurrently working on over 300 files containing over 100,000 lines of code, merging code with only minor problems. CVS was also used to merge changes made in regional prototype sessions with changes made at home at the University.

7 Managing development

Keeping the project "on track" and within the agreed time-frame was a major problem to be tackled. Project management and control was achieved in a number of ways. Development activities were managed and coordinated with BPI objectives through frequent business reviews ranging from the informal to the company's highest executive body. Up until now five different types of review, which vary both with respect to participants and with respect to purpose, have been held. A review of some kind has, on average, been held every two weeks during the five months of effective prototype development. In the second part of the project a major review of the prototype has been held approximately every second month. All reviews have actively involved relevant members of the development team. The reviews can be categorised as follows:

- Formal reviews with the project manager from the business, technical advisors from a consultancy and business representatives.
- Informal reviews with the same group.
- Reviews with the company's Regional Programme Coordinators (RPCs).
- Review with the company's executive body.
- Review with members of the company's Business Reference Group (BRG).

The purpose of the formal reviews – which were held more frequently in the beginning of the project than later on in development – was to assess whether or not the prototype was on the right track both in terms of scope and competency[8]. Informal reviews occurred in between the formal ones. They were informal in the sense that no single version of the prototype was built, frozen and presented for the occasion, rather it was a matter of the company's project manager and consultants visiting the development site and discussing work-in-progress[9]. Reviews with regional program-

---

[8] It might be noted that the "problem of culture" – academics working in a commercial context – was considered to be an issue of "high risk" by the company and its consultants; a problem resolved through frequent reviews.

[9] It should be said that for the first phase of development, the development team was located in company offices at a customer service site. While not actually located with customer service staff, access to practice was greatly facilitated. Furthermore, the transmission of knowledge was greatly facilitated through locating all the developers / perspectives in one room. This co-location supported internal awareness and coordination of development activities. It is an

me coordinators and the ethnographer, who did 'quick and dirty' studies of work (Hughes et al., 94) in Hong Kong and the US, were held to ensure that prototype kept a "global perspective" and, in their reaction to the current prototype, to get further input for development.

There has only been one review involving the company's executive body, the highest authority within the company regarding business development decisions. Following the executive review of the first major iteration of the prototype (May '97), the company decided to go ahead with developing a production version of GCSS. This decision was, amongst others, made on the basis of formal presentation of the prototype. The Business Reference Group, assembled in response to development phase two, represents the regions and is responsible for accepting features of the prototype that are to go into the production version and organising further, more "specialised" input from regional staff. By "specialised" staff is meant representatives from specific areas of the business. Although changed from time to time, one or two representatives from business have been located with the development team more or less constantly throughout design. They have been used intensively as resources on the problem domain and have also acted as coordinators between system development and BPI.

8 Concluding remarks

Returning to the question posed in the introduction, how come that the project was, and still is, successful? Based on the state of the work – still in progress – we will restrain ourselves from too firm conclusions. However, we still believe we might extract some lessons from the project so far. In the following, and we are very well aware that we are talking on the basis of one albeit comprehensive example, we will try to summarise some of the key findings in explicating some of the underlying means by which the prototype, the process, and the business results were achieved. Tentatively, and again rather simplistically, we can state that the main result seems to be the strength of an approach we might call an experimental and multiperspective approach to designing for practice.

8.1 Practice

Probably the most fundamental principle within our approach is the focus on the work practice the application has to support. One could say that practice is the subject of the analysis, a springboard for design, and the goal of the implementation. The business objective of the project as such is to design a product that fits the practice in which it is to be embedded and used, in this case customer *service*. Thus, the key feature of our approach is the focus on practice which is seen and treated as *the* fundamental resource in that it provides the possibility for grounding design,

---

organisation of work we have maintained in phase two although we are now located at the university.

identifying solutions to substantive problems, as well as providing triggers for new ideas as to how work (e.g. the *delivery* of customer service) might be achieved in the future through technological intervention.

8.2 Experimentation

In so much as design is an intervening activity very much concerned with future practice, one of the key characteristics of the whole development process is the quite comprehensive use of experimentation – i.e. the *performance* of analysis, design and implementation *in active collaboration with users.* Various methodological advise found in textbooks suggest that analysis, design and implementation should be carried out in sequence, although with iterations. The approach conducted within the Dragon Project can almost be said to go to the other extreme – there is no 'sequence' of work in the conventional sense of the word[10]. Schematically, Figure 7 depicts the approach employed and characterises experimentation.

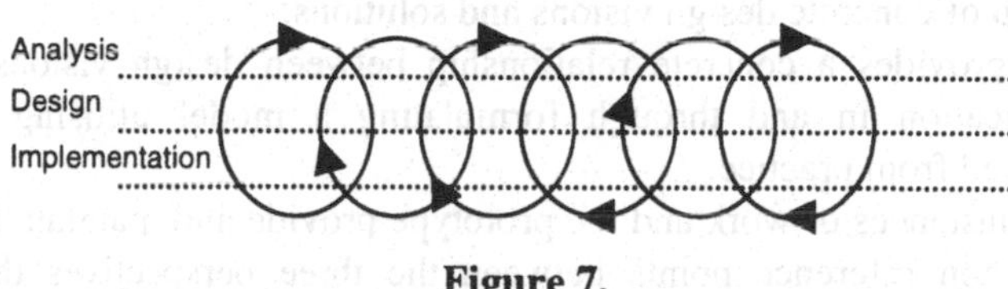

Figure 7.

In the analysis, we made extensive use of artefacts created within design and implementation. Similarly, the design activities were heavily dependent on both an in depth understanding of current practice (analysis) and a firm notion of what could actually be achieved within given constraints (implementation). Needless to say, implementation was dependent on analysis and design – notions all of which in this context are continuous, mutually elaborating and on-going: just as one starts analysing, designing and implementing in conjunction, then so one proceeds until a concrete product emerges

This 'radical parallelism' and experimentation in all phases is important and, in placing users at the centre of design activities, leads to the implementation of a prototype suitable for continuation into the product system. Just as we designed using specific experiences still keeping "the big picture" in focus, we also, and simultaneously, tried to cater for a rapid prototyping process as we developed with the

[10] Of course, in so much as this approach is iterative and in real time demands restructuring of the product, implementation of architectures supporting integration with databases, existing systems and so on, then there is a 'sequence' at work but here we are talking about the development of a technological infrastructure in contrast to the development of a functioning system that the infrastructure serves. It is in the sense of the *process of developing of functionality* (i.e. what activities the system should support) that the notion of sequence becomes redundant as analysis, design and implementation are continuous, mutually elaborative and on-going in contrast to discrete step-by-step tasks.

product system in mind – i.e. we took and take an evolutionary approach to prototyping. Central to this process were the model and the architecture, the development of which naturally requires a collection of suitable tools and techniques.

8.3 Multiperspective

In many respects the defining feature of the process is its interdisciplinary or multiperspective character. As outlined in the previous sections we have made extensive use of three very different perspectives. Although different, they share a common frame of reference – the prototype and the practice it is intended to support. Generally speaking we can say that:

- Ethnography provides a concrete understanding of work's real time accomplishment in contrast to idealisations and formal glosses.
- Cooperative design provides an understanding of the relationship between current and future practice through the experimental formulation of concrete design visions and solutions.
- OO provides a concrete relationship between design visions and the application in and through formulating a model utilising concepts derived from practice.
- The instances of work and the prototype provide and maintain important common reference points between the three perspectives throughout development.

Naturally, these perspectives do not have fixed boundaries; for all practical purposes neither seeks to exclude the other. We all need to understand the practice in question, we all need to share the design visions, as we all need to know what is realistic in terms of implementation. On the other hand, for practical purposes, we cannot all comprehend practice to the same extent. Thus, we made extensive use of overlapping competencies and foci as well as overlapping activities and responsibilities.

8.4 Implications for object-orientation

Besides these rather general lessons, we address more specific object-oriented issues. Below is a summary of some of the notions and principles applied in the current project ordered according to where they might best inform object-oriented analysis, design and implementation.

OO analysis is more than finding nouns and verb.

- Analysis is in significant part directed towards understanding current practice.
- Ethnography is a powerful approach to understanding the social organisation of activities which *is* current practice.
- Developers need concrete experiences from within practice, complementary and in addition to bringing users into the development process.
- Prototypes, mock-ups and scenarios, complement ethnographic techniques in functioning as triggers for discussions on current practice with users.

OO design is more than filling in details in the OO analysis model.

- Design is seen as an on-going process of formulating "best matches" between current work and future possibilities.
- Cooperative design bridges between current and future practice by active user involvement in a creative process of experimentation.
- Concrete representations of design visions (prototypes, mock-ups, and scenarios) provide the possibility (1) for simulating future work through hands-on-experience and (2) for (thereby) formulating concrete design-solutions.
- The central 'challenge' in design is not so much to find representative users, rather it is to find users that can challenge representations.

And to complete the list:
OO implementation is more than translating design models into code.

- Implementation is also seen as the process of realising emergent, in contrast to predefined, design visions.
- Without understanding design visions and their concrete relationship to practice, it is virtually impossible to implement or find alternatives to formal specifications.
- Implementation is in significant part constructing primary *means* for analysis and design in accomplishing evolutionary prototyping.
- The construction of robust yet readily adaptable models and architectures are crucial in implementation and depend on flexible tool support.

Naturally, the above principles do not apply to all problems in all situations. System development is, afterall, a heterogeneous enterprise not only in terms of staff but also in terms of problem domains. Up until now each of the individual perspectives outlined here have been successfully applied to a wide variety of application developments in a multiplicity of situations. Although respective disciplinary achievements suggested the strong possibility of developing a highly effective and unified approach to system development, in so much as this is the first major attempt at combining them in large-scale development, then success in a multiplicity of settings cannot be claimed for their particular association. Thus, it is difficult to assess scope, applicability, cost, etc.

What we can say, based on the experiences so far, is that the approach has been successfully applied in a situation characterised by the following features: complex human work practices, high uncertainty regarding the specifics of the potential application, large and geographically distributed organisation. In respecifying the classical working order of design from a sequential process of analysis – design – implementation to an on-going, mutually elaborative process dependent on active user involvement (experimentation), the multiperspective approach outlined here is potentially strong, both in terms of projected cost benefit and in actual terms of practical efficacy from a client's point of view, in supporting the integration of emerging information technologies into the world of work and organisation. To reiterate: we outline here an organised approach to, *not a formal method of*, work-oriented design. Finally, it might be said that in so much as we have explicated the acronym M.A.D. in what we hope is some reasonable detail, then that acronym not only captures the essence of a unique approach but also the frenetic character of rapid prototyping at work.

Acknowledgement: This work was made possible by the Danish National Centre for IT-Research (CIT, `http://www.cit.dk`), research grant COT 74.4. We would also like to express our sincere thanks to all the people within the company who made this project possible.

9 References

(Anderson et al., 89). Anderson, R.J., Hughes, J.A., Sharrock, W.W. (1989) *Working for Profit: The Social Organisation of Calculation in an Entrepreneurial Firm*, Aldershot: Avebury.

(Bannon, 91) Bannon, L.J. (1991) *From Human Factors to Human Actors: the role of psychology and human-computer interaction studies in system design*, Design at Work: Cooperative Design of Computer Systems (eds. Greenbaum, J. & Kyng, M.), pp. 25 – 44, New Jersey: Lawrence Erlbaum Associates.

(Bannon et al., 93) Bannon, L.J. & Hughes, J.A. (1993) *The Context of CSCW*, Developing CSCW Systems: Design Concepts, Report of COST 14, 'CoTech' Working Group 4 (1991-92), pp 9 – 36.

(Bjerknes et al., 87). Bjerknes, G., Ehn, P., & Kyng, M. (1987) *Computers and Democracy: A Scandinavian Challenge*, Aldershot: Avebury.

(Blomberg et al., 94). Blomberg, J., Suchman, L., Trigg, R. (1994) *Reflections on a Work-Oriented Design Project*, Proceedings of PDC '94,pp 99 – 109, Chapel Hill, North Carolina: ACM Press.

(Brandt, 93). Brandt, S., Madsen, O.L. (1994) *Object-oriented Distributed Programming in BETA*, in Lecture Notes in Computer Science, LNCS 791, Springer-Verlag 1994.

(Brandt, 94). Brandt, S. (1994) *Implementing Shared and Persistent Objects in BETA*, Progress Report, Tecnical Report, Department of Computer Science, Aarhus University.

(Bødker, 91) Bødker, S. (1991) *Through the Interface: a Human Activity Approach to User Interface Design*, Hillsdale, New Jersey: Lawrence Erlbaum Associates.

(COMIC 2.2, 93) COMIC Deliverable 2.2, Esprit Basic Research Project 6225 (1993) *Field Studies and CSCW*, (eds.) Lancaster University and Manchester University.

(Crabtree et al., 97). Crabtree, A., Twidale, M., O'Brien, J., Nichols, D.M. (1997) *Talking in the Library: Implications for the Design of Digital Libraries*, Proceedings of ACM Digital Libraries '97, Phildelphia: ACM Press

(CVS, 98). Gnu, *Concurrent Version System* (1998) ftp://archive.eu.net/gnu/.

(Damm et al., 97) Damm, C.H., Hansen, K.M., Thomsen, M. (1997) *Issues from the GCSS Prototyping Project – Experiences and Thoughts on Practice*, Department of Computer Science, Aarhus University.

(Garfinkel et al., 70) Garfinkel, H. & Sacks, H. (1970) *On Formal Structures of Practical Actions*, Theoretical Sociology: Perspectives and Developments (eds. Mckinney, J.C. & Tiryakian, E.A.), pp 337 – 366, New York: Appleton-Century-Crofts, 1970.

(Greenbaum et al., 91). Greenbaum, J., & Kyng, M. (1991) *Design at Work: Cooperative Design of Computer Systems*, Hillsdale New Jersey: Lawrence Erlbaum Associates.

(Grønbæk, 91). Grønbæk, K. (1991) *Prototyping and Active User Involvement in System Development: Towards a Cooperative Prototyping Approach.* Ph.D. Thesis, Computer Science Dept., University of Aarhus.

(Grønbæk et al., 93). Grønbæk, K., Kyng, M., & Mogensen, P. *CSCW Challenges: Cooperative Design in Engineering Projects*, Communications of the ACM 36 (6), pp 67 - 77.

(Grønbæk et al., In Press). Grønbæk, K., Kyng, M., & Mogensen, P. *Toward a Cooperative Experimental System Development Approach*, In M. Kyng & L. Mathiassen (Eds.), (In Press).

(Grudin, 89) Grudin, J. (1989) *Why Groupware Applications Fail: Problems in Design and Evaluation*, Office: Technology and People, vol. 4 (3), pp 245 – 264.

(Heath et al., 92). Heath, C. & Luff, P. (1992) *Collaboration and Control: Crisis Management and Multimedia Technology in London Underground Line Control Rooms*, JCSCW '92, vol. 1, the Netherlands: Kluwer Academic Publishers.

(Hughes et al., 92). Hughes, J., Randall, D., Shapiro, D. (1992) *Faltering from Ethnography to Design*, Proceedings of CSCW '92, pp 115 – 122, Toronto: ACM Press.

(Hughes et al., 94). Hughes, J., King, V., Rodden, T., Andersen, H. (1994) *Moving Out of the Control Room: Ethnography in System Design*, Proceedings of CSCW '94, pp 429 – 439, Chapel Hill: ACM Press.

(Hughes et al., 96). Hughes, J., Kristoffersen, S., O'Brien, J., Rouncefield, M. (1996) *When Mavis met IRIS: Ending the love affair with Organisational Memory*, Proceedings of IRIS 19 'The Future', Report 8.

(Kensing et al., 97). Kensing, F & Simonsen, J. (1997) *Using Ethnography in Contextual Design*, Communications of the ACM, 40 (7), pp 82 - 88.

(Knudsen et al., 94). Knudsen, J.L., Löfgren, M., Madsen, O.L., Magnusson, B. (1994) *Object-Oriented Environments. The Mjølner Approach*, Prentice Hall.

(Knudsen et al., 96). Knudsen, J.L., Madsen, O.L. (1996) *Using Object-Orientation as a Common Basis for System Development Education*, ECOOP '96 Teachers Symposium.

(Madsen et al., 93). Madsen, O.L., Møller-Pedersen, B., Nygaard, K. (1993) *Object-Oriented Programming in the BETA Programming Language*, ACM Press, Addison Wesley.

(Madsen, 96). O.L Madsen: Open Issues in Object-Oriented Programming (1996) – a Scandinavian perspective, Software Practice and Experience.

(Microsoft, 95). *The Component Object Model Specification*, Microsoft Corporation, 1995.

(Mogensen, 94). Mogensen, P. (1994) *Challenging Practice: an Approach to Cooperative Analysis*, Ph.D thesis, Computer Science Department, University of Aarhus, Daimi PB-465.

(Rational, 98). Rational Software Cooperation (1998) *UML Notation Guide Version 1.1*, http://www.rational.com/uml/html/notation/

(Rouncefield et al., 94). Rouncefield, M, Hughes, J.A., Rodden, T, Viller, S. (1994) *Working with "Constant Interruption": CSCW and the Small Office*, Proceedings of CSCW '94, Chapel Hill: ACM Press.

(Schmidt et al., 93) Schmidt, K. & Carstensen, P. (1993) *Bridging the Gap: Requirements Analysis for System Design*, Working Paper, COMIC-RISØ, Esprit Basic Research Project 6225, (eds.). Lancaster University and Manchester University.

(Twidale et al., 94) Twidale, M., Randall, D., Bentley, R. (1994) *Situated Evaluation for Cooperative Systems*, Proceedings of CSCW '94, pp 441 – 452, Chapel Hill, North Carolina: ACM Press.

(Weiderhold, 97) Weiderhold, J.T. (1997) *A Multi-User Persistence Framework: Building Customised Database Solutions uing the BETA Persistent Store*, MA. Thesis, Department of Computer Science, Aarhus University.

(Wiklund, 94). Wiklund, M. (1994) *Usability in Practice*, AP Professional.

(Wittgenstein, 68) Wittgenstein, L. *Philosophical Investigations*, Oxford: Basil Blackwell, 1968.

Extending the ODMG Object Model with Time

Elisa Bertino [1] *Elena Ferrari* [1] *Giovanna Guerrini* [2] *Isabella Merlo* [2]

[1] Dipartimento di Scienze dell'Informazione
Università degli Studi di Milano
Via Comelico 39/41 - I20135 Milano, Italy
{bertino,ferrarie}@dsi.unimi.it

[2] Dipartimento di Informatica e Scienze dell'Informazione
Università di Genova
Via Dodecaneso 35 - I16146 Genova, Italy
{guerrini,merloisa}@disi.unige.it

Abstract. Although many temporal extensions of the relational data model have been proposed, there is no comparable amount of work in the context of object-oriented data models. Moreover, extensions to the relational model have been proposed in the framework of SQL standards, whereas no attempts have been made to extend the standard for object-oriented databases, defined by ODMG. This paper presents T_ODMG, a temporal extension of the ODMG-93 standard data model. The main contributions of this work are, thus, the formalization of the ODMG standard data model and its extension with time. Another contribution of this work is the investigation, on a formal basis, of the main issues arising from the introduction of time in an object-oriented model.

1 Introduction

Temporal databases [16] provide capabilities for efficiently managing not only the current values of data, but also the entire history of data over time. Several database applications, such as the ones in the medical and scientific domains or the ones in the business and financial context, require support for historical data. In most cases, data of interest to those applications are meaningful only if related to time.

Most of the research and development efforts in the area of temporal databases have been carried out in the context of the relational model. A temporal extension, known as TSQL-2 [13], of the SQL-92 relational database standard, has been proposed and issues related to temporal relational data models and query languages have been extensively investigated from the theoretical point of view [17].

By contrast, research on temporal object-oriented databases is still in an early stage. Although various object-oriented temporal models have been proposed [12], there is no amount of work comparable to the work reported for the relational model. One of the main reasons for the delay in the development of temporal object-oriented data models is that, until recently, there was no standard for object-oriented databases. Recently, a proposal for an object database standard has been formulated by ODMG [4]. The ODMG standard includes a reference object model (ODMG Object Model), an object definition language (ODL) and an object query language (OQL). The definition of such a standard represents an important step toward the widespread diffusion of object-oriented DBMSs. Indeed, most of the success of relational databases, as well as of its temporal extensions, is undoubtly due to the existence of a well-accepted standard. The acceptance of the SQL standard ensures a high degree of portability and interoperability between systems, simplifies learning new relational DBMSs, and represents a wide endorsement of the relational approach.

For all the above reasons, in this paper we propose *T*_ODMG, a temporal extension of the ODMG standard object data model. Thus, the goal of our work is not to develop a new temporal object-oriented data model. Rather our goal is to incorporate temporal features into the ODMG object model. To the best of our knowledge, this is the first extensive attempt of complementing the ODMG data model with temporal capabilities.

The ODMG data model provides a very rich set of modeling primitives. Objects are characterized by a state and a behavior. The state of an object is represented by the values of its properties. Properties can be either attributes, like in most object-oriented data models, or relationships. Relationships are declared between two object types and induce a pair of traversal paths between the two types. Moreover, the ODMG data model supports the notion of key, that is, a set of properties whose values uniquely identify each object within a class extent.

The development of a temporal extension of a semantically rich data model, like the one proposed by ODMG, entails several interesting issues that we address in this paper. First the rich set of data types provided by ODMG has been complemented with a set of temporal types, which allows to handle in a uniform way temporal and non temporal domains. Then, we have added the temporal dimension to both object attributes and relationships. A relevant feature provided by *T*_ODMG is the support for temporal, immutable and static object properties. A temporal property is a property whose value may change over time, and whose values at different times are recorded in the database. An immutable property is a property whose value cannot be modified during the object lifetime, whereas a static property is a property whose value can change over time, but whose past values are not meaningful, and are thus not stored in the database. In addition, we have investigated how the notions of extent, key and object consistency should be modified to deal with the temporal dimension.

Another important property of the *T*_ODMG data model we propose is that it extends the ODMG data model in an "upward compatible" way, that is, non-temporal and temporal data coexist in an integrated way. This is very important if applications should migrate to a temporal conext.

A further contribution of this paper is that the addition of time in the ODMG standard data model has been carried out on a formal basis. This has required to first provide a formalization of the main components of the ODMG model, which was not provided in [4].

The temporal object model presented in this paper is based on the *T*_Chimera formal data model proposed by us in [3]. Such model represents the starting point of our current work. However the work reported in this paper substantially extends the previous work. First ODMG is characterized by a richer set of types with respect to the T_Chimera one. Second, ODMG supports the notions of relationship and key which are not provided by T_Chimera. Finally, the notions of temporal types and the distinction among temporal, static, immutable attributes, that are inherited from T_Chimera, obviously need to be revisited in the context of the T_ODMG model.

This paper is organized as follows. Section 2 summarizes the main features of the ODMG standard. Section 3 introduces types and values, whereas Sections 4 and 5 deal with classes and objects, respectively. Section 6 discusses existing proposals of temporal object-oriented data models. Finally, Section 7 concludes the paper.

2 The object database standard: ODMG-93

In what follows we summarize the main features of the ODMG data model. We refer the interested reader to [4] for the description of the object definition language (ODL) and the object query language (OQL).

The basic modeling concepts in the ODMG data model are the concepts of *object* and *literal*. The main difference between objects and literals is that each object has a unique identifier (*oid*), whereas a literal has no identifier. Literals are sometimes described as being constant or *immutable* since the value of a literal cannot change. By contrast, objects are described as being *mutable*. Changing the values of the attributes of an object, or the relationships in which it is involved, does not change the identity of the object.

Objects and literals can be categorized according to their *types*. Object types can be partitioned into two main groups: atomic object types and collection object types.

Atomic object types are user-defined types (e.g., `Person`, `Employee`). Collection object types represent set, bag, list and array objects. Literal types can be partitioned into three main groups: atomic literal types, collection literal types and structured literal types. Atomic literal types are numbers, characters and so on. Collection literal types represent set, bag, list and array literals. Structured literal types have a fixed number of elements, each of which has a variable name and can contain either a literal value or an object. Moreover ODMG supports user-defined structures implementing records.

The formalization of object and literal types and the differences between collection object types and collection literal types are presented in Subsection 3.1. An object is sometimes referred to as an *instance* of its type.

An object in ODMG is characterized by a *state* and a *behavior*. The state of an object is defined by the values of its *properties*. Properties can be either *attributes* of the object itself or *relationships* among the object and one or more other objects. Typically the value of an object property can change over time. The behavior of an object is defined by the set of *operations* that can be executed on or by the object. All objects of a given type have the same set of properties and the same set of defined operations.

There are two aspects in the definition of a type. A type has an *interface* specification and one or more *implementation* specifications. The interface defines the *external characteristics* of an instance of the type. That is the operations that can be invoked on the object and the state variables whose values can be accessed. By contrast, a type implementation defines the *internal aspects* of the instances of the type.

The distinction between interface and implementation is important, since the separation between these two is the approach according to which ODMG supports encapsulation. Throughout the paper we assume that a type has a single implementation specification. Therefore the terms object type, interface and class are used as synonymous. More precisely, we distinguish between object types and literal types, object interfaces and literal interfaces, while the term class is used only when dealing with objects. Moreover, implementation details are not relevant from a modeling point of view. Thus, we focus on the interface specification, disregarding the implementation specification of a type.

The attribute declarations in an interface define the abstract state of a type. An attribute value is either a literal or an object identifier. Relationships are defined between object types. The ODMG object model supports only binary relationships, i.e., relationships between two types, each of which must have instances that can be referenced by object identifiers. Therefore literal types cannot participate in relationships (since they do not have object identifiers). Relationships in the ODMG object model are similar to relationships in the entity-relationship data model [6]. A binary relationship may be one-to-one, one-to-many, or many-to-many, depending on how many instances of each type participate in the relationship. For instance, *marriage* is an example of one-to-one relationship between two instances of type `Person`. A woman can have a one-to-many *mother_of* relationship with many children. Teachers and students typically participate in many-to-many relationships.

A relationship is implicitly defined by declaring *traversal paths* that enable applications to use the logical connections between the objects participating in the relationship. For each relationship two traversal paths are declared, one for each direction of traversal of the binary relationship. For instance, the relationship between a professor and the courses he/she teaches generates two traversal paths, since a professor *teaches* courses and a course *is taught by* a professor. The **`teaches`** traversal path is defined in the interface declaration of the **`Professor`** type. The **`is_taught_by`** traversal path is defined in the interface declaration of the **`Course`** type. The fact that the **`teaches`** and **`is_taught_by`** traversal paths apply to the same relationship is indicated by an **`inverse`** clause in both the traversal path declarations.

One-to-many and many-to-many relationships can also be implemented using bags, lists and arrays.

Besides the attribute and relationship properties, the other characteristic of a type is its behavior, which is specified as a set of *operation signatures* (*method signatures*). Each signature defines the name of an operation, the name and type of each of its arguments, the types of the value(s) returned.[1] Each operation is associated with a single type and its name must be unique within the corresponding type definition. However, operations with the same name can be defined for different types. The names of these operations are said to be *overloaded*. When an operation is invoked using an overloaded name, a specific operation must be selected for execution. This selection is called *operation dispatching*. An operation may have side effects. Some operations may return no value. The ODMG object model does not include formal specification of the semantics of operations; it is highly implementation dependent. Finally *extents*, *keys* and *supertype* information can be optionally associated with a type.

The extent of a type is the set of all instances of the type within a particular database. If an object is an instance of a type `t`, than it necessarily belongs to the extent of `t`. If type `t` is a subtype of type `t'`, then the extent of `t` is a subset of the extent of `t'`.

In some cases, instances of a type can be uniquely identified by the values they carry for some property or set of properties. These identifying properties are called *keys*. The scope of uniqueness is the extent of the type, thus a type must have an extent in order to have a key.

Similar to most object models, also the ODMG object model includes inheritance based type-subtype relationships. Supertype information is one of the characteristics of types, together with extent naming and key specifications. The type-subtype relationships are commonly represented by oriented graphs; each node represents a type and there exists an arc from a node `t` to a node `t'` if `t'` is the *supertype* of `t` (*subtype*). The type/subtype relationship is sometimes called an *is-a* relationship, or simply an *ISA* relationship, or *generalization-specialization* relationship. The supertype is the more general type; the subtype is the more specialized one.

3 Types and values

In this section we formally introduce $\mathcal{T}$_ODMG types and values. First, we give a formalization of ODMG types. Then, we extend the ODMG types with temporal types. The resulting model is $\mathcal{T}$_ODMG, the temporal extension of the ODMG model. Temporal structured literal types are described in detail. Finally, we define $\mathcal{T}$_ODMG legal values. In the following we refer to Table 1 that summarizes the functions used in defining the model. For each function the table reports the name, the signature and the output.[2]

In the following we denote with $\mathcal{OI}$ a set of object identifiers, with $\mathcal{CI}$ a set of class identifiers, that is, interface names, with $\mathcal{AN}$ a set of attribute names, with $\mathcal{RN}$ a set of relationship names and with $\mathcal{MN}$ a set of method names.

[1] Moreover each signature defines the names of *exceptions* (error conditions) the operation can raise. In this context we do not consider exceptions.

[2] The meaning of each function will be clarified in the remainder of the discussion.

Name	Signature	Output
π	$\mathcal{CI} \times \mathcal{TIME} \rightarrow 2^{\mathcal{OI}}$	extent of a class at a given instant
pe_set	$\mathcal{CI} \times \mathcal{TIME} \rightarrow 2^{\mathcal{OI}}$	proper extent of a class at a given instant
type	$\mathcal{CI} \rightarrow \mathcal{T} \times \mathcal{T}$	structural property type of a class
h_type	$\mathcal{CI} \rightarrow \mathcal{T} \times \mathcal{T}$	historical property type of a class
s_type	$\mathcal{CI} \rightarrow \mathcal{T} \times \mathcal{T}$	static property type of a class
h_state	$\mathcal{OI} \times \mathcal{TIME} \rightarrow \mathcal{V} \times \mathcal{V}$	historical value of an object
s_state	$\mathcal{OI} \rightarrow \mathcal{V} \times \mathcal{V}$	static value of an object
o_lifespan	$\mathcal{OI} \rightarrow \mathcal{TIME} \times \mathcal{TIME}$	lifespan of an object
c_lifespan	$\mathcal{OI} \times \mathcal{CI} \rightarrow \mathcal{TIME} \times \mathcal{TIME}$	lifespan of an object as a member of a class

Table 1. Functions employed in defining the model

3.1 ODMG types

As we mentioned in Section 2, objects and literals can be categorized according to their types. First we give the formal definition of object types. In the remainder, ODMG$\mathcal{T}$ denotes the set of ODMG types. It is formally defined later on in this subsection.

Definition 1 (*Object Types*). The set of ODMG object types $\mathcal{OT}$ is defined as follows.

$$\mathcal{OT} = \mathcal{AOT} \cup \mathcal{AOST} \cup \mathcal{COT}$$

where:

- $\mathcal{AOT}$ is the set of ODMG *atomic object types*; it is defined as the set of class identifiers $\mathcal{CI}$;
- $\mathcal{AOST}$ is the set of ODMG *atomic object system types*; it is defined as the following set {`Object`, `Collection`, `Set`, `Bag`, `List`, `Array`};
- $\mathcal{COT}$ is the set of ODMG *collection object types*; it is defined as the following set $\mathcal{COT}$ = {`O_Set<t>` | `t` ∈ ODMG$\mathcal{T}$} ∪ {`O_Bag<t>` | `t` ∈ ODMG$\mathcal{T}$} ∪ {`O_List<t>` | `t` ∈ ODMG$\mathcal{T}$} ∪ {`O_Array<t>` | `t` ∈ ODMG$\mathcal{T}$}.[3]

□

As Definition 1 states, the ODMG object types can be partitioned into three sets. The set $\mathcal{AOT}$ denotes the simple user-defined interfaces. The set $\mathcal{AOST}$ denotes a set of predefined system types. Finally, the set $\mathcal{COT}$ denotes the types of objects of type set, bag, etc. The direct supertype of each collection object is

[3] Note that in [4] the notation for collection object types is different. For example, in case of sets `Set<t>` is used to denote both collection literal and collection object set types. We have chosen, for sake of clarity, to distinguish collection object and literal types. Therefore we use `O_Set<t>` to denote the collection object type for sets and `Set<t>` to denote the corresponding collection literal type.

the relative atomic object system type (e.g., **Set** is the direct supertype of each **O_Set<t>** such that **t** $\in$ ODMG$\mathcal{T}$). ODMG also provides collection literal types to define sets, bags, lists and arrays (Definition 2).

Note that a name in $\mathcal{CI}$ can be associated with a collection object type. For instance, the name **EmployeeSet** can be associated with the collection object type **O_Set<Employee>**. Names are associated with collection object types for an easy reference, there is, however, the complete substitutability of a collection object type and the name assigned to it.

The following definition formalizes ODMG literal types.

Definition 2 (*Literal Types*). The set of ODMG literal types $\mathcal{LT}$ is defined as follows.

$$\mathcal{LT} = \mathcal{ALT} \cup \mathcal{CLT} \cup \mathcal{SLT} \cup \mathcal{ST}$$

where:

- $\mathcal{ALT}$ is the set of ODMG *atomic literal types*; it is defined as the following set $\mathcal{ALT}$ = {**Long**, **Short**, **Unsigned long**, **Unsigned short**, **Float**, **Double**, **Boolean**, **Octet**, **Char**, **String**, **Enum**};
- $\mathcal{CLT}$ is the set of ODMG *collection literal types*; it is defined as the following set $\mathcal{CLT}$ = {**Set<t>** | **t** $\in$ ODMG$\mathcal{T}$} $\cup$ {**Bag<t>** | **t** $\in$ ODMG$\mathcal{T}$} $\cup$ {**List<t>** | **t** $\in$ ODMG$\mathcal{T}$} $\cup$ {**Array<t>** | **t** $\in$ ODMG$\mathcal{T}$};
- $\mathcal{SLT}$ is the set of ODMG *structured literal types*; it is defined as the following set $\mathcal{SLT}$ = {**Date**, **Interval**, **Time**, **TimeStamp**};[4]
- $\mathcal{ST}$ is the set of ODMG *struct literal types*; it is defined as the following set $\mathcal{ST}$ = {**Struct**{$\mathtt{t}_1\ p_1; \ldots; \mathtt{t}_n\ p_n$ }| $\mathtt{t}_i \in$ ODMG$\mathcal{T}$, $p_i \in \mathcal{AN} \cup \mathcal{RN}$, $i \in [1, n]$}.

□

An important difference between collection object types and collection literal types is that instances of collection object types have identifiers while instances of collection literal types do not have identifiers. For more details on such features of the ODMG model we refer the reader to [4].

The set of ODMG types ODMG$\mathcal{T}$ is defined as the union of the set of ODMG object types $\mathcal{OT}$ and the set of ODMG literal types $\mathcal{LT}$. Therefore:

$$\text{ODMG}\mathcal{T} = \mathcal{OT} \cup \mathcal{LT}.$$

We also recall that in the ODMG data model the type **any** stands for any type **t** $\in$ ODMG$\mathcal{T}$, and that **void** stands for "no values" and it is used for side effect operations which return no values.

[4] The interfaces of these types can be found in [4]. In the following we only specify the interfaces we are interested in, since they are relevant for our work.

3.2 *T*_ODMG types

*T*_ODMG extends the set of ODMG types with a collection of *temporal types*, introduced to handle in a uniform way temporal and non temporal domains. For each ODMG type `t`, a corresponding temporal type is defined through a special constructor *temporal*. Intuitively, instances of type *temporal*(`t`) are partial functions from instances of type **`TimeStamp`**[5] to instances of type `t`. We elaborate on this informal definition in the following section.

Definition 3 (*T*_ODMG *Temporal Types*). The set of *T*_ODMG temporal types ODMG$\mathcal{TT}$ is defined as follows.

$$\text{ODMG}\mathcal{TT} = \{temporal(\mathtt{t}) \mid \mathtt{t} \in \text{ODMG}\mathcal{T}\}.$$

□

In *T*_ODMG, temporal types can be used in the definition of collection object, literal and struct types, as stated by the following definitions. In the remainder, $\mathcal{T}$ denotes the set of *T*_ODMG types.

Definition 4 (*T*_ODMG *Object Types*). The set of *T*_ODMG object types $\mathcal{OTT}$ is defined as follows.

$$\mathcal{OTT} = \mathcal{AOT} \cup \mathcal{AOST} \cup \mathcal{COTT}$$

where:

- $\mathcal{AOT}$ is the set of ODMG *atomic object types*, as specified by Definition 1;
- $\mathcal{AOST}$ is the set of ODMG *atomic object system types*, as specified by Definition 1;
- $\mathcal{COTT}$ is the set of *T*_ODMG *collection object types*; it is defined as the following set $\mathcal{COTT} = \{\mathtt{O\_Set<t>} \mid \mathtt{t} \in \mathcal{T}\} \cup \{\mathtt{O\_Bag<t>} \mid \mathtt{t} \in \mathcal{T}\} \cup \{\mathtt{O\_List<t>} \mid \mathtt{t} \in \mathcal{T}\} \cup \{\mathtt{O\_Array<t>} \mid \mathtt{t} \in \mathcal{T}\}$.

□

Definition 5 (*T_ODMG Literal Types*). The set of *T*_ODMG literal types $\mathcal{LTT}$ is defined as follows.

$$\mathcal{LTT} = \mathcal{ALT} \cup \mathcal{CLTT} \cup \mathcal{SLTT} \cup \mathcal{STT}$$

where:

- $\mathcal{ALT}$ is the set of ODMG *atomic literal types*, as specified by Definition 2;
- $\mathcal{CLTT}$ is the set of *T*_ODMG *collection literal types*; it is defined as the following set $\mathcal{CLTT} = \{\mathtt{Set<t>} \mid \mathtt{t} \in \mathcal{T}\} \cup \{\mathtt{Bag<t>} \mid \mathtt{t} \in \mathcal{T}\} \cup \{\mathtt{List<t>} \mid \mathtt{t} \in \mathcal{T}\} \cup \{\mathtt{Array<t>} \mid \mathtt{t} \in \mathcal{T}\}$;

[5] Type **`TimeStamp`** will be described in Subsection 3.3.

- $\mathcal{SLTT}$ is the set of T_ODMG *structured literal types*; it is defined as the following set $\mathcal{SLTT} = \mathcal{SLT} \cup \{$**TimeInterval**$\}$;
- $\mathcal{STT}$ is the set of T_ODMG *struct literal types*; it is defined as the following set $\mathcal{STT} = \{\texttt{Struct}\{\texttt{t}_1\ p_1; \ldots; \texttt{t}_n\ p_n\ \} \mid \texttt{t}_i \in \mathcal{T},\ a_i \in \mathcal{AN},\ i \in [1, n]\ \}$.

□

Now we can define the set of T_ODMG types $\mathcal{T}$.

Definition 6 (*T_ODMG Types*). The set of T_ODMG types $\mathcal{T}$ is defined as follows.

$$\mathcal{T} = \text{ODMG}\mathcal{TT} \cup \mathcal{OTT} \cup \mathcal{LTT}.$$

□

In the remainder of the discussion we use ODMG$\mathcal{ST}$ to denote the set of static, that is non temporal, T_ODMG types. Formally , ODMG$\mathcal{ST} = \mathcal{T} \setminus$ ODMG$\mathcal{TT}$.

3.3 Temporal structured literals

In what follows we briefly discuss the interfaces specified for **TimeStamp**, defined as part of the ODMG standard [4], and **TimeInterval**, the new structured literal we propose. For sake of simplicity, in introducing the following interfaces we do not deal with different time zones.

As we will see in Section 6, most models support a linear discrete time structure and a single time dimension, that is, valid time. ODMG structured types provide data structures for managing time. Thus, to adhere to the ODMG model, we have chosen to support time features using the ODMG existing data structures. We will see in Subsection 3.4 that this is conceptually equivalent to supporting a linear discrete time structure.

The structured type **TimeStamp**, whose interface is described in Figure 1, provides the time granularity of our model. In what follows a time instant t is therefore represented as a pair $\langle date, time \rangle$, where *date* is a value of type **Date** that is, a year, a month and a day, whereas *time* is a value of type **Time**, that is, a particular time instant in such date, i.e., hour, minutes and seconds. In the following if **T** has type **TimeStamp** then **T.date** denotes the date and **T.time** denotes the time instant in the day, moreover **T.date.year = T.year** and so on. We do not present here the interface specifications of **Date** and **Time** for lack of space; we refer the interested reader to [4].

Note that we have chosen to model time instants as pairs $\langle date, time \rangle$. We could alternatively have chosen to employ dates as our time granularity.

In order to support time intervals, we introduce a new type **TimeInterval**, whose interface is described in Figure 2. We do not use the type interface **Interval** supplied by ODMG for intervals. Such interface does not implement our abstract notion of interval as a a set of consecutive time instants between two given instants, that is, two values of type **TimeStamp**. Rather it is only used to perform some operations on **Time** and **TimeStamp** objects. The type **TimeInterval** is

```
interface TimeStamp {
   typedef Unsigned short ushort;
   Date date();
   Time time();
   ushort year();
   ushort month();
   ushort day();
   ushort hour();
   ushort minute();
   float second();

   TimeStamp plus(in Interval an_interval);
   TimeStamp minus(in Interval an_interval);

   Boolean is_equal(in TimeStamp t);
   Boolean is_greater(in TimeStamp t);
   Boolean is_greater_or_equal(in TimeStamp t);
   Boolean is_less(in TimeStamp t);
   Boolean is_less_or_equal(in TimeStamp t);
   Boolean is_between(in TimeStamp a_t, in TimeStamp b_t);
   };
```

Fig. 1. TimeStamp interface

```
interface TimeInterval {
   TimeStamp start();
   TimeStamp end();

   TimeInterval equal(in TimeInterval I);
   Set<TimeInterval> union(in Set<TimeInterval> SI,in TimeInterval I);
   TimeInterval intersect(in TimeInterval I);

   Boolean inclusion(in TimeInterval I);
   Boolean in_interval(in TimeStamp t);
   };
```

Fig. 2. TimeInterval interface

characterized by two elements **start** and **end**, both of type **TimeStamp**, denoting the starting and ending time of the interval, respectively.

In order to simplify the notation, we use symbols, such as "=", "≤", with the obvious meaning instead of operation names. For example the symbol "=" is used to denote the equality between two structured literals; this implies that the corresponding operation, **equal**, is implemented for the type. Other examples are "≤" for **is_less_or_equal** between values of type **TimeStamp**, "∪" for **union** between time intervals etc.

Let **I** be a variable of type **TimeInterval** such that $\texttt{I.start} = \langle date_1, time_1 \rangle$ and $\texttt{I.end} = \langle date_2, time_2 \rangle$. Thus **I** denotes the set of consecutive time instants, including all time instants between t_1, that is the time instant identified by $\langle date_1, time_1 \rangle$, and t_2, that is the time instant identified by $\langle date_2, time_2 \rangle$, t_1 and t_2 included. The constraint imposed on objects of type **TimeInterval** is that $\texttt{I.start} \leq \texttt{I.end}$. A single time instant can be represented as a time interval **I** such that $\texttt{I.start} = \texttt{I.end}$, whereas if $\texttt{I.start} = \texttt{I.end} = \texttt{nil}$, **I** denotes the null interval. The operators **equal** (=), **intersect** (∩), **inclusion** (⊆) have the well-known semantics of interval operations. Moreover, function **in_interval** (∈) takes as arguments an instant t and an interval **I** and returns true if t is one of the instants denoted by interval **I**. The **union** (∪) operation takes as input an interval and a set of intervals and returns the set of intervals consisting of the given set plus the given interval. In the following, we often use a set of disjoint intervals $I = \{\texttt{I}_1, \ldots, \texttt{I}_n\}$ as a compact notation for the set of time instants included in these intervals.

3.4 *T_*ODMG values

For each predefined atomic literal type $\texttt{t} \in \mathcal{ALT}$, we postulate the existence of a non-empty set of values, denoted as $dom(\texttt{t})$. For instance, the domain of the atomic literal type **Boolean** consists of the two classical boolean values **true** and **false**. The domain of type **TimeStamp** is the set $\mathcal{TIME}$, which is a set of pairs $\langle date, time \rangle$, where *date* is a value of type **Date** and *time* is a value of type **Time**. We can say that $\mathcal{TIME}$ represents the sequence of time instants starting from the first time instant considered in the system until *now*, where *now* is the timestamp corresponding to the current date and hour according to the system clock. Such set is isomorphic to the set of natural numbers $\mathbb{N}$.

It is easy to verify that the set of values of type **Date** is isomorphic to a subset of $\mathbb{N}$ (in the following we denote with D this subset), and that the set of values of type **Time** is obviously a finite set (denoted in the following with S).[6] Therefore $\mathcal{TIME}$ is isomorphic to $D \times S$ and, since $D \times S$ is isomorphic to $\mathbb{N}$, $\mathcal{TIME}$ is then isomorphic to $\mathbb{N}$. Thus, we assume time to be discrete.

Of course, since each pair belonging to $\mathcal{TIME}$ is an instance of the ODMG type **TimeStamp**, the operations defined for type **TimeStamp** can be applied on it. Moreover the operations of the type **Date** can be applied to the first component of the pair, whereas the operations of the type **Time** can be applied to the

[6] The number of seconds in a day is a finite number.

second component of the pair. Moreover values of type `TimeInterval` are pairs where each component is of type `TimeStamp`. Then, the set of values of type `TimeInterval` is the cartesian product $\mathcal{TIME} \times \mathcal{TIME}$.

Note that in T_ODMG oids in $\mathcal{OI}$ are handled as values. Thus, an object identifier i is a value of an object type in $\mathcal{CI}$. We consider as legal values for an object type $\mathtt{t} \in \mathcal{CI}$ all the oids of objects belonging to the extent of `t` both as instances or as proper instances.[7] The set of objects instances of a class changes dynamically over time. Thus, to define the extension, that is, the set of legal values for T_ODMG object types, we introduce a function π: $\mathcal{CI} \times \mathcal{TIME} \rightarrow 2^{\mathcal{OI}}$, assigning an extent to each object type, for each instant t. For each $\mathtt{t} \in \mathcal{CI}$, $\pi(\mathtt{t}, t)$ is the set of the identifiers of objects that, at time t, belong to the extent of `t` as instances. To emphasize the fact that the interpretation of a type can only be given fixing a time instant t, we denote the set of legal values for type `t` at time t as $[\![\mathtt{t}]\!]_t$.

The following definition states the set of legal values for each T_ODMG type, denoted with $\mathcal{V}$.

Definition 7 (*Type Legal Values*). $[\![\mathtt{t}]\!]_t$ denotes the extension of type $\mathtt{t} \in \mathcal{T}$ at time t.

- $nil \in [\![\mathtt{t}]\!]_t, \forall \mathtt{t} \in \mathcal{T}$;
- $[\![\mathtt{t}]\!]_t = dom(\mathtt{t}), \forall \mathtt{t} \in \mathcal{ALT}$;
- $[\![\mathtt{TimeStamp}]\!]_t = \mathcal{TIME}$;
- $[\![\mathtt{TimeInterval}]\!]_t = \mathcal{TIME} \times \mathcal{TIME}$;[8]
- $[\![\mathtt{t}]\!]_t = \pi(\mathtt{t}, t), \forall \mathtt{t} \in \mathcal{OTT}$;
- $[\![\mathtt{Set<t>}]\!]_t = 2^{[\![\mathtt{t}]\!]_t}$;
- $[\![\mathtt{Bag<t>}]\!]_t = multiset([\![\mathtt{t}]\!]_t)$; [9]
- $[\![\mathtt{List<t>}]\!]_t = \{[v_1, \ldots, v_n] \mid n \geq 0, v_i \in [\![\mathtt{t}]\!]_t, \forall i \in [1, n]\}$;
- $[\![\mathtt{Array<t>}]\!]_t = \{[[1, v_1], \ldots, [n, v_n]] \mid n \geq 0, v_i \in [\![\mathtt{t}]\!]_t, \forall i \in [1, n]\}$;
- $[\![\mathtt{Struct}\{\mathtt{t}_1\, p_1; \ldots; \mathtt{t}_n\, p_n\}]\!]_t = \{\langle v_1 p_1, \ldots, v_n p_n \rangle \mid p_i \in \mathcal{AN} \cup \mathcal{RN},\ v_i \in [\![\mathtt{t}_i]\!]_t, \forall i \in [1, n]\}$;
- $[\![temporal(\mathtt{t})]\!]_t = \{f \mid f : \mathcal{TIME} \rightarrow \bigcup_{t' \in \mathcal{TIME}} [\![\mathtt{t}]\!]_{t'}$ is a partial function such that $\forall t'$ if $f(t')$ is defined then $f(t') \in [\![\mathtt{t}]\!]_{t'}\}$. □

Given an instant t the extensions of predefined basic value types are the elements of their corresponding domains, the extensions of classes are their explicit

[7] According to the usual terminology, an object is a *proper instance* of a class c, if c is the most specific class, in the inheritance hierarchy, to which the object belongs to. If an object is a proper instance of a class it is also an *instance* of all the superclasses of c.

[8] We do not specify the extensions of all structured literals, `Date`, `Time` and so on, since they are the obvious set of values.

[9] As specified in the definition of the model [4], `Bag` denotes unordered collections of elements that may contain duplicates. In the scientific literature, such data structures are sometimes referred to as *multisets*, thus we denote as $multiset([\![\mathtt{t}]\!]_t)$ the possible multisets whose elements are of type `t`.

extents at time t, whereas the set of legal values of the collection literal types are defined recursively in terms of the legal values of their component types. The extension of a temporal type *temporal*(`t`) is the set of partial functions from $\mathcal{TIME}$ (i.e, the set of legal values for type `TimeStamp`) to the union of the sets of legal values for type `t` for each instant t' in $\mathcal{TIME}$. The value of a variable of type *temporal*(`t`) can thus be represented as a set of pairs $(t, f(t))$, where f is a partial function, t is an element of $\mathcal{TIME}$ and $f(t)$ is the value of function f at time t. Usually, the value of a variable of type *temporal*(`t`) does not change at each instant. Therefore, its value can be, more concisely, represented as a set of pairs $\{\langle I_1, v_1\rangle, \ldots, \langle I_n, v_n\rangle\}$, where $v_1, \ldots, v_n$ are legal values for `t`, and $I_1, \ldots, I_n$ are time intervals, such that the variable assumes the value v_i for each instant in I_i, $i \in [1, n]$. We adopt this representation throughout the paper.

Example 1 Let t be an instant, $\mathtt{i}_1$ and $\mathtt{i}_2 \in \mathcal{OI}$ such that $\mathtt{i}_1$, $\mathtt{i}_2 \in \pi(\texttt{Person}, t)$.

- `10,100` $\in [\![$ `Short` $]\!]_t$;
- $\{\mathtt{i}_1, \mathtt{i}_2\} \in [\![$ `Set<Person>` $]\!]_t$;
- $\langle$ `Bob name;` $\{\langle \mathtt{I}_1, \mathtt{40}\rangle\}$ `score`$\rangle \in [\![$ `Struct{string name;` *temporal*(`Short`) `score}` $]\!]_t$

  where:

  $\mathtt{I}_1$`.start=` $\langle \langle$`1995,4,20`$\rangle, \langle$`00,00,00`$\rangle\rangle$
  $\mathtt{I}_1$`.end=` $\langle \langle$`1995,4,25`$\rangle, \langle$`00,00,00`$\rangle \rangle$

  Note that the value of type `TimeStamp` where the second component of the pair is $\langle$`00,00,00`$\rangle$ denotes the first instant of the day corresponding to the considered date. ◇

4 Classes

As we have seen in Section 2 an object type interface or, analogously, a class interface consists of a set of property (attribute and relationship) specifications, and a set of operation specifications.

Each attribute is characterized by its name, its *temporal nature* and its type. Each relationship is characterized by its name, its temporal nature, its type[10] and its inverse. T_ODMG supports properties of three different temporal kinds: temporal, immutable and static. A temporal property is a property whose value[11] may change over time, and whose values at different times are recorded in the database. An immutable property is a property whose value cannot be modified during the object lifespan, whereas a static property is a property whose value can change over time, but whose past values are not recorded in the database.

[10] Suppose that a relationship is defined between two classes C_1 and C_2, then in C_1 the type of the relationship is C_2; similarly, in C_2, the type of the inverse relationship is C_1.

[11] In this context by value of a relationship we mean the set of objects involved in the relationship.

In $T_$ODMG a *lifespan* is associated with each class, representing the time interval during which the class has existed. We assume the lifespan of a class to be contiguous.

Definition 8 (*Class Interface*). A class interface is a 6-tuple $(c, c\_type, lifespan, attr, rel, meth)$, where:

$c \in \mathcal{CI}$ is the class identifier;
$c\_type \in \mathcal{OTT} \cup \mathcal{CI}$ is the class type;
$lifespan \in (\mathcal{TIME} \times \mathcal{TIME})$ is the lifespan of the class;
$attr$ is a set containing an item for each attribute of the class. Each item is a 3-tuple $(a\_name, a\_nature, a\_type)$, where:

- $a\_name \in \mathcal{AN}$ is the attribute name;
- $a\_nature \in \{\texttt{temporal}, \texttt{static}, \texttt{immutable}\}$ is the attribute temporal nature;
- $a\_type \in \text{ODMG}\mathcal{ST}$ is the attribute domain type;

rel is a set containing an item for each relationship of the class. Each item is a 4-tuple $(r\_name, r\_nature, r\_type, r\_inv)$, where:

- $r\_name \in \mathcal{RN}$ is the relationship name;
- $r\_nature \in \{\texttt{temporal}, \texttt{static}, \texttt{immutable}\}$ is the relationship temporal nature;
- r_type can be of two different categories: $r\_type \in \mathcal{CI}$ or $r\_type \in \{\texttt{Set <t>} \mid \texttt{t} \in \mathcal{CI}\} \cup \{\texttt{Bag <t>} \mid \texttt{t} \in \mathcal{CI}\} \cup \{\texttt{List <t>} \mid \texttt{t} \in \mathcal{CI}\} \cup \{\texttt{Array <t>} \mid \texttt{t} \in \mathcal{CI}\}$;
- r_inv is a pair denoting the inverse traversal path of the relationship, that is, $r\_inv = (r\_inv\_name, r\_inv\_type)$ where:
  - $r\_inv\_name \in \mathcal{RN}$ is the inverse relationship name;
  - $r\_inv\_type \in \mathcal{OTT}$ is the inverse relationship domain type;

$meth$ is a set containing an item for each method of the class. Each item is a pair (m_name, m_sign), where:

- $m\_name \in \mathcal{MN}$ is the method name;
- m_sign is the signature of the method, expressed as:

$$p\_name_1 : \mathtt{t}_1 \times \ldots \times p\_name_j : \mathtt{t}_j \rightarrow \mathtt{t}_{j+1} \times \ldots \times \mathtt{t}_n$$

where p_name_i and $\mathtt{t}_i \in \mathcal{T}$, $i \in [1, j]$, denote names and types of input parameters and and $\mathtt{t}_i \in \mathcal{T}$, $i \in [j+1, n]$, denote types of output parameters.[12]

□

[12] Note that in the ODMG model input parameters have names, whereas output parameters do not have names. Moreover note that if n=0 the method has no parameters, the notation $p\_name_1 : \mathtt{t}_1 \times \ldots \times p\_name_j : \mathtt{t}_j \rightarrow \mathtt{void}$ denotes a method with no output parameters and, similarly, $\rightarrow \mathtt{t}_{j+1} \times \ldots \times \mathtt{t}_n$ denotes a method with no input parameters.

In $T_$ODMG the distinction between the class identifier and the class type is relevant. $T_$ODMG supports two different kinds of object types: atomic object types and collection object types. For what concerns atomic object types, the type of the class coincides with the class identifier.[13] By contrast, the class identifiers of a collection object type is the name assigned to it by the user, while its class type is a type belonging to $\mathcal{COTT}$.

Note that the *attr* and *rel* components of the interface constitute the property specification.

In order to avoid redundancy, we allow only the use of static types in the definition of attribute types and relationship domains. For example, we specify a temporal attribute a of type $temporal(\mathtt{t})$ by means of the 3-tuple $(a, \mathtt{temporal}, \mathtt{t})$ instead of by $(a, \mathtt{temporal}, temporal(\mathtt{t}))$. Given an attribute specification $(a, nat, \mathtt{t})$ we can easily derive the type $\mathtt{t}'$ of a. If $nat \in \{\mathtt{temporal}, \mathtt{immutable}\}$ then $\mathtt{t}' = temporal(\mathtt{t})$ if $nat \in \{\mathtt{temporal}, \mathtt{immutable}\}$; if $nat \in \{\mathtt{static}\}$ then $\mathtt{t}' = \mathtt{t}$. We impose the constraint, on attribute specification, that type $\mathtt{t}'$, computed with the method sketched above, must be a legal $T_$ODMG type. For instance, $(a, \mathtt{temporal}, \mathtt{Set}\langle temporal(\mathtt{t}'')\rangle)$ is an invalid attribute specification since $temporal(\mathtt{Set}\langle temporal(\mathtt{t}'')\rangle)$ is not a legal $T_$ODMG type. The same considerations hold for relationships.

We consider immutable attributes as a particular kind of temporal ones, that is, as temporal attributes whose values never change during the object lifespan. Thus, the value of an immutable attribute is modeled by means of a constant function from the temporal domain to the set of legal values for the attribute. Therefore, we can distinguish among temporal, immutable and static attributes. A temporal attribute is an attribute with a temporal type and whose value is a function from a temporal domain; an immutable attribute is an attribute with a temporal type but whose value is a *constant* function[14] from the temporal domain; finally, a static attribute is an attribute with a static type (that is, whose value is not a function from the temporal domain).

As we have seen in Section 2, a relationship can be between two types, each of which must have instances that can be referenced by object identifiers. Moreover to implement one-to-many and many-to-many relationships the relationship domain can be a set, a bag, a list or an array of objects. This is the reason why in the specification of the component *rel* of a class, *r_type* can be an object type or a collection type, whose inner type is an object type.

Similarly to attributes, relationships can be of three different types: temporal, static and immutable. If a relationship r is temporal, we are interested in recording the entire history of the relationship. This means that, for each object, we are interested in keeping track of the objects, or the set (bag, list, array) of objects, which are connected to it through r during each instant of the object lifespan. We can view the value of a temporal relationship, whose *r_type* is a type $\mathtt{t}$, as a partial function, r, from $\mathcal{TIME}$ to the union of the sets of legal values for type $\mathtt{t}$, for each instant t' in $\mathcal{TIME}$, such that if $r(t')$ is defined then

[13] We recall that $\mathcal{AOT} = \mathcal{CI}$.

[14] In both temporal and immutable attributes the function is partial.

$r(t') \in [\![\mathtt{t}]\!]_{t'}$. Thus, the value of a temporal relationship where $r\_type = \mathtt{t}$ is of type $temporal(\mathtt{t})$, where $temporal(\mathtt{t})$ is a T_ODMG legal type. The relationships **teaches** and **is_taught_by**, introduced in Section 2, are examples of temporal relationships. Usually a professor teaches different courses in different periods of his career and it could be useful to keep track of the courses a professor teaches over time. Static relationships are relationships with a static type. For what concerns this kind of relationships, we are interested only in the current value and not in recording the past values of the relationship. An example of static relationship is the relationship **live_in** between the classes **Person** and **City**. Usually one is interested in knowing the city where a person *actually* lives and not in the cities where the person has lived before. Immutable relationships are a particular type of temporal relationships. The value of an immutable relationship r, with $r\_type = \mathtt{t}$, is a constant function from $\mathcal{TIME}$ to type $\mathtt{t}$, that is, the type of an immutable relationship is $temporal(\mathtt{t})$, but the value is constant for each time instant. An example of an immutable relationship could be the relationship **son_of**, relating a person with his parents.

As we have seen in Section 2 supertype information, extent naming and specification of keys are characteristics of classes. Class characteristics can be defined as follows.

Definition 9 (*Class Characteristics*). Let C be a class and let c be its class identifier, the characteristics of C are represented as a 3-tuple $(super, extent, keys)$, where:

super is the set of class names of the direct superclasses of c;
extent is a pair (e_name, e_set), where:
- *e_name* is the extent name;
- *e_set* keeps track of the instances in the extent of C over time; it is a value of type $temporal(\mathtt{Set<c>})$;

keys is a set of pairs $(k\_nature, prop)$ where:
- $k\_nature \in \{\mathtt{absolute}, \mathtt{relative}\}$;
- $prop \in \mathcal{AN} \cup \mathcal{RN}$.

□

As in the ODMG data model these characteristics are not mandatory for a class, any of the components of the 3-tuple may be empty.

The class characteristics affected by the introduction of temporal features are *extent* and *keys*. Since we do not consider schema modifications, the set of superclasses of a given class C is invariant over time.

Usually, the extent, that is, the set of all the instances of a class, is associated with each class. In a temporal context the extent of a class can vary over time. Then, a temporal value *extent.e_set* is associated with each class C representing the objects instances of C over time: *extent.e_set* is a value of type $temporal(\mathtt{Set<c>})$, where c is the identifier of class C.

In the remainder of the discussion we use function: $pe\_set : \mathcal{CI} \times \mathcal{TIME} \rightarrow \mathcal{COT}$, which takes as argument a class identifier c and an instant t and returns the set of oids of objects for which c is the most specific type along the inheritance hierarchy at time t, that is, the set of proper instances of c. If c is the identifier of the class, the type of the value returned by *pe_set* is **Set** <c>.

Let C be the class identified by c. Then, $pe\_set(c,t) \subseteq C.extent.e\_set(t)$, $\forall t \in C.lifespan$, since all objects instances of a class at a given instant are also proper instances of the class at the same instant. Function π (cfr. Table 1), is such that, for each class name c and for each $t \in C.lifespan$, $\pi(c,t) = C.extent.e\_set(t)$.

For what concerns *keys*, each property part of a key can be of two kinds: absolute or relative. In order to clarify the meaning of these kinds of keys we have to distinguish between static, immutable and temporal properties.

- If the property is static and the key is `relative`, no two instances may have the same value for the property within the same extent.
- If the property is temporal or immutable and the key is `relative`, no two instances may have the same value for the property within the same extent for an overlapping period of time.
- If the property is static, temporal or immutable and the key is `absolute`, no two instances may have the same value for the property even if they belong to different extents and in different time periods.

Example 2 Consider a class `Person`. Suppose that objects of this class have as attributes a `ssn` and a `name` which are immutable during the object lifetime, an `address` whose variations over time are not relevant for the application at hand. Two temporal relationships `spouse` and `children` and two operations `marriage` and `move` belong to the interface, too. The corresponding T_ODMG class interface is:

$c = c\_type = \texttt{Person}$
$lifespan = [start, now]$
$attr = \{(\texttt{ssn}, \texttt{immutable}, \texttt{String}), (\texttt{name}, \texttt{immutable}, \texttt{String}),$
$\quad (\texttt{address}, \texttt{static}, \texttt{String})\}$
$rel = \{(\texttt{spouse}, \texttt{temporal}, \texttt{Person}, (\texttt{spouse}, \texttt{Person})),$
$\quad (\texttt{children}, \texttt{temporal}, \texttt{Set<Person>}, (\texttt{parents}, \texttt{Person})),$
$\quad (\texttt{parents}, \texttt{temporal}, \texttt{Set<Person>}, (\texttt{children}, \texttt{Person}))\}$
$meth = \{(\texttt{marriage}, \texttt{p} : \texttt{Person} \rightarrow \texttt{Boolean}), (\texttt{move}, \texttt{newaddress} : \texttt{String} \rightarrow)\}$

Suppose moreover that `Person` is a direct subclass of `Object`. Let $\texttt{i}_1, \ldots, \texttt{i}_4 \in \mathcal{OI}$ denote instances of type `Person`. Suppose that two instances of the class cannot have the same `ssn` whatever extent is considered, or be married to the same person in an overlapping period of time. Then, the corresponding class characteristics are:

$super = \texttt{Object}$
$extent = (\texttt{person}, \{\langle [start, now], \{\texttt{i}_1, \ldots, \texttt{i}_4\}\rangle\})$
$keys = \{\langle \texttt{absolute}, \texttt{ssn}\rangle, \langle \texttt{relative}, \texttt{spouse}\rangle\}$

◇

According to the previous definitions the class specification is defined as follows.

Definition 10 (*Class*). A class C is a 3-tuple $(int, char, impl)$ where:

int is the class interface, as specified by Definition 8;
char are the class characteristics, as specified by Definition 9;
impl is the class implementation.

□

Note that, due to space limitations, in the paper we do not give any description of class implementation. An informal definition of class implementation in ODMG can be found in [4]. To simplify the notation, given a class C we denote each component of its interface with the following dot notation: $C.c$ denotes the class identifier,[15] $C.lifespan$ denotes the class lifespan, and so on. The same simplified notation is used for class characteristics. Note that we can adopt this simplified notation because each component of a class interface and of a class characteristics has a distinct name.

We now discuss relationships between a class and its property type. The identifier c, of a class C, denotes its corresponding object type. Such object type is the type of the identifiers of the objects instances of C. Suppose that class C has as *attr* component the set: $\{attr_1, \ldots, attr_n\}$, where $attr_i = (a_i, nat_i, \mathtt{t}_i)$, $i \in [1, n]$ and as *rel* component the set: $\{rel_1, \ldots, rel_{\bar{n}}\}$, where $rel_i = (r_i, nat_i, \mathtt{d}_i, inv_i)$, $i \in [1, \bar{n}]$. The following property types can be associated with C.

- *Structural property type.* It represents the type of the attributes and relationships of instances of C. It is defined by the pair (t_attr, t_rel) where:
  $t\_attr = \mathtt{Struct}\{\mathtt{t}'_1\ a_1; \ldots; \mathtt{t}'_n\ a_n\ \}$ where $\forall i \in [1, n]$: $\mathtt{t}'_i = \mathtt{t}_i$, if nat_i=$\mathtt{static}$; $\mathtt{t}'_i = temporal(\mathtt{t}_i)$, if $nat_i \in \{\mathtt{immutable}, \mathtt{temporal}\}$;
  $t\_rel = \mathtt{Struct}\{\mathtt{d}'_1\ r_1; \ldots; \mathtt{d}'_{\bar{n}}\ r_{\bar{n}}\ \}$, where $\forall i \in [1, \bar{n}]$: $\mathtt{d}'_i = \mathtt{d}_i$, if nat_i=$\mathtt{static}$; $\mathtt{d}'_i = temporal(\mathtt{d}_i)$, if $nat_i \in \{\mathtt{immutable}, \mathtt{temporal}\}$.
- *Historical property type.* It represents the type of the temporal properties of instances of C. It is defined by the pair (t_attr, t_rel) where:
  $t\_attr = \mathtt{Struct}\{\mathtt{t}'_k\ a_k; \ldots; \mathtt{t}'_m\ a_m\}$ where $1 \leq k \leq m \leq n$ and $\{a_k, \ldots, a_m\} = \{a_i \mid a_i \in \{a_1, \ldots, a_n\}\ \wedge\ nat_i \in \{\mathtt{immutable}, \mathtt{temporal}\}\}$;
  $t\_rel = \mathtt{Struct}\{\mathtt{d}'_{\bar{k}}\ r_{\bar{k}}; \ldots; \mathtt{d}'_{\bar{m}}\ r_{\bar{m}}\ \}$, where $1 \leq \bar{k} \leq \bar{m} \leq \bar{n}$ and $\{r_{\bar{k}}, \ldots, r_{\bar{m}}\} = \{r_i \mid r_i \in \{r_1, \ldots, r_{\bar{n}}\}\ \wedge\ nat_i \in \{\mathtt{immutable}, \mathtt{temporal}\}\}$.
- *Static property type.* It represents the type of the static attributes and relationships of instances of C. It is defined by the pair (t_attr, t_rel) where:
  $t\_attr = \mathtt{Struct}\{\mathtt{t}'_j\ a_j; \ldots; \mathtt{t}'_l\ a_l\ \}$, where $1 \leq j \leq l \leq n$ and $\{a_j, \ldots, a_l\} = \{a_i \mid a_i \in \{a_1, \ldots, a_n\} \wedge\ nat_i = \mathtt{static}\}$;
  $t\_rel = \mathtt{Struct}\{\mathtt{d}'_{\bar{j}}\ r_{\bar{j}}; \ldots; \mathtt{d}'_{\bar{l}}\ r_{\bar{l}}\ \}$, where $1 \leq \bar{j} \leq \bar{l} \leq \bar{n}$ and $\{r_{\bar{j}}, \ldots, r_{\bar{l}}\} = \{r_i \mid r_i \in \{r_1, \ldots, r_{\bar{n}}\} \wedge\ nat_i = \mathtt{static}\}$.

[15] The correct notation would be *C.int.c*.

The notions of *structural*, *historical* and *static* property types of a class will be used in the next section to check object consistency. We define three functions: *type*, *h_type*, *s_type*: $\mathcal{CI} \rightarrow \mathcal{T} \times \mathcal{T}$, taking as argument a class identifier c, and returning the structural, the historical and the static property type of the class identified by c, respectively.[16]

5 Objects

$\mathcal{T}$_ODMG handles in a uniform way both historical and static objects. An object is historical if it contains at least one property with a temporal domain, it is static otherwise. Each object has a lifespan, representing the time interval during which the object exists. As for class interfaces, we assume the lifespan of an object to be contiguous. Objects can be instances of different classes during their lifetime, but we can assume that, for each instant in their lifespan, there exists at least an interface extent to which they belong to.[17] For example, an employee can be fired and rehired, but he remains instance of the class *person*, superclass of the class *employee*, till the end of its lifetime. Moreover, for each historical object the history of the most specific class to which it belongs to during its lifespan is recorded. On the contrary, for each static object, only the class identifier of the most specific class to which it currently belongs to is maintained.

Definition 11 (*Object*). An object o is a 5-tuple $(i, lifespan, v, r, class\text{-}history)$, where:

$i \in \mathcal{OI}$ is the oid of o;

$lifespan \in (\mathcal{TIME} \times \mathcal{TIME})$ is the lifespan of o;

$v \in \mathcal{V}$ is a value, containing the values of each attribute of o. It is a struct value $\langle v_1^a\ a_1, \ldots, v_n^a\ a_n \rangle$, where $a_1, \ldots, a_n \in \mathcal{AN}$ are the names of the attributes of o and $v_1^a, \ldots, v_n^a \in \mathcal{V}$ are their corresponding values;

$r \in \mathcal{V}$ is a value, containing the values of each relationship of o. It is a struct value $\langle v_1^r\ r_1, \ldots, v_n^r\ r_n \rangle$, where $r_1, \ldots, r_n \in \mathcal{RN}$ are the names of the relationships of o and $v_1^r, \ldots, v_n^r \in \mathcal{V}$ are their corresponding values;

class-history stores information about the most specific class to which o belongs to over time. It is a set $\{\langle I_1, c_1 \rangle, \ldots, \langle I_n, c_n \rangle\}$, where $I_1, \ldots, I_n$ are time intervals, $c_1, \ldots c_n$ are class identifiers, such that c_i is the class identifier of the most specific class to which o belongs to in I_i, $i \in [1, n]$. □

If o is static, *class-history* records only to the most specific class to which o currently belongs.

---

[16] Note that function *h_type* returns a null value when its argument is the identifier of a class whose instances are static, whereas function *s_type* returns a null value when its argument is a class whose instances only have temporal properties.

[17] This class is the most general class (in the inheritance hierarchy) the object has ever belonged to.

Example 3 Suppose that $\texttt{i}_1, \ldots, \texttt{i}_7 \in \mathcal{OI}$ and $\texttt{Person} \in \mathcal{CI}$. The following is an example of T_Chimera object:

$i = \texttt{i}_1$
$lifespan = I$ where $I = \langle t_1, t_2 \rangle$ and:
$t_1 = \langle\langle \texttt{1965, 3, 21}\rangle, \langle \texttt{00, 00, 00}\rangle\rangle$ $t_2 = now$
$v = \langle\ \{\langle I,\ \texttt{JS65I23}\rangle\}\ \texttt{ssn},$
$\{\langle I,\ \texttt{JohnSmith}\rangle\}\ \texttt{name},$
$\texttt{"Fifth Avenue 275 NY"}\ \ \texttt{address}\ \rangle$
$r = \langle\ \{\langle\langle t_3, t_2\rangle,\ \texttt{i}_2\rangle\}\ \texttt{spouse},\ \{\langle\langle t_4, t_5\rangle,\ \{\texttt{i}_3\}\rangle, \langle\langle t_6, t_2\rangle,\ \{\texttt{i}_3, \texttt{i}_4\}\rangle\}\ \texttt{children}\rangle,$
where:
$t_3 = \langle\langle \texttt{1990, 5, 14}\rangle, \langle \texttt{00, 00, 00}\rangle\rangle$
$t_4 = \langle\langle \texttt{1993, 12, 31}\rangle, \langle \texttt{00, 00, 00}\rangle\rangle$
$t_5 = \langle\langle \texttt{1995, 1, 17}\rangle, \langle \texttt{23, 59, 59}\rangle\rangle$
$t_6 = \langle\langle \texttt{1995, 1, 18}\rangle, \langle \texttt{00, 00, 00}\rangle\rangle$
$class\text{-}history = \{\langle I, \texttt{Person}\rangle\}$

◇

In a temporal context, several temporal constraints must be satisfied by object lifespans. To formalize these constraints we define function $o\_lifespan$: $\mathcal{OI} \rightarrow \mathcal{TIME} \times \mathcal{TIME}$, that given an oid i returns the lifespan of the object identified by i. Obviously, information about the historical extent of a class must be consistent with the class histories of the objects in the database, as stated by the following invariant.

Invariant 1 $\forall i' \in \mathcal{OI}, \forall c' \in \mathcal{CI}, \forall t \in \mathcal{TIME}$, let o be the object such that $o.i = i'$, C be the class such that $C.c = c'$, then

1. $i' \in C.e\_set(t) \Rightarrow t \in o\_lifespan(i')$;
2. $(\forall t \in I, i' \in pe\_set(c', t)) \Leftrightarrow \langle I, c'\rangle \in o.class\text{-}history.$ △

Moreover, the lifespan of an object can be partitioned into a set of intervals, depending on the object most specific class. Indeed, an object can be member of different classes during its lifetime. Therefore, we introduce function $c\_lifespan$: $\mathcal{OI} \times \mathcal{CI} \rightarrow \mathcal{TIME} \times \mathcal{TIME}$, that given an oid i and a class identifier c, returns the interval representing the set of time instants in which i was a member of the class identified by c.[18] The temporal constraints stated by the following invariant must be satisfied.

Invariant 2 $\forall i' \in \mathcal{OI}, \forall c' \in \mathcal{CI}, \forall t \in \mathcal{TIME}$, then

1. $o\_lifespan(i') = \bigcup_{c \in \mathcal{CI}} c\_lifespan(i', c)$;
2. $t \in c\_lifespan(i, c') \Leftrightarrow i \in C.e\_set(t)$, where $c' = C.c$.[19] △

[18] Note that $c\_lifespan(i, c) = \bigcup_{\langle I_i, c_i\rangle \in o.class-history,\ c_i \text{ subclass of } c} I_i$. Functions $o\_lifespan$ and $c\_lifespan$ are similar to those defined in [18].

[19] This also implies that $t \in c\_lifespan(i', c') \Leftrightarrow i' \in [\![c']\!]_t$.

5.1 Consistency notions

Because of object migrations, the most specific class to which an object belongs to can vary over time. Moreover, an object can be an instance of the same class in different, not consecutive, time instants. As an example, consider the case of an employee that is promoted to manager, (*manager* being a subclass of *employee* with some extra attributes, like *subordinates* and *official_car*). The other case is the transfer of the manager back to normal employee status. The migration of an object from a class to another can cause the addition or the deletion of some attributes from the object. For instance, the promotion of an employee to the manager status has the effect of adding the attributes *subordinates* and *official_car* to the corresponding object, while the transfer of the manager back to the employee status causes dropping the attributes *subordinates* and *official_car* from the corresponding object. If the attributes *subordinates* and *official_car* are static, they are simply deleted from the object. No track of their existence is recorded in the object when it migrates to the class *employee*. If they are temporal, the values they had when the object migrated to the class *manager* are maintained in the object, even if they are not part of the object anymore.

We require that each object must be a consistent instance of all the classes to which it belongs to. In a context where objects can have both static and temporal attributes, the notion of consistency assumes a slightly different semantics with respect to its classical definition. Verifying the consistency of an object in a temporal context requires two steps. First, the set of attributes characterizing the object for each instant t of its lifespan must be determined. Then, the correctness of their values must be checked. Note that, if we consider an instant t less than the current time, we are able to identify only the temporal attributes characterizing the object at time t, since for static attributes we record only their current values. Thus, for instants lesser than the current time, it only makes sense to check the correctness of the values of the temporal and immutable attributes of the objects. Therefore, we start by introducing the following definition.

Definition 12 (*Meaningful Temporal Properties*). Let p be a temporal[20] property of an object o. Property p is said to be meaningful for o at time t, if p is defined at time t. □

We distinguish two kinds of consistency:

- *Historical consistency.* The values[21] of the temporal properties of the object at a given instant are legal values for the temporal properties of the class.
- *Static consistency.* The values of the static attributes of the object are legal values for the static attributes of the class.

[20] From now on with temporal property we mean a property which is temporal or immutable.

[21] Given an object o, with value of a relationship we mean the object or the set of objects in relationship with o.

Consider, for instance, an object $o = (i, lifespan, v, r, \textit{class-history})$, such that $v = \langle v_1^a\ a_1, \ldots, v_n^a\ a_n\rangle$ and $r = \langle v_1^r\ r_1, \ldots, v_n^r\ r_n\rangle$. Therefore, given an instant $t \in o.lifespan$, the following values can be defined:

- *Historical value.* It is a pair (v_attr, v_rel), where v_attr represents the values of the temporal attributes meaningful for the object at time t and v_rel represents the values of the temporal relationships meaningful for the object at time t. Let $\{a_k, \ldots, a_m\}$, $1 \le k \le m \le n$, be the subset of $\{a_1, \ldots, a_n\}$ consisting of all the names of the temporal attributes meaningful for o at time t and let $\{r_j, \ldots, r_l\}$, $1 \le j \le l \le n$, be the subset of $\{r_1, \ldots, r_n\}$ consisting of all the names of the temporal relationships meaningful for o at time t. The historical value of o at time t is defined as (v_attr, v_rel) where:
  $v\_attr = \langle v_k^a(t)\ a_k, \ldots, v_m^a(t)\ a_m\rangle$, where $v_i(t)$ denotes the value of a_i at time t, $i \in [k, m]$;
  $v\_rel = \langle v_j^r(t)\ r_j, \ldots, v_l^r(t)\ r_l\rangle$, where $v_i^r(t)$ denotes the value of r_i at time t, $i \in [j, l]$.
- *Static value.* It is a pair representing the values of the static properties of the object. Its definition is analogous to that of the historical value, considering static properties instead of temporal ones.

Thus, we define two functions: *h_state*: $\mathcal{OI} \times \mathcal{TIME} \rightarrow \mathcal{V} \times \mathcal{V}$, receiving an object identifier and an instant t as input, and returning the historical value of the object at time t; *s_state*: $\mathcal{OI} \rightarrow \mathcal{V} \times \mathcal{V}$, receiving an object identifier as input, and returning the static value of the object. Note that when an object consists only of temporal properties, *h_state* returns a snapshot of the value of the object properties for a specified time instant.

We are now ready to formally introduce the notions of *historical* and *static* consistency, by making use of functions *h_type* and *s_type* (cfr. Table 1). In the following, $\Pi_i(\langle e_1, \ldots, e_n\rangle)$ denotes the i-th component of the tuple $\langle e_1, \ldots, e_n\rangle$.

Definition 13 (*Historical Consistency*). An object $o = (i, lifespan, v, r, \textit{class-history})$ is an historically consistent instance of a class c' at time t iff the following conditions hold:

- $\Pi_1(h\_state(o.i, t))$ is a legal value for the attribute specification $\Pi_1(h\_type(c'))$;
- $\Pi_2(h\_state(o.i, t))$ is a legal value for the relationship specification $\Pi_2(h\_type(c'))$.

□

Definition 14 (*Static Consistency*). An object $o = (i, lifespan, v, r, \textit{class-history})$ is a statically consistent instance of a class c', if the following conditions hold:

- $\Pi_1(s\_state(o.i, t))$ is a legal value for the attribute specification $\Pi_1(s\_type(c'))$;
- $\Pi_2(s\_state(o.i, t))$ is a legal value for the relationship specification $\Pi_2(s\_type(c'))$.

□

The consistency of an object is checked only with respect to its most specific class, since if an object is consistent with respect to its most specific class, it is also consistent with respect to all its superclasses.

Definition 15 (*Object Consistency*). An object $o = (i, lifespan, v, r, class\text{-}history)$ is consistent iff the following conditions hold:

- For each pair $\langle I, c' \rangle$ in $o.class\text{-}history$, interval I is contained in the lifespan of the class identified by c', that is, $I \subseteq C.lifespan$, where C is the class such that $C.c = c'$.
- For each instant t of the object lifespan, a class c to which the object belongs to exists and, vice versa, each instant t such that $t \in I$ where $\langle I, c \rangle \in o.class\text{-}history$ belongs to the lifespan of the object: $\bigcup_{\langle I,c \rangle \in o.class-history} I = o.lifespan$.[22]
- If a temporal property p is meaningful at time t for object o then $t \in o.lifespan$.
- For each pair $\langle I, c' \rangle$ in $o.class\text{-}history$, o is an historically consistent instance of c', for each instant $t \in I$.
- Let $\langle I, c \rangle$ be the (unique) element of $o.class\text{-}history$, such that $now \in I$. Object o must be a statically consistent instance of class c. □

The above definition states that each object, for each instant t of its lifespan, must contain a value for each temporal property of the class to which it belongs to at time t, and this value must be of the correct type and that each instant t in which a property is defined belongs to the lifespan of the considered object. Moreover, at the current time also the consistency with respect to the static properties must be checked. This notion of consistency allows to uniformly handle both static and historical objects. In the case of static objects, Definition 15 reduces to the traditional notion of consistency.

6 Related work

Table 2 compares some temporal object-oriented data models proposed in the literature. Some considered approaches are compared under a different perspective by Snodgrass [12]. In [12] the emphasis is on temporal object-oriented query languages, while we consider only data model features. Moreover, in [12] only the temporal features are compared, disregarding the object-oriented ones, whereas we consider both.

Concerning the temporal aspects, most models support a linear discrete time structure,[23] whereas only few of them model a user-defined hierarchy of time types. Two time dimensions are of interest in temporal databases: *valid* time (the time a fact was true in reality) and *transaction* time (the time the fact was stored in the database). Most models consider only the valid time. Some approaches associate a timestamp with the whole object state; others associate a timestamp with each object attribute often regarding the value of a temporal attribute as a function from a temporal domain to the set of legal values for the

[22] Note that since we do not consider objects with multiple most specific classes we have that $\bigcap_{\langle I,c \rangle \in o.class-history} I = \emptyset$.

[23] We consider time structure and time dimension as discussed in [12].

attribute. This is also the approach taken in our model. Since the ODMG object model supports both attributes and relationships, both these kinds of object properties are extended with time in our model.

Another important characteristic is whether temporal, immutable and non temporal attributes are supported. A *temporal* (or historical) attribute is an attribute whose value may change over time, and whose values at different times are recorded in the database. An *immutable* attribute is an attribute whose value cannot be modified during the object lifetime,[24] whereas a *non temporal* (or static) attribute is an attribute whose value can change over time, but whose past values are not meaningful, and are thus not stored in the database. The support for static, immutable and temporal attributes has been firstly proposed in the T_Chimera data model [2, 3]. The main difference between T_Chimera and T_ODMG are, besides the underlying object data model extended with time, that T_ODMG also supports relationships, which are not supported in T_Chimera, and that T_ODMG allows the specification of (relative and absolute) keys.

Finally, some models keep track of the dynamic links between an object and its most specific class. Indeed, an important dynamic aspect of object-oriented databases is that an object can dynamically change type, by specializing or generalizing its current one.

	[7]	[8]	[9]	[10]	[11]	[15]	[18]	[14]	Ours
o-o data model	Oodaplex	generic	Tigukat	MAD	generic	OSAM*	Oodaplex	OM	ODMG
time structure	linear discrete	linear discrete	user-def.	linear discrete	linear discrete	linear discrete	user-def.	linear discrete	linear discrete
time dimension	valid	valid	valid + trans.	valid	valid + trans.	valid	arbitrary[1]	valid	valid
values & objects	objects	objects	objects	objects	objects	objects	objects	both	objects
relationships	NO	NO	NO	NO	NO	NO	NO	YES	YES
what is timestamped	attr.	attr.	arbitrary	objects	attr.	objects	arbitrary	objects relat.	attr. relat.
temp. attr. values	funct.[2]	funct.[2]	sets of pairs	atomic valued[3]	lists of tuples	atomic valued[3]	atomic valued[3]	funct.[2]	funct.[2]
kinds of attributes	temp. + imm.	temp. + imm.	temp. + imm.	temp. + imm.	temp. + imm.	temp. + imm.	temp. + imm.	temp. + imm.	temp. + imm. + non-temp.
histories of obj. types	NO	YES	YES	NO	NO	NO[4]	YES	YES	YES

Legenda:

[1] One time dimension is considered, it can be transaction or valid time.
[2] With *funct.* we denote functions from a temporal domain.
[3] Time is associated with the entire object state.
[4] The information can be derived from the histories of object instances.

Table 2. Comparison among temporal object-oriented data models

[24] Immutable attributes can be regarded as a particular case of temporal ones, since their value is a constant function from a temporal domain.

7 Conclusions and future work

In this paper we have presented T_ODMG, a temporal extension of the ODMG object standard data model. T_ODMG supports temporal, static and immutable object properties. We have introduced the notion of temporal type and defined the set of legal values for each type. We have discussed the notion of object consistency and integrity and we have revised the notion of key in a temporal framework. A prototype implementation of the proposed model has been implemented on top of the Ode OODBMS [1], in which the histories of temporal object properties are organized as monotonic B^{+}-trees.

We plan to extend this work along several directions. First, we are investigating a temporal extension of OQL, the ODMG query language. A second relevant extension is the support for multiple time granularities and calendars. Indeed, in the current work we have prefered to keep our model of time as simple as possible and to provide a clear formalism for such model. On the top of this formalism we plan to investigate the use of multiple granularities and calendars and the problems related to the data accesses in such framework.

A third direction deals with mechanisms supporting a selective recording of past values of properties, according to the truth value of conditions associated with properties. Moreover, we plan to extend this work with time-dependent implementations. The informal idea of time-dependent implementations is that each method has a set of implementations, each referring to a different time interval. A formal treatment of temporal methods in the context of the T_Chimera model can be found in [3].

Finally, we plan to extend our work to comply with the recently published ODMG 2.0 [5] standard.

References

1. E. Bertino, M. Bevilacqua, E. Ferrari, and G. Guerrini. Approaches to Handling Temporal Data in Object-Oriented Databases. Technical Report 192-97, Dipartimento di Scienze dell'Informazione, Università di Milano, Ottobre 1997.
2. E. Bertino, E. Ferrari, and G. Guerrini. A Formal Temporal Object-Oriented Data Model. In P. Apers, editor, *Proc. Fifth Int'l Conf. on Extending Database Technology*, number 1057 in Lecture Notes in Computer Science, pages 342–356, Avignon (France), March 1996.
3. E. Bertino, E. Ferrari, and G. Guerrini. T_Chimera: A Temporal Object-Oriented Data Model. *Theory and Practice of Object Systems*, 3(2):103–125, 1997.
4. R. Cattel. *The Object Database Standard: ODMG-93.* Morgan-Kaufmann, 1996.
5. R. Cattel. *The Object Database Standard: ODMG 2.0.* Morgan-Kaufmann, 1997.
6. P. Chen. The Entity-Relationship Model - Towards a Unified View of Data. *ACM Transactions on Database Systems*, 1(1):9–36, 1976.
7. T. Cheng and S. Gadia. An Object-Oriented Model for Temporal Databases. In *Proc. of the Int'l Workshop on an Infrastructure for Temporal Databases*, 1993.
8. J. Clifford and A. Croker. Objects in Time. In *Proc. Fourth IEEE Int'l Conf. on Data Engineering*, pages 11–18, 1988.

9. I. Goralwalla and M. Özsu. Temporal Extensions to a Uniform Behavioral Object Model. In R. Elmasri, V. Kouramajian, and B. Thalheim, editors, *Proc. Twelfth Int'l Conf. on the Entity-Relationship Approach*, volume 823 of *Lecture Notes in Computer Science*, pages 110–121. Springer-Verlag, Berlin, 1993.
10. W. Käfer and H. Schöning. Realizing a Temporal Complex-Object Data Model. In M. Stonebraker, editor, *Proc. of the ACM SIGMOD Int'l Conf. on Management of Data*, pages 266–275. ACM Press, 1992.
11. E. Rose and A. Segev. TOODM - A Temporal Object-Oriented Data Model with Temporal Constraints. In *Proc. Tenth Int'l Conf. on the Entity-Relationship Approach*, pages 205–229, 1991.
12. R. T. Snodgrass. Temporal Object-Oriented Databases: A Critical Comparison. In W. Kim, editor, *Modern Database Systems: The Object Model, Interoperability and Beyond*, pages 386–408. Addison-Wesley/ACM Press, 1995.
13. R. T. Snodgrass. *The TSQL2 Temporal Query Language*. Kluwer Academic Publisher, 1995.
14. A. Steiner and M.C. Norrie. Implementing Temporal Databases in Object-Oriented Systems. In *Proc. of the Fifth International Conference on Database Systems for Advanced Applications*, pages 381–390, 1997.
15. S. Su and H. Chen. A Temporal Knowledge Representation Model OSAM*/T and its Query Language OQL/T. In G. M. Lohman, A. Sernadas, and R. Camps, editors, *Proc. Seventeenth Int'l Conf. on Very Large Data Bases*, pages 431–441, 1991.
16. A. Tansel, J. Clifford, S. Gadia, S. Jajodia, A. Segev, and R. Snodgrass. *Temporal Databases: Theory, Design, and Implementation.* Database Systems and Applications Series. Benjamin/Cummings, 1993.
17. Y. Wu, S. Jajodia, and X. S. Wang. Temporal Database Bibliography Update. Available at: http://www.isse.gmu.edu/~csis/tdb/bib97/bib97.html, 1997.
18. G. Wuu and U. Dayal. A Uniform Model for Temporal and Versioned Object-Oriented Databases. In A. Tansel, J. Clifford, S. Gadia, S. Jajodia, A. Segev, and R. Snodgrass, editors, *Temporal Databases: Theory, Design, and Implementation*, pages 230–247. Benjamin/Cummings, 1993.

Modelica - A Unified Object-Oriented Language for System Modeling and Simulation

Peter Fritzson and Vadim Engelson

PELAB, Dept. of Computer and Information Science
Linköping University, S-58183, Linköping, Sweden
{petfr,vaden}@ida.liu.se

Abstract. A new language called Modelica for hierarchical physical modeling is developed through an international effort. Modelica 1.0 [http://www.Dynasim.se/Modelica] was announced in September 1997. It is an object-oriented language for modeling of physical systems for the purpose of efficient simulation. The language unifies and generalizes previous object-oriented modeling languages. Compared with the widespread simulation languages available today this language offers three important advances: 1) *non-causal* modeling based on differential and algebraic equations; 2) *multidomain* modeling capability, i.e. it is possible to combine electrical, mechanical, thermodynamic, hydraulic etc. model components within the same application model; 3) a general type system that unifies object-orientation, multiple inheritance, and templates within a single *class* construct.

A class in Modelica may contain variables (i.e. instances of other classes), equations and local class definitions. A function (method) can be regarded as a special case of local class without equations, but including an *algorithm* section.

The equation-based non-causal modeling makes Modelica classes more reusable than classes in ordinary object-oriented languages. The reason is that the class adapts itself to the data flow context where it is instantiated and connected. The multi-domain capability is partly based on a notion of *connectors*, i.e. certain class members that can act as interfaces (ports) when connecting instantiated objects. Connectors themselves are classes just like any other entity in Modelica. Simulation models can be developed using a graphical editor for connection diagrams. Connections are established just by drawing lines between objects picked from a class library.

The Modelica semantics is defined via translation of classes, instances and connections into a flat set of constants, variables and equations. Equations are sorted and converted to assignment statements when possible. Strongly connected sets of equations are solved by calling a symbolic and/or numeric solver. The generated C/C++ code is quite efficient.

In this paper we present the Modelica language with emphasis on its class construct and type system. A few short examples are given for illustration and compared with similar constructs in C++ and Java when this is relevant.

1 Introduction

1.1 Requirements for a modeling and simulation language

The use of computer simulation in industry is rapidly increasing. This is typically used to optimize products and to reduce product development cost and time. Whereas in the past it was considered sufficient to simulate subsystems separately, the current trend is to simulate increasingly complex physical systems composed of subsystems from multiple domains such as mechanic, electric, hydraulic, thermodynamic, and control system components.

1.2 Background

Many commercial simulation software packages are available. The market is divided into distinct domains, such as packages based on block diagrams (block-oriented tools, such as SIMULINK[18], System Build, ACSL[19]), electronic programs (signal-oriented tools, such as SPICE[20], Saber), multibody systems (ADAMS[21], DADS, SIMPACK), and others. With very few exceptions, all simulation packages are strong only in one domain and are not capable of modeling components from other domains in a reasonable way. However, this is a prerequisite to be able to simulate modern products that integrate, e.g., electric, mechanic, hydraulic and control components. Techniques for general purpose physical modeling have been developed some decades ago, but did not receive much attention from the simulation market due to lacking computer power at that time.

To summarize, we currently have three following problems:

- High performance simulation of complex multi-domain systems is needed. Current widespread methods cannot cope with serious multi-domain modeling and simulation.
- Simulated systems are increasingly complex. Thus, system modeling has to be based primarily on combining reusable components. A better technology is needed in creating easy-to-use reusable components.
- It is hard to achieve truly reusable components in object-oriented programming and modeling

Disadvantage of block-oriented tools is the gap between the physical structure of some system and structure of corresponding model created by the tool. In block-oriented tools the model designer has to predict in advance in which way the equations will be used. It reduces reusability of model libraries and causes incompatibilities between blocks.

1.3 Proposed solution

The goal of the Modelica project[23] is to provide practically usable solutions to these problems, based on techniques for mathematical modeling of reusable components.

Several first generation object-oriented mathematical modeling languages and simulation systems (ObjectMath [11,13], Dymola [4], Omola [2], NMF [12], gPROMS [3], Allan [6], Smile [5] etc.) have been developed during the past few years. These languages were applied in areas such as robotics, vehicles, thermal power plants, nuclear power plants, airplane simulation, real-time simulation of gear boxes, etc.

Several applications have shown, that object-oriented modeling techniques is not only comparable to, but outperform special purpose tools on applications that are far beyond the capacity of established block-oriented simulation tools.

However, the situation of a number of different incompatible object-oriented modeling and simulation languages was not satisfactory. Therefore in the fall of 1996 a group of researchers (see Sect. 3.6) from universities and industry started work towards standardization and making this object-oriented modeling technology widely available.

The new language was called Modelica and designed for modeling dynamic behavior of engineering systems, intended to become a *de facto* standard.

Modelica is superior to current technology mainly for the following reasons:

- Object-oriented modeling. This technique makes it possible to create physically relevant and easy-to-use model components, which are employed to support hierarchical structuring, reuse, and evolution of large and complex models covering multiple technology domains.
- Non-causal modeling. Modeling is based on equations instead of assignment statements as in traditional input/output block abstractions. Direct use of equations significantly increases re-usability of model components, since components adapt to the data flow context in which they are used. This generalization enables both simpler models and more efficient simulation.
- Physical modeling of multiple domains. Model components can correspond to physical objects in the real world, in contrast to established techniques that require conversion to "signal" blocks with fixed input/output causality. In Modelica the structure of the model becomes more natural in contrast to block-oriented modeling tools. For application engineers, such "physical" components are particularly easy to combine into simulation models using a graphical editor.

1.4 Modelica view of object-orientation

Traditional object-oriented languages like C++, Java and Simula support programming with operations on state. The state of the program includes variable values and object data. Number of objects changes dynamically. Smalltalk view of object orientation is sending messages between (dynamically) created objects. The Modelica approach is different. The Modelica language emphasizes *structured* mathematical modeling and uses structural benefits of object-orientation. A Modelica model is primarily a declarative mathematical description, which allows analysis and equational reasoning. For these reasons, dynamic object creation at runtime is usually not interesting from a mathematical modeling point of view. Therefore, this is not supported by the Modelica language.

To compensate this missing feature *arrays* are provided by Modelica. An array is an indexed set of objects of equal type. The size of the set is determined once at runtime. This construct for example can be used to represent a set of similar rollers in a bearing, or a set of electrons around an atomic nucleus.

1.5 Object-Oriented Mathematical Modeling

Mathematical models used for analysis in scientific computing are inherently complex in the same way as other software. One way to handle this complexity is to use object-oriented techniques. Wegner [7] defines the basic terminology of object-oriented programming:

- *Objects* are collections of operations that share a state. These operations are often called *methods*. The state is represented by *instance variables*, which are accessible only to the operation's of the object.
- *Classes* are templates from which objects can be created.
- *Inheritance* allows us to reuse the operations of a class when defining new classes. A subclass inherits the operations of its parent class and can add new operations and instance variables.

Note that Wegner's strict requirement regarding data encapsulation is not fulfilled by object oriented languages like Simula or C++, where non-local access to instance variables is allowed.

More important, while Wegner's definitions are suitable for describing the notions of object-oriented *programming*, they are too restrictive for the case of object-oriented *mathematical modeling,* where a class description may consist of a set of equations, which implicitly define the behavior of some class of physical objects or the relationships between objects. Functions should be side-effect free and regarded as mathematical functions rather than operations. Explicit operations on state can be completely absent, but can be present. Also, causality, i.e. which variables are regarded as input, and which ones are regarded as output, is usually not defined by such an equation-based model.

There are usually many possible choices of causality, but one must be selected before a system of equations is solved. If a system of such equations is solved symbolically, the equations are transformed into a form where some (state) variables are explicitly defined in terms of other (state) variables. If the solution process is numeric, it will compute new state variables from old variable values, and thus operate on the state variables. Below we define the basic terminology of *object-oriented mathematical modeling*:

- An *object* is a collection of variables, equations, functions and other definitions related to a common abstraction and may share a state. Such operations are often called *methods*. The state is represented by *instance variables*.
- *Classes* are templates from which objects or subclasses can be created.
- *Inheritance* allows us to reuse the equations, functions and definitions of a class when defining objects and new classes. A subclass inherits the definitions of its parent class and can add new equations, functions, instance variables and other definitions.

As previously mentioned, the primary reason to introduce object-oriented techniques in mathematical modeling is to reduce complexity. To explain these ideas we use some examples from the domain of electric circuits. When a mathematical description is designed, and it consists of hundreds of equations and formulae, for instance a model of a complex electrical system, structuring the model is highly advantageous.

2 A Modelica overview

Modelica programs are built from *classes*. Like in other object-oriented languages, class contains variables, i.e. class attributes representing data. The main difference compared with traditional object-oriented languages is that instead of functions (methods) we use *equations* to specify behavior. Equations can be written explicitly, like `a=b`, or be inherited from other classes. Equations can also be specified by the **connect** statement. The statement **connect** (*v1*, *v2*) expresses coupling between variables *v1* and *v2*. These variables are called *connectors* and belong to the connected objects. This gives a flexible way of specifying topology of physical systems described in an object-oriented way using Modelica.

In the following sections we introduce some basic and distinctive syntactical and semantic features of Modelica, such as connectors, encapsulation of equations, inheritance, declaration of parameters and constants. Powerful parametrization capabilities (which are advanced features of Modelica) are discussed in Sect. 2.10.

2.1 Modelica model of an electric circuit

As an introduction to Modelica we will present a model of a simple electrical circuit as shown in Fig. 1. The system can be broken into a set of connected electrical standard components. We have a voltage source, two resistors, an inductor, a capacitor and a ground point. Models of such components are available in Modelica class libraries.

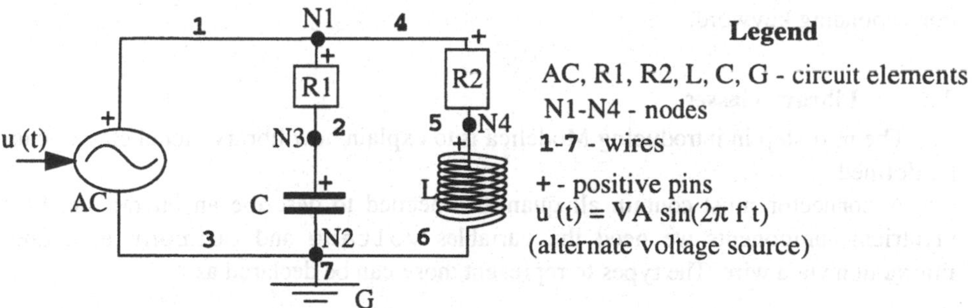

Fig. 1. A connection diagram of the simple electrical circuit example. The numbers of wires and nodes are used for reference in Table 3.1.

A declaration like one below specifies that `R1` to be of class `Resistor` and sets the default value of the resistance, `R`, to 10.

```
Resistor R1(R=10);
```

A Modelica description of the complete circuit appears as follows:

```
class circuit
   Resistor  R1(R=10);
   Capacitor C(C=0.01);
   Resistor  R2(R=100);
   Inductor  L(L=0.1);
   VsourceAC AC;
   Ground    G;
equation
   connect (AC.p, R1.p);     // Wire 1
   connect (R1.n, C.p);      // Wire 2
   connect (C.n,  AC.n);     // Wire 3
   connect (R1.p, R2.p);     // Wire 4
   connect (R2.n, L.p);      // Wire 5
   connect (L.n,  C.n);      // Wire 6
   connect (AC.n, G.p);      // Wire 7
end circuit;
```

A composite model like the circuit model described above specifies the system topology, i.e. the components and the connections between the components. The connections specify interactions between the components. In some previous object-oriented modeling languages connectors are referred to cuts, ports or terminals. The keyword **connect** is a special operator that generates equations taking into account what kind of interaction is involved as explained in Sect. 2.3.

Variables declared within classes are public by default, if they are not preceded by the keyword **protected** which has the same semantics as in Java. Additional **public** or **protected** sections can appear within a class, preceded by the corresponding keyword.

2.2 Library classes

The next step in introducing Modelica is to explain how library model classes can be defined.

A connector must contain all quantities needed to describe an interaction. For electrical components we need the variables `voltage` and `current` to define interaction via a wire. The types to represent those can be declared as

```
class Voltage = Real;
class Current = Real;
```

where `Real` is the name of a predefined variable type. A real variable has a set of default attributes such as unit of measure, initial value, minimum and maximum value. These default attributes can be changed when declaring a new class, for example:

```
    class Voltage = Real(unit="V", min=-220.0,
max=220.0);
```

In Modelica, the basic structuring element is a **class**. There are seven restricted class categories with specific keywords, such as **type** (a class that is an extension of built-in classes, such as `Real`, or of other defined types) and **connector** (a class that does not have equations and can be used in connections). In any model the **type** and **connector** keywords can be replaced by the **class** keyword giving a semantically equivalent model. Other specific class categories are **model**, **package**, **function** and **record** of which **model** and **record** can be replaced by **class**[1].

The idea of restricted classes is advantageous because the modeler does not have to learn several different concepts, but just one: the class concept. All properties of a class, such as syntax and semantic of definition, instantiation, inheritance, generic properties are identical to all kinds of restricted classes. Furthermore, the construction of Modelica translators is simplified considerably because only the syntax and semantic of a class have to be implemented along with some additional checks on restricted classes. The basic types, such as `Real` or `Integer` are built-in type classes, i.e., they have all the properties of a class. The previous definitions can be expressed as follows using the keyword **type** which is equivalent to **class**, but limits the defined type to be extension of a built-in type, record or array.

```
type Voltage = Real;
type Current = Real;
```

2.3 Connector classes

A connector class is defined as follows:

```
connector Pin
  Voltage      v;
  flow Current i;
end Pin;
```

Connection statements are used to connect instances of connection classes. A connection statement **connect**`(Pin1,Pin2)`, with `Pin1` and `Pin2` of connector class `Pin`, connects the two pins so that they form one node. This implies two equations[2],

---

1. The single syntax for functions, connectors and classes introduced by the **class** construct is a convenient way of notion unification. There is a similar approach in the BETA programming language[28] where classes and procedures are unified in the *pattern* concept.

2. The are other tools, for instance, PROLOG, where symbolic equations between terms can be written. However, in contrast to PROLOG, the Modelica environment automatically computes which variables of equations are inputs and which are outputs in corresponding context at the compilation phase. This leads to higher robustness and better performance.

namely:

```
Pin1.v = Pin2.v
Pin1.i + Pin2.i = 0
```

The first equation says that the voltages of the connected wire ends are the same. The second equation corresponds to Kirchhoff's current law saying that the currents sum to zero at a node (assuming positive value while flowing into the component). The sum-to-zero equations are generated when the prefix **flow** is used. Similar laws apply to flow rates in a piping network and to forces and torques in mechanical systems.

When developing models and model libraries for a new application domain, it is good to start by defining a set of connector classes. A common set of connector classes used in all components in the library supports compatibility of the component models.

2.4 Virtual (partial) classes.

A common property of many electrical components is that they have two pins. This means that it is useful to define an "interface" model class,

```
partial class TwoPin        "Superclass of elements
                             with two electric pins"
  Pin p, n;
  Voltage v;
  Current i;
equation
  v = p.v - n.v;
  0 = p.i + n.i;
  i = p.i;
end TwoPin;
```

that has two pins, p and n, a quantity, v, that defines the voltage drop across the component and a quantity, i, that defines the current into the pin p, through the component and out from the pin n (Fig. 2).

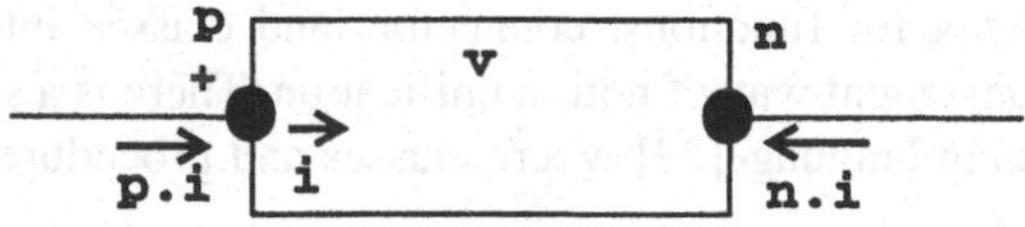

Fig. 2. Generic TwoPin model.

The equations define generic relations between quantities of a simple electrical component. In order to be useful a constitutive equation must be added. The keyword **partial** indicates that this model class is incomplete. The keyword is optional. It is meant as an indication to a user that it is not possible to use the class as it is to instantiate components. String after the class name is a comment.

2.5 Equations and non-causal modeling

Non-causal modeling means modeling based on equations instead of assignment statements. Equations do not specify which variables are inputs and which are outputs, whereas in assignment statements variables on the left-hand side are always outputs (results) and variables on the right-hand side are always inputs. Thus, the causality of equations-based models is unspecified and fixed only when the equation systems are solved. This is called non-causal modeling.

The main advantage with non-causal modeling is that the solution direction of equations will adapt to the data flow context in which the solution is computed. The data flow context is defined by telling which variables are needed as *outputs* and which are external *inputs* to the simulated system.

The non-causality of Modelica library classes makes these more reusable than traditional classes containing assignment statements where the input-output causality is fixed.

For example the equation from resistor class below:

```
R*i = v;
```

can be used in two ways. The variable `v` can be computed as a function of `i`, or the variable `i` can be computed as a function of `v` as shown in the two assignment statements below:

```
i := v/R;
v := R*i;
```

In the same way the following equation from the class `TwoPin`

```
v = p.v - n.v
```

can be used in three ways:

```
v   := p.v - n.v;
p.v := v + n.v;
n.v := p.v - v;
```

2.6 Inheritance, parameters and constants

To define a model for a resistor we exploit `TwoPin` and add a definition of **a parameter** for the resistance and Ohm's law to define the behavior:

```
class Resistor "Ideal electrical resistor"
  extends TwoPin;
  parameter Real R(unit="Ohm") "Resistance";
equation
    R*i = v;
end Resistor;
```

The keyword **parameter** specifies that the variable is constant during a simulation run, but can change values between runs. This means that **parameter** is a special kind of constant, which is implemented as a static variable that is initialized once and never changes its value during a specific execution. A **parameter** is a variable that makes it simple for a user to modify the behavior of a model.

A Modelica **constant** never changes and can be substituted inline.

The keyword **extends** specifies the parent class. All variables, **equation**s and **connect**s are inherited from the parent. Multiple inheritance is supported in Modelica.

Just like in C++ variables, equations and connections of the parent class cannot be *removed* in the subclass.

In C++ a virtual function can be *replaced* by a function with the same name in the child class. In Modelica 1.0 the equations cannot be named and therefore in general equations cannot be replaced at inheritance[1]. When classes are inherited, equations are accumulated. This makes the equation-based semantics of the child classes consistent with the semantics of the parent class.

An innovation of Modelica is that type of a variable of the parent class can be replaced. We describe this in more detail in Sect. 2.10.

2.7 Time and model dynamics

Dynamic systems are models where behavior evolves as a function of *time*. We use a predefined variable `time` which steps forward during system simulation.

A class for the voltage source can be defined as:

```
class VsourceAC "Sin-wave voltage source"
  extends TwoPin;
  parameter Voltage VA = 220 "Amplitude";
  parameter Real f(unit="Hz") = 50  "Frequency";
  constant  Real PI=3.141592653589793;
equation
  v = VA*sin(2*PI*f*time);
end VsourceAC;
```

A class for an electrical capacitor can also reuse the `TwoPin` as follows:

```
class Capacitor "Ideal electrical capacitor"
  extends TwoPin;
  parameter Real C(unit="F") "Capacitance";
equation
    C*der(v) = i;
end Capacitor;
```

1. In the ObjectMath language equations can be named and thus specialized through inheritance.

where **der**(v) means the time derivative of v.

During system simulation the variables i and v evolve as functions of time. The solver of differential equations (see Sect. 3.2) computes the values of *i(t)* and *v(t)* (*t* is time) so that *C v'(t)=i(t)* for all values of *t*.

Finally, we define the ground point as a reference value for the voltage levels

```
class Ground "Ground"
  Pin p;
equation
  p.v = 0;
end Ground;
```

2.8 Functions

Sometimes Modelica non-causal models have to be complemented by traditional procedural constructs like function calls. This is the case if a computation is more conveniently expressed in an algorithmic or procedural way. For example when computing the value of a polynomial form where the number of elements is unknown, as in the formula below:

$$y = \sum_{i=1}^{size(a)} a_i \cdot x^i$$

Modelica allows a specialization of a class called **function**, which has only public inputs and outputs (these are marked in the code by keywords **input** and **output**), one **algorithm** section and no equations:

```
function PolynomialEvaluator
    input Real a[:];// array, size defined at run time
    input  Real x;
    output Real y;
  protected
    Real   xpower;
  algorithm
    y := 0;
    xpower := 1;
    for i in 1:size(a, 1) loop
      y := y + a[i]*xpower;
      xpower := xpower*x;
    end for;
  end PolynomialEvaluator;
```

The Modelica function is side-effect free in the sense that it always returns the same outputs for the same input arguments. It can be invoked within expressions and equations, e.g. as below:

```
p = PolynomialEvaluator2(a=[1, 2, 3, 4], x=time);
```

More details on other Modelica constructs are presented in [23].

2.9 The Modelica notion of subtypes

The notion of subtyping in Modelica is influenced by type theory of Abbadi and Cardelli [1]. The notion of inheritance in Modelica is separated from the notion of subtyping. According to the definition, a class A is a *subtype* of class B if class A contains all the public variables declared in the class B, and types of these variables are subtypes of types of corresponding variables in B. The main benefit of this definition is additional flexibility in the composition of types. For instance, the class TempResistor is a subtype of Resistor.

```
class TempResistor
  extends TwoPin
  parameter Real R, RT, Tref ;
  Real T;
equation
  v=i*(R+RT*(T-Tref));
end TempResistor
```

Subtyping is used for example in class *instantiation*, *redeclarations* and function calls. If variable a is of type A, and A is a subtype of B, then a can be initialized by a variable of type B. Redeclaration is discussed in the next section.

Note that TempResistor does not inherit the Resistor class. There are different equations for evaluation of v. If equations are inherited from Resistor then the set of equations will become inconsistent in TempResistor, since Modelica currently does not support named equations and replacement of equations. For example, the specialized equation below from TempResistor:

```
v=i*(R+RT*(T-Tref))
```

and the general equation from class Resistor

```
v=R*i
```

are inconsistent.

2.10 Class parametrization

A distinctive feature of object-oriented programming languages and environments is ability to fetch classes from standard libraries and reuse them for particular needs. Obviously, this should be done without modification of the library codes. The two main mechanisms that serve for this purpose are:

- *inheritance*. It is essentially "copying" class definition and adding more elements (variables, equations and functions) to it.
- *class parametrization* (also called generic classes or types). It is replacing a generic type identifier in whole class definition by an actual type[1].

In Modelica we propose a new way to control class parametrization. Assume that a library class is defined as

```
class SimpleCircuit
  Resistor R1(R=100), R2(R=200), R3(R=300);
equation
  connect(R1.p, R2.p);
  connect(R1.p, R3.p);
end SimpleCircuit;
```

Assume that in our particular application we would like to reuse the definition of `SimpleCircuit`: we want to use the parameter values given for `R1.R` and `R2.R` and the circuit topology, but exchange `Resistor` with the temperature-dependent resistor model, `TempResistor`, discussed above.

This can be accomplished by redeclaring R1 and R2 as follows.

```
class RefinedSimpleCircuit = SimpleCircuit(
  redeclare TempResistor R1,
  redeclare TempResistor R2);
```

Since `TempResistor` is a subtype of `Resistor`, it is possible to replace the ideal resistor model. Values of the additional parameters of `TempResistor` can be added in the redeclaration:

```
redeclare TempResistor R1(RT=0.1, Tref=20.0)
```

This is a very strong modification but it should be noted that all equations that could be defined in `SimpleCircuit` are still valid.

2.10.1 Comparison with C++

The C++ language is chosen here as a common representative of an object-oriented language with a static type system. The reason to compare to C++ is to shed additional light on how the Modelica object model works in practice compared to traditional object-oriented languages. We consider the complications which arise if we attempt to reproduce Modelica class parametrization in C++.

A **`SimpleCircuit`** template class can be defined as a component of a C++ class library as follows:

1. The ObjectMath language[11] has class parametrization that allows replacing any identifier in whole class definition by an actual symbol.

```
class Resistor {
      public:
            float R;
};

template <class TResistor, class TResistor1>
    // Several template arguments can be given here
class SimpleCircuit {
  public:
    SimpleCircuit(){ R1.R=100.0; R2.R=200.0; R3.R=300.0; };
    TResistor  R1;//We should explicitly specify which two resistors will be
replaced.
    TResistor1 R2;
    Resistor R3;
    void func() {R3.R=R2.T;};};
```

Code which reuses the library classes should look like

```
class TempResistor {
      public:
            float R,T,Tref,RT;
};
class RefinedSimpleCircuit:public
    SimpleCircuit<TempResistor,TempResistor> {
    // Template parameters are passed
      RefinedSimpleCircuit(){ R1.RT=0.1; R1.Tref=20.0; }
...
};
```

To summarize we can reproduce the whole model in C++. However it is not possible to specify the `SimpleCircuit` class without explicitly specifying which data members (e.g. `R1` and `R2`) are controlled by a type parameter such as `TResistor`. The C++ template construct requires this. Therefore the possible use of type parameters in C++ always has to be anticipated by making types explicit parameters of templates. In Modelica this generality is always available by default. Therefore C++ classes typically are less general and have lower degree of reusability compared to Modelica classes.

2.10.2 Comparison with Java

Java is another object-oriented language with a static type system. There are no options for generic classes. Instead we can use explicit type casting. The same approach can be used in C++, using pointers. However, type casting gives clumsy and less readable code.

Example 1. If we permit `TempResistor` to be a subclass of `Resistor`, the code is straightforward:

```
class Resistor { public double R; };
class SimpleCircuit
{ public SimpleCircuit() {
    R1=new Resistor(); R1.R=100.0;
    R2=new Resistor(); R2.R=200.0;
    R3=new Resistor(); R3.R=300.0;};
    Resistor R1, R2, R3;
    void func(){R3.R=R1.R;};
 };

class TempResistor extends Resistor
{ public double T,Tref,RT; };
class RefinedSimpleCircuit extends SimpleCircuit
{ public
  RefinedSimpleCircuit() {
    R1=new TempResistor(); R2=new TempResistor();
   // Type casting is necessary below:

((TempResistor)R1).RT=0.1;((TempResistor)R1).TRef=20.0;}
};
```

There is no way to initialize and work further with the variables R1 and R2 without type casting.

Example 2: If we do not permit TempResistor to be a subclass of Resistor, the code is full with type casting operators:

```
class Resistor { public double R; };
class SimpleCircuit
{ public SimpleCircuit() {
    R1=new Resistor(); ((Resistor)R1).R=100.0;
    R2=new Resistor(); ((Resistor)R2).R=200.0;
    R3=new Resistor(); ((Resistor)R3).R=300.0;};
    Object R1, R2, R3;
    void func(){((Resistor)R3).R=((Resistor)R1).R;
    // This causes exception if R1 has runtime type TempResistor.
 };
};

class TempResistor
{ public double R,T,Tref,TR; };
class RefinedSimpleCircuit extends SimpleCircuit
{ public
  RefinedSimpleCircuit() {
    R1=new TempResistor(); R2=new TempResistor();
    // Type casting is necessary below
```

```
((TempResistor)R1).RT=0.1;((TempResistor)R1).TRef=20.0;}
};
```

The class `Object` is the only mechanism in Java that we can use for construction of generic classes. Since strong type control is enforced in Java, type cast operators are necessary for every access to `R1`, `R2` and `R3`. Actually we remove type control from compilation time into the run time. This should be discouraged because it makes the code design more difficult and makes the program error-prone.

To summarize we can reproduce the whole model in Java and build an almost general library. However, many explicit class casting operations make the code difficult and non-natural.

2.10.3 Final components

The modeler of the `SimpleCircuit` can state that a component cannot be redeclared anymore. We declare such component as final.

```
final Resistor R3(R=300);
```

It is possible to state that a parameter is frozen to a certain value, i.e. is not a parameter anymore:

```
Resistor R3(final R=300);
```

2.10.4 Replaceable classes

To use another resistor model in the class `SimpleCircuit`, we needed to know that there were two replaceable resistors and we needed to know their names. To avoid this problem and prepare for replacement of a set of classes, one can define a replaceable class, `ResistorModel`. The actual class that will later be used for `R1` and `R2` must have `Pins` `p` and `n` and a parameter `R` in order to be compatible with how `R1` and `R2` are used within `SimpleCircuit2`. The replaceable model `ResistorModel` is declared to be a `Resistor` model. This means that it will be enforced that the actual class will be a subtype of `Resistor`, i.e., have compatible connectors and parameters. Default for `ResistorModel`, i.e., when no actual redeclaration is made, is in this case `Resistor`. Note, that `R1` and `R2` are in this case of class `ResistorModel`.

```
class SimpleCircuit2
  replaceable class ResistorModel = Resistor;
protected
  ResistorModel R1(R=100), R2(R=200);
  final Resistor R3(final R=300);
equation
  connect(R1.p, R2.p);
```

```
    connect(R1.p, R3.p);
  end SimpleCircuit2;
```

Binding an actual model TempResistor to the replaceable class ResistorModel is done as follows.

```
    class RefinedSimpleCircuit2 =
      SimpleCircuit2(redeclare class ResistorModel =
TempResistor);
```

This construction is similar to the C++ **template** construct. ResistorModel can serve as a type parameter. However, in C++ the type parameter cannot have default value. In Modelica the class SimpleCircuit2 is complete and can be used for variable instantiation. In C++ the class SimpleCircuit2 is a template, which must be instantiated first:

```
    template <class ResistorModel>
    class SimpleCircuit2 {
        ResistorModel R1(R=100);
    ...
    }
    class RefinedSimpleCircuit2 : public
        SimpleCircuit2<TempResistor>
         { ... }
```

3 Implementation issues

3.1 Flattening of equations

Classes, instances and equations are translated into flat set of equations, constants and variables (see Table 3.1). As an example, we translate the circuit model from Sect. 2.1.

The equation v=p.v-n.v is defined by the class TwoPin. The Resistor class inherits the TwoPin class, including this equation. The circuit class contains a variable R1 of type Resistor. Therefore, we include this equation instantiated for R1 as R1.v=R1.p.v-R1.n.v into the set of equations.

The wire labelled **1** is represented in the model as **connect**(AC.p, R1.p). The variables AC.p and R1.p have type Pin. The variable v is a *non-flow* variable representing voltage potential. Therefore, the equality equation AC.p.v=R1.p.v is generated. Equality equations are always generated when non-flow variables are connected.

Notice that another wire (labelled **4**) is attached to the same pin, R1.p. This is represented by an additional connect statement: **connect**(R1.p.R2.p). The variable i is declared as a **flow**-variable. Thus, the equation AC.p.i+R1.p.i+R2.p.i=0 is generated. Zero-sum equations are always generated when connecting flow variables, corresponding to Kirchhoff's current law.

The complete set of equations generated from the `circuit` class (see Table 3.1) consists of 32 differential-algebraic equations. These include 32 variables, as well as `time` and several parameters and constants.

Table 3.1: Equations generated from the simple circuit model

AC	`0=AC.p.i+Ac.n.i`
	`AC.v=Ac.p.v-AC.n.v`
	`AC.i=AC.p.i`
	`AC.v=AC.VA*`
	`sin(2*PI*AC.f*time);`
		L	`0=L.p.i+L.n.i`
			`L.v=L.p.v-L.n.v`
			`L.i=L.p.i`
			`L.v = L.L*L.der(i)`

R1	`0=R1.p.i+R1.n.i`
	`R1.v=R1.p.v-R1.n.v`
	`R1.i=R1.p.i`
	`R1.v = R1.R*R1.i`
		G	`G.p.v = 0`

R2	`0=R2.p.i+R2.n.i`
	`R2.v=R2.p.v-R2.n.v`
	`R2.i=R2.p.i`
	`R2.v = R2.R*R2.i`
		wires	`R1.p.v=AC.p.v // wire 1`
			`C.p.v=R1.n.v  // wire 2`
			`AC.n.v=C.n.v  // wire 3`
			`R2.p.v=R1.p.v // wire 4`
			`L.p.v=R2.n.v  // wire 5`
			`L.n.v=C.n.v   // wire 6`
			`G.p.v= AC.n.v // wire 7`

C	`0=C.p.i+C.n.i`
	`C.v=C.p.v-C.n.v`
	`C.i=C.p.i`
	`C.i = C.C*C.der(v)`
		flow at node	`0=AC.p.i+R1.p.i+R2.p.i //1`
			`0=C.n.i+G.i+AC.n.i+L.n.i //2`
			`0=R1.n.i+ C.p.i //  3`
			`0 =R2.n.i + L.p.i // 4`

3.2 Solution and simulation

After flattening, all the equations are sorted. Simplification algorithms can eliminate many of them. If two syntactically equivalent equations appear only one copy of the equations is kept.

Then they can be converted to assignment statements. If a strongly connected set of equations appears, these can be transformed by a symbolic solver. The symbolic solver performs a number of algebraic transformations to simplify the dependencies between the variables. It can also solve a system of differential equations if it has a symbolic solution. Finally, C/C++ code is generated, and it is linked with a numeric solver.

The initial values can be taken from the model definition. If necessary, the user specifies the parameter values (described in Section 2.6)Sect. 2.6. Numeric solvers for differential equations (such as LSODE, part of ODEPACK[14]) give the user possibility to ask about the value of specific variable in a specific time moment. As the result a function of time, e.g. `R2.v(t)` can be computed for a time interval $[t_0, t_1]$ and displayed as a graph or saved in a file. This data presentation is the final result of system simulation.

In most cases (but not always) the performance of generated simulation code (including the solver) is similar to hand-written C code. Sometimes Modelica is more efficient than straightforward written C code, because additional opportunities for symbolic optimization are used.

3.3 Current status

Language definition. As a result from 8 meetings in the period September 1996 - September 1997 the first full definition of Modelica 1.0 was announced in September 1997 [23, 29].

Work started in the continuous time domain, since there is a common mathematical framework in the form of differential-algebraic equations and there are several existing modeling languages based on similar ideas. There is also significant experience of using these languages in various applications. It is expected that the Modelica language will become a *de-facto* standard.

Translators. A translator from a subset of Modelica to Dymola is currently available from Dynasim [8]. We are currently developing another implementation of Modelica. This version of Modelica is integrated with Mathematica [9] similarly to ObjectMath [11,13]. This tool provides both the symbolic processing power of Mathematica, the modeling capability of Modelica, as well as the integrated documentation and programming environment offered by Mathematica notebooks. The tool also supports generation of C++ code [10] for high-performance computations.

Graphical model editors. A 2D graphical model editor can be used to define a model by drawing and editing an object diagram very similar to the circuit diagram shown in Fig. 1. Such a model editor is will be implemented for Modelica based on an similar existing editor for the Dymola language, called Dymodraw. The user can place icons that represent the components and connect those components by drawing lines between their iconic representations. For clarity, attributes of the Modelica definition for the graphical layout of the composition diagram (here: an electric circuit diagram) are not shown in examples. These attributes are usually contained in a Modelica model as annotations (which are largely ignored by the Modelica translator and used by graphical tools).

The ObjectMath inheritance graph editor exemplifies another kind of model editor, which supports both display and editing of the inheritance graph. Classes and instances are represented as graph nodes and inheritance relations are shown as links between nodes. Such an editor is also planned for Modelica. A partial port of the ObjectMath editor to Modelica currently exists.

Dynamic simulation visualization. There are currently exist at least two tools for dynamic visualization and animation of Modelica simulations. One of these tools is a 3D model viewer called Dymoview [8] for Dymola and Modelica, which displays dynamic model behavior based on simulations. It can produce realistic visualizations of mechanical models constructed from graphical objects such as boxes, spheres and cylinders. The visual appearance of a class must be defined together will class definition. Simultaneously with animation any computed variables can be plotted. Another tool called MAGGIE is described in the next section.

Dynamic computational steering and animation environment. The MAGGIE (Mathematical Graphical Generated Interactive Environment) 3D model visualizer, is being developed by us. It supports automatic generation of visual appearance of objects, based on the structure of Modelica models.

Thus, a computational steering environment for the simulation application is automatically produced from the Modelica model. The user can interactively modify the structure of the automatically created 3D appearance of the model before start of visualization.

However, many parameters of the simulation and geometrical properties of the model can also be modified *during* run time, i.e. during simulation and animation. This provides immediate feedback to the user as changing model behavior and visualization. The user can specify the parameters in form-like dialog windows automatically generated based on the Modelica model. For this purpose we reuse our experience with generation of such graphical interfaces from C++ and ObjectMath data structures [24].

The simulation code, the interface for parameter control, and a graphical library based on the OpenGL toolkit are linked together into a single application which forms a computational steering environment. In contrast to traditional visualization tools this supports dynamically changing surfaces, that is useful in deformation modeling, hydrodynamics, and volume visualization. By linking all the software components into a single application we avoid saving large volumes of intermediate results on disk, which improves interactive response of our tool.

Initial experience with MAGGIE is described in [22, 25].

Checking tools. Additional information can be added to improve model consistency and reliability. One important example is the **`unit`** attribute, which provides more information in the user input forms as well as enabling more detailed consistency checking as a form of more detailed type checking. For instance, voltage can be defined as

```
type Voltage = Real(unit="V");
```

Such a checker can prevent mixing of variables with incompatible units, for example below:

```
time + position
```

where both variables have type `Real` (which are compatible), but have different units – seconds and meters – which are incompatible.

Applications. Several recent papers discussing application of Modelica in different application domains have been written: gear box modeling[15], thermodynamics[16] and mechanics[17].

3.4 Future work

The work by the Modelica Committee on the further development of Modelica and tools will continue. Current issues include definition of Modelica standard libraries. The most recent meeting was in Passau in October 1997, and next one is planned in Linköping in January 1998. Several companies and research institutes are planning development of tools based on Modelica. In our case, we focus on an interactive implementation of Modelica integrated with Mathematica to provide integration of model design and coding, documentation, simulation and graphics.

Compilation of Modelica. Modelica compilers are developed by us, by Dynasim and planned by other partners. Parser, translator and symbolic solver are developed on the basis of the experience gained with the Dymola program to convert the model equations into an appropriate form for numerical solvers with target languages C, C++, and Java. Special emphasis will be made on using symbolic techniques for generating efficient code for large models.

Parallel simulation. Part of a parallel simulation framework for high performance computers earlier developed by PELAB and SKF for bearing applications [26] will be ported and adapted for use with Modelica in order to speed up simulation.

Experimentation environment. An integrated experimentation environment is currently being designed and implemented. This integrates simulation, design optimization, parallelisation, and support documentation in the form of interactive Mathematica notebooks including Modelica models, live graphics and typeset mathematics.

Library Development. Public domain Modelica component libraries are currently under development by the Modelica design group, for example by DLR in the mecatronics area, being used in gearbox applications [15]. Several extensions to these libraries are needed in order to model complex systems. These libraries will be available for use in education and in engineering books.

3.5 Conclusion

A new object-oriented language Modelica designed for physical modeling takes some distinctive features of object-oriented and simulation languages. It offers the user a tool for expressing non-causal relations in modeled systems. Modelica is able to support physically relevant and intuitive model construction in multiple application domains. Non-causal modeling based on equations instead of procedural statements enables adequate model design and high level of reusability.

There is a straightforward algorithm translating classes, instances and connections into a flat set of equations. A number of solvers have been attached to the generated code for computation of simulation results. The experience shows that Modelica is an adequate tool for design of middle scale physical simulation models.

3.6 Acknowledgments

The Modelica definition has been developed by the Eurosim Modelica technical committee under the leadership of Hilding Elmqvist (Dynasim AB, Lund, Sweden). This group includes Fabrice Boudaud (Gaz de France), Jan Broenink (University of Twente, The Netherlands), Dag Brück (Dynasim AB, Lund, Sweden), Thilo Ernst (GMD-FIRST, Berlin, Germany), Peter Fritzson (Linköping University, Sweden), Alexandre Jeandel (Gaz de France), Kaj Juslin (VTT, Finland), Matthias Klose (Technical University of Berlin, Germany), Sven Erik Mattsson (Department of Automatic Control, Lund Institute of Technology, Sweden), Martin Otter (DLR Oberpfaffenhofen, Germany), Per Sahlin (BrisData AB, Stockholm, Sweden), Peter Schwarz (Fraunhofer Institute for Integrated Circuits, Dresden, Germany), Hubertus Tummescheit (GMD FIRST, Berlin, Germany) and Hans Vangheluwe (Department for Applied Mathematics, Biometrics and Process Control, University of Gent, Belgium). The work by Linköping University has been supported by the Wallenberg foundation as part of the WITAS project.

References

[1] Abadi M., and L. Cardelli: *A Theory of Objects*. Springer Verlag, ISBN 0-387-94775-2, 1996.

[2] Andersson M.: *Object-Oriented Modeling and Simulation of Hybrid Systems.* PhD thesis ISRN LUTFD2/TFRT--1043--SE, Department of Automatic Control, Lund Institute of Technology, Lund, Sweden, December 1994.

[3] Barton P.I., and C.C. Pantelides: *Modeling of combined discrete/continuous processes*. AIChE J., 40, pp. 966--979, 1994.

[4] Elmqvist H., D. Brück, and M. Otter: *Dymola --- User's Manual*. Dynasim AB, Research Park Ideon,Lund, Sweden, 1996.

[5] Ernst T., S. Jähnichen, and M. Klose: *The Architecture of the Smile/M Simulation Environment.* Proc.15th IMACS World Congress on Scientific Computation, Modelling and Applied Mathematics, Vol. 6, Berlin, Germany, pp. 653-658, 1997

[6] Jeandel A., F. Boudaud., and E. Larivière: *ALLAN Simulation release 3.1 description* M.DéGIMA.GSA1887. GAZ DE FRANCE, DR, Saint Denis La plaine, FRANCE, 1997.

[7] Peter Wegner. Concepts and paradigms of object-oriented programming. *OOPS Messenger,* 1 (1):9-87, August 1990.

[8] Dynasim Home page, `http://www.Dynasim.se`

[9] Mathematica Home page, `http://www.wolfram.com`

[10] Fritzson, P. Static and String Typing for Extended Mathematica, *Innovation in Mathematics*, Proceedings of the Second International Mathematica Symposium, Rovaniemi, Finland, 29 June - 4 July, V. Keränen, P. Mitic, A. Hietamäki (Ed.), pp 153-160.

[11] Peter Fritzson, Lars Viklund, Dag Fritzson, Johan Herber. High-Level Mathematical Modelling and Programming, *IEEE Software*, 12(4):77-87, July 1995.

[12] Sahlin P., A. Bring, and E.F. Sowell: *The Neutral Model Format for building simulation, Version 3.02*. Technical Report, Department of Building Sciences, The Royal Institute of Technology, Stockholm, Sweden, June 1996.

[13] ObjectMath Home Page, `http://www.ida.liu.se/labs/pelab/omath`

[14] Hindmarsh, A.C., ODEPACK, A Systematized Collection of ODE Solvers, *Scientific Computing*, R. S. Stepleman et al. (eds.), North-Holland, Amsterdam, 1983 (Vol. 1 of IMACS Transactions on Scientific Computation), pp. 55-64, also `http://www.netlib.org/odepack/index.html`

[15] Otter M., C. Schlegel, and H. Elmqvist, Modeling and Real-time Simulation of an Automatic Gearbox using Modelica. In Proceedings of ESS'97 - European Simulation Symposium, Passau, Oct. 19-23, 1997.

[16] Tummescheit H., T. Ernst and M. Klose, Modelica and Smile - A Case Study Applying Object-Oriented Concepts to Multi-facet Modeling. In Proceedings of ESS'97 - European Simulation Symposium, Passau, Oct. 19-23, 1997.

[17] Broenink J.F., Bond-Graph Modeling in Modelica. In Proceedings of ESS'97 - European Simulation Symposium, Passau, Oct. 19-23, 1997.

[18] SIMULINK 2 - Dynamic System Simulation. `http://www.mathworks.com/ products/simulink/`

[19] ACSL software. `http://www.mga.com`

[20] Jan Van der Spiegel. SPICE - A Brief Overview. http://howard.engr.siu.edu/elec/faculty/etienne/spice.overview.html, http://www.seas.upenn.edu/~jan/spice/spice.overview.html

[21] ADAMS - virtual prototyping virtually anything that moves. `http://www.adams.com`

[22] V. Engelson, P. Fritzson, D. Fritzson. Generating Efficient 3D graphics animation code with OpenGL from object oriented models in Mathematica, In *Innovation in Mathematics. Proceedings of the Second International Mathematica Symposium,* Rovaniemi, Finland, 29 June - 4 July 1997, V.Keränen, P. Mitic, A. Hietamäki (Ed.), pp. 129 - 136

[23] Modelica Home Page `http://www.Dynasim.se/Modelica`

[24] V. Engelson, P. Fritzson, D. Fritzson. Automatic Generation of User Interfaces From Data Structure Specifications and Object-Oriented Application Models. In *Proceedings of European Conference on Object-Oriented Programming (ECOOP96)*, Linz, Austria, 8-12 July 1996, vol. 1098 of Lecture Notes in Computer Science, Pierre Cointe (Ed.), pp. 114-141. Springer-Verlag, 1996

[25] V. Engelson, P. Fritzson, D. Fritzson. Using the Mathematica environment for generating efficient 3D graphics. In *Proceedings of COMPUGRAPHICS/ EDUGRAPHICS*, Vilamoura, Portugal, 15-18 December 1997 (to appear).

[26] D. Fritzson, P. Nordling. Solving Ordinary Differential Equations on Parallel Computers Applied to Dynamic Rolling Bearing Simulation. In *Parallel Programming and Applications*, P. Fritzson, L. Finmo, eds., IOS Press, 1995

[27] SIMPACK Home page `http://www.cis.ufl.edu/mpack/~fishwick/simpack.html`

[28] M. Löfgren, J. Lindskov Knudsen, B. Magnusson, O. Lehrmann Madsen *Object-Oriented Environments - The Mjølner Approach* ISBN 0-13-009291-6, Prentice Hall, 1994. See also Beta Home Page, `http://www.daimi.aau.dk/~beta/`

[29] H. Elmqvist, S. E. Mattsson: "Modelica - The Next Generation Modeling Language - An International Design Effort". In *Proceedings of First World Congress of System Simulation,* Singapore, September 1-3 1997.

Synthesizing Object-Oriented and Functional Design to Promote Re-use*

Shriram Krishnamurthi, Matthias Felleisen, and Daniel P. Friedman**

Department of Computer Science
Rice University

Abstract. Many problems require recursively specified types of data and a collection of tools that operate on those data. Over time, these problems evolve so that the programmer must extend the toolkit or extend the types and adjust the existing tools accordingly. Ideally, this should be done without modifying existing code. Unfortunately, the prevailing program design strategies do not support both forms of extensibility: functional programming accommodates the addition of tools, while object-oriented programming supports either adding new tools or extending the data set, but not both. In this paper, we present a composite design pattern that synthesizes the best of both approaches and in the process resolves the tension between the two design strategies. We also show how this protocol suggests a new set of linguistic facilities for languages that support class systems.

1 Evolutionary Software Development

Programming practice frequently confronts programmers with the following design dilemma. A recursively defined set of data must be processed by several different tools. In anticipation of future extensions, the data specification and the tools should therefore be implemented such that it is easy to

1. add a new variant of data and adjust the existing tools accordingly, and
2. extend the collection of tools.

Ideally, these extensions should not require any changes to existing code. For one, source modification is cumbersome and error-prone. Second, the source may not be available for modification because the tools are distributed in the form of object code. Finally, it may be necessary to evolve the base program in several different directions, in which case code modifications are prohibitively expensive because the required duplication would result in duplicated maintenance costs.

This dilemma manifests itself in many different application areas. A particularly important example arises in the area of programming languages. Language

* This research was partially supported by NSF grants CCR-9619756, CCR-9633109, CCR-9708957 and CDA-9713032, and a Texas ATP grant.

** Permanent address: Computer Science Department, Indiana University.

grammars are typically specified via BNFs, which denote recursively defined data sets. Language-processing tools recursively traverse sentences formed from the grammar. In this scenario, a new form of data means an additional clause in the BNF; new tools must be able to traverse all possible elements of the (extended) grammar.

Unfortunately, prevailing design strategies do not accommodate the required evolution:

- The "functional" approach, which is often realized with conventional procedural languages, implements tools as procedures on recursive types. While this strategy easily accommodates the extension of the set of tools, it requires significant source modifications when the data set needs to be extended.
- The (standard) "object-oriented" approach defines a recursive set of data with a collection of classes, one per variant (BNF clause), and places one method per tool in each class. In the parlance of object-oriented design patterns [13], this approach is known as the Interpreter pattern. The problem it poses is dual to the problem of the functional approach: variants are easy to add, while tool additions require code modifications.
- If the collection of tools is large, the designer may also use the Visitor pattern, a variant of the Interpreter pattern, which collects the code for a tool in a single class. Roughly speaking, the Visitor pattern emulates the functional approach in an object-oriented setting. As a result, it suffers from the same problem as the functional approach.

In short, the two design styles suffer from a serious problem. Each style accommodates one form of extension easily and renders the other nearly impossible.[1]

This paper presents the Extensible Visitor pattern, a new composite design pattern [28], which provides an elegant solution to the above dilemma. The composite pattern is a combination of the Visitor and Factory Method patterns. Its implementation in any class-based object-oriented programming language is straightforward. In addition, the paper introduces a linguistic abstraction that facilitates the implementation of the Visitor and Extensible Visitor patterns. The abstraction syntactically synthesizes the best of the functional and the object-oriented design approaches. Using the abstraction, a programmer only specifies the necessary pieces of the pattern; a translator assembles the pattern implementation from these pieces. We consider this approach a promising avenue for future research on pattern implementations.

Section 2 introduces a simple example of the design dilemma and briefly discusses the functional approach and the standard object-oriented approach (based on the Interpreter pattern) to extensible software. Section 3 analyzes the problems of the Visitor pattern and then develops the Extensible Visitor pattern in the context of the same running example. Section 4 describes some of the type-checking issues that arise when using this pattern. Section 5 presents a

[1] Cook [4] devotes his tutorial to this problem, which was first anticipated by Reynolds [27].

datatype Shape = $\square$ **of** num
| $\bigcirc$ **of** num
| $\cdot \rightsquigarrow \cdot$ **of** Point × Shape

Fig. 1. The Functional Approach: Types

ContainsPt : Point × Shape $\longrightarrow$ **boolean**

ContainsPt p ($\square$ s) = $\cdots$
| p ($\bigcirc$ r) = $\cdots$
| p ($\cdot \rightsquigarrow \cdot$ d s) = $\cdots$ ContainsPt p' s $\cdots$

Fig. 2. The Functional Approach: Tools

Shrink : num × Shape $\longrightarrow$ Shape

Shrink pct ($\square$ s) = ($\square$ $\cdots$)
| pct ($\bigcirc$ r) = ($\bigcirc$ $\cdots$)
| pct ($\cdot \rightsquigarrow \cdot$ d s) = ($\cdot \rightsquigarrow \cdot$ d (Shrink pct s))

Fig. 3. The Functional Approach: Adding Tools

linguistic extension that facilitates the implementation of the Visitor and Extensible Visitor patterns. Section 6 discusses the state of our implementation and our experiences. The last two sections describe related work and summarize the ideas in this paper.

2 Existing Design Approaches

To illustrate the design problem with a concrete example, we present a simplistic "geometry manager" program, derived from a US Department of Defense programming contest [15]. We discuss both the functional and the object-oriented design methods in this context and expose their failings. For this discussion, we use the term *tool* to refer to a service provided by the program, which is typically implemented as a class, function, or procedure.

Initially, our system specifies a set of data (Shape) partitioned into three subsets—squares ($\square$), circles ($\bigcirc$) and translated shapes ($\cdot \rightsquigarrow \cdot$)—and a tool that, given a shape and a point, determines whether the point is inside the shape (ContainsPt). The set of shapes is then extended with a composite shape that is the union of two others (⧉). The set of tools grows to include a shrinker that, given a number and a shape, creates a copy of that shape shrunken in its dimensions by the given percentage (Shrink).

2.1 The Functional Approach

In a functional language, recursively defined data are specified using *datatype* declarations. Such a declaration introduces a new type with one or more *variants*.

In Haskell [16] or SML [20], for example, a programmer could use the **data** or **datatype** construct, respectively, to represent the set of shapes, as shown in Fig. 1.[2] Each variant introduces a new tag to distinguish it from the other forms of data. Each variant also specifies a record-like structure with a fixed number of typed fields. The types may include the datatype being declared. In the figure, the three variants of the datatype describe the structure of the different shapes: the square is described by the length of its side (a number), a circle by its radius (a number), and a translated shape by a displacement (a Point) for the underlying shape. Values are constructed by writing the name of a variant followed by as many expressions as there are fields for that variant. For example, (□ 3) constructs a square, which is of type Shape and whose side has length 3.

Tools map variants of the Shape datatype to results. For example, Fig. 2 shows the outline of the tool ContainsPt, which determines whether a point is inside a shape. Its mathematics has been elided since it is rudimentary and not relevant to our example. The function definition uses pattern-matching: if a pattern matches, the identifiers to the left of = are bound on the right to the corresponding values of the fields. For example, the pattern (□ s) in the first line of the function matches only squares and binds s to the length of the square's side.

Since the datatype definition of a shape is recursive, the corresponding tools are usually recursive, too. The recursive calls in a tool match the recursive structure of the datatype. This template can be used to define other tools; for example, Fig. 3 shows the structure of Shrink, which takes a shrink factor (a number) and a shape, and produces the same shape but with the dimensions shrunk by the specified factor. We can add tools like Shrink without making any changes to existing tools such as ContainsPt.

In the functional style, the code for all the variants is defined within the scope of a single function. This simplifies the task of comprehending the tool. It also makes it easy to define abstractions over the code for the variants.

Unfortunately, it is impossible to add a variant to Shape without modifying existing code. First, the datatype representing shapes must be modified because most existing functional languages do not offer an extensible datatype mechanism at all or do so in a restricted manner [6, 19, 20]. Second, even if extensible datatype definitions are available, the code for each tool, such as ContainsPt, must be edited to accommodate these extensions to the datatype.[3]

In summary, the conventional functional programming methodology makes it easy to add new tools, but impossible to extend the datatype without code modification.

---

[2] In C [17], one would use (recursive) pointers, structures and unions to represent this set of constructs.

[3] Sometimes, the modifications may change the semantics of the operation. In such cases, a more sophisticated protocol is necessary, such as that specified by Cartwright and Felleisen [2].

2.2 The Object-Oriented Approach

In an object-oriented program, the data definitions for shapes and their tools are developed in parallel. Abstract classes introduce new collections of data and specify signatures for the operations that are common to all variants. Concrete classes represent the variants and provide implementations of the actual operations. This is known as the Interpreter pattern [13].[4] For instance, the SML program from Figs. 1 and 2 corresponds to the Java [14] program shown in Fig. 4. The recursive references among the collection of classes lead to corresponding recursive calls among methods, analogous to the recursion in the functional program.

In this setting, it is straightforward to extend the set of shapes. It suffices to add a new concrete class that extends Shape and whose methods specify the behavior of the existing tools for that extension. For example, Fig. 5 shows how ◫, the union of two shapes, is added to our system. Most importantly, existing tools remain unchanged.

Unfortunately, the Interpreter pattern makes it impossible to add a new tool if existing code is to stay the same. The only option is to create, for each concrete class, an extension that defines a method for the new tool. This affects every client, *i.e.*, any code that creates instances of the concrete classes. The clients must be updated to create instances of the new, extended classes instead of the old ones so that the objects they create have methods that implement the new tool.

The affected clients can include an existing tool. For example, in Fig. 6, the *shrink* method creates concrete instances of Shape that have methods for only the *containsPt* and *shrink* tools. If a tool T that is added later invokes *shrink*, the object returned by the method will not support all tools, in particular T, unless the *shrink* method is physically updated.

In summary, object-oriented programming—as represented by the Interpreter pattern—provides the equivalent of an extensible, user-defined datatype. The Interpreter pattern solves the problem of extending the set of shapes. However, this conventional design makes it difficult or, in general, impossible to extend the collection of tools without changing existing code. Furthermore, the code for each tool is distributed over several classes, which makes it more difficult to comprehend the tool's functionality. Any abstractions between the branches of a tool must reside in Shape (unless the programming language has multiple-inheritance), even though the abstraction may not apply to most tools and hence does not belong in Shape.

3 A Protocol for Extensibility and Re-Use

In any interesting system, both the (recursive) data domain and the toolkit are subject to change. Thus re-use through extensibility along both dimensions is essential.

[4] The Composite pattern [13] is sometimes used instead.

```
abstract class Shape {
  Shape shrink (double pct); }
class □ extends Shape {
  double s;
  □ (double s) { this.s = s ; }
  boolean containsPt (Point p) { ··· } }
class ○ extends Shape {
  double r;
  ○ (double r) { this.r = r ; }
  boolean containsPt (Point p) { ··· } }
class ·⇝· extends Shape {
  Point d;
  Shape s;
  ·⇝· (Point d, Shape s) { this.d = d ; this.s = s ; }
  boolean containsPt (Point p) {
    return (s.containsPt (···)) ; } }
```

Fig. 4. The Object-Oriented Approach: Basic Types and Tools

```
class □○ extends Shape {
  Shape lhs, rhs;
  □○ (Shape lhs, Shape rhs) { this.lhs = lhs ; this.rhs = rhs ; }
  boolean containsPt (Point p) {
    return (lhs.containsPt (p) ∨ rhs.containsPt (p)) ; } }
```

Fig. 5. The Object-Oriented Approach: Adding Variants

```
class Shrink□ extends □ {
  :
  Shape shrink (double pct) {
    return (new Shrink□ (···)) ; }
  :
}
```

```
class Shrink○ extends ○ { ··· }

class Shrink·⇝· extends ·⇝· { ··· }

class Shrink□○ extends □○ { ··· }
```

Fig. 6. The Object-Oriented Approach: Adding Tools

In this section, we develop a programming protocol based on object-oriented concepts that satisfies these desiderata.[5] We present the protocol in three main stages. First we explain how to represent extensible datatypes and tools via the Visitor pattern and how the Visitor pattern suffers from the same problem as the functional design strategy. Still, the Visitor pattern can be reformulated so that a programmer can extend the data domain and the toolkit in a systematic manner. Finally, we demonstrate how the protocol can accommodate extensions across multiple tools and mutually-referential data domains.

The ideas are illustrated with fragments of code written in Pizza [21], a parametrically polymorphic extension of Java. The choice of Pizza is explained in Sect. 4. In principle, any class-based language, such as C++, Eiffel, Java, or Smalltalk, suffices.

3.1 Representing Extensible Datatypes

The representation of extensible datatypes in the Visitor pattern is identical to that in the Interpreter pattern, but each class (variant) contains only one interpretive method: *process*. This method consumes a *processor*, which is an object that contains a method corresponding to each variant in the datatype. For each variant, the *process* method dispatches on that method in the processor corresponding to that variant, and returns the result of the invoked method. Figure 7 illustrates how the datatype from Sect. 2.2 is represented according to this protocol.

Since different processors return different types of results, the *process* method has the parametrically polymorphic type ShapeProcessor$\langle\alpha\rangle \longrightarrow \alpha$. That is, *process*'s argument has the parametric type ShapeProcessor$\langle\alpha\rangle$, which is implemented as an interface in Pizza. The return type is α in place of a single, fixed type. In Pizza, this type is written as $\langle\alpha\rangle\ \alpha$. For our running example, the parametric interface and the outline of the tool that checks for point containment (ContainsPt) are shown in Fig. 8.

If a processor depends on parameters other than the object to be processed, it accepts these as arguments to its constructor and stores them in instance variables. Thus, to check whether a point p is in a shape s, we create an instance of the ContainsPt processor, which is of type ShapeProcessor⟨**boolean**⟩ and which accepts the point p as an argument: **new** ContainsPt (p). This instance of ContainsPt is passed to the shape's *process* method:

$$s.process\ (\textbf{new}\ \textsf{ContainsPt}\ (p))$$

Similarly, recursion in a processor is implemented by invoking the *process* method of the appropriate object. If the processor's extra arguments do not change, *process* can be given **this**, *i.e.*, the current instance of the processor, as its argument; otherwise, a new instance of the processor is created. Consider the ContainsPt processor in Fig. 8. It deals with translated shapes by translating the

[5] A preliminary version of this protocol appears in the book by Felleisen and Friedman [9].

```
abstract class Shape {
  abstract ⟨α⟩ α process (ShapeProcessor⟨α⟩ p) ; }
class □ extends Shape {
  double s;
  □ (double s) { this.s = s ; }
  ⟨α⟩ α process (ShapeProcessor⟨α⟩ p) {
    return p.forSquare (this) ; } }
class ○ extends Shape {
  double r;
  ○ (double r) { this.r = r ; }
  ⟨α⟩ α process (ShapeProcessor⟨α⟩ p) {
    return p.forCircle (this) ; } }
class · ⇝ · extends Shape {
  Point d;
  Shape s;
  · ⇝ · (Point d, Shape s) { this.d = d ; this.s = s ; }
  ⟨α⟩ α process (ShapeProcessor⟨α⟩ p) {
    return p.forTranslated (this) ; } }
```

Fig. 7. The Visitor Pattern: Types

```
interface ShapeProcessor⟨α⟩ {
  α forSquare (□ s);
  α forCircle (○ c);
  α forTranslated (· ⇝ · t) ; }

class ContainsPt implements ShapeProcessor⟨boolean⟩ {
  Point p;
  ContainsPt (Point p) { this.p = p ; }
  public boolean forSquare (□ s) { ··· }
  public boolean forCircle (○ c) { ··· }
  public boolean forTranslated (· ⇝ · t) {
    return t.s.process (new ContainsPt (···)) ; } }
```

Fig. 8. The Visitor Pattern: Tools

point and checking it against the underlying shape. The underlined expression in the *forTranslated* method implements the appropriate recursive call by creating a new processor.

The Visitor pattern ensures that the code for each tool is localized in a single class and easily comprehensible, as in the functional approach. In the absence of a parametrically polymorphic type system, however, it is difficult to specify the types for the Visitor pattern. Section 4 discusses this issue in detail.

3.2 Adding Tools

Extending a program's tool collection based on the Visitor pattern is straightforward. For instance, a processor that shrinks shapes would implement the ShapeProcessor⟨Shape⟩ interface. This is outlined in Fig. 9. In this example, a translated shape is shrunk by shrinking the underlying shape; the shrink factor does not change for the translated figure. Hence, the recursive call uses the same processor (**this**, underlined in the figure).

3.3 Extending the Datatype: A False Start

Since concrete subclasses represent the variants of a datatype, extending a datatype description means adding new concrete subclasses. Each new class must contain the *process* method, which is the defining characteristic of Visitor-style datatypes. The actual processors are defined separately.

In parallel to the datatype extension, we must also define an extension of the interface for processors. The extended interface specifies one method per variant in the old datatype and one for each new variant. Of course, the *process* method in the new variants should only accept processors that implement the new interface. This requirement is expressed differently in different languages. In Pizza, for example, we use a runtime check; in languages that allow *process* to be overridden covariantly, any usage errors would be caught during type-checking.

To illustrate this idea, we add the union shape (◫) to the collection of shapes. The new concrete class and interface are shown in Fig. 10. A cast (underlined in the figure) requires the processor for ◫'s to implement the extended interface, UnionShapeProcessor. The extended processors can then be defined as class extensions of the existing processors for the earlier set of shapes. These extensions implement the new interface, as shown in Fig. 11.

Unfortunately, this straightforward extension of ContainsPt is incorrect. Consider the *forTranslated* method in ContainsPt. It creates a new instance of ContainsPt to process the translated shape. The new instance checks whether the "un-translated" point is in the translated shape. Since ContainsPt does not implement a *forUnion* method, a ContainsPt processor cannot process a ◫ shape. More concretely, checking whether the shape

$$\textbf{new} \cdot\!\rightsquigarrow\!\cdot\, (p,\ \textbf{new}\ ◫\ (\textbf{new}\ \square\ (\cdots),\ \textbf{new}\ \bigcirc\ (\cdots)))$$

```
class Shrink implements ShapeProcessor⟨Shape⟩ {
  double pct;
  Shrink (double pct) { this.pct = pct ; }
  public Shape forSquare (□ s) { ··· }
  public Shape forCircle (○ c) { ··· }
  public Shape forTranslated (· ⇝ · t) {
    return new · ⇝ · (t.d, t.s.process (this)) ; } }
```

Fig. 9. The Visitor Pattern: Adding Tools

```
interface UnionShapeProcessor⟨α⟩ extends ShapeProcessor⟨α⟩ {
  α forUnion (□○ u) ; }

class □○ extends Shape {
  Shape s1, s2;
  □○ (Shape s1, Shape s2) { ··· }
  ⟨α⟩ α process (ShapeProcessor⟨α⟩ p) {
    return ((UnionShapeProcessor) p).forUnion (this) ; } }
```

Fig. 10. Datatype Extension

```
class ContainsPtUnion extends ContainsPt
  implements UnionShapeProcessor⟨boolean⟩ {
  ContainsPtUnion (Point p) { super (p) ; }
  public boolean forUnion (□○ u) {
    return u.lhs.process (this) ∨ u.rhs.process (this) ; } }
```

Fig. 11. Processor Extension

```
class ContainsPt implements ShapeProcessor⟨boolean⟩ {
  Point p;
  ContainsPt (Point p) { this.p = p ; }
  ContainsPt makeContainsPt (Point p) {
    return new ContainsPt (p) ; }
  public boolean forSquare (□ s) { ··· }
  public boolean forCircle (○ c) { ··· }
  public boolean forTranslated (· ⇝ · t) {
    return t.s.process (makeContainsPt (···)) ; } }

class ContainsPtUnion extends ContainsPt
  implements UnionShapeProcessor⟨boolean⟩ {
  ContainsPtUnion (Point p) { super (p) ; }
  ContainsPt makeContainsPt (Point p) {
    return new ContainsPtUnion (p) ; }
  public boolean forUnion (◫ u) {
    return u.lhs.process (this) ∨ u.rhs.process (this) ; } }
```

Fig. 12. Extensible Visitor Processor Extension

contains some point q causes a runtime error. Specifically, when the *forTranslated* method creates a new ContainsPt processor and when this new processor is about to process the ◫ shape, the *process* method in ◫ finds that the processor does not implement the UnionShapeProcessor interface and therefore raises a runtime error.

3.4 Extending the Datatype: The Solution

The error points out that processors in the Visitor pattern are not designed to accommodate extension of the datatype. Suppose a recursive processor P can handle the variants $v_1, \ldots, v_n$. As long as the recursive call passes **this** to the datum, it does not matter whether the object is an instance of P or of a subtype of P. If, however, P creates a new instance of P for the recursive call, the new object can only handle the variants $v_1, \ldots, v_n$. When a new variant, v_{n+1}, is added, the processor provided in the recursive call can no longer process all possible inputs.

To avoid this problem, we must refrain from making a premature commitment in the recursive step. To delay making the commitment prematurely, we must delegate the decision of which processor P creates. Initially, the delegate creates instances of P. Then, when the variant v_{n+1} is added and P is extended to P', a new delegate overrides the old one to create instances of P' instead. We can encode this idea to create the *Extensible Visitor* protocol as follows:

1. The creation of new processors is performed via a separate method: a *virtual constructor* (or Factory Method [13]), called *makeContainsPt* in our example.

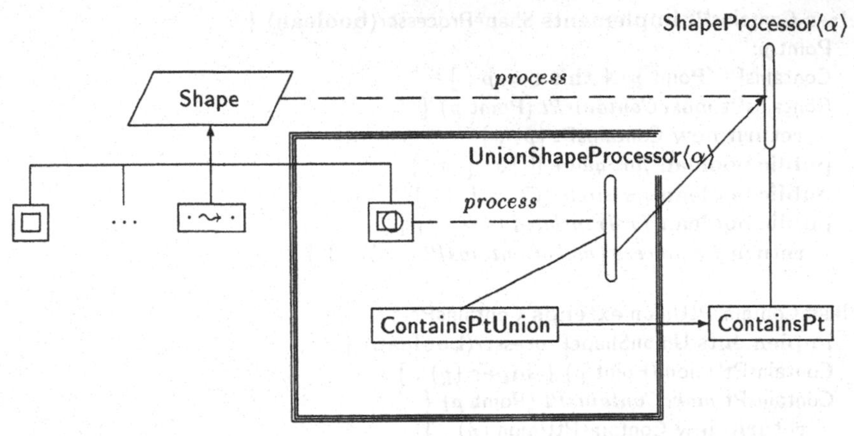

Fig. 13. Datatype and Processor Extension

2. The virtual constructor is an η-expansion of the original constructor, *e.g.*, in ContainsPt, the virtual constructor is

```
ContainsPt makeContainsPt (Point p) {
    return new ContainsPt (p) ; }
```

3. Expressions that construct processors are replaced with invocations of the virtual constructor.
4. The virtual constructor is overridden in all extensions of processors. Thus, in ContainsPtUnion, we now have

```
ContainsPt makeContainsPt (Point p) {
    return new ContainsPtUnion (p) ; }
```

The final version of the code is shown in Fig. 12.

The form of the system after the extension is shown in Fig. 13. The rectangles represent concrete classes, the parallelogram an abstract class, and the thin ovals interfaces. Solid lines with arrowheads show inheritance, while those without arrowheads indicate that a class implements an interface. Dashed lines connect classes and interfaces. The label on a dashed line names a method in the class that accepts an argument whose type is the interface. The boxed portion is the extended datatype and its corresponding processor. For a processor and datatype extension all code outside of the thick box can be re-used without any change.

3.5 Updating Dependencies Between Tools and Datatypes

The problem of updating the dependencies of processors has a general counterpart. Suppose the processors P_1, P_2, and P_3 all process the same datatype D and depend on each other as follows: P_1 creates instances of P_1 and P_2, P_2 uses

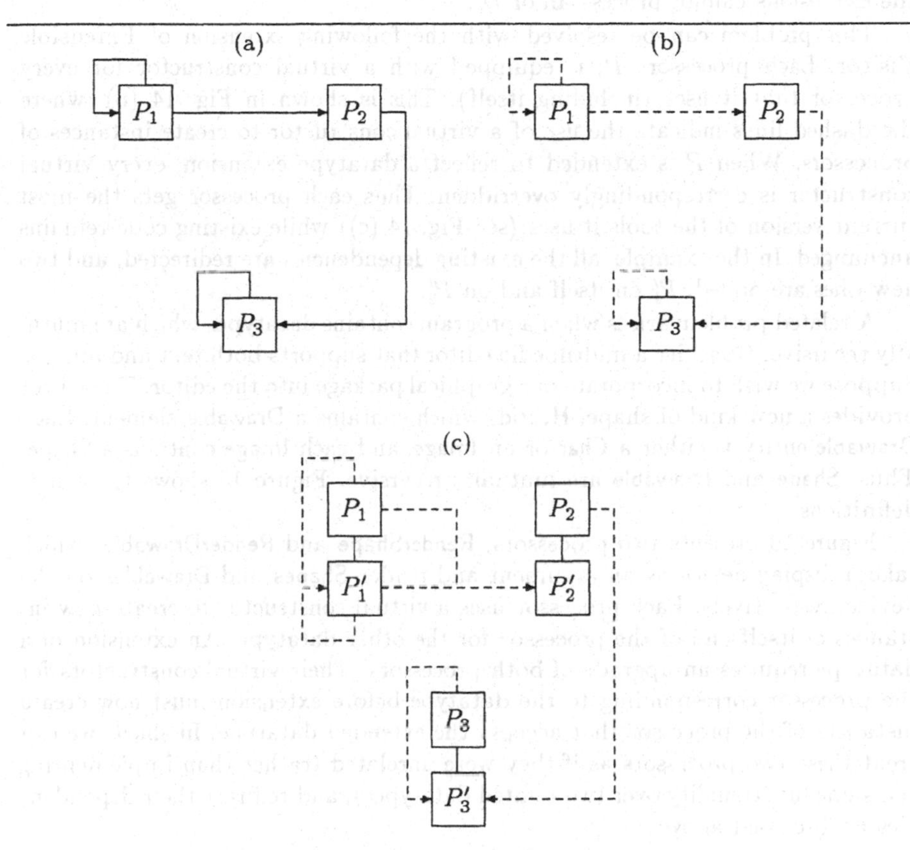

Fig. 14. **Updating Dependencies Between Tools**

P_3, and P_3 uses itself. Figure 14 (a) illustrates this situation: each processor at the tail of an arrow creates an instance of the processor at the head. When D is extended to D' with new variants, the tools are extended to P'_1, P'_2, and P'_3, respectively. If P_1, P_2, and P_3 directly create instances of each other, however, the extensions cannot process all of D'.

This problem can be resolved with the following extension of Extensible Visitor. Each processor, P, is equipped with a virtual constructor for every processor that it uses (including itself). This is shown in Fig. 14 (b), where the dashed lines indicate the use of a virtual constructor to create instances of processors. When P is extended to reflect a datatype extension, every virtual constructor is correspondingly overridden. Thus each processor gets the most current version of the tools it uses (see Fig. 14 (c)) while existing code remains unchanged. In the example, all the existing dependencies are redirected, and two new ones are added: P'_1 on itself and on P'_2.

A related problem arises when a program contains datatypes which are mutually recursive. Consider a multimedia editor that supports both text and images. Suppose we wish to incorporate our graphical package into the editor. The editor provides a new kind of shape, Hybrid, which contains a Drawable element. Each Drawable entity is either a Char or an Image, and each Image contains a Shape. Thus, Shape and Drawable are mutually recursive. Figure 15 shows these new definitions.

Figure 16 presents two processors, RenderShape and RenderDrawable, which take a display device as an argument and render Shapes and Drawables on the device, respectively. Each processor uses a virtual constructor to create new instances of itself and of the processor for the other datatype. An extension of a datatype requires an upgrade of both processors. Their virtual constructors for the processor corresponding to the datatype before extension must now create instances of the processor that accepts the extended datatype. In short, we can treat these two processors as if they were unrelated (rather than implementing the same functionality over two related datatypes), and redirect their dependencies as discussed above.

4 Types

Typed object-oriented languages can provide (at least) two kinds of polymorphism: *object polymorphism* and *parametric polymorphism*. Object polymorphism means that a variable declared to be of a particular class (type), say C, can hold instances of C or subclasses of C. In contrast, parametric polymorphism allows types to contain type variables that are (implicitly) universally quantified; for example, $list(\alpha)$ is the type of a homogenous list containing any type of element. Most typed object-oriented languages provide object polymorphism; a few offer parametric polymorphism.[6]

[6] C++'s [31] template mechanism provides a limited amount of parametric polymorphism.

```
class Hybrid extends Shape {
  Drawable d;
  ⋮ }

abstract class Drawable { ··· }
class Char extends Drawable { ··· }
class Image extends Drawable {
  Shape s;
  ⋮ }
```

Fig. 15. Mutually Recursive Datatypes

```
class RenderShape implements ShapeProcessor⟨void⟩ {
  Device d;
  RenderShape (Device d) { this.d = d ; }
  RenderShape makeRenderShape (Device d) {
    return new RenderShape (d) ; }
  RenderDrawable makeRenderDrawable (Device d) {
    return new RenderDrawable (d) ; }
  ⋮ }

class RenderDrawable implements DrawableProcessor⟨void⟩ {
  Device d;
  RenderDrawable (Device d) { this.d = d ; }
  RenderDrawable makeRenderDrawable (Device d) {
    return new RenderDrawable (d) ; }
  RenderShape makeRenderShape (Device d) {
    return new RenderShape (d) ; }
  ⋮ }
```

Fig. 16. Tools over Mutually Recursive Datatypes

Pizza's parametric polymorphism greatly facilitates the implementation of Extensible Visitors.[7] To illustrate this point in more detail, we contrast the Pizza implementation with one in Java. In Java, if *process* is expected to return values, its return type must be declared as Object. Choosing any other type C_p would force all clients to return subtypes of C_p, which is inappropriate for some clients and prevents re-use of existing libraries and classes.[8] All clients that invoke processors—including recursive invocations—must then use narrowing casts to restore the returned value to its original type. If we translate ContainsPt to return Boolean instead of **boolean**, the Java version of the *forUnion* method in ContainsPtUnion is:

> **public** Object *forUnion* (□ *u*) {
>   **return new** Boolean
>   ((((Boolean) (*u.lhs.process* (**this**))).*booleanValue* ()) ∨
>   (((Boolean) (*u.rhs.process* (**this**))).*booleanValue* ())) ; }

For the Pizza version of the same code (see Fig. 11) the compiler statically verifies that the return type of a processor is acceptable in each invoking context. Thus, in a proper implementation, the programmer gets the full benefit of type-checking, and the program incurs no runtime expense. In contrast, the Java version passes the type-checker, but the programmer is forced to specify runtime checks. These checks compromise both the program's robustness and its efficiency. A Java compiler could eliminate some of these checks, but this would rely on sophisticated flow analyses, which few compilers (if any) perform.[9]

Even Pizza requires the programmer to repeat several pieces of type information. For example, when ContainsPtUnion is defined as an extension to ContainsPt, the type parameter of UnionShapeProcessor must still be instantiated (see Fig. 12). Also, the methods inside a processor need type declarations, even though the return type is the same as the parameter of the interface. A powerful type inference mechanism, such as those of Eifrig, Smith, and Trifonov [7] and Palsberg [22], can alleviate many of these problems, especially in the context of dynamically-typed object-oriented languages.

---

[7] Thorup [33] has proposed a different style of type parameterization for Java: virtual types. To implement Extensible Visitor using virtual types, which are overrideable types in classes analogous to virtual methods, and obtain the benefits of type-checking, we need to declare *process* as follows (where α is the virtual type declared in the processor):

$$p.\alpha\ \textit{process}\ (\textsf{ShapeProcessor}\ p)$$

Unfortunately, this is currently not possible with virtual types [personal communication, August 1997]. Hence, virtual types are not yet a viable alternative for our Extensible Visitor.

[8] The choice of Object still cannot accommodate processors (such as ContainsPt) that return primitive types, which are not subtypes of any other type, including Object [14]. Such processors are forced to use the "wrapped" versions of primitive types, incurring both space and time penalties.

[9] These comments apply equally well to the Visitor protocol.

```
datatype Shape {
  variant □ (double s);
  variant ○ (double r);
  variant · ⤳ · (Point d, Shape s);
}

processor ContainsPt processes Shape
                     uses ContainsPt
                     returns boolean {
  fields (Point p);
  variant for□(s) { ··· }
  variant for○(c) { ··· }
  variant for· ⤳ ·(t) {
    return t.s.process (makeContainsPt (···)) ; }
}

datatype UnionShape extends Shape {
  variant ⊡ (Shape lhs, Shape rhs);
}

processor ContainsPtUnion extends ContainsPt
                          processes UnionShape {
  variant for⊡(u) {
    return u.lhs.process (this) ∨
           u.rhs.process (this) ; }
}
```

Fig. 17. Sample Extended Pizza Specification

5 A Language for Extensible Systems

Although the Extensible Visitor pattern solves our problem, it requires the management of numerous mundane details, such as writing class declarations to define the datatype and its variants, defining and overriding the virtual constructors, and keeping the type information consistent. Since these tasks are cumbersome and error-prone and can be managed automatically, we have also designed and implemented a language extension for specifying instances of the Visitor and Extensible Visitor patterns.

Our system, called Zodiac, provides constructs for declaring and extending datatypes and processors. Datatypes and processors are translated into collections of classes. Processors are defined with respect to a datatype. The action for each variant V of the datatype is implemented by a method m_V in the processor. The method m_V accepts one argument, which is an instance of the class used to implement the variant V.

Figure 17 illustrates how to use a Pizza-oriented version of Zodiac to specify the datatype and toolkit for our running example. At the top we define the collection of shapes, followed by the ContainsPt processor. Below that we specify UnionShape, which is Shape extended with the union of two shapes, and its corresponding processor as an extension of ContainsPt. The example uses all of Zodiac's constructs:

datatype defines a new extensible datatype or **extends** an existing one.[10] Each variant of the datatype, together with its fields, is listed following the keyword **variant**. Zodiac creates an abstract class for a new datatype, and translates each variant into a concrete subclass with a *process* method.

processor defines a processor for the datatype that is specified in the **processes** clause. The (optional) **uses** clause is followed by a list of tools that are used by the processor.[11] The processor's return type is declared after **returns**. The (optional) **fields** clause specifies the parameters of a processor, from which Zodiac determines the instance variable declarations and the constructor. The individual methods for the variants are declared with **variant**.
Zodiac creates a virtual constructor, such as *makeContainsPt* in the example, for each tool listed as a dependency. Processor extensions inherit the **returns** and **fields** declarations and the **uses** dependency of their parent. A derived processor needs to declare only the new fields and dependencies. The constructor of a processor extension accepts values for all its fields and those of its superclass, and conveys values for the inherited fields to its superclass's constructor.

Zodiac expands the Extensible Visitor specification into a collection of classes and interfaces that is α-equivalent to the code in Sect. 3.

6 Implementation and Performance

Zodiac is currently implemented as a language extension to MzScheme [12], a version of Scheme [3] extended with a Java-like object system.

A preliminary version of Zodiac has been used to implement DrScheme, a Scheme programming environment [11]. DrScheme is a pedagogically-motivated system that helps beginners by presenting Scheme as a succession of increasingly complex languages. It also supports several tools such as a syntax checker, a program analyzer, *etc.*

The largest language handled by DrScheme is the complete MzScheme language, which is many times the size of standard Scheme. Still, the language processing portions of DrScheme were developed and are maintained (part-time) by a single programmer. The preliminary implementation of Zodiac played a

[10] This datatype construct is superficially related to Pizza's algebraic data types. Pizza's data types are meant principally for creating data structures; they do not provide default visitor methods.

[11] This clause is optional since a tool may not have any dependencies to declare. This information cannot be inferred since deciding which tool dependencies should be updated is a design decision that must be made by the programmer.

significant rôle in this rapid development. It simplified the specification of the language tower, which, in turn, avoided many clerical errors and facilitated the maintenance of the software.

Our current implementation has been in use for about two years. The resulting environment is used daily in courses at Rice University and other institutions. The environment is also used to develop actual applications, and the overhead of Extensible Visitor is low enough to be practical for such use.

Zodiac is also being applied in other domains. We have used it to build Chisel, a general-purpose, extensible document construction system. This system handles "real-world" documents, and easily meets demanding performance criteria. For example, Chisel generates our entire departmental brochure (corresponding to 20-30 printed pages, or about 150 kilobytes of generated HTML) in 20 seconds on a modern workstation.

The marginal cost of using our method over the Visitor pattern is minimal. The sole difference is in the creation of processors. When the virtual constructor is not overridden, the only cost is that of a local method call, which is effectively inlined in Visitor. In many cases this overhead is avoided entirely because the current instance is re-used for recursive calls. The overall cost of this indirection depends on how often an application constructs data, and on the implementation model used for objects and methods. In our experience, this cost has been negligible.

7 Background and Related Work

Several researchers, including Cook [4], Kühne [18], Palsberg and Jay [23], and Rémy [26], have observed the trade-offs between the functional and object-oriented design approaches, and have noted the relative strengths and weaknesses of each method at datatype and toolkit extension. Of them, only Kühne [18] and Palsberg and Jay [23] suggest a solution.

Kühne's solution [18] is to replace the dispatching in the Visitor protocol with generic functions that perform double-dispatch. While Kühne's approach can accommodate legacy classes, *i.e.*, classes that do not have an explicit method for the visitor, it has the disadvantage of potentially violating the hierarchical design of the program, does not address the organization of the generic function itself, and depends on language features that support double-dispatch.

Palsberg and Jay [23] propose to use reflection to implement a Visitor-like protocol. In their protocol, all visitors are subclasses of the Walkabout class, which provides a default visitor. The default visitor examines the argument; if the argument is not a base class, the Walkabout obtains the argument's fields using Java's reflection facility [32], and then recursively visits each field.

While Palsberg and Jay's approach also scales to legacy classes, it is unclear how well their system works when the variants have instance variables unrelated to the fields of the variant, or when they have multiple fields with the same type. Their proposal also relies on the existence of reflective operators, which are not found in many languages. Finally, their system is over two orders of magnitude slower than a plain Visitor, making it unsuitable for practical use. In contrast, Extensible Visitor works with generic object-oriented languages, and incurs a negligible overhead beyond that of Visitor.

Lieberherr and his colleagues have built a system for adaptive programming [24], which addresses the structural and behavioral adaptation of systems. Using their system, Demeter, programmers write separate specifications of traversals and actions, and Demeter combines these to generate a complete program. In particular, Demeter consumes four inputs: a description of the class graph, a traversal specification for the graph, the operations to perform at each node, and some glue code for linking traversals and operations. Consequently, Demeter is only applicable when all these specifications are available for the production team to reconstruct the program. A company that wishes to distribute its product only in the form of object code to protect its proprietary algorithms would probably be unwilling to distribute its Demeter specification. In contrast, our method both assumes an open-ended program and allows the distribution and extension of object code.

The literature on design patterns contains many other attempts to define and implement patterns similar to Interpreter and Visitor. The primary presentation of the Visitor pattern [13] states that datatype extension is difficult, but does not solve the problems that arise. Baumgartner, Läufer and Russo [1] propose an implementation of Visitor based on multi-method dispatch and claim that it makes datatype and toolkit extension easy, but they do not recognize the problems that arise when extending tools or coordinating multiple tools. Seiter, Palsberg, and Lieberherr [29] describe how dynamic relationships between classes can be captured more expressively using *context relations*, which extend and override the behavior of classes and decouple behavioral evolution and inheritance hierarchies. While context relations offer a more concise way of expressing Visitor-like operations, the authors do not mention or solve the recursive instantiation problem (described in Sect. 3.3).

We can alternatively view the variants of a datatype as specifying the terms of a language, and interpreters as tools. The functional language community has been interested in the problem of creating interpreters from fragments that interpret portions of the language [2, 8, 19, 30]. These approaches are orthogonal to ours in that they can handle semantic extensions to the interpreters, but none of them consider the problem of an extensible toolkit. Most of them [2, 8, 30] do not address the problem of extending the datatype either.

Duggan and Sourelis [6], Findler [10], and Liang, Hudak, and Jones [19] describe methods for creating restricted notions of extensible datatypes. None of these approaches, however, produce datatypes that are extensible in the sense of our protocol. The programmer may specify variants of the datatype separately, but the final datatype must be assembled and "closed" before it can be used. As a result, it is not possible to extend the variants of an existing datatype. Any further additions require access to the source code.

Cartwright and Felleisen's work on extensible interpreters [2], if translated into an object-oriented framework, would probably resemble the Extensible Visitor protocol in an untyped setting.

8 Conclusions and Future Work

We have presented a programming protocol, Extensible Visitor, that can be used to construct systems with extensible recursive data domains and toolkits. It is a novel combination of the functional and object-oriented programming styles that draws on the strengths of each. The object-oriented style is essential to achieve extensibility along the data dimension, yet tools are organized in a functional fashion, enabling extensibility in the functional dimension. Systems based on the Extensible Visitor can be extended without modification to existing code or recompilation (which is an increasingly important concern).

We have also described Zodiac, a language extension for writing extensible programs. Zodiac manages the mundane and potentially error-prone administrative tasks that arise when implementing the Extensible Visitor. A variant of Zodiac has been in use for about two years in our programming environment DrScheme [11]. Through it, DrScheme is able to offer a hierarchy of language levels that facilitate a pedagogically sound introduction to programming. It supports multiple program-processing tools that operate over this range of language levels. Zodiac has also been used to build other systems, such as a document generator with multiple rendering facilities.

Our work suggests future investigations into the efficiency of the new language facilities. The current implementation of Extensible Visitor incurs an execution penalty due to dispatching. Indeed many design patterns suffer similar overheads, but their popularity suggests that users are more interested in design and extensibility considerations than in fine-grained efficiency. For example, Portner [25] reports that his use of the Interpreter pattern to implement a command language is up to 30% slower than a hand-crafted C implementation; still, he states that the low development cost far outweighs the execution penalty. Nevertheless, we believe that a compiler can exploit a Zodiac specification and assemble more efficient code than the naïve translation outlined above.

Acknowledgments

We thank Corky Cartwright, Mike Fagan, Bob Harper, Thomas Kühne, Karl Lieberherr, Jens Palsberg, and Scott Smith for helpful discussions and for comments on preliminary versions of this paper.

References

1. Baumgartner, G., K. Läufer and V. F. Russo. On the interaction of object-oriented design patterns and programming languages. Technical Report CSD-TR-96-020, Purdue University, Feburary 1996.

2. Cartwright, R. S. and M. Felleisen. Extensible denotational language specifications. In Hagiya, M. and J. C. Mitchell, editors, *Symposium on Theoretical Aspects of Computer Science*, pages 244–272. Springer-Verlag, April 1994. LNCS 789.
3. Clinger, W. and J. Rees. The revised[4] report on the algorithmic language Scheme. *ACM Lisp Pointers*, 4(3), July 1991.
4. Cook, W. R. Object-oriented programming versus abstract data types. In *Foundations of Object-Oriented Languages*, pages 151–178, June 1990.
5. Coplien, J. O. and D. C. Schmidt, editors. *Pattern Languages of Program Design*. Addison-Wesley, Reading, MA, 1995.
6. Duggan, D. and C. Sourelis. Mixin modules. In *ACM SIGPLAN International Conference on Functional Programming*, pages 262–273, May 1996.
7. Eifrig, J., S. Smith and V. Trifonov. Type inference for recursively constrained types and its application to OOP. *Mathematical Foundations of Program Semantics*, 1995.
8. Espinosa, D. Building interpreters by transforming stratified monads. Unpublished manuscript, June 1994.
9. Felleisen, M. and D. P. Friedman. *A Little Java, A Few Patterns*. MIT Press, 1998.
10. Findler, R. B. Modular abstract interpreters. Unpublished manuscript, Carnegie Mellon University, June 1995.
11. Findler, R. B., C. Flanagan, M. Flatt, S. Krishnamurthi and M. Felleisen. DrScheme: A pedagogic programming environment for Scheme. In *Ninth International Symposium on Programming Languages, Implementations, Logics, and Programs*, 1997.
12. Flatt, M. PLT MzScheme: Language manual. Technical Report TR97-280, Rice University, 1997.
13. Gamma, E., R. Helm, R. Johnson and J. Vlissides. *Design Patterns: Elements of Reusable Object-Oriented Software*. Addison-Wesley Personal Computing Series. Addison-Wesley, Reading, MA, 1995.
14. Gosling, J., B. Joy and G. L. Steele, Jr. *The Java Language Specification*. Addison-Wesley, 1996.
15. Hudak, P. and M. P. Jones. Haskell *vs.* Ada *vs.* C++ *vs.* Awk *vs.* ... An experiment in software prototyping productivity. Research Report YALEU/DCS/RR-1049, Department of Computer Science, Yale University, New Haven, CT, USA, October 1994.
16. Hudak, P., S. Peyton Jones and P. Wadler. Report on the programming language Haskell: a non-strict, purely functional language. *ACM SIGPLAN Notices*, 27(5), May 1992. Version 1.2.
17. Kernighan, B. W. and D. M. Ritchie. *The C Programming Language*. Prentice Hall, 1988.
18. Kühne, T. The translator pattern—external functionality with homomorphic mappings. In *Proceedings of TOOLS 23, USA*, pages 48–62, July 1997.
19. Liang, S., P. Hudak and M. Jones. Monad transformers and modular interpreters. In *Symposium on Principles of Programming Languages*, pages 333–343, 1992.
20. Milner, R., M. Tofte and R. Harper. *The Definition of Standard ML*. MIT Press, Cambridge, MA, 1990.
21. Odersky, M. and P. Wadler. Pizza into Java: Translating theory into practice. In *Symposium on Principles of Programming Languages*, pages 146–159, Janurary 1997.
22. Palsberg, J. Efficient inference of object types. *Information & Computation*, 123(2):198–209, 1995.

23. Palsberg, J. and C. B. Jay. The essence of the Visitor pattern. Technical Report 05, University of Technology, Sydney, 1997.
24. Palsberg, J., C. Xiao and K. Lieberherr. Efficient implementation of adaptive software. *ACM Transactions on Programming Languages and Systems*, 17(2):264–292, 1995.
25. Portner, N. Flexible command interpreter: A pattern for an extensible and language-independent interpreter system, 1995. Appears in [5].
26. Rémy, D. Introduction aux objets. Unpublished manuscript, lecture notes for *course de magistère*, Ecole Normale Supérieure, 1996.
27. Reynolds, J. C. User-defined types and procedural data structures as complementary approaches to data abstraction. In Schuman, S. A., editor, *New Directions in Algorithmic Languages*, pages 157–168. IFIP Working Group 2.1 on Algol, 1975.
28. Riehle, D. Composite design patterns. In *ACM SIGPLAN Conference on Object-Oriented Programming Systems, Languages & Applications*, pages 218–228, 1997.
29. Seiter, L. M., J. Palsberg and K. J. Lieberherr. Evolution of object behavior using context relations. *IEEE Transactions on Software Engineering*, 1998.
30. Steele, G. L., Jr. Building interpreters by composing monads. In *Symposium on Principles of Programming Languages*, pages 472–492, Janurary 1994.
31. Stroustrup, B. *The C++ Programming Language*. Addison-Wesley, 1991.
32. Sun Microsystems. Java core reflection. API and Specification, 1997.
33. Thorup, K. K. Genericity in Java with virtual types. In *European Conference on Object-Oriented Programming*, pages 444–471, 1997.

Precise Visual Specification of Design Patterns

Anthony Lauder and Stuart Kent
Division of Computing
University of Brighton, Lewes Road, Brighton, UK
A.P.J.Lauder@brighton.ac.uk
fax: +44 (0) 1273 642405, tel: +44 (0) 1273 642032
Stuart.Kent@brighton.ac.uk
fax: +44 (0) 1273 642405, tel: +44 (0) 1273 642494

Abstract. There has been substantial recent interest in captured design expertise expressed as design patterns. Prevalent descriptions of these design patterns suffer from two demerits. Firstly, they capture specific instances of pattern deployment, rather than the essential pattern itself, thus the spirit of the pattern is often lost in the superfluous details of the specific instances described. Secondly, existing pattern descriptions rely upon relatively informal diagrammatic notations supplemented with natural language annotations. This can result in imprecision and ambiguity. This paper addresses these problems by separating the specification of patterns into three models (role, type, and class). The most abstract (role-centric) model presents patterns in their purest form, capturing their essential spirit without deleterious detail. A role-model is refined by a type-model (adding usually-domain-specific constraints), which is further refined by a class-model (forming a concrete deployment). We utilise recent advances in visual modelling notation to achieve greater precision without resorting to obtuse mathematical symbols. A set-oriented view of state, operations, and instances is adopted, permitting their abstract presentation in models via this visual notation. This paper utilises these ideas in the unambiguous specification of a selection of prominent design patterns. The expectation is that precise visual pattern specification will firstly enable clear communication between domain experts and pattern writers (and ultimately pattern users), and secondly enable CASE tool support for design patterns, permitting the designer (pattern user) to operate at a higher level of abstraction without ambiguity.

1 Introduction

1.1 Design Patterns

Design patterns capture the distilled experience of expert designers. Patterns are not invented, rather they are "mined" from existing systems. The mining process involves the extraction of designs from a number of systems, looking for "patterns" in designs across those systems. The expectation is that expert designers will have utilised similar proven designs to resolve similar problems in different application domains. Patterns document these proven designs, removing domain-specific features thus specifying only their essential aspects. A documented pattern, then, is deployable in a new domain via the addition of domain-specific features to the pattern's essential aspects.

There exists a rapidly expanding body of literature documenting important design patterns [3], [5], [8], [14], [20]. The most influential of these is the "Gang of Four" text [20] (hereafter referred to as GoF) which details twenty-three fundamental patterns.

1.2 Impure Pattern Modelling

Current pattern literature (including GoF) tends to present each pattern in terms of a specific implementation of that pattern. The intent is that the reader should be able to glean from the specific implementation the essential elements (or "spirit") of the pattern, rejecting those aspects which are relevant only to the example presented. It is our belief that, although examples of pattern deployment are valuable in their own right, the essential spirit of a pattern is often lost in the superfluous details of a specific implementation. It is our assertion that example-based revelation is enhanced by the addition of precise visual specifications which retain that essential spirit.

1.3 Pure Pattern Modelling

In this paper we propose a three-model presentation of patterns. The first model (the role-model) is the most abstract and depicts only the essential spirit of the pattern, excluding inessential application-domain-specific details. The second model (the type-model) constrains the role-model with abstract state and operation interfaces forming a (usually domain-specific) refinement of the pattern. The final model (the class-model) realises the type-model, thus deploying the underlying pattern in terms of concrete classes.

1.4 Formal Modelling

A model may be viewed as a composition of constraints. Prevalent modelling notations such as Booch [2], OML [7], OMT [16], and UML [17] are not sufficiently expressive in the constraints they can represent graphically. Consequently, the designer is forced to supplement modelling diagrams with constraints specified textually. This supplementary text is typically expressed as natural language narrative. The formal methods community has argued that this combination of existing diagrammatic notations and natural language text often results in specifications which are imprecise and, therefore, ambiguous. Consequently, formal-methods mathematical notations such as Z [1] and VDM [11] have been developed to add precision to specifications. A number of contemporary object-oriented methodologies such as Syntropy [4] and Catalysis [6] replace natural language with these mathematical notations to supplement diagrammatic models with precise constraint specifications.

Formal methods research has clearly provided a strong theoretical foundation for precise specification. Research in formal methods, though, has been lacking in the area of approachability. In particular, there has been the underlying assumption that obtuse mathematical notations are necessary to achieve precision, thus alienating all but the most mathematically mature modellers. To address this problem, UML has recently been supplemented with the Object Constraint Language (OCL), a textual notation which has been developed "... to fill this gap. It is a formal language that remains easy to read and write" [19].

1.5 Visual Pattern Modelling

OCL is an important advance towards approachability. The notation, however, is founded upon the assumption that "a graphical model ... is not enough for a precise and unambiguous specification" [19]. That is, there is the underlying assumption that constraints are necessarily specified textually. Recent work by Kent [12], however, dispels this assumption by presenting an approachable diagrammatic notation with which constraints are specifiable visually with no loss of precision. Kent's notation, termed Constraint Diagrams is compatible with, and thus may supplement existing and less-expressive diagrammatic modelling notations: [2], [6], [7], [16], [17]. Note that a separate research effort is providing the formal semantics of the Constraint Diagram notation.

Current pattern literature supports diagrammatic pattern specifications with textual supplements. These textual supplements serve two purposes. The first is to reinforce diagrams with supporting information. Examples of this are descriptions of motivation for, consequences of using and known uses of the pattern. This supporting information forms a crucial and intrinsic part of any pattern description and must be retained, since a description of patterns without this supporting information would simply be an architecture without context. The second purpose of textual supplements, though, is to *disambiguate* pattern diagrams. For example, GoF presents participants and collaborations narrative to add precision and expressiveness to their structure diagram. That is, these narrative sections recognise that the diagrams presented are both ambiguous and inexpressive. We will demonstrate throughout this paper that with constraint diagram notation we are able to depict unambiguous and expressive pattern structure in a visual form, supplemented with only supporting textual information (i.e. excluding the need for narrative to disambiguate the diagrams).

In this paper we utilise constraint diagrams in combination with UML for the unambiguous specification of selected design patterns.

1.6 Selected Patterns

GoF segregates patterns into three categories: Creational Patterns (which create objects), Structural Patterns (which form composite classes and objects), and Behavioural Patterns (which partition algorithms across collaborating objects). This paper focuses upon the specification of one design pattern from each category. More specifically: Abstract Factory (Creational), Composite (Structural), and Observer (Behavioural). The first of these patterns (AbstractFactory) is the focus of the main body of the paper. The remaining patterns (Composite and Observer) are presented in the appendix.

2 Gang-of-Four Presentation of Abstract Factory Pattern

The intent of the abstract factory creational design pattern is to "Provide an interface for creating families of related or dependent objects without specifying their concrete classes" [9]

GoF presents the AbstractFactory as the single diagram, reproduced in figure 1.

Fig. 1. Gang-of-Four Presentation of Abstract Factory Pattern

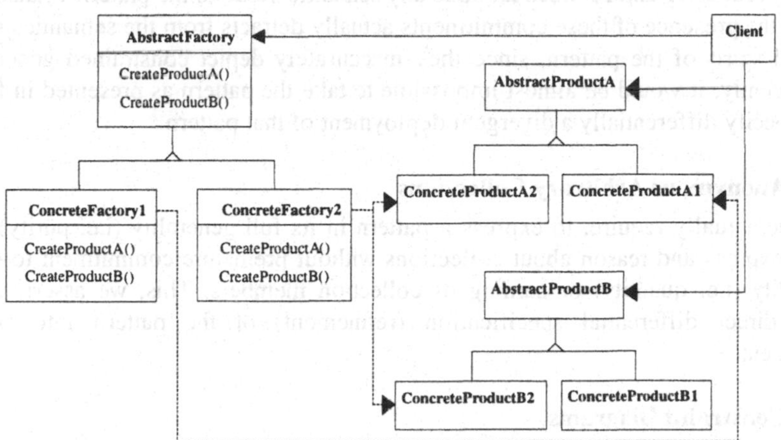

2.1 GoF Impurity

The GoF presentation of Abstract Factory, as in figure 1, suffers from the major demerit that it actually represents a single deployment of the abstract factory pattern rather than the generalised pattern itself. More specifically, the pattern as presented defines specific operation interfaces for the AbstractFactory class (CreateProductA and CreateProductB) which are realised by fixed concrete classes (ConcreteFactory1 and ConcreteFactory2). In addition, two specific abstract product classes are depicted (AbstractProductA and AbstractProductB), each further specialised by concrete product classes. This significantly reduces the general applicability of the pattern as specified. In practise, other deployments of the pattern would require different numbers of and different properties for these types and operations. The general pattern, then, is not expressed with purity in figure 1.

2.2 Collections As Named Pairs

We believe that a major cause of the lack of purity in GoF pattern diagrams is the tendancy to imply collections via the expression of fixed numbers of named instances or classes. For example, turning to figure 1 there are two concrete factory classes, and two abstract product classes each implemented by two concrete product classes. This is unsatisfactory since it forces the diagram to misrepresent quantities in the pattern (by premature commitment to a cardinality of two), and forces premature commitment to names for each of those collection elements (ProductA1, ProductA2 etc).

Similar premature commitments to named specific quantities proliferate in the GoF pattern descriptions. The behaviour of the Observer pattern, for example, is depicted via a sequence diagram depicting two concrete observer instances, whereas in reality the pattern permits any arbitrary number of observers.

Neither the commitment to fixed quantities, nor the commitment to element names such as ProductA1 and ProductA2, adds any semantic value to the pattern whatsoever. Indeed, the presence of these commitments actually detracts from the semantics of the essential spirit of the pattern, since they inaccurately depict constrained generality. Consequently, it would be almost impossible to take the pattern as presented in figure 1 and specify differentially a divergent deployment of that pattern.

2.3 Anonymous Arbitrary Collections

What we actually require, to express a pattern in its full generality (i.e. purity), is a way to express and reason about collections without premature commitment to either cardinality (i.e. quantity) or naming of collection members. This, we assert, would permit direct differential specification (refinement) of the pattern into ad-hoc deployments.

2.4 Constraint Diagrams

We choose to represent collections in terms of sets, upon which we may specify constraints applying to set members. Sets enable us to talk about collections generally (without premature commitment to cardinality or naming), and constraints enable us to talk about collections precisely. Since constraint diagrams focus upon the specification of constrained sets and set members, they constitute the ideal notation with which to depict anonymous arbitrary collections.

Constraint diagram notation is detailed initially in [12] and [13], and in an upcoming series of papers which explore both the syntax and the semantics of the notation. In the current paper we utilise a number of recent enhancements to the notation documented in the early papers. Below, we provide a brief introduction to the notation, including the recent enhancements we have utilised.

Constraint diagrams depict sets as Venn diagrams. An arbitrary member of a set is depicted via a dot within or on the edge of the set (see figure 2). Two unconnected dots are definitely distinct. Two dots connected via a spring indicates that the dots do not necessarily represent distinct set elements (i.e. they may be the same element). Two dots connected via a strut represent alternative positions for a single element (i.e. an element may reside in only one of the positions represented by the connected dots at any time).

A directed arc represents a traversable relationship between sets and set members (see figure 3).

Fig. 2. Set Membership

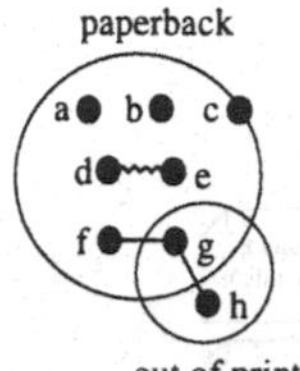

'a', 'b', and 'c' are distinct arbitrary set members.
'd' and 'e' are not-necessarily-distinct arbitrary set members
'f', 'g', and 'h' represent a single element which may exist in one, and only one, of three positions at a given time.

Fig. 3. Navigable Relationships

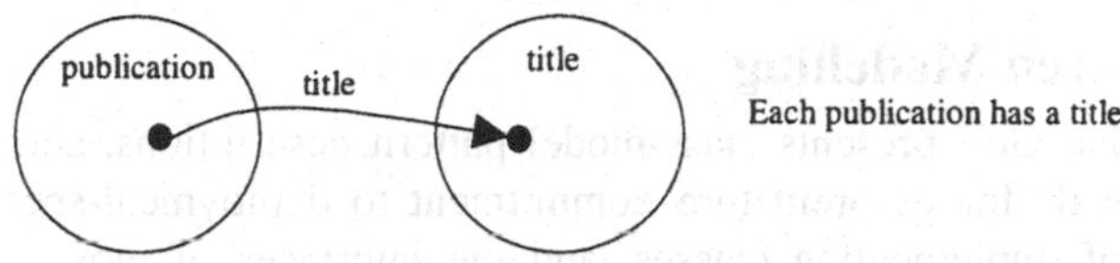

2.5 UML

In this paper we utilise constraint diagrams in conjunction with UML notation. In UML "a class is drawn as a solid-outline rectangle with 3 compartments separated by horizontal lines. The top compartment holds the class name and other general properties of the class (including stereotype; the middle list compartment holds a list of attributes; the bottom list compartment holds a list of operations" [17]. Figure 4 gives an example, depicting a publication from the perspective of a publisher:

Fig. 4. UML Class Diagram

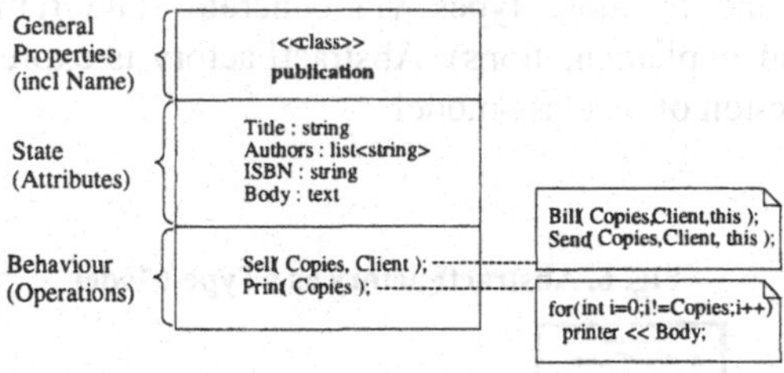

Normally, concrete instances of this class are drawn as object diagrams (which are themselves instances of their class diagram). When we wish to talk about instances in abstract terms, though, we need to represent them abstractly. Thus, we add a fourth compartment to a class, which holds abstract instances of the class, specified as a constraint diagram depicting sets and set members. In figure 5 the publication class is re-expressed with the addition of the fourth (Abstract Instance) compartment which is expressed as a constraint diagram, showing that each instance of the class has the given structure and operations. This particular constraint diagram is actually implicit in class diagrams and is elaborated here for illustration purposes only.

Fig. 5. UML Class Diagram + Abstract Instances

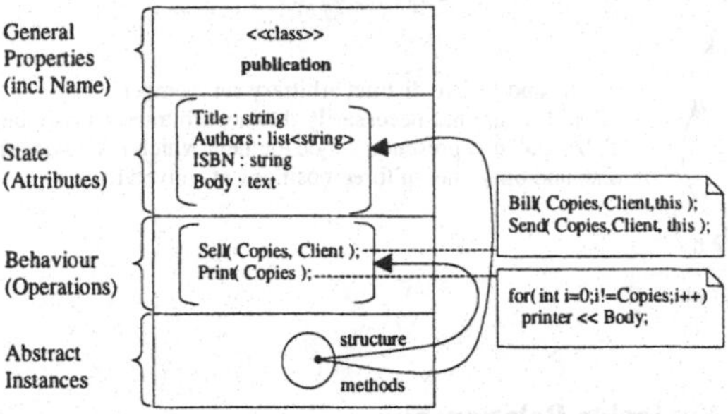

General Properties (incl Name)
<<class>>
publication
State (Attributes)
Title : string
Authors : list<string>
ISBN : string
Body : text
Behaviour (Operations)
Sell(Copies, Client);
Print(Copies);
Bill(Copies,Client,this);
Send(Copies,Client, this);
for(int i=0;i!=Copies;i++)
printer << Body;
Abstract Instances
structure
methods

3 Three Layered Modelling

We have argued that GoF presents class-model pattern descriptions, and that this is inappropriate since its forces premature commitment to deployment-specific details (such as number of implementing classes, and the interfaces of those classes). To better express the pattern in its most general terms we must present the pattern more abstractly than the class-model, to capture only its essential spirit. A deployed class-model, then, would be presented as a specific realisation of a more abstract description of the pattern.

3.1 AbstractFactory as a Type-Model

The GoF representation of the structure of AbstractFactory as a class-model may give the false impression that components of a design pattern are actually classes. It is our assertion that pattern components are better thought of in more abstract terms. Specifically, the pattern may be re-expressed as a type-model. We follow the UML tradition of defining a type as a specification of abstract state and operation interfaces. A class realises one or more types via concrete state (attributes) and concrete operations (method implementations). AbstractFactory is expressed, in figure 6, as a type-model abstraction of its class-model.

Fig. 6. AbstractFactory as aType-Model

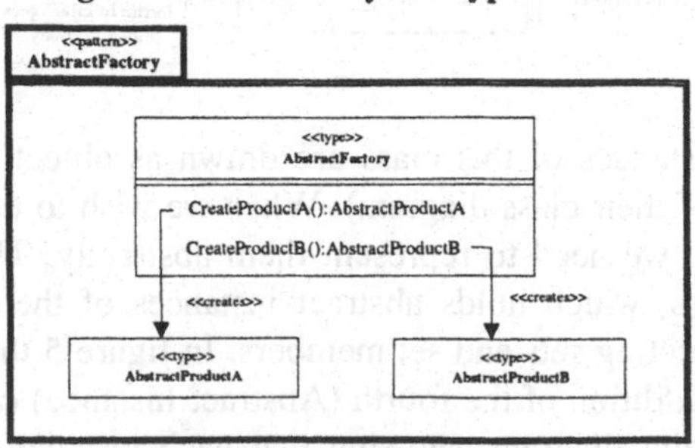

3.2 Type-Model Refinement

Note that a type-model may be refined continually into a hierarchy of derived type-models, each adding constraints to the type-model above it in the hierarchy. When a commitment is made, however, to concrete (rather than abstract) state and concrete method implementation we arrive at a class-model (which may itself be refined via inheritance into other class-models).

Deployment of the pattern depicted in figure 6 requires refinement of the type-model into a less abstract class-model, wherein classes realise the specifications within the type-model. In addition, relationships between the types may be further refined to express less abstract relationships between the classes of the class-model. In figure 7 we present a refinement of the type-model of figure 6, back to the GoF class-model of AbstactFactory as originally presented in figure 1.

Fig. 7. AbstractFactory Deployed as a Class Model

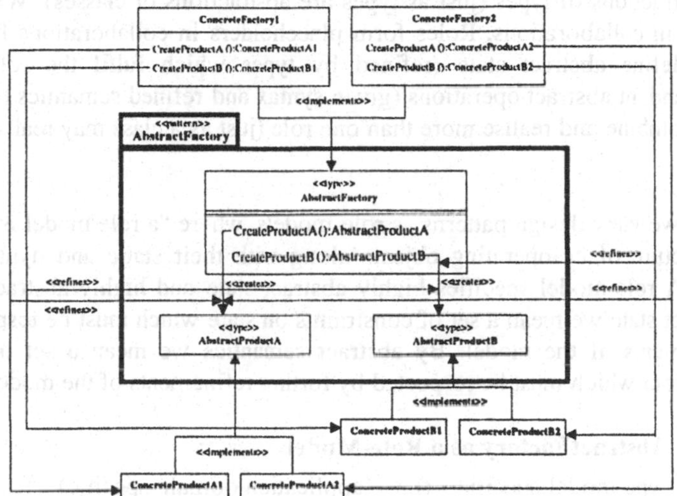

3.3 Model Generality

Figure 7 is certainly an improvement over figure 1. Its main contribution is that the type-model specifies only abstract structure for the pattern, leaving details of concrete implementation to derived class-models.

We can view the class-model in figure 7 as a specific realisation of the type-model. The type-model is sufficiently abstract to permit many other class-model realisations. However, the type-model must be viewed as an application-domain-specific refinement of the general pattern. For example, there is a commitment to a concrete operation interface, as well as a commitment to a specific number of named abstract product types. This is perfectly acceptable as a basis for further refinement within the same application domain. However, the type-model is clearly inappropriate for other application domains, which would require different abstract state and operation interfaces, and thus their own type-model specifications of the pattern. We are missing an abstraction above the type-model which expresses the pattern in an application-domain-independent way.

3.4 Patterns as Role-Models

"A role is an architectural representation of the objects occupying the corresponding positions in the object system ... Different classes can implement the same type ... Objects of the same type can, and often do, play several roles" [15]

To capture patterns more purely we must generalise our type-model further to capture only the essential spirit of the pattern, and remove non-essential features which constrain the pattern's general applicability. This is achieved by the utilisation of roles as abstractions of types (just as types are abstractions of classes). We define roles as actors in collaborations. Roles form placeholders in collaborations for types. A role may define abstract state (refined by types which fulfil the role), and syntax-independent abstract operations (given syntax and refined semantics by types). A type may combine and realise more than one role (just as a class may realise more than one type).

Thus, we view design patterns as role-models, where "a role model is a description of a structure of co-operating objects along with their static and dynamic properties" [15]. A role-model specifies highly abstract state and highly abstract semantics. By abstract state we mean a set of constraints on state which must be respected by further refinements of the model. By abstract semantics we mean a set of constraints on behaviour which must be respected by further refinements of the model.

3.5 AbstractFactory as a Role-Model

With type-model-specific (i.e. application-domain-specific) features removed, AbstractFactory is generalised to the role-model expressed in figure 8. Note that the solid start in this figure represents the creation of a set instance.

Fig. 8. AbstractFactory as a Role Model

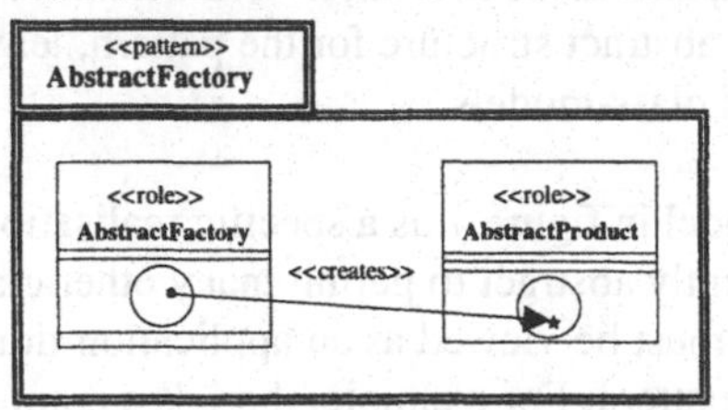

3.6 Type-Model as refinement of Role-Model

Figure 8 is a pure representation of AbstractFactory; it conveys, in terms of structure and behaviour, *the pattern, the whole pattern, and nothing but the pattern*. Naturally, a full description of the pattern would be supplemented with textual descriptions of motivation, trade-offs, known uses, etc. The figure shows that players of the AbstractFactory role share a set of semantics for operations. Each operation in that set is defined as creating a specific type of AbstractProduct. Thus, all players of the AbstractProduct role must implement a set of methods adhering to this semantics, creating via these methods the same set of AbstractProduct types. Note that we have not expressed the operation section of the AbstractFactory role in terms of concrete interfaces, rather we have expressed a constraint diagram depicting a set of semantics for the operations. We have not needed to name these operations nor specify their concrete cardinality prematurely. These would be deployment-specific issues. Instead, we have expressed meta-level constraint information which must be respected by any type-model derived from this role-model.

A role-model may be refined continually into a hierarchy of role-models. However, as soon as a commitment is made to concrete-operation syntax we have derived a type-model from the role-model. For example, we may now refine the AbstractFactory role-model to re-express the domain-specific type-model presented in figure 6. This re-expression is achieved in figure 9.

Fig. 9. AbstractFactory Role-Model to Type-Model

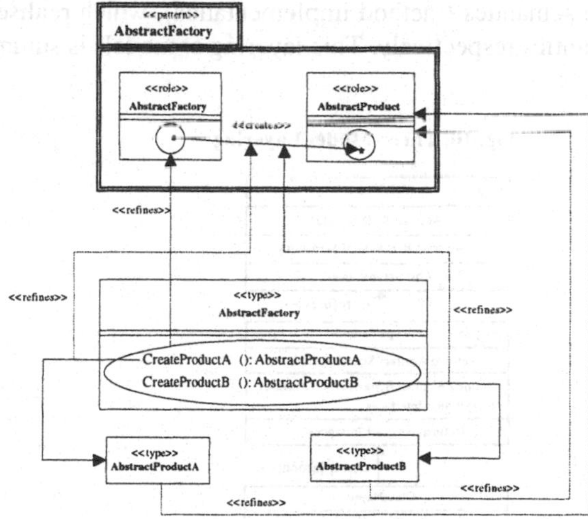

3.7 Class-Model as refinement of Type-Model

Figure 9 could be flattened (by synthesis) into the original type-model depicted in figure 1. Since both models are semantically equivalent this would be a purely cosmetic step and is unnecessary for the purposes of this paper. Consequently, we omit this step here. It is similarly easy to visualise how the concrete (class-model) deployment of the abstract factory pattern, as depicted in figure 7 may be re-expressed as a refinement of the type-model in figure 9. Again, since this is a trivial step, we omit it here.

In practise, a CASE tool supporting patterns would benefit from accommodating the flattening of derived patterns via synthesis (e.g. flattening figure 9 back to figure 1), since a valid criticism of the refinement approach is that the user can become overwhelmed by the number of levels of refinement and their interconnections. In other words, although the layering approach is valuable for building models, it is not necessarily the best approach for presenting them in an ultimate (or even intermediate) design. Tool support would presumably permit traceability between layered and synthesised models, with a mechanism for easily switching between them.

3.8 Summary of Three-Model Specification

In summary, we have argued that purity in pattern description may be achieved by employing a layered three-model specification. The first layer (the role-model) expresses the pattern purely in terms of highly abstract state and highly abstract behavioural semantics, forming a constraint set which captures the essential spirit of the pattern without dilution in non-essential (application-domain specific) details. The middle level (the type-model) refines the role-model adding usually-domain-specific refinements to the abstract state and semantics, and concrete syntax for operations described by the abstract semantics. The final layer (class-model) deploys the type-model in application-specific terms via the specification of concrete state (attributes) and concrete semantics (method implementation), which realise the abstract state and abstract semantics respectively. This layering of models is summarised in figure 10.

Fig. 10. Three-Model Layering

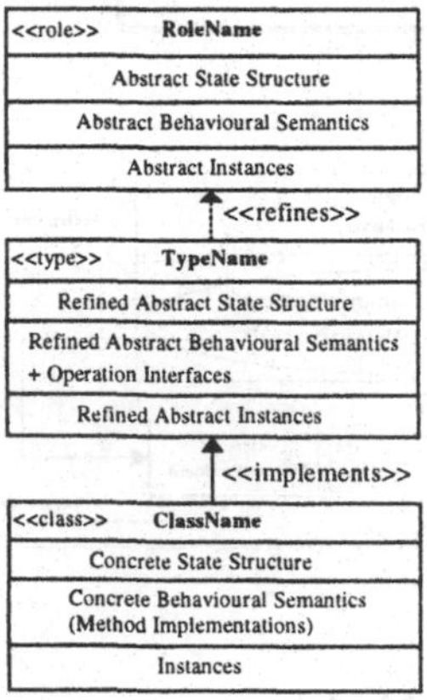

<<role>> RoleName
Abstract State Structure
Abstract Behavioural Semantics
Abstract Instances
<<refines>>
<<type>> TypeName
Refined Abstract State Structure
Refined Abstract Behavioural Semantics
+ Operation Interfaces
Refined Abstract Instances
<<implements>>
<<class>> ClassName
Concrete State Structure
Concrete Behavioural Semantics
(Method Implementations)
Instances

4 Dynamics of AbstractFactory

The previous section focused upon purity of specification by presenting patterns at multiple levels of abstraction, each refining the level above it. The focus was very much on the static properties of patterns. Our attention now turns to dynamic behaviour.

4.1 Sequence Diagrams

UML permits two overlapping forms of behavioural specification: Sequence diagrams and collaboration diagrams. The former presents time as a separate dimension but loses depiction of relationships between collaborators, whereas the latter preserves relationships but the time dimension.

Interestingly, GoF does not present AbstractFactory behaviour diagrammatically. It does, however present the behaviour of other patterns via sequence diagrams. We continue that tradition here, although we present a slightly modified form of sequence diagram, which combines the benefits of UML sequence diagrams and collaboration diagrams by bounding sequence diagrams with pre- and post-conditions expressed as constraint diagrams. That is, our diagrams show time as a separate dimension, yet still preserve relationships between collaborators. We present our diagrams in flat two-dimensional form. It is possible, however, to provide a three-dimensional rendering where each constraint diagram is tilted away into a three-dimensional image, with the time dimension running through the tilted constraint diagrams thus connecting them. This would be particularly advantageous with appropriate CASE tool support. Three-dimensional constraint diagram modelling is investigated further in [10].

4.2 Class-Model Sequence Diagrams

Typically, one or more sequence diagrams are drawn for each method in a concrete class-model. For example, we present a sequence diagram specification of ConcreteFactory1::CreateProductA() in figure 11.

Fig. 11. Class-Model-Level Sequence Diagram

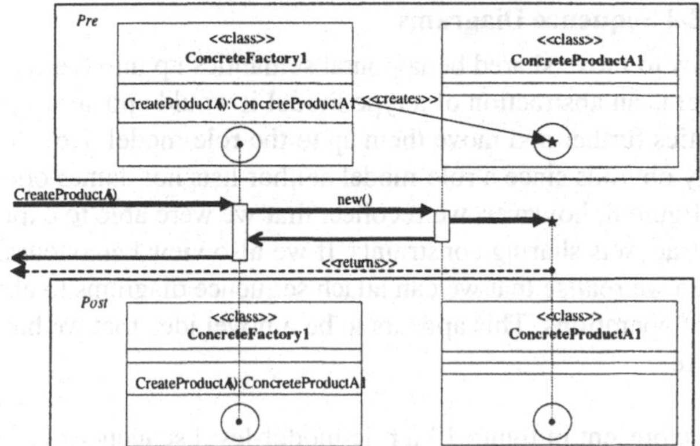

Let us examine figure 11 in detail. An instance of ConcreteFactory1 (depicted by a dot in the abstract instances compartment) is the target of the invoked operation (CreateProductA1). The invoked operation calls the 'new()' operation of ConcreteProductA1 to create an instance of that class. The created product is returned back to the client.

4.3 Type-Model Sequence Diagrams

Although it is useful to present sequence diagrams for all class-model methods, we can achieve a much cleaner view of behaviour by shifting abstract semantics up to the type-model and specifying in class-model sequence diagrams only method-specific variants of the abstract semantics. For example, all realisations of the operation AbstractFactory::CreateProductA() must respect a shared semantics, which rightly belongs as an abstract behavioural specification in the type-model. Thus, we can place shared abstract behaviour in sequence diagrams at the type-model level. An example of this is shown in figure 12.

Fig. 12. Type-Model-Level Sequence Diagram

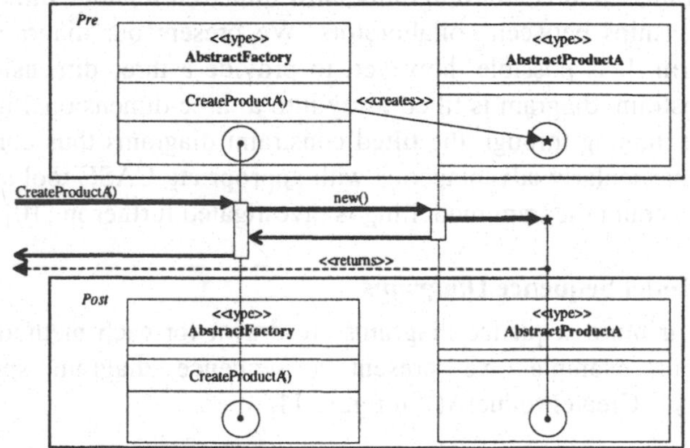

4.4 Role-Model Sequence Diagrams

We saw above how to move shared behavioural semantics up into the type-model. Since a role-model is an abstraction of a type-model it would appear useful to be able to abstract semantics further and move them up to the role-model. How to achieve this is not immediately obvious since a role-model neither lists nor names operations. Looking back at figure 8, however, we recollect that we were able to express operations as abstract sets sharing constraints. If we also view behavioural semantics as constraints, then we realise that we can attach sequence diagrams to abstract and anonymous sets of operations. This appears to be a novel idea that we have not seen explored elsewhere.

As an example, we present in figure 13 a role-model-level sequence diagram shared by all members of the set of operations to which it is attached. That sequence diagram forms the abstract semantic specification of all operations that refine the related operation set.

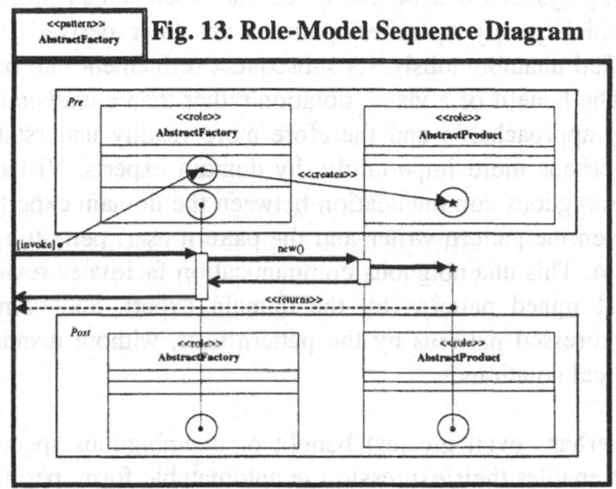

Fig. 13. Role-Model Sequence Diagram

In figure 13, the abstract operations of the AbstractFactory role are depicted as a set (of anonymous operations) each of which creates an object derived from AbstractProduct. An arbitrary operation from this set is invoked on the selected AbstractFactory compliant object. Figure 13, then, specifies semantic constraints on operations without committing to concrete syntax or implementation. Types (and subsequently classes) which refine these abstract operations must respect these constraints. Hence, abstract operations constitute the minimal specification of the (abstract) semantics of a concrete method. Types add concrete syntax (and may further refine abstract semantics) and classes add concrete implementation.

It is our assertion that figure 13 is a precise and expressive specification of the essential spirit of the AbstractFactory pattern. We have already seen in earlier sections how to refine role-model specifications into type-models and, ultimately, into class-model deployment, and hence we will not repeat those steps here.

5 Conclusions

This paper has shown visual notations can present patterns purely, precisely, and expressively. We have argued that purity, precision, and expressiveness are achieved by adopting a three-model layering of pattern descriptions, wherein the essential spirit of the pattern is represented as a role-model, further refined by a type-model, and implemented by a class-model. The essence of three-model layering is to utilise abstraction without loss of expressiveness, thus achieving maximal generality and unambiguity in pattern description. In particular, we achieve abstract-yet-precise expressiveness via the set-oriented representation of state, operations, and instances.

Since design patterns are intended for dissemination to a wider audience than ad-hoc designs, it is particularly important that they are expressed in their most general terms and communicated unambiguously. Furthermore, unambiguous specification of designs is of paramount benefit when mining existing systems for new patterns. The designs of existing systems can be examined and documented precisely as the raw material from which purely specified patterns are later derived. Unless this raw material is specified unambiguously, its subsequent refinement into pure patterns will be error-prone. The benefit of a visual notation rather than a mathematical one is that it is immediately approachable and therefore more readily understandable by other designers and, perhaps more importantly, by domain experts. Visual specifications, then, enable unambiguous communication between the domain expert and the pattern miner, and between the pattern writer and the pattern user, permitting them to speak the same language. This unambiguous communication facilitates review, verification, and correction of mined patterns by the domain expert, and comprehension and deployment of expressed patterns by the pattern user, without mandating fluency in obtuse mathematical notations.

An additional (perhaps even greater) benefit of unambiguous specification of pure patterns is that it enables their expression in automatable form, permitting automated checking of designs for inconsistency or incompleteness. Perhaps more importantly though, CASE tool support of patterns enables the designer to work at the pattern level rather that at the level of individual classes. Consequently the designer is freed to work at a higher level of abstraction. We can envision tools which enable the designer to browse purely- and precisely-specified pattern catalogues, selecting design patterns which closely match the designer's requirements, adapting selected patterns via refinement, and combining and deploying these adapted patterns as appropriate for the application domain.

The point has been raised by an early reviewer of this paper that many pattern authors will find formal specification difficult, even with a visual notation. We have to agree with this comment. However, we are constantly working at simplifying the notation, and in a more general sense at bridging the gap between formal methods work and approachability. Only time will tell whether or not we can reach widespread approachability for the modelling community. In the interim, there is, of course, no requirement that the original author of a pattern must also be the author of its formal specification. It is our belief, and indeed our current practise, that existing patterns can be 'formalised' at a time subsequent to their original publication. Clearly, formal pattern specification may not suit everybody, but for those for whom it is appropriate, we aim to provide relevant insights, notations, and tools.

6 Further Work

We have explored only one possible refinement of each role model. For example, the AbstractFactory pattern is refined (following the GoF) into a set of concrete classes implementing separate functions for each concrete product. The GoF have observed that this is just one possible implementation strategy for this pattern. Other possibilities include the use of prototype products, and also a generalised create function parameterised with the product type to be created. It is our belief that role-models are (or should be) sufficiently general to accommodate all of these alternatives. A useful short-term goal, then, is to demonstrate how these are alternatives are themselves refinements of a common role-model. This is the focus of a forthcoming paper, which will re-express completely a GoF pattern using a GoF style of presentation, including all alternatives and trade-offs, but with a layering of precise visual models at its core.

In the medium term we are describing the formal semantic underpinnings of the notation for submission to an appropriate journal, with an approachable summary submitted to a periodical of broader readership. The intent of this work is to prove that the notation forms a sound basis for formal specification.

Longer term, we are undertaking three relevant on-going research efforts: Firstly, we are exploring the applicability of these techniques to the description and refinement of other kinds of patterns (particularly analysis patterns, process patterns, and organisational patterns). Secondly, we are working with a commercial enterprise to apply these techniques in the mining of a large existing legacy system for migration to component based technology, thus demonstrating the practical application of the work. Thirdly, we intend to investigate the requirements of CASE tool support for this type of modelling.

7 Appendix

7.1 Composite Design Pattern

The intent of the Composite structural design pattern is to "Compose objects into tree structures to represent part-whole hierarchies. Composite lets clients treat individual objects and compositions of objects uniformly." [9]

In the composite design pattern a Component consists of either a leaf or a Composite which itself consists of a set of Component objects. This is depicted in figure A1.

Fig. A1. Composite Design Pattern Invariant

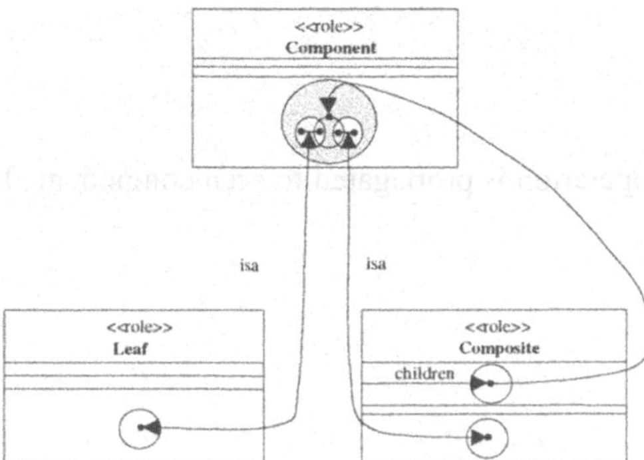

The Add() operation adds a component to a composite component. This is depicted in figure A2.

Fig. A2. Composite Design Pattern: Add()

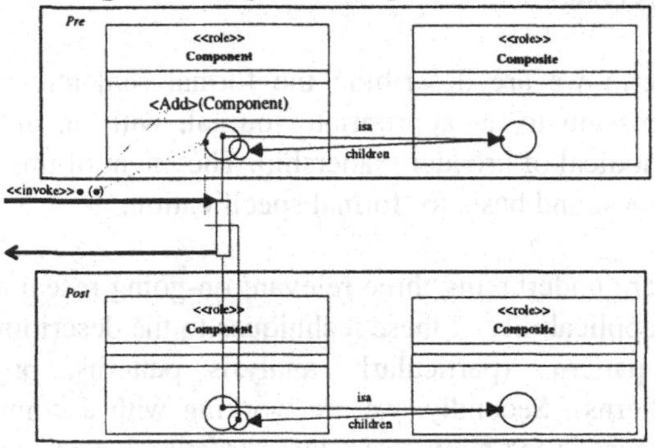

The Remove() operation removes a component from a composite component. This is depicted in figure A3.

Fig. A3. Composite Design Pattern: Remove()

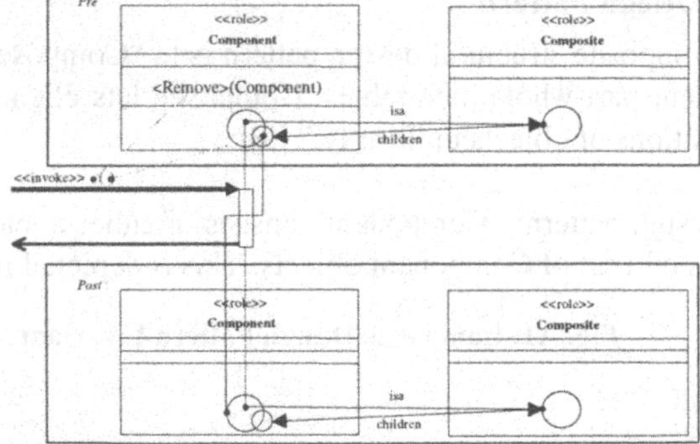

The Operation() operation is propagated to each component. This is depicted in figure A4.

Fig. A4. Composite Design Pattern: Operation()

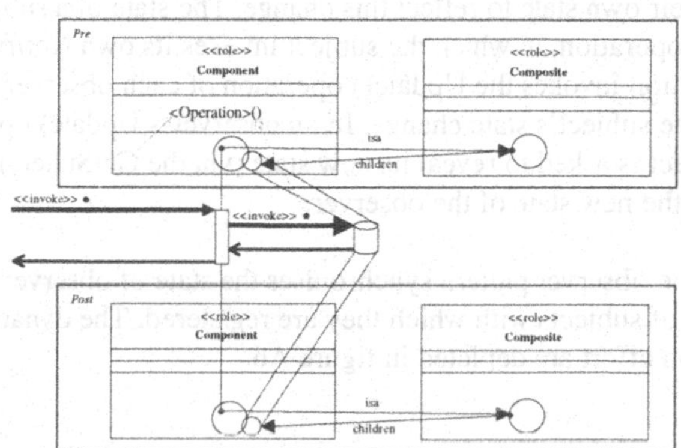

7.2 Observer Pattern

The intent of the Observer behavioural design pattern is to "Define a one-to-many dependency between objects so that when one object changes state, all its dependants are notified and updated automatically." [9]

Figure A5 presents the invariant constraints on the observer pattern. Objects with changing state are termed subjects. Observer objects are registered with subjects. Each subject, then, has a registered set of observers. Each observer is associated with only one subject. A set of concrete subjects refines the abstract specification of the subject role. A set of concrete observers refines the abstract specification of the observer role. Concrete subjects and concrete observers maintain state information.

Fig. A5. Observer Design Pattern Invariant

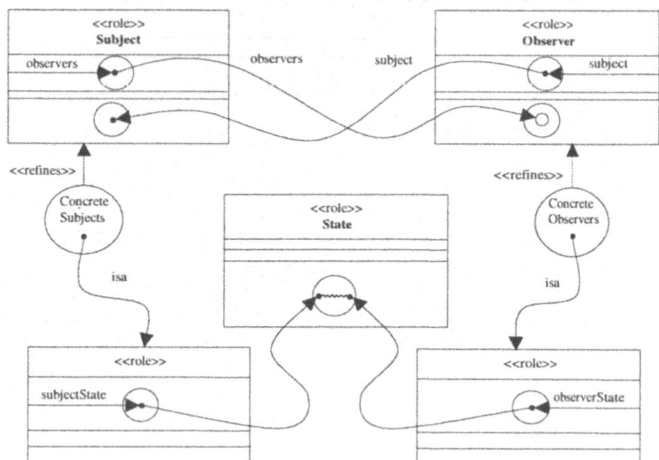

The observer pattern notifies observers when their subject's state changes, so that they may update their own state to reflect this change. The state of a subject is modified via the SetState() operation, in which the subject invokes its own Notify() operation. The Notify() operation invokes the Update() operation of each observer to inform those observers of the subject's state change. In an observer's Update) operation, the notifying subject is asked to reveal its new state (via the GetState()) operation, which then becomes the new state of the observer.

In summary, the observer pattern synchronises the state of observer objects with the evolving state of subjects with which they are registered. The dynamics of this synchronisation effort are depicted in figure A6.

Fig. A6. Observer Design Pattern: SetState()

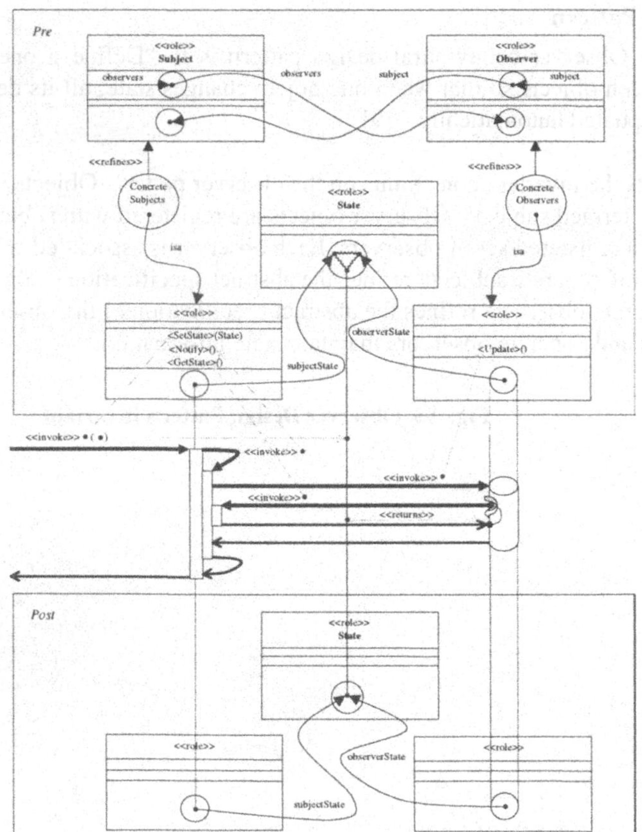

References

1. Abrial, J-R., Schuman, S., Meyer, B.: A Specification Language. On the Construction of Programs, McNaughten, R., and McKeag, R. (eds.), Cambridge University Press (1980)

2. Booch, G.: Object-Oriented Analysis and Design With Applications (2nd Edition), Benjamin/Cummings (1993)

3. Buschmann, F., Meunier, R., Rohnert, H., Sommerlad, P., Stal, M.: Pattern-Oriented Software Architecture: A System of Patterns, Wiley (1996)

4. Cook, S., and Daniels, J.: Designing Object Systems: Object-Oriented Modelling with Syntropy, Prentice-Hall (1994)

5. Coplien, J., Schmidt, D. (eds.): Pattern Languages of Program Design, Addison-Wesley (1995)

6. D'Souza, D., and Wills, A.: Objects, Components and Frameworks with UML: The Catalysis Approach, Addison-Wesley (1998)

7. Firesmith, D., Henderson-Sellers, B., Graham, I.: OPEN Modelling Language (OML) Reference Manual, SIGS Reference Library (1997)

8. Fowler, M.: Analysis Patterns: Reusable Object Models, Addison-Wesley (1997)

9. Gamma, E., Helm, R., Johnson, R., Vlissides, J.: Design Patterns: Elements of Reusable Object-Oriented Software, Addison-Wesley (1995)

10. Gil, J., and Kent, S.: Three Dimensional Software Modelling, Unpublished Manuscript (1998)

11. Jones, C.: Systematic Software Development using VDM (2nd edition), Prentice Hall (1990)

12. Kent, S.: Constraint Diagrams: Visualising Invariants in Object-Oriented Models, to appear in Procs. of OOPSLA97, ACM Press (1997)

13. Kent, S.: Visualising Action Contracts in Object-Oriented Modelling, submitted to Visual 98 (1998)

14. Pree, W.: Design Patterns for Object-Oriented Software Development, Addison-Wesley (1995)

15. Reenskaug, T., Wold, P., Lehne, O. A.: Working With Objects, Manning Publications (1996)

16. Rumbaugh, J., Blaha, M., Premerlani, W., Eddy, F., Lorensen, W.: Object-Oriented Modelling and Design, Prentice Hall (1991)

17. UML Consortium: The Unified Modelling Language Notation, version 1.1, http://www.rational.com (1997)

18. UML Consortium: The Unified Modelling Language Semantics, version 1.1, http://www.rational.com (1997)

19. UML Consortium: Object Constraint Language Specification, version 1.1, http://www.rational.com (1997)

20. Vlissides, J., Coplien, J., and Kerth, N., (eds.): Pattern Languages of Program Design 2, Addison-Wesley (1996)

Framework Design for End-to-End Optimization

Aamod Sane[1], Ashish Singhai[2,*], and Roy H. Campbell[2]

[1] Icon Computing Inc.,
11940 Jollyville Road, Suite 300N, Austin, TX 78759 USA.
E-mail: sane@iconcomp.com, Web: http://www.iconcomp.com
[2] Department of Computer Science, University of Illinois,
1304 W. Springfield Avenue, Urbana, IL 61801 USA.
E-mail: {singhai,rhc}@uiuc.edu, Web: http://choices.cs.uiuc.edu

Abstract. Framework optimizations capitalize on object dependencies, while framework flexibility and composability demand object independence. This paper shows how to balance these conflicting needs using new design techniques. These techniques embody the observation that common optimizations can be realized by reifying and tuning object interactions. Their application is illustrated for two complex frameworks: a virtual memory framework and a framework for distributed objects. A catalog of patterns that covers common optimizations is also presented.

1 Introduction

The performance of a framework depends not only on its individual objects, but also on how they interact. For example, consider a file system with a server object S that caches disk data in its buffers. Clients normally get copies of these buffers and they may modify them without affecting the server. But if a particular client C does not modify its copies, then S can allow C to directly access its buffers. This avoids a data copy and saves memory, thereby improving performance. This improvement can not be realized by individually tuning S or C because the optimization depends upon the relationship between S and C. Such optimization, based on relationships between the components of a system rather than the components themselves, will be termed end-to-end optimization.[1]

End-to-end optimization is desirable, but it increases coupling among system components. Thus, S must be changed to support a new interface, while C must be changed to use that interface to request read-only copies. As the objects become more interdependent, the framework becomes harder to understand and reuse.

In this paper, we show how to enable end-to-end optimization in frameworks without making the objects overly interdependent. Our approach is to encapsulate object interactions and then customize the interactions for performance without changing the objects themselves.

* Ashish Singhai is supported in part by the grant NSF-CDA-94-01124.

[1] The idea of whole system or end-to-end analyses originates in [24].

This scheme has several benefits. First, encapsulation localizes the changes needed for optimization. So it is easier to understand the optimizations, and to estimate how adding new objects or tasks would affect efficiency. Second, we can develop domain- or application-specific optimizations and readily realize them by customizing the interactions. Third, going beyond framework objects, we can reify and optimize interactions between multiple frameworks in an application, as well as between applications (framework users) and the framework.

The idea is effective in practice because most common optimizations can be implemented via modulation of object relationships. We present such implementations as a catalog of design patterns, documenting the applicability and implementation issues for several optimizations. This gives framework builders a method for analyzing and developing whole-framework optimizations in a systematic way.

Overview. In Sect. 2 we present examples of framework optimizations selected from a wide variety of frameworks that we have built over the years in the *Choices* operating system [4] and other projects. The frameworks include a file-system framework [40], a virtual memory framework [25], an instrumentation framework [30], and a video conferencing framework [39]. Sect. 3 analyses these examples, motivating a set of objects that make object relationships first-class. We then show that well known optimization techniques from the literature can be expressed using this approach. This leads to our catalog in pattern form.

The catalog (Sect. 4) includes several classes of optimizations: Caching, Optimize Common Tasks, Lazy Evaluation, Eager Evaluation, Using Type Information, Structure Directed Optimization, Reducing Memory Usage, Concurrency Control, and Scheduling. A set of miscellaneous optimizations is also listed. For each class, we discuss how to determine when an optimization is applicable, and how to implement it. Each catalog entry also presents several examples from the literature.

Sections 5 and 6 describe two large frameworks that we have built using this approach: a virtual memory framework [25] and a distributed object framework [37]. Section 5 also includes examples of inter-framework optimizations. After presenting related work is Sect. 7, we conclude in Sect. 8 with a discussion of future research.

2 Examples

This section presents four examples of end-to-end optimizations in the frameworks we have built. Over the years, we observed that the implementations involved manipulating object interactions in similar ways. Generalizing these observations led to this paper.

2.1 Optimizing File System and Disk-Device Interactions

A simple implementation of *File::read(offset, buffer)* is to first compute the disk address *da* for *offset*, and then invoke *DiskDriver::readDisk(da, buffer)* to get the data. This is shown in Fig. 1(a). However, in this implementation, every access incurs disk seek latency. Therefore, fast implementations *batch* requests that refer to the same track, amortizing the latency over the batch of requests [35]. Batching is implemented by changing how *File* and *DiskDriver* interact.

For instance, first we change the arguments to *read()* and *readDisk()* into *Requests* that can be sorted, queued and compacted. Next, we modify *read()* to enqueue a *Request* and wait for it to complete. Finally, implement a *Batcher* object that groups the requests, invokes *DiskDriver* to read data, and notifies waiting parties of request completion. Same optimization also applies to *write()*. The resulting implementation is shown in Fig. 1(b).[2]

Besides other objects, this optimization introduces an object that represents the exchange of data.

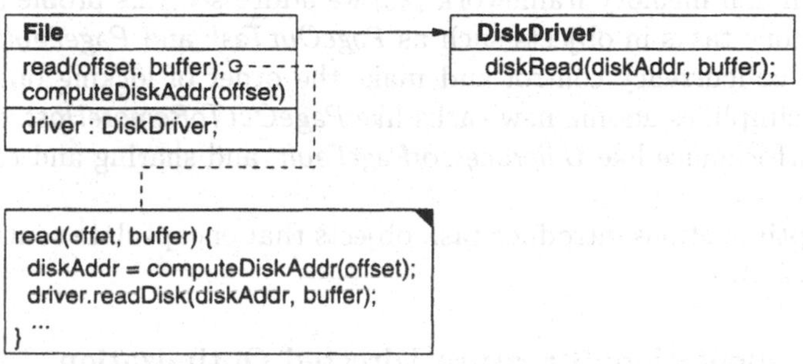

(a) Simple Implementation

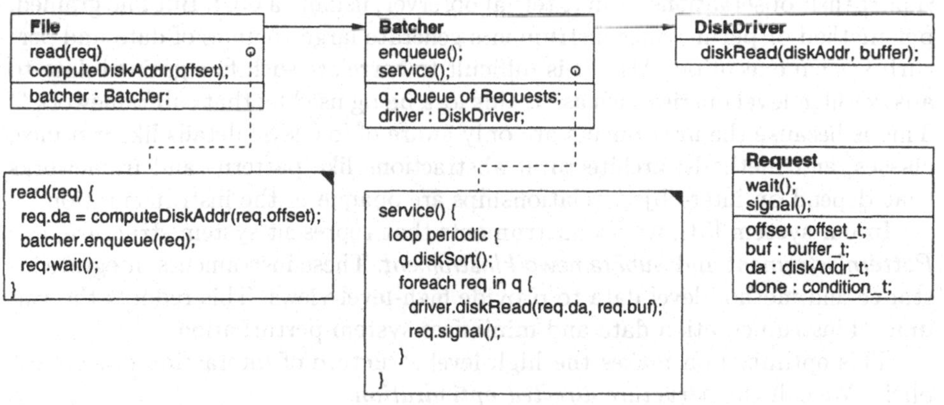

(b) Implementation with batching optimization

Fig. 1. File system example (Sect. 2.1) before and after the batching optimization

[2] To conserve space, we are presenting figures only for this example.

2.2 Changing Concurrency Control in Virtual Memory

Consider a pagefault task in a virtual memory framework [4]. The task locates the faulting virtual page using *AddressSpace*, allocates a physical page using *PhysicalPageStore*, retrieves swapped page contents from the file system, updates *VirtualMap* to make the page accessible, and updates *PhysicalMap*. A pageout task, on the other hand, locates a physical page in *PhysicalMap*, removes it from the *VirtualMap*, adds it to the kernel *VirtualMap*, and calls the file system to swap out the data.

These two tasks may execute concurrently, so they protect the objects they visit using locks. Typical implementations guidelines suggest[3] that locks be acquired and released by object methods, the lock being an instance variable. However, this hides dependencies among locks in method call sequences. Therefore it is difficult and deadlock-prone to add extensions like copy-on-write or distributed shared memory that visit and lock the same objects.

In our virtual memory framework [25] we addressed this problem by coding virtual memory tasks in objects such as *PageOutTask* and *PageFaultTask*. They encapsulate concurrency control and make the order of locking operations explicit. This simplifies adding new tasks like *PageOutToRemoteHost*, customizing tasks for performance like *UniprocessorPageFault*, and sharing and caching data across tasks.

These optimizations introduce task objects that encapsulate control flow and synchronization.

2.3 Instrumentation: Structure Directed Optimization

Instrumentation frameworks provide dynamic inspection of programs. Typically, a user associates *Instruments* with the objects and classes to be inspected, which report their observations to an external observer, usually a GUI. But fine grained, per-method or per-instance instruments generate large volumes of data and perturb system execution. Also, it is difficult to correlate such fine grained data to answer high level queries such as "is this lock being used by that subframework?" This is because the instruments are only aware of low-level details like instance, classes, and methods; architectural abstractions like patterns and frameworks that depend on inter-object relationships are opaque to the instrumentation.

In our system [31], we use instruments that represent system structure, like *PatternInstrument* and *SubFrameworkInstrument*. These instruments integrate instance and method level data to provide high-level views. This reduces the volume of instrumentation data and minimizes system perturbation.

This optimization makes the high-level structure of interacting objects explicit. We call this ***structure directed optimization.***

2.4 Video Conferencing: Control and Data Separation

In a video conferencing system that we are developing [39], *Clients* produce and consume video streams. A straightforward implementation is to let each client

[3] For example, `synchronized` methods in Java implicitly acquire and release locks.

multicast the generated streams, and receive streams generated by the others, so that they can converse with one another. But such an implementation would not scale with the number of clients. On the other hand, most clients in a conference usually listen to a single speaker, so we optimize this case.

It represents each stream as a *VideoStream* that not only abstracts video data, but also has attributes such as *isActive()* and *bitRate()*. A central *ConfControllerTask* represents the control processing for the conference. It detects active streams, inform clients about them, and throttles uninteresting streams. *Clients* need to receive and display only the stream suggested by the controller. The *ConfControllerTask* can be easily adapted to combine multiple streams (e.g., by time-sharing, or tiling) to produce a composite stream. Thus, clients would remain unchanged even if the number of active streams increased.

In this case, we arrive at an efficient implementation by encapsulating the control protocol in an object, and by exploiting the properties of video data.

3 Analyzing the Examples

In this section, we see how the optimizations from the previous section customize object interactions. We classify the interactions into those involving data, control and structure and show how to realize them using standard design patterns. A short example depicts applications of these ideas.

First, we revisit the examples from the previous section. The optimizations in these examples, summarized in Tab. 1, were implemented as follows:

Table 1. Summary of changes to examples in Sect. 2

Example	Basic Objects	Optimization	Interaction Objects
File System	File DiskDriver	Lazy Evaluation	Request Batcher
Virtual Memory	AddressSpace PhysicalMap VirtualMap PhysicalPageStore	Concurrency	PageOutTask PageFaultTask
Instrumentation	MethodInstrument InstanceInstrument ClassInstrument	Structural	PatternInstrument FrameworkInstrument
Video Conference	Client Channel	Type Based	ConfControllerTask

– In the file system example (Sect. 2.1) we reified the read and write requests into a DataObject, called *Request*, and the interaction between the file system and the disk driver into a TaskObject, called *Batcher*. This allowed us to optimize request processing by batching, i.e., rearranging the computation of requests and servicing multiple requests together.

- In the second example (Sect. 2.2), we encapsulated the concurrency control in the framework using TaskObjects like *PageFaultTask*. They localized concurrency control, and made object interactions easier to understand and customize.
- In the third example (Sect. 2.3), we made the high-level system structure explicit to reduce data that we had to store and transfer. The implementation modeled system abstractions as StructureObjects (e.g., *PatternInstrument*, *FrameworkInstrument*). This allowed us to rearrange, coalesce, and reduce computations involving large groups of framework objects.
- In the fourth example (Sect. 2.4), we decoupled data and control paths. Data communication was optimized using multicast, while control path was optimized using a centralized controller task. This resulted in a scalable video-conferencing system.

Observe that all these optimizations were implemented by specializing objects that represented different kinds of object interactions.

DataObject: DataObjects reify object interactions that exchange data.
TaskObject: TaskObjects reify control flow interactions among objects.
StructureObject: StructureObjects reify inter-object relationships such as subsystems.

Note that although we use terms like DataObject, one may use several objects to realize it. The term simply gives a common name to objects that represent data exchanged when framework objects interact.

The above analysis shows us that a framework can be made optimization-ready by introducing DataObjects, TaskObjects, and StructureObjects wherever there is a potential for exploiting object interactions. Different applications can tailor these objects in different ways, while the basic objects in the framework remain unchanged.

Implementing TaskObject, DataObject, StructureObject using patterns. Various design pattern catalogs (such as [10]) suggest patterns that can be used to implement task, data and structure objects. For instance, a TaskObject can be implemented as a COMMAND or a MEDIATOR, and may use patterns like STATE, or techniques like Object-Oriented State Machines [27]. Selection between specialized TaskObjects may be implemented as a STRATEGY. A DataObject can be implemented using PARAMETEROBJECT [26]. A StructureObject can involve a FACADE or a FACTORY augmented with interfaces for querying object structure.

Example. We recast the example of Sect. 1 in terms of TaskObject, DataObject, and StructureObject. In the example, a file framework defined *FileServers* and *Clients*. The client C accessed a server S read-only, while the client D overwrote the data it received from S. Therefore C and S could share the same data buffers.

With our new approach, the contract between *FileServer* and *Client* would be reified by a TaskObject, *ReaderTask*, that normally copies the data from server to client. If C treats its data as read only, the designer customizes the *ReaderTask* to not copy the data for the $C - S$ interaction. Alternatively, we could encapsulate the transferred data into a DataObject, *FileData*, and customize its data access methods to avoid the copy.

The remaining problem is to configure the system to use non-copying objects for $C - S$ interactions, and copying ones for $D - S$ interactions. We solve this problem using *FileSystem*, a StructureObject, which creates and maintains associations between clients and DataObjects or TaskObjects. The *FileSystem*, implemented as a FACTORY, represents the framework itself. In our instrumentation system (Sect. 2.3), it would also serve as a data aggregation point.

In the next section, we show how most common optimizations can be described as transformations of TaskObjects, DataObjects, and StructureObjects. The catalog we present gives criteria for deciding when to apply an optimization, and shows how it transforms object interactions. We describe typical implementations as combinations of TaskObjects, DataObjects, and StructureObjects. Examples from the literature are also mentioned.

4 Catalog

Catalog descriptions. In the following catalog, we describe each optimization as follows. First we describe the circumstances under which it is applicable. Then the implementation is described in terms of TaskObject, DataObject, and StructureObject. A TaskObject reifies the sequence of method calls that performs the functions supported by the framework. A DataObject encapsulates the arguments, results, and other data manipulated by a TaskObject. A StructureObject represents object groups and object associations. (See Sect. 3 for more detailed explanations). We also give a number of familiar examples of each optimization. The optimizations and some common examples are summarized in Tab. 2.

Table 2. Types of Optimizations

Optimization	Example
Inter-object caching	File Caching
Optimize common task	Inner loops
Lazy evaluation	File Access Batching
Eager evaluation	Prefetching Memory Pages
Using type information	Copy-on-write sharing
Memory Usage Optimizations	Using buffer pools
Concurrency Optimizations	Using priority locks
Structure Directed Optimizations	Multicast Trees
Miscellaneous Optimizations	Gang Scheduling

How to use the catalog. To use this catalog, first get a clear idea of the task, data, and structure relationships in your framework. Then use the applicability criteria to if they meet the requirements for a particular optimization. The implementation sections, together with the examples from Sect. 5 and Sect. 6, explain how to implement the optimizations.

4.1 Inter-Object Caching

Caching the results of methods in individual objects is common. But we are interested in caching the results of framework tasks distributed across multiple objects.

Applicability Caching is applicable when a task that computes a result may be repeated with the same arguments. We cache the computed results the first time the task executes. For subsequent executions, we return the cached results rather than repeating the computation.

Implementation If the arguments and results of tasks are kept in DataObjects, a cache can be implemented as a collection of DataObjects. In addition, TaskObjects have to be modified to:

- remember results of computations in a cache, and
- consult the cache before repeating a computation.

Caches are located in a StructureObject, where related framework objects may access it.

Examples File block caching in file systems, document caching in Web browsers, *Memoization* in functional and logic programming, index caching in databases.

4.2 Optimize Common Task

Optimizing frequently executed tasks leads to larger gains compared to optimizing tasks that may be seldom executed. In a framework, optimizing a common code path may require breaking encapsulation and refactoring.

Applicability If a task is expected to be used frequently, optimize its code. The optimizations may slow down infrequently used tasks, or compromise encapsulation.

Implementation Optimize the TaskObject for the frequently used task by inlining calls to framework methods. This eliminates the cost of indirection, but violates encapsulation. However, the violations are confined to a single TaskObject. Other ways to optimize tasks include using faster algorithms, and rearranging code to exploit processor caches. Often optimizing common code also needs optimized data access (perhaps using caching).

The optimized TaskObject is a special version of the generic TaskObject. If the framework is changed, the optimized version may be discarded or reprogrammed.

Examples Optimizing the innermost loops in numerical programs, optimizing file systems for small files because most files are small, dynamic code specialization in Synthesis [22], pointer swizzling in object databases.

4.3 Lazy Evaluation

The premise underlying lazy evaluation is that if we delay a task until its results are actually needed, more information may become available that can help optimize the task.

Applicability Lazy evaluation is applicable when all the results from a task execution are not needed immediately and when delaying the computation allows optimizing it.

Implementation TaskObject should include two methods: *prepare()*, that performs the immediate part of the task, and remembers the arguments for the delayed part; and *commit()*, that completes the execution. DataObject should have space to remember the arguments so that it can provide *commit()* with the appropriate context when it is eventually executed.

Examples Lazy write optimization in file systems (Sect. 2.1) uses *Request* to remember arguments (contents of the block and disk address) for write. The prepare part just creates a *Request*. The commit part actually writes the blocks to disk if necessary. It can avoid the write if the blocks have been overwritten, or if the file has been deleted. Even when it does write them, it batches neighboring disk blocks together and writes them using only one disk access.
Other examples: delaying marshaling of arguments in RPC until sending them and using scatter-gather hardware to collect memory fragments (see Sect. 6 for details); direct demultiplexing for network read [1].

4.4 Eager Evaluation

Eager evaluation is the dual of lazy evaluation. It computes some results that may not be needed immediately.

Applicability Eager evaluation is applicable when the incremental cost of computing another result while one result is being computed is low compared to computing it separately, and when the other result is usually needed later.

Implementation Modify the TaskObject so that when it computes the first result, it also computes the other result and saves it in the DataObject.
If the other result is an extension of the first (e.g., fetching two disk blocks, instead of one), modify arguments (e.g., change the number of blocks to read in DataObject) to get the extended result.

Examples Computing checksum of a network packet as a side effect of copying it [6], TCP header prediction [6], prefetching in databases and file systems.

4.5 Using Type Information

Data are typed, so some of their properties are known a priori. Therefore, we can substitute faster algorithms that exploit their properties.

Applicability When data input to a task have special properties, the task can be tailored to take advantage of them. Sometimes, we can instead alter data to suit a given task.

Implementation Implement several customized TaskObjects, one for each type of data. Modify StructureObjects to associate appropriate TaskObject with a given DataObject. StructureObjects usually achieve this using language level polymorphism. Let DataObjects have interfaces for querying their properties. Useful data properties are: size, order, format, location in memory, their source and destination objects, age, and application dependent properties, such as, video, audio, images, text, and large files.

Examples File systems may prefetch file data for sequentially accessed files but not for random access files. Web browsers relax security checks if the applet *source* is the local machine. Operating systems share read-only code segments among processes. Spreadsheets can use finite precision for money but arbitrary precision for other numerical data. Numerical packages supply different algorithms for different *types* of matrices [3] such as positive definite, upper triangular, symmetric, dense, and sparse. They also precondition data for algorithms. Web servers may perform lossy compression on data depending upon the client type (on-line distillation [9]).

4.6 Memory Usage Optimizations

Memory optimizations are among the most widely studied optimizations. The amount of memory available to a framework is limited, and dynamic allocations and releases are slow. Therefore, we need to optimize memory usage for improving speed and reducing the memory footprint.

Applicability Memory optimizations are often applicable to frameworks with dynamic allocations and data movement.

Implementation Most memory optimizations are implemented by tailoring TaskObjects to streamline data movement, to exploit temporal locality, and to reuse memory. Also, DataObjects should take advantage of type information to improve spatial locality, to provide fast access, and to reduce dynamic allocations. Typical memory optimizations are described below.

Avoid copies Hand off DataObject from one object to another in a TaskObject, copy on write, share read-only DataObjects.

Avoid dynamic allocation Use a pre-allocated pool of DataObjects. Pool size can be estimated using arrival rate of allocations and time between allocations and corresponding releases. Using StructureObjects, allocate related objects together instead of allocating each object individually. If allocation and release happen in the same scope, use stack allocation.

Avoid accessing memory Use pre-filled DataObject to avoid writing the common fields repeatedly, use scatter-gather I/O to collect memory fragments.

Exploit processor caching Use eager evaluation to compute multiple results on a DataObject (e.g., computing *Packet* checksum while copying it benefits from the fact that the *Packet* may be in the cache), special layout of DataObject for improved cache behavior (e.g., row major layout for matrices accessed in row major order).

Examples RPC frameworks avoid dynamic allocations using buffer pool for requests, operating systems use copy-on-write to share pages, networking frameworks use data structures like `mbuf` [16] and x-kernel messages [12] to add or remove protocol headers without copying. The resource exchanger pattern [28] combines many of these optimizations.

4.7 Concurrency Optimization

Concurrent operations on shared objects must be serialized in a framework. When serialization is implemented using locks, the framework must avoid cyclic dependencies. This involves analyzing all objects in a framework. Poor concurrency management may lead to poor performance due to contention hot-spots (many threads contending for access to same data), hard to detect race conditions, locking overhead, and deadlocks.

Applicability If a framework supports concurrent tasks that operate on shared objects, concurrency optimizations may be needed.

Implementation Use a TaskObject to localize all lock acquisition and release operations over a task. Thereafter, it can be specialized to implement different trade-offs. Hot-spot contention can be reduced by splitting critical sections, and locking overhead can be reduced by putting many objects under the protection of one lock [19]. On a uniprocessor, TaskObject can be changed to manipulate interrupts and scheduling to reduce locking overhead.

A StructureObject can associate different types of locks (e.g., read lock and read-write lock) with a DataObject for different access types, and group objects that are used together under one lock (see Sect. 6 for an example). StructureObject objects can explicitly represent lock hierarchies [19] and make them obvious and easy to understand.

DataObjects can be used as tokens for implementing mutual exclusion. If DataObjects are maintained in different memory pools and caches, contention for the global heap is reduced.

Continuations, which may reduce thread usage, can be implemented using TaskObjects and DataObjects (see Sect. 5.3 for examples).

Examples Databases use intention mode locking [21] to improve concurrency and avoid deadlock. Parts of operating systems disable interrupts to implement critical sections. Array locks [7] distribute accesses over a larger region of memory to reduce contention in multiprocessors.

4.8 Structure Directed Optimization

Just as algorithms are optimized for a given data structure, framework tasks can be optimized for a given organization of framework objects.

Applicability If the framework objects are interconnected in regular structures like rings or trees, then tasks can take advantage of the structure. If an object knows its role in the overall framework organization, it can often reduce computation or communication.

Implementation Reify the object interconnection structure in a StructureObject. TaskObjects may use methods of the StructureObjects. The particular optimizations depend on the application.

Examples The instrumentation example (Sect. 2.3) reifies structure (e.g., *PatternInstrument* and *FrameworkInstrument*) which helps reduce volume of data and minimizes system perturbation. Distributed mutual exclusion becomes easy if the processes have known structures, such as a ring. Multicast protocols use *MulticastTree* to optimize data communication among a group of processes. For other examples, see the uses of StructureObjects in Sect. 4.7.

4.9 Miscellaneous

Scheduling Scheduling optimizations are usually applicable to system level frameworks. Specialized schedulers encapsulate optimizations and StructureObjects associate applications with them.

Gang scheduling schedules a group of cooperating processes together. Different *Real-time scheduling* algorithms [17] implement policies for executing tasks so that they meet their deadlines. Priority inheritance scheduling [32] prevents unbounded priority inversion in real-time systems. *Message driven scheduling* schedules tasks when their message arrive.

Protocols Knowledge about the *type* of communication, transport medium, and data helps design custom protocols to optimize factors such as latency, buffer space, and throughput. Multimedia transmission protocols can be optimized for bursty loss in the Internet to avoid retransmissions [5]. Protocols for mobile computing are optimized to reduce expensive transmission from mobile hosts. Parallel distributed programs use protocols that exploit communication patterns [14].

Communication Optimizations In addition to protocols, communication across endpoints can also be optimized. Use asynchronous (non-blocking) communication for overlapping communication with computation. Avoid data conversion to a common format if both endpoints use same data representation. Since a DataObject encapsulates information exchanged between framework objects, they also represent the data to be exchanged across the network when a framework is extended to include communication. (E.g., *VMData* when we add distribution to virtual memory, see Sect. 5).

This completes the catalog. In the next section, we show how to use the catalog for optimizing a virtual memory framework and a distributed object framework.

5 Optimizing a Virtual Memory Framework

This section describes optimizations for the virtual memory framework[4] of the Choices operating system [25]. The virtual memory framework uses the networking framework to implement distributed shared memory. We show how our techniques help in optimizing interactions between these two frameworks.

5.1 Framework Description

The virtual memory framework provides memory management to user processes. A user process issues virtual addresses in its address space, and the virtual memory system translates them to physical addresses, retrieving memory contents from disk when necessary. A user process may also manipulate regions (ranges of addresses) of the address space. For example, a process may map files (or parts thereof) to regions with read, write, or execute permissions.

Basic Objects. These requirements suggest the following:

- *Domains* that represents the address space,
- *MemoryObjects* that represent datasets like files,
- *MemoryObjectViews* that represents parts of memory objects,
- *MemoryObjectCaches* that maintain the physical pages that hold the contents of *MemoryObjects*,
- *AddressTranslations* that manage virtual memory hardware, and
- *PageStore* that maintains unused physical pages.

These objects are tables. For example, *Domains* map virtual addresses to *MemoryObjectViews*; *MemoryObjectViews* are ranges in *MemoryObjects*. Framework operations like pagefault manipulate these tables.

A pagefault task begins with the faulting address, visits *Domain* to get the *MemoryObject* for that address, visits *MemoryObject* to locate the *MemoryObjectCache*, and reads the contents from the *MemoryObject* into a *Page*, allocating one from *PageStore* if necessary. It then updates *AddressTranslation*, mapping the *Page* to the faulting virtual address.

Interaction Objects. Ordinarily, tasks like pagefault processing are embedded in the framework as a sequence of object method calls as described above. But in our framework, we reify them as suggested in Sect. 3.

Tasks like pagefault and pageout become *PageFaultTask* and *PageOutTask*. Their parameters, results, and the objects they visit are recorded in a *VMData* object. The virtual memory system as a whole is represented by *VMSystem*, a StructureObject implemented as a FACADE [10]. *Domain* also serves as a StructureObject, representing the virtual memory objects associated with particular processes.

---

[4] The idea of optimizing via reified object relationships was developed while implementing this framework; our description pretends as if this idea was applied from the beginning.

VMSystem provides methods like *pageFault()* that initiate framework tasks. For example, *VMSystem::pageFault()* creates a new *VMData* and invokes *PageFaultTask::execute(VMData)*.

5.2 Applying Optimizations

In this section, we describe a few sample optimizations from the catalog (Sect. 4).

Caching. Multi-threaded programs exhibit page-in locality, where many processes fault on a shared page in quick succession. Therefore, store the *VMData* objects associated with recent *PageFaultTask*s in a cache. *PageFaultTask*s consult the cache before processing. Other tasks like *MMapTask*, that maps files, can also use the cache.

Common Task Optimization. Typically, *PageFaultTask* operates on a single page, and only needs to update *AddressTranslation*, or refresh the hardware cache, or change memory access levels. We optimize this by creating a special *SinglePageFaultTask*. This task directly accesses internal tables and uses locks that grant priority to single-page page faults.

Lazy Evaluation. When swapping a page out, user processes must be prevented from accessing the page. So the *AddressTranslation* hardware table entries must be removed immediately. But the page contents can be written to disk at leisure. Moreover, if the page that is to be swapped is accessed again, then we can simply map the page in, eliminating disk write and read. Therefore we use lazy evaluation for pageout. *PageOutTask* has two methods, *makePageInaccessible()* and *pageFlush()*. After executing *makePageInaccessible()*, the associated *VMData* is put in a flush queue. If the page is eventually flushed, then the pageout daemon will execute *pageFlush()*; if the page is paged in, the *VMData* information will be used to make the page accessible.

Eager Evaluation. When a virtual page is accessed, the next page is also likely to be accessed. Also, paging in two pages from disk at one time is cheaper than paging them in separately. We implement this by changing *PageFaultTask*. When *PageFaultTask* encounters a missing physical page, it allocates two pages from the *PageStore* and page them in both at once, provided both are in the same *MemoryObject*.

Using Type Information. For certain memory objects, the style of access is known. For example, pages with video data may be accessed first in first out. The user can provide such type information and policies that use the information to influence pageout. The *VMSystem* associates the memory objects and policies when the objects are initialized by the virtual memory system.

Memory Usage Optimization. The virtual memory framework uses its own heaps to avoid contention. The heap is designed for *VMData* and various table entries used by the virtual memory objects.

5.3 Extensions and Intra-Framework Optimizations

The framework described above was enhanced to support copy-on-write and distributed shared memory. Implementing these enhancements to the virtual memory framework was simplified because of the first-class relationship objects.

Copy-on-write support adds StructureObjects that represent groups of copy-on-write pages. *PageInTask* is changed to distinguish between read and write accesses, and interact with the copy-on-write objects if necessary. *PageOutTask* requires no changes, except that the policy that determines suitable pages for page out is affected.

Distributed Shared Memory requires network communication of pages. Various optimizations can be used to tune the interaction between virtual memory and network frameworks.

For example, the *VMSystem* detects if a page fault is on a distributed shared memory object. It then allocates a special *VMData* that is pre-formatted as a network packet. *PageFaultTask* hands this buffer to the network framework which uses it as its network packet. This is an optimization that uses *type information* (Sect. 4.5).

Similarly, we can reduce thread usage using TaskObjects and DataObjects to implement continuations. Normally, when a *PageFaultTask* is waiting for a network message, the thread executing it is suspended. But threads are scarce resources, so it is important to use them carefully. So *PageFaultTask* provides two methods: *getPhysicalPage()* and *installPage()*. After completing *getPhysicalPage()*, the thread executing *PageFaultTask* enqueues the corresponding *VMData* in a pending queue. When the page arrives from the network, a new thread calls *PageFaultTask::installPage(VMData)* to continue fault processing. This is a *lazy evaluation* (Sect. 4.3) and *concurrency* optimization (Sect. 4.7).

Because the concurrency control was encapsulated in the TaskObjects, it was easy to ensure that adding the new objects and changing the TaskObjects for new responsibilities did not create deadlock. The *VMData* objects suggested the network optimizations and also the generalization to use continuations. Besides interaction objects, our framework uses other ideas like object-oriented state machines [27] and resource exchanger [28] to simplify the implementation.

6 Optimizing a Distributed Object Framework

In this section we consider optimizations in *Quarterware*, a framework for distributed object computing [37].

6.1 Framework Description

A distributed object framework performs two basic tasks:

1. A local method invocation on the client side is converted into a remote request. The subtasks are: marshal the arguments to the call, make a request packet, send it over the network, then wait for the reply packet (if any), and unmarshal the reply.

2. The server side receives a request from the network and converts it to a local method invocation on the indicated server object. This task must receive a request, find the server object, unmarshal the arguments, invoke the requested method on the server, and marshal and send the reply, if any.

Basic Objects. This suggests the following basic objects for this framework (similar to TAO [29] or Orbix [13]).

- *ObjectRef*s represent remote objects locally. A client invokes methods on an *ObjectRef*.
- *ActualObjects* are server objects that implement the desired functionality. Calls on *ObjectRef*s are forwarded to the corresponding *ActualObjects*.
- *Arguments* represent the arguments to a method invocation (call).
- *Results* represent the results of a call returned by the server (*ActualObject*).
- *Channels* represent communication media.
- *MemoryAllocators* provide memory to hold *Arguments* and *Results*.

Interaction Objects. The basic objects provide methods to perform individual operations. As discussed in Sect. 3, we connect them through the following interaction objects.

- *MarshalTasks* produce network representation of *Arguments* and *Results*. They may use conventional representations such as XDR, or non-conventional marshaling mechanisms such as compression or distillation [9].
- *ClientCallTasks* implement the client side of a remote call. It involves allocating memory, invoking *MarshalTask*, sending the marshaled data on the corresponding *Channel* and doing the inverse processing for the *Result*.
- *ServiceTasks* implement the server side of a remote call. It involves receiving, unmarshaling and dispatching the request, and marshaling and returning the results.
- *CallData* encapsulates data needed for performing an invocation. It contains memory for holding *Arguments* and *Results*, references to the *Channel*, names of *ActualObject*, method to be invoked, *MarshalTask* to use, etc.
- *CallEnvironments* are StructureObjects that associate these objects with one another. For example, a *CallEnvironment* associates *MemoryAllocators*, *Channels*, *ServiceTasks*, and *ActualObjects* on the server side.

6.2 Applying Optimizations

This section illustrates a few example optimizations from the catalog (Sect. 4).

Optimizing Memory Usage. We use the *type* information for arguments, results, and *Requests* (Sect. 4.5) to optimize memory usage. Other memory usage optimizations (Sect. 4.6) [11,8] are as follows.

- Client stubs use *stack allocation* of *CallDatas* if argument sizes are known at compile time and invocation is synchronous. (*Avoid dynamic allocation, Sect. 4.6.*)

- Single threaded *ClientCallTasks* (and *ServiceTasks*) reuse the same *CallData* instance across a sequence of calls. (*Avoid dynamic allocation, Sect. 4.6.*)
- *MarshalTask* uses block copy (using `memcpy()`) for marshaling arguments that reside in contiguous memory. (*Using type information, Sect. 4.5.*)
- *ClientCallTasks* use pre-filled *CallDatas* to avoid writing the header fields such as the name of actual object. (*Avoid accessing memory, Sect. 4.5.*)
- *MemoryAllocators* provide two *types* of buffers — one for fixed size *CallDatas*, and the other for variable size *CallDatas*. Fixed size buffers incur *no dynamic allocation* overhead. (*Using type information, Sect. 4.5.*)
- *MemoryAllocators* for multi-threaded servers use a *BufferPool*. A good estimate for the *size* of the pool is the expectation of *live* requests in the system, i.e., the sum of stored (enqueued) requests and the number of active threads (each thread processes one request). (*Avoid dynamic allocation, Sect. 4.6.*)

Optimizing the Common Tasks.

- *Fuse* the *MarshalTask* and *ClientCallTask* for single threaded clients, reducing function call overhead.
- We optimize for *short requests* that have either few or no arguments, using a special *ShortCallData*. It has a small inline buffer to hold the request. This reduces dynamic allocation overhead.
- In *homogeneous systems*, data representations on the sender and receiver are identical. So *MarshalTask* for such systems does not not perform data conversion.
- With *one way requests*, the sender does not expect a reply. We modify *ClientCallTasks* and *ServiceTasks* to recognize this case and not allocate resources for the *Result*.

Structure and Concurrency Optimizations. Before executing a request, the *ServiceTask* needs to increment reference counts on *OutputChannel*, *ActualObject*, and *BufferPool*. Since these objects are shared, the reference counts increments have to be protected by locks. We can reduce the number of lock operations by incrementing the reference count on *CallEnvironment* only. Since it already groups *Channel*, *Target*, and *BufferPool*, these objects are referenced automatically (see Sect. 4.7 and 4.8).

Lazy Evaluation. Usually marshaling arguments consists of linearizing the arguments in a buffer. Marshaled arguments are then sent over the *Channel*. This involves a memory-to-memory copy. If the system supports scatter-gather I/O (e.g., Unix `sendv()` call), then we can delay linearization of arguments, and combine it with *Channel::send()*. This way we can avoid the intermediate copy.

We implement this using the *lazy evaluation* pattern (Sect. 4.3) from the catalog as follows. (See Fig. 2 for implementation.)

Specializing DataObjects Customize

- *CallData* on the client side to remember arguments rather than copying them.

– *CallData* on the server side to remember the input *Channel*.

Specializing TaskObjects Modify

– *MarshalTask::prepare()* to remember arguments.
– *MarshalTask::commit()* to linearize and write remembered arguments to the *Channel* using scatter-gather I/O.
– *ServiceTask::prepare()* to only read the request header, and remember the *InputChannel*.
– *ServiceTask::commit()*, called just before executing the request, to read the arguments from the *InputChannel* into the application memory.

```
ObjectRef::method(Argument a) {
  Result r;
  CallData cd = CDAllocator.alloc(a);
  marshaler.marshal(cd, a);
  clientCallTask.invoke(cd);
  marshaler.unmarshal(cd, r);
  return r;
}
Marshaler::marshal(CallData cd,
                   Argument a) {
  cd.buffer.copy(a.buffer);
}
ClientCallTask::invoke(
                CallData cd) {
  channel.send(cd);
  channel.receive(cd);
  return;
}
```

(a) Simple implementation

```
Marshaler::prepare(CallData cd,
                   Argument a) {
  cd.remember(a);
}
Marshaler::commit(CallData cd,
                  Channel c) {
  c.gatherSend(cd.remembered);
}
ClientCallTask::invoke(
                CallData cd) {
  marshaler.commit(cd, channel);
  channel.receive(cd);
  return;
}
```

(b) Lazy eval. on client-side

Fig. 2. Implementing lazy evaluation optimization in *Quarterware* (Sec. 6)

Optimizing Thread Usage and Scheduling. A server faces various trade-offs between response time and resource usage. For example:

– Optimize response time using more resources (threads and buffers). The extreme case is to use a new thread and a new buffer for each new request.
– Conserve resources at the cost of deteriorating response time. The extreme case is to serialize request processing using only one thread and one buffer.

– An intermediate solution is to dedicate one thread and one buffer for each client and execute requests from different clients in parallel, and those from the same clients one after the other.

We implement different versions of *ServiceTasks* to represent these trade-offs (similar to *invocation strategies* [29]). Some of the versions are:

– *STSequential* always associates the same thread with each *CallData*, i.e., task processing is sequential.
– *STMultiThreaded* creates a new thread for each task and implements thread-per-message strategy.
– *STThreadPerClient* has one thread for each client, and it uses the *inputChannel* attribute of the *CallData* to associate it with the corresponding thread.
– *STRealTime* executes real-time scheduling for requests [36]. In this case, we also have to the *Argument* format to carry additional attributes, such as, priority, and deadline.
– *STSynchronized*, like guarded commands, schedules a request subject to satisfaction of some synchronization constraints.

7 Related Work

Related work falls in two categories: work on networking optimizations and systems design, and software engineering work on reifying object relationships.

The end-to-end argument in system design was introduced by Saltzer et. al. [24]. They describe the implications of end-to-end argument for system structuring. They have argued that many system-wide properties can not be implemented without application-specific knowledge. This argument forms the basis of the insight that implementing optimizations requires changes not only to objects, but also to their interactions.

The research on Paths [20] comes closest to our work. It introduces a path as an explicit abstraction that connect the layers in an operating system and describes optimizations along a path.

Clark [6] and others describe many optimizations for network protocols. In [1] Abbot et. al. describe "Integrated Layer Processing (ILP)," their technique for optimizing protocols. ILP also relies upon fusing protocol layers to reduce copying and expediting protocol processing.

Schmidt et. al. [11] document a comprehensive set of optimizations for Object Request Brokers (ORBs). This paper is among the first works on applying networking optimizations to distributed object systems.

We distinguish our work from the above in that we show how to apply optimizations to arbitrary frameworks. Our ideas are more general than Paths [20] since we go beyond control paths: we explicitly represent data traveling along the path, as well as the structure of object interconnections. We also show how most common optimizations from the literature can be represented as transformations of control, data, and structure. In addition, we present standard techniques for describing applicability and implementations of these optimizations.

There have been many proposals to give first-class status to relationships between system components. The purpose of these proposals is to ease evolution of systems and make them easier to understand.

Reflective systems [38, 23] advocate reifying many aspects of objects. Kiczales [15] presents a design methodology, "Open Analysis and Design," which suggests incorporating reflective interfaces for customization.

Shaw [33] argues that the connections between components deserve first-class status. For example, encoding a pipe that connects two communicating programs with procedure calls obscures the data flow aspects. This paper was a starting point for our work. An architecture description language UniCon [34] and a formal description language Wright [2] explicitly model connections.

The Demeter project introduces a notation for making the structure of frameworks explicit, and express framework traversals as regular expressions [18]. This helps in framework evolution, because changes to the object structure can be expressed by changing the structure description rather than method code.

Our approach shares the advantages of reification and encapsulation with these works. However, our focus is different. We concentrate on optimizations, their representations, and their role in a framework. We use reifications as a tool to implement our optimizations.

8 Conclusion

This paper showed how to design frameworks that are easy to optimize. The design techniques allow framework users to specialize not only individual objects, but also optimize the interactions between objects. To make such customization easy, object interactions are themselves expressed as objects, and tailored using domain-specific information. Common optimizations can be expressed by modulating object relationships.

Relationship objects localize the changes required for optimization. As a result, a framework user does not have to hunt through the framework to understand the optimization. Similarly, changes to framework objects and optimizations may interact, but their interplay is made explicit by the relationship objects. This eases framework evolution and refactoring.

We also presented a catalog of optimizations that helps designers determine suitable optimizations and implement them in a systematic manner. The catalog gives designers a common vocabulary to describe optimizations and understand why and how they work. Our experience suggests that these techniques are useful in practice.

This research suggests several issues for future work. One direction is to expand the catalog of optimizations and improve the descriptions. It is remarkable that so many optimizations can be described in a uniform way by tuning object interconnections; perhaps this idea may be generalized further. It would be interesting to see whether programming languages can directly support our implementation techniques. Another possible development is to include our implementation techniques in refactoring tools.

Acknowledgments. We gratefully acknowledge help from Fabio Kon and Amitabh Dave (UIUC), John Heintz (Icon Computing), and Sharad Singhai (UMass) for their comments, and thank Monika Chandak (UIUC) for support and for loaning her machine to us.

References

1. Mark B. Abbott and Larry L. Peterson. Increasing network throughput by integrating protocol layers. *IEEE/ACM Transactions on Networking*, 1(5):600–610, October 1993.
2. Robert Allen. *A Formal Approach to Software Architecture*. PhD thesis, Department of Computer Science, Carnegie Mellon University, Pittsburgh, May 1997. CMU-CS-97-144.
3. Aart J. C. Bik and Harry A. G. Wijshoff. On automatic data structure selection and code generation for sparse computations. In *Proceedings of the Workshop on Languages and Compilers for Parallel Computing (LCPC)*, volume 768 of *Lecture Notes in Computer Science*, pages 57–75. Springer Verlag, August 1993.
4. Roy Campbell, Nayeem Islam, Peter Madany, and David Raila. Experiences designing and implementing Choices: an object-oriented system in C++. *Communications of the ACM*, 36(9):117–126, September 1993.
5. Zhigang Chen. Coding and transmission of digital video on the internet. Technical Report UIUCDCS-R-1997-2016, Department of Computer Science, University of Illinois at Urbana-Champaign, Urbana, Illinois, 1997.
6. D. Clark, V. Jocabson, J. Romkey, and M. Salwen. An analysis of TCP processing overhead. *IEEE Communications Magazine*, 27(6):23–29, Jun 1989.
7. A. Dave, N. Islam, and R. H. Campbell. A low-latency scalable locking algorithm for shared memory multiprocessors. In *Proceedings of the 6th Symposium on Parallel and Distributed Processing*, pages 10–17. IEEE Computer Society Press, October 1994.
8. Eric Eide, Kevin Frei, Bryan Ford, Jay Lepreau, and Gary Lindstrom. Flick: A flexible, optimizing IDL compiler. In *ACM SIGPLAN '97 Conference on Programming Language Design and Implementation (PLDI)*, pages 44–56, June 1997.
9. Armando Fox, Steven D. Gribble, Eric A. Brewer, and Elan Amir. Adapting to network and client variability via on-demand dynamic distillation. In *Proceedings of the 7th International Conference on Architectural Support for Programming Languages and Operating Systems*, pages 160–170. ACM, October 1996.
10. Erich Gamma, Richard Helm, Ralph Johnson, and John Vlissides. *Design Patterns: Elements of Reusable Object-Oriented Software*. Addison Wesley, 1994.
11. A. Gokhale and D. C. Schmidt. Principles for optimizing corba internet inter-orb protocol performance. In *Proceedings of the 31st Hawaii International Conference onf System Sciences*, pages 375–386, January 1998. (to appear).
12. N. C. Hutchinson and Larry L. Peterson. The *x*-kernel: An architecture for implementing network protocols. *IEEE Transactions on Software Engineering*, 17(1):64–76, January 1991.
13. IONA Technologies. *The Orbix Architecture*, November 1996. Available at `http://www.iona.com/Products/Orbix/Architecture/index.html`.
14. N. Islam, A. Dave, and R. H. Campbell. Communication compilation for unreliable networks. In *Proceedings of the 16th International Conference on Distributed Computing Systems*, pages 188–195, May 1996.

15. Gregor Kiczales, John Lamping, Cristina Videira Lopes, Anurag Mendhekar, and Gail Murphy. Open implementation design guidelines. In *Proceedings of the 19th International Conference on Software Engineering*, pages 481–490, May 1997.
16. S. J. Leffler, M. K. McKusick, M. J. Karels, and J. S. Quaterman. *The Design and Implementation of the 4.3 BSD UNIX Operating System.* Addison Wesley, 1988.
17. C. L. Liu and J. W. Layland. Scheduling algorithms for multiprogramming in hard real-time environment. *Journal of the ACM*, 20(1):46–61, January 1973.
18. Cristina Videira Lopes and Karl Lieberherr. Abstracting process-to-function relations in concurrent object-oriented applications. In *Proceedings of the 8th European Conference on Object-Oriented Programming (ECOOP)*, volume 821 of *Lecture Notes in Computer Science*, pages 81–99. Springer Verlag, July 1994.
19. Paul E. McKenney. Selecting locking primitives for parallel programming. *Communications of the ACM*, 39(10):75–82, October 1996.
20. David Mosberger and Larry L. Peterson. Making paths explicit in the scout operating system. In *2nd Symposium on Operating Systems Design and Implementation (OSDI '96)*, pages 153–167. USENIX, October 1996.
21. Nathan Goodman Philip A. Bernstein, Vassos Hadzilacos. *Concurrency Control and Recovery in Database Systems.* Addison Wesley, 1987.
22. Calton Pu, Henry Massalin, and John Ioannidis. The synthesis kernel. *Computing Systems*, 1(1):11–32, Winter 1988.
23. *Reflection'96*, San Francisco, CA, April 1996.
24. J. H. Saltzer, D. P. Reed, and D. D. Clark. End-to-end arguments in system design. *ACM Transactions on Computer Systems*, 2(4):277–288, November 1984.
25. Aamod Sane. *Techniques for Developing Correct, Fast, and Robust Implementations of Distributed Protocols.* PhD thesis, Department of Computer Science, University of Illinois, Urbana-Champaign, December 1997.
26. Aamod Sane and Roy Campbell. Composite messages: A structural pattern for communication among software components. In *OOPSLA'95 Workshop on Design Patterns in Concurrent, Distributed, and Parallel Object-Oriented Systems*, 1995.
27. Aamod Sane and Roy Campbell. Object-oriented state machines: Subclassing, composition, delegation, and genericity. In *Proceedings of the OOPSLA*, pages 17–32. ACM, October 1995.
28. Aamod Sane and Roy Campbell. Resource exchanger: A behavioral pattern for low overhead concurrent resource management. In *Pattern Languages of Program Design.* Addison Wesley, 1996.
29. Douglas C. Schmidt and Chris Cleeland. Applying patterns to develop extensible and maintainable orb middleware. Available at `http://www.cs.wustl.edu/\~schmidt/ORB-patterns.ps.gz`.
30. Mohlalefi Sefika. *Design conformance management of software systems: An architecture-oriented approach.* PhD thesis, Department of Computer Science, University of Illinois, Urbana-Champaign, August 1996. UIUCDCS-R-96-1974.
31. Mohlalefi Sefika, Aamod Sane, and Roy H. Campbell. Architecture-oriented visualization. In *Proceedings of the Conference on Object-Oriented Programming Systems, Languages, and Applications (OOPSLA)*, volume 31(10) of *ACM SIGPLAN Notices*, pages 389–405, October 1996.
32. L. Sha, R. Rajkumar, and J. P. Lehoczky. Priority inheritance protocols: An approach to real-time synchronization. *IEEE Transactions on Computers*, 39(9):1175–1185, September 1990.
33. M. Shaw. Procedure calls are the assembly language of software interconnections: Connectors deserve first class. In D. Lamb, editor, *Studies of Software Design*,

volume 1078 of *Lecture Notes in Computer Science*, pages 17–32, Baltimore, Md, May 1993. Springer Verlag.

34. Mary Shaw, Robert DeLine, Daniel V. Klein, Theodore L. Ross, David M. Young, and Gregory Zelesnik. Abstractions for software architecture and tools to support them. *IEEE Transactions on Software Engineering*, 21(4):314–335, April 1995.
35. Abraham Silberschatz and Peter B. Galvin. *Operating System Concepts*. Addison Wesley, 1997.
36. Ashish Singhai, Aamod Sane, and Roy Campbell. Reflective ORBs: Support for robust, time-critical distribution. In *Proceedings of the ECOOP'97 Workshop on Reflective Real-Time Object-Oriented Programming and Systems*, volume (to appear) of *Lecture Notes in Computer Science*. Springer Verlag, June 1997.
37. Ashish Singhai, Aamod Sane, and Roy Campbell. Quarterware for middleware. In *Proceddings of the 18th International Conference on Distributed Computing Systems (ICDCS)*. IEEE, May 1998.
38. Brian C. Smith. *Reflection and Semantics in A Procedural Language*. PhD thesis, Massachusetts Institute of Technology, January 1982. MIT-LCS-272.
39. Habanero project, 1997. Available at: `http://http://www.ncsa.uiuc.edu/SDG/Software/Habanero/`.
40. Lim Swee. *Adaptive Caching in a Distributed File System*. PhD thesis, Department of Computer Science, University of Illinois, Urbana-Champaign, November 1995.

Flexible Alias Protection

James Noble[1], Jan Vitek[2], and John Potter[1]

[1] Microsoft Research Institute, Macquarie University, Sydney
kjx,potter@mri.mq.edu.au

[2] Object Systems Group, Université de Genève, Geneva.
Jan.Vitek@cui.unige.ch

Abstract. Aliasing is endemic in object oriented programming. Because an object can be modified via any alias, object oriented programs are hard to understand, maintain, and analyse. *Flexible alias protection* is a conceptual model of inter-object relationships which limits the visibility of changes via aliases, allowing objects to be aliased but mitigating the undesirable effects of aliasing. Flexible alias protection can be checked statically using programmer supplied *aliasing modes* and imposes no runtime overhead. Using flexible alias protection, programs can incorporate mutable objects, immutable values, and updatable collections of shared objects, in a natural object oriented programming style, while avoiding the problems caused by aliasing.

1 Introduction

I am who I am; I will be who I will be.

Object identity is the foundation of object oriented programming. Objects are useful for modelling application domain abstractions precisely because an object's identity always remains the same during the execution of a program — even if an object's state or behaviour changes, the object is always the same object, so it always represents the same phenomenon in the application domain [30].

Object identity causes practical problems for object oriented programming. In general, these problems all reduce to the presence of *aliasing* — that a particular object can be referred to by any number of other objects [20]. Problems arise because objects' state can change, while their identity remains the same. A change to an object can therefore affect any number of other objects which refer to it, even though the changed object itself may have no information about the other objects.

Aliasing has a large impact on the process of developing object oriented software systems. In the presence of aliases, understanding what a program does becomes more complex, as runtime information about topology of the system is required to understand the effects of state changes. Debugging and maintaining programs with aliasing is even more difficult, because a change to one part of a program can affect a seemingly independent part via aliased objects.

In this paper, we present *flexible alias protection*, a novel conceptual model for enforcing alias encapsulation and managing the effects of aliasing. Flexible alias protection rests on the observation that the problems caused by aliasing are not the result of either aliasing or mutable state in isolation; rather, problems result from the interaction between them, that is, when aliases make state changes visible. We propose a prescriptive technique for enforcing flexible alias protection based on programmer-supplied *aliasing mode declarations* which relies on static mode checking to verify the aliasing properties of an object's implementation. The mode checking is modular, allowing implementations to be checked separately, and is performed entirely at compile-time, with no additional run-time cost.

Flexible alias protection is closely related to the work of Hogg [19] and Almeida [2]. Our proposal differs from these in two main respects. Most importantly, flexible alias protection allows objects to play a number of different roles, which reflect the ways in which objects are used in common object oriented programming styles. For example, a container's *representation* objects may be read and written, but must not be exposed outside their enclosing container, while a container's *argument* objects may be aliased freely, but a container may not depend upon their mutable state. Flexible alias protection does not require the complex abstract interpretation of Almeida's Balloon types, and is thus more intuitive for programmers and less sensitive to small changes in the implementations of the protected objects.

This paper is organised as follows. Section 2 presents the problems created by aliasing in object oriented programs, and Section 3 discusses related work. Section 4 then introduces the concepts underlying flexible alias protection, and Section 5 presents a model for static mode checking. Section 6 discusses future work, and Section 7 concludes the paper. We begin by describing the problem caused by aliasing in object oriented programs.

2 Aliasing and Encapsulation

Aliases can cause problems for object oriented programs whenever a program abstraction is implemented by more than one object in the target program. That is, when there is one *aggregate object* representing the whole of an abstraction and providing an encapsulated interface to it, and encapsulating one or more other objects implementing the abstraction represented by the aggregate object. We say the objects implementing the aggregate objects are members of the aggregate object's *aliasing shadow*[1].

Aliasing can cause problems whenever references into an aggregate object's shadow exists from outside the shadow. Messages can be sent to that shadow object via the alias, bypassing the aggregate, and modify the state of the subsidiary objects, and thus of the whole abstraction implemented by the aggregate object, see Figure 1. References to an aggregate object's shadow can arise in two

[1] An aggregate object's shadow is similar to Wills' *demesnes* [41], or the objects in an Island [19] or Balloon [2]. In this paper, we use the term *shadow* to denote the intrinsic nature of this set of objects, and other terms to denote particular aliasing control mechanisms

ways: either an object which is referenced from outside can be added into the shadow, or a reference from within the shadow can be passed out.

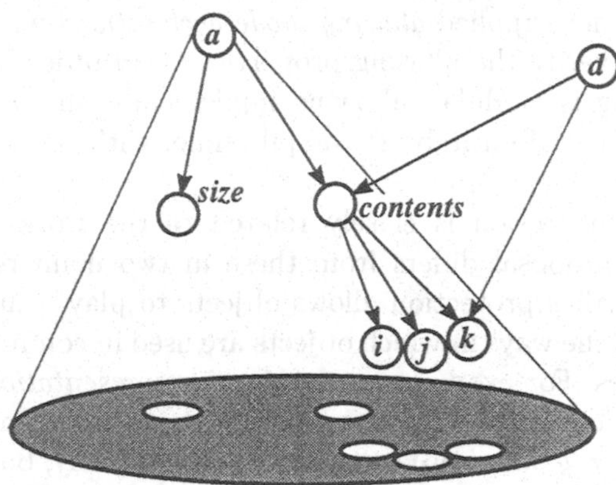

Fig. 1. *Unconstrained Aliasing.* The hash table a has a shadow composed of representation objects *size* and *contents*, and some argument objects contained in the table, i, j, and k. Both *contents* and k are seen from the outside by d. Thus, d is able to change the state of a's implementation without going through a.

The breaches of encapsulation caused by aliasing may affect correctness of the aggregate objects, causing the program to err, or, perhaps even more seriously, opening security holes in the application. We illustrate these problems with two examples.

Consider an object implementing a simple hash table (see Figure 2). The hash table object has two components: an array of table entries and an integer, stored as variables named contents and size. The hash table object is an aggregate, its shadow contains the integer, the array, and the table entry objects in the array. If a reference to the contents array exists from outside the hash table object (that is, if the array is aliased) the contents of the hash table can be modified by sending a message directly to the array object, without sending a message to the hash table object itself.

Aliases to the hash table's elements can arise in a number of ways. For example, if references to the key and item objects are retained outside the hashtable, the hash table elements will be aliased. Alternatively, a hash table operation (such as get) can directly return a reference to an object stored in a hash table, and this will immediately create an alias.

Aliases to the array object making up the hashtable's internal representation may also be created. Typically, representation objects are created within the aggregate object of which they are a part, and so preexisting references from outside the aggregate are unlikely. An operation upon the aggregate can, however, return a reference to one of the internal representation objects just as easily

```
class Hashtable<Hashable,Item> {

        private Array<HashtableEntry<Hashable,Item>> contents;
        private int size;

        public void put(Hashable key, Item val);
        public Item get(Hashable key);

        public Array<HashtableEntry<Hashable,Item>>
            expose() {
                return contents;
        };
}
```

Fig. 2. A Simple Hashtable

as it can return a reference to one of the elements — for example, Figure 2 shows how a hashtable could include an expose operation which would return the entire array.

Exposing internal representation may have security implications if objects are used as capabilities [13,16]. Viewing an object's interface as a capability is appealing, because it leverages the safety property guaranteed by a strong type system to turn it into a protection mechanism for implementing access control. In effect, the type system prevents access to operations not explicitly listed in an object's interface. The danger with this model is that, as there are no strong protection domains between entities, it surprisingly easy to open an aggregate object to attacks [39]. Aliasing plays an important role here as it can be exploited to gain access to the trusted parts of an abstraction. A case in point is the recent defect in an implementation of SUN's digital signatures for Java applets which permitted any applet to become trusted, simply because an alias to the system's internal list of signatures was being returned, instead of a copy of that list.

This paper is concerned with a programming discipline which simultaneously prevents aliases to the internal representation of an abstraction from escaping the abstraction's scope, and protects an abstraction from existing aliases to objects it receives as argument, while preserving many common object oriented programming styles. We will start by reviewing known approaches to this problem.

3 Related Work

3.1 Aliasing and Programming Languages

The traditional solution adopted by programming languages to encapsulate references (and thus aliases) is to provide *access modes* which control how names can be used within programs. For example, consider the *private* and *protected* modes of Java and C++ which restrict access to the names of variables and methods.

An aggregate object's shadow can be stored within the aggregate object's protected local state, but this is not enough to protect the shadow objects from aliasing [2, 19, 20]. As we have already seen, a method attached to an aggregate object can return a reference to a shadow object. An aggregate object can also store objects created outside itself into nominally private state, and these objects may have been aliased before they become members of the shadow. An object's encapsulation barrier protects only that individual object, and that object's private local state: the members of an aggregate object's shadow are not effectively encapsulated. That is to say, access modes protect local state by restricting access to the names of the local state, rather than to the objects to which the names refer.

In practice, many programming languages do not provide even this level of encapsulation. In languages such as C++ and Java, the language access modes provide protection on a *per-class* basis, so any object can retrieve a private reference from any other object of the same class, thus instantly creating an alias into another object's shadow. Eiffel includes *expanded types* which are always passed by value rather than reference. Unfortunately, subcomponents of expanded types can be passed by reference, and so can be aliased.

Rather than rely on access modes, it is sometimes suggested that aliasing can be controlled using private classes — that is, a private object should be an instance of a private class, rather than stored in a private variable. Private classes are not a general solution, however, since they also protects names rather than objects. For example, private classes are typically shared among all instances of the class where they are declared. More importantly, if a private class is to be used with existing libraries or frameworks, it will have to inherit from a well known public class, and so dynamic type casts can be used to access the private class as if it were its public superclass.

Garbage collection (or at least a restricted form of explicit memory management) is required to support all forms of aliasing control. If a program can delete an object while references to it are retained, and that object's memory is then reallocated to a new object, the new object will be aliased by the retained pointers to the nominally deleted object.

In practice, then, careful programming and eternal vigilance are the only defences against aliasing problems in current object oriented languages.

3.2 Full Alias Encapsulation

In recent years there have been a number of proposals to address aliasing in object oriented languages. For example, expressions can be analysed statically to determine their *effects*, described in terms of the memory regions they can change or depend upon [35, 28], whole programs can be analysed directly to detect possible aliasing [26, 10, 22], or hints may be given to the compiler as to probable aliasing invariants [18]. Objects can be referred to by tracing *paths* through programs, rather than by direct pointers, so that aliased objects will always have the same name [3,6,5], or pointers can be restricted to point to a particular set of objects [38]. Copying, swapping, destructive reads, or destructive assignments can replace regular reference assignment in programs, so that each object is only referred to by one *unique* or *linear* pointer [4,8,32,17,27]. Finally, languages can provide an explicit notion of aggregation, object containment, or ownership [19,2,9,24,11,15]. Unfortunately, these proposals forbid many common uses of aliasing in object oriented programs.

In this section, we review two of the most powerful proposals: John Hogg's Islands [19] and Paulo Sergio Almeida's Balloons [2]. Although they differ greatly in detail and mechanism — Islands use aliasing mode annotations attached solely to object's interfaces, while Balloons use sophisticated abstract interpretation — both these proposals have a common aim, which we term *full alias encapsulation*. Essentially, these proposals statically prevent external references into an object's shadow. This restriction ensures that Islands and Balloons can never suffer from problems caused by aliasing — their representations cannot be exposed, they cannot accept aliased objects from outside, and they cannot depend transitively upon other aliased objects. These restrictions apply only at the interface between Islands and Balloons and the rest of the system, so objects may be aliased freely inside or outside a Balloon or Island. Similarly, aliasing of normal objects is unrestricted within Islands and Balloons. This allows Islands and Balloons to encapsulate complex linked structures while still providing aliasing guarantees to the rest of the system.

Unfortunately, full encapsulation of aliasing is too restrictive for many common design idioms used in object oriented programming. In particular, an object cannot be a member of two collections simultaneously if either collection is fully encapsulated against aliases. A collection's member is part of the collection's shadow, and as such cannot be part of another fully encapsulated collection.

Islands and Balloons have mechanisms which mitigate against this restriction, generally by distinguishing between static and dynamic aliases — a static alias is an alias caused by reference from a long-lived variable (an object's instance variable or a global variable) while a dynamic alias is caused by a short-lived, stack allocated variable. Unfortunately, these distinctions also cause problems. Both Islands and Transparent Balloons allow dynamic aliases to any member of an aggregate object's shadow. This allows collection elements to be acted upon when they are within the collection, provided no static references are created. Unfortunately, this also allows objects which are part of an aggregate's private internal representation to be exposed.

Islands restrict dynamic aliases to be read only, that is, Islands enforce *encapsulation* but not *information hiding*. Transparent Balloons impose no such restriction, so in a transparent Balloon, an internal representation object can be dynamically exposed and modified externally. Almeida also describes Opaque Balloons which forbid any dynamic aliases. That is, transparent balloons control static aliasing, but provide neither information hiding nor encapsulation, while opaque balloons completely hide and encapsulate everything they contain.

4 Flexible alias protection

Although aliasing has the potential to cause a great many problems in object oriented programs, it is demonstrably the case that these problems do not manifest themselves in the vast majority of programs. That is, although paradigmatic object oriented programming style uses aliasing, it does so in ways which are benign in the majority of cases.

This situation parallels that of programming in untyped languages such as BCPL or assembler. Although untyped languages leave a wide field open for gratuitous type errors, programmers can (and generally do) successfully avoid type errors, in effect imposing a type discipline upon the language. Of course, it is almost certain that type problems will arise over time, especially as programs are maintained by programmers unaware of the uses and constraints of the types in the program. As a result, more formal static typing mechanisms have evolved to protect the programmer against type errors. The success and acceptance of a type system in practice depends on the extent to which it supports or constrains idiomatic programming style [25].

Our aim is to use techniques similar to type checking to provide guarantees about programs' aliasing properties, but without compromising typical object oriented programming styles. In particular, we aim to support many benign uses of aliasing, including objects being contained within multiple collections simultaneously, while still providing significant protection against aliasing problems. This requires that some form of aliasing be permitted, but that aliasing must be restricted to where it is appropriate.

Some objects can always be aliased freely without affecting the program's semantics. These objects are instances of *value types* which represent primitive values, such as machine level integers, characters or booleans. Since instances of value types are *immutable* (they never change, although variables holding them can change) they cause no problems when they are shared between various aggregate objects[2]. Functional languages have always used aliasing to implement immutable referentially transparent values — the great advantage being that precisely because these objects are immutable, any aliasing is completely invisible to the programmer.

The observation that value types can be aliased indiscriminately without compromising safety, because their state does not change, suggests an alternative formulation of the aliasing problem: the problem is not the presence of aliases, but the visibility of non-local changes caused by aliases. This suggests a different approach to dealing with aliasing: rather than trying to restrict aliases by constraining the references between objects, we should restrict the visibility of changes to objects. Aliasing can certainly be permitted, provided any changes within aliased objects are invisible.

This bears out the experience that many object oriented programs have been written in spite of aliasing — aliasing *per se* causes no problems for object

---

[2] Almeida describes how value types can be implemented as a specialisation of Balloons, and Hogg mentions immutable objects in passing.

oriented programming: the problem is the unexpected changes caused by aliasing. Object oriented programs which employ aliasing must do so in ways which avoid critical dependencies on mutable properties of objects.

To address these aliasing issues and to develop a programming discipline that may help preventing the problems described in previous section, we introduce the notion of an *alias-protected container* as a particular kind of aggregate object which is safe from the undesirable effects of aliasing. The remainder of this section is devoted to specifying the characteristics of alias-protected containers. The following section introduces *alias mode checking* which provides the means to enforce alias protection in object oriented languages by using aliasing modes and roles.

4.1 Alias-Protected Containers

We propose to protect containers from aliasing by dividing the elements of a container's shadow into two categories — the container's private *representation* and the container's public *arguments.* A container's representation objects are private and should not be accessible from outside. A container may freely operate upon (or depend upon) its representation objects — it may create new representation objects, change their state, and so on, but never expose them.

A container's arguments can be publicly accessed from elsewhere — in particular, an object can be an argument of more than one container. Because these objects are available and modifiable outside the container, the container may only depend upon argument objects inasmuch as they are immutable, that is, a container can never depend upon any argument object's mutable state. It is important to realise that the dependency is on the *interface* presented by the element objects to the collection. Provided all the operations in this interface do not rely upon mutable state, no changes in the element object can be visible to collection, and the element objects can be freely aliased and mutated outside the collection. This restriction protects the container's integrity against changes in elements caused via aliases.

For example, a hash table typically depends on element objects understanding a message which returns their hash code. If an element's hash code changes (presumably caused by another part of the program modifying the element via an alias) the integrity of the hash table will be compromised, but if the hash codes never change, the hash table will function correctly, even if other aspects of the elements change frequently.

Because a container's argument and representation objects have different aliasing and mutability restrictions — representation objects must remain inside the container, but can be read and written, while argument objects must be treated as immutable but can be referenced from outside the container — the implementation of the container needs to keep the two sets completely separate. If a representation object is accidently treated as an argument, it can be exposed outside the container, typically by being explicitly returned as the result of a method. If an argument object is treated as part of the representation, the containers implementation can become susceptible to problems caused by pre-existing aliases to the argument. Figure 3 illustrates how the objects referred to by a hash table (from Figure 2) are either part of the hash table's representation or arguments.

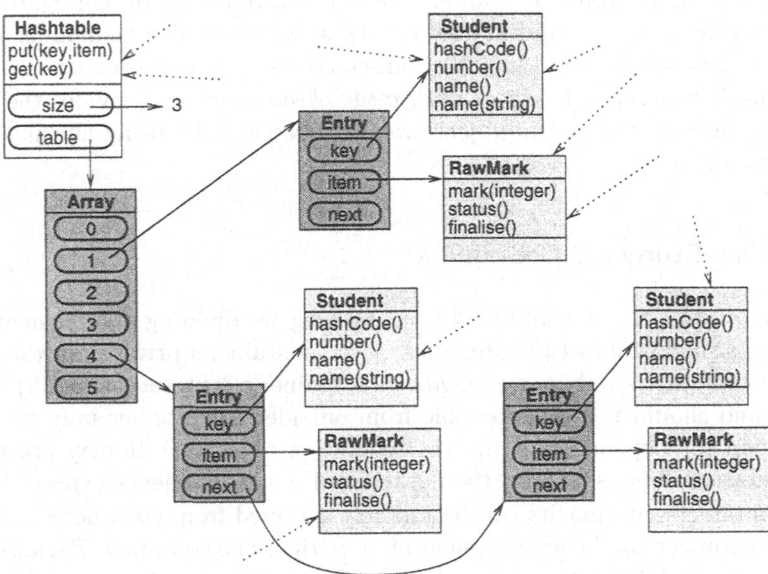

Fig. 3. A hashtable's internal Array and Entry objects are part of its representation (dark grey) while student and RawMark objects are stored as the hashtable's arguments (light grey). Representation objects can only be referenced from within the hashtable aggregate (solid arrows) while arguments objects can be referenced from outside (dotted arrows).

Alias protected containers themselves may be aliased, in fact they may even be mutually aliased. For instance, a container may be passed as argument to itself. This does not cause problems, however, as a container cannot depend upon the mutable state of its argument objects.

One very important aspect for the usability of any definition of alias-protected containers is their composability — that is whether alias-protected containers can be implemented out of simpler containers.

4.2 Composing Containers

Complex aggregate objects should be able to be composed from simpler objects — that is, containers need to be able to use other objects as part of their implementations. This is easily accommodated within our container model — a container can certainly have another object (which could be a container) as part of its representation. Provided the internal object does not expose its own representation or depend upon its arguments, the composite container will provide the same level of aliasing protection as an individual container object.

Sometimes, however, a composite container may need to use an internal container to store some of its argument or representation objects. For example, a university student records system may need to record the students enrolled in each course and the raw marks each student has received. Each course object can use a hash table to keep track of its students and their marks, however students will be part of the course's arguments (since a single student could be enrolled in multiple courses) while each student's raw marks will be part of the course's representation, since only weighted final marks should actually be presented to students. As far as the internal hash table is concerned, both the student objects and mark objects are its arguments — the students being the hash table's keys and the raw marks the hash table's items. The hash table will also have its own representation objects, which must be completely encapsulated inside it.

To maintain flexible alias protection, a container's representation objects and argument objects must be kept completely separate. This requirement holds no matter how a container is implemented. When a container uses an internal collection, this requirement must be enforced on the internal collection also. If a representation object could be passed into the internal collection, then retrieved and treated as if it were an argument, then the composite container's representation could be exposed. Similarly, if an argument could be retrieved from an inner collection and treated as part of the composite container's representation, the composite container would become susceptible to its arguments aliasing.

To avoid breaching encapsulation, composite containers have to be restricted in how they can pass objects to internal objects. We consider that each object has one or more *argument roles*, which describe how the object uses its arguments. An object must keep its various argument roles separated — in particular, it may only return an argument as a particular role from some message if the argument was passed into the object as the same role. For example, a simple collection, such as a set, bag, or list, will have only one argument role, while an indexed collection, such as a hash table mapping keys to items, will have two roles, one for its keys and one for its items. A composite container may only store one kind of object (argument or representation) in any given inner object's role. Thus, an enclosing container can store part of its representation in an inner container and retrieve it again, sure that the inner container has not substituted an argument object or an object which is part of the inner container's representation.

Reconsidering the university course example, the hash table will have a key role and an item role. The course object stores its argument Student objects in the hash table's key role, and its representation objects representing the students' marks in the hash table's item role (see Figure 4).

4.3 Summary

We have introduced flexible alias protection to provide a model of aliasing which supports typical object oriented programming styles involving aggregate con-

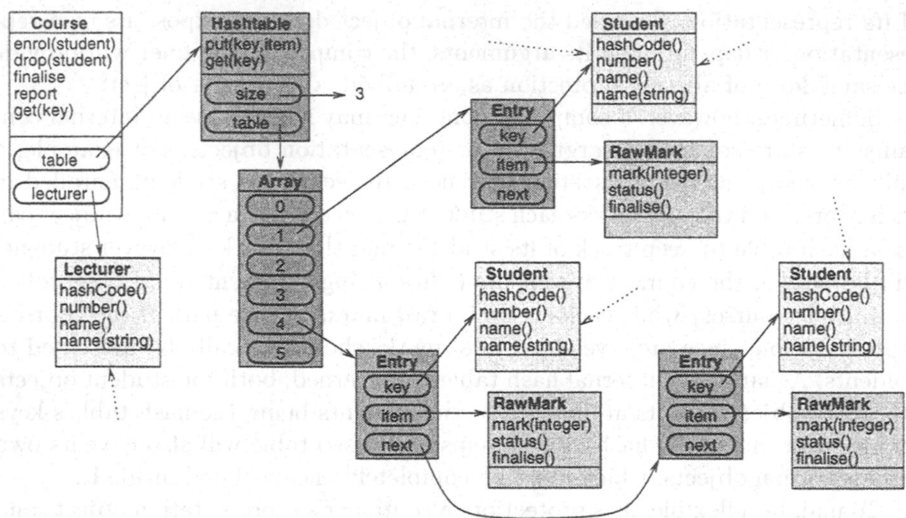

Fig. 4. A Course uses a hashtable as part of its representation (dark grey) while Student and Lecturer objects are the course's arguments (light grey). The hashtable also stores RawMark objects for each student, and these are arguments to the hashtable but part of the Course's representation (mid gray), so cannot be accessed from outside the Course (dotted arrows).

tainer objects. Flexible alias encapsulation separates the objects within an aggregate container into two categories — representation objects which can be modified within the container but not exported from it, and argument objects which can be exported from the container but which the container must treat as immutable. Argument objects can be further divided into subcategories, each representing a different argument *role*. Just as a container's representation objects must be kept separate from its argument objects, so each role must be kept independent.

These restrictions can be expressed in the following invariants:

- F_1 **No Representation Exposure** — A container's mutable representation objects should only be accessible via the container object's interface. No dynamic or static references to representation objects should exist outside the container.
- F_2 **No Argument Dependence** — A container should not depend upon its arguments' mutable state. That is, a container should use arguments only insofar as they are immutable.
- F_3 **No Role Confusion** — A container should not return an object in one role when it was passed into the container in another role.

In the next section we describe how *aliasing modes* ensure these three invariants can be checked statically for a variety of container types.

5 Aliasing Modes

We have developed a set of *aliasing modes* and a simple technique, *aliasing mode checking*, to statically ensure invariants $F_1 \ldots F_3$ hold, so that a container can defend itself against possible aliasing problems. Aliasing mode checking aims to preserve as much as possible of the paradigmatic object-oriented style, including the benign use of aliasing, while making program's aliasing properties explicit. Aliasing mode checking is based on declarations of *aliasing modes*, which are similar to the modes used in Islands [19] or the `const` mode used in C++ [36]. An aliasing mode is essentially a tag which annotates the definition of a local name, and restricts the operations which can be performed upon objects through that name. Modes are purely static entities, having no runtime representation. Like the C++ `const` attribute, and unlike Island's modes, our aliasing modes can decorate every type constructor in a type expression, and are propagated through the expressions in the program, just as types are. Also like C++ or Islands' modes, our modes are relational in that they restrict access only through the name they annotate — if an object is aliased by another name, the aliases may have different modes and allow different operations to be performed on the object. Unlike C++'s `const`, modes may not be cast away.

Aliasing mode checking verifies an object's aliasing properties to a similar extent that a static type checker verifies an object's typing properties. Working from declarations supplied by the programmer, an aliasing mode checker propagates aliasing modes through expressions. The resulting modes are then checked for consistency within the defining context. Like most type checking, aliasing mode checking is conservative, so it should not accept programs which do not have the required aliasing properties, but it may reject programs which actually have the required properties if it cannot verify them statically. Also like type checking, aliasing mode checking is enforced by a set of simple, local rules, designed to be easy for programmers to understand and to debug. Note that although they are similar, aliasing mode checking and type checking are completely orthogonal. An expression's aliasing mode correctness implies nothing about its type correctness, and vice versa.

The aliasing mode system comprises the following modes: *arg*, *rep*, *free*, *var*, and *val*. These modes decorate the type constructors in a language's type expressions, resulting in *moded type expressions*. The *arg* and *var* modes optionally also have a *role tag* $\mathcal{R}$, which is used to distinguish between similar modes which play different roles. The first two modes, *rep* and *arg*, are the most important, and identify expressions referring to the representation and argument objects of containers. The *free* mode is used to handle object creation, the *val* mode is syntactic sugar for value types, and the *var* mode provides a loophole for auxiliary objects which provide weaker aliasing guarantees. To separate argument objects from representation objects and argument objects in other roles, different modes are not assignment compatible, except that expressions of *free* mode can be assigned to variables of any other mode (assuming type compatibility).

The modes attached to the parameters of the messages in an object's interface (including the receiver, self) determine the aliasing properties for the object as a whole. For example, if an object uses only modes *arg*, *free*, and *val*, it will be a "*clean*" immutable object, that is, it will implement a referentially transparent value type. If all of an object's method's parameters and return values (except the implicit self parameter) are restricted to *arg*, *free*, or *val*, the object will be an alias-protected container with flexible alias protection, and if in addition it has no variables of *arg* mode, the object will provide full alias encapsulation. The modes of an object's internal variables are used to check that the aliasing properties of the object's implementation match those of the declarations, as follows:

rep A *rep* expression refers to an object which is part of another object's representation. Objects referred to by *rep* expressions can change and be changed, can be stored and retrieved from internal containers, but can never be exported from the object to which they belong.

arg $\mathcal{R}$ A *arg* expression refers to an object which is an argument of an aggregate object. Objects referred to by *arg* expressions can never change in a way which is visible via that expression — that is, *arg* expressions only provide access to the immutable interface of the objects to which they refer. There are no restrictions upon the transfer or use of *arg* expressions around a program.

free A *free* expression holds the only reference to an object in the system, so objects referred to by a *free* expression cannot be aliased. In particular, the mode of the return values of constructors is *free*. Expressions of mode *free* can be assigned to variables of any other mode, provided that any given *free* expression is always assigned to variables of the same other mode.

val A *val* expression refers to an instance of a value type. The *val* mode has the same semantics as the *arg* mode, however, we have introduced a separate *val* mode so that explicit *arg* roles are not required for value types. The *val* mode is the only mode which implies a constraint upon the *type* of the expression to which it is bound, and can be automatically attached to all expressions of value types where no other mode is supplied.

var $\mathcal{R}$ The *var* mode refers to a mutable object which may be aliased. Expressions with mode *var* may be changed freely, may change asynchronously, and can be passed into or returned from messages sent to objects. This mode is basically the same as the reference semantics of most object oriented programming languages, or the *var* mode in Pascal, except that it obeys the assignment (in)compatibility rules of the other modes.

Note that modes and roles are not specific to a particular object oriented language, but do require a strong static type system. Our examples use an idealisation of Java with parametric polymorphism, based on Pizza [34], For pedagogical reasons, in places we use more explicit role annotations on variables and parameters than is strictly necessary.

5.1 Modes and Invariants

The purpose of aliasing modes is to enforce the flexible alias encapsulation invariants F_1 to F_3. The invariants are enforced by recasting them in terms of the modes of expressions, rather than sets of objects, and then restricting the operations permissible on expressions of various modes. This results in three mode invariants, each corresponding to one flexible alias encapsulation invariant. The semantics of these invariants are implicit in the semantics of the modes described above, but we will consider each separately, as follows:

- M_1 **No Representation Exposure** — No expression containing mode *rep* may appear in an object's interface. An aggregate object's representation should remain encapsulated within that object. In the mode system, component objects which make up an object's representation will have mode *rep*, so they should not be returned from that object. Expressions including mode *rep* should not be accepted as arguments, due to the possibility of preexisting aliases. We take an object's interface to include all external variables or functions visible within an object, so this restriction (together with the composition rules below, §5.4) also stops objects exposing their representation through a "back door".
- M_2 **No Argument Dependence** — No expression of mode *arg* may be sent a message which visibly changes or depends upon any mutable state. Objects referred to by expressions of mode *arg* may be freely aliased throughout the system, so containers may not depend upon their mutable state. To enforce this restriction, we forbid messages sent to *arg* expressions which access any mutable state. The only messages which may be sent to *arg* expressions are those which are purely functional — we call them *clean* expressions. For the same reason, *arg* expressions may only be passed to other functions as mode *arg*.
- M_3 **No Role Confusion** — No expression of any mode except *free* may be assigned to a variable of any other mode. Objects subject to mode checking must keep objects of different roles separate. This can be implemented fairly simply by forbidding assignment between expression of different modes.

Immutable Interfaces Rule M_2 for avoiding argument dependencies requires that messages sent to expressions of mode *arg* should not depend upon mutable state, or cause any side effects. We call these types of messages *clean* messages, and they should be identified by an annotation on method declarations. One simple definition of a *clean* message is that it is made up only of *clean* expressions, where a *clean* expression either reads a variable of mode *arg* or *val*, or sends a *clean* message — the only modes which may appear in a *clean* method definition are *arg*, *val*, or *free*, and a clean method cannot modify variables. More complex definitions of *clean* could be formulated to have the same effect, but with fewer practical restrictions.

However it is defined, *clean* will impose restrictions on the way a container can use its arguments, but these restrictions are not as severe as they may seem. This is because aliasing mode checking distinguishes between *clean interfaces* and *clean objects*. A *clean* interface provides access to the immutable properties of an otherwise mutable object, while a *clean* object implements an immutable value type. A mode *arg* reference to a mutable object restricts the use of that object to the *clean* portion of its interface — if the object is aliased elsewhere via *rep* or *var*mode, those references can make full use of the object. Completely *clean* objects are only required when value semantics (mode *val* expressions) are to be used, and should be identified by annotations on objects' definitions.

5.2 Example: A Simple Hashtable

To illustrate the use of modes and roles Figure 5 shows a simple example of a naïve hashtable class completely annotated with mode declarations — compare with Figure 2. The hashtable is represented using an array of hashtable entries which hold the keys and items stored in the table.

This example uses three modes — *arg*, *val*, and *rep*. Argument items to be contained within the hashtable are declared as mode "*arg k*" or mode "*arg i*" — that is, mode *arg* with role tag *k* for keys or *i* for items. The modes are identified both in the declarations of method parameters and return values, and within the definition of the `table` representation array. The representation array object holding the hashtable entries is mode *rep*, because it needs to be changed by the hashtable (to store and retrieve entries). The entries themselves are similarly mode *rep*. Because the table contains argument objects (which are mode *arg*), the table's full moded type is **rep** `Array<HashtableEntry<`**arg k** `Hashable,` **arg i** `Item>>`. Finally, integers are used to return `size` of the hashtable. Since integers are value types, these are mode *val*.

```
class Hashtable<arg k Hashable, arg i Item> {
    private rep
        Array<rep HashtableEntry<arg k Hashable, arg i Item>>
            contents;
    private val int size;

    public void put(arg k Hashable key, arg i Item value);
    public arg i Item get(arg k Hashable key);
}
```

Fig. 5. A Hashtable with Aliasing Mode Declarations

5.3 Mode Checking

In this section we give an intuitive overview of mode checking, as a formal definition is beyond the scope of this paper. A method is mode checked by first determining the modes of its constituent expression's terms, then propagating modes through expressions. Determining the mode of the terms in an expression is generally quite simple — aliasing modes are attached to terms in the environment. Propagating modes through compound subexpressions is more complicated, but assuming moded type information for operators is available in the environment, parameter modes can be checked against the environment definitions, and then the operator's result mode from the environment can be taken as the mode of the whole subexpression.

Figure 6 shows the definition of the hashtable's **get** method. The figure includes an *arg k* mode declaration on the method's **key** parameter, and is annotated with the modes of the most crucial terms in the method.

```
arg i Item get(arg k Hashable key ) {
    val int hash = key.hashCode();
    val int index =
      (hash & 0x7FFFFFFF) % contents.length;
    rep HashtableEntry<arg k Hashable, arg i Item> e;
    for (e = contents[index]; e != null ; e = e.next) {
          // all rep HashtableEntry<arg k Hashable, arg i Item>
      if ((e.key.hashCode() == hash) && e.key.equals(key)) {
          // hashCode and equals must be clean
        return e.item;
      //...
```

Fig. 6. The Hashtable Get Method

The most important message send in the **get** method occurs on the first line, in `int hash = key.hashCode()`. The mode of `key` is *arg*, and only *clean* messages may be sent to expressions of mode *arg*. Provided the `hashCode` method is *clean*, it may be sent to the `key` parameter object. Since `hashCode` returns an integer, its return value has mode *val* and so can be assigned to a mode *val* variable. The arithmetic on the second line is simple: arithmetic operators on mode *val* expressions return mode *val*.

The expressions within the `for` loop are more complex to check, as these involve a number of propagations. First, the mode of `contents[index]` must be determined. This is a index operation on the `contents` array. Since the array has the mode **rep Array<rep HashtableEntry<arg h Hashable, arg i Item>>**, the result of an index operation will be the mode of the hash table entries — **rep HashtableEntry<arg h Hashable, arg i Item>**. This is the same as the mode of the `e` variable, so the assignment can proceed. Since this is a *rep* mode, the fields of `e` (and other `HashtableEntries` which also have mode *rep*) can be read and assigned to. The `HashtableEntry` objects have two fields, `key` and `item` with modes *arg k* and *arg i* respectively. Since *arg k* objects support *clean* `hashCode` and `equals` methods, these two sends can proceed even though they are sent to the mode `arg` expression `e.key`. Finally, `e.item` can be returned since it has mode *arg i*.

5.4 Composing Moded Types

Mode checking in the context of a single method is quite simple, and is adequately covered by the rules and invariants described above. In fact, the above rules apply within a single static type environment, such as a module or package, even if this involves more than one class. For example, the hash table above actually involves a number of objects (the hash table itself, its component array, and the hash table entries) but does so solely from the perspective of the hash table.

Mode checking which crosses scope boundaries is somewhat more complex. When an aggregate object is composed from a number of other objects, the modes in the aggregate object must be unified with the externally visible modes of its subsidiary objects — that is, the subsidiary objects' *arg* and *var* roles. We call this process *aliasing mode parameter binding*, and it is analogous to the binding of type parameters when instantiating generic types. The complexity arises when containers are composed inside other objects, as any mode must be able to be bound to mode *arg* moded type parameters of encapsulated containers.

For example, imagine the hash table being used to represent the relationship between `Student` objects and `RawMark` objects representing the enrolment in a university course (see Figure 7). The `Student` objects have mode *arg*, because they do not belong to the `Course` object — in particular, one student can be enrolled in a number of courses. The `RawMark` objects are part of the `Course` object's representation (i.e. mode *rep*), to ensure that they are encapsulated within the `Course`, and also so that they can be sent messages which change their state to record each `Student`'s raw marks. These *rep* `RawMark` objects need to be stored within the `Hashtable`, that is, passed to variables and retrieved as results which were declared as mode *arg* (see Figure 5).

```
class Course<arg s Student> {
   private rep Hashtable<arg s Student, rep RawMark> marks =
         new Hashtable();
      ...
   public void enrol (arg s Student s) {
      rep RawMark r = new RawMark();
      marks.put(s, r);
   }
   public void
      recordMarkFor(arg s Student s, val String workUnit, val int mark) {
      marks.get(s).recordMarkFor(workUnit, mark);
   }
   public void finalReport (arg s Student s) {
      marks.get(s).finalReport();
   }
}
```

Fig. 7. A Course represented by a Hashtable

Aliasing mode parameter binding occurs when generic types are instantiated and their parameters bound. A sequence of actual moded types (containing the client's roles) must be bound to a sequence of formal moded types (containing the server's roles), resulting in a mapping from formal to actual moded type parameters. Each moded type parameter is considered individually, in two stages. First, the parameter roles are bound, and then the aliasing modes in the bindings are checked.

Each formal role in the server must map to one actual role in the client. One actual role may be mapped by more than one formal role, however. The most important feature of these mappings is that they must be consistent, that is there must be only one mapping for each object within any given scope, and whenever parameters are passed to or results retrieved from a particular object, the *same* mappings must be used.

The aliasing mode bindings in these mappings are then checked depending upon the modes within the server's formal parameters. Formal parameters may have either mode *arg* or mode *var* (since mode *rep* is encapsulated within components, and modes *free* and *val* are global so do not need to be bound). Formal mode parameters of mode *arg* can be bound to any actual mode, and formal parameters of mode *var* can be bound to any actual mode except *arg*.

These binding rules are designed to ensure that the flexible alias encapsulation invariants of an outer container are maintained, assuming they are maintained by an inner container. The interesting cases occur when objects which are parts of an outer container are passed to an inner encapsulated container, since the basic rules encapsulate aliasing in each individual container.

The outer container's representation is protected against exposure (F_1 is maintained) because the inner container can only return the outer container's representation objects back to the outer container, as the inner container is part of the outer container's representation. An inner container cannot depend upon any of the outer container's arguments, because the outer container's arguments can only be bound to mode *arg* in an inner container. Thus F_2 for the whole container is supported by M_2 in the inner container.

Similarly, the role binding rules and M_3 in an inner container ensure that the enclosing container's roles are not confused, maintaining F_3. Each formal role in the inner container can only be bound to at most one of the outer container's roles, so objects cannot be inserted into the inner container under one outer container role and retrieved as another. Several inner container roles may be bound to one outer container role, but this simply means the inner container makes a finer distinction within the outer container's roles.

5.5 Choice of Modes

Our choice of aliasing modes may seem somewhat idiosyncratic. While some of the modes (*var*, *rep*, *val*) are hopefully noncontroversial, and others taken directly from previous work (*free* from Islands [19]), the *arg* mode is novel. We have also omitted several modes from other work, including *read* and *unique* modes [19, 2]. This section presents some of the rationale for our choice of modes.

Mode *val* The *val* mode is in a strict sense redundant, as its semantics are essentially the same as *arg* mode, and could be replaced by *arg* mode without weakening the system. We have retained *val* mode for a number of reasons, foremost of which is that we share a sense of the overall importance of value types [2, 29, 23].

A separate *val* mode provides an additional cue to the programmer when used to describe a component of a container's representation. Reading the moded type declaration **rep** `Foo<`**arg** *a* `Shape>` a programmer can conclude that the *arg a* components of `Foo` are "real" arguments which may be aliased elsewhere. In contrast, the similar declaration **rep** `Foo<`**val** `Shape>` makes clear that the `Shape` components are pure value types. More practically, an explicit *val* mode greatly reduces the number of roles programmers must consider when designing objects, because all expressions which handle *clean* objects can have mode *val*.

The Restrictions on Mode *arg* The restrictions we have placed on mode *arg* are particularly tight. Mode *arg* combines the restrictions of modes like C++'s `const`, which prevents modifications to objects, and a strong transitive sense of referential transparency, so no changes are visible through *arg* mode references. The second part of this restriction is certainly necessary to guarantee the flexible aliasing encapsulation invariants, in particular F_2. The first part of this restriction is less necessary, because the aliasing invariants implicitly assume that a container's arguments may be changed asynchronously via aliases at any time, so no mode safety would be lost by allowing changes via an *arg* reference (at least in sequential systems). We have imposed this restriction as a matter of taste, to keep the mode system as simple as possible, and because widespread use of a `writeonly` mode seems quite counterintuitive [37].

***read* and *unique* Modes** Islands [19] make great use of a *read* mode, which can be seen as a transitive version of C++'s `const`. These *read* mode expressions cannot be used to change mutable state, and cannot be stored in object's instance variables, but are not referentially transparent, so the objects upon which they depend may be changed "underfoot" via aliases.

We have omitted a *read* mode for three reasons. First, *read* expressions are used to dynamically expose objects which are part of Islands. Since argument objects within flexibly encapsulated containers can be statically or dynamically aliased outside, a *read* mode is much less necessary. Second, to be useful, a *read* mode must constrain Islands' *clients*, and we have tried to avoid modes which propagate upwards, out of containers into their context. Third, especially because of the restrictions on storing *read* expressions into objects' variables, *read* does not fit well with typical object oriented programming styles.

Islands also introduced a *unique* mode [19], and similar ideas are used in Balloons [2] and have been proposed by others [32, 8, 17]. A *unique* variable is *linear* — it holds the only reference to an object [4]. We have not introduced a *unique* mode for much the same reasons we have omitted *read*. Like a *read* mode, a *unique* mode is useful in some cases, for example, a *unique* mode allows objects to be inserted to and removed from encapsulated containers without copying or aliasing. Like a *read* mode, a *unique* mode extends its protection "upwards", requiring respect from containers' clients. Also, a *unique* mode may not provide as much protection as might be imagined, since *unique* objects can be shared via non-*unique* "handle" objects [32]. Unfortunately, making effective use of *unique* objects seems to require programming language support, such as a destructive read [19], copy assignment [2], or swapping [17]. Finally, our *free* mode reduces the need for a *unique* mode, although at the cost of requiring extra object copying in some circumstances.

Upwards and Downwards Mode Restrictions Most of our aliasing modes are anchored at a particular object, and propagate *downwards* into the implementation of that object, restricting the ways it can use other objects. This is in contrast to modes like *read* and *unique* which work *upwards*, giving rise to restrictions on objects' clients, Mode *arg* is a downward mode *par excellence* — *arg* imposes a great many restrictions on a container's implementations, but none on a container's client. We prefer downward modes to upward modes for several reasons. We assume objects with flexible alias encapsulation will form part of a traditional, alias-intensive object oriented system, and we aim to support a paradigmatic object oriented programming style, so we cannot make assumptions about programs' global aliasing behaviour. We don't want programmers to have to rewrite code to conform to mode restrictions. We imagine aliasing modes infiltrating the systems bottom up — our flexible alias encapsulation is particularly suitable for describing properties of existing collection libraries, for example. Containers with flexible alias encapsulation must defend *themselves* against aliasing problems: they cannot rely on the rest of the program "doing it for them" by obeying mode restrictions.

The only assumption we do accept about the "rest of the program" is that any methods or expressions claiming to be *clean* or *free* are in fact *clean* or *free*. In a way, this constraint also flows downwards, from the interface of the external objects to their implementation, rather than upwards out of a container to its elements. We view *clean* and *free* as *descriptions* of the properties of external objects in the program, which restricts the operations which flexible alias encapsulated containers can do with those external objects, rather than restrictions on the external objects.

5.6 Object Oriented Idioms

We conclude the presentation of aliasing modes by showing how they can be used to capture the aliasing properties of a number of common object oriented programming idioms.

Flyweights as *clean* objects Flyweight objects [12] contain no mutable intrinsic state, that is, a Flyweight object is an instance of a value type. A Flyweight can be described using the mode system as a *clean* object, that is, an object which provides only a *clean* interface. A *clean* object is restricted to expressions of modes *arg*, *free*, and *val* — in particular, the mode of self is *arg*, which prevents assignment to any instance variables. For example, a simple Glyph flyweight could be implemented as a clean object:

```
clean class Glyph {
   private val Font font;
   private val int size;
   public free Glyph( val Font _font, val int _size) {
      font = _font; size = _size;
      //...
```

Although *clean* objects cannot normally access mutable state, they must still be constructed and initialised. Aliasing modes model construction explicitly, by treating constructors as special methods which return mode *free*. This allows objects' instance variables to be initialised within constructors, because *free* does not have the *clean*-message only restriction of mode *arg*. A *clean* object's variables could even be initialised after construction, for example to cache the results of a *clean* method, modelling language constructs such as Java's blank finals [14] or Cecil's per-object field initialisers [7].

Collections and Facades with Full Alias Encapsulation Collections and Facades are usually modelled as containers with flexible alias protection, that is, as objects where only *arg*, *val*, and *free* modes may appear in their method interfaces (including constructors) and any variables with scope larger than an object may only be read as mode *arg*. Aliasing modes can enforce the kind of full alias encapsulation provided by Islands [19] or Balloons [2]. In addition to the restrictions for flexible alias protection, instance variables of fully encapsulated containers may not have mode *arg* subcomponents. This allows aliased objects to be passed into a container, but not stored directly within it — to store an object it must first be copied, producing a *free* object which can then be passed to a mode *free* parameter and assigned to a mode *rep* variable. For example, a fully encapsulated TupperwareSet could be implemented using a Set with flexible alias protection as follows:

```
class TupperwareSet {
   private
      rep Set<rep Object> storage; // no arg subcomponents.
   public
      void add(free Object _o) {
         rep Object o; // for clarity
         o = _o.; // assign free copy to rep
         storage.add(o);
      }
```

If the _o argument was mode *arg* rather than mode *free*, it could not be added to the *rep* storage set.

Iterators for Collections Iterators [12] are commonly used to provide sequential access to collections. Unfortunately, by their very nature, iterators must alias the collections they iterate over, indeed, iterators often need direct access to containers' private implementations for efficiency reasons. This aliasing is made explicit in the moded type declarations, where an extra *var* role is required to indicate that implementations and iterators are aliased.

```
class FastVector<var a Array<arg i Item>> {
  private
    var a Array<arg i Item> table; // note var
  public
    free FastVectorIterator<var a Array<arg i Item >>
      newIterator() {
        FastVectorIterator(this.table);
          // hand in internal table
      }
  }

class FastVectorIterator<var a Array<arg i Item>> {
  public
    free FastVectorIterator<var a Array<arg i Item>>
      FastVectorIterator(var a Array<arg i Item >>) {
      // direct access to Array implementation
      // via var  parameter inside constructor ...

class IteratorClient {
  private
    var FastVector<var a Array<rep Elem e>> arr;
  public
    void iterate() {
      var FastVectorIterator<var a Array<rep Elem e>> it;
      rep Elem e;
      for (it=arr.newIterator(); it.hasNext; e = it.next) {
        e.use();
        //...
```

In the example, the iterator and vector have mode *var* in their moded types, so they cannot be exported from the `IteratorClient` object, if the `IteratorClient` is to be an alias-protected container.

6 Discussion

In this section we discuss further aspects of flexible alias protection and aliasing mode checking, and describe the current status of our work.

6.1 Usability

Because object identity is such a fundamental part of the object orientation paradigm, problems with aliasing cannot really be "solved". Any attempt to address the aliasing program for practical object oriented programming must be evaluated as an engineering compromise: how much safety does it provide, at what cost, and, most importantly, how usable are the mechanisms by typical programmers doing general purpose programming.

The crucial question is how natural (or how contrived) a programming style is required by the proposed aliasing mode checking. Obviously aliasing mode declarations impose a syntactic overhead, but this at most doubles the cost of the kind of static type declarations used in Eiffel or C++, even if all type declarations must be annotated with modes. In return for the extra syntax, flexible alias encapsulation imposes significantly weaker restrictions on program design than other types of alias encapsulation [2, 19, 24], while still providing protection against common aliasing problems. In particular, flexible encapsulation allows container arguments to be aliased, permitting many programming idioms which cannot be used when aliases are fully encapsulated.

Making aliasing modes explicit has advantages when checking aliasing modes and reporting aliasing errors. Like type checking, aliasing mode checking only needs information which is in the scope of the expression to be checked. Methods can be checked individually and incrementally, and because alias modes are visible to the programmer in the program's text, errors can be reported in terms which programmers should be able to understand.

This is in contrast to the sophisticated static analysis required to check Balloon types, which may need to check the implementation of a number of different classes as a unit, and which reports errors in terms of possible runtime aliasing states, rather than syntactic properties of the program [2].

The ability to present comprehensible error messages points towards an important secondary benefit of programmer-supplied aliasing declarations. Making alias modes explicit should help provide a conceptual language within which programmers can think about the aliasing properties of their programs and designs, in the same way that type systems promote awareness of program's type properties.

6.2 Inheritance and Subtyping

Aliasing issues are generally considered to be orthogonal to subtyping and inheritance [19, 2], so alias mode checking should be orthogonal to type checking and subtyping. In practice, there can be interplay between objects' aliasing properties, subtyping, and inheritance.

Subtyping is defined by the substitution principle — that an instance of a subtype can be used wherever an instance of a supertype is acceptable [1]. Considering aliasing, substitution requires that a subtype's aliasing guarantees cannot be weaker than its supertype's. The precise rules can be derived from the aliasing mode invariants (particularly M_3), expressed in the mode binding rules in section 5.4. A subtype's aliasing modes must be able to be bound wherever its supertype's modes can be bound. The main consequence of this rule is that a type's *clean* interface must be a subtype of its supertype's *clean* interface, for *all* types in the program.

Alias mode checking depends upon inheritance, at least, it treats objects as if inheritance had been flattened. Modes introduce dependencies which make subclasses more dependent upon details of their superclasses, exacerbating the fragile base class problem. As with typing, visibility declarations can offer subclasses some protection against changes to superclasses mode definitions, by restricting the scope of the changes. If inheritance is used for code reuse, a subclass may require different modes to its superclass, giving rise to inheritance anomalies similar to those found in concurrent systems [31].

6.3 Concurrency

Flexible alias protection and aliasing modes provide a good foundation within which object oriented languages can support concurrent execution. Flexibly encapsulated objects can be units of concurrency control, that is, a container can manage concurrent access to itself and its representation objects. The M_1 invariant guarantees that no process is able to access a *rep* object without first passing through its enclosing container, and thus being subject to the container's concurrency control regime. Containers and their *rep* objects can be internally multi-threaded (providing intra-object concurrency) and they must manage this concurrency internally.

The accessing modes map particularly well onto the *Aspects of Synchronisation* model of concurrency control [21]. This model divides concurrency constraints into three *aspects* — *exclusion* constraints which protect objects against conflicting threads, *state* constraints which allow access to an object only when is it in a particular state, and *coordination* constraints which can depend upon multiple unrelated objects. Exclusion and state constraints are local to individual objects, that is, a container and any *rep* subcomponents. Transaction constraints involve multiple independent objects, so apply to objects which use mode *var* expressions.

Finally, *clean* objects and interfaces do not require any form of concurrency control, because they do not involve mutable state. This is particularly useful in conjunction with flexible alias encapsulation, because multiple concurrent processes and multiple concurrent containers can safely store and access shared elements via mode *arg* or mode *val* without any concurrency control, because *arg* and *val* mode references only provide access to *clean* interfaces.

6.4 Mode Polymorphism and Inference

Our system of aliasing modes is more restrictive than it needs to be. This is because the programmer is forced to choose a specific mode declaration for every argument and variable, even though more than one declaration may be consistent within the context of the whole program. Unfortunately, once a mode has been chosen for a particular method or variable, other uses of that method which would require different modes are rejected by aliasing mode checking.

What is required here is some form of *mode polymorphism* — a single definition of a method, variable, object, or interface needs to be interpreted with different generic bindings for modes, in the same way a type-generic module can be instantiated with different concrete types. In our development of aliasing mode checking to date, we have not investigated mode polymorphism deeply.

Aliasing mode *inference* could also reduce the need for programmers to be overly specific about their program's aliasing modes. By analogy with type inference, aliasing mode inference would infer possible aliasing modes by analysing the source text of the program, automatically adding mode declarations to programs without them. We have only addressed inference in as much as mode checking's propagation of modes through expressions is the basis for inference.

6.5 Immutability and Change Detection

Our aliasing mode system is also restrictive because it is based around immutable properties of objects — properties which are set when objects are created (or initialised lazily) but do not subsequently change. Some objects' otherwise "immutable" state may remain unchanged for long periods of time, but then change on rare occasions. For example, a student's name is generally immutable, but may be changed by deed poll or marriage. If names may possibly change, they cannot be part of the student objects' clean interface, so student objects cannot be sorted or indexed based upon their names. Rather, some other attribute of students must be used to access them. Most academic institutions introduce student numbers for just this purpose, of course, and these typically meet the all the requirements for being part of a clean interface. The use of aliasing modes supports the practice of assigning these kind of "account numbers" during program analysis and design [40].

Alternatively, dynamic change detection techniques could be employed to handle changes in objects which would otherwise be treated as immutable. In this approach, the programming language or runtime system is extended to detect when a container depends upon the properties of one of its arguments, that is, when a container sends a message to another object through a mode *arg* reference. When such a dependency is detected, it can be recorded by the change detection system, which can then monitor the state of the "*subject*" object which is being depended upon. Using a mechanism such as the Observer pattern, when the subject's state changes, the dependent container can be notified of the change and can update its internal state [12]. We plan to extend our previous work on dynamic change detection to incorporate flexible alias protection and aliasing modes [33].

6.6 Current Status

In this paper, we have presented a conceptual model of flexible alias protection. We have also developed formal models of flexible alias protection which are not presented here due to space restrictions. We are currently working on an extension of the Pizza compiler [34] to extend Java with aliasing modes and mode checking — indeed, all the examples in this paper are written using our moded Pizza (mmmPizza) syntax. Because aliasing mode checking is carried out purely at compile time, mmmPizza generates exactly the same code as the original Pizza compiler. We considered building a preprocessor to implement aliasing mode checking, however we believed it would be easier to modify an existing compiler than to build a mode checker from scratch. We are also working on the implementation of alias protected class libraries which we shall use in real applications. At that point, we will be able to asses more precisely the impact of aliasing modes on programming style.

7 Conclusion

One man's constant is another man's variable.
Alan Perlis, Epigrams on Programming.

Aliasing is endemic in object oriented programming. Indeed, given that object oriented programming is based strongly on object identity, perhaps *alias oriented* programming would be a better term than object oriented programming! We have presented flexible alias encapsulation, a conceptual model for managing the effects of aliasing, based on the observation that aliasing *per se* is not the major problem — rather, the problem is the visibility of changes caused via aliases. This model uses explicit aliasing modes attached to types to provide static guarantees about the creation and use of object aliases. As a result, the model prevents exposure of object's representations, limits the dependence of containers upon their arguments, and separates different argument roles.

Acknowledgements

We would like to thank Doug Lea for his pertinent comments on various drafts, Eydun Eli Jacobsen for his observation on protecting names versus protecting objects, David Holmes for his comments on aliasing and concurrent object systems, David Clarke for his perspectives from the evolving formal theory and implementation, John Boyland for his discussions about modes and promises, and Martin Odersky for the Pizza compiler. We also thank Bjorn Freeman-Benson and the anonymous reviewers for their careful consideration. This work was supported by Microsoft Pty. Ltd., Australia.

References

1. Martín Abadi and Luca Cardelli. *A Theory of Objects*. Springer-Verlag, 1996.
2. Paulo Sérgio Almeida. Balloon Types: Controlling sharing of state in data types. In *ECOOP Proceedings*, June 1997.
3. Pierre America and Frank de Boer. A sound and complete proof system for SPOOL. Technical Report Technical Report 505, Philips Research Laboratories, 1990.

4. Henry G. Baker. 'Use-once' variables and linear objects – storage management, reflection and multi-threading. *ACM SIGPLAN Notices*, 30(1), January 1995.
5. Edwin Blake and Steve Cook. On including part hierarchies in object-oriented languages, with an implementation in Smalltalk. In *ECOOP Proceedings*, 1987.
6. Alan Borning. The programming language aspects of ThingLab, a constraint-oriented simulation laboratory. *ACM Transactions on Programming Languages and Systems*, 3(4), October 1981.
7. Craig Chambers. The Cecil language: Specification & Rationale. Technical Report Version 2.7, University of Washington, March 1997.
8. Edwin C. Chan, John T. Boyland, and William L. Scherlis. Promises: Limitied specifications for analysis and manipulation. In *IEEE International Conference on Software Engineering (ICSE)*, 1998.
9. Franco Civello. Roles for composite objects in object-oriented analysis and design. In *OOPSLA Proceedings*, 1993.
10. Alain Deutsch. Interprocedural May-Alias Analysis for Pointers: Beyond k-limiting. In *Proceedigns of the ACM SIGPLAN'94 Conference on Programming Language Design and Implementation*, June 1994.
11. Jin Song Dong and Roger Duke. Exclusive control within object oriented systems. In *TOOLS Pacific 18*, 1995.
12. Erich Gamma, Richard Helm, Ralph E. Johnson, and John Vlissides. *Design Patterns*. Addison-Wesley, 1994.
13. T. Goldstein. The gateway security model in the Java electronic commerce framework. Technical report, Sun Microsystems Laboratories – Javasoft, December 1996.
14. James Gosling, Bill Joy, and Guy Steele. *The Java Language Specification*. Addison-Wesley, 1996.
15. Peter Grogono and Patrice Chalin. Copying, sharing, and aliasing. In *Proceedings of the Colloquium on Object Orientation in Databases and Software Engineering (COODBSE'94)*, Montreal, Quebec, May 1994.
16. Daniel Hagimont, J. Mossière, Xavier Rousset de Pina, and F. Saunier. Hidden software capabilities. In *16th International Conference on Distributed Computing System*, Hong Kong, May 1996. IEEE CS Press.
17. Douglas E. Harms and Bruce W. Weide. Copying and swapping: Influences on the design of reusable software components. *IEEE Transactions on Software Engineering*, 17(5), May 1991.
18. Laurie J. Hendren and G. R. Gao. Designing programming languages for analyzability: A fresh look at pointer data structures. In *Proceedings of the IEEE 1992 International Conference on Programming Languages*, April 1992.
19. John Hogg. Islands: Aliasing protection in object-oriented languages. In *OOPSLA Proceedings*, November 1991.
20. John Hogg, Doug Lea, Alan Wills, Dennis deChampeaux, and Richard Holt. The Geneva convention on the treatment of object aliasing. *OOPS Messenger*, 3(2), April 1992.
21. David Holmes, James Noble, and John Potter. Aspects of synchronisation. In *TOOLS Pacific 25*, 1997.
22. Neil D. Jones and Steven Muchnick. Flow analysis and optimization of LISP-like structures. In Steven Muchnick and Neil D. Jones, editors, *Program Flow Analysis: Theory and Applications*. Prentice Hall, 1981.
23. Stuart Kent and John Howse. Value types in Eiffel. In *TOOLS 19*, Paris, 1996.
24. Stuart Kent and Ian Maung. Encapsulation and aggregation. In *TOOLS Pacific 18*, 1995.

25. Brian Kernighan. Why Pascal is not my favourite programming language. Technical Report 100, Bell Labs, 1983.
26. William Landi. Undecidability of static analysis. *ACM Letters on Programming Languages and Systems*, 1(4), December 1992.
27. K. Rustan M. Leino and Raymie Stata. Virginity: A contribution to the specification of object-oriented software. Technical Report SRC-TN-97-001, Digital Systems Research Center, April 1997.
28. John M. Lucassen and David K. Gifford. Polymorphic effect systems. In *Proceedings of the Eighteenth Annual ACM SIGACT-SIGPLAN Symposium on Principles of Programming Languages*, January 1988.
29. B. J. MacLennan. Values and objects in programming languages. *ACM SIGPLAN Notices*, 17(12), December 1982.
30. Ole Lehrmann Madsen, Birger Møller-Pedersen, and Kirsten Nygaard. *Object-Oriented Programming in the BETA Programming Language.* Addison-Wesley, 1993.
31. S. Matsuoka, K. Wakita, and A. Yonezawa. Sychronisation constraints with inheritance: What is not possible? — so what is? Technical report, Dept. of Information Science, University of Tokyo, 1990.
32. Naftaly Minsky. Towards alias-free pointers. In *ECOOP Proceedings*, July 1996.
33. James Noble and John Potter. Change detection for aggregate objects with aliasing. In *Australian Software Engineering Conference*, Sydney, Australia, 1997. IEEE Press.
34. Martin Odersky and Philip Wadler. Pizza into Java: Translating theory into practice. In *Proc. 24th ACM Symposium on Principles of Programming Languages*, January 1997.
35. John C. Reynolds. Syntatic control of interference. In *5th ACM Symposium on Principles of Programming Languages*, January 1978.
36. Bjarne Stroustrup. *The C++ Programming Language.* Addison-Wesley, 1986.
37. Bjarne Stroustrup. *The Design and Evolution of C++.* Addison-Wesley, 1994.
38. Mark Utting. Reasoning about aliasing. In *The Fourth Australasian Refinement Workshop*, 1995.
39. Jan Vitek, Manuel Serrano, and Dimitri Thanos. Security and communication in mobile object systems. In J. Vitek and C. Tschudin, editors, *Mobile Object Systems: Towards the Programmable Internet.*, LNCS 1222. Springer-Verlag, April 1997.
40. William C. Wake. Account number: A pattern. In *Pattern Languages of Program Design*, volume 1. Addison-Wesley, 1995.
41. Alan Cameron Wills. *Formal Methods applied to Object-Oriented Programming.* PhD thesis, University of Manchester, 1992.

Predicate Dispatching: A Unified Theory of Dispatch

Michael Ernst, Craig Kaplan, and Craig Chambers

Department of Computer Science and Engineering
University of Washington
Seattle, WA, USA 98195-2350
{mernst,csk,chambers}@cs.washington.edu
http://www.cs.washington.edu/research/projects/cecil/

Abstract. *Predicate dispatching* generalizes previous method dispatch mechanisms by permitting arbitrary predicates to control method applicability and by using logical implication between predicates as the overriding relationship. The method selected to handle a message send can depend not just on the classes of the arguments, as in ordinary object-oriented dispatch, but also on the classes of subcomponents, on an argument's state, and on relationships between objects. This simple mechanism subsumes and extends object-oriented single and multiple dispatch, ML-style pattern matching, predicate classes, and classifiers, which can all be regarded as syntactic sugar for predicate dispatching. This paper introduces predicate dispatching, gives motivating examples, and presents its static and dynamic semantics. An implementation of predicate dispatching is available.

1 Introduction

Many programming languages support some mechanism for dividing the body of a procedure into a set of cases, with a declarative mechanism for selecting the right case for each dynamic invocation of the procedure. Case selection can be broken down into tests for *applicability* (a case is a candidate for invocation if its guard is satisfied) and *overriding* (which selects one of the applicable cases for invocation).

Object-oriented languages use overloaded methods as the cases and generic functions (implicit or explicit) as the procedures. A method is applicable if the run-time class of the receiver argument is the same as or a subclass of the class on which the receiver is specialized. Multiple dispatching [BKK+86,Cha92] enables testing the classes of all of the arguments. One method overrides another if its specializer classes are subclasses of the other's, using either lexicographic (CLOS [Ste90]) or pointwise (Cecil [Cha93a]) ordering.

Predicate classes [Cha93b] automatically classify an object of class A as an instance of virtual subclass B (a subclass of A) whenever B's predicate (an arbitrary expression typically testing the runtime state of an object) is true. This creation of virtual class hierarchies makes method dispatching applicable even in cases where the effective class of an object may change over time. Classifiers [HHM90b] and modes [Tai93] are similar mechanisms for reclassifying an object into one of a number of subclasses based on a case-statement-like test of arbitrary boolean conditions.

Pattern matching (as in ML [MTH90]) bases applicability tests on the run-time datatype constructor tags of the arguments and their subcomponents. As with classifiers and modes, textual ordering determines overriding. Some languages, such as Haskell [HJW+92], allow arbitrary boolean guards to accompany patterns, restricting applicability. Views [Wad87] extend pattern matching to abstract data types by enabling them to offer interfaces like various concrete datatypes.

Predicate dispatching integrates, generalizes, and provides a uniform interface to these similar but previously incomparable mechanisms. A method declaration specifies its applicability via a *predicate expression*, which is a logical formula over class tests (i.e., tests that an object is of a particular class or one of its subclasses) and arbitrary boolean-valued expressions from the underlying programming language. A method is applicable when its predicate expression evaluates to *true*. Method m_1 overrides method m_2 when m_1's predicate logically implies that of m_2; this relationship is computed at compile time. Static typechecking verifies that, for all possible combinations of arguments to a generic function, there is always a single most-specific applicable method. This ensures that there are no "message not understood" errors (called "match not exhaustive" in ML) or "message ambiguous" errors at run-time.

Predicate expressions capture the basic primitive mechanisms underlying a wide range of declarative dispatching mechanisms. Combining these primitives in an orthogonal and general manner enables new sorts of dispatching that are not expressible by previous dispatch mechanisms. Predicate dispatching preserves several desirable properties from its object-oriented heritage, including that methods can be declared in any order and that new methods can be added to existing generic functions without modifying the existing methods or clients; these properties are not shared by pattern-matching-based mechanisms.

Section 2 introduces the syntax, semantics, and use of predicate dispatching through a series of examples. Section 3 defines its dynamic and static semantics formally. Section 4 discusses predicate tautology testing, which is the key mechanism required by the dynamic and static semantics. Section 5 surveys related work. Section 6 concludes with a discussion of future directions for research.

2 Overview

This section demonstrates some of the capabilities of predicate dispatching by way of a series of examples. We incrementally present a high-level syntax which appears in full in Fig. 6; Fig. 1 lists supporting syntactic domains. Words and symbols in **boldface** represent terminals. Angle brackets denote zero or more comma-separated repetitions of an item. Square brackets contain optional expressions.

E	$\in$ *expr*	The set of expressions in the underlying programming language
Body	$\in$ *method-body*	The set of method bodies in the underlying programming language
T	$\in$ *type*	The set of types in the underlying programming language
c	$\in$ *class-id*	The namespace of classes
m	$\in$ *method-id*	The namespace of methods and fields
f	$\in$ *field-id*	The namespace of methods and fields
p	$\in$ *pred-id*	The namespace of predicate abstractions
v, w	$\in$ *var-id*	The namespace of variables

Fig. 1. Syntactic domains and variables. Method and field names appear in the same namespace; the *method-id* or *field-id* name is chosen for clarity in the text.

Predicate dispatching is parameterized by the syntax and semantics of the host programming language in which predicate dispatching is embedded. The ideas of predicate dispatching are independent of the host language; this paper specifies only a predicate dispatching sublanguage, with *expr* the generic nonterminal for expressions in the host language. Types and signatures are used when the host language is statically typed and omitted when it is dynamically typed.

2.1 Dynamic dispatch

Each method implementation has a predicate expression which specifies when the method is applicable. Class tests are predicate expressions, as are negations, conjunctions, and disjunctions of predicate expressions.

method-sig	::=	**signature** *method-id* (⟨ *type* ⟩) : *type*	
method-decl	::=	**method** *method-id* (⟨ *formal-pattern* ⟩) [**when** *pred-expr*] *method-body*	
formal-pattern	::=	*var-id*	
pred-expr	::=	*expr* @ *class-id*	succeeds if *expr* evaluates to an instance of *class-id* or one of its subclasses
	|	**not** *pred-expr*	negation
	|	*pred-expr* **and** *pred-expr*	conjunction (short-circuited)
	|	*pred-expr* **or** *pred-expr*	disjunction (short-circuited)

Predicate expressions are evaluated in an environment with the method's formal arguments bound (see Sect. 3 for details). An omitted **when** clause indicates that the method handles all (type-correct) arguments.

Method signature declarations give the type signature shared by a family of method implementations in a generic function. A message send expression need examine only the corresponding method signature declaration to determine its type-correctness, while a set of overloaded method implementations must completely and unambiguously implement the corresponding signature in order to be type-correct.

Predicate dispatching can simulate both singly- and multiply-dispatched methods by *specializing* formal parameters on a class (via the "@*class-id*" syntax).

Specialization limits the applicability of a method to objects that are instances of the given class or one of its subclasses. More generally, predicate dispatching supports the construction of arbitrary conjunctions, disjunctions, and negations of class tests. The following example uses predicate dispatching to implement the **Zip** function which converts a pair of lists into a list of pairs:[1]

```
type List;
  class Cons subtypes List { head:Any, tail:List };
  class Nil subtypes List;

signature Zip(List, List):List;
method Zip(l1, l2) when l1@Cons and l2@Cons {
    return Cons(Pair(l1.head, l2.head), Zip(l1.tail, l2.tail)); }
method Zip(l1, l2) when l1@Nil or l2@Nil { return Nil; }
```

The first **Zip** method applies when both of its arguments are instances of **Cons** (or some subclass). The second **Zip** method uses disjunction to test whether either argument is an instance of **Nil** (or some subclass). The type checker can verify statically that the two implementations of **Zip** are mutually exclusive and exhaustive over all possible arguments that match the signature, ensuring that there will be no "message not understood" or "message ambiguous" errors at run-time, without requiring the cases to be put in any particular order.

There are several unsatisfactory alternatives to the use of implication to determine overriding relationships. ML-style pattern matching requires all cases to be written in one place and put in a particular total order, resolving ambiguities in favor of the first successfully matching pattern. Likewise, a lexicographic ordering for multimethods [Ste90] is error-prone and unnatural, and programmers are not warned of potential ambiguities. In a traditional (singly- or multiply-dispatched) object-oriented language without the ability to order cases, either the base case of **Zip** must be written as the default case for all pairs of **List** objects (unnaturally, and unsafely in the face of future additions of new subclasses of **List**), or *three* separate but identical base methods must be written: one for **Nil**×**Any**, one for **Any**×**Nil**, and a third for **Nil**×**Nil** to resolve the ambiguity between the first two. In our experience with object-oriented languages (using a pointwise, not lexicographic, ordering), these triplicate base methods for binary messages occur frequently.

As a syntactic convenience, class tests can be written in the formal argument list:

formal-pattern ::= [*var-id*] [@ *class-id*]   like *var-id* @ *class-id* in *pred-expr*

The class name can be omitted if the argument is not dispatched upon, and the formal name can be omitted if the argument is not used elsewhere in the predicate or method body.

The first **Zip** method above could then be rewritten as

---

[1] **Any** is the top class, subclassed by all other classes, and **Pair** returns an object containing its two arguments.

```
method Zip(l1@Cons, l2@Cons) {
  return Cons(Pair(l1.head, l2.head), Zip(l1.tail, l2.tail)); }
```

This form uses an implicit conjunction of class tests, like a multimethod.

2.2 Pattern matching

Predicates can test the run-time classes of components of an argument, just as pattern matching can query substructures, by suffixing the @*class* test with a record-like list of field names and corresponding class tests; names can be bound to field contents at the same time.

pred-expr ::= ...
  | *expr* @ *specializer*
specializer ::= *class-id* [{ ⟨ *field-pat* ⟩ }]
field-pat ::= *field-id* [= *var-id*] [@ *specializer*]

A *specializer* succeeds if all of the specified fields (or results of invoking methods named by *field-id*) satisfy their own *specializers*, in which case the *var-ids* are bound to the field values or method results. As with *formal-pattern*, the formal name or specializer may be omitted.

Our syntax for pattern matching on records is analogous to that for creating a record: `{ x := 7, y := 22 }` creates a two-component record, binding the `x` field to 7 and the `y` field to 22, while `{ x = xval }` pattern-matches against a record containing an `x` field, binding the new variable `xval` to the contents of that field and ignoring any other fields that might be present. The similarity between the record construction and matching syntaxes follows ML. Our presentation syntax also uses curly braces in two other places: for record type specifiers (as in the declaration of the `Cons` class, above) and to delimit code blocks (as in the definitions of the `Zip` methods, above).

The following example, adapted from our implementation of an optimizing compiler, shows how a `ConstantFold` method can dispatch for binary operators whose arguments are constants and whose operator is integer addition:

```
type Expr;
  signature ConstantFold(Expr):Expr;
  -- default constant-fold optimization: do nothing
  method ConstantFold(e) { return e; }

  type AtomicExpr subtypes Expr;
    class VarRef subtypes AtomicExpr { ... };
    class IntConst subtypes AtomicExpr { value:int };
    ... -- other atomic expressions here

  type Binop;
    class IntPlus subtypes Binop { ... };
    class IntMul subtypes Binop { ... };
    ... -- other binary operators here
```

```
class BinopExpr subtypes Expr { op:Binop, arg1:Expr, arg2:Expr, ... };
  -- override default to constant-fold binops with constant arguments
  method ConstantFold(e@BinopExpr{ op@IntPlus, arg1@IntConst, arg2@IntConst }) {
    return new IntConst{ value := e.arg1 + e.arg2 }; }
... -- more similarly expressed cases for other binary and unary operators here
```

The ability in pattern matching to test for constants of built-in types is a simple extension of class tests. In a prototype-based language, @ operates over objects as well as classes, as in "*answer* @ 42".

As with pattern matching, testing the representation of components of an object makes sense when the object and the tested components together implement a single abstraction. We do not advocate using pattern matching to test components of objects in a way that crosses natural abstraction boundaries.

2.3 Boolean expressions

To increase the expressiveness of predicate dispatching, predicates may test arbitrary boolean expressions from the underlying programming language. Additionally, names may be bound to values, for use later in the predicate expressions and in the method body. Expressions from the underlying programming language that appear in predicate expressions should have no externally observable side effects.[2]

pred-expr ::= ...		
	| **test** *expr*	succeeds if *expr* evaluates to *true*
	| **let** *var-id* := *expr*	evaluate *expr* and bind *var-id* to its value; always succeeds

The following extension to the `ConstantFold` example illustrates these features. Recall that in `{ value=v }`, the left-hand side is a field name and the right-hand side is a variable being bound.

```
-- Handle case of adding zero to anything (but don't be ambiguous
-- with existing method for zero plus a constant).
method ConstantFold(
        e@BinopExpr{ op@IntPlus, arg1@IntConst{ value=v }, arg2=a2 })
  when test(v == 0) and not(a2@IntConst) {
  return a2; }
method ConstantFold(
        e@BinopExpr{ op@IntPlus, arg1=a1, arg2@IntConst{ value=v } })
  when test(v == 0) and not(a1@IntConst) {
  return a1; }

... -- other special cases for operations on 0,1 here
```

[2] We do not presently enforce this restriction, but there is no guarantee regarding in what order or how many times predicate expressions are evaluated.

2.4 Predicate abstractions

Named predicate abstractions can factor out recurring tests and give names to semantically meaningful concepts in the application domain. Named predicates abstract over both tests and variable bindings — the two capabilities of inline predicate expressions — by both succeeding or failing and returning a record-like set of bindings. These bindings resemble the fields of a record or class, and similar support is given to pattern matching against a subset of the results of a named predicate invocation. Predicate abstractions thus can act like views or virtual subclasses of some object (or tuple of objects), with the results of predicate abstractions acting like the virtual fields of the virtual class. If the properties of an object tested by a collection of predicates are mutable, the object may be given different virtual subclass bindings at different times in its life, providing the benefits of using classes to organize code even in situations where an object's "class" is not fixed.

pred-sig ::= **predsignature** *pred-id* (⟨ *type* ⟩)
  [**return** { ⟨ *field-id* : *type* ⟩ }]
pred-decl ::= **predicate** *pred-id* (⟨ *formal-pattern* ⟩)
  [**when** *pred-expr*] [**return** { ⟨ *field-id* := *expr* ⟩ }]
pred-expr ::= ...
  | *pred-id* (⟨ *expr* ⟩) [=> { ⟨ *field-pat* ⟩ }] test predicate abstraction
specializer ::= *class-spec* [{ ⟨ *field-pat* ⟩ }]
class-spec ::= *class-id* *expr* @ *class-id* is a class test
  | *pred-id* *expr* @ *pred-id* [{... }] is alternate syntax for *pred-id*(*expr*) [=>{... }]

A predicate abstraction takes a list of arguments and succeeds or fails as determined by its own predicate expression. A succeeding predicate abstraction invocation can expose bindings of names to values it computed during its evaluation, and the caller can retrieve any subset of the predicate abstraction's result bindings. Predicate signatures specify the type interface used in typechecking predicate abstraction callers and implementations. In this presentation, we prohibit recursive predicates.

Simple predicate abstractions can be used just like ordinary classes:

```
predicate on_x_axis(p@point)
  when (p@cartesianPoint and test(p.y == 0))
    or (p@polarPoint and (test(p.theta == 0) or test(p.theta == pi)));

method draw(p@point) { ... }        -- draw the point
method draw(p@on_x_axis) { ... }    -- use a contrasting color so point is visible
```

In the following example, taken from our compiler implementation, `CFG_2succ` is a control flow graph (CFG) node with two successors. Each successor is marked with whether it is a loop exit (information which, in our implementation, is dynamically maintained when the CFG is modified) and the innermost loop it does not exit. It is advantageous for an iterative dataflow algorithm to propagate values along the loop exit only after reaching a fixed point within the loop; such an algorithm would dispatch on the **LoopExit** predicate. Similarly, the algorithm could switch from iterative to non-iterative mode when exiting the outermost loop, as indicated by **TopLevelLoopExit**.

```
predsignature LoopExit(CFGnode)
  return { loop:CFGloop };
predicate LoopExit(n@CFG_2succ{ next_true = t, next_false = f })
  when test(t.is_loop_exit) or test(f.is_loop_exit)
  return { loop := outermost(t.containing_loop, f.containing_loop) };
predicate TopLevelLoopExit(n@LoopExit{ loop@TopLevelScope });
```

Only one definition per predicate abstraction is permitted; App. B relaxes this restriction.

Because object identity is not affected by these different views on an object, named predicate abstractions are more flexible than coercions in environments with side-effects. Additionally, a single object can be classified in multiple independent ways by different predicate abstractions without being forced to define all the possible conjunctions of independent predicates as explicit classes, relieving some of the problems associated with a mix-in style of class organization [HHM90b,HHM90a].

2.5 Classifiers

Classifiers [HHM90b] are a convenient syntax for imposing a linear ordering on a collection of predicates, ensuring mutual exclusion. They combine the state testing of predicate classes and the total ordering of pattern matching. An optional **otherwise** case, which executes if none of the predicates in the classifier evaluates to true, adds the guarantee of complete coverage. Multiple independent classifications of a particular class or object do not interfere with one another.

classifier-decl ::= **classify** (⟨ *formal-pattern* ⟩)
⟨ **as** *pred-id* **when** *pred-expr* [**return** { ⟨ *field-id* := *expr* ⟩ }] ⟩
[**as** *pred-id* **otherwise** [**return** { ⟨ *field-id* := *expr* ⟩ }]]

Here is an example of the use of classifiers:

```
class Window { ... }

classify(w@Window)
  as Iconified when test(w.iconified)
  as FullScreen when test(w.area() == RootWindow.area())
  as Big when test(w.area() > RootWindow.area()/2)
  as Small otherwise;

method move(w@FullScreen, x@int, y@int) { }           -- nothing to do
method move(w@Big, x@int, y@int) { ... }             -- move a wireframe outline
method move(w@Small, x@int, y@int) { ... }           -- move an opaque window
method move(w@Iconified, x@int, y@int) { ... }       -- modify icon coordinates

-- resize, maximize, and iconify similarly test these predicates
```

method-sig	::= **signature** *method-id* (⟨ *type* ⟩) : *type*	
method-decl	::= **method** *method-id* (⟨ *var-id* ⟩) **when** *pred-expr method-body*	
pred-sig	::= **predsignature** *pred-id* (⟨ *type* ⟩) **return** { ⟨ *field-id* : *type* ⟩ }	
pred-decl	::= **predicate** *pred-id* (⟨ *var-id* ⟩) **when** *pred-expr* **return** { ⟨ *field-id* := *expr* ⟩ }	
$P, Q \in$ *pred-expr*	::= *var-id* @ *class-id*	succeeds if *var-id* is an instance of *class-id* or a subclass
	| **test** *var-id*	succeeds if *var-id*'s value is *true*
	| **let** *var-id* := *expr*	evaluate *expr* and bind *var-id* to that value; always succeeds
	| *pred-id* (⟨ *var-id* ⟩) => { ⟨ *field-id* = *var-id* ⟩ }	test predicate abstraction
	| **true**	always succeeds
	| **not** *pred-expr*	negation
	| *pred-expr* **and** *pred-expr*	conjunction (short-circuited)
	| *pred-expr* **or** *pred-expr*	disjunction (short-circuited)

Fig. 2. Abstract syntax of the core language. Words and symbols in **boldface** represent terminals. Angle brackets denote zero or more comma-separated repetitions of an item. Square brackets contain optional expressions. The text uses parentheses around *pred-exprs* to indicate order of operations. Each predicate may be defined only once (App. B relaxes this restriction), and recursive predicates are forbidden.

Classifiers introduce no new primitives, but provide syntactic support for a common programming idiom. To force the classification to be mutually exclusive, each case is transformed into a predicate which includes the negation of the disjunction of all previous predicates (for details, see App. A). Therefore, an object is classified by some case only when it cannot be classified by any earlier case.

3 Dynamic and static semantics

The rest of this paper formalizes the dynamic and static semantics of a core predicate dispatching sublanguage. Figure 2 presents the abstract syntax of the core sublanguage which is used throughout this section. Appendix A defines desugaring rules that translate the high-level syntax of Fig. 6 into the core syntax.

In the remainder of this paper, we assume that all variable names are distinct so that the semantic rules can ignore the details of avoiding variable capture.

3.1 Dynamic semantics

This section explains how to select the most-specific applicable method at each message send. This selection relies on two key tests on predicated methods: whether a method is applicable to a call, and whether one method overrides another.

$\alpha, \beta \in$ *value*	Values in the underlying programming language
$b \in \{$*true*, *false*$\}$	Mathematical booleans
$K \in$ (*var-id* $\rightarrow$ *value*) $\cup$ (*pred-id* $\rightarrow$ *pred-decl*)	Environments mapping variables to values and predicate names to predicate declarations

$\text{lookup}(v, K) \rightarrow \alpha$	Look up variable v in environment K, returning the value α.
$K[v := \alpha] \rightarrow K'$	Bind name v to value α in environment K, resulting in the new environment K'. Any existing binding for v is overridden.
$\text{eval}(E, K) \rightarrow \alpha$	Evaluate expression E in environment K, returning the value α.
$\text{instanceof}(\alpha, c) \rightarrow b$	Determine whether value α is an instance of c or a subclass of c.
$\text{accept}(\alpha) \rightarrow b$	Coerce arbitrary program values to *true* or *false*, for use with **test**.

Fig. 3. Dynamic semantics domains and helper functions. Evaluation rules appear in Fig. 4. The host programming language supplies functions eval, instanceof, and accept.

A method is applicable if its predicate evaluates to *true*. Predicate evaluation also provides an extended environment in which the method's body is executed. Bindings created via **let** in a predicate may be used in a method body, predicate **return** clause, or the second conjunct of a conjunction whose first conjunct created the binding. Such bindings permit reuse of values without recomputation, as well as simplifying and clarifying the code. Figures 3 and 4 define the execution model of predicate evaluation.

Predicate dispatching considers one method m_1 to override another method m_2 exactly when m_1's predicate implies m_2's predicate and not vice versa. Section 4 describes how to compute the overriding relation, which can be performed at compile time.

Given the evaluation model for predicate expressions and the ability to compare predicate expressions for overriding, the execution of generic function invocations is straightforward. Suppose that generic function m is defined with the following cases:

$$\begin{array}{l} \textbf{method}\, m(v_1, \ldots, v_n)\ \textbf{when}\, P_1\ \textit{Body}_1 \\ \textbf{method}\, m(v_1, \ldots, v_n)\ \textbf{when}\, P_2\ \textit{Body}_2 \\ \vdots \\ \textbf{method}\, m(v_1, \ldots, v_n)\ \textbf{when}\, P_k\ \textit{Body}_k \end{array}$$

To evaluate the invocation $m(E_1, \ldots, E_n)$ in the environment K, first obtain $\alpha_i = \text{eval}(E_i, K)$ for all $i = 1, \ldots, n$. Then, for $j = 1, \ldots, k$, obtain a truth value b_j and a new environment K_j through $\langle P_j, K[v_1 := \alpha_1, \ldots, v_n := \alpha_n]\rangle \Rightarrow \langle b_j, K_j\rangle$, as in the predicate invocation rules of Fig. 4.[3]

Now let I be the set of integers i such that $b_i = \textit{true}$, and find $i_0 \in I$ such that P_{i_0} overrides all others in $\{P_i\}_{i \in I}$. The result of evaluating $m(E_1, \ldots, E_n)$

[3] Since we assume that all variable names are distinct and disallow lexically nested predicate abstractions, we can safely use the dynamic environment at the call site instead of preserving the static environment at the predicate abstraction's definition point.

$$\frac{}{\langle \mathbf{true}, K\rangle \Rightarrow \langle \mathit{true}, K\rangle}$$

$$\frac{\mathrm{lookup}(v, K) = \alpha \qquad \mathrm{instanceof}(\alpha, c) = b}{\langle v \mathbin{@} c, K\rangle \Rightarrow \langle b, K\rangle}$$

$$\frac{\mathrm{lookup}(v, K) = \alpha \qquad \mathrm{accept}(\alpha) = b}{\langle \mathbf{test}\ \ v, K\rangle \Rightarrow \langle b, K\rangle}$$

$$\frac{\mathrm{eval}(E, K) = \alpha \qquad K[v := \alpha] = K'}{\langle \mathbf{let}\ \ v := E, K\rangle \Rightarrow \langle \mathit{true}, K'\rangle}$$

$$\frac{\begin{array}{c}\forall i \in \{1,\ldots,n\} \quad \mathrm{lookup}(v_i, K) = \alpha_i \\ \mathrm{lookup}(p, K) = \mathbf{predicate}\ p(v'_1,\ldots,v'_n)\ \mathbf{when}\ P\ \mathbf{return}\ \{f_1 := w'_1,\ldots,f_m := w'_m,\ldots\} \\ \langle P, K[v'_1 := \alpha_1,\ldots,v'_n := \alpha_n]\rangle \Rightarrow \langle \mathit{false}, K'\rangle\end{array}}{\langle p(v_1,\ldots,v_n) \texttt{=>} \{f_1 = w_1,\ldots,f_m = w_m\}, K\rangle \Rightarrow \langle \mathit{false}, K\rangle}$$

$$\frac{\begin{array}{c}\forall i \in \{1,\ldots,n\} \quad \mathrm{lookup}(v_i, K) = \alpha_i \\ \mathrm{lookup}(p, K) = \mathbf{predicate}\ p(v'_1,\ldots,v'_n)\ \mathbf{when}\ P\ \mathbf{return}\ \{f_1 := w'_1,\ldots,f_m := w'_m,\ldots\} \\ \langle P, K[v'_1 := \alpha_1,\ldots,v'_n := \alpha_n]\rangle \Rightarrow \langle \mathit{true}, K'\rangle \\ \forall i \in \{1,\ldots,m\} \quad \mathrm{lookup}(w'_i, K') = \beta_i \\ K[w_1 := \beta_1,\ldots,w_m := \beta_m] = K'' \quad (*)\end{array}}{\langle p(v_1,\ldots,v_n) \texttt{=>} \{f_1 = w_1,\ldots,f_m = w_m\}, K\rangle \Rightarrow \langle \mathit{true}, K''\rangle}$$

$$\frac{\langle P, K\rangle \Rightarrow \langle b, K'\rangle}{\langle \mathbf{not}\, P, K\rangle \Rightarrow \langle \neg b, K\rangle}$$

$$\frac{\langle P, K\rangle \Rightarrow \langle \mathit{false}, K'\rangle}{\langle P\ \mathbf{and}\ Q, K\rangle \Rightarrow \langle \mathit{false}, K\rangle}$$

$$\frac{\langle P, K\rangle \Rightarrow \langle \mathit{true}, K'\rangle \qquad \langle Q, K'\rangle \Rightarrow \langle \mathit{false}, K''\rangle}{\langle P\ \mathbf{and}\ Q, K\rangle \Rightarrow \langle \mathit{false}, K\rangle}$$

$$\frac{\langle P, K\rangle \Rightarrow \langle \mathit{true}, K'\rangle \qquad \langle Q, K'\rangle \Rightarrow \langle \mathit{true}, K''\rangle}{\langle P\ \mathbf{and}\ Q, K\rangle \Rightarrow \langle \mathit{true}, K''\rangle}$$

$$\frac{\langle P, K\rangle \Rightarrow \langle \mathit{true}, K'\rangle}{\langle P\ \mathbf{or}\ Q, K\rangle \Rightarrow \langle \mathit{true}, K\rangle}$$

$$\frac{\langle P, K\rangle \Rightarrow \langle \mathit{false}, K'\rangle \qquad \langle Q, K\rangle \Rightarrow \langle \mathit{true}, K''\rangle}{\langle P\ \mathbf{or}\ Q, K\rangle \Rightarrow \langle \mathit{true}, K\rangle}$$

$$\frac{\langle P, K\rangle \Rightarrow \langle \mathit{false}, K'\rangle \qquad \langle Q, K\rangle \Rightarrow \langle \mathit{false}, K''\rangle}{\langle P\ \mathbf{or}\ Q, K\rangle \Rightarrow \langle \mathit{false}, K\rangle}$$

Fig. 4. Dynamic semantics evaluation rules. Domains and helper functions appear in Fig. 3. We say $\langle P, K\rangle \Rightarrow \langle b, K'\rangle$ when the predicate P evaluates in the environment K to the boolean result b, producing the new environment K'. If the result b is *false*, then the resulting environment K' is ignored. Bindings do not escape from **not** or **or** constructs; App. B relaxes the latter restriction. The starred hypothesis uses K, not K', to construct the result environment K'' because only the bindings specified in the **return** clause, not all bindings in the predicate's **when** clause, are exposed at the call site.

is then the result of evaluating $Body_{i_0}$ in the environment K_{i_0}, so that variables bound in the predicate can be referred to in the body. If no such i_0 exists, then an exception is raised: a "message not understood" error if I is empty, or a "message ambiguous" error if there is no unique most specific element of I.

An implementation can make a number of improvements to this base algorithm. Here we briefly mention just a few such optimizations. First, common subexpression elimination over predicate expressions can limit the computation done in evaluating guards. Second, precomputed implication relationships can prevent the necessity for evaluating every predicate expression. If a more specific one is true, then the less specific one is certain to be satisfied; however, such satisfaction is irrelevant since the more specific predicate will be chosen. Third, clauses and methods can be reordered to succeed or fail more quickly, as in some Prolog implementations [Zel93].

3.2 Static semantics and typechecking

The operational model of predicate dispatch described in Sect. 3.1 can raise a run-time exception at a message send if no method is applicable or if no applicable method overrides all the others. We extend the typechecking rules of the underlying language to guarantee that no such exception occurs.

Figure 5 presents the static semantic domains, helper functions, and typechecking rules for the core predicate dispatching sublanguage. The return type for a predicate invocation is an unordered record. Bindings do not escape from **not** or **or** constructs (App. B makes bindings on both sides of a **or** disjunct visible outside the disjunct).

We can separate typechecking into two parts: *client-side*, which handles all checking of expressions in the underlying language and uses method signatures to typecheck message sends, and *implementation-side*, which checks method and predicate implementations against their corresponding signatures. Only implementation-side checking is affected by predicate dispatching.

Implementation-side typechecking must guarantee *completeness* and *uniqueness*. Completeness guarantees that no "message not understood" error is raised: for every possible set of arguments at each call site, some method is applicable. Let P_m be the disjunction of the predicates of all of m's implementations, and let P_s be a predicate expressing the set of argument classes that conform to the types in the method signature. (See below for the details of predicate P_s; a class c conforms to a type T if every object which is an instance of that class has type T or a subtype of T.) If P_s implies P_m, then some method is always applicable. Uniqueness guarantees that no "message ambiguous" error is raised: for no possible set of arguments at any call site are there multiple most-specific methods. Uniqueness is guaranteed if, for each pair of predicates P and Q attached to two different implementations, either P and Q are disjoint (so their associated methods can never be simultaneously applicable) or one of the predicates implies the other (so one of the methods overrides the other). Section 4 presents implication and disjointness tests over predicate expressions.

$T \leq T'$	Type T is a subtype of T'.
conformant-type(T, c)	Return the most-specific (with respect to the subtyping partial order) type T' such that every subclass c' of c that conforms to T also conforms to T'. This helper function is supplied by the underlying programming language.
$\Gamma + \Gamma' = \Gamma''$	Overriding extension of typing environments. For each $v \in \mathrm{dom}(\Gamma')$, if $\Gamma' \models v : T'$, then $\Gamma'' \models v : T'$; for each $v \in \mathrm{dom}(\Gamma) \setminus \mathrm{dom}(\Gamma')$, if $\Gamma \models v : T$, then $\Gamma'' \models v : T$.

$$\frac{}{\Gamma \vdash \textbf{signature } m(T_1, \ldots, T_n) : T_r \Rightarrow \Gamma + \{m : (T_1, \ldots, T_n) \rightarrow T_r\}}$$

$$\frac{\Gamma \models m : (T_1, \ldots, T_n) \rightarrow T_r \qquad \Gamma + \{v_1 : T_1, \ldots, v_n : T_n\} \vdash P \Rightarrow \Gamma' \quad \Gamma' \models Body : T_b \quad T_b \leq T_r}{\Gamma \vdash \textbf{method } m(v_1, \ldots, v_n) \textbf{ when } P \; Body \Rightarrow \Gamma}$$

$$\frac{}{\begin{array}{c}\langle \Gamma, \textbf{predsignature } p(T_1, \ldots, T_n) \textbf{ return } \{f_1 : T_1^r, \ldots, f_m : T_m^r\}\rangle \\ \Rightarrow \Gamma + \{p : (T_1, \ldots, T_n) \rightarrow \{f_1 : T_1^r, \ldots, f_m : T_m^r\}\}\end{array}}$$

$$\frac{\begin{array}{c}\Gamma \models p : (T_1, \ldots, T_n) \rightarrow \{f_1 : T_1^r, \ldots, f_m : T_m^r, \ldots\} \\ \Gamma + \{v_1 : T_1, \ldots, v_n : T_n\} \vdash P \Rightarrow \Gamma' \\ \forall i \in \{1, \ldots, m\} \quad \Gamma' \models v_i' : T_i' \wedge T_i' \leq T_i^r\end{array}}{\Gamma \vdash \textbf{predicate } p(v_1, \ldots, v_n) \textbf{ when } P \textbf{ return } \{f_1 := v_1', \ldots, f_m := v_m'\} \Rightarrow \Gamma}$$

$$\frac{}{\Gamma \vdash \textbf{true} \Rightarrow \Gamma}$$

$$\frac{\Gamma \models v : T \qquad \textit{conformant-type}(c, T) = T'}{\Gamma \vdash v \,@\, c \Rightarrow \Gamma + \{v : T'\}}$$

$$\frac{\Gamma \models v : Bool}{\Gamma \vdash \textbf{test } \; v \Rightarrow \Gamma}$$

$$\frac{\Gamma \models expr : T}{\Gamma \vdash \textbf{let } \; v := expr \Rightarrow \Gamma + \{v : T\}}$$

$$\frac{\begin{array}{c}\Gamma \models p : (T_1, \ldots, T_n) \rightarrow \{f_1 : T_1^r, \ldots, f_m : T_m^r, \ldots\} \\ \Gamma \models v_1 : T_1' \quad \ldots \quad \Gamma \models v_n : T_n' \quad T_1' \leq T_1 \quad \ldots \quad T_n' \leq T_n\end{array}}{\Gamma \vdash p(v_1, \ldots, v_n) \Rightarrow \{f_1 = v_1', \ldots, f_m = v_m'\} \Rightarrow \Gamma + \{v_1' : T_1^r, \ldots, v_m' : T_m^r\}}$$

$$\frac{\Gamma \vdash P \Rightarrow \Gamma'}{\Gamma \vdash \textbf{not } P \Rightarrow \Gamma}$$

$$\frac{\Gamma \vdash P_1 \Rightarrow \Gamma' \qquad \Gamma' \vdash P_2 \Rightarrow \Gamma''}{\Gamma \vdash P_1 \textbf{ and } P_2 \Rightarrow \Gamma''}$$

$$\frac{\Gamma \vdash P_1 \Rightarrow \Gamma' \qquad \Gamma \vdash P_2 \Rightarrow \Gamma''}{\Gamma \vdash P_1 \textbf{ or } P_2 \Rightarrow \Gamma}$$

Fig. 5. Typechecking rules. The hypothesis $\Gamma \models E : T$ indicates that typechecking in typing environment Γ assigns type T to expression E. The judgment $\Gamma \vdash P \Rightarrow \Gamma'$ represents extension of typechecking environments: given type environment Γ, P typechecks and produces new typechecking environment Γ'.

Completeness checking requires a predicate P_s that expresses the set of tuples of values $v_1, \ldots, v_n$ conforming to some signature's argument types $T_1, \ldots, T_n$; this predicate depends on the host language's model of classes and typing. If classes and types are the same, and all classes are concrete, then the corresponding predicate is simply v_1 @ T_1 **and**... **and** v_n @ T_n. If abstract classes are allowed, then each v_i @ T_i is replaced with v_i @ T_{i1} **or** ... **or** v_i @ T_{im}, where the T_{ij} are the top concrete subclasses of T_i. If inheritance and subtyping are separate notions, then the predicates become more complex.

Our typechecking need not test that methods conform to signatures, unlike previous work on typechecking multimethods [CL95]. In predicate dispatching, a method's formal argument has two distinct types: the "external" type derived from the signature declaration, and the possibly finer "internal" type guaranteed by successful evaluation of the method's predicate. The individual @ tests narrow the type of the tested value to the most-specific type to which all classes passing the test conform, in a host-language-specific manner, using *conformant-type*. The *conformant-type* function replaces the more complicated conformance test of earlier work.

4 Comparing predicate expressions

The static and dynamic semantics of predicate dispatching require compile-time tests of implication between predicates to determine the method overriding relationship. The static semantics also requires tests of completeness and uniqueness to ensure the absence of "message not understood" errors and "message ambiguous" errors, respectively. All of these tests reduce to tautology tests over predicates. Method m_1 with predicate p_1 overrides method m_2 with predicate p_2 iff p_1 implies p_2 — that is, if (**not** p_1) **or** p_2 is true. A set of methods is complete if the disjunction of their predicates is true. Uniqueness for a set of methods requires that for any pair of methods, either one's predicate overrides the other's, or the two predicates are logically exclusive. Two formulas are mutually exclusive exactly if one implies the negation of the other.

Section 4.1 presents a tautology test over predicate expressions which is simple, sound, and complete up to equivalence of arbitrary program expressions in **test** constructs, which we treat as black boxes. Because determining logical tautology is NP-complete, in the worst case an algorithm takes exponential time in the size of the predicate expressions. For object-oriented dispatch, this is the number of arguments to a method (a small constant). Simple optimizations (Sect. 4.2) make the tests fast in many practical situations. This cost is incurred only at compile time; at run time, precomputed overriding relations among methods are simply looked up.

We treat expressions from the underlying programming language as black boxes (but do identify those whose canonicalizations are structurally identical). Tests involving the run-time values of arbitrary host language expressions are undecidable. The algorithm presented here also does not address recursive predicates. While we have a set of heuristics that succeed in many common, practical cases, we do not yet have a complete, sound, and efficient algorithm.

4.1 The base algorithm

The base algorithm for testing predicate tautology has three components. First, the predicate expression is canonicalized to macro-expand predicate abstractions, eliminate variable bindings, and use canonical names for formal arguments. This transformation prevents different names for the same value from being considered distinct. Second, implication relations are computed among the atomic predicates (for instance, x @ **int** implies x @ **num**). Finally, the canonicalized predicate is tested for every assignment of atomic predicates to truth values which is consistent with the atomic predicate implications. The predicate is a tautology iff evaluating it in every consistent truth assignment yields *true*.

Canonicalization Canonicalization performs the following transformations:

- Expand predicate calls inline, replacing the => clause by a series of **let** bindings.
- Replace **let**-bound variables by the expressions to which they are bound, and replace **let** expressions by **true**.
- Canonically rename formal parameters according to their position in the formal list.

After canonicalization, each predicate expression is a logical formula over the following atoms with connectives **and**, **or**, and **not**.

pred-atom ::= **true**
| **test** *expr*
| *expr* @ *class-id*

Canonicalized predicates are a compile-time construct used only for predicate comparison; they are never executed. Canonicalized predicates bind no variables, and they use only global variables and formal parameters.

In the worst case, canonicalization exponentially blows up expression sizes. For instance, in

$$\textbf{let}\ x_1 = x{+}x\ \textbf{and}\ \textbf{let}\ x_2 = x_1{+}x_1\ \textbf{and}\ \textbf{let}\ x_3 = x_2{+}x_2\ \textbf{and} \ldots \textbf{and}\ \textbf{test}\ x_n = y\ ,$$

the final x_n is replaced by an expression containing 2^n instances of x. Inline expansion of predicate abstractions similarly contributes to this blowup. As with ML typechecking [KM89], which is exponential in the worst case but linear in practice, we anticipate that predicates leading to exponential behavior will be rare.

In what follows, we consider two expressions identical if, after canonicalization, they have the same abstract syntax tree.

Omitting the canonicalization step prevents some equivalent expressions from being recognized as such, but does not prevent the remainder of the algorithm from succeeding when results are named and reused rather than the computation repeated.

Truth assignment checking We present a simple exponential-time algorithm to check logical tautology; because the problem is NP-complete, any algorithm takes exponential time in the worst case. Let there be n distinct predicate atoms in the predicate; there are 2^n different truth assignments for those atoms. Not all of those truth assignments are consistent with the implications over predicate atoms: for instance, it is not sensible to set **a @ int** to *true* but **a @ num** to *false*, because **a @ int** implies **a @ num**. If every consistent truth assignment satisfies the predicate, then the predicate is a tautology. Each check of a single truth assignment takes time linear in the size of the predicate expression, for a total time of $O(n2^n)$.

The following rules specify implication over (possibly negated) canonical predicate atoms.

$$\begin{aligned} E_1 \mathbin{@} c_1 \Rightarrow E_2 \mathbin{@} c_2 \quad & \text{iff} \quad (E_1 \equiv E_2) \text{ and } (c_1 \text{ is a subclass of } c_2) \\ E_1 \mathbin{@} c_1 \Rightarrow \mathbf{not}(E_2 \mathbin{@} c_2) \quad & \text{iff} \quad (E_1 \equiv E_2) \text{ and } (c_1 \text{ is disjoint from } c_2) \\ a_1 \Rightarrow a_2 \quad & \text{iff} \quad \mathbf{not}\, a_2 \Rightarrow \mathbf{not}\, a_1 \\ a_1 \Rightarrow \mathbf{not}\, a_2 \quad & \text{iff} \quad a_2 \Rightarrow \mathbf{not}\, a_1 \end{aligned}$$

Two classes are disjoint if they have no common descendant, and **not not** $a = a$.

4.2 Optimizations

The worst-case exponential-time cost to check predicate tautology need not prevent its use in practice. Satisfiability is checked only at compile time. When computing overriding relationships, the predicates tend to be small (linear in the number of arguments to a method). We present heuristics that reduce the costs even further.

Logical simplification — such as eliminating uses of **true**, **false**, a **and not** a, and a **or not** a, and replacing **not not** a by a — can be performed as part of canonicalization to reduce the size of predicate expressions.

Unrelated atomic predicates can be treated separately. To determine whether **method** $m_1(f_1@c_1, f_2@c_2)\{...\}$ overrides **method** $m_1(f_1@c_3, f_2@c_4)\{...\}$ it is sufficient to independently determine the relationship between c_1 and c_3 and that between c_2 and c_4. Two tests with a smaller exponent replace one with a larger one, substantially reducing the overall cost. This technique always solves ordinary single and multiple dispatching overriding in time constant and linear in the number of formals, respectively, by examining each formal position independently. The technique also applies to more complicated cases, by examining subsets of formal parameters which appear together in tests from the underlying programming language.

It is not always necessary to completely expand predicate abstraction calls as part of canonicalization. If relations between predicate abstractions or other predicate expressions are known, then the tautology test can use them directly. As one example, different cases of a classifier are mutually exclusive by definition.

The side conditions on atomic predicate values (their implication relationships) usually prevent the need to check all 2^n different truth assignments for a predicate containing *n* atomic predicates. When **a @ int** is set to *true*, then all truth assignments which set **a @ num** to *false* can be skipped without further consideration.

Finally, it may be possible to achieve faster results in some cases by recasting the tautology test. Rather than attempting to prove that every truth assignment satisfies a predicate expression, it may be advantageous to search for a single truth assignment that satisfies its negation.

5 Related work

5.1 Object-oriented approaches

In the model of predicate dispatching, traditional object-oriented dispatching translates to either a single class test on the receiver argument or, for multiple dispatching, a conjunction of class tests over several arguments. Full predicate dispatching additionally enables testing arbitrary boolean expressions from the underlying language, accessing and naming subcomponents of the arguments, performing tests over multiple arguments, and arbitrarily combining tests via conjunction, disjunction, and negation. Also, named predicate abstractions effectively introduce new virtual classes and corresponding subclassing links into the program inheritance hierarchy. Predicate dispatching preserves the ability in object-oriented languages to statically determine when one method overrides another and when no message lookup error can occur. Singly-dispatched object-oriented languages have efficient method lookup algorithms and separate typechecking, which depend crucially on the absence of any separate modules that dispatch on other argument positions. Multiply-dispatched object-oriented languages have more challenging problems in implementation [KR89,CTK94,AGS94] and typechecking [CL95], and predicate dispatching in its unrestricted form shares these challenges.

Predicate classes [Cha93b] are an earlier extension of object-oriented dispatching to include arbitrary boolean predicates. A predicate class which inherits from class A and has an associated predicate expression *guard* would be modeled as a named predicate abstraction that tests @A **and** *guard*. Predicate dispatching is more general, for example by being able to define predicates over multiple arguments. Predicate dispatching exploits the structure of **and**, **or**, and **not** to automatically determine when no message lookup error can occur, while typechecking of predicate classes relies on uncheckable user assertions about the relations between the predicate classes' guard expressions.

Classifiers in Kea [HHM90b,HHM90a,MHH91] let an instance of a class be dynamically reclassified as being of a subclass. A classifier for a class is composed of a sequence of predicate/subclass pairs, with an object of the input class automatically classified as being of the subclass with the first successful predicate. Because the sequence of predicates is totally ordered and the first successful predicate takes precedence over all later predicates, a classifier provides a concise syntax for a set of mutually exclusive, exhaustive predicate abstractions. Predicate abstractions are more general than classifiers in many of the ways discussed above, but they also provide syntactic support for this important idiom. Kea is a purely functional language, so classifiers do not need to consider the semantics of reclassifying objects when the values of predicates change; predicate dispatching addresses this issue by (conceptually) performing reclassification as needed as part of message dispatching.

Modes [Tai93] are another mechanism for adding dynamic reclassification of a class into a subclass. Unlike predicate classes and classifiers, the modes of a class are not first-class subclasses but rather internal components of a class that cannot be extended externally and that cannot exploit inheritance to factor shared code. Mode reselection can be done either explicitly at the end of each method or implicitly after each assignment using a declaratively specified classification.

5.2 Pattern matching approaches

Predicate dispatching supports many of the facilities found in pattern matching as in ML [MTH90] and Haskell [HJW+92], including tests over arbitrary nested structure, binding of names to subcomponents, and arbitrary boolean guard expressions. Predicate dispatching additionally supports inheritance (its class tests are more general than datatype constructor patterns), disjunctions and negations of tests and conjunctions of tests on the same object, and named predicate abstractions to factor out common patterns of tests and to offer conditional views of objects extended with virtual fields. The patterns in a function are totally ordered, while predicate dispatching computes a partial order over predicates and warns when two patterns might be ambiguous. Finally, new methods can be added to existing generic functions without changing any existing code, while new patterns can be added to a function only by modifying it.

Views [Wad87] extend pattern matching to abstract data types by allowing an abstract data type to offer a number of views of itself as a concrete datatype, over which pattern matching is defined. Predicate dispatching supports "pattern matching" over the results of methods (by **let**-binding their results to names and then testing those names, just as field contents are bound and tested), and those methods can serve as accessor functions to a virtual view of the object, for instance `rho` and `theta` methods presenting a polar view of a cartesian point. Views must be isomorphisms, which enables equational reasoning over them; by contrast, named predicate abstractions provide conditional views of an object without requiring the presence of both in and out views.

Pizza [OW97] supports both algebraic datatypes (and associated pattern matching) and object-oriented dispatching, but the two mechanisms are largely distinct. The authors argue that datatypes are good for fixed numbers of representations with extensible operations, while classes are good for a fixed set of operations with extensible representations. By integrating pattern matching and dispatching, including multimethods, predicate dispatching achieves extensibility in both dimensions along with the syntactic convenience of pattern matching. Predicate dispatching faces more difficult implementation and separate typechecking challenges with the shift to multimethod-like dispatching.

6 Conclusions

Many language features express the concept of selecting a most-specific applicable method from a collection of candidates, including object-oriented dispatch, pattern matching, views, predicate classes, and classifiers. Predicate dispatching integrates and generalizes these mechanisms in a single framework, based on a core language of boolean expressions over class tests and arbitrary expressions, explicit binding forms to generalize features of pattern matching, and named predicate abstractions with result bindings. By providing a single integrated mechanism, programs can take advantage of various styles of dispatch and even combine them to create applicability conditions that were previously either impossible or inconvenient to express.

We have implemented predicate dispatching in the context of Dubious, a simple core multiply-dispatched object-oriented programming language. The implementation supports all the examples presented in this paper, although for clarity this paper uses a slightly different presentation syntax. The implementation supports the full core language of Sect. 3 and many of the syntactic sugars of App. A. This implementation was helpful in verifying our base design. We expect that it will also provide insight into the advantages and disadvantages of programming with predicate dispatching, as well as help us to evaluate optimization strategies. The implementation is available from `http://www.cs.washington.edu/research/projects/cecil/www/Gud/`.

So far, we have focused on developing the static and dynamic semantics for predicate dispatching. Two unresolved practical issues that we will address in the future are efficient implementation techniques and separate typechecking support for predicate dispatching. We anticipate that efficient implementations of unrestricted predicate dispatching will build upon work on efficient implementation of multimethod dispatching and on predicate classes. In addition, static analyses that factor a collection of predicates to avoid redundant tests and side-effect analyses that determine when predicates need not be re-evaluated appear to be promising lines for future research. Similarly, separate typechecking of collections of predicated methods will build upon current work to develop modular and incremental methods for typechecking multimethods [CL95].

Acknowledgments

Todd Millstein, Vassily Litvinov, Wilson Hsieh, David Grove, and the anonymous referees made helpful comments on a draft of this paper. This research is supported in part by an NSF grant (number CCR-9503741), an NSF Young Investigator Award (number CCR-9457767), a grant from the Office of Naval Research (contract number N00014-94-1-1136), an IBM graduate fellowship, an FCAR graduate scholarship, and gifts from Sun Microsystems, IBM, Xerox PARC, Pure Software, and Edison Design Group.

References

[AGS94] Eric Amiel, Olivier Gruber, and Eric Simon. Optimizing multi-method dispatch using compressed dispatch tables. In *Proceedings OOPSLA '94*, pages 244–258, Portland, OR, October 1994.

[BKK+86] Daniel G. Bobrow, Ken Kahn, Gregor Kiczales, Larry Masinter, Mark Stefik, and Frank Zdybel. Commonloops: Merging lisp and object-oriented programming. In *Proceedings OOPSLA '86*, pages 17–29, November 1986. Published as ACM SIGPLAN Notices, volume 21, number 11.

[Cha92] Craig Chambers. Object-oriented multi-methods in Cecil. In O. Lehrmann Madsen, editor, *Proceedings ECOOP '92*, LNCS 615, pages 33–56, Utrecht, The Netherlands, June 1992. Springer-Verlag.

[Cha93a] Craig Chambers. The Cecil language: Specification and rationale. Technical Report UW-CSE-93-03-05, Department of Computer Science and Engineering. University of Washington, March 1993.

[Cha93b] Craig Chambers. Predicate classes. In O. Nierstrasz, editor, *Proceedings ECOOP '93*, LNCS 707, pages 268–296, Kaiserslautern, Germany, July 1993. Springer-Verlag.

[CL95] Craig Chambers and Gary T. Leavens. Typechecking and modules for multi-methods. *ACM Transactions on Programming Languages and Systems*, 17(6):805–843, November 1995.

[CTK94] Weimin Chen, Volker Turau, and Wolfgang Klas. Efficient dynamic look-up strategy for multi-methods. In M. Tokoro and R. Pareschi, editors, *Proceedings ECOOP '94*, LNCS 821, pages 408–431, Bologna, Italy, July 1994. Springer-Verlag.

[HHM90a] J. Hamer, J.G. Hosking, and W.B. Mugridge. A method for integrating classification within an object-oriented environment. Technical Report Auckland Computer Science Report No. 48, Department of Computer Science, University of Auckland, October 1990.

[HHM90b] J.G. Hosking, J. Hamer, and W.B. Mugridge. Integrating functional and object-oriented programming. In *Technology of Object-Oriented Languages and Systems TOOLS 3*, pages 345–355, Sydney, 1990.

[HJW+92] Paul Hudak, Simon Peyton Jones, Philip Wadler, Brian Boutel, Jon Fairbairn, Joseph Fasel, Maria Guzman, Kevin Hammond, John Hughes, Thomas Johnsson, Dick Kieburtz, Rishiyur Nikhil, Will Partain, and John Peterson. Report on the programming language Haskell, version 1.2. *SIGPLAN Notices*, 27(5), May 1992.

[KM89] Paris C. Kanellakis and John C. Mitchell. Polymorphic unification and ML typing. In ACM-SIGPLAN ACM-SIGACT, editor, *Conference Record of the 16th Annual ACM Symposium on Principles of Programming Languages (POPL '89)*, pages 105–115, Austin, TX, USA, January 1989. ACM Press.

[KR89] Gregor Kiczales and Luis Rodriguez. Efficient method dispatch in PCL. Technical Report SSL 89-95, Xerox PARC Systems Sciences Laboratory, 1989.

[MHH91] Warwick B. Mugridge, John Hamer, and John G. Hosking. Multi-methods in a statically-typed programming language. In P. America, editor, *Proceedings ECOOP '91*, LNCS 512, pages 307–324, Geneva, Switzerland, July 15-19 1991. Springer-Verlag.

[MTH90] Robin Milner, Mads Tofte, and Robert Harper. *The Definition of Standard ML*. MIT Press, 1990.

[OW97] Martin Odersky and Philip Wadler. Pizza into Java: Translating theory into practice. In *Conference Record of the 24th ACM SIGPLAN-SIGACT Symposium on Principles of Programming Languages*, pages 146–159, January 1997.

[Ste90] Guy L. Steele Jr. *Common Lisp: The Language.* Digital Press, Bedford, MA, 1990. Second edition.

[Tai93] Antero Taivalsaari. Object-oriented programming with modes. *Journal of Object-Oriented Programming*, pages 25–32, June 1993.

[Wad87] Philip Wadler. Views: A way for pattern matching to cohabit with data abstraction. In *Proceedings of the Fourteenth Annual ACM Symposium on Principles of Programming Languages*, pages 307–313, Munich, Germany, January 1987.

[Zel93] John M. Zelle. Learning search-control heuristics for logic programs: Applications tospeed-up learning and languageacquisitions. Technical Report AI93-200, University of Texas, Austin, May 1, 1993.

A Desugaring rules

The following rewrite rules desugar the high-level syntax of Fig. 6 into the core abstract syntax of Fig. 2. The rules are grouped by their intention, such as providing names for arbitrary expressions or breaking down compound predicate abstractions.

For brevity, we omit the rewrite rules which introduce defaults for omitted optional program fragments: dummy variables for pattern variables, "`@Any`" specializers, empty field pattern sets in specializers, and "**when true**" and "**return { }**" clauses. Additional rules may be introduced to simplify the resulting formula, such as converting "v @ `Any`" to "**true**" and performing logical simplification.

For brevity, we use $\bigwedge_{i=1}^{n} \{P_i\}$ to stand for the conjunction of the terms: P_1 **and**... **and** P_n. When $n = 0$, $\bigwedge_{i=1}^{n} \{P_i\}$ stands for **true**. Variables v' and v'_i are new variables which do not appear elsewhere in the program. Ceiling braces $\lceil\cdot\rceil$ surround (potentially) sugared expressions; application of the rewrite rules eliminates those braces.

A.1 Declarations

These rules move specializers from formal lists into **when** clauses.

$\lceil$**method** $m(v_1 \mathbin{@} S_1, \ldots, v_n \mathbin{@} S_n)$ **when** P *Body*$\rceil$

  $\Longrightarrow$ **method** $m(v_1, \ldots, v_n)$ **when** $\bigwedge_{i=1}^{n} \{\lceil v_i \mathbin{@} S_i\rceil\}$ **and** $\lceil P\rceil$ *Body*

$\lceil$**predicate** $p(v_1 \mathbin{@} S_1, \ldots, v_n \mathbin{@} S_n)$ **when** P **return** $\{f_1 := E_1, \ldots, f_m := E_m\}\rceil$

  $\Longrightarrow$ **predicate** $p(v_1, \ldots, v_n)$

    when $\bigwedge_{i=1}^{n} \{\lceil v_i \mathbin{@} S_i\rceil\}$ **and** $\lceil P\rceil$ $\lceil$**return** $\{f_1 := E_1, \ldots, f_m := E_m\}\rceil$

method-sig	::=	**signature** *method-id* (⟨ *type* ⟩) : *type*	
method-decl	::=	**method** *method-id* (⟨ *formal-pattern* ⟩) [**when** *pred-expr*] *method-body*	
pred-sig	::=	**predsignature** *pred-id* (⟨ *type* ⟩) [**return** { ⟨ *field-id* : *type* ⟩ }]	
pred-decl	::=	**predicate** *pred-id* (⟨ *formal-pattern* ⟩) [**when** *pred-expr*] [**return** { ⟨ *field-id* := *expr* ⟩ }]	
classifier-decl	::=	**classify** (⟨ *formal-pattern* ⟩) ⟨ **as** *pred-id* **when** *pred-expr* [**return** { ⟨ *field-id* := *expr* ⟩ }] ⟩ [**as** *pred-id* **otherwise** [**return** { ⟨ *field-id* := *expr* ⟩ }]]	
$P, Q \in$ *pred-expr*	::=	*expr* @ *specializer*	succeeds if *expr* evaluates to a value that satisfies *specializer*
	|	**test** *expr*	succeeds if *expr* evaluates to *true*
	|	**let** *var-id* := *expr*	evaluate *expr* and bind *var-id* to its value; always succeeds
	|	*pred-id* (⟨ *expr* ⟩) [=> { ⟨ *field-pat* ⟩ }]	test predicate abstraction
	|	**true**	always succeeds
	|	**false**	never succeeds
	|	**not** *pred-expr*	negation
	|	*pred-expr* **and** *pred-expr*	conjunction (short-circuited)
	|	*pred-expr* **or** *pred-expr*	disjunction (short-circuited)
formal-pattern	::=	[*var-id*] [@ *specializer*]	like *var-id*@*specializer* in *pred-expr*
$F \in$ *field-pat*	::=	*field-id* [= *var-id*] [@ *specializer*]	
$S \in$ *specializer*	::=	*class-spec* [{ ⟨ *field-pat* ⟩ }]	
$C \in$ *class-spec*	::=	*class-id*	*expr* @ *class-id* is a class test
	|	*pred-id*	*expr* @ *pred-id* [{ ... }] is sugar for *pred-id*(*expr*) [=>{ ... }]
	|	**not** *class-spec*	succeeds if *class-spec* does not
	|	*class-spec* & *class-spec*	succeeds if both *class-specs* do
	|	*class-spec* | *class-spec*	succeeds if either *class-spec* does

Fig. 6. Full extended abstract syntax for predicate dispatching. The syntax is as presented incrementally in Sect. 2, with the addition of the **true** and **false** predicate expressions and the **not**, &, and | class specializers. Words and symbols in **boldface** represent terminals. Angle brackets denote zero or more comma-separated repetitions of an item. Square brackets contain optional expressions. Each predicate may be defined only once (App. B relaxes this restriction), and recursive predicates are forbidden.

A.2 Naming of non-variable expressions

The core language permits arbitrary expressions only in **let** bindings and uses variable references elsewhere. These rules introduce **let** bindings and are intended to fire only once (alternately, only if one of the E expressions is not a mere variable reference), lest the @ and predicate application rules cause an infinite loop in desugaring.

$$\lceil E \mathbin{@} S \rceil \Longrightarrow \textbf{let } v' := E \textbf{ and } \lceil v' \mathbin{@} S \rceil$$

$\lceil$**test** $E\rceil \Longrightarrow$ **let** $v' := E$ **and test** v'
$\lceil p(E_1, \ldots, E_n)$ **=>** $\{F_1, \ldots, F_m\}\rceil$
$\Longrightarrow \bigwedge_{i=1}^{n} \{$**let** $v'_i := E_i\}$ **and** $\lceil p(v'_1, \ldots, v'_n)$ **=>** $\{F_1, \ldots, F_m\}\rceil$
$\lceil$**return** $\{f_1 := E_1, \ldots, f_m := E_m\}\rceil$
$\Longrightarrow$ **and** $\bigwedge_{i=1}^{m} \{$**let** $v'_i := E_i\}$ **return** $\{f_1 := v'_1, \ldots, f_m := v'_m\}$

A.3 Compound predicate expressions

These rules show how to desugar **false** and compound predicate expressions.

$$\lceil \textbf{false} \rceil \Longrightarrow \textbf{not true}$$
$$\lceil \textbf{not } P \rceil \Longrightarrow \textbf{not } \lceil P \rceil$$
$$\lceil P_1 \textbf{ and } P_2 \rceil \Longrightarrow \lceil P_1 \rceil \textbf{ and } \lceil P_2 \rceil$$
$$\lceil P_1 \textbf{ or } P_2 \rceil \Longrightarrow \lceil P_1 \rceil \textbf{ or } \lceil P_2 \rceil$$

A.4 Field bindings

Pattern matching permits arbitrarily nested tests and simultaneous matching on fields of objects, fields of predicate results, and results of arbitrary method invocations. These rules separate these varieties of record patterns and flatten tests.

We introduce the concept of a class specializer *generating* a field. A class name generates the fields in the class; a predicate name generates the fields in the predicate's **return** clause; a conjunction generates the fields generated by either of its conjuncts; and a disjunction generates the fields generated by both of its disjuncts.

If F_i is generated by $C \neq c$ for $1 \leq i \leq m < n$:
$\lceil v$ **@** $C\ \{F_1, \ldots, F_m, \ldots, F_n\}\rceil$
$\Longrightarrow \lceil v$ **@** $C\ \{F_1, \ldots, F_m\}\rceil$ **and** $\lceil v$ **@** Any $\{F_{m+1}, \ldots, F_n\}\rceil$
$\lceil v$ **@** $c\ \{f_1 = v_1$ **@** $S_1, \ldots, f_n = v_n$ **@** $S_n\}\rceil$
$\Longrightarrow v$ **@** c **and** $\bigwedge_{i=1}^{n} \{$**let** $v_i := v.f_i$ **and** $\lceil v_i$ **@** $S_i\rceil\}$
$\lceil v$ **@** $p\ \{f_1 = v_1$ **@** $S_1, \ldots, f_n = v_n$ **@** $S_n\}\rceil$
$\Longrightarrow p(v)$ **=>** $\{f_1 = v_1, \ldots, f_n = v_n\}$ **and** $\bigwedge_{i=1}^{n} \{\lceil v'$ **@** $S_i\rceil\}$

A.5 Compound predicate abstractions

These rules simplify compound predicate abstractions.

$$\lceil v \textbf{ @ not } C\{F_1, \ldots, F_m\}\rceil \Longrightarrow \textbf{not } \lceil v \textbf{ @ } C\{F_1, \ldots, F_m\}\rceil$$

If F_i, $m+1 \leq i \leq n$, is generated by C_2 (& rule only):
$\lceil v$ **@** C_1 **&** $C_2\{F_1, \ldots, F_m, \ldots, F_n\}\rceil \Longrightarrow \lceil v$ **@** $C_1\{F_1, \ldots, F_m\}\rceil$
and $\lceil v$ **@** $C_2\{F_{m+1}, \ldots, F_n\}\rceil$
$\lceil v$ **@** $C_1 \mid C_2\{F_1, \ldots, F_m\}\rceil \Longrightarrow \lceil v$ **@** $C_1\{F_1, \ldots, F_m\}\rceil$
or $\lceil v$ **@** $C_2\{F_1, \ldots, F_m\}\rceil$

A.6 Classifiers

Sequential ordering over classifier cases is enforced by creating extra predicates d_i such that d_i is true if any c_j, $j \leq i$, is true. Each c_i is true only if d_{i-1} is not (that is, no previous conjunct was true).

$$\left\lceil \begin{array}{l} \textbf{classify}(v_1 \mathbin{@} S_1, \ldots, v_m \mathbin{@} S_m) \\ \quad \textbf{as } c_1 \textbf{ when } P_1 \textbf{ return } \{f_{1,1} := v'_{1,1}, \ldots, f_{1,m_1} := v'_{1,m_1}\} \\ \quad \vdots \\ \quad \textbf{as } c_n \textbf{ when } P_n \textbf{ return } \{f_{n,1} := v'_{n,1}, \ldots, f_{n,m_n} := v'_{n,m_n}\} \\ \quad \textbf{as } c_{n+1} \textbf{ otherwise return } \{f_{n+1,1} := v'_{n+1,1}, \ldots, f_{n+1,m_{n+1}} := v'_{n+1,m_{n+1}}\} \end{array} \right\rceil$$

$$\Longrightarrow \left\lceil \begin{array}{l} \textbf{predicate } c_1(v_1 \mathbin{@} S_1, \ldots, v_m \mathbin{@} S_m) \textbf{ when } P_1 \\ \qquad \textbf{return } \{f_{1,1} := v'_{1,1}, \ldots, f_{1,m_1} := v'_{1,m_1}\}; \end{array} \right\rceil$$

$$\lceil \textbf{predicate } d_1(v_1 \mathbin{@} S_1, \ldots, v_m \mathbin{@} S_m) \textbf{ when } P_1; \rceil$$

$$\left\lceil \begin{array}{l} \textbf{predicate } c_2(v_1 \mathbin{@} S_1, \ldots, v_m \mathbin{@} S_m) \textbf{ when } P_2 \textbf{ and not } d_1(v_1, \ldots, v_m) \\ \qquad \textbf{return } \{f_{2,1} := v'_{2,1}, \ldots, f_{2,m_2} := v'_{2,m_2}\}; \end{array} \right\rceil$$

$$\lceil \textbf{predicate } d_2(v_1 \mathbin{@} S_1, \ldots, v_m \mathbin{@} S_m) \textbf{ when } d_1(v_1, \ldots, v_m) \textbf{ or } P_2; \rceil$$

$$\vdots$$

$$\left\lceil \begin{array}{l} \textbf{predicate } c_n(v_1 \mathbin{@} S_1, \ldots, v_m \mathbin{@} S_m) \textbf{ when } P_n \textbf{ and not } d_{n-1}(v_1, \ldots, v_m) \\ \qquad \textbf{return } \{f_{n,1} := v'_{n,1}, \ldots, f_{n,m_n} := v'_{n,m_n}\}; \end{array} \right\rceil$$

$$\lceil \textbf{predicate } d_n(v_1 \mathbin{@} S_1, \ldots, v_m \mathbin{@} S_m) \textbf{ when } d_{n-1}(v_1, \ldots, v_m) \textbf{ or } P_n; \rceil$$

$$\left\lceil \begin{array}{l} \textbf{predicate } c_{n+1}(v_1 \mathbin{@} S_1, \ldots, v_m \mathbin{@} S_m) \textbf{ when not } d_n(v_1, \ldots, v_m) \\ \qquad \textbf{return } \{f_{n+1,1} := v'_{n+1,1}, \ldots, f_{n+1,m_{n+1}} := v'_{n+1,m_{n+1}}\}; \end{array} \right\rceil$$

B Bindings escaping "or"

In the static and dynamic semantics presented in Sect. 3, bindings never escape from **or** predicate expressions. Relaxing this constraint provides extra convenience to the programmer and permits more values to be reused rather than recomputed. It is also equivalent to permitting overloaded predicates or multiple predicate definitions—so far we have permitted only a single definition of each predicate. With appropriate variable renaming, multiple predicate definitions that rely on a dispatching-like mechanism to select the most specific applicable method can be converted into uses of **or**, and vice versa.

For example, the two `ConstantFold` methods of Sect. 2.3 can be combined into a single method. Eliminating code duplication is a prime goal of object-oriented programming, but the previous version repeated the body twice. Use of a helper method would unnecessarily separate the dispatching conditions from the code being executed, though a helper predicate could reduce code duplication in the predicate expression.

```
-- handle case of adding zero to a non-constant
method ConstantFold(e@BinopExpr{ op@IntPlus, arg1=a1, arg2=a2 })
   when (a1@IntConst{ value=v } and test(v == 0)
        and not(a2@IntConst) and let res := a2)
    or (a2@IntConst{ value=v } and test(v == 0)
        and not(a1@IntConst) and let res := a1) {
   ... -- increment counter, or do other common work here
   return res; }
```

As another example, the **LoopExit** example of Sect. 2.4 can be extended to present a view which indicates which branch of the **CFG_2succ** is the loop exit and which the backward branch. When performing iterative dataflow, this is the only information of interest, and in our current implementation (which uses predicate classes [Cha93b]) we generally recompute this information after discovering that an object is a **LoopExit**. Presenting a view which includes this information directly would improve the code's readability and efficiency.

```
predsignature LoopExit(CFGnode)
  return { loop:CFGloop, next_loop:CFGedge, next_exit:CFGedge };
predicate LoopExit(n@CFG_2succ{ next_true: t, next_false: f })
  when (test(t.is_loop_exit) and let nl := t and let ne := f)
    or (test(f.is_loop_exit) and let nl := f and let ne := t)
  return { loop := nl.containing_loop, next_loop := nl, next_exit := ne };
```

Permitting bindings which appear on both sides of **or** to escape requires the following changes to the dynamic semantics of Fig. 4. (The third rule is unchanged from Fig. 4 but included here for completeness.)

$$\frac{\langle P, K\rangle \Rightarrow \langle \mathit{true}, K'\rangle}{\langle P \textbf{ or } Q, K\rangle \Rightarrow \langle \mathit{true}, K'\rangle}$$

$$\frac{\langle P, K\rangle \Rightarrow \langle \mathit{false}, K'\rangle \qquad \langle Q, K\rangle \Rightarrow \langle \mathit{true}, K''\rangle}{\langle P \textbf{ or } Q, K\rangle \Rightarrow \langle \mathit{true}, K''\rangle}$$

$$\frac{\langle P, K\rangle \Rightarrow \langle \mathit{false}, K'\rangle \qquad \langle Q, K\rangle \Rightarrow \langle \mathit{false}, K''\rangle}{\langle P \textbf{ or } Q, K\rangle \Rightarrow \langle \mathit{false}, K\rangle}$$

These execution rules do not reflect that only the bindings appearing on both sides, not all those appearing on the succeeding side, should escape; however, the typechecking rules below guarantee that only the appropriate variables are referenced.

The static semantics of Fig. 5 are modified to add two helper functions and replace a typechecking rule:

$T \sqcup T' = T''$	Least upper bound over types. T'' is the least common supertype of T and T'.
$\sqcup_{\text{env}}(\Gamma, \Gamma') = \Gamma''$	Pointwise lub over typing environments. For each $v \in \text{dom}(\Gamma'') = \text{dom}(\Gamma) \cap \text{dom}(\Gamma')$, if $\Gamma \models v : T$ and $\Gamma' \models v : T'$, then $\Gamma'' \models v : T \sqcup T'$.

$$\frac{\Gamma \vdash P_1 \Rightarrow \Gamma' \qquad \Gamma \vdash P_2 \Rightarrow \Gamma'' \qquad \sqcup_{\text{env}}(\Gamma', \Gamma'') = \Gamma'''}{\Gamma \vdash P_1 \textbf{ or } P_2 \Rightarrow \Gamma'''}$$

Finally, canonicalization must account for the new semantics of **or**. In order to permit replacement of variables by their values, we introduce a new compile-time-only ternary conditional operator ?: for each variable bound on both sides of the predicate. The first argument is the predicate expression on the left-hand side of the **or** expression; the second and third arguments are the variable's values on each side of the **or**.

Canonicalizing this new ?: expression requires ordering the tests canonically; any ordering will do. This may necessitate duplication of some expressions, such as transforming $b\ ?\ e_1 : (a\ ?\ e_2 : e_3)$ into $a\ ?\ (b\ ?\ e_1 : e_2) : (b\ ?\ e_1 : e_3)$ so that those two expressions are not considered distinct. With these two modifications, the tautology test is once again sound and complete.

Orthogonal to the Java Imperative *

Suad Alagić, Jose Solorzano, and David Gitchell

Department of Computer Science
Wichita State University
Wichita, KS 67260-0083, USA
alagic@cs.twsu.edu

Abstract. Three nontrivial limitations of the existing Java^{TM} technology are considered from the viewpoint of object-oriented database technology. The limitations are: lack of support for orthogonal persistence, lack of parametric (and in fact bounded and F-bounded) polymorphism and lack of an assertion (constraint) language. These limitations are overcome by leaving Java as it is, and developing a declarative (query in particular) component of the Java technology. This declarative language is implemented on top of the Java Virtual Machine, extended with orthogonal and transitive persistence. The model of persistence also features complex name space management.
Keywords: Declarative languages, orthogonal persistence, F-bounded polymorphism, Java Virtual Machine.

1 Introduction

In spite of the fact that Java^{TM} [17] is a product of good language design, it exhibits several serious limitations with respect to object-oriented database management. A perfectly valid justification is that it was probably never conceived as a database programming language. Yet, some of these database-critical features are important for object-oriented programming in general.

The first such limitation is, of course, the lack of support for persistence. Persistence is a key feature of object-oriented database technology [10].

The second limitation is the absence of parametric polymorphism. This limitation is particularly critical in database management because most database technologies rely heavily on collections. Static typing of collections in Java is impossible, and so is static typing of queries. Awkward type casts and extensive dynamic type checks are required, affecting both efficiency and reliability.

The third limitation is the lack of an assertion language. Such declarative capabilities for expressing preconditions, postconditions and class invariants are important for object-oriented programming in general ([24], [22], [25]). Moreover, constraints and other declarative language features (including queries) are critical for any viable database technology.

* This material is based upon work supported in part by the U.S. Army Research Office under grant no. DAAH04-96-1-0192.

Several projects are under way, extending the Java technology with persistence [11], parametric polymorphism ([27], [9]) and even queries [15].

The projects extending the language with parametric polymorphism necessarily require changing the language, but they do not necessarily change the Java Virtual Machine.

Java OQL [15] does not change the language, but supporting queries as methods and as objects requires run-time reflection [3] where the standard notion of static typing is extended to dynamic compilation. In addition, persistence capabilities are required in the underlying architecture.

PJama (formerly PJAVA) [11] provides orthogonal persistence without changing the language, but it requires an extension of the Java Virtual Machine. The Java Virtual Machine is specified in [23].

The approach that we take in extending the Java technology with database capabilities is different from any of the above. We do not change the language in spite of its limitations. We leave Java as it is. But we develop a declarative language with all the desired features discussed above and make it fit into the existing Java technology. An extension of the Java Virtual Machine is still required in order to support a sophisticated and orthogonal model of persistence in order to implement this declarative language.

The declarative language *MyT* presented in this paper makes it possible to express preconditions, postconditions and class invariants. This addresses the problem of the lack of assertions in Java. But the constraint language goes further in allowing declarative specification of methods.

The constraint language has its limitations in expressiveness ([2], [4]). Just like data languages, it is not computationally complete. But it covers a variety of non-trivial applications [6] and it is integrated into the Java programming environment by allowing references to Java classes.

On the other hand, Java classes can access persistent objects and their classes, which are created by *MyT*. Java classes can also naturally create persistent classes and objects without any references to *MyT* facilities. This is done by simply relying on PJama, and possibly on our name space management extension.

Java is not a persistent programming language. *MyT* features an orthogonal model of persistence and transitive persistence (persistence by reachability). Unlike all other approaches, persistence capabilities in this model are associated with the root (top) class. This way all classes are persistence capable. The model is naturally based on reachability. In addition, this model of persistence features hierarchical name space management, extending the existing Java mechanism based on packages. Such complex name space management is lacking in persistent supporting Java extensions, such as PJama [11].

Collection classes are critical for object-oriented database technologies. Typing generic collection classes in Java has well-known problems. The best we can do is to specify generic collection classes whose elements are of type *Object*. Accessing such collections requires type casts, which means dynamic type checks.

Thus static type checking of typical declarative constructs, queries in particular, cannot be performed in the Java type system.

Because of this, the constraint language supports parametric polymorphism, thus overcoming this serious drawback of Java in database applications [3]. The form of parametric polymorphism is F-bounded [14], so it allows proper typing of ordered collections and indices ([8], [3]).

Unlike the existing Java preprocessor systems, this system is a real compiler that generates Java byte code. In addition, a real novelty of this compiler is that it generates methods from declarative constraints. This in particular includes proper treatment of preconditions, postconditions and class invariants in the generated code.

A class in the declarative constraint language is translated into a Java class file. This must be done in such a way that the generated file passes the Java verification test. This test was designed to recognize class files that are generated by a possibly hostile compiler. This is precisely one of the reasons why several Java extending projects are based on preprocessors. Our compiler generates Java class files directly.

The constraint language naturally supports queries. Queries refer to persistent collections. They can be statically type checked, which would not be possible in the type system underlying Java or Java OQL ([15], [3]). The run-time support includes algorithms that operate on the complex implementation architecture for persistent collections. This architecture includes access paths implemented via extendible hashing, or as indices.

The paper is organized as follows. In section 2 we introduce the constraint language, its logic basis, collection classes and queries. In section 3 we introduce advanced typing techniques available in *MyT* (bounded and F-bounded type quantification). In section 4 we introduce our model of persistence, and name space management as supported by environments. In section 5 we describe the underlying persistence implementation architecture. In section 6 we describe our implementation techniques for F-bounded polymorphism, along with the specifics of Java class file representation. Section 7 deals with compilation issues, which include proper management of Java class files and Java byte code generation from the constraint language.

2 The constraint language

2.1 The logic basis

The declarative language *MyT* has a logic basis that is in fact temporal [4]. This point is not particularly significant for the main results of this paper. Other logic basis are also possible, and the results would apply to many of those. However, the logic basis should be able to express typical types of assertions in object-oriented programming, such as preconditions, postconditions, class invariants, history properties, etc.

The underlying temporal paradigm is intentionally simple. It is based on the notion of time, that is discrete and linear, extending infinitely to the future.

This paradigm and the full-fledged temporal constraint language are elaborated in full detail in separate papers ([2], [4]).

Illustrative examples of classes presented in this paper make use of only two temporal operators. The operator *always* is denoted as $\Box$. If C is a constraint, then $\Box C$ is true in the current state iff C evaluates to true in all object states, starting with the current one. The operator *nexttime* is denoted as $\bigcirc$. The constraint $\bigcirc C$ is true in the current state iff the constraint C is true in the next object state.

The constraints are expressed by temporal Horn clauses. Standard Horn clauses have the form $A \leftarrow B_1, B_2, ..., B_n$, where A is the head, $B_1, B_2, ..., B_n$ is the body of the clause, $A, B_1, B_2, ..., B_n$ are atomic predicates, $\leftarrow$ denotes implication and comma denotes conjunction. The constraint language, in addition, allows the temporal operators to appear in temporal Horn-clauses.

There are restrictions on the usage of the temporal operators in the constraint language. These rules limit the expressive power of the language, but at the same time they guarantee the existence of the execution model of the language, and its formal semantics [5]. In spite of its limitations, the language allows a wide variety of database oriented applications to be handled in a high-level, declarative manner.

2.2 Collection classes

The constraint language will be illustrated by samples of collection classes. The class *Collection* given below is equipped with a predicate method *belongs* indicating whether its argument belongs to a collection object, the receiver of the message. Messages of this type are called *observers*. The corresponding Java term is *accessor methods*. These messages allow inspection of the underlying hidden object state.

The *Collection* class is equipped with two mutator methods *insert* and *delete* that change the underlying object state. The constraint section specifies the effect of the mutator messages on the only observer of the collection object state. The constraints illustrate how *preconditions* and *postconditions* are specified in the constraint language.

Class Collection[T]
Observers
belongs(T)
Mutators
insert(T); delete(T)
Constraints
ForAll X:T;
$\Box$(self.belongs(X) $\leftarrow$ self.delete(X)),
$\Box$($\bigcirc$self.belongs(X) $\leftarrow$ self.insert(X))
End Collection.

The *precondition* for deletion of an element X is that the element X belongs to the collection, hence the constraint $\Box$(self.belongs(X) $\leftarrow$ self.delete(X)). The *postcondition* for inserting X into the collection is that after the insertion X belongs to the collection. This is expressed using the next state operator ◯ in the constraint □(◯self.belongs(X) ← self.insert(X)). The always operator □ is used because these constraints apply to all object states.

Consider now a class *Bag* derived by inheritance from the class *Collection*. *Bag* has an additional observer method *occurs* which specifies how many times the first argument of this method belongs to the underlying *Bag* object. In addition, *Bag* introduces two constructor methods *union* and *intersect*.

The *initial constraint* new(Bag[T]).occurs(X,0) ← specifies the initial state of a bag object when its is created by a new message.

The constraint $\Box(self.belongs(X) \leftarrow self.occurs(X, N), N.gtr(0))$ is a *class invariant*. It involves the observer methods only. It applies to all object states and thus the only temporal operator used is always.

The *transition constraints* □(◯self.occurs(X, N.succ()) ← self.occurs(X, N), self.insert(X)) and □(◯self.occurs(X, N.pred()) ← self.occurs(X, N), self.delete(X)) specify the effect of the inherited mutators *insert* and *delete* on the newly introduced observer *occurs*.

Finally, the *constructor constraints* □(self.union(B).occurs(X, M.max(N)) ← self.occurs(X, M), B.occurs(X,N)) and □(self.intersect(B).occurs(X, M.min(N)) ← self.occurs(X, M), B.occurs(X, N)) specify the observer *occurs* of the bag object constructed by the *union* and *intersect* methods.

Class Bag[T]
Inherits Collection
Observers
occurs(T, Natural)
Constructors
union(Bag[T]): Bag[T],
intersect(Bag[T]): Bag[T]
Constraints
ForAll B: Bag[T]; X:T; M, N: Natural;
new(Bag[T]).occurs(X,0) ←,
□(self.belongs(X) ← self.occurs(X, N), N.gtr(0)),
□(◯self.occurs(X, N.succ()) ← self.occurs(X, N), self.insert(X)),
□(◯self.occurs(X, N.pred()) ← self.occurs(X, N), self.delete(X)),
□(self.union(B).occurs(X, M.max(N)) ← self.occurs(X, M), B.occurs(X,N)),
□(self.intersect(B).occurs(X, M.min(N)) ← self.occurs(X, M), B.occurs(X, N))
End Bag.

2.3 Queries

It should come as no surprise that queries are objects in this system. By way of comparison, incorporating OQL query capabilities into Java comes with nontrivial problems [3]. These problems are manifested by Java OQL [15], which requires run-time reflection (or dynamic compilation) as an implementation technique.

The type of reflective techniques required for a type safe implementation of Java OQL have been developed for other persistent object systems ([16], [12]).

But these techniques are by no means trivial, and go beyond the bounds of the usual static type checking techniques. *MyT* queries can be statically type checked, as one would naturally expect.

The core of the query capabilities is the predefined parametric class Query[T] equipped with an observer *qualification* and a constructor *eval*. The latter takes the queried collection as its argument and produces the collection which represents the result of the query. The objects that appear in the result of the query are those that satisfy *qualification*. This is easily expressed in the constraint section of this class.

Class Query[T]
Observers
qualification(T)
Constructors
eval(Collection[T]): Collection[T]
Constraints
ForAll X: T; S: Collection[T];
□(self.eval(S).belongs(X) ← S.belongs(X), self.qualification(X))
End Query.

A specific query is obtained by instantiating the above class, as in the example given below:

Class MyQuery[Employee]
Inherits Query[Employee]
Constraints
ForAll X: Employee; N: Real;
□(self.qualification(X) ← X.job("programmer"), X.salary(N), N.gtr(70,000.00))
End MyQuery.

3 The type system

The type system consists of three levels. The third (topmost) level consists of a single object *Class*. Instances of *Class* are classes. These are second-level objects. Instances of classes are first-level objects. This view fits the Java type system. In addition, it fits the orthogonal model of persistence which supports reachability.

The formal development of the type system is not the topic of this paper. It is given in a separate paper [4] together with a proof of its type safety. The type system of full-fledged *MyT* is based on self types ([1], [13]). The type system underlying this paper is more restrictive in order to make it compatible with the Java type system. Self types and multiple dispatch required for their type-safe implementation are thus omitted.

3.1 Bounded type quantification

A simple form of parametric polymorphism used in the above sample collection classes does not cover very important situations required in most database technologies. Queries often produce ordered collections and query evaluation algorithms often require ordered collections. A typical access path used in query evaluation is an index. Persistent collections in database systems thus may be ordered and equipped with indices. Proper typing of such collections requires bounded type quantification (constrained genericity in Eiffel ([24], [25])) and even F-bounded type quantification ([14], [8], [3]) in the type parameter section of a class.

An ordered collection may be specified using bounded type quantification as follows:

Class OrderedCollection[T **Inherits** Ordered]
Inherits Collection[T]
...
End OrderedCollection.

The class *Ordered* used to constraint the type parameter of the class *OrderedCollection* is given below:

Class Ordered
Observers
lessThan(Any)
...
End Ordered.

3.2 F-bounded polymorphism

Using *Any* as the type of the argument of the ordering method *lessThan* obviously leads to dynamic type checking. Static typing of ordered collections is accomplished by making the class *Ordered* parametric:

Class Ordered[T]
Observers
lessThan(T)
...
End Ordered.

An ordered collection may now be defined using F-bounded polymorphism as follows:

Class OrderedCollecton[T **Inherits** Ordered[T]]
Inherits Collection[T]
...
End OrderedCollection.

Proper and static typing of the *Index* class involves both bounded and F-bounded type quantification [3].

Class Index[T0 **Inherits** Ordered[T0], T **Inherits** T0]
Constructors
select(T0): Collection[T]
...
End Index.

In the above class $T0$ denotes the type of the search attributes. $T0$ must be equipped with an ordering method *lessThan*, hence the F-bounded condition $T0$ **Inherits** *Ordered*[$T0$]. T stands for the type of elements of the indexed collection, hence the bounded condition T **Inherits** $T0$. The constructor *select* returns the set of all objects of the underlying collection with the given value of the search attributes supplied as the argument of the *select* method.

A technique related to F-bounded polymorphism is called matching [1], and it is perhaps more intuitive and easier to grasp. It should be noted that these more advanced typing notions come with a price. The underlying type system becomes more complex [18], and it may even be undecidable [28].

4 Persistence

4.1 Model of orthogonal persistence

The underlying model of persistence has the following fundamental properties:

- *Persistence is orthogonal to the class hierarchy.* Objects of any level and of any type may be persistent.
- *Persistence is transparent to clients.* This means that clients do not move objects to and from stable storage, nor do they deal with files, etc.
- *Persistence is per-object based.* Objects of a particular class may be persistent or transient, and in fact there may be in general objects of both kinds for a given class.
- *Persistence is based on message-passing.* An object is promoted to persistence by sending a *persists* message to that object.
- *Persistence is complete with respect to observable properties of objects.* This property is known as *reachability* or *transitive persistence.* It guarantees that all observable properties of a persistent object are well-defined even though they may in fact refer to other objects.
- *The model of persistence guarantees type safety.*

Orthogonal persistence is accomplished by *placing message based persistence capabilities in the root class Any*. This is a distinctive feature of this model of persistence. This model is truly object-oriented, as it is based on *message passing and inheritance*, unlike other published models that we are aware of.

We mention another project that shares similar ideas on the model of persistence for Java [21]. Although JavaSPIN does not associate the method *persist* with the class *Object*, its Java preprocessor accomplishes this effect by incorporating this method in the generated classes.

A partial specification of the predefined class *Any* is:

Class Any
Observers
persistent()
Mutators
persists()
Constraints
$\square(\bigcirc$self.persistent() $\leftarrow$ self.persists())
End Any.

The same message based passing mechanism applies to classes, instances of the class *Class*.

4.2 Environments

The second component of the model of persistence allows name space management based on environments. As persistence is orthogonal to the type (class) hierarchy, name space management is controlled by an orthogonal mechanism. This is in sharp contradistinction to Napier [26], which has a type **env**, and Eiffel [24], which has a class ENVIRONMENT. In addition, Napier is not object-oriented, and the support for persistence in Eiffel is low-level, and not part of the language.

Name space management is controlled in Java by packages. But a package is a collection of related classes. An environment is more general in that it may contain both objects and classes. This is exactly what is needed in persistent and database applications. It is also a consequence of orthogonality. In particular, a database schema is an environment. Indeed, it contains both types and objects (typically collections) of those types.

An environment is simply a set of (*identifier*,*object*) bindings. Objects may belong to any level, i.e., they may be classes or objects. All identifiers in an environment are, of course, distinct. Predefined bindings that cannot be changed include those that apply to *Class*, *Any*, standard primitive types, collection classes, query class, etc. The root of persistence is the environment *Main* which cannot be dropped. *Main* always contains bindings for *Class* and *Any*.

An environment establishes a *scope* which can be dynamically created, extended or shrunk. When an object is promoted to longevity by a *persists* message, a new binding is introduced for this object in the currently valid scope. Scopes can be nested in such a way that the classical scoping rules apply: bindings in an inner scope are invisible in its outer scope, and bindings in the outer scope are visible (unless redefined) in the inner scope.

When an environment is open, all its bindings are made visible, so that objects in the environment can be referred to just by their names. There is no difference in referencing transient objects declared in a class and persistent objects.

Opening a scope is accomplished by a **With** block which is illustrated below. **With** block is also a unit of user interaction with the environment consisting of a collection of objects and their classes. Similar effects are accomplished in Java by package import clauses.

```
With Main
    Class ThreeDObject
    ...
    End ThreeDObject;
    Class MovingObject
    Inherits ThreeDObject
    ...
    End MovingObject;
    Environment MyEnvironment;
    With MyEnvironment
    Class Shuttle
    Inherits Moving Object
    ...
    End Shuttle;
    MyShuttle: Shuttle
    End MyEnvironment
End Main.
```

The outer **With** block opens the main environment. It then creates two classes *ThreeDObject* and *MovingObject* in the main environment, the second one derived by inheritance from the first. Another environment *MyEnvironment* is also created within the main environment. The inner **With** block introduces two bindings in the inner environment. *Shuttle* is bound to a class derived from the class *MovingObject* and *MyShuttle* is bound to an object of class *Shuttle*.

5 Persistence implementation architecture

Compiled *MyT* code runs on the PJama Virtual Machine. The PJama Virtual Machine is an extension of the Java Virtual Machine with persistence capabilities. PJama ([11], [20]) provides an interface *PJStore* and its implementation for managing persistent objects in Java. A simplified *PJStore* interface has the following form:

```
interface PJStore
{   ...
    public static PJStore getStore();
    public void newPRoot(String,Object);
    public void setPRoot(String,Object);
    public Object getPRoot(String);
}
```

In order to make an object persistent, an object representing the persistent store must be first made available by the method *getStore*. The method *newPRoot* is then invoked on this *PJStore* object. Its arguments are the name of the object and the object itself. The effect of invoking *newPRoot* is to introduce a binding of the argument name to the argument object in the persistent store. This promotes the argument object to persistence and makes it accessible by the name provided as the first argument of *newPRoot*. Furthermore, all objects referred to directly or indirectly by the newly promoted object are also promoted to longevity. PJama thus supports ***persistence by reachability*** or ***transitive persistence.***

PJama's model of persistence is ***orthogonal.*** However, the model of persistence in *MyT* is more sophisticated. Its distinctive features include ***persistence capabilities in the root class*** and ***hierarchical name space management.*** The name space management model allows references to transient and persistent objects without differentiation. This more sophisticated model of persistence has been implemented by developing a library of classes which is, of course, not only useful as part of *MyT*'s runtime system, but also as an addition to PJama.

The limitation of the PJama's flat name-space has been overcome by mostly ignoring its naming scheme altogether. For all practical purposes, we make PJama aware of only one named object, an instance of class *Environment* we call *Main. Environment* is *not* a public class. The underlying persistence implementation architecture is naturally completely hidden from *MyT* users.

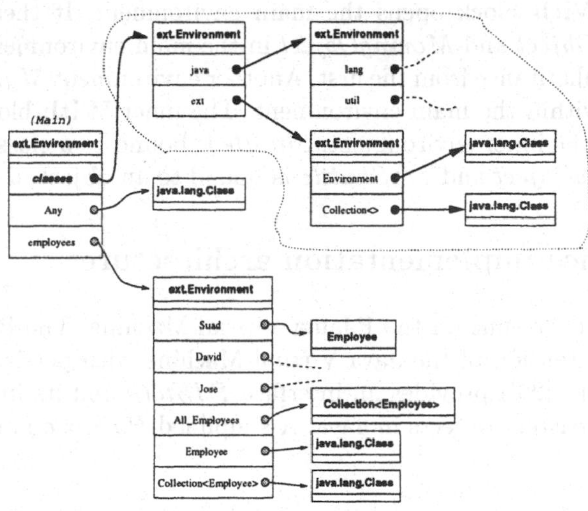

Fig. 1. ***Illustration of a hypothetical environment graph of persistent objects in the MyT naming scheme***

In order to implement the class *Environment*, we use one of Java's well-known classes, *Hashtable*. PJama's reachability capabilities take care of the rest; that is, anything reachable from *Main* is, of course, persistent.

Figure 1 illustrates what a hypothetical naming graph may look like in this scheme. Note that standard Java classes appear in the *Main* environment except that their names reflect Java conventions related to packages. Other classes intended for general use, such as *Collection*, should also be in *Main*.

```
class Environment
{   Environment getParent();
    boolean isParent (Environment env);
    boolean isRoot();
    void addBinding (String name, Object obj);
    void removeBinding (String name);
    Object lookup (String name);
    void with(); // open a scope
    void close(); // close a scope
    private Hashtable aHashtable;
}
```

The class *Environment* is not directly accessible to the users. The methods of the class *Environment* are invoked indirectly through static methods of another class, called *Scoping*, which is public.

The implementation of *Environment* is actually quite straightforward. Methods *addBinding* and *removeBinding* simply invoke *Hashtable.add* and *Hashtable.remove*, respectively. Method *getParent* returns a reference to the parent environment, or *null* if invoked on the main environment. Method *lookup* is implemented recursively as follows:

```
public Object lookup (String name)
{ Object obj = aHashtable.get(name);
   if (obj == null && isRoot() == false)
         obj=getParent().lookup (name);
   return obj;
}
```

A Java programmer would normally use the *PJStore* interface to manage persistent objects. In the underlying persistent implementation architecture, objects are made persistent by invoking the method *Scoping.addBinding*. In the *MyT* user model, persistence capabilities are associated with the root class *Any*. The class *Any* has a method named *persists* which promotes its receiver object to longevity. The method *persists* is implemented simply as follows.

```
void persists (String name)
{ Scoping.addBinding (name, this);
}
```

6 Implementing F-bounded polymorphism

6.1 The technique

There are several general techniques for implementing parametric polymorphism in an object oriented programming language:

- Creation of specialized code for each instantiated class. This is also known as a *heterogeneous translation* [27].

- Creation of generic code shared by all instantiated classes. The code is ready to be executed without modification. This is also known as a *homogeneous translation* [27].
- Creation of generic code with tags. The code is modified upon class loading of instantiated classes. This approach has been reported in [9] and it is referred to as *load-time expansion* or *load-time instantiation*.

C++ uses the first technique through substitution of the actual type (class) parameters in the template source code during compilation. It is arguable whether Java or *MyT* could ever implement any form of textual substitution, since the design philosophy of both languages does not require the source code of external classes to be available during compilation. Nevertheless, a heterogeneous translation can be achieved in these systems by having the compiler create a specialized class file from a template every time a generic class is instantiated. An obvious shortcoming of this approach is that it may unnecessarily clutter up the file system with an excessive number of files that differ only in the actual type parameters.

The designers of Pizza — a superset of Java with parametric polymorphism and other features — claim that they have achieved both homogeneous and heterogeneous translations in their system [27]. It seems, however, that the current distribution supports a homogeneous translation only. This is in fact the preferred approach since it only requires modification of the compiler (which is always necessary) and does not generate redundant class files.

A homogeneous translation is accomplished in Pizza by generating a valid Java class file from a parametric class with the bound type in place of the type parameter. This technique is possible because Java is based on single dispatch, so that the types of arguments of a message do not affect the selection of the method at run-time.

Load-time instantiation, which is the proposal found in [9], is attractive because of its simple implementation. The changes to the compiler are in all likelihood minimal, as well as the extensions of the *ClassLoader* class. Furthermore, this approach does not clutter up the file system. Note that the Java technology allows the *ClassLoader* class to be extended so that it can deal with class files representing parametric classes. This feature has been used in [9], in our project, and in other Java extending projects.

The main problem of load-time instantiation as used in [9] is that it requires class files extended with appropriately encoded type constraints. These class files are not valid Java class files, and are transformed into valid Java class files by the extended loader. There are many potential problems with two forms of class files, one of which is not legal.

The technique presented in this paper offers two advantages with respect to the above two. Class files generated from parametric classes are always valid Java class files, as in Pizza. In addition, the type information about instantiated generic classes is specific and available at run-time, which is not the case in Pizza.

In the source code of a *MyT* class specification, both persistent and transient (local) objects are treated equally. That is, objects are referred to by their names, and there is no need to invoke a method that retrieves an object from the store. In PJama the programmer must explicitly invoke a method named *getPRoot* to retrieve an object from the store [11]. All a Java compiler can assume is that the object returned by this method is an instance of *Object*.

In *MyT* the compiler must be aware of the precise types of persistent objects in order to type-check the source code correctly. This is not a problem with instances of non-generic classes, as each object always refers to the class from which it was instantiated. But for objects of ***instantiated parametric classes*** the compiler must be aware not only of the generic class, but also of the instantiation parameters, or else proper type-checking cannot be carried out.

Of course, the Pizza compiler also requires this information to be available, but the difference lies in how the actual parameters are known to the compiler. In Pizza, the instantiation parameters are obtained from the source code being compiled. In fact, only the bound type is available from the class file.

In *MyT*, the source code of an instantiation is not necessarily available for persistent objects. This type-specific information is available for the instantiated parametric classes from their class objects in the persistent store. This is the crucial difference between Pizza and *MyT*. *MyT* has been designed with a persistent store in mind, and Pizza has not. This is why *MyT* solves the problem of specific type information without affecting the validity of the Java class file representation.

In our implementation, for every parametric class the *MyT* compiler creates a generic ***abstract*** class file. In this file, each formal type parameter is substituted by its bound type, as is done in Pizza. The class file also contains information about the actual position of each formal type parameter, which is required by the compiler to be able to correctly type-check instantiations of the generic class.

For classes obtained by instantiation of the parametric class, this technique also includes the information about the actual type parameters. This information is included in the ***class name***.

The Java *ClassLoader* is extended as in [9] to read the generic class file and create appropriately instantiated class objects as explained below. This technique allows implementation of both bounded and F-bounded parametric polymorphism.

A significant difference between our approach and that of Pizza is that each instance of a generic type refers to a class whose name contains the actual type parameters of the instantiation. In Pizza, there is really no way to know — at run-time — what the actual type parameters are. Only the upper bound is available.

6.2 Class file representation

A Java class file marked ***abstract*** is generated by the compiler. This class file is used as a kind of template for the classes instantiated from the parametric class. This technique was chosen for two reasons.

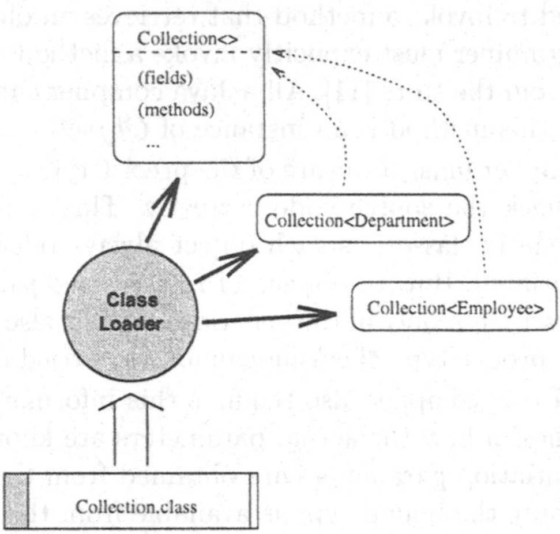

Fig. 2. ***Extended class loader handles parametric classes***

- Abstract class files are available in the Java Virtual Machine. A class file representing an abstract class is generated from a generic class substituting the bound types for the type parameters. This way we obtain a perfectly valid class file.
- Abstract classes cannot be instantiated, and thus our particular representation has no effect on the execution model of the Java Virtual Machine.

None of the actual methods in this abstract class are *in fact* abstract. These methods are completely implemented by instantiation using the bound types in place of the type parameters.

The extended class loader is used to create specific class objects from the abstract template class. These class objects can take one of two possible forms, depending upon whether it is more desirable to optimize memory usage or speed of execution.

- The first form (see fig. 3) is a nearly empty subclass of the abstract class with specific type information for the actual parameters contained in the name of this extended class.
- The second form (see fig. 4) is a complete instantiation of the parametric abstract class file, with the name of the class as in the first method, and with abstract flags cleared.

The first version has the disadvantage that it adds one level of hierarchical look-up to all messages passed to an object of an instantiated parametric class, slowing execution at run time. The second implementation version has a performance advantage over the first form by eliminating the extra level of look-up in method dispatch. It has a disadvantage over the first form because it requires more space for Java class objects. This could be a particular disadvantage if the

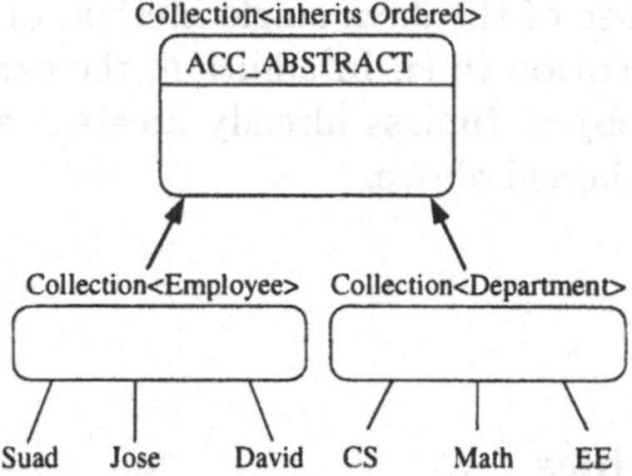

Fig. 3. *Space efficient implementation of parametric polymorphism*

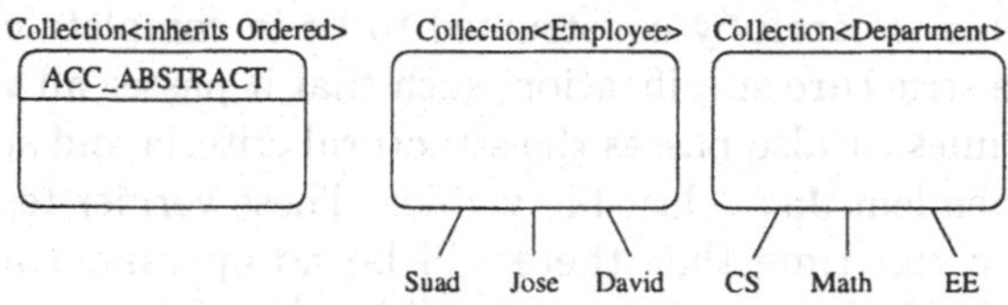

Fig. 4. *Time efficient implementation of parametric polymorphism*

same parametric class were to have numerous specific classes instantiated from it, each with different actual type parameters.

Note that class files for instantiated parametric classes are never constructed; only the class file of the parametric class exists. This is obviously an advantage of this technique. In addition, because of the technique for providing the actual type parameters for instantiated parametric classes, such files would not be valid Java class files.

The actual type information is provided in the name of the instantiated parametric class, as one might naturally expect. For example, if the name of a parametric class file is *Collection.class*, this name will appear in the class object created by the extended loader as "*Collection* <>". An example of the name of a specific instantiation of this class is "*Collection* < *Employee* >", where *Employee* is the actual type parameter. If the bound type of the type parameter of the class *Collection* is *Ordered*, the compiler will, of course, check that *Employee* extends *Ordered*. The fact that these names are not standard Java class files names for the Java compiler does not matter, as these names will be reflected only in the main memory and in the persistent store.

Consider now the actions of the extended class loader. The class loader is invoked to load a class with a given name. The standard loader must be extended in order to recognize the names of instantiated parametric classes. When such a name is detected, the abstract file representing the parametric class is loaded. This is a perfectly valid class file, as the bound type appears in place of the formal parameter. Because of the Java single method dispatch mechanism, this fact has no effect at execution time. In addition, the extended class loader also creates a specific class object (unless already created) according to one of the two possible options explained above.

7 The compiler

7.1 Managing class files

The *MyT* compiler has a collection of classes for managing Java class files. These classes allow the compiler to interpret the contents of Java class files, as well as to construct them. The latter includes byte code generation for methods.

A Java class file is carefully constructed to be in complete compliance with the Java class file structure specification, such that it passes all verification tests at load and run times. It also passes the structural criteria and static constraints tests of the independent Java class file verifier. These verifier tests are stringent and ensure before run time that there will be no operand stack overflows or underflows, that loads from and stores to all local variables are valid, and that only valid types of arguments are used for all Java Virtual Machine instructions.

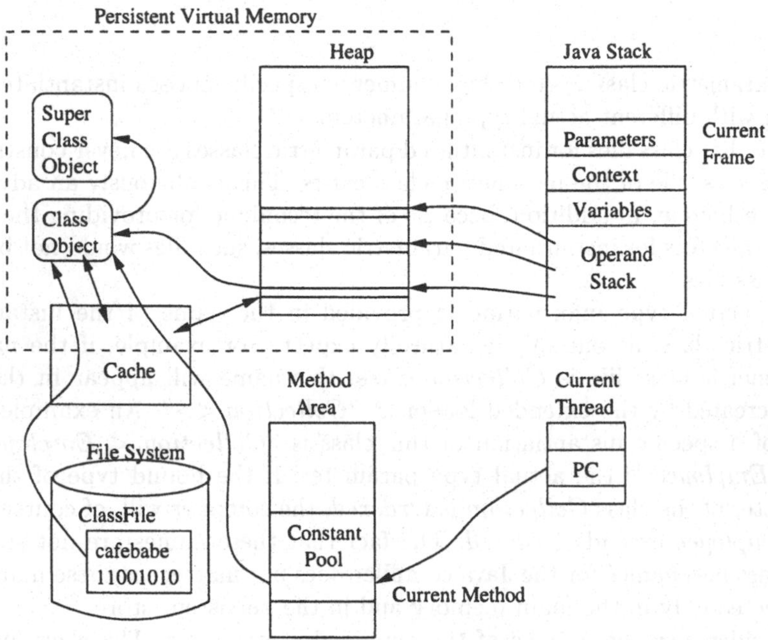

Fig. 5. *The overall architecture of the MyT system*

In PJama there exist both persistent *Class* objects and class files. The reason for this redundancy is compatibility with the Java Virtual Machine. In our system, accessing the *Class* object from the persistent store is attempted first. If the persistent *Class* object in fact exists, Java Core Reflection [19] is used to access the information on fields, methods and constructors of this class. Otherwise, the associated Java class file is located and the required information is collected from the file.

7.2 Run-time model

The run-time model for constraint evaluation is stack-oriented. It makes use of the Java stacks. A method invocation creates a new stack frame. A stack frame contains an operand stack, which is used in evaluating constraints as explained below. The run-time architecture of the system is presented in figure 5.

In a message $a.f(a_1, a_2, ..., a_n)$, $a, a_1, a_2, ..., a_n$ are terms which, when evaluated, produce object identifiers on the top of the operand stack. Before the selected method for f is invoked, $n+1$ object identifiers (the receiver and n arguments) are placed on the operand stack. Method lookup is based on the Java single dispatch mechanism. If f is a constructor, the result of method invocation will be the object identifier of the constructed object placed on the top of the operand stack after removal of $n+1$ top-level entries. If f is an observer, boolean (in fact Java int) is placed on the top of the operand stack.

Unary observers in most cases correspond to the fields of the underlying object state. n-ary observers are more subtle to implement. For collection classes (those derived from a predefined class *Collection*), an n-ary observer is implemented as a relation associated with the collection object. This relation is called an access relation [2] and consists of tuples of object identifiers for which the observer evaluates to true. Updates to the underlying collection must therefore be reflected in the associated access relations. A compressed representation of an access relation may be a dynamic index. Further details are elaborated in [2].

7.3 Evaluating constraints

- *Initial constraints*
  The simplest form of a constraint is the *initial* constraint, with the form $self.p(a_1, a_2, ..., a_n) \leftarrow$, where p is an observer and $a_1, a_2, ..., a_n$ are ground terms (i.e. terms with no variables). This form merely provides the values for setting the underlying state of the observer in the head of the implication.

- *Class invariants*
  Class invariants test whether the state of the object is acceptable. They are of the form:

  $\Box(self.p(a_1, a_2, ..., a_n) \leftarrow$
  $self.p_1(a_{11}, a_{12}, ..., a_{1n}),\ self.p_2(a_{21}, a_{22}, ..., a_{2n}),\ ...,\ self.p_k(a_{k1}, a_{k2}, ..., a_{kn}))$

  where $p, p_1, p_2, ..., p_k$ are observers.

- *Preconditions*
  Precondition constraints check that the state of the object is acceptable for the execution of a mutator, given a list of arguments to that mutator. They are of the form

  $$\Box(self.p(a_1, a_2, ..., a_n) \leftarrow self.m(a_{m1}, a_{m2}, ..., a_{mn}))$$

  where p is an observer and m is a mutator.
- *Postconditions*
  Postcondition constraints test whether the final state of the object is acceptable following the execution of a mutator, given the set of arguments to that mutator. They are of the form

  $$\Box(\bigcirc self.p(a_1, a_2, ..., a_n) \leftarrow self.m(a_{m1}, a_{m2}, ..., a_{mn}))$$

  where p is an observer and m is a mutator.
  The final state of the object following execution of a mutator must also meet the criteria of the *class invariants*, which are tested before the constraints are tested.
- *Transition constraints*
  Transition constraints actually specify changes of the state of an object, provided that the changes pass the criteria of the *precondition*, *postcondition* and *class invariant* constraints, as well as the criteria specified by the *transition* constraint itself. The form of a *transition* constraint is:

  $$\Box(\bigcirc\ self.p(a_1,\ a_2,\ ...,\ a_n) \leftarrow self.m(a_{m1}, a_{m2}, ..., a_{mn}),\ self.p_1(a_{11}, a_{12}, ..., a_{1n}),\ self.p_2(\ a_{21},\ a_{22},\ ...,\ a_{2n}),\ ...,\ self.p_k(a_{k1},\ a_{k2},\ ...,\ a_{kn}))$$

  where p, p_1, p_2, ..., p_k are observers, and m is a mutator.

Due to space limitations, we describe briefly just the evaluation of a transition constraint. When evaluating a transition constraint, the observers in the body of a transition clause are invoked in turn. If any observer returns *false*, then the transition fails. If all observers return *true*, then a temporary clone of the object is created, and the state of the observer in the head of the implication is set appropriately. The *class invariant* constraint and *postcondition* constraint methods are invoked on the clone object. If any of these constraints return *false*, then the transition fails. If all return *true*, then the transition is committed, and the state of the observer in the head of the implication in the original object is set accordingly. Of course, the overall result of a constraint evaluation is also pushing the Java integer representation of the computed logical value on top of the operand stack.

8 Conclusions

Our goal was to investigate whether the existing Java technology can be suitably extended by very non-traditional components targeted to applications in which the Java language itself has serious limitations. Our targeted application areas are database and persistent object systems. Java itself has problems in dealing with such applications since it does not support persistence, parametric polymorphism and assertions (constraints). Our goal was to accomplish this extension without changing the Java language and its Virtual Machine.

The component extending the Java technology designed and implemented in this project is in fact a statically typed, declarative object-oriented language *MyT*. The language features a high-level model of persistence, with orthogonality and reachability. Its type system is much more sophisticated than the Java type system. In particular, it supports F-bounded polymorphism. The language is in fact a constraint language, sufficiently expressive to allow assertions typical for object-oriented languages (preconditions, postconditions, class invariants, history properties). The language allows references to Java interfaces and Java classes. It supports name space management which extends similar facilities both in Java and in its persistent extensions such as PJama.

This result shows that the Java Virtual Machine is in fact a suitable implementation platform even for very non-traditional object-oriented languages. However, an extension of the Java Virtual Machine is still required in order to support persistence.

Specific techniques presented in the paper for implementing a high-level model of persistence and F-bounded polymorphism are in our opinion of general interest. The advantages of the model of persistence is that it is truly object-oriented because it is based on message passing and inheritance. It is also high-level, and naturally supports orthogonality and transitivity of persistence. In particular, the name space management model gives the impression that there is no difference between users' references to transient and persistent objects.

The advantages of the implementation technique for bounded and F-bounded polymorphism is that it makes use of valid Java class files and provides specific type information for classes obtained by instantiating parametric classes. This specific type information, missing in some other techniques, is important for systems that make use of Java Core Reflection [19]. It is also important for models of persistence that are equipped with a high-level model of name space management, like the one proposed in this paper. Last but not least, more sophisticated (multiple) method dispatch techniques will benefit from this technique.

We expect that the idea to generate Java byte code from constraints will be of interest to implementors of declarative (query in particular) object-oriented languages on top of the Java Virtual Machine. Java OQL [15] would be a particularly important example.

Parametric polymorphism is not the only desirable feature missing from the Java type system. A more expressive type system based on self types avoids problems in expressing binary methods in a natural manner ([1], [13]). The type system of the full-fledged *MyT* is in fact more general than the type system presented in this paper because it supports self types. Type safety is accomplished using a technique called constrained matching [4]. Unlike the techniques of type systems, constrained matching delegates problems that cannot be handled by the type system to the temporal constraint system. In addition, its run-time model is based on a limited form of multiple dispatch.

Although Java is based on single dispatch, the Java Virtual Machine makes it possible to implement the form of multiple dispatch technique required to support self types. This is due to the wealth of information (type information in particular) contained in a Java class file. But integrating this extension with the Java environment causes nontrivial problems in order to avoid corrupting the Java type system. This issue is left as an open problem for future research.

Due to space limitations, the implementation architecture for persistent collections has not been elaborated in this paper. A persistent collection may be equipped with multiple access paths (access relations [2]) that are implemented using dynamic indices or extensible hashing. Orthogonal persistence and persistence by reachability are thus a must in order to be able to manage correctly this complex structure of collection objects.

References

1. Abadi, M., Cardelli, L.: On Subtyping and Matching, Proceedings of ECOOP '96, *Lecture Notes in Computer Science* **1098**. Springer-Verlag (1996) 145-167.
2. Alagić, S.: A Temporal Constraint System for Object-Oriented Databases, Constraint Databases and Applications, Proceedings of CDB '97 and CP '96 Workshops, *Lecture Notes in Computer Science* **1191**. Springer-Verlag (1997) 208-218.
3. Alagić, S.: The ODMG Object Model: Does it Make Sense? Proceedings of the OOPSLA '97 Conference. ACM (1997) 253-270.
4. Alagić, S.: Constrained Matching is Type Safe, Proceedings of the 6th Database Programming Language Workshop (DBPL), 1997, *Lecture Notes in Computer Science*. Springer-Verlag (1998) (to appear).
5. Alagić, S., Alagić, M.: Order-Sorted Model Theory for Temporal Executable Specifications, *Theoretical Computer Science* **179** (1997) 273-299.
6. Alagić, S.: A Statically Typed, Temporal Object-Oriented Database Technology, *Transactions on Information and Systems* **78**. IEICE (1995) 1469-1476.
7. Alagić, S., Sunderraman, R., Bagai, R.: Declarative Object-Oriented Programming: Inheritance, Subtyping and Prototyping, Proceedings of ECOOP '94, *Lecture Notes in Computer Science* **821**. Springer-Verlag (1994) 236-259.
8. Alagić, S.: F-bounded Polymorphism for Database Programming Languages, Proceedings of the 2nd East-West Database Workshop, *Workshops in Computing*. Springer-Verlag (1994) 125-137.
9. Agesen, O., Freund, S., Mitchell, J. C.: Adding Type Parameterization to Java, Proceedings of the OOPSLA '97 Conference. ACM (1997) 49-65.
10. Atkinson, M., Bancilhon, F., DeWitt, D., Dittrich, K., Zdonik, S.: The Object-Oriented Database System Manifesto, Proceedings of the First Object-Oriented and Deductive Database Conference, Kyoto (1989) 223-240.
11. Atkinson, M., Daynes, L., Jordan, M. J., Printezis, T., Spence, S.: An Orthogonally Persistent Java^{TM}, ACM SIGMOD Record **25** (4) (1996) 68-75.
12. Atkinson, M., Morrison, R.: Orthogonally Persistent Object Systems, *VLDB Journal* **4** (1995) 319-401.
13. Bruce, K., Schuett, A., van Gent, R.: PolyTOIL: a Type-Safe Polymorphic Object Oriented Language, Proceedings of ECOOP '95, *Lecture Notes in Computer Science* **952**. Springer-Verlag (1996) 27-51.

14. Canning, P., Cook, W., Hill, W., Olthoff, W., Mitchell, J. C.: F-bounded Polymorphism for Object-Oriented Programming, Proceedings of the ACM Conference on Functional Programming Languages and Computer Architecture. ACM (1989) 273-280.
15. Cattell, R. G. G., Barry, D., Bartels, D., Berler, M., Eastman, J., Gamerman, S., Jordan, D., Springer, A., Strickland, H., Wade, D.: *The Object Database Standard: ODMG 2.0.* Morgan Kaufmann (1997).
16. Cooper, R., Kirby, G.: Type-Safe Linguistic Run-time Reflection: A Practical Perspective, Proceedings of the 6th Int. Workshop on Persistent Object Systems, *Workshops in Computing.* Springer-Verlag (1994) 331-354.
17. Gosling, J., Joy, B., Steele, G.: *The Java^{TM} Language Specification.* Addison-Wesley (1996).
18. Gawecki, A., Matthes, F.: Integrating Subtyping, Matching and Type Quantification: A Practical Perspective, Proceedings of ECOOP '96, *Lecture Notes in Computer Science* **1098**. Springer-Verlag (1996) 25-47.
19. Java Core Reflection, JDK 1.1, Sun Microsystems (1997).
20. Jordan, M.: Early Experiences with Persistent Java^{TM}, Proceedings of the First Int. Workshop on Persistence and Java, SUN Microsystems Laboratories (1996).
21. Kaplan, A., Myrestrand, G. A., Ridgeway, J. V. E., Wileden, J. C.: Our SPIN on Persistent Java^{TM}, Proceedings of the First Int. Workshop on Persistence and Java, SUN Microsystems Laboratories (1996).
22. Liskov, B., Wing, J. M.: A Behavioral Notion of Subtyping, *ACM Transactions on Programming Languages and Systems* **16** (1994) 1811-1841.
23. Lindholm, T., Yellin, F.: *The Java^{TM} Virtual Machine Specification.* Addison-Wesley (1996).
24. Meyer, B.: *Eiffel: the Language.* Prentice-Hall (1992).
25. Meyer, B.: *Object-Oriented Software Construction.* Prentice-Hall (1997).
26. Morrison, R., Brown, A. L., Connor, R., Dearle, A.: Napier88 Reference Manual, Universities of Glasgow and St. Andrews Technical Report PPRR-77-89 (1989).
27. Odersky, M., Wadler, P.: Pizza into Java: Translating Theory into Practice, Proceedings of the POPL Conference. ACM (1997) 146-159.
28. Pierce, B. C.: Bounded Quantification is Undecidable, Proceedings of the POPL Conference. ACM (1993) 305-315.

Modelling a Distributed Cached Store for Garbage Collection: The Algorithm and Its Correctness Proof*

Paulo Ferreira[1] and Marc Shapiro[2]

[1] INESC/IST, R. Alves Redol N° 9, Lisboa, Portugal
paulo.ferreira@inesc.pt
[2] INRIA Rocquencourt, B.P. 105, 78153 Le Chesnay Cedex, France
marc.shapiro@inria.fr

Abstract. Caching and persistence support efficient, convenient and transparent distributed data sharing. The most natural model of persistence is persistence by reachability, managed automatically by a garbage collector (GC). We propose a very general model of such a system (based on distributed shared memory) and a scalable, asynchronous distributed GC algorithm. Within this model, we show sufficient and widely applicable correctness conditions for the interactions between applications, store, memory, coherence, and GC.
The GC runs as a set of processes (local to each participating machine) communicating by asynchronous messages. Collection does not interfere with applications by setting locks, polluting caches, or causing I/O; this requirement raised some novel and interesting challenges which we address in this article. The algorithm is safe and live; it is not complete, *i.e.* it collects some distributed cycles of garbage but not necessarily all.

1 Introduction

We present a system, Larchant, which provides a distributed and persistent store, intended for interactive cooperative tasks. A program shares data with others, possibly running at different sites and at different times, by mapping the Larchant store in memory via a Distributed Shared Memory (DSM) mechanism [18]. Programmers may concentrate on application development; low-level issues related to distribution, replication, coherence, input/output, and memory management are handled automatically. Thus, we call Larchant a Persistent Distributed Store; it consists essentially of a large-scale DSM that is persistently backed to disk and garbage collected.

1.1 Motivation

In a centralized program, sharing consists simply of using a pointer. So-called Single Address Space Operating Systems (SASOS) such as Monads [15], Opal

* This work was supported in part by the Esprit Project PerDiS N° 22533.

[8] or Grasshopper [10] extend this simple model elegantly to distribution and persistence. In a SASOS, an object is mapped at the same address in every process ever accessing it, ensuring that pointers remain valid across address spaces and time. It uses DSM techniques to ensure consistency of distributed replicas, and memory is mapped to backup storage for persistence. However the SASOS design has two flaws. First, since every object has a fixed address for all eternity, fragmentation of the store is a serious risk. Second, it relies on programmer discipline to deallocate objects properly.

Relying on programmer discipline to deallocate objects may lead to the deletion of an object that is still referenced. This would make the store *unsafe:* some other program may fail mysteriously when using the remaining reference, possibly much later in time. Such errors are very hard to detect, and when they are, it is too late. Furthermore, failure to delete unreachable objects causes memory leaks, which clog up the store persistently.

The deallocation problem is fixed by the model of *Persistence By Reachability* [3]. Programs have access to a *persistent root* (*e.g.*, a name server), from which they can *navigate* the pointer graph. Those objects that are transitively reachable from the persistent root must remain in persistent memory; any others are garbage and must be reclaimed. This is the task of the GC algorithm. Then, the fragmentation problem is solved by recycling storage and using a compacting GC.

GC techniques are well known in centralized systems [29]. Many researchers have proposed GC extensions to message-passing distributed systems [25]. In contrast, there is little previous work applicable to the problem of supporting PBR in a distributed cached store [1, 17, 19, 30] such as Larchant. This is a hard problem because:

- Applications modify the pointer graph concurrently by simply performing a pointer assignment. This is a very frequent operation, which should not be slowed down (by inserting reference counting code, for instance).
- Replicas are not instantly coherent. Observing a consistent image of the graph is difficult and costly.
- The pointer graph may be very large and distributed. Much of it resides on disk. Tracing the whole graph in one blow is unfeasible.
- A localized change to the pointer graph can affect remote portions of the graph. This has consequences on the global ordering of operations.
- The GC should not compete with applications. For instance, it should not take locks, cause coherence operations, or cause I/O.

GC in a large-scale distributed system is hard, especially with replication. It is tempting to apply standard consistency algorithms to the GC problem. For instance, one could layer a centralized GC algorithm above a coherent DSM, but this approach ignores the scalability and non-competition issues.

Some object-oriented databases run their collector as a transaction; this essentially blocks all useful work for the duration of the collection, and ignores the scalability issue. Another possible approach would be to collect a consistent snapshot [7] off-line; this is correct because being garbage is a stable property; unfortunately it is an expensive and non-scalable solution.

1.2 Overview

The main goals of our distributed GC algorithm are correctness, scalability, low overhead, and independence from a particular coherence algorithm. Secondary goals are avoiding source code and compiler changes.

Our approach divides the global GC into small, local, independent pieces, that run asynchronously, hence can be deferred and run in the background:

- The store is partitioned (each partition is called a bunch; more details in Section 2.2), and partitions are replicated. GC is a hybrid of tracing within a partition and counting across partitions.
- Each site runs a collector with a standard tracing algorithm [29] that works in one or more partitions (on that site) at the same time.
- The cooperation protocol between collectors enables them to run without any mutual synchronization.
- A collector examines only the local portion of the graph, without causing any I/O or taking locks.
- A collector may run even when local replicas are not known to be coherent.

This paper presents a distributed GC algorithm and a set of five simple rules ensuring its correctness. In particular, we show that, in this context, GC is safe if it conforms to the following rules (presented here informally):

- No collector may reclaim data until it has been declared unreachable at all replicas.
- A collector sends constructive (reachability) information before destructive (reclamation) information.
- All constructive information is sent.
- This information is received in the same order by remote collectors.
- The coherence protocol may propagate modified data only after it has been scanned by the local collector.

We prove our algorithm is safe, *i.e.* no reachable data is reclaimed; it is also live, *i.e.* some garbage is eventually reclaimed. Unfortunately, it is not *complete*, *i.e.* not all garbage is reclaimed (in particular, some distributed cycles) because completeness is at odds with scalability. An evaluation of the amount of unreclaimed garbage is the subject of on-going research [24]).

The contributions of this paper are the following. (i) A very simple, general model of a cached distributed shared store. (ii) Sufficient safety rules for GC in this context, in particular, for the interactions between coherence and GC. (iii) A distributed GC algorithm which is adapted to the model, avoids compiler modifications, is widely applicable, correct, scalable and efficient.

The outline of this paper is as follows. Section 2 presents our model of a distributed cached store. Section 3 describes the distributed GC algorithm and

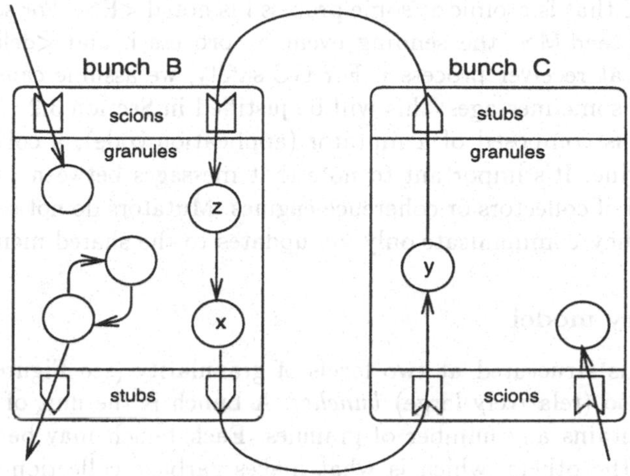

Fig. 1. *Two bunches containing granules, stubs, and scions.*

a set of safety rules for tracing garbage collection in the presence of replication. Section 4 compares our solution with related work. We summarize our contributions and future work in Section 5. Appendix A complements the main text; it provides a proof for the safety and liveness of the distributed GC algorithm.

For brevity, this paper omits some material without compromising its readability and correctness. For a more extensive treatment see Ferreira[12].

2 System model

In this section we present a general model for a garbage-collected distributed cached store, with sub-models for: network and processes, memory, coherence, mutator (application), and garbage collection. It incorporates only those elements that are relevant to the distributed garbage collection problem. It is extremely stylized with respect to any actual implementation.

Our model is based on a minimal set of coherence operations that are the same for any replicated memory. It does not dictate when such operations take place. (In a practical system, these operations are related to mutator activity.)

The model is also independent of the local garbage collection algorithm, pointer representation, or secondary storage technology. It applies to a large number of distributed sharing architectures, for instance a DSM, a SASOS, a client-server or peer-to-peer object-oriented database, or a client-server CORBA system.

2.1 Network and process model

The distributed system is composed of a set of sequential processes, communicating only by messages.

An event E that is atomic at some process i is noted $<E>_i$. For some message M, we note $<\textsf{send.M}>_i$ the sending event at process i, and $<\textsf{deliver.M}>_j$ the delivery of M at receiver process j. For GC safety, we assume causally-ordered delivery [5] of some messages; this will be justified in Section 3.2.

A process is composed of a mutator (application code), a collector, and a coherence engine. It's important to note that messages between processes flow only on behalf of collectors or coherence engines. Mutators do not send messages directly, *i.e.* they communicate only via updates to the shared memory. [3]

2.2 Memory model

The memory is structured at two levels of granularity (see Figure 1). (i) It is partitioned into (relatively large) *bunches*. A bunch is the unit of caching and tracing; it contains any number of granules. Each bunch may be traced independently of the others, which is what makes garbage collection scalable. (ii) The (rather small) *granule* is the unit of allocation, deallocation, identification, and coherence.[4] A granule resides entirely within a single bunch and allows fine-grained coherence.

A granule may contain any number of references, pointing to other granules. A reference may also be null (represented here as value zero), *i.e.* not pointing to anything. The model does not constrain the representation of references; for instance a raw pointer is supported.Hereafter, we indifferently use the words reference or pointer.

Bunches are noted X, Y, etc.; granules are noted x, y, etc. When x contains the address of y, x is said to point to y. To simplify the presentation, and without loss of generality, this article only considers pointers that cross bunch boundaries; the mechanisms for intra-bunch pointers are similar.

2.3 Coherence model

Bunches and granules are replicated in processes. The image of X (resp. x) in process i, noted X_i (resp. x_i), is called i's replica of X (resp. x). An invalidated replica is modeled by the null value.

In each process, a *coherence engine* provides the shared memory abstraction, by managing replicas of granules. The coherence engine sends and receives messages according to some coherence algorithm.

A process may disseminate the value of x to other processes, by sending **propagate** messages. Event $<\textsf{send.propagate(x)}>_i$ puts the current value of x_i in the message; event $<\textsf{deliver.propagate(x)}>_j$ assigns x_j with the value from the message. There is no assumption to which process, if any, or in what order **propagate** messages are delivered.

---

[3] If mutators were allowed to exchange messages, the pointers they contain must be taken into account by the GC algorithm. This is probably straightforward, using techniques such as SSP Chains [26], but has not been considered yet.

[4] It is convenient to think of a granule as an object, but note that granules are not necessarily the same as language-level objects, which can be larger or smaller.

After a granule replica changes value, either by assignment or by being the target of a propagate, it is said *GC-dirty*. A replica remains GC-dirty until it is subjected to a scan operation (see Section 2.5).

Many coherence algorithms define a *owner* process for a granule. Ownership does not appear in our model; however, in such coherence algorithms, the "Union Rule" (presented in Section 3.1) can make use of the properties of owners for a more efficient implementation.

The coherence model presented above is unconstrained enough to apply to any cached or replicated architecture. For concreteness, we show the mapping of entry consistency [4], the coherence protocol used in the current implementation of Larchant, to the model just described.

Mapping entry consistency to the coherence model Entry consistency uses *tokens* to schedule access to shared data and to ensure its consistency. A program precedes every use of a shared variable with an acquire primitive, and follows it with the corresponding release. Acquire asks for a token, and is parameterized with the type of access, either read or write; the protocol maintains a single writer, multiple readers semantics.

At any point in time, each granule has a single *owner* which is defined as the process that holds the write token or was the last one to hold it.

Sending a token also sends the most current version of the granule. Only the owner may send the write token. Sending a write token (i) invalidates the sender's replica and any reader tokens and replicas, (ii) sends the current value, and (iii) transfers ownership to the receiver. The owner may transform its write token into a read token. Any holder of a read token may send another read token (along with the granule value) to another process.

In this protocol, acquire messages, invalidation messages, and their replies are all modeled by a propagate. More precisely, the sending of an acquire message and the corresponding reply, is modeled as a single propagate (from the owner to the acquiring process) in which the granule's data is sent within the message. Invalidation of a replica is equivalent to a propagate message in which the granule's contents is null; thus, once a granule replica becomes invalid it contains no pointer (it is equivalent to a spontaneous, local assignment of the whole granule's data to the value zero).

2.4 Mutator model

For the purpose of GC, the only relevant action of the mutator is *pointer assignment*, which modifies the reference graph, possibly causing some granules to become unreachable. An application may arbitrarily assign a pointer with any legal reference value.

Suppose x points to t and y points to z. The result of assignment $<\mathsf{x} := \mathsf{y}>_\mathsf{i}$ is that x now also points to z, and the previous pointer to t is lost. (The replica that appears on the left-hand side of an assignment thereafter becomes GC-dirty.) This operation is atomic at process i, which only means that the model

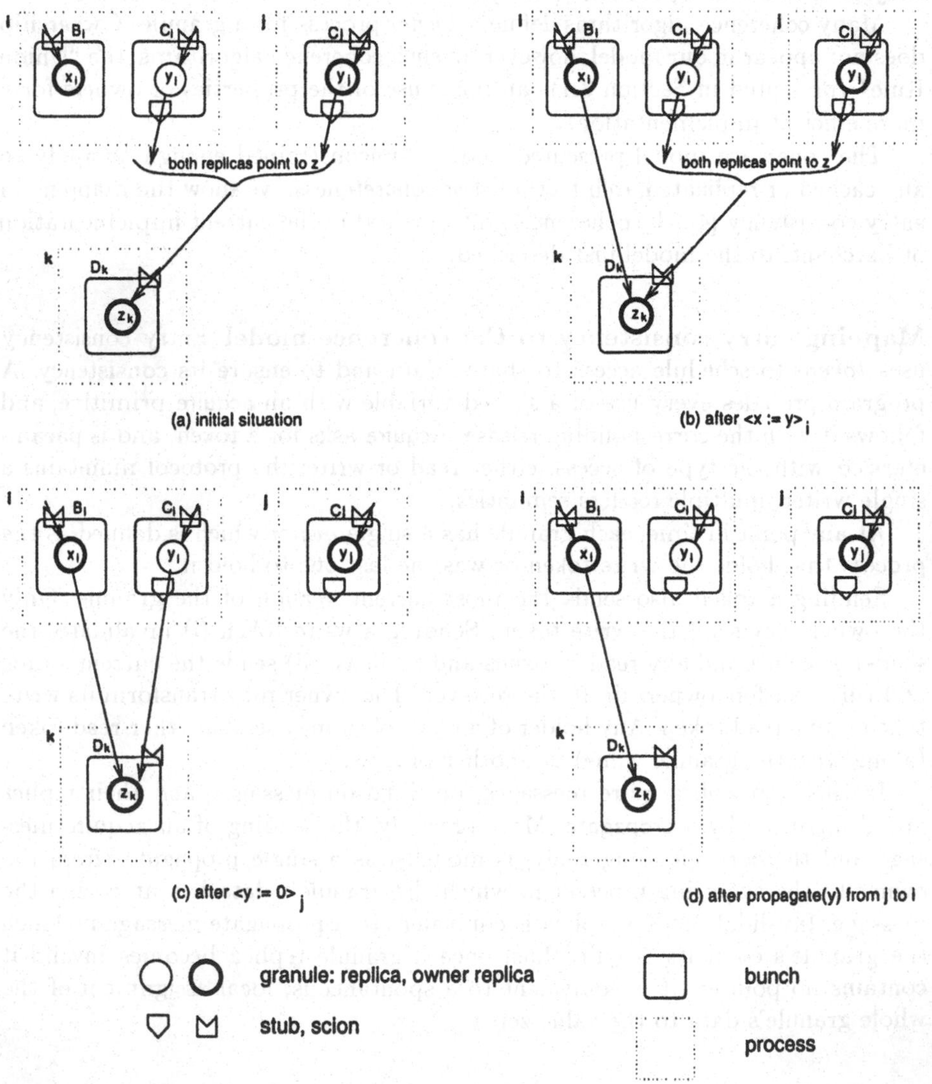

Fig. 2. *Prototypical example of mutator execution. Note that the stubs and scions become temporarily inconsistent with the pointers. However, as described in the paper, this does not compromise safety.*

does not allow hidden pointers. Granule creation (by some primitive similar to Unix malloc) is taken as a special case of pointer assignment.

Our reasoning is based on the following *prototypical example* (see Figure 2). Consider two granules x and y located in bunches X and Y, respectively. Initially x is null and y points to granule z located in bunch Z. Now, mutators within processes i and j execute the following operations: <x := y>$_i$, <y := 0>$_j$, such that at the end x points to z and all the replicas of y are null.

2.5 GC model

There are two well-known families of GC algorithms [29]. The first, counting, is invoked each time a reference is assigned; it scales well because it only involves the process performing the assignment, and the granule(s) referred to. It is considered expensive and non-portable because the counting operation is inserted inline by the compiler; furthermore it does not reclaim cycles of garbage. The second, tracing, is a global operation on the whole memory, and therefore scales poorly.

Many distributed GCs [25] are hybrids, in an attempt to combine the best of both worlds. Hybrid GCs partition the memory: they trace references internal to a partition, and count references that cross partition boundaries. This replaces the unfeasible global trace with the weaker problem of tracing each partition.[5]

In previous distributed GCs, a partition was often identified with a process [26]. This is a natural design option as those GCs were conceived for distributed systems based on RPC (Remote Procedure Call) in which cross-partition pointers were tracked at the process border. However, Larchant is based on DSM, therefore, memory partitioning is different: (i) a bunch may be replicated in multiple processes; (ii) a trace partition contains multiple bunches, in order to reclaim cross-bunch cycles of garbage; (iii) it will do so opportunistically in order to avoid input/output. This article focuses on the issues associated with point (i) with emphasis on the algorithm and its safety; points (ii) and (iii) have been studied in previous articles [13, 27] and are out of the scope of this paper. Fault-tolerance is also out of the scope; however, there are well known solutions that can be applied to our system [20].

In order to make the tracing of a bunch independent from other bunches, each bunch replica is provided with data structures that describe the references that cross its boundaries (see Figure 1): a *stub* describes an outgoing reference, a *scion* an incoming one; scions have an associated counter that counts references to some granule.[6] Note that Larchant's stubs and scions are not indirections participating in the mutator computation, but auxiliary data structures of the collector.

---

[5] Of course, the weaker formulation does not allow to collect cross-partition cycles of garbage.

[6] For simplicity, we speak of reference counting. In reality, we use the "reference listing" variant: instead of just a count, there is a list of scions, one per bunch containing a pointer to this granule, that records the identity of the originating bunch. This makes the increment messages idempotent, *i.e.* redundant increments have no effect.

A granule x in bunch X is said *protected* if and only if x is pointed directly or indirectly by a scion in X.

In the case of a reference from x contained in X, to z contained in Z, the stub is noted stub(Xx, Zz) and the corresponding scion scion(Xx, Zz).

The elementary collection operation is **scan**. At times a single granule replica x_i is scanned. Operation $\mathsf{scan}_i(x)$ returns the list of granules z, t, ..., that are pointed to by x_i. At other times, a whole bunch replica X_i is traced, noted $\mathsf{trace}_i(X)$, scanning all reachable granules that it contains. The roots of the trace are the scions in X_i.

A trace of X_i produces: (i) a set of granules contained in X_i, transitively reachable from its scions, and (ii) a set of stubs describing the outgoing pointers of the set of granules (mentioned in the previous point). Then, this generated set of stubs can be compared to the previous set (before the trace) in order to find which scions should have its counter incremented or decremented. This will be addressed with more detail in Section 3.2.

A GC-dirty replica remains GC-dirty until scanned. Then, *i.e.* after being scanned, it becomes GC-clean.

For concreteness, now we show the mapping of a mark-and-sweep collector [22], one of the GC algorithms used in the current implementation of Larchant, to the model just described.

Mapping mark-and-sweep to the GC model A mark-and-sweep collector has two phases: *(i)* trace the pointer graph starting from the root and mark every granule found, and *(ii)* sweep (*i.e.*, examine) all the heap reclaiming unmarked granules.

During the mark phase every reachable granule is marked (setting a bit in the granule's header, for example) and scanned for pointers. This phase ends when there are no more reachable granules to mark.

During the sweep phase the collector detects which granules are not marked and inserts their memory space in the free-list. When the collector finds a marked granule it unmarks it in order to make it ready for the next collection. This phase ends when there is no more memory to be swept.

Our model describes this algorithm through the operations **scan** and **trace**. The first operation models the scanning for pointers on each reachable granule, during the mark phase. The second operation, **trace**, models the entire mark phase in which all reachable granules are found (*i.e.*, marked and scanned).

3 GC algorithm and safety rules

Having exposed our model, we now turn to the solution of the main issues. This section describes the distributed GC algorithm, *i.e.* tracing a bunch and counting references that cross bunch boundaries, and the corresponding safety rules.

Tracing a bunch causes stubs to be created or deleted; the purpose of the counting algorithm is to adjust scions accordingly. As a simplification, we address the tracing of a single bunch, ignoring the fact that a partition may in fact contain any number of bunches in order to collect cross-bunch cycles of garbage [27].

When a mutator performs an assignment such as <x := y>$_i$, up to three processes are involved in the corresponding counting. Say granules x, y, z and t are located in bunches X, Y, Z and T respectively. Suppose that prior to the assignment, x pointed to z and y pointed to t. As a consequence of the above assignment operation, the collector of process i increments the reference count for t by performing the local operation <**create.stub**(Xx, Tt)>$_i$ and sending message **increment.scion**(Xx, Tt) to the collector in some process j, managing T. In addition, it decrements the reference count for z by performing the local operation **delete.stub**(Xx, Zz), and sending message **decrement.scion**(Xx, Zz) to the collector in some process k, managing Z.

An obvious solution to perform reference counting would be to instrument applications in order to track every pointer assignment. However, this solution would be extremely expensive in terms of performance because pointer assignment is a very frequent operation and counting might imply remote communication. This leads us to a fundamental insight of our design: instead of instrumenting the application, as suggested above, we observe that *counting may be deferred to a later tracing.* This removes counting from the application path, avoids reliance on compiler support, and enables batching optimizations. It in turn puts requirements on tracing, which will be addressed in the following sections.

3.1 Tracing in the presence of replicas: the union rule

Each process runs a standard centralized tracing collector. The issue we raise now is how collectors cooperate, in order to take replication into account. It is desirable that a collector remain independent, both of remote collectors, and of the coherence algorithm. In our design, a collector may scan a local replica, even if it is not known to be coherent, and independently of the actions of remote collectors.

Thus, the collector at process i might observe x_i to be pointing to z, whereas collector at process j concurrently observes x_j to be pointing to t. The coherence protocol will probably eventually make both replicas equal, but the collector cannot tell which value of x is correct. In the absence of better information, the collector must accept all replicas as equally valid, and never reclaim a granule until it is observed unreachable in the union of all replicas. This is captured by the following rule.

Safety Condition I: Union Rule. *If some replica* x_i *points to* z, *and some replica* x_j *is reachable, then* z *is reachable.*

The above rule makes reachable some granule pointed only by an unreachable replica x_i, if some other replica x_j is reachable. This very conservative formulation is necessary in the absence of knowledge of the coherence algorithm.

It's worthy to note that, instead of adopting the Union Rule, we could consider each replica as a separate granule, implicitly connected to its peer replicas.

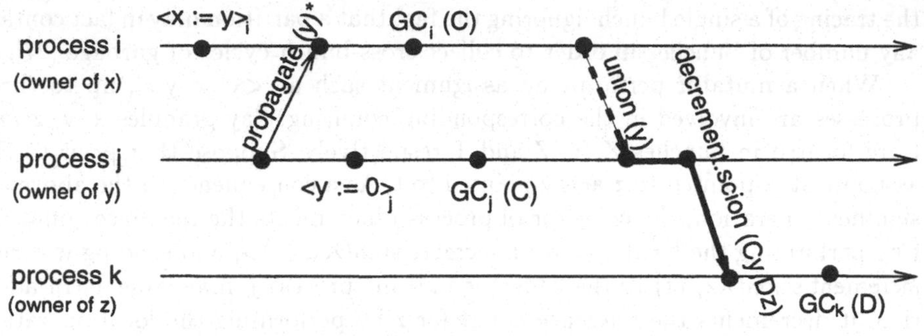

Fig. 3. *Prototypical example of Figure 2 restrained to the case of entry consistency.*

Pointers from different replicas would be counted separately. For instance, suppose x has three replicas, two of which point to z; then the reference count of z is at least 2. However, this solution has the drawback that every replica of x must send a number of counting messages.

A simpler and more efficient solution applies to coherence protocols where a granule has a single owner process (such as entry consistency, for example). The collectors centralize the information about pointers from x at the owner of x, using what we call union messages. In other words, a process holding replica x_j sends a union message, to x's owner, after detecting a change in the pointers from x_j. (Note that this detection is achieved by tracing x_j's enclosing bunch.)

Now, suppose that x points to z, and x is assigned a new value (for instance 0). It is only when all the replicas of x have the new value, and the corresponding collectors have informed x's owner (by sending it a union message) that there are no pointers from x to z, that the owner of x sends a message to the owner of z, to decrement the corresponding scion's reference count. This technique moves some of the responsibility for reference counting to the owner of the granules where references originate.

For concreteness, in the next section we show how the Union Rule can be enforced in a system supporting a specific coherence protocol, entry consistency.

Adapting the union rule to entry consistency In some DSM coherence protocols (for instance, sequential consistency and entry consistency) only the current owner of granule x is allowed to assign to x. In this case, a non-owner replica x_i cannot cause a granule unreachable from x_i to become reachable (because to do so would require assigning to x_i). Then, the implementation of the Union Rule is straightforward as explained now.

Consider Figure 3; it illustrates the prototypical example of Figure 2 re-

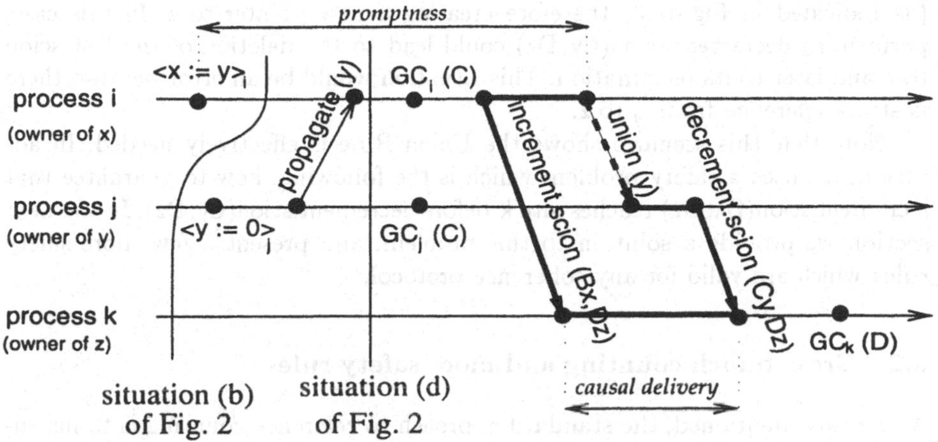

Fig. 4. *Timeline showing the effect of some of the safety rules for the prototypical example of Figure 2. On site* i, *the sending of* increment.scion(Bx, Dz) *may be delayed at most until sending* union(y). *Note the causal dependence (indicated by the thick lines) between the* increment.scion *and* decrement.scion *messages, carried by the* union *message.*

strained to a system with the entry consistency coherence protocol. The owner of y (site j) maintains a *copy-count* for each stub corresponding to a pointer originating in y. Let us consider the stub for a pointer from y to z; the stub's copy-count is equal to the number of replicas of y. Now, suppose the mutator at j performs <y := 0>$_j$. Note that, given the entry consistency protocol, previous to this assignment all replicas of y have been invalidated (in particular, y_i). Later, on site i, when the collector discovers that y_i does not point to z (because the invalidation has nulled the whole data of y_i), it sends a union message to j. This decrements the corresponding stub's copy-count. After all the collectors (whose processes cache a replica of y) have sent their union message to j, the stub's copy-count at j is zero; therefore, a decrement.scion(Cy, Dz) is sent from j to the owner of z (site k) in order to decrement the reference count of scion(Cy, Dz).

An attentive reader could argue that there is a simpler solution, in which the Union Rule is not needed, because as soon as a granule replica is invalidated we safely know that such a replica does not point to any other granule. We now describe this (apparent) solution and show why it is wrong.

When the mutator at j performs <y := 0>$_j$ all the other replicas of y are invalid, thus they contain no pointer to any granule, in particular y_i does not point to z anymore. For this reason, as soon as <y := 0>$_j$ is performed, the collector at j could safely reach the conclusion that there is no replica of y that still points to z. This is in fact true. However, note that this does not mean that decrement.scion(Cy, Dz) can be safely sent from j to k. The reason is that on site i, before y_i has became invalid, the mutator might have performed <x := y>$_i$

(as indicated in Figure 3) therefore creating a new pointer to z. In this case, performing decrement.scion(Cy, Dz) could lead to the deletion of the last scion to z and later to its reclamation. This situation would be an error because there is still a reference from x_i to z.

Note that this scenario shows the Union Rule is effectively needed. In addition, it raises a safety problem which is the following: how to guarantee that increment.scion(Bx, Dz) reaches site k before decrement.scion(Cy, Dz). In the next section we provide a solution to this problem, and present a few more safety rules which are valid for any coherence protocol.

3.2 Cross-bunch counting and more safety rules

As already mentioned, the standard approach to reference counting is to instrument assignments in order to immediately increment/decrement the corresponding counts. This approach requires compiler modification, and is expensive when assignments are frequent and counting is a remote operation, as is the case in Larchant.

Our solution consists of deferring the counting to a later tracing. In fact, the counts need not be adjusted immediately. Consider assignment $<x := y>_i$, where y points to z. At the time of the assignment, z is reachable by definition, and is guaranteed to remain reachable as long as y_i is not modified and remains reachable. It is not necessary for (a process managing) x to increment z's reference count, as long as (some process managing) y does not decrement it.

Let us return to the prototypical example of Figure 2. At the time of $<x := y>_i$, granule z is reachable (from both replicas of y) and is protected by some scion, say scion(Tt, Zz); presumably, but not necessarily, T = Y and t = y. As long as z's scion has a non-zero count, it is safe to delay the increment (possibly, the creation) of scion(Bx, Dz). (Recall that, in our system, it is the trace of bunch X which updates X's set of stubs, that causes the corresponding scions count to be adjusted.)

There is a problem with this approach, however. In the prototypical example, once situation (d) has been reached, it is possible that decrement.scion(Cy, Dz) reaches site k before increment.scion(Bx, Dz); then z could be incorrectly reclaimed. To avoid this unsafe situation, it suffices to give precedence to increment.scion over decrement.scion and union messages. This is illustrated in Figure 4: the interval named *promptness*, shows how much the message increment.scion(Bx, Dz) can be delayed w.r.t. the moment when the corresponding assignment operation ($<x := y>_i$) has been performed.

The following rules say how late counting can be deferred, while still sending messages in a safe order.

Safety Condition II: Increment Before Decrement Rule. *Scanning a granule (i.e., making it GC-clean) causes the corresponding* increment.scion *messages to be sent immediately.*

Safety Condition III: Comprehensive Tracing Rule. *When process* i *sends a* union *or* decrement.scion *message, all replicas at* i *must be GC-clean.*

Safety Condition IV: Clean Propagation Rule. *When process* i *sends* propagate(x), x_i *must be GC-clean.*

Safety Condition V: Causal Delivery Rule. *Garbage-collection messages (*increment.scion, union *and* decrement.scion*) are delivered in causal order.*

Rule II allows a granule replica to be scanned at any time; scanning a granule that contains a new pointer immediately sends an increment.scion message to the referent. It's important to mention that any message is asynchronous, so its actual transmission might take place later, as long as messages are delivered in the order sent (more on this later).[7]

Rule III ensures that union and decrement.scion messages are sent after increment.scion messages. In conjunction with Rule II, it ensures all increment.scion messages that the unions and decrement.scions might depend on have indeed been sent.

Rule IV ensures that when a process receives a new granule via a propagate operation, any increment.scions corresponding to its new value have already been sent.

If delivery order is no better than FIFO, races can appear between increment.scion and decrement.scion messages. Rule V solves this problem. Note that coherence messages do not need causal delivery, thus limiting the cost.

Rules I through V are sufficient for the safe coexistence of replicated data and a hybrid garbage collector. They are independent of the coherence and tracing algorithms, and impose very few interactions between collection and coherence.

In the following sections we explain these rules in more detail, and provide some examples in which their need is clear and easily understandable.

Comprehensive tracing rule This section provides an explanation of the Comprehensive Tracing Rule. We show the need for this rule by giving an example of what happens when this rule is not enforced.

Consider Figures 2 and 4 after mutators have executed <x := y>$_i$, <y := 0>$_j$, and y propagated to site i, *i.e.* once situation (d) has been reached. (Note that scion(Bx, Dz) has not been created yet.) Suppose that trace_i(C) runs and the Comprehensive Tracing Rule is not fulfilled. This means that the collector sends a union message to j (owner of y) indicating that stub(Cy, Dz) has disappeared in process i, but scan_i(x) is not performed; therefore increment.scion(Bx, Dz) is not sent. As a result, j applies the Union Rule and <send.decrement.scion(Cy, Dz)>$_j$ is executed. Thus, scion(Cy, Dz) is deleted in k. Then, if trace_k(D) runs, granule z is unsafely reclaimed.

---

[7] In fact, sending a message immediately means put it in the sending queue.

The Comprehensive Tracing Rule prevents the above scenario as it forces x_i to be GC-cleaned before i sends the union message to j. Then, according to the Increment Before Decrement Rule, <send.increment.scion(Bx, Dz)>$_i$ is performed before the union message is sent (and j applies the Union Rule and executes <send.decrement.scion(Cy, Dz)>$_j$). Since we assumed causal delivery (Rule V) scion(Bx, Dz) is created before scion(Cy, Dz) is deleted. Consequently, z is not reclaimed by trace_k(D).

Clean propagation rule This section provides an explanation of the role of the Clean Propagation Rule, by describing an example of what occurs if this rule is not enforced.

Consider Figures 2 and 4 after the mutator has executed <x := y>$_i$ and before <y := 0>$_j$, *i.e.* once situation (b) has been reached. Now, suppose that granule x_i is propagated to some process w in the absence of the Clean Propagation Rule, *i.e.* without performing scan_i(x). Then, x_i is assigned in such a way that it no longer points to z (*e.g.*, <x := 0>$_i$). At this moment, the only scion that protects z is scion(Cy, Dz). Suppose that both replicas of y are modified in processes i and j such that they no longer point to z. Hence, by the collection algorithm, scion(Cy, Dz) is deleted. Thus, z may be unsafely reclaimed by trace_k(D) (x_w still points to z).

The Clean Propagation Rule prevents the above scenario as it forces x_i to be GC-cleaned. Thus, by Rule II, <send.increment.scion(Bx, Dz)>$_i$ is performed immediately, *i.e.* before x_i is propagated to site w.

Causal delivery rule This section shows the need for the Causal Delivery Rule by giving an example of what happens when this rule is not enforced.

Consider the prototypical example of Figure 2 after mutators have executed <x := y>$_i$, <y := 0>$_j$, and y propagated to site i, *i.e.* once situation (d) has been reached. (Note that scion(Bx, Dz) has not been created yet.) Then, the collectors on sites i and j perform as follows: i executes <send.increment.scion(Bx, Dz)>$_i$, while j executes <send.decrement.scion(Cy, Dz)>$_j$. In an asynchronous system, the former may be delivered after the latter, causing z to be incorrectly reclaimed. In fact, there is a hidden causality relation through the shared variable y. In our algorithm, this causal relation is captured by the union message, as apparent in Figure 4. Thus, given the Causal Delivery Rule, there is at all times at least a scion protecting z from being reclaimed.

4 Related work

The concept of persistence by reachability (PBR) was first proposed by Atkinson [3] in the early 1980's. EOS [14] is an early example of a DSM providing PBR. It has a copying GC that takes into account user placement hints to improve locality. However, its GC is quite complex and has not been implemented.

Much previous work in distributed garbage collection, such as SSP Chains [26] or Network Objects [6], considers processes communicating via RPC, and uses a hybrid of tracing and counting. Each process traces its internal pointers; references across process boundaries are counted as they are sent/received in messages.

Some object-oriented databases (OODB) use a similar approach [1, 9, 23, 30] *i.e.* a partition can be collected independently from the rest of the database. In particular, Thor [20, 21] is a research OODB with PBR. In Thor, data resides at a small number of servers and is cached at workstations for processing. A Thor server counts references contained in objects cached at a client. Thor defers counting references originating from some object x cached at a client, until x is modified at the server. However, their work does not address the issue of GC interaction with coherence and replication in a DSM based system.

The work most directly related to ours is Skubiszewski and Porteix's GC-consistent cuts [28]. They consider asynchronous tracing of an OODB; however they consider neither distribution nor replication. The collector is allowed to trace an arbitrary database page at any time, subject to the following ordering rule. For every transaction accessing a page traced by the collector, if the transaction copies a pointer from one page to another, the collector either traces the source page before the write, or traces both the source and the destination page after the write. The authors prove that this is a sufficient condition for safety and liveness.

It's worthy to note that the solutions mentioned above do not consider a DSM based system, such as Larchant, in which cross-partition pointers are created by a simple assignment operation.

Most previous work on garbage collection in shared memory deals either with multiprocessors [2, 11] or with a small-scale DSM [17]. These authors make strong coherence assumptions, and they ignore the issues of scale and of persistence.

Yu and Cox [31] describe a conservative collector for the TreadMarks [16] DSM system. It uses partitioned GC on a process basis; all messages are scanned for possible contained pointers. Like Larchant, their GC does not rely on coherence. However, their solution is specific to TreadMarks, *i.e.* it is not widely applicable.

5 Conclusion

Larchant is a Cached Distributed Shared Store based on the model of a DSM with Persistence By Reachability. Data is replicated in multiple sites for performance and availability. Reachability is assessed by tracing the pointer graph, starting from the persistent root, and reclaiming unreachable data. This is the task of Garbage Collection.

This paper focused on the interactions between garbage collection on the one hand, and caching and replication on the other. We show that both the tracing and the distributed counting garbage collector run independently of coherence. Garbage collection does not need coherent data, never causes coherence messages nor input/output, and it does not compete with applications' locks or working sets. However, coherence messages must at times be scanned before sending.

Using an extremely stylized model of an application (reduced to unconstrained pointer assignments) and of a coherence protocol (reduced to unconstrained propagation messages), we give rules for the safe coexistence of garbage collection with replication.

Our GC is a hybrid (or partitioned) algorithm. It combines tracing within a partition, with reference-counting across partition boundaries. Each process may trace its own replicas, independently of one another and of other replicas. Counting at some process is asynchronous to other processes, and asynchronous to the local mutator. In addition, counting is deferred and batched.

We presented five safety rules that guarantee the correctness of the distributed reference-counting algorithm. Along with these rules, we provided a proof that the algorithm is safe and live (see Appendix A). These safety rules are minimal and generally applicable given the asynchrony to applications, and the minimum assumptions we made concerning coherence:

- Union Rule: a granule may be reclaimed only if it is unreachable from the union of all replicas (of the pointing granules);
- Increment before Decrement Rule: when a granule is scanned, the corresponding increment.scion messages must be sent immediately (*i.e.*, put them in the sending queue);
- Comprehensive Tracing Rule: when a union or a decrement.scion message is sent, all replicas (on the sending site) must be GC-clean;
- Clean Propagation Rule: a granule must be scanned before being propagated; and
- Causal Delivery Rule: GC messages must be delivered in causal order.

Measurements of our first (non-optimized) implementation, which can be found in Ferreira[12], show that the cost of tracing is independent of the number of replicas, and that there is a clear performance benefit in delaying the counting.

Causal delivery, imposed by Rule V, is non-scalable in the general case; however, we do not consider this to be a serious problem in real implementations because causality can be ensured by taking advantage of the specific coherence protocols. For example, in our current implementation (supporting entry consistency) causal delivery is ensured by a mixture of piggy-backing and acknowledgments.

We are currently working on a follow-up of Larchant in Esprit Project PerDiS [24], where it will be used for a large-scale cooperative engineering CAD application. This will enable us to measure and characterize the behaviour of real persistent applications, to fully study the performance of the distributed GC algorithm and to evaluate its completeness in a real-world environment. A first prototype of the PerDiS implementation is freely available in http://www.perdis.esprit.ec.org.

References

1. L. Amsaleg, M. Franklin, and O. Gruber. Efficient Incremental Garbage Collection for Client-Server Object Database Systems. In *Proc. of the 21th VLDB Int. Conf.*, Zürich, Switzerland, September 1995.

2. Andrew W. Appel. Simple Generational Garbage Collection and Fast Allocation. *Software Practice and Experience*, 19(2):171–183, February 1989.
3. M. P. Atkinson, P. J. Bailey, K. J. Chisholm, P. W. Cockshott, and R. Morrison. An approach to persistent programming. *The Computer Journal*, 26(4):360–365, 1983.
4. B. Bershad, M. J. Zekauskas, and W. A. Sawdon. The Midway distributed shared memory system. In *Proc. of the 1993 CompCon Conf.*, 1993.
5. Kenneth Birman, Andre Schiper, and Pat Stephenson. Lightweight causal and atomic group multicast. *ACM Transactions on Computer Systems*, 9(3):272–314, August 1991.
6. Andrew Birrell, Greg Nelson, Susan Owicki, and Edward Wobber. Network objects. *Software Practice and Experience*, S4(25):87–130, December 1995. http://gatekeeper.dec.com/pub/DEC/SRC/research-reports/abstracts/src-rr-115.html.
7. K. Mani Chandy and Leslie Lamport. Distributed snapshots: determining global states of distributed systems. *ACM Transactions on Computer Systems*, 3(1):63–75, February 1985.
8. J. S. Chase, H. E. Levy, M. J. Feely, and E. D. Lazowska. Sharing and adressing in a single address space system. *ACM Transactions on Computer Systems*, 12(3), November 1994.
9. Jonathan E. Cook, Alexander L. Wolf, and Benjamin G. Zorn. Partition selection policies in object database garbage collection. In *Proc. Int. Conf. on Management of Data (SIGMOD)*, pages 371–382, Minneapolis MN (USA), May 1994. ACM SIGMOD.
10. Alan Dearle, Rex di Bona, James Farrow, Frans Henskens, Anders Lindström, John Rosenberg, and Francis Vaughan. Grasshopper: An orthogonally persistent operating system. *Computing Systems*, 7(3):289–312, 1994.
11. Damien Doligez and Xavier Leroy. A concurrent, generational garbage collector for a multithreaded implementation of ML. In *Proc. of the 20th Annual ACM SIGPLAN-SIGACT Symp. on Principles of Programming Lang.*, pages 113–123, Charleston SC (USA), January 1993.
12. Paulo Ferreira. *Larchant: ramasse-miettes dans une mémoire partagée répartie avec persistance par atteignabilité.* Thèse de doctorat, Université Paris 6, Pierre et Marie Curie, Paris (France), May 1996. http://www-sor.inria.fr/SOR/docs/ferreira_thesis96.html.
13. Paulo Ferreira and Marc Shapiro. Garbage collection and DSM consistency. In *Proc. of the First Symposium on Operating Systems Design and Implementation (OSDI)*, pages 229–241, Monterey CA (USA), November 1994. ACM. http://www-sor.inria.fr/SOR/docs/GC-DSM-CONSIS_OSDI94.html.
14. Olivier Gruber and Laurent Amsaleg. Object grouping in EOS. In *Proc. Int. Workshop on Distributed Object Management*, pages 184–201, Edmonton (Canada), August 1992.
15. James Leslie Keedy. Support for objects in the MONADS architecture. In J. Rosenberg, editor, *Proc. Workshop on persistent object systems*, pages 202–213, Newcastle NSW (Australia), January 1989.
16. P. Keleher, A. Cox, and W. Zwaenepoel. TreadMarks: Distributed shared memory on standard workstations and operating systems. *Proceedings of the 1994 Winter USENIX Conference*, January 1994.
17. T. Le Sergent and B. Berthomieu. Incremental multi-threaded garbage collection on virtually shared memory architectures. In *Proc. Int. Workshop on Memory*

Management, number 637 in Lecture Notes in Computer Science, pages 179–199, Saint-Malo (France), September 1992. Springer-Verlag.

18. Kai Li and Paul Hudak. Memory coherence in shared virtual memory systems. *ACM Transactions on Computer Systems*, 7(4):321–359, November 1989.
19. Barbara Liskov, Mark Day, and Liuba Shrira. Distributed object management in Thor. In *Proc. Int. Workshop on Distributed Object Management*, pages 1–15, Edmonton (Canada), August 1992.
20. Umesh Maheshwari and Barbara Liskov. Fault-tolerant distributed garbage collection in a client-server, object database. In *Proc. Parallel and Dist. Info. Sys.*, pages 239–248, Austin TX (USA), September 1994. ftp://pion.lcs.mit.edu/pub/thor/dgc.ps.gz.
21. Umesh Maheshwari and Barbara Liskov. Partitioned garbage collection of a large object store. In *Proc. Int. Conf. on Management of Data (SIGMOD)*, Montreal, Canada, 1996.
22. John McCarthy. Recursive functions of symbolic expressions and their computation by machine. *Communications of the ACM*, 3(4):184–195, April 1960.
23. J. Eliot B. Moss, David S. Munro, and Richard L. Hudson. PMOS: A complete and coarse-grained incremental garbage collector for persistent object stores. In *Proc. of the 6th Int. Workshop on Persistent Object Systems*, Cape May NJ (USA), May 1996.
24. PerDiS ESPRIT Project - LTR 22533. The PerDiS project: a Persistent Distributed Store, 1997. http://www.perdis.esprit.ec.org.
25. David Plainfossé and Marc Shapiro. A survey of distributed garbage collection techniques. In *Proc. Int. Workshop on Memory Management*, Kinross Scotland (UK), September 1995. http://www-sor.inria.fr/SOR/docs/SDGC_iwmm95.html.
26. Marc Shapiro, Peter Dickman, and David Plainfossé. SSP chains: Robust, distributed references supporting acyclic garbage collection. Rapport de Recherche 1799, Institut National de Recherche en Informatique et Automatique, Rocquencourt (France), November 1992. http://www-sor.inria.fr/SOR/docs/SSPC_rr1799.html.
27. Marc Shapiro and Paulo Ferreira. Larchant-RDOSS: a distributed shared persistent memory and its garbage collector. In J.-M. Hélary and M. Raynal, editors, *Workshop on Distributed Algorithms (WDAG)*, number 972 in Springer-Verlag LNCS, pages 198–214, Le Mont Saint-Michel (France), September 1995. http://www-sor.inria.fr/SOR/docs/LRDSPMGC_wdag95.html.
28. Marcin Skubiszewski and Patrick Valduriez. Concurrent garbage collection in O_2. In *24th International Conference on Very Large Data Bases*, Athens, Greece, 1997.
29. Paul R. Wilson. Uniprocessor garbage collection techniques. In *Proc. Int. Workshop on Memory Management*, number 637 in Lecture Notes in Computer Science, Saint-Malo (France), September 1992. Springer-Verlag. ftp://ftp.cs.utexas.edu/pub/garbage/bigsurv.ps.
30. V. Yong, J. Naughton, and J. Yu. Storage reclamation and reorganization in client-server persistent object stores. In *Proc. Data Engineering Int. Conf.*, pages 120–133, Houston TX (USA), February 1994.
31. Weimin Yu and Alan Cox. Conservative garbage collection on distributed shared memory systems. In *16th Int. Conf. on Distributed Computing Syst.*, pages 402–410, Hong Kong, May 1996. IEEE Computer Society.

A Proofs of safety and liveness

This appendix provides a proof that the distributed GC algorithm is safe and live.

A.1 Safety

To understand this proof, note that:

- the phrase "scion(Xx, Yy) exists" means that the reference count of the scion is non-zero;
- event <deliver.decrement.scion(Xx, Yy)>$_j$ deletes scion(Xx, Yy) at j if and only if the scion's counter becomes zero as a result of the decrement.scion message;
- event <deliver.increment.scion(Xx, Yy)>$_j$ creates scion(Xx, Yy) at j if and only if that scion does not exist yet; otherwise, it increments that scion's counter;
- a granule is created with an initial scion (this is guaranteed by the granule creation primitive) in order to ensure that the Base Case assumptions, in our proofs, are always verified;
- we assume a coherence protocol in which each granule has a owner as defined in Section 2.3; and
- we represent a pointer from granule x in bunch B to granule z in bunch D as $\mathsf{Bx} \rightarrow \mathsf{Dz}$.

The distributed GC algorithm must satisfy the following obvious safety invariant:

Safety Invariant 1 *No reachable granule is reclaimed.*

Since we are considering only cross-bunch pointers, the above invariant is equivalent to:

Safety Invariant 2 *:*

$$(\forall \mathsf{B}, \forall \mathsf{x} \in \mathsf{B} : \exists \mathsf{Bx} \rightarrow \mathsf{Dz}) \Rightarrow (\exists \mathsf{T}, \exists \mathsf{t} \in \mathsf{T} : \exists \mathsf{scion}(\mathsf{Tt}, \mathsf{Dz}))$$

This reads "if a granule x in B points to z in D, then some scion protects z." Note that this is weaker than the more intuitive "if x points to z, then scion-(Bx, Dz) exists"; indeed, the scion that protects z does not need to match the pointer.

We prove the safety of the distributed GC algorithm by showing that it maintains the above safety invariant. We start by proving two lemmas; these will be needed to prove a theorem.

Lemma 1 *Let n different granules $\mathsf{x}^1, \ldots, \mathsf{x}^n$ located respectively in bunches $\mathsf{B}^1, \ldots, \mathsf{B}^n$, all cached in process p, be the set of all protected granules pointing to $\mathsf{z} \in \mathsf{D}$ cached in process k. Then, $\forall i, 1 \leq i \leq n$:*

- x^i *is GC-clean* $\wedge\ \exists$ scion($\mathsf{B}^i\mathsf{x}^i$, Dz), *or*
- $\exists j, 1 \leq j \leq n$, x^i *is GC-dirty* $\wedge\ \exists$ scion($\mathsf{B}^j\mathsf{x}^j$, Dz)

This lemma says that as long as there is a granule pointing to z, cached in some process p, there exists at least a scion protecting z. We prove this lemma by induction over the size of the set containing granules pointing to z, for a single process.

Base case:
Initially a single protected granule x^1 points to z: $x^1 \in B^1$ cached in process p, and scion(B^1x^1, Dz) exists. Let $x^2 \in B^2$, also cached in p, initially not pointing to z This initial situation obviously verifies the lemma as x^1 is GC-clean and scion(B^1x^1, Dz) exists.

Now, consider that $<x^2 := x^1>_p$ is performed (now x^2 also points to z); therefore $x^{\ 2}$ is GC-dirty. If x^1 is not assigned to thereafter, the lemma remains trivially true since x^2 is GC-dirty and scion(B^1x^1, Dz) exists.

Therefore consider that x^1 is changed by an assignment such as $<x^1 := 0>_p$. (The actual value of the right-hand side does not matter for the proof, except that when the right-hand side is a pointer to z it is as if the assignment did not take place.) Hence, $x^{\ 1}$ is GC-dirty. Until a bunch tracing takes place at p, no <send.increment.scion> or <send.decrement.scion> is performed at p, and the lemma remains trivially true since x^2 is GC-dirty and scion(B^1x^1, Dz) exists.

When a bunch tracing does execute in process p, both x^2 (containing the new pointer) and x^1 (previously containing the pointer to z) are GC-cleaned (they were both GC-dirty); therefore stub(B^2x^2, Dz) is created and stub(B^1x^1, Dz) disappears (*i.e.*, it is no longer in the new set of stubs).

According to Rule II (Increment Before Decrement) and Rule III (Comprehensive Tracing), <send.increment.scion(B^2x^2, Dz)>$_p$ precedes <send.decrement.-scion(B^1x^1, Dz)>$_p$.

We assumed that messages are delivered in causal order (Rule V), hence <deliver.increment.scion(B^2x^2, Dz)>$_k$ precedes <deliver.decrement.scion(B^1x^1, D-z)>$_k$. Thus, at any moment, there exists at least a scion protecting z: either scion(B^1x^1, Dz), or scion(B^2x^2, Dz), or both.

Induction case:
Assume a set of different granules $x^1, \ldots, x^j$ located respectively in bunches $B^1, \ldots, B^j$ all cached in process p, pointing to z with the corresponding scions already created. Consequently, granule x^l, $1 \leq l \leq j$, points to z: $x^l \in B^l$ cached in process p, and scion(B^lx^l, Dz) exists. This initial situation obviously verifies the lemma as x^l is GC-clean and scion(B^lx^l, Dz) exists.

Let $x^{j+1} \in B^{j+1}$, also cached in p, initially not pointing to z. Now, consider that $<x^{j+1} := x^l>_p$ is performed (thus, x^{j+1} also points to z) therefore $x^{\ j+1}$ is GC-dirty. If x^l is not assigned to thereafter, the lemma remains trivially true since x^{j+1} is GC-dirty and scion(B^lx^l, Dz) exists.

Therefore consider that x^l is changed by an assignment such as $<x^l := 0>_p$. (The actual value of the right-hand side does not matter for the proof, except that when the right-hand side is a pointer to z it is as if the assignment did not take place.) Hence, $x^{\ l}$ is GC-dirty. Until a bunch tracing takes place at p, no <send.increment.scion> or <send.decrement.scion> is performed at p, and the lemma remains trivially true since x^{j+1} is GC-dirty and scion(B^lx^l, Dz) exists.

When a bunch tracing does execute in process p, both x^{j+1} (containing the new pointer) and x^l (previously containing the pointer to z) are GC-cleaned (they were both GC-dirty); therefore stub($B^{j+1}x^{j+1}$, Dz) is created and stub($B^l x^l$, Dz) disappears (*i.e.*, no longer in the new set of stubs).

According to Rule II (Increment Before Decrement) and Rule III (Comprehensive Tracing), event <send.increment.scion($B^{j+1}x^{j+1}$, Dz)>$_p$ precedes <send.-decrement.scion($B^l x^l$, Dz)>$_p$.

We assumed that messages are delivered in causal order (Rule V), hence <deliver.increment.scion($B^{j+1}x^{j+1}$, Dz)>$_k$ precedes <deliver.decrement.scion($B^l x^l$,-Dz)>$_k$. Thus, at any moment, there exists at least a scion protecting z: either scion($B^l x^l$, Dz), or scion($B^{j+1}x^{j+1}$, Dz), or both.

This terminates the induction over the size of the set containing granules pointing to z, for a single process. □

Now, we present the second lemma.

Lemma 2 *Let n different granules* $x^1, \ldots, x^n$ *be the set of all protected granules, located in bunch* B, *pointing to* z ∈ D *owned by* k. *Let m different processes* $p^1, \ldots, p^m$ *be the set of all processes caching a replica of* x^i. *Then,* $\forall i, 1 \leq i \leq n$:

- x^i *is GC-clean* ∧ ∃ scion(Bx^i, Dz), *or*
- $\exists j, 1 \leq j \leq n$, x^i *is GC-dirty* ∧ ∃ scion(Bx^j, Dz)

This lemma says that, as long as there is a replica of some granule x located in B, pointing to z, cached in some process, there exists a scion protecting z. We prove this lemma by induction: *(i)* over the size of the set containing granules pointing to z, and *(ii)* over the size of the set containing processes caching replicas of the granules pointing to z.

Base case:
Initially there is a single granule $x^1 \in$ B pointing to z, x^1 is owned by process p^1, scion(Bx^1, Dz) exists, $x^2 \in$ B does not point to z and is also owned by p^1, and neither x^1 nor x^2 are cached in p^2. This initial situation obviously verifies the lemma as x^1 is GC-clean and scion(Bx^1, Dz) exists.

Now, perform <$x^2 := x^1$>$_{p^1}$; thus, x^2 points to z and is GC-dirty. If x^1 is not assigned to thereafter, the lemma remains trivially true as x^1 is GC-clean and scion(Bx^1, Dz) exists.

Therefore, consider that x^1 is changed by an assignment such as <$x^1 := 0$>$_{p^1}$. (The actual value of the right-hand side does not matter for the proof, except that when the right-hand side is a pointer to z it is as if the assignment did not take place.) Hence, x^1 is GC-dirty. Until a bunch tracing or a propagate operation takes place at p^1, no <send.increment.scion> or <send.decrement.scion> is performed at p^1, and the lemma remains trivially true since x^2 is GC-dirty and scion(Bx^1, Dz) exists. We examine these two cases now: bunch tracing and propagate operation, both performed at p^1.

When a bunch tracing does execute in process p^1, both x^2 (containing the new pointer) and x^1 (previously containing the pointer to z) are GC-cleaned (they were both GC-dirty); therefore stub(Bx^2, Dz) is created and stub(Bx^1, Dz) disappears (*i.e.*, no longer in the new set of stubs).

According to Rule II (Increment Before Decrement) and Rule III (Comprehensive Tracing), event <send.increment.scion(Bx^2, Dz)>$_{p^1}$ precedes <send.decrement.scion(Bx^1, Dz)>$_{p^1}$.

We assumed that messages are delivered in causal order (Rule V), hence <deliver.increment.scion(Bx^2, Dz)>$_k$ precedes <deliver.decrement.scion(Bx^1, Dz)>$_k$. Thus, at any moment, there exists at least a scion protecting z: either scion(Bx^1, Dz), or scion(Bx^2, Dz), or both. Therefore, the lemma remains true when a bunch collection occurs in process p^1.

Now, we consider a propagate operation. Before a <send.propagate(x^2)>$_{p^1}$ (possibly sent to p^2) takes place,[8] according to Rule IV (Clean Propagation), x^2 is GC-cleaned. Therefore x^2 is scanned, stub(Bx^2, Dz) is created and <send.increment.scion(Bx^2, Dz)>$_{p^1}$ is performed. Therefore, the lemma remains true as x^2 is GC-clean and scion(Bx^2, Dz) exists.

Induction case:
Let h different process $p^1, \ldots, p^h, 1 \leq h \leq m$ be the only processes caching granules $x^1, \ldots, x^j, 1 \leq j \leq n$, all $\in$ B, all pointing to z $\in$ D owned by k. The scions for the pointers from $x^1, \ldots, x^j$ to z do exist. Granule x^j is owned by p^w, $1 \leq w \leq m$. Let granule x^{j+1} owned by p^w, initially not pointing to z, and process p^{h+1} initially not caching any granule pointing to z. This initial situation obviously verifies the lemma as x^j is GC-clean and scion(Bx^j, Dz) exists.

Now, perform <$x^{j+1} := x^j$>$_{p^w}$; thus, x^{j+1} points to z and is GC-dirty. If x^j is not assigned to thereafter, the lemma remains trivially true as x^j is GC-clean and scion(Bx^j, Dz) exists.

Therefore, consider that x^j is changed by an assignment such as <$x^j := 0$>$_{p^w}$. (The actual value of the right-hand side does not matter for the proof, except that when the right-hand side is a pointer to z it is as if the assignment did not take place.) Hence, x^j is GC-dirty. Until a bunch tracing or a propagate operation takes place at p^w, no <send.increment.scion> or <send.decrement.scion> is performed at p^w, and the lemma remains trivially true since x^{j+1} is GC-dirty and scion(Bx^j, Dz) exists. We examine these two cases now: bunch tracing and propagate operation, both performed at p^w.

When a bunch tracing does execute in process p^w, x^{j+1} (containing the new pointer) and x^j (previously containing the pointer to z) are GC-cleaned (they were both GC-dirty); therefore stub(Bx^{j+1}, Dz) is created and stub(Bx^j, Dz) disappears (*i.e.*, no longer in the new set of stubs).

According to Rule II (Increment Before Decrement) and Rule III (Comprehensive Tracing), event <send.increment.scion(Bx^{j+1}, Dz)>$_{p^1}$ precedes <send.decrement.scion(Bx^j, Dz)>$_{p^1}$.

We assumed that messages are delivered in causal order (Rule V), hence <deliver.increment.scion(Bx^{j+1}, Dz)>$_k$ precedes <deliver.decrement.scion(Bx^j, Dz)>$_k$. Thus, at any moment, there exists at least a scion protecting z: either scion(Bx^j, Dz), or scion(Bx^{j+1}, Dz), or both. Therefore, the lemma remains true when a bunch tracing occurs at process p^w.

[8] Note that the propagation of x^1 is not relevant because it does not lead to the sending of any GC specific message, in particular no decrement.scion is performed.

Now, we consider a propagate operation. Before a <send.propagate(x^{j+1})>$_{p^w}$ takes place, according to Rule IV (Clean Propagation), x^{j+1} is GC-cleaned. Therefore x^{j+1} is scanned, stub(Bx^{j+1}, Dz) is created and <send.increment.scion-(Bx^{j+1}, Dz)>$_{p^w}$ is performed. Therefore, the lemma remains true as x^{j+1} is GC-clean and scion(Bx^{j+1}, Dz) exists.

This terminates the induction over the size of the set containing granules pointing to z, and over the size of the set containing processes caching replicas of the granules pointing to z. □

Now, we prove the following theorem:

Theorem 1 *Let n different granules* $x^1, \ldots, x^n$ *be the set of all protected granules pointing to* $z \in D$ *owned by process* k, *located respectively in bunches* $B^1, \ldots, B^n$. *Let m different processes* $p^1, \ldots, p^m$ *be the set of all processes caching a replica of all bunches mentioned above. Then,* $\forall i, 1 \leq i \leq n$, scion($B^i x^i$, Dz) *exists at* k.

This theorem implies Safety Invariant 2. Whereas the latter states that, whatever number of cross-bunch pointers point to $z \in D$, at least one scion protects z, Theorem 1 is stronger, saying that at least one scion per bunch containing a pointer to z, protects z. Note that it does not say whether this scion effectively corresponds to an existing pointer to z.

We prove this theorem by induction: *(i)* over the size of the set containing granules pointing to z in a single process, and *(ii)* over the size of the set of processes caching replicas of granules pointing to z.

Base case:
Assume that initially $x^1 \in B^1$ and $x^2 \in B^2$ are both owned by p^1, only x^1 points to $z \in D$ owned by k, scion(B^1x^1, Dz) exists, and process p^2 does not cache any granule pointing to z. This initial situation obviously verifies the theorem as scion(B^1x^1, Dz) exists.

Now, consider that <$x^2 := x^1$>$_{p^1}$ is performed (thus, x^2 also points to z); therefore x^2 is GC-dirty. If x^1 is not assigned to thereafter, the theorem remains trivially true, since scion(B^1x^1, Dz) exists.

Therefore, consider an assignment such as <$x^1 := 0$>$_{p^1}$. (The actual value of the right-hand side does not matter for the proof, except that when the right-hand side is a pointer to z it is as if the assignment did not take place.) Until a bunch tracing or a propagate operation takes place at p^1, no <send.increment.-scion> or <send.decrement.scion> is performed, and the theorem remains trivially true.

Now, suppose a bunch tracing does occur at p^1; by Lemma 1 we have that at any moment, there exists at least a scion protecting z: either scion(B^1x^1, Dz), or scion(B^2x^2, Dz), or both.

Suppose a propagate(x^1) occurs at p^1; by Lemma 2 we have that scion(B^2x^2, Dz) exists before <send.propagate(x^2)>$_{p^1}$.

Induction case:
Let j different granules $x^1, \ldots, x^j$, located in bunches $B^1, \ldots, B^j, 1 \leq j \leq n$, all pointing to z, all owned by $p^h, 1 \leq h \leq m$. Initially, $x^{j+1} \in B^{j+1}$, owned by p^h does not point to z, scion(B^jx^j, Dz) exists, and process p^{h+1} does not cache

any granule pointing to z. This initial situation obviously verifies the theorem as scion(B^jx^j, Dz) exists.

Now, consider that $<x^{j+1} := x^j>_{p^h}$ is performed (thus x^{j+1} also points to z), therefore x^{j+1} is GC-dirty. If x^j is not assigned to thereafter, the theorem remains trivially true as scion(B^jx^j, Dz) exists.

Therefore, consider an assignment such as $<x^j := 0>_{p^h}$ (again, the actual value of the right-hand side does not matter for the proof). Until a bunch tracing or a propagate operation takes place at p^h, no <send.increment.scion> or <send.-decrement.scion> is performed at p^h, and the theorem remains trivially true (scion(B^jx^j, Dz) still exists).

In the first case, *i.e.* when a bunch tracing takes place at p^h, by Lemma 1 we have that at any moment, there exists at least a scion protecting z: either scion(B^jx^j, Dz), or scion($B^{j+1}x^{j+1}$, Dz), or both.

In the second case, *i.e.* when event <send.propagate(x^{j+1})>$_{p^h}$ happens, by Lemma 2 we have that scion($B^{j+1}x^{j+1}$, Dz) exists. □

A.2 Liveness

Our distributed GC algorithm is clearly not complete because it does not reclaim all cross-bunch cycles of garbage. Thus, we only consider the existence of acyclic cross-bunch garbage.

We assume that: *(i)* every bunch is eventually traced, *(ii)* intra-bunch tracing is complete w.r.t. that bunch, and *(iii)* increment.scion, decrement.scion, and union messages are eventually delivered in causal order.

We will not present here the full proof of liveness given its lack of interest. We simply show the conditions that must hold and how they are ensured.

The obvious liveness condition is:

Liveness Condition 1 *A granule not reachable is eventually reclaimed.*

Given that we are considering cross-bunch collection, Liveness Condition 1 implies:

Liveness Condition 2 *A granule not protected by any scion is eventually reclaimed.*

This condition is obviously ensured by the assumptions that every bunch is eventually traced, and bunch tracing is complete w.r.t. that bunch.

Note that, for liveness we must ensure that if a granule is no longer reachable from any incoming cross-bunch pointer, eventually no scion protects it. Thus, the following liveness condition must hold:

Liveness Condition 3 *A granule no longer reachable is eventually not protected.*

This condition is obviously ensured because: *(i)* we assumed that every bunch is eventually traced and bunch tracing is complete w.r.t. that bunch, therefore eventually there will be no stubs for disappearing outgoing pointers, and *(ii)* we assumed that both messages for deletion of scions and union messages are eventually delivered.

Therefore, a scion representing a incoming cross-bunch pointer no longer existing will be eventually deleted, and the corresponding object reclaimed.

Cyclic Distributed Garbage Collection with Group Merger

Helena Rodrigues* and Richard Jones

Computing Laboratory, University of Kent, Canterbury, Kent CT2 7NF, UK
Tel: +44 1227 827943, Fax +44 1227 762811
email: {hccdr,R.E.Jones}@ukc.ac.uk
http://www.cs.ukc.ac.uk/people/staff/rej/

Abstract. This paper presents a new algorithm for distributed garbage collection and outlines its implementation within the Network Objects system. The algorithm is based on a *reference listing* scheme augmented by *partial tracing* in order to collect distributed garbage cycles. Our collector is designed to be flexible thereby allowing efficiency, expediency and fault-tolerance to be traded against completeness. Processes may be dynamically organised into groups, according to appropriate heuristics, in order to reclaim distributed garbage cycles. Unlike previous group-based algorithms, multiple concurrent distributed garbage collections that span groups are supported: when two collections meet they may either merge, overlap or retreat. The algorithm places no overhead on local collectors and suspends local mutators only briefly. Partial tracing of the distributed graph involves only objects thought to be part of a garbage cycle: no collaboration with other processes is required.

Keywords: distributed systems, garbage collection, termination detection

1 Introduction

With the continued growth of distributed systems, designers are turning their attention to garbage collection [35, 30, 24, 22, 23, 7, 26, 27, 25, 14, 31, 15, 33, 20, 28, 18], prompted by the complexity of memory management and the desire for transparent object management. The goals of an ideal distributed garbage collector are that:

safety: only garbage should be reclaimed.
completeness: all garbage, including distributed cycles, at the start of a collection cycle should be reclaimed by its end.
concurrency: neither mutator nor local collector processes should be suspended; distinct distributed collection processes should run concurrently.
promptness: garbage should be reclaimed promptly.
efficiency: time and space costs should be minimised.

* Work supported by JNICT grant (CIENCIA/BD/2773/93-IA) through the *PRAXIS XXI* Program (Portugal).

locality: inter-process communication should be minimised.
expediency: garbage should be reclaimed despite the unavailability of parts of the system.
scalability: it should scale to networks of many processes.
fault tolerance: it should be robust against message delay, loss or replication, or process failure.

Inevitably compromises must be made between these goals. For example, scalability, fault-tolerance and efficiency may only be achievable at the expense of completeness, and concurrency introduces synchronisation overheads. Unfortunately, many solutions in the literature have never been implemented so there is a lack of empirical data for the performance of distributed garbage collection algorithms to guide the choice of compromises. For this reason we add a further goal:

flexibility: the collector should be configurable, guided by heuristics or hints from either the programmer or compiler.

Distributed garbage collection algorithms generally follow one of two strategies: tracing or reference counting. Tracing algorithms visit all 'live' objects [17, 13]; global tracing requires the cooperation of all processes before it can collect any garbage. This technique does not scale, is not efficient and requires global synchronisation. In contrast, distributed reference counting algorithms have the advantages for large-scale systems of fine interleaving with mutators, and locality of reference (and hence low communication costs). Although standard reference counting algorithms are vulnerable to out-of-order delivery of reference count manipulation messages, leading to premature reclamation of live objects, many distributed schemes have been proposed to handle or avoid such race conditions [6, 39, 16, 29, 36, 7, 26].

On the other hand, reference counting algorithms cannot collect cycles of garbage, although cyclic connections between objects in distributed systems are fairly common. For example, objects in client-server systems may hold references to each other, and often this communication is bi-directional [40]. Many distributed systems are typically long running (e.g. distributed databases), so floating garbage is particularly undesirable as even small amounts of uncollected garbage may accumulate over time to cause significant memory loss [27]. Although inter-process cycles of garbage can be broken by explicitly deleting references, this leads to exactly the error-prone scenario that garbage collection replaces.

Systems using distributed reference counting as their primary distributed memory management policy must reclaim cycles by using a complementary tracing scheme [22, 24, 21, 25, 33, 28, 18], or by migrating objects until an entire garbage cyclic structure is eventually held within a single process where it can be collected by the local collector [35, 27]. However, migration is communication-expensive and existing complementary tracing solutions require global synchronisation and the cooperation of all processes in the system [22], place additional overhead on the local collector and application [25], rely on cooperation from the local collector to propagate necessary information [24], or are not fault-tolerant [24, 25].

This paper presents an algorithm and outlines its implementation for the Network Objects system [8]. A fuller description and a proof of its correctness is to be found in [34]. Our algorithm is based on a *reference listing* [7], augmented by *partial tracing* in order to collect distributed garbage cycles [21, 33]. Our algorithm preserves our primary goals of efficient reclamation of local and distributed acyclic garbage, low synchronisation overheads, and avoidance of global synchronisation. In brief, our aim is to match rates of collection against rates of allocation of data structures. Objects only reachable from local processes have very high allocation rates, and must be collected most rapidly. The rate of creation of references to remote objects that are not part of distributed cycles is much lower, and the rate of creation of distributed garbage cycles is lower still and hence should have the lowest priority for reclamation.

To these ends, we permit some degree of completeness and efficiency in collecting distributed cycles to be traded, although eventually all these cycles will be reclaimed. We use heuristics to form groups of processes *dynamically* that cooperate to perform partial traces of subgraphs suspected of being garbage. Our earlier work offered only limited support for multiple, independently-initiated distributed garbage collections, as we imposed the restriction that no two distributed garbage collections could overlap; that is, no object could be simultaneously a member of more than one group and hence subject to more than one garbage collection [33]. This restriction prevented the collection of garbage cycles that spanned groups. In this paper, we lift this restriction and furthermore offer considerable flexibility to the programmer/compiler over how groups interact.

The paper is organised as follows. Section 2 introduces the computational model: the distributed system, mutator processes, visibility of objects across the network, reference passing and liveness. Section 3 introduces our partial tracing algorithm before Sect. 4 describes multiple, independently initiated, distributed garbage collections and deals with the problem of cycles that span groups. Section 5 introduces the problems of concurrency between mutators and collectors, and explains how the collectors are synchronised and termination achieved. Section 6 outlines a proof of correctness, and Sect. 7 maps our abstract description of our collector onto a concrete implementation using Modula-3's Network Objects system. Section 8 identifies the parameters that determine the cost of our algorithm and discusses how heuristics may be used to tune the collector. Finally we discuss related work in Sect. 9, and conclude in Sect. 10.

2 Computational Model

A distributed system is considered to consist of a collection of *processes*, organised into a network, that communicate by exchange of *messages*. Each process can be identified unambiguously, and we identify processes by upper-case letters, e.g. A, B, ..., and objects by lower-case letters (subscripted by the identifier of their owner), e.g. x_A, x_B, ...

From the garbage collector's point of view, *mutator* processes perform computations independently of other mutators in the system (although they may periodically exchange messages) and allocate objects in local heaps. The state of the distributed computation is represented by a *distributed graph* of objects. Objects may contain references to objects in the same or another process. Each process also contains a set of *local roots* that are always accessible to the local mutator. Objects that are reachable by following from a root a path of references held in other objects are said to be *live*. Other objects are said to be *garbage*, to be reclaimed by a *collector*. A collector that operates solely within a local heap is called a *local collector*.

For the moment, we abstract away from the details of the implementation by considering each process to maintain two tables. The *in-table* of a process lists all the remotely referenced *in-objects* belonging to the process. Only in-objects may be shared by processes. The process accessing an in-object for which it holds a reference is called the *client*, and the process containing the network object is called its *owner*. Clients and owners may run on different processes within the distributed system. Objects cannot migrate from one process to another.

A client cannot directly access an in-object but can only invoke the methods of a corresponding *out-object*, which in turn makes remote procedure calls to the owner. Associated with each entry in an in-table is a reference list, or *client set*, of the processes holding out-objects for the in-object. The *out-table* of each process lists all its out-objects and the remote in-objects to which they refer. A process holds at most one out-object for a given in-object and all references in the process to the remote object point to the corresponding out-object.

The heap of a process is managed by garbage collection. Local collections are based on tracing from process roots — the stack, registers, global variables and also the in-table. The in-table is considered a root by the local collector in order to preserve objects reachable only from other processes. In-table entries are managed by the distributed memory manager.

Remote references may be deleted or copied from one process to another either as arguments or results of methods. If the process receiving a reference is not the owner of the in-object, then the process may need to create a local out-object. In order to marshal a reference to another process, the sender process needs either to be the owner of the object or to have a out-object for that object. This operation must preserve a key invariant: whenever there is a out-object for an in-object x_P belonging to owner P at client C, then $C \in x_P.clientSet$.

Out-objects unreachable from their local root set are reclaimed by local collectors, in which case the corresponding owner is informed that the reference should be removed from its client set. When an in-object's client set becomes empty, the object is removed from the in-table so that it can be reclaimed subsequently by its owner's local collector. The invariants necessary to avoid race conditions and prevent premature reclamation of in objects are maintained in the standard way [7].

3 The Basic Algorithm

Our algorithm is based on the premise that distributed garbage cycles exist but are less common than acyclic structures. Thus reclamation of distributed cyclic garbage may be performed more slowly than that of local or distributed acyclic data. One consequence is that it is important that collectors — whether local or distributed — should not unduly disrupt mutator activity. We rely on local data being reclaimed by a tracing collector [20], whilst distributed acyclic structures are managed by reference listing [7]. We augment these mechanisms with an incremental, three-phase, partial trace to reclaim distributed garbage cycles. Our implementation does not halt local collectors at all, and suspends mutators only briefly. Local collectors reclaim garbage independently and expediently in each process. The partial trace merely identifies garbage cycles without reclaiming them. Consequently, both local and partial tracing collector can operate independently and concurrently. To simplify exposition, we start by describing the basic mechanisms, restricting our discussion to the collection of garbage within a single group of cooperating processes. We add multiple, independent but co-operating, distributed collectors in Sect. 4 and discuss concurrency and termination in Sect. 5.

Our algorithm operates in three phases [11, 33]. The first, *mark-red*, phase identifies a distributed subgraph that may be garbage, to which subsequent efforts are confined. The mark-red phase also identifies *dynamically* groups of processes that will collaborate to reclaim distributed cyclic garbage. A group is simply the set of processes visited by mark-red. Group collection is desirable for fault-tolerance, decentralisation, flexibility and efficiency. Fault-tolerance and efficiency are achieved by requiring the cooperation of only those processes forming the group: progress can be made even if other processes in the system fail. Decentralisation is achieved by partitioning the network into groups, with multiple groups simultaneously but independently active for garbage collection: communication is only necessary between members of the group.

The second, *scan*, phase determines whether members of this subgraph are actually garbage. This phase must also detect that any other collections upon which this collection depends have also terminated. Finally the *sweep* phase makes any garbage objects available for reclamation by local collectors.

The distributed collector requires that each item in processes' in- and out-tables has a *colour* — red, green or none — and that initially all objects are uncoloured (i.e. colour 'none'). In-objects also have a *red set* of process names, akin to their client set.

Partial tracing is initiated at *suspect* objects: out-objects suspected of belonging to a distributed garbage cycle (any distributed cycle must contain some out-object). A new partial trace may be initiated by any process not currently part of a trace. There are several reasons for choosing to initiate such an activity: the process may be idle, a local collection may have reclaimed insufficient space, the process may not have contributed to a distributed collection for a long time, or the process may simply choose to start a new distributed collection whenever it discovers a suspect object. Suspects should be chosen with care both to maximise the amount of garbage reclaimed and to minimise redundant computation or communication. A naïve view is to consider an out-object to be suspect if it is not referenced locally, other than through the in-table. This information is provided by the local collector — any out-object that has not been marked is suspect. This heuristic is very simplistic and may lead to undesirable wasted and repeated work. For example, it may repeatedly identify an out-object as a suspect even though it is reachable from a remote root. Rather, our algorithm should be seen as a framework: any better heuristic could be used [26]. In Section 8 we show how more sophisticated heuristics improve the algorithm's discrimination and hence its efficiency.

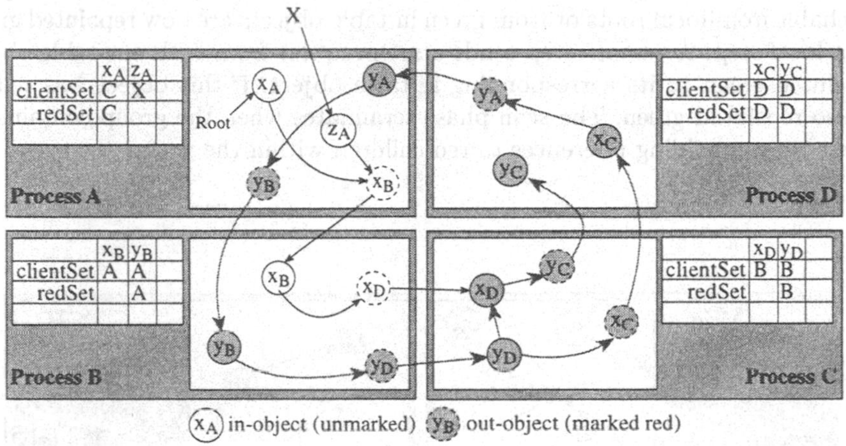

Fig. 1. mark-red identifies a subgraph suspect of being garbage

The **mark-red phase** paints the transitive referential closure of suspect out-objects red. It proceeds by a series of alternating local and remote steps. A *local step* forwards a colour from an object i in a process' in-table to all objects in its out-table reachable from i. A *remote step* sends a request from an out-table object to its corresponding in-table object, in this case reddening the in-object and inserting the name of the sending process into the red-set to indicate that this client is a member of the suspect subgraph[1]. Thus red-sets can be thought of as the 'dual' of client-sets: client-sets list all references to an in-object but red-sets list only those references believed to be dead.

The example in Fig. 1 illustrates a mark-red process. The figure contains a garbage cycle: $y_A y_B y_D x_C y_A$. Process A has initiated a partial trace; y_B is a suspect because it is not reachable from a local root (other than through the

[1] Notice that cooperation from the acyclic collector and the mutator would be required if, instead, mark-red removed references from client sets or copies of client sets (see [21]). Red sets avoid this need for cooperation as well as allowing the algorithm to identify which processes have sent mark-red requests.

in-table). The mark-red process paints the suspect's transitive closure red, and constructs the red sets. Note that objects x_D and y_C are not garbage although they have been painted red: their liveness will be detected by the scan phase.

At the end of the mark-red phase, a group of processes has been formed that will cooperate for the **scan-phase**. The aim of this phase is to determine whether any member of the red subgraph is reachable from outside that subgraph. It is executed concurrently on each process in the group. The first step is to compare the client- and red-sets of each red in-table object. If does not have a red-set (e.g. x_D in Fig. 1), or the difference between its client- and red-sets is non-empty, the object must have a client outside the suspect red graph. In this case the object is painted green to indicate that it may be live. Again, the scan phase proceeds by a series of alternating local and remote steps. All red in- and out-table objects reachable from local roots or from green in-table objects are now repainted green by a local step. A remote step sends a scan-request from each out-table object repainted green to its corresponding in-table object. If this object was red, it is also repainted green. The scan phase terminates when the group contains no green objects holding references to red children within the group.

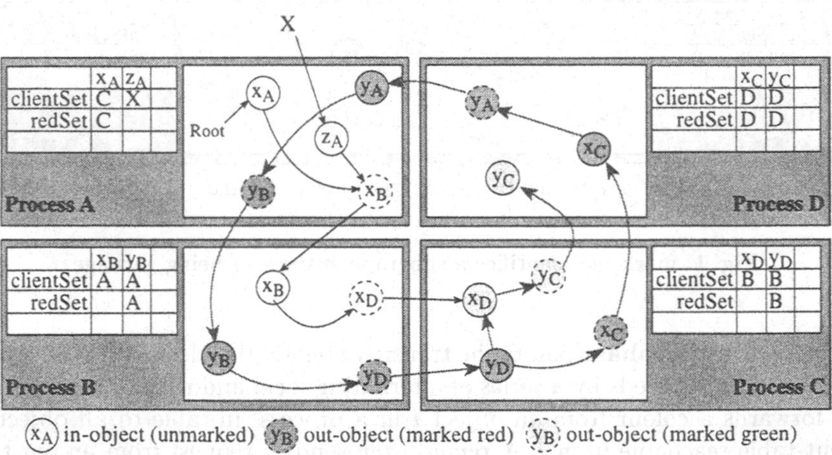

Fig. 2. the scan phase 'rescues' any red objects that may be live

Figure 2 shows the result of the scan phase. x_D in process D has no red-set so is painted green and becomes a root for the local step. y_C is reachable from x_D and so is also repainted green[2]. Note that the only inter-process edge traversed in the scan phase is that between the y_C.

[2] Notice that other group-based partial tracing schemes do not consider public objects internal to the group to be roots [24]. In our example that would require extra messages to be sent from A to B and from B to D in order to preserve x_D.

At the end of the scan phase, all live objects are green[3]. Any remaining red objects must be part of inaccessible cycles, and can thus be safely reclaimed. The **sweep phase** is executed in each process independently: at the next local collection, red in-table objects are not considered to be roots, and thus their (garbage) descendents will be reclaimed. The reclamation of an out-table item causes the reference listing mechanism to send a delete message to the owner of the corresponding in-table object: when its client-set becomes empty, that object will also be reclaimed.

4 Multiple Group Collection

Very few studies have measured the performance of distributed garbage collection algorithms and behaviour of the programs they support. In particular, comparatively little is known about the topology or demographics of distributed object systems —for example, how common are distributed cycles, how large are they, how long lived are they? A deficiency of many proposals for group-based distributed collectors, including our earlier work [33], is the treatment of inter-group garbage cycles.

Our new algorithm allows different collecting groups to cooperate for garbage collection. Scalability demands that distributed garbage collections may be initiated independently, but this raises the possibility that two independently initiated groups may meet in one or more processes. There are two ways in which distributed structures, hence groups identified by mark-red, may overlap. First, a *process* may be a member of more than one group despite there being no reference from any object in one group to any object in any other group. Consequently no object will visited by more than one group. Alternatively, an *object* may be referenced by objects in more than one group. It is this more interesting and challenging alternative that we address now; the simpler problem is also solved by our algorithm.

There are three possible strategies for resolving this matter. First, all interaction between two independent distributed garbage collections could be prohibited whilst nevertheless permitting inter-group references [33]. This has the advantage of simplicity as it eliminates all interaction between distributed collectors, and obviates any need for synchronisation either to assure correctness and termination, or to bound the size of a collection. However, it fails to collect garbage cycles that span groups.

The second strategy is to allow both collections to proceed, but to ignore one another. In effect, the groups retain their own identity but *overlap*. This requires that the collectors do not share any state (the colour and red-set information held in the in- and out-tables). This could be achieved by maintaining one copy of this state information for each collection group, and having all garbage collection messages signed with the identity of their group (i.e. the identity of their initiating process). The obvious drawback is that, while this is scalable and complete, it is neither time- nor space-efficient as it leads to repeated work.

[3] Note that the converse, *i.e.* that all green objects are live, is not necessarily true.

The third strategy is to *merge* the two collecting groups into a single group, thereby giving completeness and efficiency albeit at the cost of greater complexity. To collect garbage data structures that span two groups, some form of synchronisation must exist between the groups. One group maybe be *dependent* on the other, and unable to determine that the structure it is holding is garbage until the other has also determined that its portion of the structure is garbage. In the example in Fig. 3, the group containing processes A and B cannot detect that its structure is garbage until the CD group has completed its scan phase.

4.1 Partial Tracing Objects

Our algorithm records this dependency information explicitly. Each in- and out-object holds (in addition to the colour) a *marks* list of groups that have visited the object; the head of this list is called the *mark.*

The Network Objects library handles all communication between network objects through a special object in each process [8]. We adopt the same approach to support our partial tracing mechanisms by constructing a new partial tracing object (pto) PT_{id} when a collection for group *id* visits a participant process for the first time in this collection cycle:

$$PT_{id} = (id,\ participants,\ ins,\ outs,\ guardians,\ dependents)$$

id is a unique identifier. A distributed garbage collection can be identified by its initiating process and the set of suspect objects from which it starts. For simplicity we shall usually assume *id* and the initiator to be synonymous.

participants the members of the group collaborating to collect garbage.

ins, outs in- and out-objects in this process visited by this group.

dependents pto's that are dependent on this object.

guardians pto's that are guardians of this object.

For convenience, we denote the colour of an object with mark A by red_A, $green_A$, etc. Most communication between groups is handled through these local pto's (ambassadors, maybe?) without exchanging messages across the network.

4.2 Merging Mark-red

The mark-red phase is initiated from a suspect out-object (e.g. v_C in Fig. 3) by creating a pto identified by this process, say D. This *initiating pto* is said to be *active-disquiet.* The suspect is reddened and its *mark* set to PT_D. The pto then executes alternate local and remote steps, colouring objects that it reaches. It performs a local mark-red step from each in-object i newly marked red_D to colour each out-object o reachable from i as follows:

(ML.1) If o has not been coloured, then it is reddened and its mark set to PT_D: it is red_D.

(ML.2) If o is already red_D, then no further action is necessary.

(ML.3) If o is ***red***$_A$ and $A \neq D$, then two groups have met in the same phase. We merge the groups and say that A is ***dependent*** on D and D is a ***guardian*** for A. PT_D is appended to ***o.marks***, PT_D is added to the ***guardians*** set of the pto PT_A, and PT_A to the ***dependents*** set of pto PT_D. Both these interactions take place between the pto's in this process — no messages are sent.

(ML.4) If o is green, it must have been marked by another group operating in a later phase so the red wave-front retreats from this object.

Remote steps executed by PT_D propagate colours from out-objects o in a process P to in-objects i in a remote process Q. A new PT_D pto is constructed in Q to represent this group (unless one already exists for this group as a result of an earlier mark-red request in this collection cycle).

(MR.1) If i is uncoloured or ***red***$_D$, P is added to its red set and i is marked ***red***$_D$.

(MR.2) If i is ***red***$_A$ and $A \neq D$, P is still added to i's red set. Once again two groups have met and, as in the local step, PT_D is appended to ***i.marks*** and to PT_A***.guardians***, PT_A to PT_D***.dependents*** in process Q; no messages are exchanged.

(MR.3) If i is green, no further action is taken.

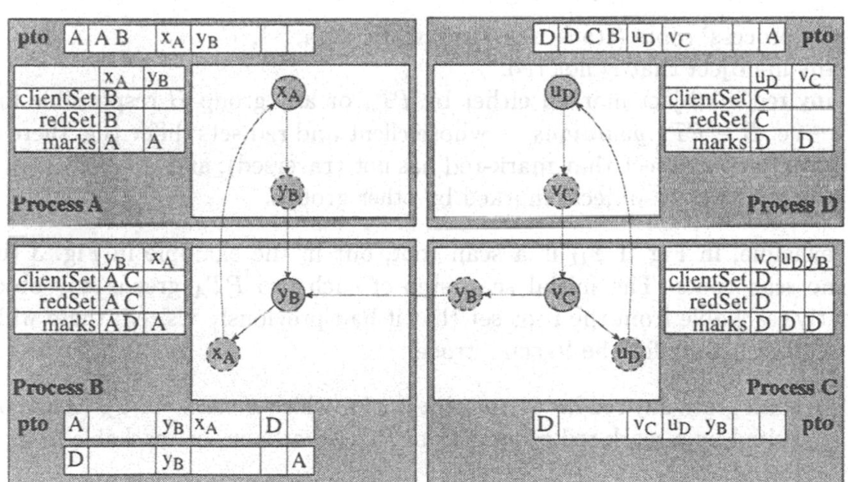

Fig. 3. end of the mark-red phase

When a pto has no more local steps to perform and has received acknowledgements for all the tracing requests that it has sent, the pto returns an acknowledgement to the pto whose remote step caused it to be created. The acknowledgement contains a list of the participating processes that it and its children have visited. It is now said to be ***passive-quiet*** but may be re-awakened by further mark-red requests (in which case it becomes ***passive-disquiet***). No further synchronisation is needed between the mark-red phases of each group[4]. At the end of the mark-red phase, each initiating pto will know the participants in its group, and objects in these participant processes reachable from suspects will have been painted red (with their *marks* list identifying all the groups of which they are members). Figure 3 shows an example in which two processes, A and D, have initiated independent distributed collections which have met at y_B. Note that process B contains pto's for both groups A and D.

4.3 Scanning Merged Groups

The aim of the merging collector is now to identify those objects that are not reachable from a root or from outside the merged super-group. A component group cannot make such a decision in isolation. Thus each initiating pto must determine that (a) it and all the participants in its group, and (b) all the groups upon which it depends, have completed their scan phase.

On termination of its mark-red phase, the initiator instructs all participants in its group to start the scan phase. In this phase, each pto will 'rescue' any live objects that it had inadvertently marked red. Again, after an initial step to colour green any in- or out- object reachable from the local roots, the scan phase proceeds by an alternating series of local and remote steps. The roots of the scan phase for a pto PT_A are:

- the process' roots (stack, registers, static area...),
- any in-object that is not red,
- any red in-object marked either by PT_A or any group B responsible for it — i.e. $B \in PT_A.guardians$ — whose client and red sets differ (i.e. there is a path to this object that mark-red has not traversed), and
- any other red in-objects marked by other groups.

For example, in Fig. 1 x_D is a scan root, but in the example in Fig. 3 there are no scan roots. The initial scan step of each pto PT_A greens any objects directly reachable from the root set that it had previously visited: these will be the starting points for the 'rescue' trace.

(SI.1) Mark green any red in- or out-object x for which $x.mark = PT_A$ (x had been visited by a mark-red request from PT_A) that is in, or reachable from, the root set.

The local scan phase step for PT_A propagates the green colour from a $green_A$ in-object i to those out-objects o in the same process reachable from i that PT_A had previously visited in the mark-red phase:

(SL.1) Green o if it is *red* and $A \in o.marks$.

The remote step from a $green_A$ out-object o propagates the green colour to the corresponding in-object i:

[4] The termination of each phase is discussed in more detail in Sect. 5.

(SR.1) If i is red and $PT_A \in i.marks$, mark i green.
(SR.2) If i is red but $PT_A \notin i.marks$, retreat.
(SR.3) If i is not red, retreat.

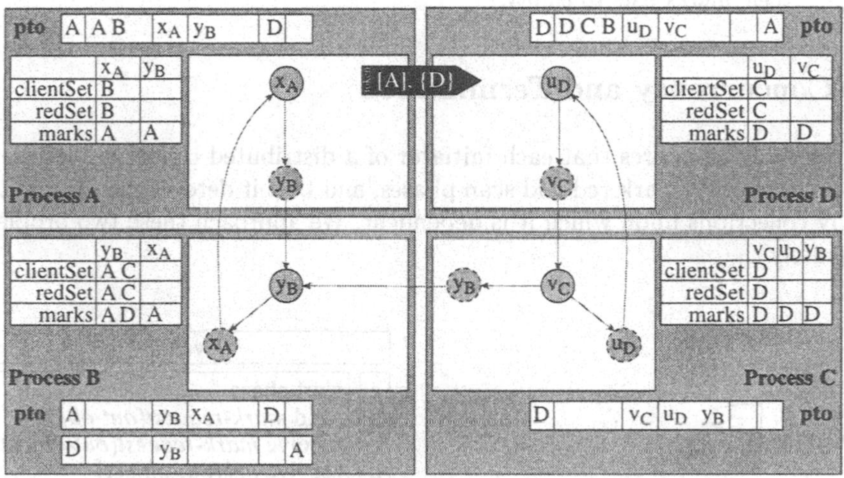

Fig. 4. end of the scan phase

Remote steps do not invoke local steps directly. Rather, the pto that 'owns' the in-object (identified by its *mark*) will execute a local step once it has started its scan phase. Note that an in-object may be part of more than one group (the length of its *marks* list is greater than one). If a pto receives a scan-request before it receives the instruction to start the scan phase, it simply marks the in-object green but does not yet take a local step.

As before, a pto PT_A becomes passive-quiet in the scan phase when it has no more local steps to perform and has received acknowledgements for all the remote steps that it has executed. It returns to its parent tracing object a list of all the groups upon which it is dependent, $PT_A.guardians$[5].

$$PT_A.guardians = \bigcup_{i.mark=A} i.marks$$

Figure 4 shows the example at the end of the scan phase. PT_A in process B has reported to the process A that initiated the collection that the collection is dependent on D.

4.4 Sweep Phase

The scan phase of a group cannot terminate as long as it is possible for a member of that group to receive further scan requests. We describe our termination

[5] A group A may be a guardian for group B and vice-versa.

mechanism in Sect. 5.4 below. At the end of the scan phase, any red_A objects are unreachable from process roots either within or without this group. First we give the single step taken by the sweep phase for PT_A in each process concurrently:

(SW.1) Remove all red_A from the in-table; repaint as uncoloured all $green_A$, setting their *marks* lists to empty.

5 Concurrency and Termination

The algorithm requires that each initiator of a distributed collection detect the termination of its mark-red and scan phases, and that it detects the termination of any collections upon which it is dependent. We approach these two problems separately.

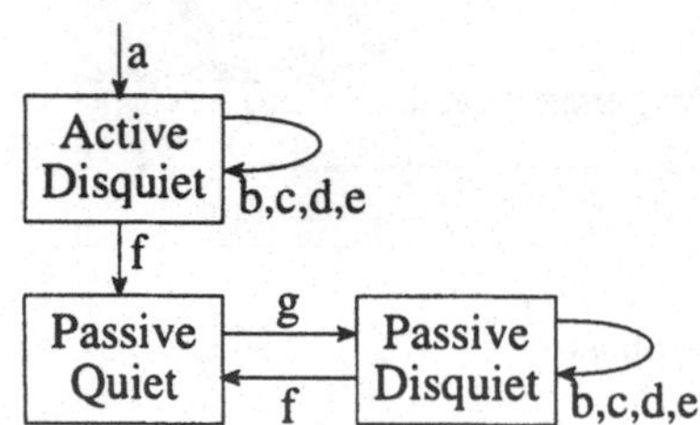

	Events
a	start phase
b	send *mark-request(out-object)*
c	receive *mark-request(out-object)*
d	receive *ack(out-object)*
e	perform *local step*
f	all acks received
g	receive *mark-request(out-object)*

Fig. 5. state transitions for termination detection. An additional initial state required by pto's that receive a scan-request before the instruction to start the scan phase is omitted for simplicity.

5.1 Group Termination

For termination of each group, we use an acknowledgement-based termination detection protocol for both the mark-red and the scan phases that does not require processes to be known at the start of distributed garbage collection [38]. Following Augusteijn [2], we introduce three possible states for a process (see Diagram and Table 5): *active-disquiet*, *passive-disquiet* and *passive-quiet*.

- A process initiating a phase is active-disquiet.
- The receipt of a tracing request causes a passive-quiet process to become passive-disquiet.
- Requests have no effect on the *state* of an active-disquiet process — the request is simply added to the process' work-list.
- When a process has no more work to do — no local steps to perform and it has received acknowledgements for all its tracing requests — the process becomes passive-quiet.

- On becoming passive-quiet, processes return an acknowledgement, identifying themselves and those identified by any tracing requests that they have in turn exported. Requests to active-disquiet processes on the other hand are acknowledged immediately[6].

From this it can be seen that there is always an active-disquiet process responsible for any passive-disquiet process. It therefore suffices to detect the termination of the active processes alone. In the mark-red phase, this is particularly simple as there is just one active process: the initiator; in the scan phase however there may be many active disquiet processes.

5.2 Mark-red Phase

Within a single group, the mark-red phase is initiated by a single active-disquiet process. As soon as this process has received acknowledgements from all the mark-red processes that it has exported, it becomes passive-quiet: the mark-red phase is complete and the membership of the group is known.

Our collector does not need to visit the complete transitive referential closure of suspect out-objects. The purpose of the mark-red phase is simply to determine the scope of subsequent phases and to construct red-sets. Early termination of this phase can be used to trade *conservatism* (tolerance of floating garbage) for expediency, and bounds on the size of the graph traced (and hence on the cost of the trace). We believe that our approach also shows promise for other NUMA problems that use partitioned address spaces, such as distributed object-oriented databases and persistent storage systems [34]. Importantly, this conservativism allows the phase to be executed concurrently with mutators without need for synchronisation and so permits cheap termination of this phase.

5.3 Scan Phase

The scan phase is initiated concurrently on each participant process holding part of the red, suspect subgraph. The pto's representing this group collection in each participant process are set to active-disquiet on receipt of the instruction from the initiating pto to start this phase. Group scan phase termination is detected by the protocol described above. Each of the active-disquiet pto's for this group informs the initiating pto as soon as it becomes passive-quiet.

In contrast to the mark-red phase, the scan phase must be complete with respect to the red subgraph, since it must ensure that all live red objects are repainted green. As with other concurrent marking schemes, this requires synchronisation between mutator and collector. We consider the effect of mutator actions on first scan phase local steps and then scan phase remote steps.

Termination detection requires that scan phase local steps must be able to detect any change to the connectivity of the graph made by a mutator. A local mutator may only change this connectivity by overwriting references to objects.

---

[6] We piggy-back collector acknowledgements on the back of RPC acknowledgements.

Such writes can be detected by a *write barrier* [41] — our implementation is described in Sect. 7. Once a process has no more local scan steps to perform, any red in-object *o* and its red descendents are isolated from the green subgraph held in that process — they cannot become reachable through actions of the local mutator. However their reachability can still be changed if:

(a) a remote method is invoked on *o*; or
(b) a new out-object corresponding to *o* is created in some other process;
(c) another object in the same process receives a reference to *o* from a remote process.

None of these events can occur unless the red out-object is still alive. Correct termination detection requires that each scan-request (and subsequent scan) has an active-disquiet process ultimately responsible for it. Trapping mutator messages with a 'snapshot-at-the-beginning' barrier preserves this invariant. If a client invokes a remote method from a red out-object, or copies the reference held by a red out-object to another process, a scan-request is sent to the corresponding in-object, along with the mutator message[7]. The scan-request paints the in-object, and any local out-objects reachable from it, green in an atomic local-step operation before the mutator message is handled.

The mutator operation that sprung the trap cannot have been made from a passive-quiet process. If it were, the red out-object would have been unreachable from the client process' roots unless a prior external mutator action had caused the object to become locally reachable. But in this case the out-object would have been repainted green by the write barrier. Thus, an active-disquiet process is always responsible for the scan-request generated by the barrier. If the owner of the in-object is also active-disquiet, an acknowledgement is returned immediately and this process takes over responsibility for any consequent scan-requests. If it is passive, the scan-request is not acknowledged until all the descendents have been scanned; the client process cannot become quiet until it has received this acknowledgement.

5.4 Super-group Termination

The scan phase of an individual group cannot terminate as long as it is possible for a member of the group to receive further scan requests. Our modification of Augusteijn's algorithm resolves this for members of a single group, but a group may also receive scan-requests from members of other groups in its super-group. We note however that there will be an active-disquiet process responsible for these requests, and say that a process is *stable* if it is not active-disquiet. Once a process becomes stable it can never become active-disquiet again: although it may perform scan steps these will be on behalf of other active-disquiet processes. We say that a group is *partially terminated* if all its participants are stable. Our termination property for a single group is that all groups (initiating pto's) on which it depends are partially terminated. We define a relation *Dependent*:

[7] In our implementation, we send both messages in the same remote procedure call.

Definition 1. *∀ pto's PT_A, PT_D in a process, Dependent(PT_A, PT_D) ≡ $PT_D \in PT_A$.guardians*

and we calculate its reflexive transitive closure, *Dependent**. We adopt the simple protocol of passing tokens around a ring formed by initiator members of the super group [32], so that when a token has returned to the initiator that created it, the scan phase of that group is complete. As soon as an initiator A partially terminates, it constructs a token. The token has two parts:

terminated a list of the groups in ring that are known to have partially terminated; initially this holds A alone.

next a set of initiators not yet visited; initially this holds the groups responsible for A, A.*guardians*.

Propagation of the token around the ring is simple. An initiator process A retains the token until all members of its group are stable, i.e. the group is partially terminated. If the head of the token's *terminated* list is A then the scan phase has fully terminated. Otherwise A (i) removes itself from the *next* set to the end of to the *terminated* list, (ii) inserts any of its guardian groups that are not members of the *terminated* list in the *next* set, and (iii) passes the token to any member of the *next* set. If this set is empty, all the *Dependent*(A)* groups have terminated and the token is returned to its owner, the head of the *terminated* list. Figure 4 shows the token sent by A to its guardian, D; D will return the token with an empty *next*-set to the head of the *terminated*-list, A. As D has an empty *guardians* set, it does not need to wait for any other group to terminate.

6 Safety

The safety requirement for our algorithm is that live objects are never reclaimed. First we note that the system of acknowledgements ensures that marking requests are guaranteed to be delivered to their destination unless either the client or owner process fails before the message is safely delivered and acknowledged. Although it is possible that messages might be duplicated, marking is an idempotent operation (*cf.* reference listing, above).

To demonstrate that the merging algorithm is correct, we briefly outline how it can be shown that, if a pto PT_B is in its sweep phase, then no red_B objects in the same process can receive a scan request, and hence that no red_B object can be live in B's sweep phase. First, we conservatively define an object x to be *live* if

$$(\exists P \in supergroup \wedge \exists r \in Roots(P) \wedge path(r,x)) \quad \vee$$
$$(\exists Q \notin supergroup \wedge \exists o \in out\text{-}table(Q) \wedge path(o,x))$$

Suppose that x is live but erroneously reclaimed by pto PT_B in process P. By (SW.1), $red_B(x) \wedge live(x)$. Thus

$$(\exists i \in in\text{-}table(P) \wedge path(i,x) \wedge live(i)) \vee (\exists r \in Roots(P) \wedge path(r,x))$$

There cannot have been such a path from a local root before PT_B took its initial scan step — since (SI.1) would have greened x — so only a subsequent remote method invoked from an out-object o' on an in-object i' from which x is reachable could have created this path. If o' was red_B, x would have been repainted green by o''s barrier. If it was $green_B$, a scan request has been sent to repaint i and hence x green (if the scan-request acknowledgement has not been received then the request will be sent again, with the mutator message). If o' had not been visited by B, then i would have been a scan root for PT_B.

So x must have been reachable from i when PT_B took its initial scan step, and this i cannot have been a local scan root (SI.1). Hence

$$red(i) \wedge (i.redSet = i.clientSet) \wedge (i.mark = PT_B \vee i.mark \in PT_B.guardians)$$

All out-objects o (i.e. $o \in i.clientSet$) from which i is reachable must be red (MR.1 or MR.2), and by hypothesis, at least one such red_A, for some group A, must be live. We need to show that group A has completed its scan phase and hence that o can never become green.

If $A = B$ then the pto's responsible for both x and o are members of the same group. Hence o's pto has completed its scan phase and so cannot generated further scan requests. Alternatively, $A \neq B$ in which case $A \in PT_B.guardians$ (MR.1 or MR.2) and hence a member of the *guardians* set of the initiator of group B (the final action of a pto in the scan phase is to return a list of guardian groups to its initiator). The scan phase termination for group B must send a token to, *inter alia*, the initiator of group A (since $A \in PT_B.guardians$). Group B does not enter the sweep phase until A (and other guardian groups) have returned the token, but group A will not do so until all its members are passive-quiet. No scan request can be generated from within group A.

Neither can a scan request originate from a group in *Dependent*(A)* as all pto's within *Dependent*(A)* are partially terminated by the time that A has received its token back. Any request must be from an out-object o'' in a third group, $C \notin$ *Dependent*(A)*. Since the in-object was red, its red set contained o'' and hence its *marks* contained C, i.e. C is a guardian for group B. But this means that $C \in$ *Dependent*(A)*. Thus no such scan request can occur. Hence group A has completed its scan phase and the red objects cannot be live.

7 Mapping the Algorithm onto Network Objects

Our algorithm is built on top of the reference listing mechanism provided by the Network Objects distributed memory manager, albeit slightly modified [8]. The Network Objects collector is resilient to communication failures or delays, and to process failures. Object migration is not supported. In this section we describe how our algorithm is mapped onto the Network Objects system. In particular we are bound to account for the collection of local and acyclic distributed garbage, and synchronisation between mutators and collectors

Network Objects is a distributed object library for Modula-3, a garbage-collected language [10]. Our local collector is a slightly modified version of the

SRC Modula-3 incremental, mostly copying collector [4]. Synchronisation between the mutator and the local collector is provided by a page-wise read-only barrier supported by the operating system [1].

Network Objects uses reference lists rather than counts: any client process holds at most one *surrogate* for any given network, or *concrete*, object. Our in-table is represented by that part of (a modified version of) the Network Objects' *object table*, that contains references, or *wireReps*, to concrete network objects, and our out-table is that part that contains references to surrogate objects.

Communication failures are detected by a system of acknowledgements. However, a process that sends a message but does not receive an acknowledgement cannot know whether that message was received or not. Unlike reference counting, reference listing operations are idempotent and so resilient to duplication of messages. Network Objects' dirty call mechanism also prevents out-of-order delivery of messages from causing the premature reclamation of objects.

An owner of a network object can also detect the termination of any client process. Any client that has terminated is removed from the client set of the corresponding concrete object, allowing objects to be reclaimed even if the client terminates abnormally. Unfortunately, communication delay may be misinterpreted as process failure, in which case an object may be prematurely reclaimed. Proof of the safety and liveness of the Network Objects system may be found in [7].

Unlike the mark-red phase, scan phase tracing must be accurate with respect to the red subgraph in order to ensure that it reaches all red objects that are live. Mostly Parallel garbage collection [9] uses operating system support to detect those objects modified by mutators (actually pages that have been updated within a given interval). When the local scan phase process has visited all objects reachable from its starting points, the mutator is halted while the graph is retraced from roots any modified objects. Because most of the scanning work has already been done, it is expected that this retrace will terminate promptly (the underlying assumption is that the rate of allocation of network objects, and of objects reachable from those network objects, is low). In any event, this retrace may be interrupted and restarted later.

Scan-requests caused by mutator action are asynchronous and these may require the out-object descendents of the receiving in-object to be repainted green atomically. The simplest method of propagating marks from in- to out-objects is to 'stop the world' in that process and perform a standard recursive trace from the in-object. We claim that this does not cause excessive delay as this event is unlikely to occur if our heuristic for finding suspects is good, and moreover it is likely that objects reachable from a live in-object are already known to be live.

8 Costs and Heuristics

The costs associated with our algorithm can be divided into two categories: those associated with the RPC calls exchanged between processors and those common to any incremental collector caused by running scan phase local steps concurrently with mutators. We analyse the former here.

Call the number of inter-process edges in the subgraph visited by mark-red e, and the number of participants in this group n. Note that $e \leq$ the number of edges in the transitive referential closure of the suspect objects.

- The mark-red phase for each group issues e mark-request RPC calls, by definition.
- The number of mark-red acknowledgement calls depends on whether the request is sent to a quiet or a disquiet pto, and this in turn depends on the topology (degree of sharing) of the subgraph. An acknowledgement from a disquiet pto can be piggy-backed onto the RPC acknowledgement; that from a quiet process requires a separate call. Thus, between $n-1$ (one acknowledgement for each pto-creating request) and e (one per edge) calls are required.
- Each acknowledgement message has a length $\leq n$, the maximum number of processes to which the request message can have been forwarded.

Thus the number of RPC calls C_{MR} caused by mark-red is:

$$e + n - 1 \leq C_{MR} \leq 2e$$

- Scan phase initiation requires $n-1$ messages to participating pto's.
- The number of scan requests sent depends on the accuracy with which suspects are identified. In the best case, no requests will be sent but each pto must report termination to the initiator; in the worst case, the number of RPC calls is the same as that for mark-red[8]. Let p be the probability that our suspect identification heuristic is accurate.
- Super group termination requires d_A calls for each group A where $d_A = |Dependent^*(A)|$.

Thus the expected number of RPC calls C_{SC} caused by the scan phase is:

$$(1-p)e + 2(n-1) + d \leq C_{SC} \leq 2(1-p)e + (1+p)(n-1) + d$$

- The sweep phase requires $n-1$ messages.

The total number of RPC calls C required is:

$$(2-p)e + 4(n-1) + d \leq C \leq 2(2-p)e + (2+p)(n-1) + d$$

The cost of our algorithm is determined by the parameters n, e, d and p. p depends on our choice of suspect; n, e and d are partly determined by the topology of the subgraph and the dynamics of distributed collections but can also be controlled by policy decisions on the extent of mark-red's coverage of the graph. Because little is known of the demographics of distributed objects,

[8] The intermediate case occurs when a subset of the red sub-graph is found to be live.

flexibility is a key goal of our collector. Our collector can be seen as a framework within which policy decisions can be implemented. Policy guides the choice of suspects, the choice of processes forming each group and the merger of groups.

A new partial trace may be initiated by any process not currently part of a trace. There are several reasons for choosing to initiate such an activity: the process may be idle, a local collection may have reclaimed insufficient space, the process may not have contributed to a distributed collection for a long time, or the process may simply choose to start a new distributed collection whenever it discovers a suspect object. A very simple heuristic would be to use the local collector alone to identify those surrogates only reachable from the object table but the better the heuristic the greater the chance p that our algorithm traces only garbage subgraphs thereby decreasing the number of times a partial trace is run, limiting the mark-red trace to garbage and reducing the number of scan phase messages to the best case, and decreasing the chance of wasted and repeated work.

A more sophisticated heuristic is to estimate an object's minimum distance from a root, measured by inter-process references — the *distance heuristic* [26]. The distance heuristic requires each in-object to periodically propagate an estimate of its distance from a root to its children, who use this estimate to adjust their own distance estimate. The insight is that the estimate for objects in a garbage cycle will increase without bound; once a threshold value is reached for an object's distance, we have some confidence, but no guarantee, that the object is garbage. A drawback of the distance heuristic is that several objects in a garbage cycle may attain the threshold together, leading to multiple collections in the same cycle (increasing both d and the number of pto's in processes where the collections meet). By only propagating distances over a certain threshold with mark-red requests we can reduce the risk of multiple distributed collections in the same garbage cycle and therefore reduce the overheads of our algorithm. However, even with a simplistic heuristic, a probability of being garbage can be assigned to each suspect object that has survived a partial tracing. For example, we could take a round-robin approach by tracing only from the suspect that was least recently traced.

p and n can be controlled by bounding the amount of work done by mark-red. Recall that this phase needs only make a conservative estimate of the transitive referential closure of suspect objects — it need not visit the whole closure. This policy decision can be taken statically by prior negotiation or dynamically by mark-red. It may be determined by the collector itself or by the user program, globally or on a per-process or even per-object basis. Heuristics based on geography, process identity, distance from the suspect originating the collection, minimum distance from any object known to be live, or time constraints may be used to restrict the extent of mark-red or the decision whether to merge with, overlap or retreat from other distributed collections. In the absence of knowledge of the problem being computed, it is unclear what action should be taken when two groups meet. A merger may not always be desirable. Instead it may be preferable to run multiple overlapping groups. For example the best compromise may be to combine simultaneously occasional long-running but complete collections over very large groups with more frequent faster completing collections over small groups. Our algorithm offers the implementer the choice between completeness and promptness at the level of groups, processes and individual objects. Groups can decide whether or not to merge, processes can decide whether to allow groups to merge, to overlap or to retreat from one another, and objects can decide on merger or retreat.

The cost of distributed collection is comparatively robust against the rate of modification of references held in objects. The cost to the local scan step depends, as with any incremental uniprocessor collector, on how it is synchronised with the mutator [20]. Modifications caused by exchange of mutator messages trigger the barrier, causing the collector to do work, only on the first occasion in a collection cycle that a message is sent from a red out-object. Indeed, the frequency of messages sent to an object that would otherwise be considered suspect is a useful measure of whether that object should be considered as a root for a distributed collection.

9 Related Work

Distributed reference counting can be augmented in various ways to collect distributed garbage cycles. Juul and Jul [22], periodically invoke global marking to collect distributed garbage cycles, tracing the whole graph before any cyclic garbage can be collected. Even though some degree of concurrency is allowed, this technique cannot make progress if a single process has crashed, even if that process does not own any part of the distributed garbage cycle. This algorithm is complete, but it needs global cooperation and synchronisation, and thus does not scale.

Maeda *et al.* [25] present a solution also based on earlier work by Jones and Lins using partial tracing with weighted reference counting [21]. Weighted reference counting is resilient to race conditions, but cannot recover from process failure or message loss. As suggested by Jones and Lins, they use secondary reference counts as auxiliary structures. Thus they need a weight-barrier to maintain consistency, incurring further synchronisation costs.

Maheshwari and Liskov [27] describe a simple and efficient way of using object migration to allow collection of distributed garbage cycles, that limits the volume of the migration necessary. The *distance heuristic* estimates the length of the shortest path from any root to each object. This heuristic allows the identification of objects belonging to a garbage cycle, with a high probability of being correct. These objects are migrated directly to a selected destination process to avoid multiple migrations. However, this solution requires support for object migration (not present in Network Objects). Moreover, migrating an object is a communication-intensive operation, not only because of its inherent overhead but also because of the time necessary to prepare an object for migration and to install it in the target process [37]. In a recent paper Maheshwari and Liskov use the same distance heuristic to identify suspect objects from which they start a back trace in an attempt to discover a root [28]. They employ similar reference listing and barriers schemes to those presented here. Unlike [15], their algorithm provides an efficient method of calculating back-references and takes account of concurrency.

Lang *et al.* [24] also presented an algorithm for marking within groups of processes. Their algorithm uses standard reference counting, and so inherits its inability to tolerate message failures. It relies on the cooperation from the local collector to propagate necessary information. This algorithm is difficult to evaluate because of the lack of detail presented. However, the main differences between this and our algorithm is that we trace only those subgraphs suspected of being garbage and that we use heuristics to form groups opportunistically. In contrast, Lang's method is based on Christopher's algorithm [11]. Consequently it repeatedly scans the heap until it is sure that it has terminated. This is less efficient than simply marking nodes red. For example, concrete objects referenced from outside the suspect subgraph are considered as roots by the scan phase, even if they are only referenced inside the group. In the example of Fig. 1 and 2 our algorithm would need a total of 6 messages (5 for mark-red phase and 1 for scan phase), against a total of 10 messages (7 for the initial marking and 3 for the global propagation) for Lang's algorithm. Objects may also have to repeat traces on behalf of other objects (i.e. a trace from a 'soft' concrete object may have to be repeated if the object is hardened). Their 'stabilisation loop' may also require repeated traces. Finally, failures cause the groups to be completely reorganised, and a new group garbage collection restarted almost from scratch.

Hudson *et al.* have adapted their Mature Object Space 'train' algorithm for distributed garbage collection [19, 18]. While their new algorithm collects all garbage, including distributed garbage, it requires an *object substitution protocol* to ensure that all old references to an object are updated to refer to the new copy. Detecting that a train has no external references is also more complex in a distributed environment than in a uniprocessor one: they use a similar token ring technique to that we use for detecting super group termination.

10 Conclusions and Future Work

This paper has outlined a solution for collecting distributed garbage cycles, designed for the Network Objects system but applicable to other systems — a complete treatment will be found in [34]. Our algorithm is based on a *reference listing* scheme [7], augmented by *partial tracing* in order to collect distributed garbage cycles [21]. *Groups* of processes are formed *dynamically* to collect cyclic garbage. Processes within a group cooperate to perform a partial trace of only those subgraphs suspected of being garbage. If necessary, groups can cooperate to collect garbage cycles that span them.

Our memory management system is highly *concurrent*: mutators, local collectors, the acyclic reference collector and distributed cycle collectors operate mostly in parallel. Local collectors are never delayed, and mutators are only halted by a distributed partial tracing to complete a local scan.

Our system reclaims garbage *efficiently*: local and acyclic collectors are not hindered. The efficiency of the distributed partial tracing can be increased by restricting the size of groups, thereby trading *completeness* for *promptness*. The use of the acyclic collector and groups also permits *scalability* whereas the ability to merge groups ensures *completeness*.

Our collector provides a *flexible* framework for the implementation of policy decisions directing the collection of garbage. Heuristics may be applied to govern the choice of suspects, the extent of the subgraph to be traced and whether to allow independent collections that meet to merge, overlap or retreat. Our algorithm therefore offers the implementer the choice between completeness and promptness at the level of groups, processes and individual objects.

Our distributed collector is *fault-tolerant*: it is resilient to message delay, loss and duplication, and to process failure. *Expediency* is achieved by the use of groups.

Early versions of our algorithm have been implemented. In particular, some choices for cooperation with the mutator require further study and depend mainly on experimental results and measurements. We are also interested in heuristics for suspect identification and group formation. Finally, we would like to thank the anonymous referees for their helpful comments on the earlier draft of this paper.

References

[1] Andrew W. Appel, John R. Ellis, and Kai Li. Real-time concurrent collection on stock multiprocessors. *ACM SIGPLAN Notices*, 23(7):11–20, 1988.

[2] Lex Augusteijn. Garbage collection in a distributed environment. In de Bakker et al. [12], pages 75–93.

[3] Henry Baker, editor. *International Workshop on Memory Management*, volume 986 of *Lecture Notes in Computer Science*, Kinross, Scotland, September 1995. Springer-Verlag.

[4] Joel F. Bartlett. Compacting garbage collection with ambiguous roots. Lisp Pointers 1, 6 (April–June 1988), pp. 2–12.

[5] Yves Bekkers and Jacques Cohen, editors. *International Workshop on Memory Management*, volume 637 of *Lecture Notes in Computer Science*, St Malo, France, 16–18 September 1992. Springer-Verlag.

[6] David I. Bevan. Distributed garbage collection using reference counting. In *PARLE Parallel Architectures and Languages Europe*, volume 259 of *Lecture Notes in Computer Science*, pages 176–187. Springer-Verlag, June 1987.

[7] Andrew Birrell, David Evers, Greg Nelson, Susan Owicki, and Edward Wobber. Distributed garbage collection for network objects. Technical Report 116, DEC Systems Research Center, December 1993.

[8] Andrew Birrell, Greg Nelson, Susan Owicki, and Edward Wobber. Network objects. Technical Report 115, DEC Systems Research Center, February 1994.

[9] Hans-Juergen Boehm, Alan J. Demers, and Scott Shenker. Mostly parallel garbage collection. *ACM SIGPLAN Notices*, 26(6):157–164, 1991.

[10] Luca Cardelli, James Donahue, Lucille Glassman, Mick Jordan, Bill Kalsow, and Greg Nelson. Modula-3 report (revised). Research Report PRC–131, DEC Systems Research Center and Olivetti Research Center, 1988.

[11] T. W. Christopher. Reference count garbage collection. *Software Practice and Experience*, 14(6):503–507, June 1984.

[12] Jacobus W. de Bakker, L. Nijman, and Philip C. Treleaven, editors. *PARLE'87 Parallel Architectures and Languages Europe*, volume 258/259 of *Lecture Notes in Computer Science*, Eindhoven, The Netherlands, June 1987. Springer-Verlag.

[13] Margaret H. Derbyshire. Mark scan garbage collection on a distributed architecture. *Lisp and Symbolic Computation*, 3(2):135 - 170, April 1990.

[14] Paulo Ferreira and Marc Shapiro. Asynchronous distributed garbage collection in the Larchant cached shared store. Available from Marc Shapiro, May 1996.

[15] Matthew Fuchs. Garbage collection on an open network. In Baker [3].

[16] Benjamin Goldberg. Generational reference counting: A reduced-communication distributed storage reclamation scheme. In *Conference on Programming Languages Design and Implementation*, volume 24(7) of *ACM SIGPLAN Notices*, pages 313–320, Portland, June 1989.

[17] Paul R. Hudak and R. M. Keller. Garbage collection and task deletion in distributed applicative processing systems. In *Symposium on Lisp and Functional Programming*, pages 168–178, Pittsburgh, August 1982. ACM Press.

[18] Richard L. Hudson, Ron Morrison, J. Eliot B. Moss, and David S. Munro. Garbage collecting the world: One car at a time. In *Conference on Object-Oriented Systems, Languages and Applications — Twelth Annual Conference*, volume 32(10) of *ACM SIGPLAN Notices*, pages 162–175. ACM Press, October 1997.

[19] Richard L. Hudson and J. Eliot B. Moss. Incremental garbage collection for mature objects. In Bekkers and Cohen [5].

[20] Richard E. Jones. *Garbage Collection: Algorithms for Automatic Dynamic Memory Management.* Wiley, July 1996. With a chapter on Distributed Garbage Collection by R. Lins.

[21] Richard E. Jones and Rafael D. Lins. Cyclic weighted reference counting without delay. *Parallel Architectures and Languages Europe*, volume 694 of *Lecture Notes in Computer Science.* Springer-Verlag, June 1993.

[22] Neils-Christian Juul and Eric Jul. Comprehensive and robust garbage collection in a distributed system. In Bekkers and Cohen [5].

[23] Rivka Ladin and Barbara Liskov. Garbage collection of a distributed heap. In *International Conference on Distributed Computing Systems*, Yokohama, June 1992.

[24] Bernard Lang, Christian Quenniac, and José Piquer. Garbage collecting the world. In *Symposium on Principles of Programming Languages*, ACM SIGPLAN Notices, pages 39–50. ACM Press, January 1992.

[25] Munenori Maeda, Hiroki Konaka, Yutaka Ishikawa, Takashi Tomokiyo, Atsushi Hori, and Jorg Nolte. On-the-fly global garbage collection based on partly mark-sweep. In Baker [3].

[26] Umesh Maheshwari. Fault-tolerant distributed garbage collection in a client-server object-oriented database. In *Conference on Parallel and Distributed Information Systems, Austin*, September 1994.

[27] Umesh Maheshwari and Barbara Liskov. Collecting cyclic distributed garbage by controlled migration. In *Principles of Distributed Computing*, 1995.

[28] Umesh Maheshwari and Barbara Liskov. Collecting cyclic distributed garbage by back tracing. In *Principles of Distributed Computing*, 1997.

[29] José M. Piquer. Indirect reference counting: A distributed garbage collection algorithm. In *Parallel Architectures and Languages Europe*, volume 505 of *Lecture Notes in Computer Science.* Springer-Verlag, June 1991.

[30] David Plainfossé and Marc Shapiro. Experience with fault-tolerant garbage collection in a distributed Lisp system. In Bekkers and Cohen [5].

[31] David Plainfossé and Marc Shapiro. A survey of distributed garbage collection techniques. In Baker [3].

[32] S. P. Rana. A distributed solution to the distributed termination problem. *Information Processing Letters*, 17:43–46, July 1983.

[33] Helena C. C. D. Rodrigues and Richard E. Jones. A cyclic distributed garbage collector for Network Objects. In *International Workshop on Distributed Algorithms WDAG'96*, Bologna, October 1996.

[34] Helena C.C.D. Rodrigues. *Cyclic Distributed Garbage Collection*. PhD thesis, Computing Laboratory, The University of Kent at Canterbury, 1998. In preparation.

[35] Marc Shapiro. A fault-tolerant, scalable, low-overhead distributed garbage collection protocol. In *Symposium on Reliable Distributed Systems*, Pisa, September 1991.

[36] Marc Shapiro, Peter Dickman, and David Plainfossé. SSP chains: Robust, distributed references supporting acyclic garbage collection. Rapports de Recherche 1799, Institut National de la Recherche en Informatique et Automatique, November 1992.

[37] N.G. Shivaratri, P. Krueger, and M. Singhal. Load distributing for locally distributed systems. *Computer*, 25(12):33–44, December 1992.

[38] Gerard Tel and Friedmann Mattern. The derivation of distributed termination detection algorithms from garbage collection schemes. *ACM Transactions on Programming Languages and Systems*, 15(1), January 1993.

[39] Paul Watson and Ian Watson. An efficient garbage collection scheme for parallel computer architectures. In de Bakker et al. [12], pages 432–443.

[40] Paul Wilson. Distr. gc general discussion for faq. gclist mailing list (gclist@iecc.com), March 1996.

[41] Paul Wilson. Garbage collection and memory hierarchy. In Bekkers and Cohen [5].

Experiences Developing a Virtual Shared Memory System Using High-Level Object Paradigms

J. Cordsen, J. Nolte, W. Schröder-Preikschat[†]

GMD FIRST
Rudower Chaussee 5
D-12489 Berlin, Germany
{jc,jon}@first.gmd.de

†University of Magdeburg
Universitätsplatz 2
D-39106 Magdeburg, Germany
wosch@cs.uni-magdeburg.de

Abstract. Shared-memory programming is still a common and popular way of utilizing parallel machines for high-performance computing. Virtual shared memory (VSM) systems promote a gentle migration path allowing the execution of shared-memory programs on distributed-memory machines. Such kind of systems are both complex and extremely sensitive to performance issues. Therefore many VSM systems still handle distribution aspects manually by means of low-level message-passing operations to gain maximum performance. In contrast, in the PEACE operating system family almost *all* distribution aspects have been covered conveniently and yet efficiently by so-called *dual objects*. In this paper the VSM subsystem, called VOTE, of PEACE is presented as a case study for complex systems services that claim for high-level but lightweight object models with an efficient implementation.

1 Introduction

Shared-memory programming is still a common and popular way of utilizing parallel machines for high-performance computing. This programming style is based on a well-known methodology and supported by high-quality programming environments (e.g. compilers and debuggers) and matured libraries. It will be still dominant in the near future due to the lack of other accepted and pioneering approaches to parallel programming. Consequently, during the last decade large efforts were spent applying the shared-memory paradigm to distributed-memory parallel machines. This led to the development of various (hardware- and/or software-supported) *virtual shared memory* (VSM) systems. Examples are IVY[15], Midway[2], Munin[4], or DASH[13].

By means of architectural transparency, VSM systems promote a gentle migration path allowing the execution of shared-memory programs on distributed-memory machines. The particular motivation behind VOTE was to support a symbiosis of architectural transparency *and* efficiency.

As an extension to the PEACE parallel operating system[22], VOTE benefits from the advantages offered by problem-oriented kernels being tailored to particular application demands. Following the pattern of PEACE, the design and implementation of VOTE was strongly influenced by the program family concept[21]. Rather than providing a single consistency protocol which manages the replicated VSM data for all kinds of shared-memory programs, users are offered problem-oriented solutions by a *family of consistency protocols*[7].

Both, VOTE and PEACE exhibit a lightweight system structure, resulting in a high-performance software backplane for parallel computing. The lightweight structure is not only a result of having applied the family concept in the system software design process. It is also the result of the exploitation of an optimized high-level object paradigm in the implementation process. This object paradigm is found by *dual objects* supporting object-oriented (system) programming in a distributed environment[20].

This paper describes the dual-object-based implementation of the VOTE system and gives a performance analysis of both the VOTE system as well as the dual object implementation. It is organized as follows: Section 2 briefly discusses the design principles and basic architecture of PEACE. Section 3 introduces the notion of dual objects and describes language-level support as well as implementation; Section 4 presents a brief insight into the VOTE system describing its building blocks and their interactions; Section 5 makes a performance analysis; Section 6 concludes the paper.

2 PEACE

PEACE is a *framework* for (distributed) parallel applications dedicated to run on distributed memory (massively) parallel architectures. Although specifically designed to support high performance parallel computing, this framework is also suitable for constructing (microkernel-based) distributed operating systems with real-time capabilities as well as object-oriented parallel computing platforms for workstation networks.

2.1 Design Principles

Parallel operating systems must exhibit a lightweight or even *featherweight system structure* that is adaptable to the individual needs of both an application program and the hardware architecture. The approach followed by PEACE is to understand a parallel operating system as a *program family*[21] and to use *object orientation*[24] as the fundamental implementation discipline. The former concept (program families) helps prevent the design of a monolithic system organization, while object orientation enables the efficient implementation of a highly modular system structure.

The program family concept distinguishes between a *minimal subset of system functions* and *minimal system extensions*. It does not dictate any particular implementation technique. The minimal subset of system functions defines a platform of fundamental abstractions serving to implement minimal system extensions. These extensions, then, are made on the basis of an *incremental system design*[10], with each new level being a new minimal basis (i.e., *abstract machine*) for additional higher-level system extensions. A true application-oriented system evolves, since extensions are only made on demand, namely, when needed to implement a specific system feature that supports a specific application. Design decisions are postponed as long as possible. In this process, system construction takes place bottom-up but is controlled in a top-down (application-driven) fashion.

In its last consequence, applications become the final system extensions. The traditional boundary between application and operating system disappears. The operating system extends into the application, and vice versa. Inheritance is the appropriate technique to either introduce new system extensions or replace existing system extensions by alternate implementations. Either case, the system extensions are customized with respect to specific user demands and will be present at runtime only in coexistence with the corresponding application. Thus, applications are not forced to pay for (operating system) resources that will never be used.

2.2 Functional Decomposition

The global architecture assumes that a member of the PEACE parallel operating system family is constructed from three major building blocks. These building blocks are the ***nucleus***, the ***kernel***, and POSE, the ***Parallel Operating System Extension*** (Fig. 1). In addition to the system components, the ***application*** is considered as the fourth integral part of this architecture. The application largely determines the complexity of a family member and the distribution of the building.

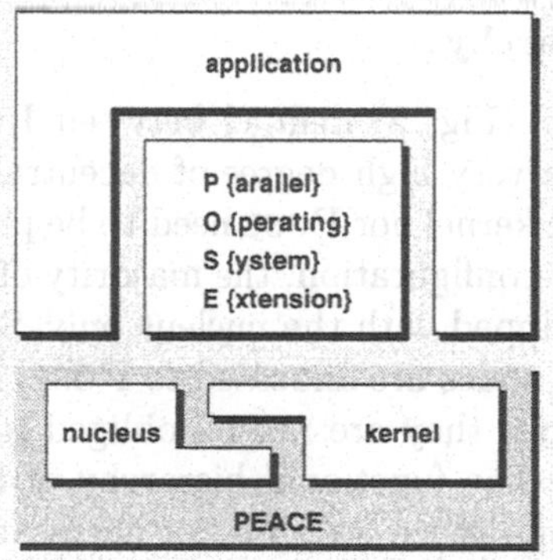

Fig. 1. Building blocks

The nucleus implements system-wide interprocess communication and provides a runtime executive for the processing of threads. It is part of the kernel domain, with the kernel being a multi-threaded system component that encapsulates minimal nucleus extensions. These extensions implement device abstractions, dynamic creation and destruction of process objects, the association of process objects with naming domains and address spaces, and the propagation of exceptional events (traps, interrupts). Application-oriented services such as naming, process and memory management, file handling, I/O, and load balancing are performed by POSE.

Kernel and POSE services are built by dual objects. As will be discussed later, the dual objects are managed by so called *clerks*. Since a clerk is implemented as an active object, the two building blocks kernel and POSE are made from active objects managing dual objects. In contrast, the nucleus is an ensemble of passive objects that schedule active objects.

An active object is implemented by a ***lightweight process***. A number of these objects may share the same address space, thus constituting a *team* of lightweight processes, i.e., a ***heavyweight process***. Each service that is provided by both POSE and the kernel is implemented by such a team and represents a PEACE *entity*. Entities are system extensions. They are loaded on demand and (in most cases) can be arbitrarily distributed.

The dividing line between user and supervisor mode as shown in Figure 1 is a logical boundary only. It depends on the actual representation of the interactions specified by the *functional hierarchy*[10] (and of the hardware architecture) whether this boundary is physically present.

VOTE is an autonomous POSE component. It serves as a minimal kernel extension, in particular the address space management subsystem. The PEACE family members implementing only virtual shared memory will consist of a single POSE component, i.e. VOTE, a scaled-down kernel encapsulating both the MMU driver and threads management, and the nucleus.

2.3 Functional Hierarchy

The functional hierarchy (Fig. 2) defined between POSE, the kernel, and the nucleus makes possible a very high degree of decentralization. From the design point of view, neither the kernel nor POSE need to be present on every node, only the nucleus. In a specific configuration, the majority of the nodes of a massively parallel machine are equipped with the nucleus only. Some nodes are supported by the kernel, and a few nodes are allocated to POSE. All nodes can be used for application processing, but they are not all obliged to be shared between user tasks and system tasks. The functional hierarchy of the three building blocks expresses the logical design of PEACE, but not necessarily the physical representation.

Nucleus services are made available to the application via *Nearby Object Invocation* (NOI). The logical design assumes a separation of the nucleus from the application (and POSE), which calls for the use of traps to invoke the nucleus and for address space isolation. This is the place where *cross domain calls* may happen. The nucleus is "nearby" the using entity. It shares with the entity the same node, but not necessarily the same address space segment. In addition to

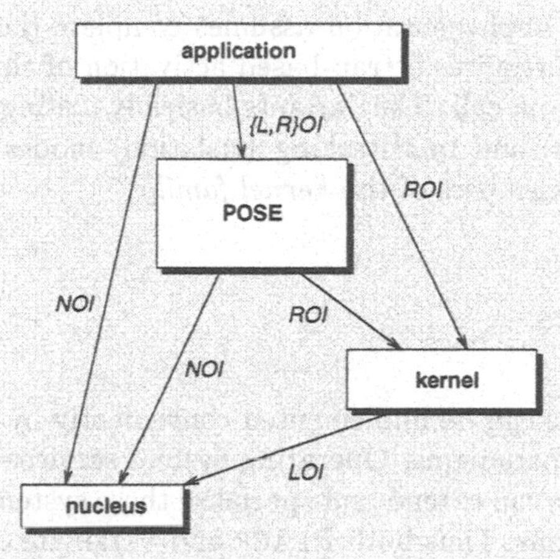

Fig. 2. Invocation scheme

that, there are nucleus configurations which totally sacrifice the trap interface, defining a single address space that lodges possibly all four building blocks.

The kernel resides with the nucleus in the same address space. Together they constitute the ***kernel entity***. The kernel therefore performs *Local Object Invocation* (LOI) to request nucleus services. Kernel services are made available via *Remote Object Invocation* (ROI)[14]. The ROI scheme always implies context switching, but not necessarily address space switching. A separate thread of control is used to execute the requested method (i.e., service). In contrast to that, NOI (logically) implies the activation/deactivation of the nucleus address space via local system call traps. The implementation of ROI takes advantage of the network-wide message passing services provided by the nucleus and, thus, is based on NOI.

Services of POSE are requested via LOI and ROI. The former scheme is used to interact with the POSE runtime system library whereas the latter is used to interact with the POSE active objects. In certain situations the POSE library directly transforms the issued LOI into one or more ROI requests to the kernel. The POSE service then is not provided by an active object, but entirely on a library basis (i.e., passive object).

Although the functional hierarchy assumes NOI for the interaction between application (POSE) and nucleus, the LOI scheme is used for those members of the PEACE family that place their focus on performance. The entrance to the nucleus is represented as an abstract data type with two implementations. The first implementation sacrifices vertical and horizontal isolation. Thus, there is neither a separation between the user and supervisor modes of operation (vertical isolation) nor a separation between competing tasks (horizontal isolation). In this case, NOI actually means LOI. Horizontal isolation means that user/system entities have a private address space, that is, operate in a private protection domain. The second implementation assumes complete (i.e., vertical and horizontal) isolation and requires a trap-based activation of the nucleus. NOI then becomes a cross-domain call. The variants basically distinguish between single-tasking (no isolation) and multitasking (isolation) modes of operation. They implement different members of the *kernel family*.

3 Dual Objects

Family based systems can be implemented conveniently by means of object oriented programming paradigms. Operating system services are implemented as classes then and users can extend and specialize these system classes by means of inheritance mechanisms. Thus both PEACE and VOTE are entirely implemented in C++. In VOTE inheritance is used to introduce specialized members of the family of consistency protocols and customize the building blocks to various user demands.

In theory this scenario is sound and straight forward but in practice the conceptual advantages of object orientation are *extremely* hard to exploit without suitable object models and language-level support for object-oriented implementation techniques in distributed contexts. In order to implement VSM semantics, instances of the VOTE classes are to be allocated to different nodes of a distributed-memory parallel computer. As a consequence, these instances need to be accessed network-wide.

When users extend and specialize e.g. PEACE or VOTE classes by means of inheritance mechanisms, class hierarchies need to be extended across address spaces as well as network boundaries and objects can be fragmented across address spaces. This in turn can lead to serious performance penalties caused by frequent remote invocations, when application classes closely interact with their system-level base classes. On the other hand it is obvious that client classes cannot have full access to system-level state information to avoid forgery and ease resource sharing amongst many clients. Implementing system services as fragmented objects[17] would have supported independence as well as encapsulation of object fragments allocated in different address spaces. Nevertheless we considered that model already too complex for those very lightweight system structures we were aiming at, because the fragmented object model partially relied on group communication mechanisms and did not support inheritance-based fragmentation.

Having such problems in mind we designed a general object model for system programming. This model transposes the classical coarse grained user/supervisor memory model of monolithic systems to very small objects of language-level granularity. So-called *dual objects*[20] implement system services and encapsulate both user-level and system-level state information in a single object context. Clients are allowed to control the user-level part of a dual object directly and efficiently within their address spaces, whereas system servers have transparent access to both parts during service invocations. Thus much closer interactions between user and system classes are possible as in conventional object models and the model remains simple enough to be implemented efficiently.

3.1 Language-level Support

Dual objects are described by annotated C++ classes[1] that specify user-level and system-level class members. To retain a strong backward compatibility to original C++, all `public` and `protected` members are considered to be user-level, whereas all `private` members belong to the system-level. Thus the weak language-level protection of private class members in C++ is enforced by strong encapsulation of private data in the (remote) address-space of the server.

Fig. 3 shows a much simplified example of the dual `Adviser` class that controls consistency protocols in the VOTE system. Dual classes are identified using a `/*!dual!*/` annotation following the closing bracket of the class declaration. The private member slots belong to the system-level whereas all `protected` members are user-level data members. Thus the methods `indicateWS()`, `setMode()`, `setProt()` and `setCap()` can be executed directly within the client's address space as indicated by the `/*!local!*/` annotation whereas methods like `handle()` are executed remotely under the control of the server using remote object invocation techniques (ROI)[14]. During invocations the user-level members are made available for the server. Thus the `handle()` method has transparent access to the actual `cap`, `mode`, `protocol`, `high` and `low` members.

Methods and parameters are annotated in an IDL-like style to specify parameter functionality and remote invocation semantics. Parameters to remote methods are passed by value by default. Pointers have to be annotated to specify e.g. input (`in`) or output (`out`) parameters[2].

Generic bulk data is not automatically handled through language-level parameter passing but by explicit remote `fetch()` and `store()` operations provided by the PEACE nucleus. These two primitives provide fast end-to-end data transfers between (remote) address spaces. An address-space capability (`Ticket`) is required to apply these methods. Thus in the `Adviser` example, `handle()` uses the user-level `cap` member to perform bulk data transfers between the client's and the server's address spaces.

Dual classes can be composed by (even remote) inheritance mechanisms and thus important C++ features like multiple inheritance are retained. These classes are fed to a *dual object generator* (DOG) to transform them into functionally enriched C++ classes capable of dealing with the distribution aspects of dual objects. Client and server representations of a dual object are generated. The

[1] Basing on annotated C++ was more a pragmatic than a conceptual decision. At the time starting the PEACE development, it was fairly hard to convince users to better employ C++ rather than Fortran for parallel programming. It would have been even harder, if not impossible, to come up with some sort of interface definition language different from C++ and Fortran. Thus, annotating C++ was seen to be the best possible compromise at that point in time.

[2] For a complete description of annotations see[19, 20].

```
class Adviser : ... {
    private:                    // system-level
        Actor** actors;
        Actor*  my_actor;
        int num_actors;
    protected:                  // user-level
        Ticket   cap;
        AccMode  mode;
        VSMProt  protocol;
        Addr     low;
        Addr     high;
    public:
        // local methods
        void indicateWS (int high, int low) /*!local!*/
        {
            this->high = high;
            this->low = low;
        }

        void setMode (AccMode mode) /*!local!*/
        {
            this->mode = mode;
        }

        void setProt (VSMProt prot) /*!local!*/
        {
            this->protocol = prot;
        }

        void setCap (Ticket cap) /*!local!*/
        {
            this->cap = cap;
        }

        // remote methods
        int  handle (int page, Addr addr, AccFault type);
}/*!dual!*/;
```

Fig. 3. The Dual Adviser class

same holds for the stub methods used for remote invocation. An additional preprocessor version of the DOG integrates the dual object model into standard C++ to ease the implementation of distributed and parallel system services (as well as C++ applications).

3.2 Resource Sharing

A client (or a server) can grant access to its resources by creating clones of its dual object instances and transferring these clones to other processes. Whenever a dual object is cloned, only the user-level part is copied, whereas the system-level part is (transitively) shared amongst all clones. Thus in the `Adviser` example (fig. 3) the private system-level members are shared amongst all instances transitively cloned from the same origin. In contrast all `protected` user-level members are independent copies that will be manipulated or initialized independently from each other (fig. 4). The user-level part of a dual object then becomes a client-specific context that is implicitly provided to servers during

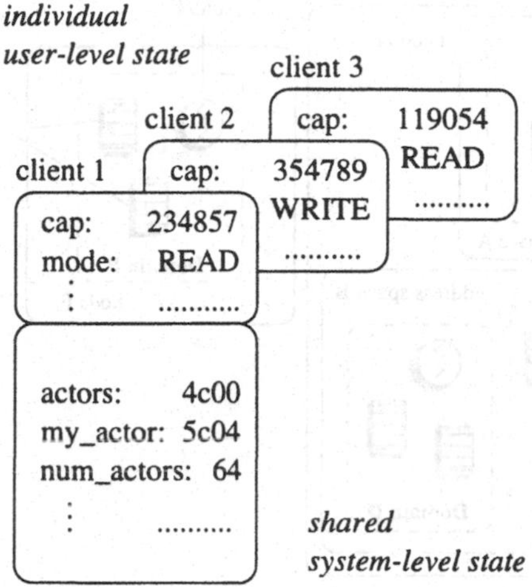

Fig. 4. Resource Sharing with Dual Objects

service invocations. Thus the `cap`, `mode`, `protocol`, `high` and `low` members (fig. 4) will always refer to the user-level part of the client actually calling a specific `Adviser` instance.

As a result servers are not enforced to maintain client-specific data themselves. Robustness of services is therefore enhanced and system-level data can be shared conveniently and economically amongst many clients. In fact, these resource sharing facilities are comparable to delegation based models[16, 25] with the major difference that the sharing facilities of dual objects are statically defined through classes whereas common delegation schemes allow dynamic sharing.

3.3 Runtime Model and Implementation Issues

Dual objects have two representations at runtime, one for clients and one for servers. We call instances of the client's representations *likenesses* and instances of the server's representation *prototypes*. A likeness reflects the public interface of a dual class and consists of public and protected members only, whereas the prototype consists of all members. Furthermore, the likeness holds a (remote) reference to its prototype. Thus a likeness is both an object that can be manipulated locally as well as a proxy[23] for a remote prototype.

Prototypes are passive C++ objects that are kept in so-called *domains*[18]. Domains are a concept for local object spaces that are managed by active server objects we call *clerks*. These clerks are able to instantiate new prototypes upon request and control access to all objects within their domains. Many domains may share an address space or may have separate address spaces either on the same machine or somewhere in a network to constitute a global distributed object space (fig. 5). Furthermore, a domain may either be sequential or concurrent.

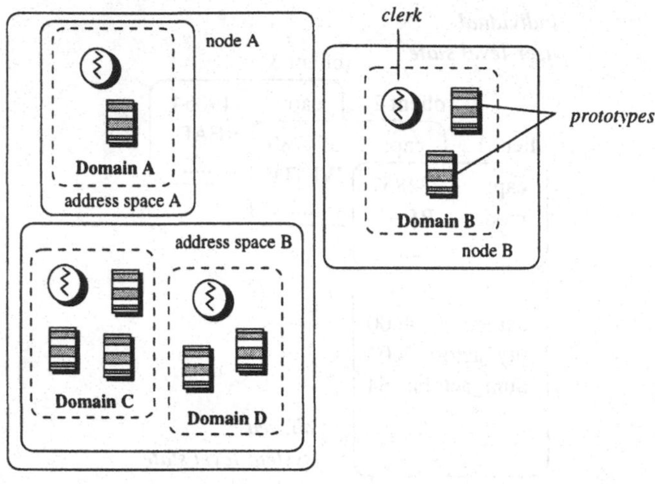

Fig. 5. Domains

Sequential domains are monitors and allow exactly one object in the domain to be manipulated at a time. Concurrent domains manage a dynamic thread pool and implement read/write monitors on single object instances.

When a dual object is created, an instantiation request is sent to the clerk of the domain selected to host the new prototype. Domains are selected either by name contacting a name service or by a *unique identifier* denoting the communication address of the clerk controlling the domain. The clerk in turn creates the prototype and executes its constructor. After initialization all user-level parts of the prototype are extracted and sent back to the requesting client. Here a likeness is initialized with the user-level data and the remote reference to the newly created prototype. In fact, any time a client declares a new likeness instance which is not a clone of an existing likeness, the instantiation procedure described above is transparently executed.

Methods that access user-level data only are executed locally on the likeness leaving the prototype untouched. All methods that are executed on the likeness that involve system-level data will in fact be remote object invocations on a remote prototype. Since the user-level part may have been changed by previous local calls, it is transmitted along with the arguments of the call (fig.6). The receiving clerk then will update the prototype by means of the actual user-level data before the method is executed[3]. When the method returns the user-level part is extracted and sent back to the client along with the results of the method. The likeness in turn is updated with the actual data. This protocol causes some additional overhead for those methods which access both user-level and system-level data simultaneously. Since that overhead is comparable to implicit parame-

[3] This is necessary because we use standard C++ compilers as back-end. Otherwise user-level members could be referenced differently from system-level members.

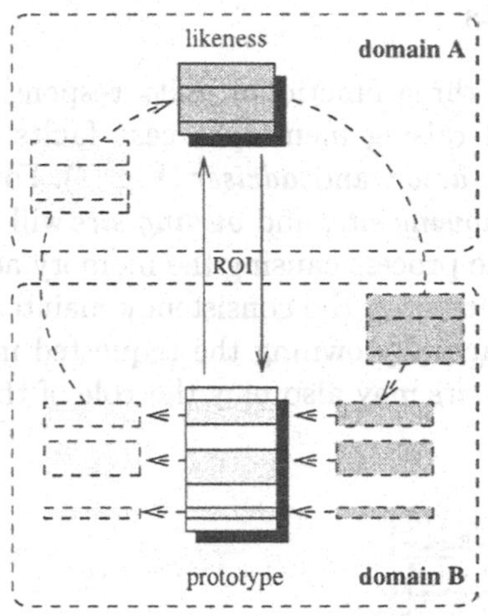

Fig. 6. Remote Invocation

ter passing it can be neglected if the transfer costs of user-level state information is small compared to the execution time of the method (fig. 3). Other methods are either not affected or even executed locally at the client site if no system-level data is accessed at all.

4 The VOTE System

A shared-memory program running on top of VOTE is executed in a multiple reader/single writer (MRSW) sequential consistency model[12] to ensure architectural transparency. At any time, the program may change the consistency maintenance, keeping on execution by virtue of a different memory consistency model. VOTE supports a number of performance enhancement techniques. These techniques help avoiding sequences of read/write memory access faults, pre-paging and releasing address ranges, and to provide support for one-sided communication in order to propagate data to each process in a specified set of destinations. A fine-grained multiple writer model allows (within a page) modifying accesses with a subsequent restoration scheme[7] in order to unify a sequential consistent result. Furthermore, VOTE also supports message-passing communication functions which operate in coexistence to the demand paging of sequential consistency.

A detailed description of the VOTE system, its performance enhancement techniques, and studies about efficiency and scalability of parallel VSM applications can be found in[8]. This paper concentrates on the VOTE core only to show how dual objects have been exploited to construct an efficient VSM system.

4.1 Functional Units

VOTE is distinguishing three functional units responsible for handling consistency maintenance and raising memory access faults. These three functional units are called *catcher*, *actor*, and *adviser* (Fig. 7). For the sake of clarity, the terms *requesting site*, *knowing site*, and *owning site* will be used in the following. The *requesting site* is the process causing the memory access fault. The *knowing site* is the process implementing the consistency maintenance, whereas the *owning site* is the process actually owning the requested memory page. In specific situations, the *knowing site* may also play the role of the *owning site*.

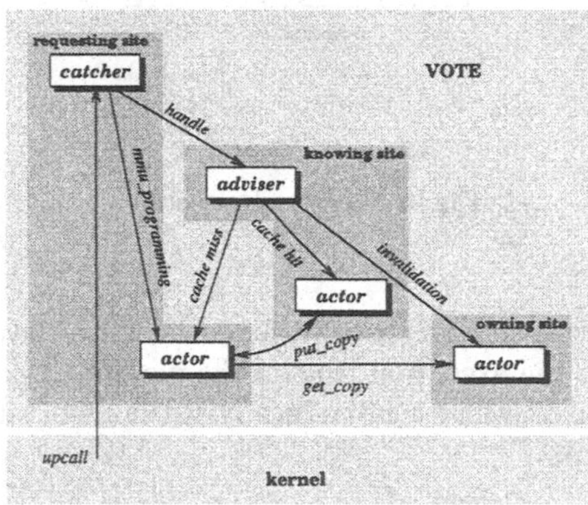

Fig. 7. VOTE building blocks

An application process using the global address space of VOTE will be associated with an exception handler (*catcher*). In case of a memory access fault, the *catcher* is invoked (via an upcall) by the PEACE kernel. The *catcher* determines the consistency maintenance instance relevant for handling the access fault. For this purpose, a pre-determined (user-directed) mapping from memory pages to consistency maintenance objects is used. Upon this information, the *catcher* calls the *adviser* at the *knowing site*.

The *adviser* object implements the consistency maintenance for the requested memory page. This instance maintains directory information about the distribution of the memory pages it has taken responsibility for. Each *adviser* is supplemented by a set of so called *actor* objects. When a VSM variable is declared to be maintained by a specific *adviser*, an associated *actor* will be created in the address space of the declaring application process. Thus, using several *adviser* objects in order to maintain different memory pages will result in the same number of *actor* instances associated to each of the application processes. The *adviser* itself creates an *actor* for the purpose of caching VSM pages and to optimize access fault handling.

The purpose of an *actor* is to provide to its *adviser* an interface controlling the memory management and the movement of VSM memory pages. The functional encapsulation of, on the one hand, consistency maintenance by the *adviser* and, on the other hand, memory management and data transfer by the *actor* enables VOTE to make use of idle processors or dedicated system processors. State-of-the-art consistency maintenance operates with a dynamic distributed ownership-based protocol. Due to the ownership approach, this scheme is restricted to operate only on processors running application tasks. Because of this disadvantage, VOTE rejects the dynamic distributed consistency maintenance and uses the highly optimized fixed distributed scheme instead.

4.2 Interactions of the Functional Units

If an application causes a memory access fault, kernel-based trap handling saves the current context and activates the *catcher* being in charge of raising the memory access fault. The *catcher* allocates a memory region, determines the responsible *knowledge site* and calls `handle()` (Fig.3) with the requested page number, address of the allocated memory region, and information about the access fault type (i.e. protection or access violation) as arguments. When an *adviser* receives the request to handle a memory access fault, the access fault type, the directory information, and client specific information determines the further processing.

The most simple case of consistency maintenance is a protection violation, that is the *requesting site* already owns a copy of the memory page with a read-only access permission. Then the *adviser* sends invalidation messages to the set of *owning sites*, updates the directory information and replies to the *requesting site* in order to upgrade its memory access permission.

If the access fault was an access violation, the *knowing site* checks if the requested memory page has been cached. In case of a cache hit, the page is transfered directly to the *knowing site* using `put_copy()`.[4] If the access violation was due to a write access, the *knowing site* invalidates the set of copy holders before the directory information is updated. In contrast, a read access violation requires only adding the *requesting site* to the set of copy holders. Afterwards, the *requesting site* is sent a reply for local MMU programming.

The final two cases handle access violations if a cache miss for the requested page was detected at the *knowing site*. In this situation the *adviser* calls the *actor* of the *requesting site* with the information where to get a copy of the memory page. Then, data is copied from the *owning site* to the *requesting site* using `get_copy()`. At the *requesting site*, the desired access permission is defined. If the page has read-only access permission, a copy of the page is sent to the *knowing site* as well (using `put_copy()`). As described above, caching these pages at the *knowing site* results in a prompt handling of future read access faults with respect to the same pages. Finally, control returns to the *adviser*. If a write access

[4] The description is simplified for reasons of clarity. To ensure sequential consistency, VOTE uses a distributed locking protocol.

violation is to be handled, invalidations are sent to the set of *owning sites*. The directory information is updated and the *requesting site* is sent a reply.

5 Exploiting Dual Objects

The entire VOTE software architecture is implemented using the high-level object paradigm of dual objects. The three function units *catcher*, *actor* and *adviser* are implemented as dual classes. Hence, the interactions taking place between the instances of these classes (i.e. the dual objects) are to be carried out on a ROI-basis mostly.

```
class Catcher : public Guardian {
    private:
        Adviser* adviser;
        ...
    public:
        Catcher (/*!in!*/Adviser* adviser);
        void exception(LogAdr loc, LogAdr pc, MemFault cause)
        {
            ...
            adviser->handle(loc.Index() ...); // remote call
            ...
        }
}/*!dual!*/;
```

Fig. 8. The Catcher class

Fig. 8 shows the definition of the dual `Catcher` class that reacts on page-faults and propagates these to an appropriate `Adviser` instance for VSM protocol handling. The `Catcher` class is derived from a dual `Guardian` class. This class gives access to low-level memory management of the PEACE kernel and propagates traps (even across the network) to higher-level abstractions. Method `exception()` redefines a virtual `Guardian` method and implements application-specific fault handling. For performance reasons we place `Catcher` instances in a local domain sharing the local address space of the process, whose traps need to be caught. Nevertheless, in principal these faults could also be handled at any place in the network transparently to the nucleus detecting the fault because dual objects provide location transparency.

Upon an access fault, the `exception()` method of a `Catcher` instance will be called by the nucleus and executed in the domain where the `Catcher` actually resides. The `exception()` method then performs local VSM processing such as memory allocation before it contacts the `Adviser` instance responsible for the memory region in question. This call is carried out on a ROI-basis invoking the `handle()` method of the dual `Adviser` object (fig. 3). The *catcher* is unaware of the actual location of its *adviser* and the `Adviser` instance can be located anywhere in the network.

The same holds for instances of the dual class `Actor` that implements methods like `put_copy()` and `get_copy()` for remote page transfers as well as methods for remote MMU handling (fig.9).

```
class Actor : ... {
    private:
        VSMInfo*  info;
    public:
        ...
        // remote methods for page transfer
        int  put_copy (int page, /*!in!*/VSMPage* data);
        int  get_copy (int page, /*!out!*/VSMPage* data);
        ...
        // remote methods for address space handling transfer
        int  invalidate (int page);
}/*!dual!*/;
```

Fig. 9. The Actor class

The complete dual `Actor` class sketched here very briefly implements in fact more than 35 different methods for remote page and MMU handling, that optimize several access cases and allow remote control of address space management. Although these remote methods could have been implemented manually by means of low-level message passing operations, these numbers indicate that language-level ROI support can improve software productivity significantly. This is especially true during prototyping phases when interfaces quite often change and experimentation consumes a lot of the total development time. We estimate that a manual implementation would have consumed at least several hours up to a few days of additional error prone work that was performed reliably by an automatic tool in a fraction of a second.

The dual `Actor` class basically uses the ROI capabilities provided by dual classes. The dual `Adviser` class (fig. 3) intensively applies the extended resource sharing model provided by dual objects. The private system-level part contains references to a set of `Actor` instances (data members `actors` and `num_actors`). Data member `my_actor` points to the local *actor*. This variable is used to optimize the handling of read access faults in case of a cache hit for the requested VSM page. The user-level data members (`protocol`, `low`, `high`, and `mode`) are used to customize the consistency maintenance with respect to the specific memory access characteristics of an application. Each process belonging to the parallel application gets a clone of the dual `Adviser` instance controlling a VSM segment shared by these processes. Recall that in the case of dual objects only user-level parts are cloned, whereas the system-level part is implicitly shared amongst all clones (refer to section 3.2). Therefore it is possible to individually specify the current working set of an application process defining the members `low` and `high` to minimize page-faults and false sharing, when several processes operate on the same page but on disjoint locations within the page. Furthermore, the `mode` and `protocol` members provide information about the required memory consistency models and expected page-access patterns. Thus each process belonging to the parallel application can customize its individual access patterns and consistency requirements through efficient local operations, that only manipulate user-level state. Upon a memory access fault, the *catcher* invokes the *adviser* thereby automatically providing the customized user-level state information of the faulting process.

Without the dual object model we either would have to perform costly remote invocations to optimize page access or store this information locally in a different kind of object and pass this information explicitly as additional parameters upon any access fault. The first case would be extremely inefficient and virtually discards its intended optimization effect completely. The second case would require clumsy workarounds and unclear interfaces since the user-level data would to be passed as extra arguments to the methods of the `Adviser` class. The dual object model keeps all related data in a uniform context and effectively hides distribution aspects.

6 Performance Analysis

The VOTE performance was measured on a multi-node MANNA system. Every dual-processor MANNA node consists of two 50-MIPS RISC processors (i860XP) sharing the memory and the I/O units attaching peripherals to the node; they also share the bidirectional communication link. This link connects the node with a byte-wide 16×16 crossbar switch, providing a throughput of 2×47.68 MB/s. The effective memory access rate is 381.47 MB/s.

6.1 Dual Objects

The high-level dual object model eases the design and implementation of the VOTE system. Reusability, extensibility, and efficient use of system resources are enhanced to a high extent. Table 1 shows the basic timings for elementary communication costs as well as remote object invocation times. The PEACE nucleus provides synchronous and asynchronous packet-based mechanisms (64 bytes) for inter process communication (IPC) as well as primitives for end-to-end bulk data transfer (`fetch()`, `store()`). The ROI mechanisms are built upon these mechanisms. When the argument size (including the user-level part of a dual object) exceeds an IPC-packet, bulk data transfer primitives are automatically applied to transmit bigger messages.

The typical ROI overhead is in the vicinity of 8μsec and drops to less than 5μsec in case of local communication that implies a better cache utilization[5]. Notably we cannot measure significant differences with varying parameter sizes up to the size of a packet. The DOG generates statically typed message formats for most methods and thus marshaling costs for simple data types and aggregate

[5] The generated code as well as the code in the ROI runtime system is the same in both the local and the remote case.

Operation	Time (μsec)
Inter Process Communication (IPC)	157
Async. IPC	18
bulk data transfer (fetch)	122
bulk data transfer (store)	28
ROI with argument size not exceeding an IPC packet	165-168
async. ROI	ca. 26
ROI with implicit bulk data transfer	308
remote object creation	266

Table 1. Performance of basic operations

types are *extremely* low. Only array data types and aggregate data types that contain arrays require significant improvement (see also table 2).

Table 2 shows the overheads of memory allocation and copying when executing `get_copy()` (refer to Fig. 7). The benchmarks were run using dual objects of different utilization, with variable sized data sets, and exploiting different compilers (Metaware, Portland).[6]

Size (KB)	Metaware compiler					Portland compiler				
	Copy granularity				Basic	Copy granularity				Basic
	char	int	double	memcpy	costs	char	int	double	memcpy	costs
4	1793	807	607	463	369	1545	691	552	478	376
8	3325	1350	946	658	483	2834	1107	816	667	489
16	6477	2503	1743	1071	701	5539	2084	1504	1100	701
32	13572	4995	3610	1936	1151	10999	4061	2922	1978	1166
64	26969	9807	7115	3691	2058	21848	7986	5702	3724	2065

Table 2. Overhead of memory allocation and copy efforts (μs)

The execution of `get_copy()` requires calling the *owning site* and transferring a page containing the requested data. Since `get_copy()` is a method applied to a dual `Actor` object, the call is carried out on a ROI-basis. In this particular case, (1) a remote rendezvous between client and server takes place and (2) a data transfer is initiated to get the requested page in place. These two steps make up

[6] The Metaware compiler is a product of MetaWare Inc, version Rel 2.1e. The Portland compiler is a product of The Portland Group, Inc., version Rel 3.1-1. The Metaware compiler is strong achieving a better MIPS rate, whereas the Portland compiler results in better FLOPS rates. Consequently, an operating system is best supported by the Metware compiler while "number crunching" applications are best supported by the Portland compiler.

the basic communication costs of remote memory-to-memory paging in VOTE. Depending on the compiler in use, Table 2 lists the sum of both times.

As indicated in Table 2, VOTE cannot make full use of the parameter passing mechanisms of the dual object model to come close to the basic communication costs. Rather, VOTE allocates and transfers the data itself. The effects of implicit parameter passing are shown in the columns `char`, `int`, and `double`. In these cases, following the typical use pattern of a C++ VSM programmer, the requested memory page is a typed array of the plain data types `char`, `int`, and `double`, respectively. Many of these pages may constitute some sort of matrix used by the (numerical) application program.

Invoking `get_copy()`, the ROI stubs linearize the typed page into a typed message before communication becomes effective. Similar holds for the receiving site, where a typed page is rebuilt from the received typed message. For each page, this causes a local memory-to-memory copy overhead in addition to the basic (page) data transfer. As shown, the copy overhead varies depending on the actual plain data types of the page. This is because copying is performed in a (high-level language) loop created by the DOG and containing assignments to either of `char`, `int`, or `double` instances.

Table 2 shows that the copying overhead dominates the total execution time of the data transfer and is not acceptable for performance critical services. Even the use of a highly optimized memory-to-memory copying routine (`memcpy()`) considerably defects the overall performance. Compared to the basic communication costs, in the best case the VOTE consistency maintenance would increase by 25.5 % (using the Metaware compiler and a `memcpy()` of 4 KB pages) and in the worst case the runtime would grow as much as 1210.5 % (using the Metaware compiler and performing a `char` copy loop to transfer 64 KB pages). Here are the limits of straightforward language-level support for parameter passing. Although the DOG is perfectly able to pass objects with multi dimensional arrays as parameters, this feature could not be used for performance reasons. Thus pages needed to be treated like bulk data and needed to be handled manually by means of `fetch()` and `store()` methods that do not require internal copies. On the other hand, most remote synchronization and consistency protocol handling could be performed flawlessly and transparently using dual objects and the language-level support provided by the DOG. Therefore the most complex parts of the VOTE system could be designed and implemented with a minimum of development overhead. After this work was completed, the manual optimization of the page transfers was straightforward and easy to accomplish by means of the PEACE data transfer primitives.

In VOTE, access violation has been especially optimized with respect to a read access fault on a page cached by the *adviser*. The optimization took advantage from specific data-transfer features provided by the PEACE nucleus, in particular the asynchronous write of an arbitrarily sized data segment into remote memory[22].

The breakdown into the basic activities of trap handling, packet communication (IPC), dual object overhead (ROI), data transfer (HVDT), MMU pro-

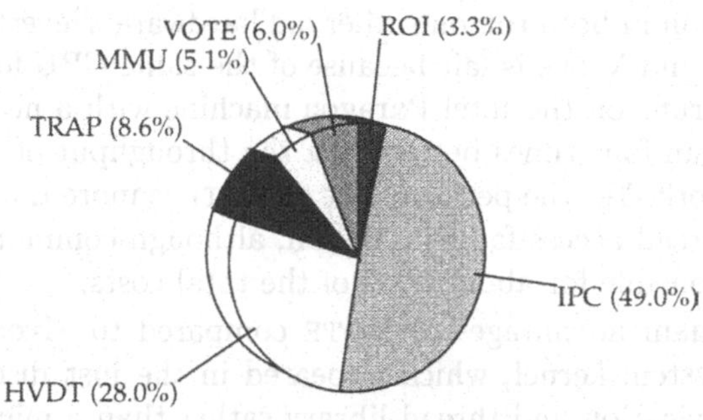

Fig. 10. Percentages of system functions during consistency maintenance

gramming, and maintenance activities in VOTE shows that communication is the dominating issue (Fig. 10). About 80% of the time spent by VOTE for access fault handling is devoted to communication, that is ROI, IPC, and HVDT. Therefore, a high-performance communication facility is of great importance for VOTE. Dual objects make the handling of the VOTE classes much easier and, used in an appropriate way, add an negligible overhead to the basic message-passing mechanisms.

6.2 Related Works

Considering the implementation of VOTE and the resulting performance, the dual object paradigm proved to be the right decision for the design and development of the VSM subsystem of PEACE. Making a cost/profit analysis, the additional overhead of dual objects is very low and can be neglected when running real-world applications. As outlined by Table 3, the end-user performance of VOTE compared to other VSM systems applying very low-level message passing layers for implementation appears to be very good.

System	Platform	CPU	Network	Time (ms)
Mether	SunOS4.0	25 MHz MC68020	1.2 MB/s	70-100
Munin	V	25 MHz MC68020	1.2 MB/s	13-31
Myoan	OSF/1 + NX	50 MHz i860XP	200 MB/s	4.068
VOTE	PEACE + dual objects	50 MHz i860XP	47.68 MB/s	0.667

Table 3. Comparison of read-fault handling in different VSM systems

Mether and Munin both run on rather old hardware. Nevertheless, a comparison of Myoan[3] and VOTE is fair because of the same CPU foundation in both systems. Myoan runs on the Intel Paragon machine with a network throughput which is more than four times better than the throughput of the MANNA communication network. Yet the performance of VOTE is more than six times better than handling a read access fault in Myoan, although communication and data transfer are responsible for about 80 % of the total costs.

One of the main advantages of VOTE compared to Myoan is the specialized operating-system kernel, which appeared in the just discussed case to be "only" a communication and thread library rather than a microkernel with additional user-level and problem-oriented communication support. In order to partly overcome the performance problems, Myoan is even using the low-level NX communication library for inter-node communications bypassing the underlying microkernel. This reduces the communication time (for 8 bytes) from 1909 μs, when exploiting the IPC functions of the OSF microkernel, to about 329 μs.

In VOTE we hadn't to go down to such low levels mainly because dual objects both provide a suitable high-level system programming paradigm and a very efficient implementation at the same time. Thus implementation issues are significantly improved and the lightweight system structure of PEACE is not compromised by complex middleware layers.

Other high-level approaches from the distributed systems area such as CORBA[9] tend to "eat up" the performance of lower layers for the sake of convenient heterogeneous computing and interoperability issues. In the high performance systems area more recent parallel C++ versions such as CC++[5], ICC++[6], Mentat[1] and MPC++[11] seem to be promising. Nevertheless, system programming still needs significantly more control over runtime issues than languages designed for application level programming usually provide. MPC++ and EUROPA C++[26] provide powerful meta-level programming facilities that could have beneficial impact on system programming in the near future.

7 Conclusion

Family based operating system services such as the VOTE VSM system are hard to implement without suitable high-level paradigms and language-level support. Design and implementation of VOTE, as well as PEACE, was strongly influenced by the concept of dual objects. This object model transposes the classical coarse grained user/supervisor memory model of monolithic systems to very small objects of language-level granularity. Therefore dual objects encapsulate both user-level and system-level state information in a single object context to encourage much closer interactions between user and system classes as in conventional object models. Servers are not enforced to maintain client-specific data themselves. Robustness of services is therefore enhanced and system-level data can be shared conveniently and economically amongst many clients.

By providing a highly abstract and yet efficient object-oriented programming environment, the (system) programmer is relieved from dealing with the peculiarities of distributed-memory parallel machines. The VOTE performance figures show that high-level object paradigms do not impose a general bottleneck for both complex and performance critical operating system services.

References

1. A.Grimshaw. Easy-to-use parallel processing with Mentat. *IEEE Computer*, 26(5), May 1993.
2. B. N. Bershad and J. M. Zekauskas. Midway: Shared Memory Parallel Programming with Entry Consistency for Distributed Memory Multiprocessors. Technical Report CMU-CS-91-170, Carnegie-Mellon University, 1991.
3. G. Cabillic, T. Priol, and I. Puaut. Myoan: An Implementation of the Koan Shared Virtual Memory on the Intel Paragon. Technical Report 812, Irisa, Rennes, 1994.
4. J. B. Carter. *Efficient Distributed Shared Memory Based on Multi-Protocol Release Consistency.* PhD thesis, Rice University, 1993.
5. K. M. Chandy and C. Kesselman. CC++: A Declarative Concurrent Object-Oriented Programming Notation. In *Research Directions in Concurrent Object-Oriented Programming.* MIT Press, 1993.
6. A. Chien, U.S. Reddy, J.Plevyak, and J. Dolby. ICC++ – A C++ Dialect for High Performance Parallel Computing. In *Proceedings of the 2nd JSSST International Symposium on Object Technologies for Advanced Software, ISOTAS'96*, Kanazawa, Japan, March 1996. Springer.
7. J. Cordsen. Basing Virtually Shared Memory on a Family of Consistency Models. In *Proceedings of the IPPS Workshop on Support for Large-Scale Shared Memory Architectures*, pages 58–72, Cancun, Mexico, April 26th, 1994.
8. J. Cordsen, Th. Garnatz, A. Gerischer, M. D. Gubitoso, U. Haack, M. Sander, and Schröder-Preikschat. VOTE for PEACE — Implementation and Performance of a Parallel Operating System. *IEEE Concurrency*, 5(2):16–27, 1997.
9. Object Management Group Document. The Common Object Request Broker: Architecture and Specification 2.0. Technical report, OMG.
10. A. N. Habermann, L. Flon, and L. Cooprider. Modularization and Hierarchy in a Family of Operating Systems. *Communications of the ACM*, 19(5):266–272, 1976.
11. Yutaka Ishikawa, Atsushi Hori, Mitsuhisa Sato, Motohiko Matsuda, Jörg Nolte, Hiroshi Tezuka, Hiroki Konaka, Munenori Maeda, and Kazuto Kubota. Design and Implementation of Metalevel Architecture in C++ – MPC++ Approach –. In *Reflection '96*, 1996.
12. L. Lamport. How to make a Multiprocessor Computer that Correctly Executes Multiprocessor Programs. *IEEE Transactions on Computers*, C–28(9):241–248, September 1979.
13. D. Lenoski, J. Laudon, T. Joe, D. Nakahira, L. Stevens, A. Gupta, and J. Hennessy. The DASH Prototype: Implementation and Performance. In *Proceedings of the 19th Annual International Symposium on Computer Architecture*, pages 92–103, Gold Coast, Australia, May 19–21, 1992.
14. Henry M. Levy and Ewan D. Tempero. Modules, Objects, and Distributed Programming: Issues in RPC and Remote Object Invocation. *Software—Practice and Experience*, 21(1):77–90, January 1991.

15. K. Li. *Shared Virtual Memory on Loosely Coupled Multiprocessors.* PhD thesis, Yale University, 1986.
16. H. Lieberman. Using Prototypical Objects to Implement Shared Behavior in Object–Oriented Systems. In *Special Issue of SIGPLAN notices*, volume 21, pages 214–223. ACM, November 1986.
17. Mesaac Makpangou, Yvon Gourhant, Jean-Pierre Le Narzul, and Marc Shapiro. Structuring Distributed Applications as Fragmented Objects. Rapport de recherche 1404, Institut National de la Recherche en Informatique et Automatique, Rocquencourt (France), January 1991.
18. O. M. Nierstrasz. Active Objects in Hybrid. In *Special Issue of SIGPLAN notices*, volume 22, pages 243–253. ACM, December 1987.
19. J. Nolte. Language Level Support for Remote Object Invocation. Arbeitspapiere der GMD 654, Gesellschaft für Mathematik und Datenverarbeitung, St. Augustin, Germany, June 1992.
20. J. Nolte and W. Schröder-Preikschat. An Object-Oriented Computing Surface for Distributed Memory Architectures. In *Proceedings of the Twenty-Sixth Annual Hawaii International Conference on System Sciences*, volume 2, pages 134–143, Maui, Hawaii, January 5–8, 1993. IEEE Computer Society Press.
21. D. L. Parnas. Designing Software for Ease of Extension and Contraction. *IEEE Transactions on Software Engineering*, SE-5(2), 1979.
22. W. Schröder-Preikschat. *The Logical Design of Parallel Operating Systems.* Prentice Hall International, 1994. ISBN 0-13-183369-3.
23. M. Shapiro. Structure and Encapsulation in Distributed Systems: the Proxy Principle. In *Proceedings of the 6th International Conference on Distributed Computing Systems*, pages 198–204, Cambridge, MA, 1986.
24. P. Wegner. Classification in Object-Oriented Systems. *SIGPLAN Notices*, 21(10):173–182, 1986.
25. Peter Wegner. Dimensions of Object–Based Language Design. *Special issue of SIGPLAN Notices*, 22(12):88–97, October 1987.
26. The Europa WG. EUROPA Parallel C++ Specification. Technical report, http://www.dcs.kcl.ac.uk/EUROPA, 1997.

Binary Component Adaptation

Ralph Keller and Urs Hölzle[1]

Abstract. Binary component adaptation (BCA) allows components to be adapted and evolved in binary form and on-the-fly (during program loading). BCA rewrites component binaries before (or while) they are loaded, requires no source code access and guarantees release-to-release compatibility. That is, an adaptation is guaranteed to be compatible with a new binary release of the component as long as the new release itself is compatible with clients compiled using the earlier release. We describe our implementation of BCA for Java and demonstrate its usefulness by showing how it can solve a number of important integration and evolution problems. Even though our current implementation was designed for easy integration with Sun's JDK 1.1 VM rather than for ultimate speed, the load-time overhead introduced by BCA is small, in the range of one or two seconds. With its flexibility, relatively simple implementation, and low overhead, binary component adaptation could significantly improve the reusability of Java components.

1 Introduction

Object-oriented programming promises to improve programmer productivity by fostering component reuse. Ideally, new programs are mostly composed of existing components which can be adapted to the specific purpose by using language mechanisms such as polymorphism and inheritance. Thus, relatively little time is spent creating entirely new code, and most of the programming effort lies in combining or specializing existing reusable components [Cox86]. In other words, the main activity associated with software development is not the origination of new programs, but the integration, modification, and evolution of existing ones [Win79].

Unfortunately, this vision cannot always be realized in environments that cannot be centrally managed and coordinated. In particular, combining independently developed components can be difficult [Höl93], as can be the evolution of components over time. Even if small (trivial) changes could rectify a problem, source code changes may be impossible for a variety of reasons. Therefore, interoperability between software components is a major issue in software development [Weg96].

Binary component adaptation (BCA) [KH97] allows more flexible object couplings by shifting many small but important decisions (e.g., method names or explicit subtype relationships) from component production time to component integration time, thus enabling programmers to adapt even third-party binary components to their needs. BCA rewrites component binaries before (or while) they are loaded. This rewriting is possible if binaries contain enough symbolic information (as do Java class files, for example). Component adaptation takes place *after* the component has been delivered to the programmer, and the internal structure of a component is directly modified *in place* in order to make changes. Rather than creating new classes such as wrapper classes, the

[1] Dept. of Computer Science, Univ. of California, Santa Barbara, CA 93106, {ralph,urs}@cs.ucsb.edu.

definition of the original class is modified. By directly rewriting binaries, BCA combines the flexibility of source-level changes without incurring its disadvantages. In particular, binary component adaptation

- requires no source code access, so that it can be used on third-party libraries;
- preserves release-to-release compatibility, so that compatibility problems only arise in situations where they would also arise with unmodified components;
- is very flexible, allowing a wide range of modifications (including method addition, renaming, and changes to the inheritance or subtyping hierarchy);
- can be deferred until load-time, so that the adaptations can be distributed and performed "just in time"; and
- introduces only a small load-time overhead.

We have implemented a working prototype of BCA for Java using Sun's JDK 1.1.3 virtual machine (VM). After reviewing some background, we describe our implementation in detail in section 3. In section 4 we present example uses of BCA and analyze its overhead.

1.1 Overview

The general structure of a binary component adaptation system is quite simple. Component adaptation takes place after the component has been delivered to the programmer, and the internal structure of a component is directly modified *in place* in order to make changes. Rather than creating new classes such as wrapper classes, BCA modifies the definition of the original class.

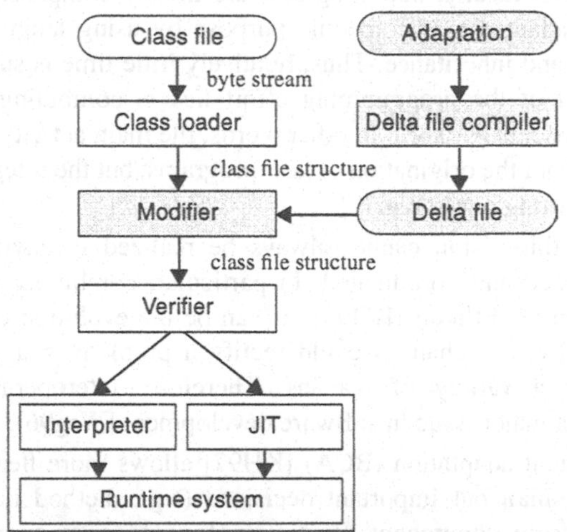

Figure 1. Overview of a binary component adaptation system

Figure 1 illustrates the general structure of BCA system integrated into a Java Virtual Machine (JVM) implementation. The class loader reads the original binary representation of a class (the *class file*); this file was previously compiled from source code by a standard Java compiler and appears in the standard format (i.e., the JVM class file format [LY96]). The class file is retrieved from either a file system or network as an unstructured stream of bytes. It contains enough high-level information about the underlying program to allow inspection and modification of its structure. The file includes code (*bytecodes*) and a symbol table, as well as other ancillary information required to support key features such as safe execution (verification of untrusted binaries), dynamic loading, linking, and reflection. Unlike other object file formats, type information is present for the complete set of object types that are included in a class file. These properties include the name and signature of methods, name and type of fields (class or instance variables), and their corresponding access rights. All references to classes, interfaces, methods, and fields are symbolic and are resolved at load time or during execution of the program. Most of this symbolic information is present because it is required for the safe execution of programs. For example, the JVM requires type information on all methods so that it can verify that all potential callers of a method indeed pass arguments of the correct type. Similarly, method names are required to enable dynamic linking.

The loader parses the byte stream of the class file and constructs an internal data structure to represent the class. In a standard implementation of the JVM, this internal representation would be passed on to the verifier. With BCA, the loader hands the data structure to the modifier which applies any necessary transformations to the class. The modifications are specified in a *delta file* that is read in by the modifier at start-up of the VM. (We call it *delta file* since the file contains a list of differences or *deltas* between the standard class file and the desired application-specific variant.) The user defines the changes in form of an *adaptation specification*, which is compiled to a binary format (delta file) in order to process it more efficiently at load time.

After modification, the changed class representation is passed on to the verifier which checks that the code does not violate any JVM rules and therefore can safely be executed. After successful verification, the class representation is then handed over to the execution part of the JVM (e.g., an interpreter and/or compiler). BCA does not require any changes to either the verifier or the actual JVM implementation.

To ensure consistency, the adaptation system must have access to the complete program, (i.e., all class files that could possibly be affected by modifications). If the complete set of classes can be determined statically, *off-line (static) binary component adaptation* could simply read the transitive closure of all classes and transform them all off-line, producing a new set of class files that forms the complete modified application. Off-line adaptation has the disadvantage that it physically duplicates class files and thus increases disk space usage since each application potentially needs its own copy of every class in every library. In return, off-line adaptation completely eliminates any runtime overhead since no modifications are needed at load time or during program execution. Furthermore, off-line adaptation also allows delivery of a complete application to a customer without requiring any changes in the customer's setup (i.e., using the customer's existing, standard virtual machine).

Alternatively, *online (dynamic) binary component adaptation* performs all adaptations dynamically, (i.e., as classes are loaded during execution, as shown above). Online adaptation may impose a certain runtime overhead during the loading phase, but code will execute at full speed afterwards. Also, online BCA requires delta files to be distributed with the application, and users must use a BCA-aware runtime system. However, this disadvantage can be compensated for a number of advantages. First, online adaptation requires no additional disk space beyond the space required for the delta file. Second, it does not require *a priori* knowledge of the set of classes loaded and thus can handle the full Java language including constructs for explicit dynamic class loading. For example, Java's Class.forName method allows a class to be looked up by name, causing the class to be loaded dynamically if it is not already present. Since the argument to the call can be an arbitrary string expression, it is not possible in general to determine the transitive closure of classes for a program containing such calls, so that static component adaptation would not be sufficient.

In the remainder of this paper, we discuss our implementation of online BCA for the JDK 1.1.3 Java implementation. Before going into implementation details, section 2 reviews the motivation for BCA, (i.e., what problems BCA is intended to solve). Section 3 then describes our particular implementation, including some of the trickier aspects an online BCA system must resolve. Section 4 then evaluates the performance of our prototype implementation, (i.e., the load-time overhead imposed by performing adaptations on-the-fly).

2 The Problem

Component reusers face two main problems, integration and evolution. In this section, we review these problems and show how binary component adaptation can solve them. The discussion is kept brief for space reasons and summarizes the more detailed description found in [KH97].

2.1 The Integration Problem

Assume an application using components A and B, each obtained from a different vendor or organization. The simplified class interfaces of these types are as follows (in reality both classes would define additional methods):

```
class A {
        public void output(PrintStream os);
}

class B {
        public void print();
}
```

Note that both classes define support for printing, although the details (method names and signatures) differ slightly. Unfortunately, these minor differences suffice to make the two classes hard to integrate into the same program. For example, suppose a programmer wanted to store components derived from A and B in a list in the application and later iterate over the list to print all objects:

```
Enumeration e;
while (e.hasMoreElements()) {
        Printable p = (Printable)e.nextElement();
        p.print();
}
```

However, this usage is impossible because of two superficial problems. First, in class A the print method is called output and expects a stream as a parameter. If the programmer had access to source code, it would be possible to add a print method to A; its implementation would simply call output(System.out). But source code access is unlikely since the component was bought from an independent vendor.

Even after solving the first problem, the two components still cannot be combined because of a second problem: A and B have no common superclass or supertype. This problem could be resolved by adding an implements Printable clause to both classes, indicating that both support the interface Printable. Again, this change requires source code access and a recompilation.

Alternatively, the component user could try to solve integration problems using wrapper objects or other programming techniques. However, such attempts can introduce significant additional programming effort, runtime overheads, and difficult subtyping problems [Höl93] and thus we do not consider them a satisfactory general solution.

One could argue that integration would be seamless if components were "well-designed" right from the beginning. However, we believe that it is highly doubtful that such perfection would be common in an open, large-scale component market [Höl93]. Components cannot be viewed in isolation; even if all components are internally consistent and well-designed, their combination may not be consistent. Programs are likely to combine many different components or component frameworks, making perfect harmony unlikely.

Sometimes "imperfection" is present by design. For example, while it might be very desirable for some applications that the standard class String contain encrypt and decrypt methods, such functionality may have been considered too specialized by the designers and thus was deliberately not included in order to keep the class interface simple. Other component programmers may well have different or even conflicting requirements and therefore would choose a different interface. Even if a component producer could anticipate all possible uses *a priori*, the resulting interface would be too complicated, and most programmers would be overwhelmed by a multitude of methods, most of which they never need.

In summary, minor incompatibilities prevent pervasive reuse because a few details do not match: for example a method is misnamed, parameters may appear in a different order, a method requires a slightly different argument type, a component does not fit into a type hierarchy. Therefore, components must be adapted in some manner before they can be successfully integrated into an application.

Binary component adaptation allows classes to be modified on a per-application basis; a *delta file* describes the differences between the standard classes and the application-specific variant. To integrate components A and B, both classes require a common supertype Printable; in addition, class A needs a print method. These changes result in the following adaptation specification:

```
delta class A {
        add interface Printable;
        add method public void print() { output(System.out); }
}
delta class B {
        add interface Printable;
}
```

Both changes retain binary compatibility: Adding a new method cannot affect existing components since they do not refer to this method, and adding an interface is similarly transparent to code that does not use this interface.

2.2 The Evolution Problem

Evolution represents the continuous cycle of activities involved in the development, use, and maintenance of software systems. Software systems evolve over time in response to numerous requirements including bug fixes, user demands for greater functionality, and especially support changes in related software [Som92]. Because such change is inevitable, mechanisms must be developed for evaluating, controlling, and making modifications.

In widely distributed and relatively loosely coordinated environments like the Internet, it is impractical or impossible to automatically recompile pre-existing binaries that depend on a component that is evolving. Thus, component evolution should preserve binary compatibility with pre-existing applications. A change is *binary compatible* with pre-existing client binaries if these binaries that previously executed without linkage errors continue to execute without linkage errors. Linkage errors are type errors detected at link time (e.g., missing method or mismatched method signatures) or at runtime (e.g., invoking an abstract method). Of course, the actual intention of binary compatibility is to ensure that existing binaries continue to run *correctly* with the new component version, but such strong semantic guarantees cannot be verified by a compiler.

Therefore, the evolution of a class library distributed over the Internet is only practical if changes do not abandon support for the already compiled applications. In other words, a library vendor must maintain release-to-release binary compatibility [F+95].

2.2.1 Interface Evolution

The requirement for binary compatibility places stringent restrictions even on the use of simple language constructs such as Java's interfaces. For example, assume an interface Enumeration as shown below which provides a uniform way to iterate through various collections:

```
interface Enumeration {
    boolean hasMoreElements();
    Object nextElement();
}
```

The method hasMoreElements checks for the end of the iteration and the method nextElement returns the next element of the collection.

After this interface was released, suppose we would like to extend it with a method that returns the last element:

```
Object lastElement();
```

However, adding a new member to an interface requires all classes conforming to the interface to provide an implementation for the new method. That is, existing classes that implement Enumeration must implement lastElement because a client may depend on the modified interface. Therefore, this change to the interface does not preserve binary compatibility.

Note that the new method can be expressed by the functionality already provided by the public interface, with an implementation like this:

```
Object lastElement() {
        Object o = null;
        while (hasMoreElements()) o = nextElement();
        return o;
}
```

While it is easy in theory to write a default implementation of lastElement for all classes that need it, this approach is impractical. The basic problem is that interface changes must be reflected *immediately* by all classes that implement a specific interface. But these classes are generally not known to the interface developer since they were developed independently by others, and thus they cannot be changed or recompiled.

Interfaces are widely used and generally considered good programming practice, and thus the interface evolution problem is severe. Since any change abandons the support for already compiled code, interfaces are essentially unevolvable. In other words, the interface designer gets "only one chance to do it right."

This problem is easy to solve with binary component modification as well. To add the lastElement method to the Enumeration interface, we just need to provide a default implementation in the delta file, to be added to any class supporting the old interface:

```
delta interface Enumeration
        add method public Object lastElement() { /* code omitted, see above */ }
}
```

This adaptation specification extends interface Enumeration with the additional method declaration and implicitly performs an add method adaptation to every class that supports Enumeration (or any subinterface of Enumeration).

2.2.2 Evolution of Class/Interface Hierarchies

The requirement for binary compatibility also makes it difficult to change a class or interface hierarchy. For example, during the transition from Sun's JDK 1.1.beta3 to the final JDK 1.1, the class java.security.Key was transformed into an interface. This change did not preserve compatibility with pre-existing binaries that depend on Key even though the functionality defined by the interface was exactly the same as in the class (i.e., no methods were added or changed). Nevertheless, the change made it illegal to inherit from Key since it was no longer a class. (In Java, a class can inherit only code from another class but not from an interface.)

In this particular case, the change was possible since it was a change to a beta release that was understood to be unfinished, (i.e., programmers did not expect complete binary compatibility with subsequent versions). Had class Key already been distributed widely, the change would have been impossible.

2.2.3 Changed Specifications

Changing a semantic specification poses a major problem for component evolution. Consider a minor specification faux-pas in Java's Date class which provides a system-independent abstraction of dates and times. While days are numbered from 1 to 31, months are numbered from 0 to 11; i.e., 0 is January, and so on. In retrospect, this numbering scheme was probably a poor design decision. Unfortunately, correcting this flaw would introduce major incompatibility problems, since applications that were constructed for the old Date class would no longer work correctly. To prevent these problems, the specification will probably never be updated, and programmers will have to deal with the unintuitive definition indefinitely; this is a solution which is not entirely satisfactory. As a slight improvement, one could add a new function that returns the "correct" month number. But the most intuitive name for this function is already taken, and the presence of multiple functions for the same functionality could further confuse programmers.

This problem is better solved with binary component adaptation. The basic idea is to rename the old definition to obsolete_getMonth and then to add the new definition of getMonth:

```
delta class Date {
        rename method getMonth to obsolete_getMonth;
        add method public int getMonth() { return obsolete_getMonth() + 1; }
}
```

A complication arises because the original and new getMonth methods have identical signatures. Therefore, it is unclear whether a particular call site should be redirected to obsolete_getMonth or whether it was compiled with the new definition. Section 3.7.1 describes how our system uses versioning information to solve this problem.

2.3 Discussion

The presence of a flexible and effective adaptation mechanism like binary component adaptation affects both component producers and consumers. Producers benefit from component adaptation because it makes their components more reusable and therefore more valuable. The increased number of situations in which a specific component can be used may also broaden the market for this component, further benefiting the producer. Furthermore, component adaptation may reduce the maintenance and technical support overhead of the producer since fewer customers will request minor changes. Also, the producer benefits from facilitated component evolution as discussed above. Finally, all these advantages are available without delivering source code to the customers.

Component reusers benefit equally. With binary component adaptation, third-party components are almost as malleable as self-written code. In fact, BCA is arguably better than source code modification, even in situations where source code availability is not a problem. In particular, BCA handles evolution better guaranteeing compatibility with future versions of the base component. In contrast, source-based versioning tools are much more fragile since simple changes such as reformatting or rearranging source code may prevent the automatic incorporation of adaptations into a new version. In addition, online BCA handles open systems including programs that dynamically load unknown classes that must be adapted.

3 Implementing Binary Component Adaptation

In this section we will discuss binary component adaptation and its implementation in detail. We will discuss a Java implementation only, but the concepts should transfer to other languages in a straightforward way.

3.1 Modifications in Java

The range of possible adaptations is limited by three constraints: the amount of symbolic information available in binaries, the amount of optimization applied to binaries, and the desire to enforce binary compatibility. In the case of Java, class files contain enough symbolic information to allow virtually any change so that the first constraint does not apply. Some optimizations such as method inlining can prevent certain modifications. Fortunately, this problem does not appear to be severe for Java programs, partially because Java's security model prevents many optimizations at the bytecode level. For example, methods accessing private or protected instance variables cannot be inlined into methods from unrelated classes because the resulting bytecodes do not pass bytecode verification since they contain direct references to private fields.

Table 1 lists a range of useful changes to a Java class or interface; all of them are supported by our current implementation. Note that by composition more complicated modifications can be constructed. For example, reimplementing an existing method can be accomplished by first renaming the method and then adding a method with the original name. In addition, a number of other modifications could be implemented whose usefulness is currently less clear. For example, visibility attributes (private, public, etc.) can be changed, although some changes may not preserve binary compatibility. One could also add new parameters to an existing method, providing default values to be passed from existing call sites.

	Modification	Parameters	Description
Class	renameClass	<new class name>	rename a class
	renameClassRef	<new class name>	rename a symbolic reference to a class
	changeSuperClass	<new superclass name>	change the super class
Interface	addInterface	<interface name>	add an interface to the implements clause
	changeInterface	<interface name, new name>	change the implements list
Method	addMethod	<method name, signature, byte codes>	add a method to a class
	renameMethod	<method name, signature, new name>	rename a method structure
	renameMethodRef	<method name, signature, new name>	rename a symbolic reference to a method
Field	addField	<field name, initial value>	add a field to a class
	renameField	<field name, new name>	rename a field structure
	renameFieldRef	<field name, new name>	rename a symbolic reference to a field

Table 1. Modifications supported by BCA

3.2 Modifying the Class File

An online binary component adaptation system rewrites components while they are loaded. The modifier operates on the internal representation of the class that the loader builds. The class loader parses the Java class file and stores the various components into an object hierarchy. Each component of the class file format [LY96], such as fields, methods, attributes, and various other entries of the constant pool, is represented by a C++ class.

Figure 2 shows the high-level representation of a class and its type information. In particular, the class representation contains the name of the class and superclass, the class access rights, a list of implemented interfaces, a method and field table, attributes and a constant pool. Each method can have various optional attributes. A Code attribute holds

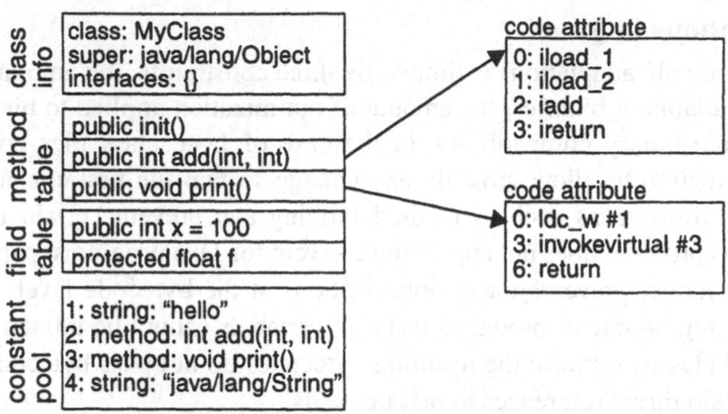

Figure 2. Intermediate class file representation

byte codes and auxiliary information (e.g., exception handler table), and instructions refer to the constant pool for their operand (e.g., lcd_w #1 refers to the string "hello"). An Exceptions attribute is used to indicate which checked exceptions a method may throw. Fields are listed in a table as well, but unlike methods, they contain no code. Since a class points to the superclass, the complete type hierarchy can be reconstructed if needed. Knowing the type hierarchy is useful for changes such as moving class members to the superclass, splitting a class, or merging two classes.

Modifying the class structure involves adding new parts (methods, fields, interfaces) and changing or deleting existing ones. Adding an instance or class variable (field) to the class is straightforward; the modifier extends the field table by a new field structure. This field structure contains constant pool references to the field name and descriptor, and optionally an initial value attribute. The modifier looks up the field name and descriptor in the constant pool (or adds them if not present) and sets the indices in the field structure.

A class, field, method, or interface is renamed by changing the reference to the constant pool containing that name. To preserve consistency, the modifier must update all references from other classes. Therefore, the constant pool of each loaded class is examined for a reference to the renamed object and rewritten to use the new symbolic name; the same operation is performed on any class loaded in the future.

3.3 Delta Files

The delta file contains the changes the modifier must perform at load time. The format should be a compact representation of the adaptation specification so that the modifier can handle it efficiently during class loading. In general, an adaptation specification includes Java source code for added or reimplemented methods. The delta file compiler translates the source code fragments into JVM byte codes and stores them in the delta file.

The delta includes a list of differences, each represented by a pair *<precondition, modification>*. The precondition defines the property the class must satisfy in order to perform the corresponding modification. For example, to add a method to classes implementing a given interface, the precondition requires that the class indeed lists the interface in the implements clause. In our implementation, possible preconditions include a specific class name, implements clause, or simply *true* if every class needs modification (e.g., to update references after renaming).

The component programmer can generate a delta file by specifying the adaptations using a specialized tool (i.e., graphical editor) or by creating a textual adaptation specification that is subsequently compiled into a delta file.

3.4 Delta File Compilation

Figure 3 depicts the process of compiling an adaptation specification into a delta file. The delta file compiler generates a byte code format that is independent of the constant pool since the constant pool layout of the target class is unknown. Each instruction that refers to the constant pool is annotated with the explicitly resolved constant. A table stores the byte offset of the missing constant pool index together with the resolved constant.

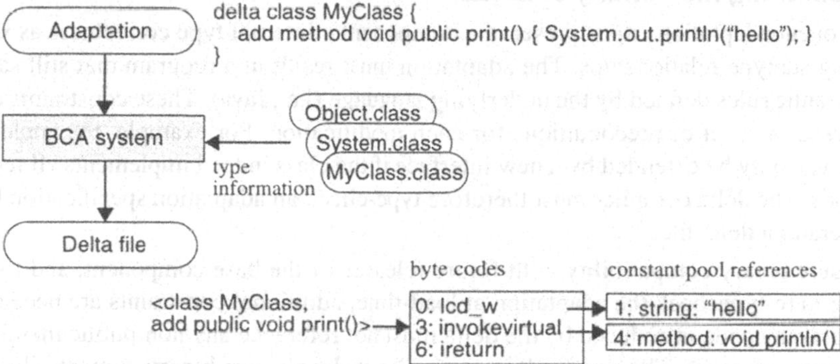

Figure 3. Delta file generation from an adaptation specification

For simplicity, our current implementation uses javac, the standard Java compiler, to generate byte codes for a new method. To add a method to a class, the delta file compiler parses the binary class file, looks up the class and super class names, interface list, and access rights, and inspects the variable and method tables. It then generates a textual Java declaration for that class and extends it by the new method. (To add a method to an interface, we create a declaration for a concrete class that conforms to the interface.) The delta compiler then invokes javac to compile the file into a binary class file from which it extracts the new byte codes.

Since the byte codes are specific to the constant pool for the compiled class, the delta compiler must transform them into a constant pool independent format in order to plug them into any destination class file. For that reason, the delta file compiler resolves every constant pool reference and stores the location of the missing constant pool entry together with the constant in a table. During class loading, the modifier updates all missing constant pool indices and adds constants to the constant pool if required.

We must also ensure that the modifier can indeed patch every instruction operand referring to the constant pool during loading. The JVM supports both one- and two-byte constant pool addressing. Updating a one-byte constant pool reference may lead to a conflict if the constant pool already has 255 or more entries. Instruction widening (e.g., ldc is converted into ldc_w) eliminates this restriction but requires an additional byte for addressing of the constant pool. Inserting bytes into the code may invalidate jump targets, and therefore jump addresses may need corrections. Furthermore, instructions requiring 4-byte operand alignment (e.g., tableswitch and lookuptable) may need pad byte adjustments.

To prevent these problems, we require that any code added to a class use two-byte constant pool references. In fact, the only instruction using a one-byte constant pool reference is ldc; replacing it with ldc_w guarantees that constant pool references can always be patched during class loading. Because of this restriction, the modifier can avoid instruction widening, jump target translation, and realignment of instruction operands, greatly simplifying the addition of new code to a class. At runtime, the modifier simply walks through a table of constant pool references and updates each two-byte index with the actual index into the constant pool of the modified class.

3.5 Checking the Validity of Deltas

Component adaptations must preserve a component's internal type correctness as well as existing subtype relationships. The adaptation must result in a program that still satisfies all semantic rules defined by the underlying language (i.e., Java). These constraints can be expressed by a set of preconditions for each modification. For example, the implements clause can only be extended by a new interface if the class indeed implements all required methods. The delta compiler must therefore type-check an adaptation specification before it generates a delta file.

To ensure binary compatibility with future releases of the base component, and to avoid having to re-typecheck the adaptation at load-time, additional constraints are needed. For example, any code introduced by the delta must not reference any non-public members of the base component. The exact rules are similar to Java's own binary compatibility rules [LY96, GJS96], with the exception that some name clashes are legal as described further below in section 3.7. (Java faces a similar problem because classes can be independently recompiled, and the Java Language Specification [GJS96] contains an extensive section defining binary compatible changes.)

3.6 Compiling Against Adapted Classes

New source code that uses an adapted class must compile correctly and link against adapted classes. For example, assume that a client uses a class that is modified by a delta to include a new method. The compiler must know the changes introduced by the delta in order to call the new method. In other words, each class that the compiler loads must reflect the changes from the deltas. For that reason, the compiler passes every class it loads to the adaptation system before it parses it to retrieve type information.

We integrated BCA into the standard Java compiler javac by modifying its class loader (Figure 4). Whenever the class being compiled references another class, javac loads the corresponding class file. We modified javac to call the BCA system whenever such a class file is loaded. Integrating the adaptation system was simple and required only a few extra lines that invoke the modifier via a native method call. (We wrapped the modifier, which is written in C++, into a Java class containing a single native method.) The adaptation logic is the same as for the VM class loader, and thus both can use the same dynamic library.

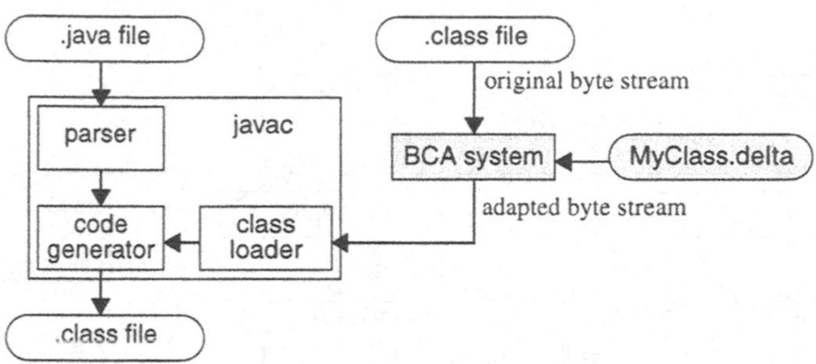

Figure 4. Integration of our BCA system into javac

3.7 Enabling Binary Compatibility

Component adaptations should preserve binary compatibility, unless the programmer is willing to forgo its advantages. Binary compatibility requires that adaptations depend only on the public items (classes, variables, methods, etc.) of a component, so that the adaptation can be applied to any compatible future release of the component and at least as compatible with future releases as ordinary clients would be. However, even if adaptations access only public members, one complication remains.

3.7.1 Disambiguation

With component adaptation, classes are subject to changes via two independent paths, namely *evolution* and *adaptation*. This situation poses a new problem: Changes introduced by evolution may interfere with changes made by adaptation. Figure 5 illustrates this point: If a programmer adds a method print to component A through a delta Printable, then the delta could introduce a conflict when applied to a future release of the component A' that added a print method with the same signature. Since there are two identical method declarations, we have a name clash. Fortunately, this conflict is simple to detect when a class is loaded. Renaming can resolve the conflict as long as the BCA system can identify for each call site which of the two method it calls. The BCA system transparently renames one of the methods (including all affected calls) to resolve the conflict without any programmer intervention.

But how can the system tell whether a particular call site was compiled against the new component version (and thus refers to the new method introduced by the component producer) or was compiled against the adaptation created by the component consumer?

3.7.2 Marking Classes

To solve this problem, we require each client of an adapted binary to record this relationship. The relationship is expressed by an attribute that is automatically added to every class compiled against an adapted component. Thus, when a name clash occurs, the system can inspect the Deltafile attribute of every class containing an ambiguous call. If the Deltafile attribute is absent, the class was compiled against an unadapted component and any calls to print from this class must refer to the print method introduced by the producer.

In Figure 5 the compiler marked class C with the Printable delta, since it was compiled against an adapted class A. On the other hand, class D includes no marker since it uses A',

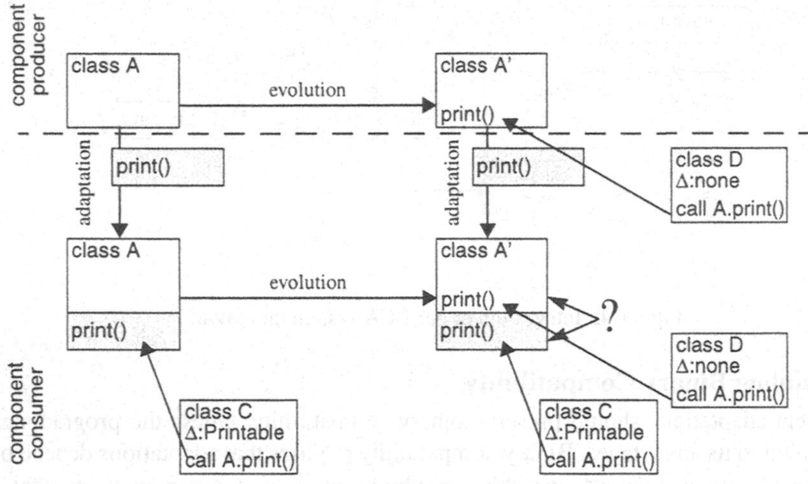

Figure 5. Disambiguation of a name clash

the evolved version of class A. Even when the adaptation is applied to the evolved A' (as shown in the lower right part of Figure 5), the adaptation system can still resolve the print call in class C to the code introduced by the adaptation because C includes a marker. Likewise, the print reference in class D must refer to the unadapted code since no marker is present in D.

No class can contain calls to both methods, since such a class would have been compiled against both the adaptation and the new component release. If a programmer needs to write a class that uses both the adaptation and the new (conflicting) features of the new release, he or she must first resolve the conflict by renaming the method in the adaptation, (i.e., by creating a new delta).

3.8 Composition of Delta Files

Pushing the idea of integrating independently developed components one step further, it is natural to assume that programmers would also be faced with the problem of integrating independently developed deltas. While space restrictions prevent a full discussion here, we will briefly discuss the main issues.

First, conflicts between deltas only need to be resolved by the application programmer and not by application users. The reason is simple: in our model, deltas are bundled with complete applications, (i.e., each application comes with its finite set of deltas). Therefore, the application programmer can resolve any conflicts between deltas, and no new conflicts will appear during actual use of the application since the set of deltas is fixed.

Composing deltas is quite useful because it allows deltas to be reused and combined. For example, a delta that adds printing may be combined with a delta that offers serialization. Deltas that operate on a distinct set of class items (e.g., methods, fields) are non-conflicting and can therefore be composed arbitrarily (i.e., the order of the composition does not matter). Renaming can resolve many conflicts (e.g., both deltas add a method foo). But some conflicts must be resolved manually; for example, if both deltas "wrap" an existing method (similar to the example in section 2.2.3), the order of composition may be important and must be determined by the programmer.

3.9 Security Issues

Since all code must pass the bytecode verifier, the BCA system cannot be used to circumvent the language-level security checks. But this fact itself does not guarantee that the security model is preserved. For example, a delta could replace all methods of the SecurityManager class with methods that allow any access. Clearly, the use of deltas must therefore be governed by security policies. For example, a simple policy is to allow modifications to untrusted classes only (i.e., to classes loaded over the network); modifications of standard library classes such as java.lang.String would therefore be prohibited. A more flexible policy could use digital signatures or mechanisms similar to those already implemented in Java's SecurityManager.

4 Experiments

Binary component adaptation introduces a certain overhead during the class loading phase, but code executes at full speed afterwards. Since class loading is part of the total runtime, the rewriting of classes must be efficient. In this section we show some example uses of BCA and analyze their execution performance.

We designed our implementation for easy integration with Sun's JDK 1.1 VM rather than for ultimate speed. In the current implementation we modify class files before they are passed on to the native JDK loader (Figure 6). This organization is simple to implement since the presence of modifications is invisible to the standard virtual machine (VM), and thus the VM needs only minor modifications in order to insert BCA into the loading process.

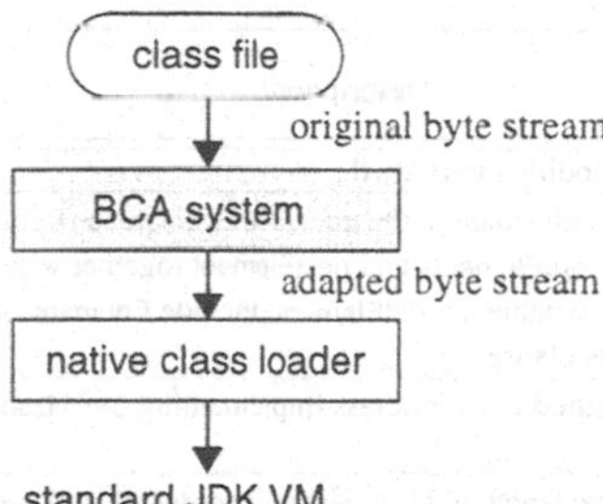

Figure 6. Integration of our BCA system into JDK VM

The main disadvantage of this approach is its higher overhead; the class file is parsed twice, once by the modifier and once by the native class loader. That is, the BCA system first parses the class file and builds its internal representation. Then it modifies this representation and writes a new class file into a memory buffer from which the native class loader loads the modified class. We will quantify the extent of this redundant parsing and unparsing further below.

4.1 Benchmarks

We chose a variety of Java applications written in pure Java containing no native methods. Since BCA introduces a certain overhead during class loading but not while byte codes are executed, we expect BCA to perform better on applications that run for a longer period of time since the relative load time overhead is smaller. To measure this effect, both short- and long-running programs were tested. Table 2 shows the Java applications used for our benchmarks. All applications are realistic programs that typically consist of more than 100 classes.

Application	Input data	Description	#loaded classes	Kbytes of byte codes
javac	javac source files	Sun Java compiler compiling its own sources	219	754
JLex 1.2	sample.lex	lexical analyzer generator	71	251
Pizza 1.1	Main.pizza	Pizza language extensions compiler	171	748
SunCC 0.7pre5	Corba-IDL specification	Java compiler-compiler	115	682
JCUP	parser.cup	parser generator	107	391
Appletviewer	curtime.class	loading and displaying applet, then quitting	225	675

Table 2. Description of benchmark programs

We also developed delta files intended to be typical BCA uses. BCA performance depends primarily on two parameters, namely the kind of modifications made and the number of classes affected. To examine the behavior depending on the number of rewritten classes, we designed deltas that mutate no class at all, one class, a few classes, and many classes. To study the overhead introduced by the BCA system, all deltas rewrite the applications in a way that does not produce a semantically different program (e.g., no new methods are called). Mutating the control flow would lead to side effects and could therefore distort the results. Table 3 shows the deltas and their file size.

Delta file	Description	Size (bytes)	Affected classes
Empty	contains no modifications at all	6	no class
VectorEnumeration	make Vector conformant to the interface Enumeration by adding methods hasMoreElements and nextElement together with a new instance variable currentElement; include Enumeration in the implements clause	299	class Vector
AddPrintSerializable	add a print method to every class implementing Serializable	218	classes implementing interface Serializable
RenameStringLength	rename method length in class String to newlength and update all references in all existing classes	112	class String; all classes are checked for existing references

Table 3. Delta files

The Empty delta file performs no changes at all. This delta is useful to get an idea of the base overhead introduced by our prototype implementation due to class file conversion. An ideal BCA implementation would be as fast as Sun's VM for this delta. The VectorEnumeration delta complements class Vector with two missing methods and an instance variable so that it conforms to the interface Enumeration. Deltas can also rewrite classes that are not explicitly mentioned by name. For example, AddPrintSerializable changes all classes implementing Serializable by adding a print method. This may affect a large number of classes, depending on how many classes that conform to Serializable are loaded. The delta RenameStringLength renames the method length in class String and updates all references in existing classes.

4.2 Measurements

Table 4 shows absolute execution times in seconds for Sun's JDK 1.1.3 VM and our modified VM. We ran each benchmark five times on an otherwise idle 40MHz SPARCstation-10 and reported the sum of user and system time of the fastest run.

Application	Sun's JDK VM	BCA-enabled VM							
		Empty		VectorEnumeration		AddPrintSerializable		RenameStringLength	
	time	time	%	time	%	time	%	time	%
javac	56.6	56.5	-0.3%	57.3	1.1%	57.2	1.0%	57.9	2.3%
JLex	28.8	30.1	4.7%	31.0	8.1%	29.7	3.4%	30.3	5.4%
Pizza	4.2	6.9	66.7%	6.8	62.8%	6.9	66.2%	7.0	67.6%
SunCC	26.2	27.6	5.3%	28.0	6.8%	27.9	6.3%	28.0	6.6%
CUP	7.7	9.1	18.3%	9.3	20.1%	9.2	19.6%	9.1	18.2%
Appletviewer	8.0	10.4	29.1%	10.7	33.8%	10.7	33.2%	10.7	33.7%

Table 4. Benchmark execution times (in seconds)

Overall, the load-time overhead introduced by BCA is small in absolute terms, even though we designed our implementation for easy integration with Sun's JDK VM rather than for ultimate speed. The base loading overhead (Empty delta) is about 1-2 seconds for the benchmarks above. As explained in section 4.1, an implementation that integrated the modifier into the native loader (as illustrated in Figure 1) would not incur this overhead. The table also reveals some random variations which are probably caused by cache effects or network activity. For example, javac executes slightly faster than Sun's VM when using the Empty delta file. In other words, the base overhead of BCA is so small that it can be obscured by random variations in execution time, especially for long-running programs.

The overhead of the other deltas is not much higher than the base overhead incurred by Empty; the largest difference is 0.9 seconds (VectorEnumeration for JLex). To find out how much of the overhead is actually spent modifying the class data structures (rather than parsing and unparsing the class files), we profiled our BCA implementation with gprof. Table 5 shows the number of changes that the modifier performed on the class files and the percentage of the runtime overhead used to make modifications.

Clearly, modifications contribute only a minor part to the overhead. In other words, the overhead of our current implementation is dominated by the (unnecessary) reading and writing of the class file. The actual modifications typically take only about 10% of the overall time, indicating that an order-of-magnitude speedup may be possible with an implementation that avoided the extra reads and writes. In the worst case, the modifications consume about one quarter of the overall overhead in the case of AddPrintSerializable which adds a print method to each class implementing Serializable.

Application	VectorEnumeration					AddPrintSerializable					RenameStringLength				
	#add method	#add field	#rename method	#rename method ref	modification overhead	#add method	#add field	#rename method	#rename method ref	modification overhead	#add method	#add field	#rename method	#rename method ref	modification overhead
javac	2	1	-	-	0.2%	12	-	-	-	9.0%	-	-	1	219	12.8%
JLex	2	1	-	-	2.6%	9	-	-	-	15.0%	-	-	1	71	13.0%
Pizza	-	-	-	-	0%	10	-	-	-	9.4%	-	-	1	171	10.7%
SunCC	2	1	-	-	1.1%	11	-	-	-	7.1%	-	-	1	115	12.4%
CUP	2	1	-	-	1.0%	17	-	-	-	19.7%	-	-	1	107	17.2%
Appletviewer	2	1	-	-	0.3%	33	-	-	-	26.7%	-	-	1	225	12.8%

Table 5. Relative overhead of BCA

4.3 Discussion

Rewriting class files while they are loaded is efficient and imposes only a minor load time cost. Clearly, the performance of our implementation could be improved significantly, but we have not yet optimized it because even the unoptimized version appears to be fast enough, and we did not want to lose the ease of integration into existing VMs (e.g., porting BCA to newer versions of the JDK). We measured the overhead on a relatively slow SPARCstation-10 to improve the accuracy of our data through longer program executions. On current machines such as a 200MHz Pentium Pro, the typical overhead of 1-2 seconds measured above drops to a few tenths of a second (i.e., the CPU overhead is negligible). For such machines, the dominating cost of BCA will most likely be the extra file I/O to read the deltas files from disk or over a network. Since delta files are highly encoded and small compared to the base class files, this I/O overhead is likely to be very small as well. In fact, BCA could actually reduce the I/O overhead, for example, when adding a method to a group of classes. Without BCA, such a change would increase the file size of each class, whereas with BCA the method is read only once. In summary, we believe there is strong evidence that BCA will impose only a very small execution penalty on a BCA-aware system.

4.4 Status and Future Work

We have developed a working prototype of dynamic BCA for Java that implements a wide range of the adaptations. Our system includes a BCA-aware Java virtual machine, a delta file compiler to generate deltas from an adaptation specification, and a modified version of javac in order to compile programs that use adapted components. We plan to make this implementation publicly available in order to facilitate experimentation with binary component adaptation.

We are currently working on an easy-to-use delta file compiler that translates an adaptation specification into a binary delta file. The delta file compiler contains a lexer, parser, and code generator and is written purely in Java. In the near future, we plan to support additional modifications for refactorings (e.g., split a class, merge two classes, move a method upwards in the type hierarchy). The delta compiler currently does not include a type checker yet but relies on javac to report errors in methods added by deltas.

5 Related Work

Much previous work has viewed the problems of component adaptation and evolution as a programming language problem, and several language features have been proposed that can address some (but not all) problems. *Descriptive classes* [San86] allowed the programmer to create supertypes after the fact, solving part of the example problem in section 2.1. The usefulness of creating new superclasses for existing classes was discussed in detail by Pedersen [Ped89] and implemented in Cecil [Cha93a]. *Predicate classes* [Cha93b] offer yet another way to extend and adapt objects, although they were conceived for a different purpose. In languages allowing multiple dispatch (e.g., CLOS and Cecil) new methods can be attached to existing classes.

Horn's *enhancive types* [Hor87] do not alter types (classes) directly but instead allow a base type to be coerced into another type (the enhanced type) that offers additional methods implemented in terms of the base type's public interface. Unlike BCA, enhancive types do not allow the addition of instance variables or the renaming of methods or classes. Remarkably, enhancive types respect compatibility. No existing code needs re-typechecking because of the enhancements, and thus they can be applied to future versions of the code without problems. Since existing code is left untouched, however, the range of permissible modifications is much smaller than with BCA.

Objective-C's *categories* are named collections of method definitions that are added to an existing class [ObjC96]. Rather than defining a subclass to extend an existing class, category methods are added directly to the class. As with subclassing, there is no need for source code for the extended class. Thus, categories allow class adaptations similar to binary component adaptation. However, changes are limited to adding and overriding methods; a category can't declare any new instance or class variables or rename a method. When a category method overrides an existing method, the new version cannot invoke the method it replaces. Finally, the Objective-C compiler cannot guarantee compatibility with future versions of the class.

In previous work [Höl93], Hölzle discussed the shortcomings of language-based solutions to component integration and observed that many problems could be solved if types could be modified in place. He also proposed to deliver executables in a higher-level format to allow such modifications, but since no language supported a standardized high-level executable file format at the time the idea seemed impractical.

Palsberg and Schwartzbach recognized similar problems with traditional reuse mechanisms and proposed a type substitution mechanism aimed at maximizing code reuse [PS90]. However, for adaptation purposes, their solution is both too general and too restricted: too general because in the presence of subtype polymorphism it may require the re-typechecking of a component's implementation, and too restricted because it does not allow adding new methods or renaming methods.

Nimble [PA91] is a tool for procedural languages that allows programmers to transform actual procedure parameters at run-time. A map defines the rules of parameter conversion and is used to generate an adaptor which is linked into the application. At run-time the adaptor performs the parameter translation. Although Nimble does not require source code and can bridge simple interface mismatches, it is much more restricted than BCA since it only addresses parameter type conversions.

Bracha [Bra92] presents a framework for modularity in programming languages by viewing inheritance as a mechanism for module manipulation. Bracha proposes *mixins* which are a more powerful form of inheritance since a mixin is not inextricably bound to a parent. A mixin is a function from classes to classes that is parametrized by a parent which it is modifying. In our context, a delta can be regarded as a mixin which is then applied to a class. Unlike mixins, deltas modify the class in place rather than producing a new class. Even though Java does not support mixins at the language level, they could be simulated using binary component adaptation.

An alternative adaptation strategy to BCA, *dynamic interface adaptation* [MS97] dynamically loads adaptors (wrappers) to bridge interface mismatches between Smalltalk components. Adaptors (or wrappers) implement a mapping function between call-out and call-in interfaces of components. If the interfaces between components show mismatches, the run-time system looks up an appropriate adaptor and configures it on demand. Yellin and Strom [YS97] define adaptors that in addition to interface mismatches can also bridge sequencing constraints (protocols). Unlike BCA, adaptors do not modify classes in place and usually slow down calls to adapted components.

BCA could be used to support program refactoring. For example, Opdyke [Opd92] defines a set of restructuring operations (refactorings) to support the design, evolution and reuse of object-oriented application frameworks. Refactorings do not by themselves change the behavior of a program, but they restructure it in a way that makes the software easier to extend and reuse. Similarly, Hürsch [Hür95] presents a framework for evolution that automatically maintains the overall consistency of an object-oriented system. Both systems could operate on binaries using BCA instead of transforming source code.

Forman et. al. [F+95] discuss release-to-release binary compatibility between class libraries and its importance for software distribution. IBM's System Object Model (SOM) guarantees that new methods and classes can be added to a SOM library without recompiling client applications. SOM also supports evolution of class libraries through a large number of compatibility-preserving transformations, but all the transformations require source code. However, it would be conceivable to construct a BCA system for SOM binaries.

Adaptable binaries [G+95] also allow direct transformations on a binary, but unlike BCA the adaptation is performed at the instruction level (i.e., it ignores the programming language semantics). Its main applications are quite different from BCA and include software-fault isolation (software memory protection), machine-retargeting, and optimizations.

A number of higher-level binary distribution formats (e.g., ANDF [OSF91], Omniware [A+96], Slim Binaries [FK96], and BRISC [E+97]) could be extended to support BCA. In addition to a description of all classes and types, the object files need enough information to allow dependent code to be updated (e.g., because dispatch tables or object sizes changed).

Harrison and Ossher [HO93] as well as Smith and Ungar [SU96] argue for subject-oriented programming, an object model that allows multiple different perspectives of the same object. Ideally, different (subjective) views of the same object can coexist simultaneously in a single application. Binary component adaptation does not go quite that far, allowing only one application-specific version of a class. Subject programming also assumes full source-level access at integration time, does not necessarily preserve binary compatibility, and views subjectivity more as a programming language level mechanism than as a binary rewriting tool.

6 Conclusions

Component producers and consumers spend considerable effort on integrating and evolving components. Binary Component Adaptation (BCA) can reduce this effort by enabling the reuser to more effectively customize components to the needs of the particular application and by supporting predictable and non-predictable component evolution.

BCA differs from most other techniques in that it rewrites component binaries before (or while) they are loaded. Since component adaptation takes place *after* the component has been delivered to the programmer, BCA shifts many small but important decisions (e.g., method names or explicit subtype relationships) from component production time to component integration time, thus enabling programmers to adapt even third-party binary components to their needs. By directly rewriting binaries, BCA combines the flexibility of source-level changes without incurring its disadvantages:

- It allows adaptation of any component without requiring source code access.
- It provides release-to-release binary compatibility, guaranteeing that the modifications can successfully be applied to future releases of the base component.
- It can perform virtually all legal modifications (at least for Java), such as adding or renaming methods or fields, extending interfaces, and changing inheritance or subtyping hierarchies. Several of these changes (e.g., extending an existing interface) would be impossible or impractical without BCA since they would break binary compatibility.
- BCA handles open, distributed systems well because the programmer can specify adaptations for an open set of classes (e.g., all subclasses of a certain class) even though the exact number and identity of the classes in this set is not known until load time.
- Since binary adaptations do not require the re-typechecking of any code at adaptation time, BCA is efficient enough to be performed at load time.

To our knowledge, no other mechanism combines all of these advantages.

We described an efficient implementation of BCA for Java using Sun's JDK 1.1 VM. The implementation requires only minimal changes to the virtual machine and the Java compiler. No changes to the JVM class file format are required, nor any change to the bytecode verifier or any other part of the JVM definition. Therefore, it can easily be integrated into other JVM implementations and is upwardly compatible with existing VMs.

Even though our current implementation was designed for easy integration with an existing VM rather than for ultimate speed, our measurements show that the load-time overhead introduced by BCA is small, in the range of one or two seconds of execution time. A more efficient implementation that is more tightly integrated with the basic VM would substantially reduce this overhead further.

We believe that with its flexibility, relatively simple implementation, and low overhead, binary component adaptation could significantly improve the reusability of Java components by enabling the reuser to more effectively customize components to the needs of the particular application.

Acknowledgments. This work was supported in part by National Science Foundation CAREER grant CCR-9624458 and by Sun Microsystems.

7 References

[A+96] Ali-Reza Adl-Tabatabai, Geoff Langdale, Steven Lucco, Robert Wahbe. Efficient and Language-Independent Mobile Programs. *PLDI '96 Proceedings*, pp. 127-136, Philadelphia, Pennsylvania, May 1996.

[Bra92] Gilad Bracha. *The Programming Language Jigsaw: Mixins, Modularity and Multiple Inheritance.* Ph.D. Thesis, University of Utah Computer Science Department, March 1992.

[Cha93a] Craig Chambers. *The Cecil Language—Specification and Rationale.* Technical Report 93-03-05, Computer Science Department, University of Washington, Seattle 1993.

[Cha93b] Craig Chambers. Predicate Classes. *ECOOP '93 Conference Proceedings*, Kaiserslautern, Germany, July 1993.

[Cox86] Brad Cox. *Object-Oriented Programming: An Evolutionary Approach.* Addison-Wesley, Reading, MA 1986.

[E+97] Jens Ernst, William Evans, Christopher W. Fraser, Steven Lucco, Todd A. Proebsting. Code Compression. *PLDI '97 Proceedings*, pp. 358-365, Las Vegas, Nevada, June 15-18, 1997.

[FK96] M. Franz and T. Kistler. Slim Binaries. *Technical Report No. 96-24*, Department of Information and Computer Science, University of California, Irvine, June 1996.

[F+95] Ira R. Forman, Michael H. Conner, Scott H. Danforth, Larry K. Raper. Release-to-Release Binary Compatibility in SOM. *Proceedings of OOPSLA '95, ACM SIGPLAN Notices,* Volume 30, Number 10, October 1995.

[GJS96] James Gosling, Bill Joy and Guy Steele. *The Java Language Specification*. Addison-Wesley, 1996.

[G+95] Susan L. Graham, Steven Lucco, Robert Wahbe. Adaptable Binary Programs. *USENIX*, Winter 1995, pp. 315-325.

[HO93] William Harrison and Harold Ossher. Subject-Oriented Programming. *OOPSLA '93 Conference Proceedings*, Washington DC, October 1993.

[Hür95] Walter L. Hürsch. *Maintaining Consistency and Behavior of Object-Oriented Systems during Evolution.* Ph.D. Thesis, College of Computer Science of Northeastern University, August 1995.

[Hor87] Chris Horn. Conformance, Genericity, Inheritance and Enhancement. *ECOOP '87 Conference Proceedings,* pp. 223-233, Paris, France, June 1987. Published as Springer Verlag LNCS 276, Berlin, Germany 1987.

[Höl93] Urs Hölzle. Integrating Independently-Developed Components in Object-Oriented Languages. *Proceedings of ECOOP'93*, Springer Verlag LNCS 512, 1993.

[KH97] Ralph Keller and Urs Hölzle. Supporting the Integration and Evolution of Components Through Binary Component Adaptation. *Technical Report TRCS97-15*, Department of Computer Science, University of California, Santa Barbara, September 1997.

[LY96] Tim Lindholm and Frank Yellin. *The Java Virtual Machine Specification*, Addison-Wesley, September 1996.

[MS97] Kai-Uwe Mätzel and Peter Schnorf. Dynamic Component Adaptation. *Ubilab Technical Report 97.6.1*, Union Bank of Switzerland, Zürich, Switzerland, June 1997.

[ObjC96] Apple Computers. *Object-Oriented Programming and the Objective-C Language*. http://devworld.apple.com/dev/SWTechPubs/Documents/OPENSTEP/ObjectiveC/objctoc.htm.

[Opd92] William F. Opdyke. *Refactoring Object-Oriented Frameworks*. Ph.D. Thesis, University of Illinois at Urbana-Champaign, 1992.

[OSF91] Open Systems Foundation. *OSF Architecture-Neutral Distribution Format Rationale*. Open Systems Foundation, June 1991.

[PA91] Purtilo J. and Atlee J. Module Reuse by Interface Adaptation. *Software Practice and Experience*, Vol. 21, No. 6, 1991.

[Ped89] Claus H. Pedersen. Extending ordinary inheritance schemes to include generalization. *OOPSLA '89 Conference Proceedings*, pp. 407-417, New Orleans, LA.

[PS90] Jens Palsberg and Michael Schwartzbach. Type substitution for object-oriented programming. *ECOOP/OOPSLA '90 Conference Proceedings*, pp. 151-160, Ottawa, Canada, October 1990.

[San86] David Sandberg. An Alternative to Subclassing. *OOPSLA '86 Conference Proceedings*, pp. 424-428, Portland, OR, October 1986. Published as *SIGPLAN Notices 21(11)*, November 1986.

[Som92] Ian Sommerville. *Software Engineering*. 4th ed., Addison-Wesley, 1992.

[SU96] Randall B. Smith and David Ungar. A Simple and Unifying Approach to Subjective Objects. *Theory and Practice of Object Systems 2(3)*:161-178, 1996.

[Weg96] Peter Wegner. Interoperability. *ACM Computing Surveys*, Vol. 28, No. 1, 1996.

[Win79] Terry Winograd. Beyond programming languages. *Communications of the ACM*, 22:7, pages 391-401, July, 1979.

[W+93] Robert Wahbe, Steven Lucco, Thomas E. Anderson, Susan L. Graham. Efficient Software-Based Fault Isolation. *SOSP 1993*, pp. 203-216.

[YS97] Daniel M. Yellin and Robert E. Strom. Protocol Specifications and Component Adaptors. IBM T.J. Watson Research Center. *ACM Transactions on Programming Languages and Systems*, Vol. 19, No. 2, March 1997, pages 292-333.

Object-Oriented Architectural Support for a Java Processor

N. Vijaykrishnan[1], N. Ranganathan[1] and R. Gadekarla[2*]

[1] Center for Microelectronics Research, Department of Computer Science & Engg., University of South Florida, Tampa, FL 33620

[2] Bell South Communications, Birmingham, Alabama.

Abstract. In this paper, we propose architectural support for object manipulation, stack processing and method invocation to enhance the execution speed of Java bytecodes. First, a virtual address object cache that supports efficient manipulation and relocation of objects is presented. The proposed scheme combines the serialized handle and object lookup into a single lookup. Next, the extended folding optimization that combines the execution of a sequence of bytecodes is proposed. This eliminates the redundant loads and stores of local variables associated with stack architectures. Also, three cache-based schemes: hybrid cache, hybrid polymorphic cache and two-level hybrid cache to implement virtual method invocations are presented. These schemes utilize the receiver type locality at call sites and eliminate the need for creating dispatch tables used in current JVM implementations.

1 Introduction

Java's object oriented nature along with its distributed nature makes it a good choice for network computing. The secure, dynamic, multi-threaded and portable nature of Java along with its support for garbage collection meets most of the current software requirements. This along with its compact object code makes it as the language of choice for the burgeoning embedded processor market. Applications in Java are compiled into the byte code format to execute in the Java Virtual Machine (JVM). The core of the JVM implementation is the execution engine that executes the byte codes. This can be implemented in four different ways (Figure 1):

1. An interpreter is a software emulation of the virtual machine. It uses a loop that fetches, decodes and executes the byte codes until the program ends. The Java interpreter due to the software emulation has an additional overhead of executing more instructions than just the byte codes. Also, it suffers from the penalty of inefficient use of micro-architectural features like cache and branch prediction. The software decoder is normally implemented using a large switch statement that affects the locality of the Instruction cache. Both the Java byte codes (instructions) and the associated data become data when the interpreter is executed thereby resulting in more data misses [13].

* This work was done when the author was at University of South Florida

2. A Just-in-time (JIT) compiler is an execution model which tries to speed up the execution of interpreted programs. It compiles a Java method into native instructions on the fly and caches the native sequence. On future references to the same method, the cached native method can be executed directly without the need for interpretation. JIT compilers have been released by many vendors like Borland, Symantec [26], Microsoft, and Softway [25]. Compiling during program execution, however, inhibits aggressive optimizations because compilation must only incur a small overhead. This constraint makes the JIT compilers intrinsically slower than direct-native code execution. Further, the quality of the generated code critically depends on the specific features of the target processor. Hence, porting these compilers requires a large amount of work. Another disadvantage of JIT compilers is the two to three times increase in the object code, which becomes critical in memory constrained embedded systems. There are many ongoing projects in developing JIT compilers that aim to achieve C++ like performance, such as CACAO [14]. Recently, performance analysis and tuning environments to improve the performance of JIT compilers on specific-platforms like Intel-based systems have been developed.
3. Off-line bytecode compilers can be classified into two types: those that generate native code and those that generate an intermediate language like C. J2C [27], Jolt [28] Harissa [29], Turbo J [22] and Toba [24] are compilers that generate a C code from byte codes. The choice of C as the target language permits the reuse of extensive compilation technology available in different platforms to generate the native code. In bytecode compilers that generate native code directly like NET [13], Asymetrix SuperCede [23] portability becomes extremely difficult. In general, only applications that operate in a homogeneous environment and those that undergo infrequent changes benefit from this type of execution.
4. A Java processor is an execution model that implements the JVM directly on silicon. It not only avoids the overhead of translation of the byte codes to another processor's native language, but also provides support for Java runtime features. It can be optimized to deliver much better performance than a general purpose processor for Java applications by providing special support for stack processing, multi-threading, garbage collection, object addressing and symbolic resolution. It can also make efficient use of the processor resources like the cache and branch prediction unit unlike the interpreters. Java processors can be cost-effective to design and deploy in a wide range of embedded applications such as telephony and web tops. It is estimated that Java specific processors could capture half the total available micro controller market by 1999 [33].

The various features of Java that make it suitable for software applications also add performance overheads. The use of polymorphic methods, garbage collection, context switching, dynamic loading and symbolic resolution contribute to the slow execution speed of Java code. Implementations of other languages such as Smalltalk and Forth have attempted to reduce some of these overheads.

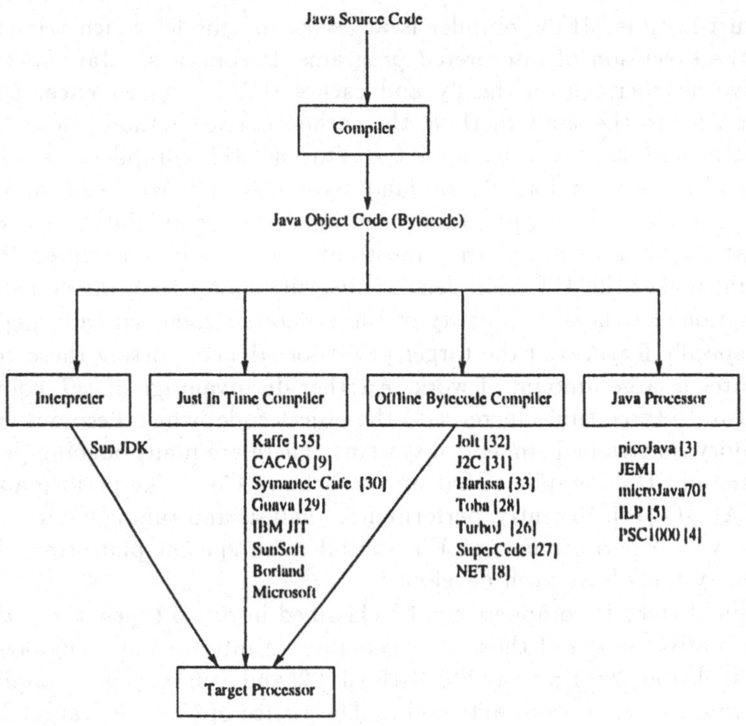

Fig. 1. Executing Java byte codes

Smalltalk systems such as SOAR and Mushroom provide architectural support for efficient object addressing and dynamic dispatches [16], [10]. Further, various Forth machines that are stack based like the JVM include various features to enhance performance of stack operations [30]. The proposed Java architecture is a stack machine executing bytecodes directly on silicon. Sun's microJava, picoJava-I [3] and the Patriot Scientific PSC1000 [4] are other stack-based Java processors. In microJava and picoJava, the JVM instruction set forms the native language of the processor. On the other hand, the PSC1000's stack based instruction set is different but similar to the JVM instruction set. Further, Java processors based on the picoJava core such as Rockwell's JEM1 have been developed. A different approach to Java processors is used in the ILP machine proposed in [5]. Unlike the stack based processors, it is based on an incremental compilation model and involves code expansion and translation overhead. The Java processors have been reported to execute bytecodes much faster than other execution models. picoJava-I was reported to execute bytecodes 15 to 20 times faster than an interpreter running on Intel 486 and five times faster than a JIT compiler running on Pentium [3]. In this paper, we investigate the various aspects of Java execution and identify architectural features that would improve Java's speed of execution. Based on this investigation, a new processor architecture is proposed to execute the JVM instructions with better runtime efficiency. The proposed architecture includes support for object addressing, virtual method invocation and extended folding.

In the next section, the proposed Java processor architecture is described. The processor organization and instruction set are explained in this section. In Section 3, the instruction cache design for the Java processor is investigated. The architectural support for object addressing, extended folding and dynamic dispatch are explained in Sections 4, 5 and 6 respectively. Finally, conclusions are presented in Section 7.

2 Proposed Architecture

The implementation of the JVM on hardware provides the dual benefits of running the byte codes as a native language of the processor and also provides support for its runtime features. In this section, a new processor architecture that executes Java byte codes directly on hardware is described.

2.1 Processor Organization

The Java processor architecture shown in Figure 2 consists of the following functional units: the stack unit, the instruction fetch and program counter(PC) control unit, the variable length instruction decoder, arithmetic unit, memory and I/O interface unit, control unit, and the method inlining unit. The processor includes a 4K direct mapped instruction cache, a 4K direct mapped data cache and an 8K virtually addressed object cache. The processor core consists of a four-stage pipeline: instruction fetch, decode, execute and write-back. The Java bytecodes are initially fetched from the instruction cache by the instruction fetch and PC control unit. These bytecodes are then decoded by the variable length decoding unit. Simple instructions are executed directly on hardware, while the more complex instructions such as object creations are handled by the trap handler. The execution of object manipulation instructions utilizes the virtually addressed object cache. The data is accessed from the object cache using the object reference in the stack unit and the offset field. The offset field is either a part of the instruction or present in the stack unit. The method inlining unit is used to implement the dynamic dispatch associated with virtual method invocations. This unit contains a hybrid cache that caches the method location and receiver types at the call sites. The hybrid cache is indexed using the call site location contained in the PC to obtain the method location for the invoked virtual method. The cached method location is communicated to the instruction fetch and PC control unit when the current receiver type and cached receiver type match. The hybrid cache scheme used to implement the virtual method calls is explained in detail later. The Branch Target Buffer (BTB) is used to predict the branch direction and notify the fetch unit whenever a branch instruction is decoded. This predictor contains a 1K 1-bit prediction history table. The arithmetic and logical instructions are executed by the integer and floating point units. These units communicate with the stack unit to obtain inputs and to write back the outputs. The integer unit consists of a 32-bit ALU and a 32-bit multiplier. The FPU supports both double and floating point arithmetic operations as well as some of the conversion operations. In order to reduce the complexity of the processor, division is performed using microcode. The memory and I/O interface unit serves as the interface for off-chip communication.

The stack unit forms the core of the processor and contains the stack cache, the stack addressing unit, the stack cache manager and some special purpose registers. The stack cache unit contains two register sets that store the top most elements of the stack frames corresponding to two threads of execution. Each register set contains thirty-two 32-bit registers which can be accessed randomly. Additionally, there are two special registers, the top on stack register (TOS) and next on stack register (NOS) corresponding to each thread. These registers serve as the input for the arithmetic and logical operations. Further, the TOS register is used during object manipulation and method invocation operations. The special purpose registers in the stack unit store the current frame pointer, the local variable base and the stack pointer. These registers are used by the stack cache addressing unit to generate the addresses required to access the data in the stack cache. The random, single cycle access of the local variables in the register set using this addressing support enables the extended folding optimization. This optimization eliminates the requirement to move the data from the local variables to the TOS and NOS register before computation. The stack cache manager prevents underflows and overflows in the stack cache by shuttling data to and from the data cache. The processor also uses a by-pass logic to allow the execute stage to continue without the write back stage having to complete. This is important as most instructions depend on the value of the TOS.

The processor implements the JVM instruction set, the quick format variants and additional instructions to facilitate system calls and resolution operations. The instruction set makes use of a fixed length opcode of 8 bits, but instructions vary in length. The instruction set of the Java processor can be classified into seven classes: load and store, arithmetic and conversion, operand stack management, control transfer, object manipulation, method invocation and system instructions. In the later sections, we will focus more on the object addressing and method invocation instructions.

3 Instruction Cache Behavior

In this section, the instruction cache behavior of the Java bytecodes and the equivalent C code is studied. This analysis is used in designing the instruction cache for the proposed Java processor. First, the experimental model and tools that were used to obtain the traces are explained. Then, the effect of block and cache size variation on the miss rates of the instruction cache are investigated. The interpreter in Java Soft's JDK 1.0.2 version for Solaris running on a Sparc-20 was modified to obtain the traces for performing the Java byte code cache analysis. The byte code addresses were generated by executing the benchmarks using the modified interpreter. The traces obtained were then analyzed using the dineroIII cache simulator [7]. The trace patterns for the C code were obtained

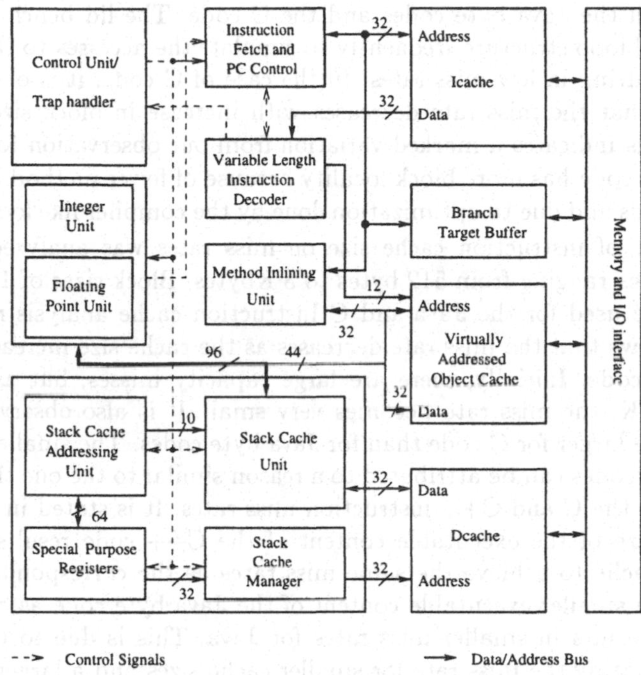

Fig. 2. Processor Architecture

using qpt2, a quick profiler [7] running on a Sparc-20 processor using Solaris. The cache analysis on this trace was again done using the dineroIII cache simulator. The programs selected for comparing C and Java byte codes included some Open Software Foundations Java Test Suite programs [11]: (i) Dhrystone, (ii) RSA Security, Inc. MD5 Message-Digest Algorithm (MDA), (iii) Logical disk simulation (lld), (iv) Hanoi and (v) the Line count utility.

The changes in the instruction miss rate for different block and cache sizes are investigated. For Java byte codes, the effect of block size variation for an 8K direct mapped instruction cache was studied. Figure 3(a) shows that for Hanoi and Dhrystone, when the block size increases from 4 bytes to 8 bytes the instruction cache miss rate decreases. After attaining the best miss rate for an 8-byte or a 16-byte block, the miss rate increases again for larger blocks. Initially, the small blocks fail to capture the locality in full resulting in more misses and hence miss rate decreases with increase in block size. The subsequent increase in miss rates can be attributed to the small locality of the Java byte codes. The frequent invocation of many small methods results in a decrease in locality with an increase in block size. The basic block size of the Java byte code was found to be around 5 (4.9 for Dhrystone) instructions. Smaller the instruction length, more the number of instructions that can fit in a block of fixed size. This results in a smaller locality for the Java byte codes whose average instruction length is around 1.8. Also, it is observed that the lld and MDA benchmarks have low miss rates for both the Java byte codes and the C code. The lld benchmark makes use of a small loop structure frequently to simulate the accesses to the segments of a disk resulting in low miss rates. In the case of C code, it is observed from Figure 3(b) that the miss rate decreases with increase in block size from 4 to 64 bytes. This indicates a marked variation from our observation for Java byte codes. The C code has more block locality because of fewer method invocations, larger methods and due to optimization done by the compiler like loop unrolling.

The effect of instruction cache size on miss rates was analyzed for direct mapped caches ranging from 512 bytes to 8 Kbytes. Block sizes of 16-bytes and 64-bytes were used for the Java and C Instruction cache analysis respectively. Figures 4 shows that the miss rate decreases as the cache size increases for both Java and C code. Initially, there are large capacity misses, but as cache size approaches 8K, the miss rate becomes very small. It is also observed that the miss rates are larger for C code than for Java byte codes. The smaller miss rates for Java byte codes can be attributed to a reason similar to the one that explains differences in the C and C++ instruction miss rates. It is stated in [2] that the larger text size of the executable content of the C++ code results in the use of a larger cache to achieve the same miss rates as the corresponding C code. Similarly, the smaller executable content of the Java byte code as compared to the C code results in smaller miss rates for Java. This is due to the capacity misses dominating the miss rate for smaller cache sizes and a larger executable size causing capacity misses for larger caches.

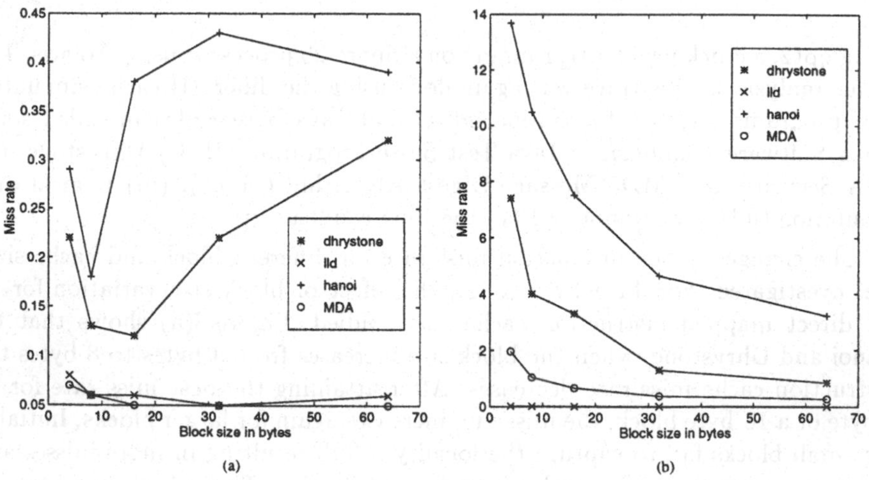

Fig. 3. Effect of varying block size on an 8K Icache for (a) Java byte codes (b) C code

It was observed that the block size of the cache has a significant impact on the performance of a Java processor. It was also noticed that the miss rates of Java

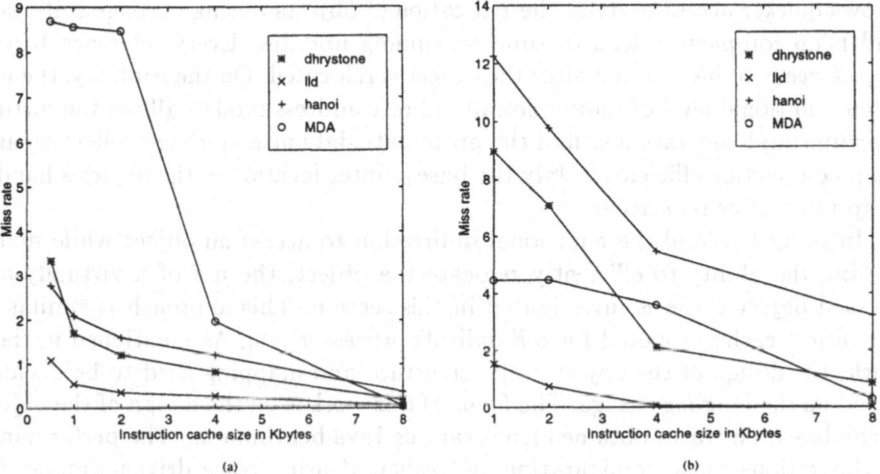

Fig. 4. Effect of varying Icache size for (a) Java byte codes (b) C code

byte codes are less than that of C code. Based on this analysis, an instruction cache of 4Kbytes with a block size of 16 bytes was utilized in the proposed Java processor.

4 Object Addressing Support

Java is an object-oriented language that operates on variable sized contiguous lists of words called objects. Objects, in turn, are comprised of many fields. The fields of the object are accessed and manipulated using the object manipulation instructions of the JVM. The location of the field is determined by adding the base location of the object in which the field is contained with its offset within the object. The number of indirections required to obtain the object's base location varies based on the object representation.

Object representation models used in various JVM implementations can be classified as those that use indirect or direct addressing. In the indirect address object models, the object reference does not point directly to the instance data. Instead, they point to a handle that contains a pointer to the base location of the object. Thus, all references to the object in the code are pointers to the handle. Java Soft's JDK uses an indirect address object model shown in Figure 5. The handle location contains pointers to the object's location in the heap and a pointer to the object's method table. Using this representation, two levels of indirection, one to the handle and another to the object field, are required for each field access. In order to avoid the cost of two levels of indirection for each object access, systems such as NET compiler and CACAO use a direct address object model [14]. In the direct address object model, the object reference directly points to the base location of the object. Though this allows quicker access to data, the relocation of objects during garbage collection and heap compaction lead to time consuming updates. Every reference to the object needs to be updated after the object is relocated. On the contrary, the use of an additional level of indirection in indirect address models allows the virtual machine implementation to find the up-to-date data after garbage collection and heap compaction efficiently. Only the base pointer location in the object's handle is updated after relocation.

In order to avoid the additional indirection to access an object while maintaining the ability to efficiently relocate the object, the use of a virtually addressed object cache is investigated in this section. This approach is similar to the object cache proposed for a Smalltalk processor [10]. As mentioned in their work, the design of the object cache structure and mapping need to be decided based on the language usage. The focus of this work is on the design of the object cache based on traces obtained from various Java benchmarks. The performance of the various cache configurations is evaluated using trace driven simulations along with an analytical timing model for the cache. The analytical timing model enables to take into account the impact of cache and block size on cache cycle costs unlike the fixed cycle cost used in [10].

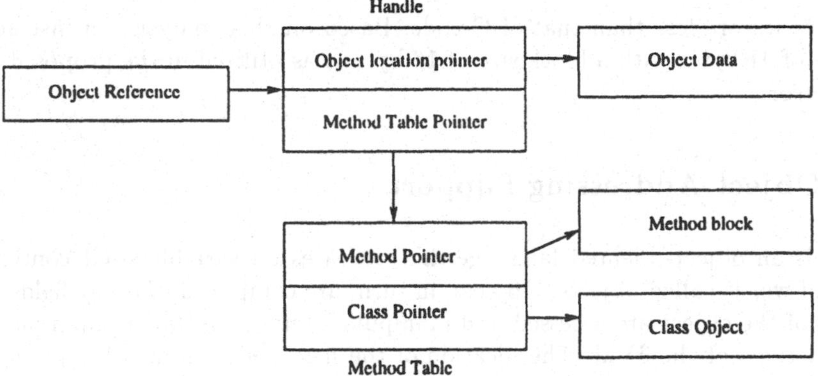

Fig. 5. Sun JVM Object Representation

4.1 Object Manipulation Instructions

The object manipulation instructions of the JVM operate on both class instances and arrays. Distinct sets of instructions are used to manipulate class instances and arrays. However, all these instructions locate the field for manipulation by adding the fields offset with the base location of the object. These instructions constitute around 12% of instructions executed by the JVM. Hence the execution of these instructions has a significant impact on overall performance of the Java code. While the static class objects are manipulated by the *getstatic* and *putstatic* instructions, the object instances are manipulated by the *getfield* and *putfield* instructions of the JVM. The fields of these objects are initially addressed symbolically in these instructions and are converted into a quick format variation after symbolic resolution. The instance variable manipulation instructions are converted into two forms of quick format instructions based on the size of the field offset. When the offset of the field being accessed is less than 256, the object manipulation instructions are converted to quick format instructions like *getfield_quick* and *getfield2_quick*. In these quick format instructions, the field offset is contained within the instruction format. If the offset is greater than 255, the quick format variation of the instruction contains an index to the constant pool. This index is used to access the offset and type of the field from the constant pool. Due to the small size of the objects used in the benchmark programs, it was found that after resolution about 99% of the object manipulation instructions were converted to a quick format variation, which contains the field offset within the instruction format. Figure 6(a) illustrates the operation of the *getfield_quick* instruction using a handle representation. The instance field is accessed by adding the field's offset present in the instruction with the base location of the object. The base location of the object is obtained from the handle of the object. The object reference on the top of the stack (TOS) is used to locate the object's handle. Array components are accessed using instructions such *iaload* and *iastore*. Both the object reference and the offset are obtained from the stack unit for these instructions.

4.2 Virtual Address Object Cache

In the handle representation, each (object reference,offset) pair maps to a unique memory location. This observation indicates that there would be no aliasing problems in a cache which is virtually addressed using this pair. In the virtually addressed cache, the object reference and the offset are used to access the field directly. This eliminates the additional indirection involved with the indirect object access models. Further, the offset addition operation involved with both the direct and indirect object access models are eliminated. The (object reference,offset) pair, which is used to address the virtually addressed cache, is partitioned to form the block index, block offset and the tag bits. The block index is used to select the appropriate block within the cache which may contain the data, the block offset indicates the displacement into the selected block and the tag bits are used to verify that a hit has occurred.

The virtual address used to index the object cache consists of a 32-bit object reference and a 32-bit field offset. The 64-bit (object reference,offset) pair results in a large overhead for maintaining the tag bits. In order to reduce the tag overhead, the object sizes in various Java benchmarks were analyzed. The profiling results for the various benchmarks indicate that the average object size is around 30 bytes. While an offset of 8 bits would be sufficient for around 99% of all non-array objects, an offset of 12 bits would be useful for array components. Thus, the virtual address to access a field consists of a 32-bit object reference and a 12-bit field. Larger offsets could be handled explicitly using the real address available in the object tables or larger objects could be broken into smaller objects by the compiler. An object table that maintains the handles of the recently used objects is used to handle the virtual address cache misses. This table is used to find the actual address of the object in the memory. Whenever an object is relocated in memory, the corresponding object table entry is updated. Though the actual address of the object changes, the (object reference, offset) pair associated with the field remains the same. Thus, the entries map to the same location in the virtual address cache after object relocation. The use of the virtually addressed cache avoids additional indirection in accessing objects, while permitting easy relocation of objects.

Cache interference occurs when more than one address maps onto the same cache location. Thus the partitioning of the address to choose the tag bits, block index bits and the block offset bits is critical to the performance of the cache. Poor choice of the block index bits would result in frequent cache interference. Figure 7 shows three ways in which the block offset and block index bits were selected. Schemes 1 and 2, suffer from high cache interference and hence cause high miss rates. In scheme 1, the most significant bits (MSB) of the object references are used to index the block. Since object references were assigned sequentially, most of the references map onto the same block resulting in high miss rates. In scheme 2, a part of the least significant bits(LSB) of the object reference and the most significant bits of the offset is used as block index. Since most objects are small there is a lot of redundancy in the MSB bits of the offset. Hence the miss rates still remain high due to cache interference. In scheme 3, the LSB of the object reference is used as the block index and the LSB of the offset is used as offset. Since there is little redundancy in the block index bits, this scheme provides hit rates that range around 90%. However, the frequent use of large objects results in high cache interference due to the mapping of the various fields of the object onto the same block. Due to the small average size of objects, most of the object accesses hit in the object cache.

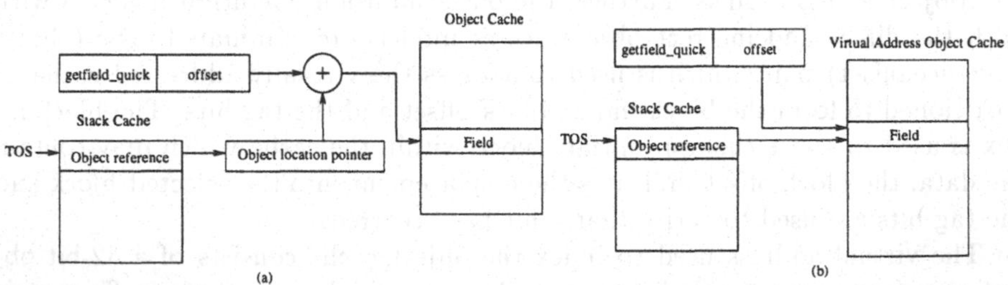

Fig. 6. Field access (a) without a virtual address cache (b) with a virtual address cache

4.3 Performance Analysis

The various configurations of the virtual address object cache were evaluated using the benchmarks described in Table 1. Scheme 3 was used as the mapping strategy to index the object cache and an 1K entry direct mapped object table

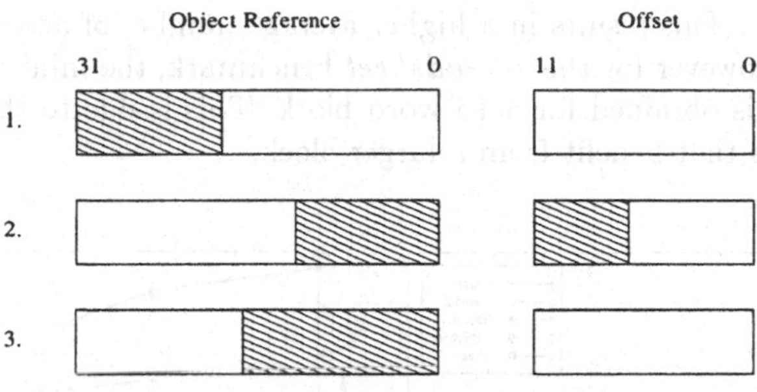

Fig. 7. Virtual Addressing Mapping Strategies

Table 1. Description of Benchmarks and size of dispatch tables

Benchmark	Description	T1	T2
Javac	Java compiler [18]	3932	22488
Javadoc	Documentation generator for Java source [18]	2784	20820
Disasmb	Java class disassembler	988	3380
Sprdsheet	Spreadsheet applet [18]	3304	14396
JLex	Lexical analyzer generator written for Java [20]	1752	10092
Espresso	Java compiler [21]	1836	10224
Lisp	A Lisp interpreter [8]	1120	4788
GUI	A graphical user interface applet [18]	4572	24740
Heap	Garbage collection applet[18]	4336	30496

T1 - DTS size in bytes; T2 - VTBL size in bytes

was used to handle the object cache misses for all the configurations. The average number of cycles required for each object access was studied by varying the cache and block size, associativity and write policies. The access times of the various cache configurations are based on a 0.8μ technology and were obtained using modifications to *cacti* [9]. Further, the number of cycles per object access is based on a 10ns clock used for the processor. The number of cycles per object access also includes the block transfer time, a 70ns latency for each object cache miss, cycles for handling object table misses on an object cache miss and the object cache access time.

Figure 8(a) shows the variation in average number of cycles per object access with change in block size. It was observed that a block size of 8 words resulted in the minimum average number of cycles per object access for all benchmarks except for *spreadsheet*. Since hit rates increase with increase in block size, the average number of cycles decrease when the block size changes from 4 to 8 words. However, the miss penalty also increases for larger blocks. When the block size increases to 16 words, the miss penalty dominates the improvement obtained by higher hit rates. This results in a higher average number of access cycles for 16 word blocks. However for the *spreadsheet* benchmark, the minimum number of average cycles is obtained for a 16 word block. This is due to the frequent use of large objects that benefit from a larger block.

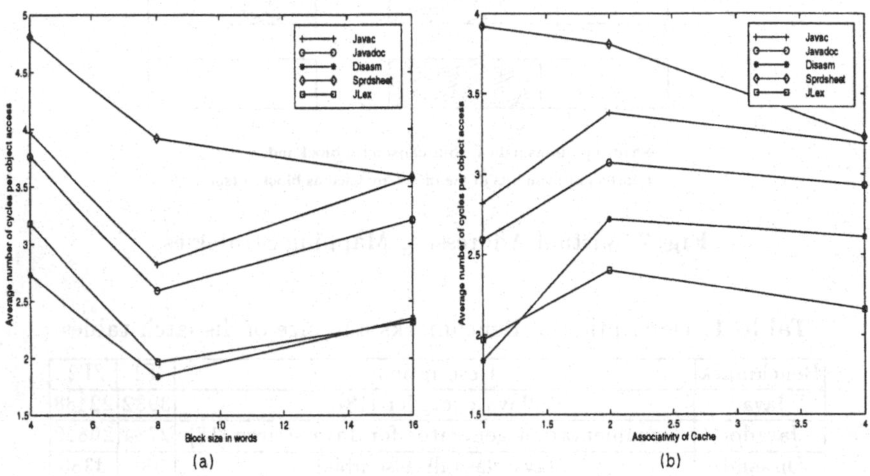

Fig. 8. (a) Variation in average number of cycles per access with block size. A direct mapped, 8K word virtual address object cache that utilizes a write back with dirty replacement scheme is used. (b) Variation in average number of cycles per access with associativity. An 8K word virtual address object cache with an 8 word block that utilizes a write back with dirty replacement scheme is used.

Figure 8(b) shows the effect of the degree of cache associativity on the performance. It was observed that the hit rates are higher for a higher degree of associativity. However, the increase in cache access time with associativity dominates this benefit. Thus, it can be observed that the direct-mapped configuration (associativity = 1) provides faster object access than the two-way and four-way associative mappings. However for the *spreadsheet* benchmark, the improvement in hit rate with increase in associativity dominates the increase in cache access time. Thus, the four-way associative mapping performs the best.

The effect of varying the size of the virtual address object cache is shown in Figure 9(a). It was observed that the access speed improves with increase in cache size due to the reduction in cache interference misses. It was also observed that the rate of improvement reduces as the cache size keeps increasing. The effect of three write policies on the cache performance was also studied. Figure 9(b) shows that the write back with dirty replacement scheme provides the best performance among the three schemes. Among the write through schemes, the write allocate on a write miss performs better than the no allocation on a write miss scheme.

Figure 10 shows the average number of access cycles required for object manipulation instructions with and without the use of a virtual address object

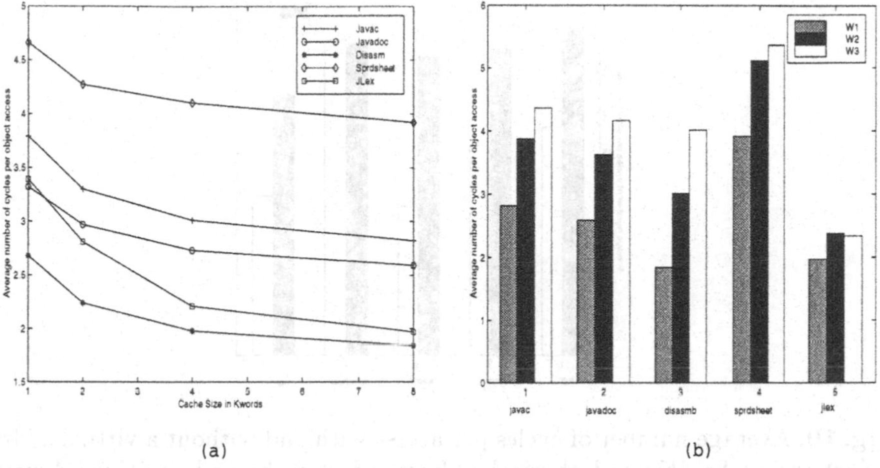

Fig. 9. (a) Variation in average number of cycles per access with cache size. A direct mapped virtual address object cache with 8 word blocks that utilizes a write back with dirty replacement scheme was used. (b) Effect of write schemes on the performance of the Cache. W1 refers to the flagged write back scheme, W2 refers to the write through with write allocate and W3 refers to write through with no write allocate. A direct mapped virtual address object cache of 8K words with 4 word blocks was used for all schemes.

cache. These are referred as R2 and R1. Without the use of a virtual address object cache (R1), a handle lookup followed by an offset addition is required before an object lookup. The virtual address object cache combines the serialized handle lookup, offset addition and object lookup into a single lookup. An 1K word object cache and an 1K word virtually address object cache with 4 word blocks were used for the two schemes, R1 and R2 respectively. Further, the write back policy and LRU replacement strategy are used for the comparison. An 1K entry object table was used to maintain the handles in both the schemes. It was observed that the virtual address cache requires lesser number of average cycles than the indirect object address model for four of the benchmarks. For the *disassembler* benchmark, the direct mapped 4K entry virtual object cache with a block size of 4 words reduces 1.95 cycles for each object access compared to the indirect object access using R1. It was also observed that the high cache interference due to the virtual address mapping scheme results in poor performance for the *spreadsheet* benchmark.

5 Extended Folding

In stack implementations, the operation of bringing local variables of the current frame to the top of the stack and storing the results back consumes a large amount of time. The example expression a = (b - c) + (d - e) translates into

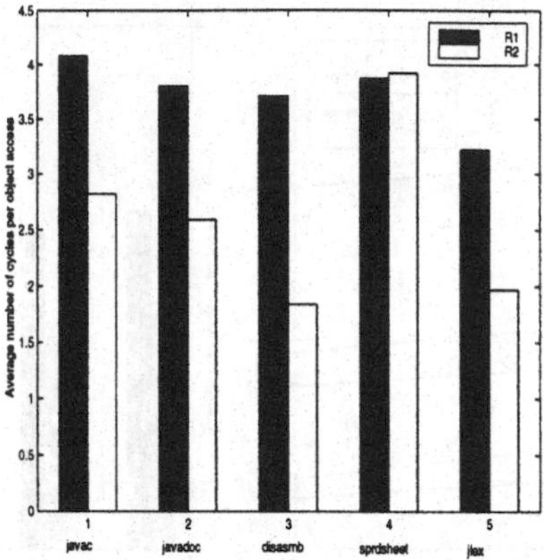

Fig. 10. Average number of cycles per access with and without a virtual address object cache. An 8K word physical address object cache and an 8K word virtual address object cache both with 8 word blocks were used for the two schemes, R1 and R2 respectively.

the byte codes sequence shown in Figure 11(a). The picoJava processor uses the folding optimization to boost the performance by combining an instruction which loads from a stack frame followed by an arithmetic operation or a pushing of a simple constant followed by an arithmetic operation into a single operation. The resulting byte code after folding is given in Figure 11(b). The mapping of the top most elements of the stack onto a register array permit the random access to the local variables. This eliminates the separate step required for loading the local variable onto the top of the stack. However, this optimization is not possible in case the local variable is not present in the register array.

In our processor, we further enhance this folding process to combine other patterns of instructions. Among the various combinations considered, only the (load,load,arithmetic), (load,arithmetic,store), (arithmetic,store) sequences occurred frequently. Other sequences including (pop,pop),(dup,load,arithmetic) were also tried but their frequency was too low to consider implementation. The load includes instructions that load data from a local variable or push a constant. The store operations are those which write back results into the local variables. The extended folding optimization is disabled whenever the local variables are not available in the stack cache. This disabling, however, occurs infrequently due to the small average number of local variables (3.2 for Javac) and the small average size of the maximum operand stack (4.5 for Javac) used by Java methods. This results in the availability of the local variables in the stack cache for most accesses.

The example expression reduces to the code shown in 11(c) after the extended folding optimization Like the folding optimization, the random single cycle access to the registers in the stack cache permits the extended folding optimization. However, the instruction decoder and the frame addressing support required for folding need to be enhanced to support extended folding. The instruction decoder has been modified to identify the new patterns of byte code that have to be combined using extended folding. Further, the extended folding optimization requires access to an additional local variable in the stack cache over the folding optimization. The frame addressing support has been enhanced to provide the locations of two local variables in the stack cache simultaneously. An adder has been included to add the offset of the local variable to the local variable base pointer in order to access the additional local variable. The additional support required for extended folding over folding has a negligible impact on the cycle time. However, there is a significant reduction in number of execution cycles due to the extended folding optimization. The reduction in number of cycles due to extended folding optimization for the various patterns combined is given in Table 2.

(a)	(b)	(c)
iload b	iload b	iload b, iload c, isub
iload c	iload c, isub	iload d, iload e, isub
isub	iload d	iadd, istore a
iload d	iload e, isub	
iload e	iadd	
isub	istore a	
iadd		
istore a		
# of cycles = 8	# of cycles = 6	# of cycles = 3

Fig. 11. Extended folding optimization

6 Virtual Method Invocation

One of the major objectives of an object-oriented programming language like Java is to allow easy reuse and modification of the existing software components. Unfortunately, the characteristics of this programming style result in large runtime overhead due to the frequent use of dynamic dispatches. The invokevirtual instruction, which is the most frequently used method invocation statement in Java bytecodes, uses dynamic dispatch. The appropriate code for execution at a virtual method call site is determined by the object reference (receiver) on the top of JVM's stack. The most effective way of reducing the dynamic dispatch overhead based on the receiver type would be to eliminate the virtual method invocation and bind the call statically at compile time. Various static analysis techniques can be used to eliminate the virtual method invocations [12]. However, only a portion of the virtual calls can be eliminated due to the difficulty in

Table 2. Folding Enhancements Effectiveness

Benchmark	Instructions	P1	P2	P3	P4	I1	I2
Dhrystone	1802073	3429	10564	15352	17021	18781	35802
Lisp Interpreter	798415	1138	3498	59	1643	1197	2840
Ticker Applet	390690	4709	7479	309	2537	5018	7555
Class Disassembler	3776589	28856	33233	8584	216	37440	37656
Linpack	8040994	712186	7681	115	20500	712301	732801
Javac	8428348	181390	154497	11991	69715	193381	263096
Javadoc	6593825	139905	119269	3637	57463	143542	201005
Espresso	6685308	232478	152656	12604	5580	245082	250662
Javalex	754182	512	15487	17	216	529	745

P1 - (load,load,arithmetic) P2 - only (load,arithmetic) P3 - (load arith store) P4 - only (arith store) I1 - Number of three instruction optimizations I2 - Improvement over picoJava folding

deciding the call sites that can be safely bound statically. In this work, we focus on handling the calls that cannot be eliminated by these techniques.

Dispatch Table Search (DTS) is the simplest technique to implement the virtual method invocation. When a virtual method is invoked, a search for the invoked method is performed in the class of the current object. If no method is found, the search proceeds in the superclass(es). The DTS mechanism is best option in terms of space cost. However the search penalty renders the mechanism very slow. Table based or cache based schemes can be used to efficiently implement dynamic dispatch. Dispatch table based techniques have been used in various JVM implementations such as Sun's JDK and CACAO [14]. These tables are based on the principle of using a fixed index for each method that a class understands, in such a way that the method will have the same index in all subclasses. This permits table based schemes to provide a constant time dynamic dispatch. However, dispatch table schemes such as VTBL, RD and SC require significantly more data space than DTS because they duplicate information. This is due to each class storing all methods that it understands instead of all methods it defines. Thus, all the inherited methods contribute to the additional entries found in these schemes. Since, many embedded applications are memory constrained the additional data space is a concern. Various compaction techniques like selector coloring and compact tables can be used to reduce the size of these tables [19]. However, most of the compaction schemes have to recompute the dispatch table every time a new class is loaded [6]. This renders the compaction schemes unsuitable in Java's dynamically linked environment.

Cache-based schemes eliminate the need to create and maintain the dispatch tables. Three cache-based schemes: Hybrid Cache (HC), Hybrid Polymorphic Cache (HPC) and Two-level Hybrid Cache (THC) to support virtual method invocation in the Java processor are investigated in this section. The method inlining unit can contain one these three variations based on the performance/cost tradeoffs.

6.1 Hybrid Cache

Each entry in the hybrid cache consists of the class of the object and a method location pointer. Whenever a virtual method instruction is decoded, the n least significant bits of the program counter (the call site address) are used to index into the hybrid cache. The other bits of the program counter (PC) serve as the tag bits for the cache. The comparison of the tag and the comparison of the class of the current object with the cached class entry are performed concurrently. If the tags and class types match, the cached method location entry is used to locate and execute the invoked method. On a cache miss, dispatch table search (DTS) is used as the backup strategy to update the entries of the cache. The case when the tag and receiver hit for the HC scheme is illustrated in Figure 14. The entry (R1,M1) in the HC corresponds to the receiver type R1 and the location of method M1 corresponding to the class of receiver R1.

The HC scheme is similar to other inline cache schemes proposed for Smalltalk systems [15], [16]. The proposed scheme makes use of the receiver type locality at the call sites like the inline cache mechanisms. However, unlike an inline cache mechanism that inserts the receiver type checking the prologue to each method, type checking is performed in hardware in the proposed processor. The sequence of operations involved with the method call shown in Figure 13 are microcoded to implement the invokevirtual instruction of the Java processor. This eliminates the space overhead associated with inserting prologue code. It must also be observed that the proposed scheme is different from the global lookup cache technique [17]. In the global look-up cache, each entry consists of the class of the object, method name and the method location pointer. The method name at call site combined with the class of the object hashes into an index in the cache. If the current class and method name match those in the cached entry, the code at the method location pointer is executed. The computation of the hash function at each dispatch renders the Look-up cache scheme slow. Using HC, the hashing function is eliminated and only the call site location is used to index into the cache.

Unlike an inline cache where misses occur only when the receiver type at the call site changes, the hybrid scheme is also affected by cache interference. Cache interference is the effect of entries of two different call sites mapping onto the same cache location. Thus the mapping strategy used is critical to the performance of the hybrid cache. The results of direct and two-way associative mapping are presented later. Further, the dispatch speed of the hybrid cache mechanism depends on the type locality exhibited at the call-sites by the program. The type locality at the call sites for various Java applications is shown in Figure 12. The call sites are shown as monomorphic sites (single receiver type), polymorphic sites of degree two and three (two and three receiver types) and call sites with a higher degree of polymorphism. It is observed that the number of different receiver classes actually appearing at a particular call site is very small. The number of monomorphic call sites constitutes more than 40% of the call sites for all the benchmarks. The entry in the hybrid cache always has a hit for such call sites in the absence of cache interference. Further, most of the polymorphic call sites have a degree of two and less than 15% of call sites have more than two receiver types.

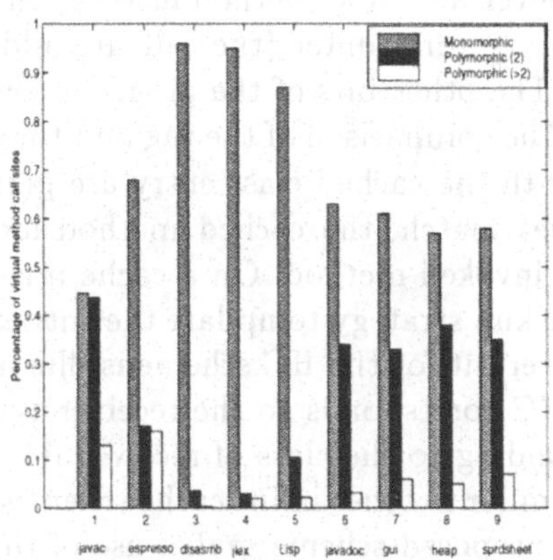

Fig. 12. Type locality at Call Sites

```
Proposed Hybrid Scheme
Call Site Location: invokevirtual object.method
Computation at call site
  entry = cache[PC[1:n]]
  if (entry.class == object->class and cache[entry].tag == PC[32:n+1])
       jump to entry.method_location
  else
       call DTS
  Computation in called method: None
```

Fig. 13. Virtual method invocation using hybrid cache

6.2 Hybrid Polymorphic Cache

The hybrid cache with a single entry performs well for all monomorphic call sites. However, the penalty due to misses at polymorphic call sites increases the average dispatch time. Since most polymorphic call sites have a degree of two as observed in Figure 12, the use of a per-call-site two entry hybrid polymorphic cache (HPC) to reduce the miss penalty is investigated. Each entry in the HPC contains the

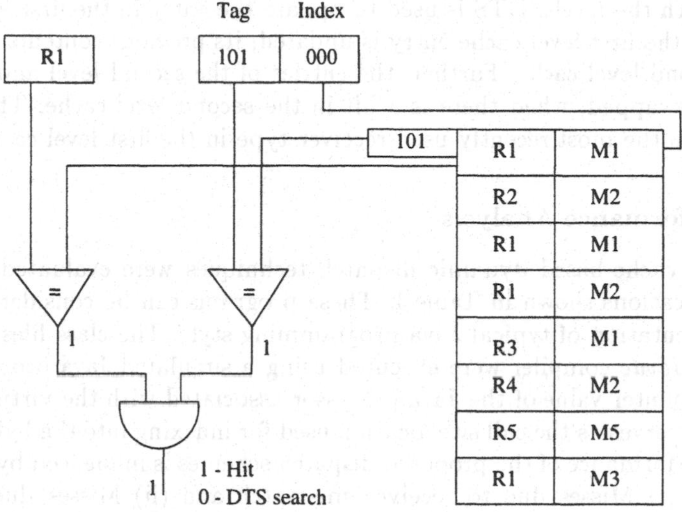

Fig. 14. Hybrid Cache: Tag and receiver hit. Tags are present for all entries but is shown only for the indexed entry

class type and method location pointer of two different receiver types. The class of the current object is compared with both the cached classes simultaneously. On a match, the corresponding method location pointer is utilized to invoke the virtual method. DTS is used to update the least recently used cache entry and perform the dynamic dispatch on a miss. The HPC scheme is similar to the Polymorphic inline cache used as an extension to inline cache mechanism [32].

6.3 Two Level Hybrid Cache

HPC improves the performance at polymorphic call sites by providing two receiver types. However, the large number of monomorphic call sites present in Java code do not utilize the additional receiver type entry associated with the HPC. Hence, the use of a two level single-entry hybrid cache, with a larger first level cache and a smaller second level cache is investigated. The two level scheme enables to provide more than one receiver type for the call sites like the HPC while achieving the space efficiency of the hybrid cache for monomorphic call sites. Polymorphic call sites can benefit from this scheme by allowing two receiver types, one at each cache level. Further, effects of cache interference may reduce as tags are associated with each level of cache. This has an effect similar to increasing the associativity of the hybrid cache. However, the scheme requires extra hardware to compare the tag bits at both the levels simultaneously. On a virtual method invocation, the least significant bits of the program counter index into both levels of the hybrid cache in parallel. If the tag and the receiver of the current object match the cached entry in either level of cache, the corresponding method location is used to perform the method call. If the tag or receiver miss at both the levels, DTS is used to update the entry in the first level cache. Whenever the first level cache entry is updated, its previous contents are copied to the second level cache. Further, the entries of the second level and first level cache are swapped, when there is a hit in the second level cache. This enables to maintain the most recently used receiver type in the first level cache.

6.4 Performance Analysis

The three cache-based dynamic dispatch techniques were evaluated using the Java applications shown in Table 1. These programs can be considered to be a fair representation of typical Java programming style. The class files generated using the *Javac* compiler were executed using a simulated Java processor. The program counter value of the Java processor associated with the virtual method invocation serves as the call site location used for indexing into the hybrid cache.

The performance of the proposed dispatch schemes is influenced by two types of misses: (i) Misses due to receiver mismatch and (ii) Misses due to cache interference. Figure 15 shows the miss rates corresponding to the two types of misses for the various benchmarks. It was observed that the HPC performance better than the HC due to the substantial reduction in receiver misses. For *Jlex*, the receiver misses decrease from 4.52% to 0.0010%. Correspondingly, the average number of cycles required for dispatch reduces from 9.7 to 5.66. Further, it was observed that the THC performs better than the HPC scheme. While the receiver misses increase in the THC when compared with HPC, the misses due to cache interference reduces significantly for most of the benchmarks. For *Javac*, the receiver misses increase from 1.9% for a HPC to 2.4% for THC. The misses due to cache interference on the other hand reduce from 4.6% to 3.8%.

Figure 16(a) shows the effect of varying HC size and its associativity on the hit rates at the call sites. The figure shows that the hit rates increase with cache size due to the decrease in cache interference. Also, it can be observed that the 2-way associative HC performs better than a direct mapped HC with same number of words. Hit rates range from 86.3% to 96.3% for the various configurations shown in the figure. It was observed that HPC performs similar to HC for variation in associativity and cache size. For Javac, the hit rate improves from 89.8% for a 256 entry direct mapped HPC to 97.4% for an 1K 2-way associative HPC.

Figure 16(b) shows the comparative hit rates for the HC and HPC. Due to the extra receiver type and method location present in the HPC, the HPC should be compared with HC with twice the number of entries present in HPC. It can be observed that the 512 entry 2-way associative HPC has a hit rate of 96.3% for *javac* compared to the hit rate of 93.4% for an 1K entry 2-way associative HC. Thus, HPC was found to have higher hit rates than a HC with equivalent overhead.

Since dispatch speed is a better measure of performance, the average number of cycles required per dispatch was compared. Five cycles are required by the Java processor on a cache hit to perform the dynamic dispatch. It requires two cycles to obtain the current object's class, one cycle to obtain the call site entry from the cache, one cycle to perform the tag and receiver type comparisons, and another cycle to branch to the method location. The miss penalty involves the DTS search. DTS requires 10 cycles for checking each method within a class and requires 3 cycles for moving to the super class. Thus, the miss penalty would vary based on the number of methods and levels searched before DTS finds the appropriate method. The average number of cycles required for performing the dynamic dispatch using a direct mapped HC and HPC is shown in Figure 17(a). It can be observed that the HPC has a better dispatch speed than HC.

Figure 17(b) shows the average number of cycles required per dispatch for various configurations of the HPC. It can be observed that dispatch speed improves with associativity and cache size. The average number of cycles is a function of both hit rate and the penalty associated with DTS. It was observed that the 2-way associative 1K HPC for the *Javac* and *Espresso* have almost the same hit rates. However, *Javac* requires more number of cycles for effecting a dispatch (9.9 cycles) compared to *Espresso* (6.6 cycles). The deeper hierarchy and more number of methods associated with *Javac* increases the number of cycles required for DTS.

Figure 18(a) shows the effective hit rate using the two-level scheme with a first level 256 entry two-way associative hybrid cache. It can be observed that the increase in associativity for the second level cache does not always improve the performance. For *Javadoc*, the hit rate for a 64 entry direct mapped second level cache is 96.7% whereas it is 96.1% for a 64 entry 2-way associative cache. This is due to the small size of the second-level cache where the misses are mainly due to capacity misses. The capacity misses increase with increase in associativity and hence the observed behavior. Further, it can be observed that the variation in the second-level cache size has no impact on the hit rates of *JLex* due to the very high hit rates for all configurations.

Figure 18(b) compares the dispatch speed of the three schemes with equal overhead. It can be observed that the THC scheme performs the best. This is because a two-level cache can use the second level cache either to reduce cache interference at the first level or improve performance at polymorphic call sites.

7 Conclusions

Architectural support for object addressing, stack processing and method invocation in a Java processor was proposed and evaluated. A virtual address object cache that supports efficient manipulation and relocation of objects was presented. The proposed scheme reduces up to 1.95 cycles per object access compared to the serialized handle and object lookup scheme. Next, the extended folding optimization that combines the execution of a sequence of bytecodes was investigated. This eliminates redundant loads and stores operations that constitute up to 9% of the instructions. Also, three cache-based schemes: hybrid cache, hybrid polymorphic cache and two-level hybrid cache to implement virtual method invocations were presented. These schemes utilize the receiver type

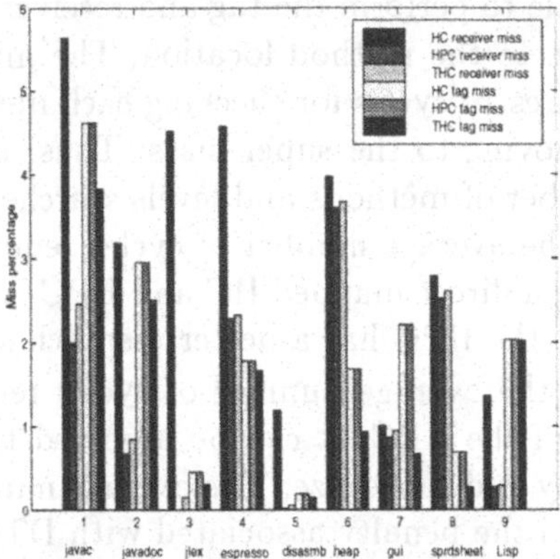

Fig. 15. Receiver and tag misses for HC, HPC and THC; HC and HPC use 256 entry two-way associative cache; THC has a 256 entry two-way associative first level cache and a 128 entry direct mapped second level cache

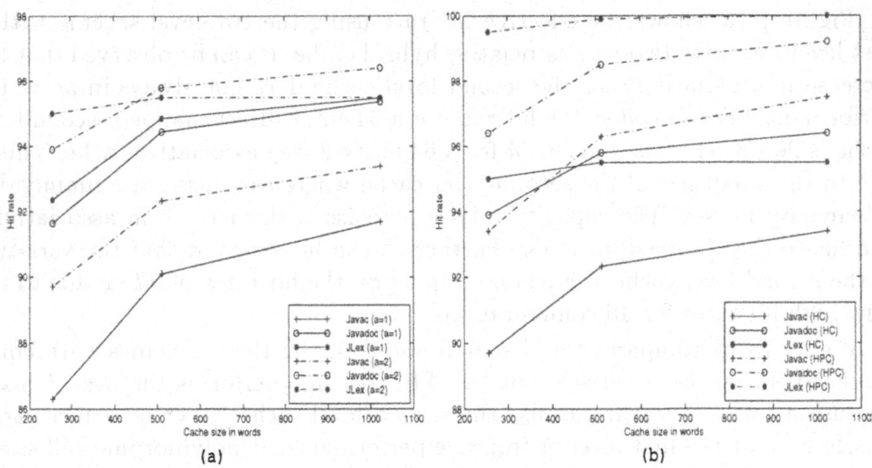

Fig. 16. (a) Variation in hit rate with cache size and associativity in a HC (b) Variation in hit rate for direct mapped HC and HPC

locality at call sites and eliminate the need for creating dispatch tables used in current JVM implementations.

References

1. T. Lindholm, F. Yellin, The Java Virtual Machine Specification, Addison Wesley, 1997.
2. B. Calder, D. Grunwald, and B. Zorn, " Quantifying Behavioral Differences Between C and C++ Programs", Journal of Programming Languages, Vol. 2., Num 4, 1994.

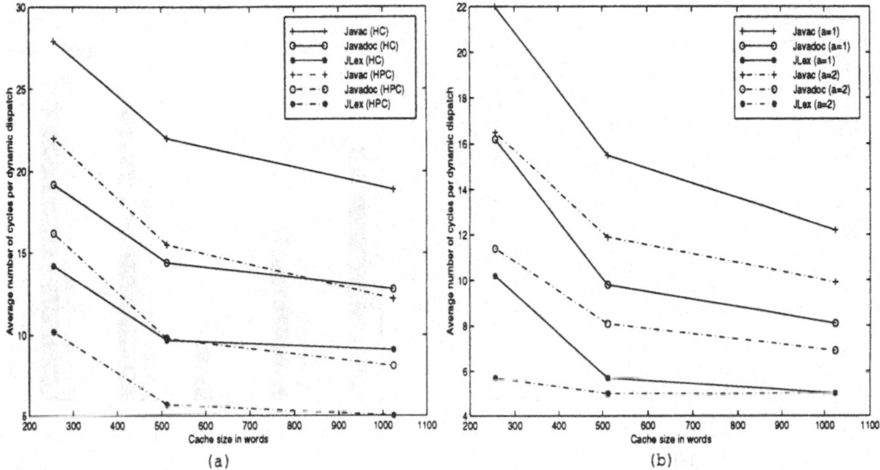

Fig. 17. (a) Average number of cycles per dynamic dispatch for direct mapped HC and HPC (b) Variation in average number of cycles per dynamic dispatch for HPC with associativity and cache size

3. J. Michael O'Connor, M. Tremblay, "picoJava-I: The Java Virtual Machine in Hardware", IEEE *Micro*, March/April 1997, pp. 45-53.
4. Patriot Scientific Corporation, the PSC1000 Processor, www.ptsc.com/PSC1000.
5. K. Ebcioglu, E. Altman, E. Hokenek, "A JAVA ILP Machine Based on Fast Dynamic Compilation", International Workshop on Security and Efficiency Aspects of Java, Eilat, Israel, January 9-10, 1997
6. K. Driesen, U. Hoelzle and J. Vitek, "Message Dispatch on Pipelined Processors", proc. ECOOP' 95, 1995.
7. WARTS: The Wisconsin Architectural Research Tools Set, University of Wisconsin, Madison.
8. J. R. Jackson, Java by example, SunSoft Press, 1997.
9. N. P. Jouppi and S. J. E. Wilton, "An Enhanced Access and Cycle Time Model for On-Chip Caches", DEC- WRL Technical Report, 93.5, July 1994.
10. I. W. Williams, Object-Based Memory Architecture, PhD thesis, Department of Computer Science, University of Manchester, May 1989.
11. Open Group Research Institute Java Test Suite, http://www.gr.osf.org/java/testsuite/html/.
12. J. A. Dean, Whole-Program Optimization of Object-Oriented Languages, Ph.D Thesis, University of Washington, 1996.
13. C. A. Hsieh, et. al., "Optimizing NET Compilers for Improved Java Performance", Computer, June 1997, pp. 67-75.
14. A. Krall and R. Grafl, "CACAO - A 64 bit JavaVM Just-in-Time Compiler", PPoPP '97 JAVA workshop.
15. Deutsch and Schiffman, " Efficient implementation of the Smalltalk-80 system", proc. 11th ACM Symposium on the Principles of Programming Languages, Jan 1984, pp. 297-302.

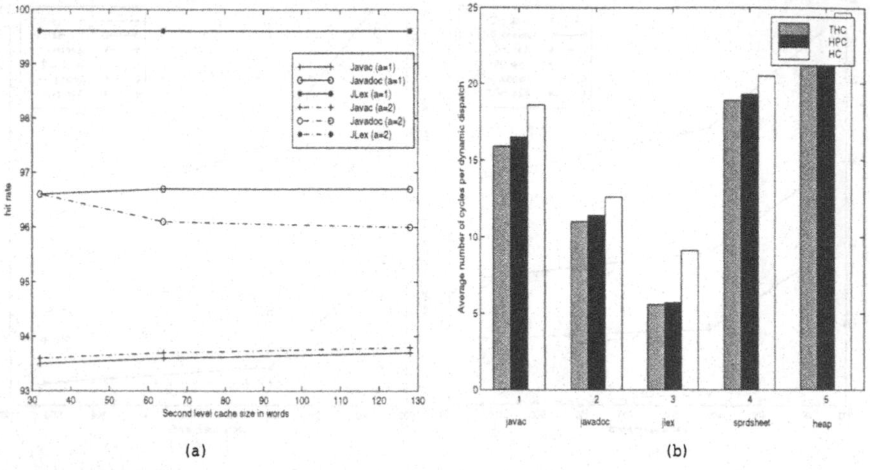

Fig. 18. (a) Variation in THC hit rates with change in second level cache size and associativity (b) Comparison of a 512 entry 2-way associative HC, 256 entry 2-way associative HPC and a 256 entry 2-way associative first level and 128 entry direct mapped second level THC

16. D. Ungar, The Design and Evaluation of a High-Performance Smalltalk System, MIT Press, Cambridge, MA, 1987.
17. A. Goldberg and D. Robson, Smalltalk-80: The Language and its Implementation, Second Edition, Addision-Wesley, reading, MA, 1985.
18. JavaSoft Home page, http:/www.javasoft.com/
19. J. Vitek, "Compact Dispatch Tables for Dynamically Typed Programming Languages", Object Applications,ed. D. Tzichritzis, Univ. of Geneva, Centre Universitaire d'Informatique, Aug. 1996.
20. JLex, http://www.cs.princeton.edu/ appel/modern/java/JLex/.
21. EspressoGrinder, wwwipd.ira.uka.de/ espresso
22. Turbo J Compiler, http://www.osf.org/www/java/turbo/.
23. Asymetrix SuperCede, www.asymetrix.com/products/supercede/.
24. Toba: A Java-to-C Translator, www.cs.arizona.edu/sumatra/toba/.
25. Guava JIT compiler, guava.softway.com.au/index.html.
26. Symantec Cafe, www.symantec.com/cafe/index_product.html.
27. J2C, www.webcity.co.jp/info/andoh/java/j2c.html.
28. Jolt: Converting bytecode to C, www.blackdown.org/kbs/jolt.html.
29. G. Muller, B. Moura, F. Bellard and C. Consel, "Harissa: a Flexible and Efficient Java Environment Mixing Bytecode and Compiled Code", proc. COOTS '97.
30. A. Arvindam, The design and behavioral model of an enhanced FORTH architecture, Masters Thesis, Univ. of S. Florida, 1995.
31. KAFFE, www.kaffe.org
32. U. Hoelzle, C. Chambers and D. Ungar, "Optimizing Dynamically-Typed Object-Oriented Languages with Polymorphic Inline Caches", proc. ECOOP'91, July 1991.
33. "The Unprecedented Opportunity for Java Systems", Whitepaper 96-043, Sun Microelectronics.

A Study of The Fragile Base Class Problem

Leonid Mikhajlov[1] and Emil Sekerinski[2]

[1] Turku Centre for Computer Science,
Lemminkäisenkatu 14A, Turku 20520, Finland;
lmikhajl@aton.abo.fi
[2] McMaster University,
1280 Main Street West, Hamilton, Ontario, Canada, L8S4K1;
emil@ece.eng.mcmaster.ca

Abstract. In this paper we study the fragile base class problem. This problem occurs in open object-oriented systems employing code inheritance as an implementation reuse mechanism. System developers unaware of extensions to the system developed by its users may produce a seemingly acceptable revision of a base class which may damage its extensions. The fragile base class problem becomes apparent during maintenance of open object-oriented systems, but requires consideration during design. We express the fragile base class problem in terms of a flexibility property. By means of five orthogonal examples, violating the flexibility property, we demonstrate different aspects of the problem. We formulate requirements for disciplining inheritance, and extend the refinement calculus to accommodate for classes, objects, class-based inheritance, and class refinement. We formulate and formally prove a flexibility theorem demonstrating that the restrictions we impose on inheritance are sufficient to permit safe substitution of a base class with its revision in presence of extension classes.

1 Introduction

The name *fragile base class problem* gives a good intuitive understanding of the problem. Classes in the foundation of an object-oriented system can be fragile. The slightest attempt to modify these foundation classes may damage the whole system.

The problem does not depend on the system implementation language. However, systems employing code inheritance as an implementation reuse mechanism along with self-recursion [28] are vulnerable to it. Such systems are delivered to users as a collection of classes. The users can reuse the functionality provided by the system by inheriting from system classes. Moreover, when the system is an object-oriented framework, the users can extend the system functionality by substituting its classes with derived ones. In general, system developers are unaware of extensions developed by the users. Attempting to improve functionality of the system, the developers may produce a seemingly acceptable revision of system classes which may damage the extensions. In a closed system all extensions are under control of system developers, who, in principle, can analyze the effect of certain base class revisions on the entire system. Although possible in principle, in practice this becomes infeasible [29, 23]. In an open system the fragile base class problem requires consideration during design [32].

We have encountered several different interpretations of the problem in the technical literature on this topic. Often, during a discussion of component standards, the name is used to describe the necessity to recompile extension and client classes when base classes are changed [15]. While being apparently important, that problem is only a technical issue. Even if recompilation is not necessary, system developers can make inconsistent modifications. Another interpretation is the necessity to guarantee that objects generated by an extension class can be safely substituted for objects of the corresponding base class [32]. Only in this case, the extension class can be safely substituted for the base class in all clients. However, objects of the extension class can be perfectly substitutable for objects of the base class even if the latter is fragile.

At first glance the problem might appear to be caused by inadequate system specification or user assumptions of undocumented features, but our study reveals that it is more involved. We consider an example which illustrates how concealed the problem can be.

We take a more formal look on the nature of the problem. We abstract the essence of the problem into a flexibility property and explain why unrestricted code inheritance violates this property. By means of five orthogonal examples violating the flexibility property, we demonstrate different aspects of the problem. Then we formulate requirements disciplining inheritance. We extend the refinement calculus [8, 19, 20] with notions of classes, objects, class-based inheritance, and refinement on classes. For the formalization of inheritance we adopt a model suggested by Cook and Palsberg in [10]. We formulate, prove, and explain a flexibility theorem showing that the restrictions we impose on inheritance are sufficient to permit substituting a base class with its revision in presence of extension classes. Finally, we discuss related work and draw some conclusions.

2 Fragile Base Class Problem

We assume a fairly standard model of object-oriented programming employing objects, classes, and single inheritance. A class is a template that defines a set of instance variables and methods. Instantiating a class creates a new object with instance variables initialized with initial values and method bodies defined by the class. A subclass inherits instance variables and method definitions from a superclass. All methods are dynamically bound. Every method has an implicit parameter *self*, which must be referred explicitly when a method of the class calls another method of the same class. Methods of a subclass can refer to methods of a superclass through another implicit parameter *super*. As the problem does not depend on the implementation language, we use a simple language-independent notation in our examples.

```
Bag = class                              CountingBag = class
    b : bag of char                          inherits Bag
                                             n : int
    init ≙ b := ⟦⟧                           init ≙ n := 0; super.init
    add(val x : char) ≙                      add(val x : char) ≙
        b := b ∪ ⟦x⟧                             n := n + 1; super.add(x)
    addAll(val bs : bag of char) ≙
        while bs ≠ ⟦ ⟧ do
            begin var y | y ∈ bs·
                self.add(y);
                bs := bs − ⟦y⟧
            end
        od
    cardinality(res r : int) ≙               cardinality(res r : int) ≙
        r := |b|                                 r := n
end                                      end

        Bag′ = class
            b : bag of char
            init ≙ b := ⟦ ⟧
            add(val x : char) ≙ b := b ∪ ⟦x⟧
            addAll(val bs : bag of char) ≙ b := b ∪ bs
            cardinality(res r : int) ≙ r := |b|
        end
```

Fig. 1. Example of the fragile base class problem

2.1 Example of the Fragile Base Class Problem

We begin with an example, presented in Fig. 1, which gives an intuitive understanding of the problem and shows how disguised the fragile base class problem can be.[1] Suppose that a class *Bag* is provided by some object-oriented system, for example, an extensible container framework. In an extensible framework user extensions can be called by both the user application and the framework. The class *Bag* has an instance variable b : *bag of char*, which is initialized with an empty bag. It also has methods *add* inserting a new element into b, *addAll* invoking the *add* method to add a group of elements to the bag simultaneously, and *cardinality* returning the number of elements in b.

Suppose now that a user of the framework decides to extend it. To do so, the user derives a class *CountingBag*, which introduces an instance variable n, and overrides *add* to increment n every time a new element is added to the bag. The user also overrides the *cardinality* method to return the value of n which should be equal to the number of elements in the bag. Note that the user is obliged to verify that *CountingBag* is substitutable for *Bag* to be safely used by the framework.

After some time a system developer decides to improve the efficiency of the class *Bag* and releases a new version of the system. An "improved" *Bag′* im-

[1] This example is adopted from [26]

plements *addAll* without invoking *add*. Naturally, the system developer claims that the new version of the system is fully compatible with the previous one. It definitely appears to be so if considered in separation of the extensions. However, when trying to use *Bag'* instead of *Bag* as the base class for *CountingBag*, the framework extender suddenly discovers that the resulting class returns the incorrect number of elements in the bag.

Here we face the fragile base class problem. Any open system applying code inheritance and self-recursion in an ad-hoc manner is vulnerable to this problem.

2.2 Failure of the Ad-Hoc Inheritance Architecture

Let us analyze the reasons for the failure in modifying a system relying on ad-hoc code inheritance. Assume that we have a base class C and an extension class E inheriting from it. We say that E is equivalent to $(M\ \mathbf{mod}\ C)$[2], where M corresponds to the extending part of the definition of E, and the operator **mod** combines M with the inherited part C. We refer to M as a *modifier* [31]. Therefore, we have that C belongs to the system, while $(M\ \mathbf{mod}\ C)$ represents a user extension of this system. The model of single inheritance employing the notion of modifiers was proved by Cook and Palsberg in [10] to correspond to the form of inheritance used in object-oriented systems.[3] For instance, in our previous example M has the form:

$$
\begin{aligned}
M \;=\; & \mathbf{modifier} \\
& \quad n : \mathit{int} := 0 \\
& \quad \mathit{add}(x : \mathit{char}) \mathrel{\widehat{=}} n := n + 1; \mathit{super.add}(x) \\
& \mathbf{end}
\end{aligned}
$$

We accept the view that a base class and a modifier initialize their own instance variables.

When system developers state that the new version of their system is fully compatible with the previous one, they essentially say that a revision class C' is a *refinement* of C. We say that a class C *is refined by* a class C', if the externally observable behavior of objects generated by C' is the externally observable behavior of objects generated by C or an improvement of it. In other words, objects generated by C' must be substitutable for objects generated by C in any possible context. Ensuring substitutability of the user extension $(M\ \mathbf{mod}\ C)$ for the framework class C amounts to verifying that C *is refined by* $(M\ \mathbf{mod}\ C)$.

Thus, all participating parties, i.e. the system developers and its extenders, rely on a *flexibility property* :

$$
\begin{aligned}
&\text{if } C \textit{ is refined by } C' \text{ and } C \textit{ is refined by } (M\ \mathbf{mod}\ C) \\
&\text{then } C \textit{ is refined by } (M\ \mathbf{mod}\ C')
\end{aligned}
$$

[2] We read **mod** as modifies.

[3] In their paper modifiers are referred to as wrappers. We prefer the term modifier, because the term wrapper is usually used in the context of object aggregation.

Unfortunately, the flexibility property does not hold in general, as demonstrated by our example. In our opinion, this fact constitutes the essence of the fragile base class problem. This consideration brings us to the question, what are the shortcomings of inheritance and what are the restrictions we need to make in order to evade the problem.

3 Aspects of the Problem

Now let us consider five examples invalidating the flexibility property and illuminating the shortcomings of inheritance. [4] Note that if we regard the definition of a base class as the specification of its functionality, we cannot blame modifier developers for relying on undocumented features and, therefore, inducing the problem. The examples are orthogonal to each other, meaning that all of them illustrate different aspects of the problem.

Let us first briefly introduce the used terminology. A call of a method through the implicit parameter self is referred to as a *self-call*. Analogously, we refer to an invocation of a method through the implicit parameter super as a *super-call*. When an extension class invokes a base class method, we say that an *up-call* has occurred; when a base class invokes a method of a class derived from it, we refer to such an invocation as a *down-call*.

3.1 Unanticipated Mutual Recursion

Suppose that C describes a class with a state x, initially equal to 0, and two methods m and n, both incrementing x by 1. A modifier M overrides n so that it calls m. Now, if a revision C' reimplements m by calling the method n, which has an implementation exactly as it was before, we run into a problem.

$$
\begin{array}{lll}
C \;=\; \textbf{class} & M \;=\; \textbf{modifier} & C' \;=\; \textbf{class} \\
\quad x : \mathit{int} := 0 & & \quad x : \mathit{int} := 0 \\
\quad m \mathrel{\widehat{=}} x := x + 1 & & \quad m \mathrel{\widehat{=}} \mathit{self}.n \\
\quad n \mathrel{\widehat{=}} x := x + 1 & \quad n \mathrel{\widehat{=}} \mathit{self}.m & \quad n \mathrel{\widehat{=}} x := x + 1 \\
\textbf{end} & \textbf{end} & \textbf{end}
\end{array}
$$

When the modifier M is applied to C', the methods m and n of the resulting class (M **mod** C') become mutually recursive. Apparently, a call to either one leads to a never terminating loop.

This example demonstrates that the problem might occur due to unexpected appearance of mutual recursion of methods in the resulting class.

[4] As we tried to keep these examples as concise as possible, they might appear slightly artificial.

3.2 Unjustified Assumptions in Revision Class

To illustrate the next shortcoming of inheritance, it is sufficient to provide only the specification of a base class. The base class C calculates the square and the fourth roots of a given real number. Its specification is given in terms of **pre** and **post** conditions which state that, given a non-negative real number x, the method will find such r that its power of two and four respectively equals x.

A modifier M overrides the method m so that it would return a negative value.[5] Such an implementation of m is a refinement of the original specification, because it reduces nondeterminism.

$$
\begin{array}{ll}
C = \textbf{class} & M = \textbf{modifier} \\
\quad m(\textbf{val}\ x : \mathit{real}, \textbf{res}\ r : \mathit{real}) \mathrel{\widehat=} & \quad m(\textbf{val}\ x : \mathit{real}, \textbf{res}\ r : \mathit{real}) \mathrel{\widehat=} \\
\qquad \textbf{pre}\ x \geq 0 & \qquad r := -\sqrt{x} \\
\qquad \textbf{post}\ r^2 = x & \\
\quad n(\textbf{val}\ x : \mathit{real}, \textbf{res}\ r : \mathit{real}) \mathrel{\widehat=} & \\
\qquad \textbf{pre}\ x \geq 0 & \\
\qquad \textbf{post}\ r^4 = x & \\
\textbf{end} & \textbf{end}
\end{array}
$$

A revision C' of the base class implements the specification of the square root by returning a positive square root of x. The implementation of the fourth root relies on this fact and merely calls m from itself twice, without checking that the result of the first application is positive. Note that C' is a refinement of C.

$$
\begin{array}{l}
C' = \textbf{class} \\
\quad m(\textbf{val}\ x : \mathit{real}, \textbf{res}\ r : \mathit{real}) \mathrel{\widehat=} \\
\qquad r := \sqrt{x} \\
\\
\quad n(\textbf{val}\ x : \mathit{real}, \textbf{res}\ r : \mathit{real}) \mathrel{\widehat=} \\
\qquad \mathit{self.m}(x, r); \mathit{self.m}(r, r) \\
\textbf{end}
\end{array}
$$

Suppose now that we have an instance of a class (M **mod** C'). The call to n will lead to a failure, because the second application of the square root will get a negative value as a parameter.

This example demonstrates that the problem might occur due to an assumption in the revision class that, while a self-call, the body of a method, as defined in the revision class itself, is guaranteed to be executed. However, due to inheritance and dynamic binding this assumption is not justified.

3.3 Unjustified Assumptions in Modifier

Participants of this example are rather meaningless; however, from the more formal point of view, they are composed from legal constructs, and therefore,

[5] By convention $\sqrt{x}$ returns a positive square root of x.

should satisfy our flexibility property. We use an assertion statement $\{p\}$, where p is a state predicate. If p is true in a current state, the assertion skips, otherwise it aborts. Thus, the assertion statement can be seen as an abbreviation for the corresponding conditional.

$$
\begin{array}{ll}
C = \textbf{class} & M = \textbf{modifier} \\
\quad l(\textbf{val}\ v : \mathit{int}) \mathrel{\widehat{=}} \{v \geq 5\} & \quad l(\textbf{val}\ v : \mathit{int}) \mathrel{\widehat{=}} \textbf{skip} \\
\quad m(\textbf{val}\ v : \mathit{int}) \mathrel{\widehat{=}} \mathit{self}.l(v) & \\
\quad n(\textbf{val}\ v : \mathit{int}) \mathrel{\widehat{=}} \textbf{skip} & \quad n(\textbf{val}\ v : \mathit{int}) \mathrel{\widehat{=}} \mathit{self}.m(v) \\
\textbf{end} & \textbf{end}
\end{array}
$$

$$
\begin{array}{l}
C' = \textbf{class} \\
\quad l(\textbf{val}\ v : \mathit{int}) \mathrel{\widehat{=}} \{v \geq 5\} \\
\quad m(\textbf{val}\ v : \mathit{int}) \mathrel{\widehat{=}} \{v \geq 5\} \\
\quad n(\textbf{val}\ v : \mathit{int}) \mathrel{\widehat{=}} \textbf{skip} \\
\textbf{end}
\end{array}
$$

Let us compute full definitions of the classes (M **mod** C) and (M **mod** C').

$$
\begin{array}{ll}
(M\ \textbf{mod}\ C) = \textbf{class} & (M\ \textbf{mod}\ C') = \textbf{class} \\
\quad l(\textbf{val}\ v : \mathit{int}) \mathrel{\widehat{=}} \textbf{skip} & \quad l(\textbf{val}\ v : \mathit{int}) \mathrel{\widehat{=}} \textbf{skip} \\
\quad m(\textbf{val}\ v : \mathit{int}) \mathrel{\widehat{=}} \mathit{self}.l(v) & \quad m(\textbf{val}\ v : \mathit{int}) \mathrel{\widehat{=}} \{v \geq 5\} \\
\quad n(\textbf{val}\ v : \mathit{int}) \mathrel{\widehat{=}} \mathit{self}.l(v) & \quad n(\textbf{val}\ v : \mathit{int}) \mathrel{\widehat{=}} \{v \geq 5\} \\
\textbf{end} & \textbf{end}
\end{array}
$$

It is easy to see that while C is refined by (M **mod** C), the class C is not refined by (M **mod** C'). Due to the presence of assertion $\{v \geq 5\}$ in the method n of (M **mod** C'), its precondition is stronger than the one of the method n of C, while to preserve refinement its precondition could have only been weakened.

Therefore, the problem might occur due to an assumption made in a modifier that in a particular layout base class self-calls are guaranteed to get redirected to the modifier itself. However such an assumption is unjustified, because the revision class can modify the self-calling structure.

3.4 Direct Access to the Base Class State

Developers of a revision C' may want to improve the efficiency of C by modifying its data representation. The following example demonstrates that, in general, C' cannot change the data representation of C in presence of inheritance.

A base class C represents its state by an instance variable x. It declares two methods m and n increasing x by 1 and 2 respectively. A modifier M provides a harmless (as it appears by looking at C) override of the method n, which does exactly what the corresponding method of C does, i.e. increases n by 2.

$$
\begin{array}{ll}
C = \textbf{class} & M = \textbf{modifier} \\
\quad x : \mathit{int} := 0 & \\
\quad m \mathrel{\widehat{=}} x := x + 1 & \\
\quad n \mathrel{\widehat{=}} x := x + 2 & \quad n \mathrel{\widehat{=}} x := x + 2 \\
\textbf{end} & \textbf{end}
\end{array}
$$

A revision C' introduces an extra instance variable y, initialized to 0. Methods m and n increase x and y by 1 and by 2, but indirectly via y. Therefore, the methods of C' implicitly maintain an invariant, $x = y$.

$$
\begin{array}{l}
C' \;=\; \textbf{class} \\
\qquad x : int := 0; y : int := 0 \\
\qquad m \mathrel{\widehat{=}} y := y + 1; x := y \\
\qquad n \mathrel{\widehat{=}} y := y + 2; x := y \\
\textbf{end}
\end{array}
$$

Now, if we consider an object *obj* to be an instance of class (M **mod** C'), obtained by substituting C' for C, and the sequence of method calls *obj.n;obj.m*, we face the problem. By looking at C, we could assume that the sequence of method calls makes x equal to 3, whereas, in fact, x is assigned only 1.

An analogous problem was described by Alan Snyder in [23]. He notices that "Because the instance variables are accessible to clients of the class, they are (implicitly) part of the contract between the designer of the class and the designers of descendant classes. Thus, the freedom of the designer to change the implementation of a class is reduced". In our example, since M is allowed to modify the instance variables inherited from C directly, it becomes impossible to change the data representation in C'.

3.5 Unjustified Assumption of Binding Invariant in Modifier

A class C has an instance variable x. A modifier M introduces a new instance variable y and binds its value to the value of x of the base class the modifier is supposed to be applied to. An override of the method n verifies this fact by first making a super-call to the method l and then asserting that the returned value is equal to y.

$$
\begin{array}{ll}
C \;=\; \textbf{class} & M \;=\; \textbf{modifier} \\
\qquad x : int := 0 & \qquad y : int := 0 \\
\qquad l(\textbf{res}\; r : int) \mathrel{\widehat{=}} r := x & \\
\qquad m \mathrel{\widehat{=}} x := x + 1; \mathit{self.n} & \qquad m \mathrel{\widehat{=}} y := y + 1; \mathit{super.m} \\
 & \qquad\qquad \textbf{begin var}\; r \cdot \\
\qquad n \mathrel{\widehat{=}} \textbf{skip} & \qquad n \mathrel{\widehat{=}} \qquad \mathit{super.l}(r); \{r = y\} \\
 & \qquad\qquad \textbf{end} \\
\textbf{end} & \textbf{end}
\end{array}
$$

It is easy to see that before and after execution of any method of (M **mod** C) the predicate $x = y$ holds. We can say that (M **mod** C) maintains the invariant $x = y$. The full definition of the method m in an instance of the class (M **mod** C) effectively has the form $y := y + 1; x := x + 1; \{x = y\}$, where the assertion statement skips, since the preceding statements establish the invariant.

Now, if a revision C' reimplements m by first self-calling n and then incrementing x as illustrated below, we run into a problem.

$$\begin{aligned} C' \;=\; & \textbf{class} \\ & \quad x : \mathit{int} := 0 \\ & \quad l(\textbf{res}\; r : \mathit{int}) \mathrel{\widehat{=}} r := x \\ & \quad m \mathrel{\widehat{=}} \mathit{self}.n; x := x + 1 \\ & \quad n \mathrel{\widehat{=}} \textbf{skip} \\ & \textbf{end} \end{aligned}$$

The body of the method m in an instance of the class (M **mod** C') is effectively of the form $y := y + 1; \{x = y\}; x := x + 1$, and, naturally, it aborts.

When creating a modifier, its developer usually intends it for a particular base class. A common practice is an introduction of new variables in the modifier and binding their values with the values of the intended base class instance variables. Such a binding can be achieved even without explicitly referring to the base class variables. Thus the resulting extension class maintains an invariant binding values of inherited instance variables with the new instance variables. Such an invariant can be violated when the base class is substituted with its revision. If methods of the modifier rely on such an invariant, a crash might occur.

3.6 Discussion

The presented examples demonstrate different aspects of the fragile base class problem. However, this list of aspects is by no means complete. We have chosen these aspects, because in our opinion they constitute the core of the problem. Also among these basic aspects of the problem there are some which were apparently overlooked by other researchers, as we discuss in our conclusions.

Further on in this paper we confine the fragile base class problem in a number of ways. First, we consider a class to be a closed entity. This means that method parameters and instance variables that are objects of some other classes are textually substituted with definitions of the corresponding classes. Therefore, without loss of generality we consider method parameters and instance variables to be of simple types. Second, we consider the case when a base class revision and extension have as many methods as the corresponding base class. Third, for the time being we consider only functional modifiers, i.e. modifiers that do not have instance variables of their own. Modeling modifiers with state adds considerable complexity and constitutes a topic of current separate research. We also assume that a base class does not have recursive and mutually recursive methods. As we have stated above, our language provides only for single inheritance.

The first four shortcomings of inheritance illustrated above lead to the formulation of the four requirements disciplining it:

1. **"No cycles" requirement:** ***A base class revision and a modifier should not jointly introduce new cyclic method dependencies.***

2. **"No revision self-calling assumptions" requirement:** *Revision class methods should not make any additional assumptions about the behavior of the other methods of itself. Only the behavior described in the base class may be taken into consideration.*
3. **"No base class down-calling assumptions" requirement:** *Modifier methods should disregard the fact that base class self-calls can get redirected to the modifier itself. In this case bodies of the corresponding methods in the base class should be considered instead, as if there were no dynamic binding.*
4. **"No direct access to the base class state" requirement:** *An extension class should not access the state of its base class directly, but only through calling base class methods.*

We claim that if disciplining inheritance according to these four requirements, we can formulate and prove a flexibility theorem which permits substituting a base class with its revision in presence of extension classes. In the next section we consider a formal basis necessary for formulating this theorem.

4 Formal Basis

4.1 Refinement Calculus Basics

This section is based on the work by Back and von Wright as presented in [3, 6–8]. The behavior of a program statement can be characterized by Dijkstra's weakest precondition predicate transformer [11]. For a statement S and a predicate p, the weakest precondition $wp(S, p)$ is such that the statement S terminates in a state satisfying the postcondition p. Since the relation between pre- and postconditions is all we are interested in for a statement, we can identify the statement with a function mapping postconditions to preconditions.

The predicates over a state space (type) Σ are the functions from Σ to *Bool*, denoted $\mathcal{P}\Sigma$. The relations from Σ to Γ are functions from Σ to a predicate (set of values) over Γ, denoted by $\Sigma \leftrightarrow \Gamma$. The predicate transformers from Σ to Γ are the functions mapping predicates over Γ to predicates over Σ, denoted $\Sigma \mapsto \Gamma$ (note the reversion of the direction):

$$\begin{aligned} \mathcal{P}\Sigma &\mathrel{\hat=} \Sigma \to Bool \\ \Sigma \leftrightarrow \Gamma &\mathrel{\hat=} \Sigma \to \mathcal{P}\Gamma \\ \Sigma \mapsto \Gamma &\mathrel{\hat=} \mathcal{P}\Gamma \to \mathcal{P}\Sigma \end{aligned}$$

The entailment ordering $p \subseteq q$ on predicates $p, q : \mathcal{P}\Sigma$ is defined by universal implication:

$$p \subseteq q \mathrel{\hat=} (\forall \sigma : \Sigma \cdot p\ \sigma \Rightarrow q\ \sigma)$$

The predicates *true* and *false* over Σ map every $\sigma : \Sigma$ to the boolean values T and F, respectively. Conjunction $p \wedge q$, disjunction $p \vee q$, and negation $\neg p$ are all defined by pointwise extension of the corresponding operations on *Bool*.

The cartesian product of state spaces Σ_1 and Σ_2 is written $\Sigma_1 \times \Sigma_2$. For relations $P_1 : \Sigma_1 \leftrightarrow \Gamma_1$ and $P_2 : \Sigma_2 \leftrightarrow \Gamma_2$, their *product* $P_1 \times P_2$, is a relation of type $(\Sigma_1 \times \Sigma_2) \leftrightarrow (\Gamma_1 \times \Gamma_2)$, where for $\sigma_1 : \Sigma_1$, $\sigma_2 : \Sigma_2$, $\gamma_1 : \Gamma_1$ and $\gamma_2 : \Gamma_2$, we have:

$$(P_1 \times P_2)\ (\sigma_1, \sigma_2)\ (\gamma_1, \gamma_2)\ \hat{=}\ (P_1\ \sigma_1\ \gamma_1)\ \wedge\ (P_2\ \sigma_2\ \gamma_2)$$

The relational product operator is right associative.

The *identity relation*, $Id : \Sigma \leftrightarrow \Sigma$, is defined for $\sigma_1, \sigma_2 : \Sigma$ as follows:

$$Id\ \sigma_1\ \sigma_2\ \hat{=}\ \sigma_1 = \sigma_2$$

A predicate transformer $S : \Sigma \mapsto \Gamma$ is said to be *monotonic* if for all predicates p and q, $p \subseteq q$ implies $S\ p \subseteq S\ q$. Statements from Σ to Γ are identified with monotonic predicate transformers from Σ to Γ. Statements of this kind may be concrete, i.e. executable, or abstract, i.e. specifications, and may have different initial and final state spaces.

The sequential composition of statements $S : \Sigma \mapsto \Gamma$ and $T : \Gamma \mapsto \Delta$ is modeled by their functional composition. Let q be a predicate over Δ, then

$$(S;T)\ q\ \hat{=}\ S\ (T\ q).$$

Meet of (similarly-typed) predicate transformers is defined pointwise:

$$(S \sqcap T)\ q\ \hat{=}\ (S\ q\ \wedge\ T\ q)$$

Meet of statements models *nondeterministic choice* between executing statements S and T. It is required that both alternatives establish the postcondition. For predicate transformers $S_1 : \Sigma_1 \mapsto \Gamma_1$ and $S_2 : \Sigma_2 \mapsto \Gamma_2$, their product $S_1 \times S_2$ is a predicate transformer of type $\Sigma_1 \times \Sigma_2 \mapsto \Gamma_1 \times \Gamma_2$ whose execution has the same effect as simultaneous execution of S_1 and S_2:

$$(S_1 \times S_2)\, q\ \hat{=}\ (\cup q_1, q_2 \mid q_1 \times q_2 \subseteq q \cdot S_1\, q_1 \times S_2\, q_2)$$

The **abort** statement does not guarantee any outcome or termination, therefore, it maps every postcondition to *false*. The **magic** statement is *miraculous*, since it is always guaranteed to establish any postcondition. The **skip** statement leaves the state unchanged. For any predicate $q : \mathcal{P}\Sigma$

$$\begin{aligned} \textbf{abort}\ q\ &\hat{=}\ \mathit{false} \\ \textbf{magic}\ q\ &\hat{=}\ \mathit{true} \\ \textbf{skip}\ q\ &\hat{=}\ q. \end{aligned}$$

For a predicate $p : \mathcal{P}\Gamma$, the assertion $\{p\}$ it behaves as **abort** if p does not hold, and as **skip** otherwise. The *guard* statement $[p]$ behaves as **skip** if p holds, otherwise it behaves as **magic**. Let q be a predicate over Γ, then:

$$\begin{aligned} \{p\}\ q\ &\hat{=}\ p \wedge q \\ [p]\ q\ &\hat{=}\ p \Rightarrow q \end{aligned}$$

Given a relation $P : \Sigma \leftrightarrow \Gamma$, the *angelic update* statement $\{P\} : \Sigma \mapsto \Gamma$ and the *demonic update* statement $[P] : \Sigma \mapsto \Gamma$ are defined by:

$$\begin{aligned} \{P\}\ q\ \sigma\ &\hat{=}\ (\exists \gamma : \Gamma \cdot (P\ \sigma\ \gamma)\ \wedge\ (q\ \gamma)) \\ [P]\ q\ \sigma\ &\hat{=}\ (\forall \gamma : \Gamma \cdot (P\ \sigma\ \gamma)\ \Rightarrow\ (q\ \gamma)) \end{aligned}$$

When started in a state σ, both $\{P\}$ and $[P]$ choose a new state γ such that $P\ \sigma\ \gamma$ holds. If no such state exists, then $\{P\}$ aborts, whereas $[P]$ can establish any postcondition.

A statement S is said to be conjunctive if

$$S\ (\wedge i \in I \cdot p_i) \ = \ (\wedge i \in I \cdot S\ p_i),$$

where $I \neq \emptyset$. An arbitrary conjunctive statement can be represented by a sequential composition $\{q\};[Q]$ for some predicate q and relation Q.

Assignment can be modeled as an update statement. If the state space Σ is partitioned by variables $x : T$ and $y : U$, i.e. $\Sigma = T \times U$, then

$$x := e \ \hat{=} \ [R], \text{ where } R\ (x,y)\ (x',y') = (x' = e \wedge y' = y).$$

A specification statement with a precondition over the initial state space and a postcondition relating initial and final state spaces is defined by a sequential composition of assertion and demonic update:

$$\textbf{pre}\ p\ \textbf{post}\ q \ \hat{=} \ \{p\};[R], \text{where } q\ (x,y) = \forall (x',y') \cdot R\ (x,y)\ (x',y')$$

For statements S and T of the same type and a predicate p, the conditional is defined by:

$$\textbf{if}\ p\ \textbf{then}\ S\ \textbf{else}\ T\ \textbf{fi} \ \hat{=} \ ([p];S) \sqcap ([\neg p];S)$$

The refinement ordering $S \sqsubseteq T$, read S *is refined by* T, on statements $S,T : \Sigma \mapsto \Gamma$ is defined as a universal entailment:

$$S \sqsubseteq T \ \hat{=} \ (\forall q : \mathcal{P}\Gamma \cdot S\ q \subseteq T\ q)$$

For example, a specification statement is refined if its precondition is weakened and the postcondition is strengthened:

$$\textbf{pre}\ p\ \textbf{post}\ q \sqsubseteq \textbf{pre}\ p'\ \textbf{post}\ q'$$
$$\text{if } p \subseteq p' \text{ and } q' \subseteq q$$

Other rules for refinement of specifications into programs and transforming programs are given in [3, 19, 12].

An iteration statement is defined by the least fixed point of a function F with respect to the refinement ordering:

$$\textbf{while}\ p\ \textbf{do}\ S\ \textbf{od} \ \hat{=} \ \mu\ F,$$
$$\text{where } F\ X = \textbf{if}\ p\ \textbf{then}\ S; X\ \textbf{else skip fi}$$

According to the theorem of Knaster-Tarski [30], a monotonic function has a unique least fixed point in a complete lattice. Statements form a complete lattice with the refinement ordering $\sqsubseteq$, and the statement **if** $p(x)$ **then** $S; X$ **else skip fi** is monotonic with respect to $\sqsubseteq$ in X, therefore, $\mu\ F$ exists and is unique. Intuitively, defining iteration in this way implies that a non-terminating loop behaves as **abort**.

A *block* construct allows temporary adding a new *local* state component to the present *global* state. An entry statement **enter** adds a new state component to the present state and initializes it in accordance with a given predicate p. An exit statement **exit** removes the added state component.

$$\begin{array}{l} \mathbf{enter}\, z \,|\, p \;\hat{=}\; [P], \\ \quad \text{where } P\ (x,y)\ (z',x',y') = (x' = x \wedge y' = y \wedge p\ (z',x',y')) \\ \mathbf{exit}\, z \;\hat{=}\; [Q], \\ \quad \text{where } Q\ (z,x,y)\ (x',y') = (x' = x \;\wedge\; y' = y) \end{array}$$

Accordingly, the block construct is defined as follows:

$$\mathbf{begin\ var}\, z \,|\, p \cdot S\, \mathbf{end} \;\;\hat{=}\;\; \mathbf{enter}\, z \,|\, p; S; \mathbf{exit}\, z$$

In general, different state spaces can be coerced using *wrapping* and *unwrapping* operators. Statements S and S' operating on state spaces Σ and Σ' respectively can be combined using a relation $R : \Sigma' \leftrightarrow \Sigma$ which, when lifted to predicate transformers, gives the update statements $\{R\} : \Sigma' \mapsto \Sigma$ and $[R^{-1}] : \Sigma \mapsto \Sigma'$. We use these statements to define *wrapping* and *unwrapping* operators as follows:

$$\begin{array}{ll} \textit{unwrapping}: & S{\downarrow}R \;\hat{=}\; \{R\}; S; [R^{-1}] \\ \textit{wrapping}: & S'{\uparrow}R \;\hat{=}\; [R^{-1}]; S'; \{R\} \end{array}$$

Thus, after wrapping we have that $S{\downarrow}R$ and $S'{\uparrow}R$ operate on the state spaces Σ' and Σ respectively. Sometimes it is necessary to wrap a statement operating on an extended state into a relation R. In this case we consider the relation R to be automatically extended into $Id \times R$ or $R \times Id$. For example, to wrap a statement $S : \Sigma \times \Gamma \mapsto \Sigma \times \Gamma$, the relation $R : \Sigma' \leftrightarrow \Sigma$ is extended to $R \times Id$.

The wrapping and unwrapping operators are left associative and have the lower precedence than the relational product. Further on, we make use of the following

$$\textit{wrapping rule}: \quad S{\uparrow}R{\downarrow}R \sqsubseteq S$$

For tuples of statements we have:

$$\begin{array}{lll} (S_1, ..., S_n){\uparrow}R & \hat{=} & (S_1{\uparrow}R, ..., S_n{\uparrow}R) \\ (S_1, ..., S_n){\downarrow}R & \hat{=} & (S_1{\downarrow}R, ..., S_n{\downarrow}R) \end{array}$$

4.2 Formalization of Classes and Modifiers

We model classes as self referential structures as proposed by Cook and Palsberg in [10]. This model applies to most mainstream object-oriented languages like C++, Java and Smalltalk. However, in our formalization classes have internal state, unlike in their model.

For simplicity, we model method parameters by global variables that both methods of a class and its clients can access. We precede a formal method parameter with a keyword **val** to indicate that the method only reads the value of this parameter without changing it. Similarly, we precede the formal parameter with **res** to indicate that the method returns a value in this parameter.

In practice a call of a method m_j by a method m_i of the same class has the form *self*.m_j. Due to inheritance and dynamic binding such a call can get redirected to a definition of m_j in an extension class. We model the method m_i as a function of an argument *self*.m_j. In general, a method of a class may invoke all the other methods of the same class. Thus if there are n methods in the class we have

$$m_i = \lambda(x_1, ..., x_n).c_i,$$

where c_i is a statement representing the body of the method m_i and x_j stands for *self*.m_j. Accordingly, we define a class C by

$$C \;=\; (c_0, cm), \text{where } cm = \lambda self \cdot (c_1, ..., c_n),$$

and where $c_0 : \Sigma$ is an initial value of the internal class state and *self* is an abbreviation for the tuple $x_1, ..., x_n$. We assume that cm is monotonic in the *self* parameter. For our purposes it suffices to model the state space of all parameters of all methods as an extra component Δ of the class state space. Thus cm has the type

$$((\Sigma \times \Delta \mapsto \Sigma \times \Delta) \times ... \times (\Sigma \times \Delta \mapsto \Sigma \times \Delta)) \to$$
$$((\Sigma \times \Delta \mapsto \Sigma \times \Delta) \times ... \times (\Sigma \times \Delta \mapsto \Sigma \times \Delta)).$$

We declare the class C, defined in this way, as follows:

$$C \;=\; \textbf{class}\ c := c_0,\ m_1 \;\widehat{=}\; c_1, ..., m_n \;\widehat{=}\; c_n\ \textbf{end}$$

A class can be depicted as in Fig. 2. The incoming arrow represents calls to the class C, the outgoing arrow stands for self-calls of C.

In our model classes are used as a templates for creating objects. Objects have all of the self-calls resolved with the methods of the same object. Modeling this formally amounts to taking the least fixed point of the function cm. For tuples of statements $(c_1, .., c_n)$ and $(c_1', ..., c_n')$, where c_i and c'_i are of the same type, the refinement ordering is defined elementwise:

$$(c_1, ..., c_n) \sqsubseteq (c'_1, ..., c'_n) \;\widehat{=}\; c_1 \sqsubseteq c'_1 \wedge \;...\; \wedge c_n \sqsubseteq c'_n$$

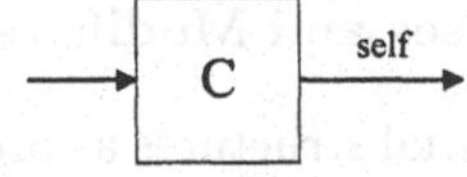

Fig. 2. Illustration of a class

Statement tuples form a complete lattice with the above refinement ordering. Also *cm* is monotonic in its argument. These two conditions are sufficient to guarantee that the least fixed point of the function *cm* exists and is unique. We define the operation of taking the least fixed point of a class by taking initial values of its instance variables and taking the least fixed point of its methods *cm*:

$$\mu\, C \;\widehat{=}\; (c_0, \mu\, cm)$$

Fig. 3 illustrates taking the fixed point of the class C.

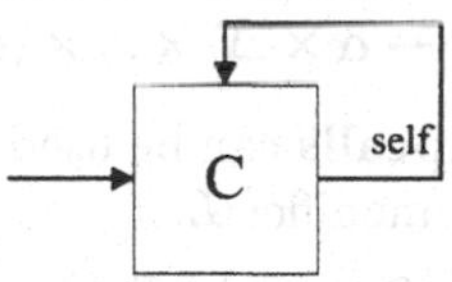

Fig. 3. Illustration of taking a fixed point of C

If we model objects as tuples of instance variable values and method bodies, then taking the least fixed point of the class C corresponds to creating an object of this class:

$$create\; C \;\widehat{=}\; \mu\, C$$

It suffices to consider only those modifiers which redefine all methods of the base class. In case some method should remain unchanged, the corresponding method of the modifier calls the former via *super*.

A modifier $L =$ **modifier** $m_1 \;\widehat{=}\; l_1, ..., m_n \;\widehat{=}\; l_n$ **end** is modeled by a function

$$L = \lambda self \cdot \lambda super \cdot (l_1, ..., l_n),$$

where *self* and *super* are abbreviations of the tuples $x_1, ..., x_n$ and $y_1, ..., y_n$ respectively. We assume that L is monotonic in both arguments. See Fig. 4 for an illustration of modifiers. As with the class diagram, the incoming arrow represents calls to methods of the modifier, whereas the outgoing arrows stand for self and super-calls of the modifier.

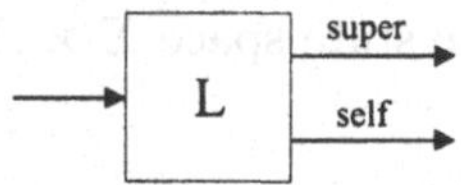

Fig. 4. Illustration of modifiers

Under the condition that the signatures of modifier methods match those of the base class, the modifier can be applied to an arbitrary base class. The modifier does not access the state of the base class directly, but only by making super-calls. As the state space of the base class is unknown until modifier application, we say that the methods of the modifier L operate on the state space $\alpha \times \Delta$, where α is a type variable to be instantiated with the type of the internal state of the base class while modifier application, and Δ is a type of the state component representing all parameters of all methods of the modifier. Hence, the type of L is as follows:

$$\begin{array}{l} ((\alpha \times \Delta \mapsto \alpha \times \Delta) \times \ldots \times (\alpha \times \Delta \mapsto \alpha \times \Delta)) \to \\ \quad ((\alpha \times \Delta \mapsto \alpha \times \Delta) \times \ldots \times (\alpha \times \Delta \mapsto \alpha \times \Delta)) \to \\ \quad\quad ((\alpha \times \Delta \mapsto \alpha \times \Delta) \times \ldots \times (\alpha \times \Delta \mapsto \alpha \times \Delta)) \end{array}$$

Two operators **mod** and **upcalls** can be used for creating an extension class from the base class C and the modifier L:

$$\begin{array}{ll} L \ \mathbf{mod}\ C & \widehat{=} \ (c_0,\ \lambda \mathit{self} \cdot \ \mathit{lm}\ \mathit{self}\ (\mathit{cm}\ \mathit{self})) \\ L \ \mathbf{upcalls}\ C & \widehat{=} \ (c_0,\ \lambda \mathit{self} \cdot \ \mathit{lm}\ \mathit{self}\ (\mu\ \mathit{cm})) \end{array}$$

In both cases the modifier L is said to be applied to the base class C. See Fig. 5 for an illustration of modifier application. Note that in case of the **mod** operator self-calls of C become down-calls; whereas, with the **upcalls** operator self-calls of C remain within C itself.

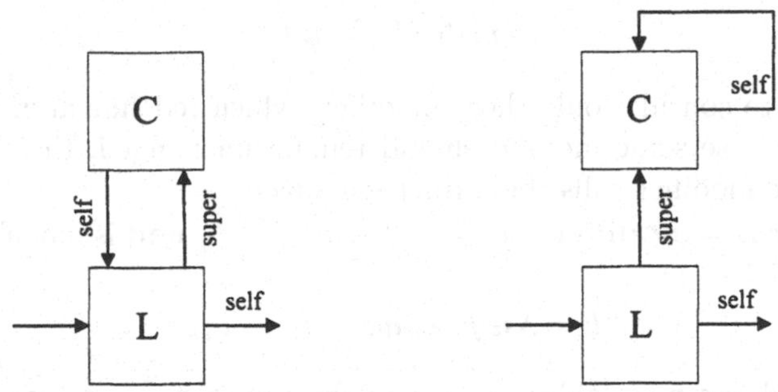

Fig. 5. Illustration of operators **mod** and **upcalls**

Application of the modifier L instantiates its type variable α with the type Σ of the base class C. Hence, the classes created by the application of L to C have methods operating on the state space $\Sigma \times \Delta$.

4.3 Refinement on Classes

Before defining refinement of classes, we first consider data refinement of statements. Let $S : \Sigma \mapsto \Sigma$ and $S' : \Sigma' \mapsto \Sigma'$ be statements and $R : \Sigma' \leftrightarrow \Sigma$ a relation between the state spaces of these statements. We define data refinement between S and S' as in [8]:

$$S \sqsubseteq_R S' \ \widehat{=}\ S \sqsubseteq S' \uparrow R \text{ or, equivalently,}$$
$$S \sqsubseteq_R S' \ \widehat{=}\ S \downarrow R \sqsubseteq S'$$

We can express class refinement in terms of refinement on abstract data types [14, 4, 12]. An abstract data type T can be represented in the form

$$T = (t_0, tp),$$

where t_0 is an initial value of an internal state of type Σ, and tp is a tuple of procedures modifying this internal state. The procedures are of type $(\Sigma \times \Delta) \mapsto (\Sigma \times \Delta)$, where Δ is the state space component representing all parameters of all procedures. We say that the abstract data type $T = (t_0, tp)$ is data refined by an abstract data type $T' = (t'_0, tp')$ via a relation $R : \Sigma' \leftrightarrow \Sigma$ if initialization establishes R and all procedures preserve R:

$$T \sqsubseteq_R T' \ \widehat{=}\ R\ t'_0\ t_0 \ \wedge\ tp \sqsubseteq_{R \times Id} tp'$$

By convention, when R is equal to Id, the subscript on the refinement relation is omitted.

Now class refinement can be defined as follows. Let C be as defined in the previous section and $C' = (c'_0, cm')$, where $cm'\ self = (c'_1, ..., c'_n)$, and $R : \Sigma' \leftrightarrow \Sigma$, then

$$C \sqsubseteq_R C' \ \widehat{=}\ \mu\, C \sqsubseteq_R \mu\, C'.$$

Class refinement ensures that all objects of the refining class are safely substitutable for objects of the refined class. This notion of class refinement allows the instance variables of C' extend those of C or to be completely different. The refinement relation can be also applied to a pair of abstract or concrete classes.

5 Flexibility Theorem

Recall that the flexibility property has the form

if C *is refined by* (L **mod** C) and C *is refined by* D
then C *is refined by* (L **mod** D),

where C is a base class, L a modifier and D a revision of the class C. As was illustrated in the previous sections, this property does not hold in general. In the following sections we formulate, prove, and explain a flexibility theorem, which provides for safe substitutability of C with (L **mod** D) by strengthening the premises of the flexibility property, following the requirements formulated in Sec. 3.6.

5.1 Formulating and Proving Flexibility Theorem

Consider classes C, D and a modifier L, such that $C = (c_0, cm)$ with $cm = \lambda self \cdot (c_1, ..., c_n)$, $D = (d_0, dm)$ with $dm = \lambda self \cdot (d_1, ..., d_n)$, and $L = \lambda self \cdot \lambda super \cdot (l_1, ..., l_n)$. As we have assumed that the classes and the modifier do not have recursive and mutually recursive methods, it is always possible to rearrange their methods in linear order so that each method calls only previous ones. We assign an index to every method with respect to this order. We assume that the corresponding methods in C, D and L receive the same index. Without loss of generality, we can consider the case when for every distinct index there is only one method. We represent methods by functions of the called methods:

$$\begin{array}{ll} C_1 = \lambda() \cdot c_1, & ...\, C_n = \lambda(x_1, ..., x_{n-1}) \cdot c_n \\ D_1 = \lambda() \cdot d_1, & ...\, D_n = \lambda(x_1, ..., x_{n-1}) \cdot d_n \\ L_1 = \lambda() \cdot \lambda(y_1) \cdot l_1, & ...\, L_n = \lambda(x_1, ..., x_{n-1}) \cdot \lambda(y_1, ..., y_n) \cdot l_n \end{array}$$

There are no free occurrences of *self* and *super* in C_i, D_i and L_i. Thus, for example, for the class C we have that:

$$cm = \lambda self \cdot (C_1\ (), C_2\ (x_1), ..., C_n\ (x_1, ..., x_{n-1}))$$

Let $R : \Sigma' \leftrightarrow \Sigma$ be a relation coercing the state space component Σ' of the revision D to the component Σ of the base class C. Now we can formulate the *flexibility theorem*:

Flexibility Theorem *Let C, D be the classes, L the modifier, and R the state coercing relation as defined above. Then the following holds:*

$$\begin{array}{l} \mu\, C \sqsubseteq_R (d_0,\ dm\ ((\mu\ cm) \downarrow (R \times Id))) \ \wedge\ \mu\, C \sqsubseteq \mu\ (L\ \textbf{upcalls}\ C) \ \Rightarrow \\ \qquad \mu\, C \sqsubseteq_R (L\ \textbf{mod}\ D) \end{array}$$

Proof In accordance with the definition of abstract data type refinement, we first need to show that $R\ d_0\ c_0 \ \Rightarrow\ R\ d_0\ c_0$, which is trivially true.

Next we need to show the following goal:

$$\begin{array}{l} snd(\mu\ C) \sqsubseteq_{R \times Id} dm\ ((\mu\ cm) \downarrow (R \times Id)) \ \wedge\ snd(\mu\ C) \sqsubseteq snd(\mu\ (L\ \textbf{upcalls}\ C)) \ \Rightarrow \\ \qquad snd(\mu\ C) \sqsubseteq_{R \times Id} snd(\mu\ (L\ \textbf{mod}\ D)) \end{array}$$

Note that in this goal data refinement relations connect tuples of predicate transformers, which correspond to the method bodies with all self and super-calls resolved with the methods of the same class. Thus, we can rewrite this goal as

$$\begin{array}{l} (\mathcal{C}_1, \ldots, \mathcal{C}_n) \sqsubseteq_{R \times Id} (\mathcal{D}_1, \ldots, \mathcal{D}_n) \ \wedge\ (\mathcal{C}_1, \ldots, \mathcal{C}_n) \sqsubseteq (\mathcal{L}_1, \ldots, \mathcal{L}_n) \ \Rightarrow \\ \qquad (\mathcal{C}_1, \ldots, \mathcal{C}_n) \sqsubseteq_{R \times Id} (\mathcal{M}_1, \ldots, \mathcal{M}_n), \end{array}$$

where $\mathcal{C}$, $\mathcal{D}$, $\mathcal{L}$, and $\mathcal{M}$ are defined as follows:

$$\begin{array}{ll} \mathcal{C}_1 = C_1\ (), & ...\ \mathcal{C}_n = C_n\ (\mathcal{C}_1, ..., \mathcal{C}_{n-1}) \\ \mathcal{D}_1 = D_1\ () \downarrow (R \times Id), & ...\ \mathcal{D}_n = D_n\ (\mathcal{C}_1, ..., \mathcal{C}_{n-1}) \downarrow (R \times Id) \\ \mathcal{L}_1 = L_1\ ()\ \mathcal{C}_1, & ...\ \mathcal{L}_n = L_n\ (\mathcal{L}_1, ..., \mathcal{L}_{n-1})\ (\mathcal{C}_1, ..., \mathcal{C}_n) \\ \mathcal{M}_1 = L_1\ ()\ \mathcal{T}_1, & ...\ \mathcal{M}_n = L_n\ (\mathcal{M}_1, ..., \mathcal{M}_{n-1})\ (\mathcal{T}_1, ..., \mathcal{T}_n) \\ \mathcal{T}_1 = D_1\ (), & ...\ \mathcal{T}_n = D_n\ (\mathcal{M}_1, ..., \mathcal{M}_{n-1}) \end{array}$$

Here $\mathcal{C}$ are the method bodies of the methods $C_1, ..., C_n$ with all self-calls recursively resolved with $\mathcal{C}$. The statements $\mathcal{D}$ represent *dm* $((\mu\ cm){\downarrow}(R \times Id))$, where each $\mathcal{D}_i$ is a method body of the method D_i with all self-calls resolved with properly coerced $\mathcal{C}$. The statements $\mathcal{L}$ represent the least fixed point of (L **upcalls** C) methods. Note how $\mathcal{M}$ and $\mathcal{T}$ jointly represent the least fixed point of (L **mod** D) methods. The statements $\mathcal{M}$ stands for the methods of the modifier L with calls to *self* resolved with $\mathcal{M}$ themselves and calls to *super* resolved with $\mathcal{T}$. On the other hand, the statements $\mathcal{T}$ represent methods of the revision D with calls to *self* resolved with $\mathcal{M}$.

Rather than proving the goal above, we prove the stronger goal

$$(\mathcal{C}_1, \ldots, \mathcal{C}_n) \sqsubseteq_{R \times Id} (\mathcal{D}_1, \ldots, \mathcal{D}_n) \ \wedge\ (\mathcal{C}_1, \ldots, \mathcal{C}_n) \sqsubseteq (\mathcal{L}_1, \ldots, \mathcal{L}_n) \ \Rightarrow \\ (\mathcal{L}_1, \ldots, \mathcal{L}_n) \sqsubseteq_{R \times Id} (\mathcal{M}_1, \ldots, \mathcal{M}_n) \ \wedge\ (\mathcal{D}_1, \ldots, \mathcal{D}_n) \sqsubseteq (\mathcal{T}_1, \ldots, \mathcal{T}_n)$$

from which the target goal follows by transitivity. For proving this stronger goal we need the *wrapping theorem*

$$L_i\ (\mathcal{M}_1, \ldots, \mathcal{M}_{i-1}){\uparrow}(R \times Id)\ (\mathcal{D}_1, \ldots, \mathcal{D}_i){\uparrow}(R \times Id) \sqsubseteq \\ (L_i\ (\mathcal{M}_1, \ldots, \mathcal{M}_{i-1})\ (\mathcal{D}_1, \ldots, \mathcal{D}_i)){\uparrow}(R \times Id)$$

proved in Appendix.

We prove the goal by induction on the index of methods. Here we only present the inductive step of the proof, because the base step can be proved similarly. The inductive assumption for the inductive case states that when the participating entities have n methods, the goal holds. After transformations, our proof obligation for the case of $n+1$ methods is:

$$(\mathcal{C}_1, \ldots, \mathcal{C}_{n+1}) \sqsubseteq_{R \times Id} (\mathcal{D}_1, \ldots, \mathcal{D}_{n+1}) \ \wedge\ (\mathcal{C}_1, \ldots, \mathcal{C}_{n+1}) \sqsubseteq (\mathcal{L}_1, \ldots, \mathcal{L}_{n+1}) \ \wedge \\ (\mathcal{L}_1, \ldots, \mathcal{L}_n) \sqsubseteq_{R \times Id} (\mathcal{M}_1, \ldots, \mathcal{M}_n) \ \wedge\ (\mathcal{D}_1, \ldots, \mathcal{D}_n) \sqsubseteq (\mathcal{T}_1, \ldots, \mathcal{T}_n) \ \Rightarrow \\ \mathcal{L}_{n+1} \sqsubseteq_{R \times Id} \mathcal{M}_{n+1} \ \wedge\ \mathcal{D}_{n+1} \sqsubseteq \mathcal{T}_{n+1}$$

We prove this goal as follows:

$$\mathcal{L}_{n+1} \sqsubseteq_{R \times Id} \mathcal{M}_{n+1} \ \wedge\ \mathcal{D}_{n+1} \sqsubseteq \mathcal{T}_{n+1}$$

$= \{$ *definitions, definition of data refinement* $\}$

$$L_{n+1}\ (\mathcal{L}_1, \ldots, \mathcal{L}_n)\ (\mathcal{C}_1, \ldots, \mathcal{C}_{n+1}) \sqsubseteq \\ (L_{n+1}\ (\mathcal{M}_1, \ldots, \mathcal{M}_n)\ (\mathcal{T}_1, \ldots, \mathcal{T}_{n+1})){\uparrow}(R \times Id) \ \wedge\ \mathcal{D}_{n+1} \sqsubseteq \mathcal{T}_{n+1}$$

$\Leftarrow \left\{\begin{array}{l} \textit{monotonicity of } L_{n+1}, \textit{assumption } (\mathcal{L}_1, \ldots, \mathcal{L}_n) \sqsubseteq (\mathcal{M}_1, \ldots, \mathcal{M}_n){\uparrow}(R \times Id), \\ \textit{assumption } (\mathcal{C}_1, \ldots, \mathcal{C}_{n+1}) \sqsubseteq (\mathcal{D}_1, \ldots, \mathcal{D}_{n+1}){\uparrow}(R \times Id), \textit{wrapping theorem} \end{array}\right\}$

$$L_{n+1}\ (\mathcal{M}_1, \ldots, \mathcal{M}_n){\uparrow}(R \times Id)\ (\mathcal{D}_1, \ldots, \mathcal{D}_{n+1}){\uparrow}(R \times Id) \sqsubseteq \\ L_{n+1}\ (\mathcal{M}_1, \ldots, \mathcal{M}_n){\uparrow}(R \times Id)\ (\mathcal{T}_1, \ldots, \mathcal{T}_{n+1}){\uparrow}(R \times Id) \ \wedge\ \mathcal{D}_{n+1} \sqsubseteq \mathcal{T}_{n+1}$$

$\Leftarrow \{$ *monotonicity of* L_{n+1} $\}$

$$(\mathcal{D}_1, \ldots, \mathcal{D}_{n+1}){\uparrow}(R \times Id) \sqsubseteq (\mathcal{T}_1, \ldots, \mathcal{T}_{n+1}){\uparrow}(R \times Id) \ \wedge\ \mathcal{D}_{n+1} \sqsubseteq \mathcal{T}_{n+1}$$

$\Leftarrow \{$ *monotonicity of wrappers, assumption* $(\mathcal{D}_1, \ldots, \mathcal{D}_n) \sqsubseteq (\mathcal{T}_1, \ldots, \mathcal{T}_n)\}$

$\mathcal{D}_{n+1} \sqsubseteq \mathcal{T}_{n+1}$

$= \{$ *definitions* $\}$

$D_{n+1}\ (\mathcal{C}_1, \ldots, \mathcal{C}_n){\downarrow}(R \times Id) \sqsubseteq D_{n+1}\ (\mathcal{M}_1, \ldots, \mathcal{M}_n)$

$\Leftarrow \left\{ \begin{array}{l} \textit{monotonicity of } D_{n+1}, \textit{assumption } (\mathcal{C}_1, \ldots, \mathcal{C}_{n+1}) \sqsubseteq (\mathcal{L}_1, \ldots, \mathcal{L}_{n+1}) \textit{ then} \\ \textit{assumption } (\mathcal{L}_1, \ldots, \mathcal{L}_n) \sqsubseteq (\mathcal{M}_1, \ldots, \mathcal{M}_n){\uparrow}(R \times Id) \end{array} \right\}$

$D_{n+1}\ (\mathcal{M}_1, \ldots, \mathcal{M}_{n+1}){\uparrow}(R \times Id){\downarrow}(R \times Id) \sqsubseteq D_{n+1}\ (\mathcal{M}_1, \ldots, \mathcal{M}_n)$

$\Leftarrow \{$ *wrapping rule* $\}$

$D_{n+1}\ (\mathcal{M}_1, \ldots, \mathcal{M}_n) \sqsubseteq D_{n+1}\ (\mathcal{M}_1, \ldots, \mathcal{M}_n)$

$= T$

□

5.2 Interpretation and Implications of Flexibility Theorem

Let us consider how the requirements of Sec. 3.6 are reflected in the flexibility theorem and what are the consequences of this theorem.

In our formalization the "no cycles" requirement is handled by the fact that we have rearranged methods in the participating classes and the modifier in linear order, and assigned the same index to the corresponding methods. Thus mutual recursion of methods cannot appear. In practice the unanticipated mutual recursion can be avoided if methods of a revision class and a modifier do not introduce self-calls to the methods which are not self-called in the corresponding methods of the base class.

The "no revision self-calling assumptions" requirement states that, while reasoning about the behavior of a revision class method, we should not assume the behavior of the methods it self-calls, but should consider instead the behavior described by the base class. This requirement together with the first assumption of the flexibility property is formalized as the first conjunct in the antecedent of the flexibility theorem, $\mu\ C \sqsubseteq_R (d_0,\ dm\ ((\mu\ cm){\downarrow}(R \times Id)))$. As we have explained above, the application of dm to the properly coerced $(\mu\ cm)$ returns a tuple of methods of D with all self-calls redirected to methods of C.

The "no base class down-calling assumptions" requirement states that, while reasoning about the behavior of modifier methods, we should not assume the behavior of those modifier methods to which self-calls of the base class can get redirected. Instead we should consider the corresponding methods of the base class. This requirement along with the second assumption of the flexibility property is handled by the second conjunct in the antecedent of the flexibility theorem, $\mu\ C \sqsubseteq \mu\ (L\ \textbf{upcalls}\ C)$. As we have explained earlier, if a modifier is applied to the base class using the **upcalls** operator, self-calls of the base class remain within the base class itself.

The "no direct access to the base class state" requirement is addressed by our formalization of modifiers. As we have stated above, methods of a modifier always skip on the α component of the state space, thus excluding the possibility of direct access to the base class state.

The refinement calculus allows for reasoning about correctness of refinement between statements or programming constructs in general. In this respect it does not differentiate between abstract specification statements and executable ones. Therefore, our results are applicable to any group consisting of a base class, its extension, and a modification of the base class. In particular, two scenarios are of interest:

- A base class C is a specification class, i.e. its methods contain specification statements, and C' is its implementation;
- A base class C is an executable class and C' is its revision.

The fragile base class problem was first noticed while framework maintenance, and corresponds to the second scenario. However, this problem applies to the first scenario as well.

6 Related Work and Conclusions

The fragile base class problem is of particular importance for object-oriented software development. As soon as one defines a base class, an extension, and wants to change the base class, one faces this problem. Even in case of a large closed system this problem becomes non-trivial and painful to deal with. In case of an open system it becomes crucial.

The name fragile base class problem was introduced while discussing component standards [32, 15], since it has critical significance for component systems. Modification of components by their developers should not affect component extensions of their users in any respect. Firstly, recompilation of derived classes should be avoided if possible [15]. This issue constitutes a syntactic aspect of the problem. While being apparently important, that problem is only a technical issue. Even if recompilation is not necessary, component developers can make inconsistent modifications. This aspect of the problem was recognized by COM developers [32] and led them to the decision to abandon inheritance in favor of forwarding as the reuse mechanism. Although solving the problem, this approach comes at the cost of reduced flexibility. On the other hand, inheritance proved to be a convenient mechanism for code reuse. This consideration brought us to the following question: "How can we discipline code inheritance to avoid the fragile base class problem, but still retain a significant degree of flexibility in code reuse?"

We have encountered several research directions which are related to ours. The first direction combines research on semantics of object oriented languages with ensuring substitutability of objects. Hense in [13] gives a denotational semantics of an object-oriented programming language. His model provides for classes with state, self-referencing, and multiple inheritance. The latter is described using wrappers of Cook and Palsberg [10]. However, a number of notions crucial for our purposes, such as, e.g. refinement ordering on classes, are not defined. Various approaches to substitutability of objects are presented in [1, 17, 18]. However, they do not model self-calls in classes in presence of inheritance and dynamic binding.

The second direction of related research is oriented towards developing a methodology for specifying classes to make code reuse less error prone. The key idea of extending a class specification with specification of its *specialization interface* was presented first by Kiczales and Lamping in [16]. This idea was further developed by Steyaert et al. in [26]. In fact the second paper considers the fragile base class problem in our formulation (although they do not refer to it by this name). The authors introduce *reuse contracts* "that record the protocol between managers and users of a reusable asset". Acknowledging that "reuse contracts provide only syntactic information", they claim that "this is enough to firmly increase the likelihood of behaviorally correct exchange of parent classes". Such syntactic reuse contracts are, in general, insufficient to guard against the fragile base class problem.

Our first example is, in fact, adopted from [26]. They blame the revision *Bag′* of the base class for modifying the structure of self-calls of *Bag* and, therefore, causing the problem. They state that, in general, such method inconsistency can arise only when a revision chooses to eliminate a self-call to the method which is overridden in a modifier. From this one could conclude that preserving the structure of self-calls in a revision would safeguard against inconsistencies. Our examples demonstrate that this is not the case.

Our analysis reveals different causes of the *Bag/CountingBag* problem. The extension class *CountingBag* relies on the invariant $n = |b|$ binding values of the instance variable n with the number of elements in the inherited instance variable b. This invariant is violated when *Bag* is substituted with *Bag′* and, therefore, the *cardinality* method of the resulting class returns the incorrect value. Apparently, this problem is just an instance of the "unjustified assumption of the binding invariant in modifier" problem presented in Sec. 3.5.

As a potential solution to this problem one can specify methods *add* and *addAll* as *consistent methods* as was first suggested in [16]. This means that the extension developers would be disallowed to override one without overriding the other. However, recommendations of Kiczales and Lamping are based only on empirical expertise, thus it is not clear whether they apply in the general case. We believe that such methodology should be grounded on a mathematical basis, and developing such methodology constitutes the ultimate goal of our research.

Stata and Guttag in [24, 25] elaborate the idea of specialization interfaces by providing a mathematical foundation in behavioral subtyping style [1, 17]. They introduce *class components*, which combine a substate of a class and a set of methods responsible for maintaining that state, as units of modularity for the specialization interface. Such class components are overridable, i.e. an extension class may provide its own implementation of an entire class component. Even though they do not consider substitution of a base class with a revision in presence of extensions, many of their findings are related to ours. However, they specify methods in terms of pre and post conditions which in our opinion is not expressive enough to capture the intricacies of the example in Sec. 3.5. Furthermore, Stata in [25] states that class components are independent if "the instance variables of a component may be accessed only by the methods in the component", and one component "depends only on the specification of the other component, not on its implementation". It is possible to construct an example, similar to the one presented in Sec. 3.5, which has two class components independent according to the independence requirement above, yet overriding in a subclass one of these components, following its specification, leads to a crash.

The application of formal methods to analyzing the fragile base class problem gives us an opportunity to gain a deeper insight into the problem, which was impossible without it. In fact, only the "direct access to base class state" problem was known from the literature. The other problems where noticed while attempting to formally prove the flexibility property. The correspondence between the requirements we formulate and good programming style guidelines is not incidental. We believe that our theory provides a mathematical foundation for the empirical expertise.

Application of the refinement calculus to formalizing classes makes our class semantics more succinct. The refinement calculus also gives us a mathematical framework for formal reasoning about substitutability of objects. Note also that we express class refinement through abstract data type refinement which is a well established theory. This allows applying a large collection of refinement laws for verification.

By formulating the problem in terms of the flexibility property and formally proving it, we demonstrate that the restrictions imposed on inheritance are sufficient to circumvent the problem.

The analysis of the fragile base class problem has revealed that the inheritance operator **mod** is not monotonic in its base class argument. The monotonicity property

$$\text{if } C \textit{ is refined by } C' \text{ then } (M \textbf{ mod } C) \textit{ is refined by } (M \textbf{ mod } C')$$

is stronger than the flexibility property. If inheritance were monotonic, not only the fragile base class problem would be avoided, but also the extension $(M \textbf{ mod } C)$ would be fully substitutable with the new extension $(M \textbf{ mod } C')$, whenever C is substitutable with C'. Extra restrictions should be imposed on inheritance to make it monotonic. Examining these restrictions is the subject of our future research. Effects of disciplining inheritance, the way we propose, on component and object-oriented languages and systems require separate consideration and also constitute the subject of future research. The other research direction is in generalizing the results by relaxing the confinements on the problem that we have made and weakening the restrictions we have imposed on the inheritance mechanism.

Acknowledgments

We would like to thank Ralph Back, Joakim von Wright, Anna Mikhajlova, Jim Grundy, Wolfgang Weck, Martin Büechi, and Linas Laibinis for a lot of valuable comments.

References

1. P. America. Designing an object-oriented programming language with behavioral subtyping. *Foundations of Object-Oriented Languages, REX School/Workshop, Noordwijkerhout, The Netherlands, May/June 1990*, volume 489 of Lecture Notes in Computer Science, pp. 60–90, Springer–Verlag, 1991.
2. Apple Computer, Inc. OpenDoc programmer's guide. *Addison-Wesley Publishing Company,* Draft. Apple Computer, Inc., 9/4/95.
3. R.J.R. Back. Correctness preserving program refinements: proof theory and applications.*vol. 131 of Mathematical Center Tracts.* Amsterdam: Mathematical Center, 1980.
4. R.J.R. Back. Changing data representation in the refinement calculus. *21st Hawaii International Conference on System Sciences*, 1989.
5. R.J.R. Back and M.J. Butler. Exploring summation and product operators in the refinement calculus. *Mathematics of Program Construction, 1995*, volume 947 of Lecture Notes in Computer Science, Springer–Verlag, 1995.
6. R. J. R. Back, J. von Wright. Refinement Calculus I: Sequential Nondeterministic Programs. In *Stepwise Refinement of Distributed Systems*, pp. 42–66, Springer–Verlag, 1990.
7. R. J. R. Back, J. von Wright. Predicate Transformers and Higher Order Logic. In *REX Workshop on Semantics: Foundations and Applications*, the Netherlands, 1992
8. R.J.R. Back, J. von Wright. Refinement Calculus, A Systematic Introduction. *Springer–Verlag*, April 1998.
9. L. Cardelli and P. Wegner. On understanding types, data abstraction, and polymorphism. *Computing Surveys,* 17(4):471–522, 1985.
10. W. Cook, J. Palsberg. A denotational semantics of inheritance and its correctness. *OOPSLA'89 Proceedings*, volume 24 of SIGPLAN Notices, pp. 433–443, October 1989.
11. E.W.Dijkstra, A discipline of programming. *Prentice-Hall International*, 1976.
12. P.H.B. Gardiner and C.C. Morgan. Data refinement of predicate transformers. *Theoretical Computer science*, 87:143-162, 1991.
13. A. V. Hense. Denotational semantics of an object-oriented programming language with explicit wrappers. Volume 5 of *Formal Aspects of Computing*, pp. 181.207, Springer–Verlag, 1993.
14. C.A.R. Hoare. Proofs of correctness of data representation. *Acta informatica,* 1(4), 1972.
15. IBM Corporation. IBM's System Object Model (SOM): Making reuse a reality. *IBM Corporation, Object Technology Products Group,* Austin, Texas.
16. G. Kiczales, J. Lamping. Issues in the design and specification of class libraries. *OOPSLA'92 Proceedings*, volume 27 of SIGPLAN Notices, pp. 435–451, October 1992.
17. B. Liskov and J. M. Wing. A behavioral notion of subtyping. *ACM Transactions on Programming Languages and Systems*, 16(6):1811–1841, November 1994.

18. A. Mikhajlova, E. Sekerinski. Class refinement and interface refinement in object-oriented programs. *FME'97: Industrial Applications and Strengthened Foundations of Formal Methods*, volume 1313 of Lecture Notes in Computer Science, Springer–Verlag, 1997.
19. C. C.Morgan. Programming from specifications. *Prentice-Hall,* 1990.
20. J. M. Morris. A theoretical basis for stepwise refinement and the programming calculus. *Science of Computer Programming,* 9, 287–306, 1987.
21. C. Pfister, C. Szyperski. Oberon/F framework. Tutorial and reference. *Oberon microsystems, Inc.*, 1994.
22. D. Pountain, C. Szyperski. Extensible software systems. *Byte Magazine,* 19(5): 57–62, May 1994. http://www.byte.com/art/9405/sec6/art1.html.
23. A. Snyder. Encapsulation and Inheritance in Object-Oriented Programming Languages. *OOPSLA '86 Proceedings*, volume 21 of SIGPLAN Notices, pp. 38–45, 1986.
24. R. Stata, J. V. Guttag. Modular reasoning in the presence of subtyping. *OOPSLA '95 Proceedings*, volume 30 of SIGPLAN Notices, pp. 200–214, 1995.
25. R. Stata. Modularity in the presence of subclassing. *SRC Research Report 145*, Digital Systems Research Center, 1997.
26. P. Steyaert, Carine Lucas, Kim Mens, Theo D'Hondt. Reuse contracts: managing the evolution of reusable assets. *OOPSLA'96 Proceedings*, volume 31 of SIGPLAN Notices, pp. 268–285, 1996.
27. B. Stroustrup. The C++ programming language. *Addison-Wesley,* 1986.
28. C. Szyperski. Independently extensible systems. Software engineering potential and challenges. *Proceedings of the 19th Australasian Computer Science Conference* Melbourne, Australia, February 1996.
29. D. Taenzer, M. Gandi, S. Podar. Problems in object-oriented software reuse. *Proceedings ECOOP'89, S. Cook (Ed.), Cambridge University Press* Nottingham, July 10-14, 1989, pp. 25–38.
30. A. Tarski. A Lattice Theoretical Fixed Point Theorem and its Applications. volume 5 of *Pacific J. Mathematics*, pp. 285–309, 1955.
31. P. Wegner, S. B. Zdonik. Inheritance as an incremental modification mechanism or what like is and isn't like. *Proceedings ECOOP'88*, volume 322 of Lecture Notes in Computer Science, pp. 55–77, Springer-Verlag, Oslo, August 1988.
32. S. Williams and C. Kinde. The Component Object Model: Technical Overview. *Dr. Dobbs Journal,* December 1994.

Appendix

Before proving the wrapping theorem, we first need to consider a number of theorems and laws of the refinement theory.

Without loss of generality, an arbitrary statement calling procedures $m_1, ..., m_n$ can be rewritten as

$$\textbf{begin var } l \mid p \cdot \textbf{do } g_1 \to m_1; S_1 \, [] \, ... \, [] \, g_n \to m_n; S_n \textbf{ od end}$$

which, using the **while** statement, is equivalently expressed as

$$\textbf{begin var } l \mid p \cdot \textbf{while } (g_1 \vee ... \vee g_n) \textbf{ do } [g_1]; m_1; S_1 \sqcap ... \sqcap [g_n]; m_n; S_n \textbf{ od end}$$

for some initialization predicate p, guards g_i, and conjunctive statements S_i. Further on we write S_i **for** $i = 1..n$ as an abbreviation for $S_1 \sqcap ... \sqcap S_n$.

In particular, we can represent the body of an arbitrary method m_i of a modifier in the following form:

$$
\begin{array}{l}
m_i = \textbf{begin var } l \mid p\cdot \\
\quad\quad \textbf{while } g_1 \vee \ldots \vee g_{i-1} \vee g'_1 \vee \ldots \vee g'_i \textbf{ do} \\
\quad\quad\quad\quad [g_j]; x_j; S_j \textbf{ for } j = 1..i-1 \sqcap \\
\quad\quad\quad\quad [g'_j]; y_j; S'_j \textbf{ for } j = 1..i \\
\quad\quad \textbf{od} \\
\quad \textbf{end}
\end{array}
$$

for some local variables l, initialization predicate p, guards $[g_i]$, $[g'_i]$, and conjunctive statements S_i, S'_i.

We make use of the following rules for data refinement of sequential composition of statements, nondeterministic choice of statements, and **while** statement presented in [8]:

$$
\begin{array}{ll}
;\ \textit{rule}: & (S_1; S_2){\downarrow}R \sqsubseteq (S_1{\downarrow}R); (S_2{\downarrow}R) \\
\sqcap\ \textit{rule}: & (S_1 \sqcap S_2){\downarrow}R \sqsubseteq (S_1{\downarrow}R \sqcap S_1{\downarrow}R) \\
\multicolumn{2}{l}{\textit{while rule}: \textbf{while } g \textbf{ do } S \textbf{ od}{\downarrow}R \sqsubseteq \textbf{while } \{R\}\ g \textbf{ do } [[R]\ g]; (S{\downarrow}R) \textbf{ od}}
\end{array}
$$

We define an *indifferent statement* [8] as a statement that does not refer to components of the state coerced by a data refinement relation. We say that the statement $S : \Gamma \times \Delta \mapsto \Gamma \times \Delta$, which modifies only the Δ component of the state, is indifferent to $R : \Gamma \times \Delta \leftrightarrow \Sigma \times \Delta$, which modifies only the Γ component of the state. We employ the following result for calculating a data refinement of an indifferent statement:

$$\textit{indifference rule}: \quad S{\downarrow}R \sqsubseteq S, \textit{ where } S \textit{ is conjunctive and indifferent to } R$$

In case when a guard g of the **while** statement is indifferent towards a relation R, it is possible to show that the while-loop rule can be slightly modified:

$$\textit{indifferent while rule}: \ \textbf{while } g \textbf{ do } S \textbf{ od}{\downarrow}R \sqsubseteq \textbf{while } g \textbf{ do } S{\downarrow}R \textbf{ od}$$

Wrapping Theorem *Let $L, \mathcal{M}, \mathcal{T}$ and R be as defined in Sec. 5, then*

$$
\begin{array}{l}
L_i\ (\mathcal{M}_1, \ldots, \mathcal{M}_{i-1}){\uparrow}(R \times \mathit{Id})\ (\mathcal{T}_1, \ldots, \mathcal{T}_i){\uparrow}(R \times \mathit{Id}) \sqsubseteq \\
\quad\quad\quad\quad (L_i\ (\mathcal{M}_1, \ldots, \mathcal{M}_{i-1})\ (\mathcal{T}_1, \ldots, \mathcal{T}_i)){\uparrow}(R \times \mathit{Id})
\end{array}
$$

Proof If we denote $(R \times \mathit{Id})$ by P, we can rewrite our goal as was described above:

$$
\left(\begin{array}{l}
\textbf{begin var } l \mid p\cdot \\
\quad \textbf{while } g_1 \vee \ldots \vee g_{i-1} \\
\quad\quad \vee\, g'_1 \vee \ldots \vee g'_i \textbf{ do} \\
\quad\quad [g_j]; \mathcal{M}_j{\uparrow}P; S_j \textbf{ for } j = 1..i-1 \sqcap \\
\quad\quad [g'_j]; \mathcal{T}_j{\uparrow}P; S'_j \textbf{ for } j = 1..i \\
\quad \textbf{od} \\
\textbf{end}{\downarrow}P
\end{array}\right)
\sqsubseteq
\left(\begin{array}{l}
\textbf{begin var } l \mid p\cdot \\
\quad \textbf{while } g_1 \vee \ldots \vee g_{i-1} \\
\quad\quad \vee\, g'_1 \vee \ldots \vee g'_i \textbf{ do} \\
\quad\quad [g_j]; \mathcal{M}_j; S_j \textbf{ for } j = 1..i-1 \sqcap \\
\quad\quad [g'_j]; \mathcal{T}_j; S'_j \textbf{ for } j = 1..i \\
\quad \textbf{od} \\
\textbf{end}
\end{array}\right)
$$

Consider the typing of the participating constructs. If the type of the local variable l is Λ, then state predicates p, g_j, g'_j and statements S_j are working on the state space $\Lambda \times \Sigma \times \Delta$, but they skip on the state component of type Σ. Thus, application of the appropriately extended relation P effectively coercing Σ' into Σ cannot influence these constructs, in other words, they are indifferent to P.

We prove the theorem by refining the left hand side to match the right hand side:

$$
\begin{array}{l}
\quad \mathbf{begin\ var}\ l \mid p \cdot \\
\quad\quad \mathbf{while}\ g_1 \vee ... \vee g_{i-1} \vee g'_1 \vee ... \vee g'_i\ \mathbf{do} \\
\quad\quad\quad [g_j]; \mathcal{M}_j \uparrow P; S_j\ \mathbf{for}\ j = 1..i-1\ \sqcap \\
\quad\quad\quad [g'_j]; \mathcal{T}_j \uparrow P; S'_j\ \mathbf{for}\ j = 1..i \\
\quad\quad \mathbf{od} \\
\quad \mathbf{end}{\downarrow}P \\
= \{\ \textit{definition of block}\ \} \\
\quad (\mathbf{enter}\, l \mid p; \\
\quad \mathbf{while}\ g_1 \vee ... \vee g_{i-1} \vee g'_1 \vee ... \vee g'_i\ \mathbf{do} \\
\quad\quad [g_j]; \mathcal{M}_j \uparrow P; S_j\ \mathbf{for}\ j = 1..i-1\ \sqcap \\
\quad\quad [g'_j]; \mathcal{T}_j \uparrow P; S'_j\ \mathbf{for}\ j = 1..i \\
\quad \mathbf{od}; \\
\quad \mathbf{exit}\, l) {\downarrow}P \\
\sqsubseteq \{\ ;\ \textit{rule}\ \} \\
\quad (\mathbf{enter}\, l \mid p) {\downarrow}P; \\
\quad \mathbf{while}\ g_1 \vee ... \vee g_{i-1} \vee g'_1 \vee ... \vee g'_i\ \mathbf{do} \\
\quad\quad [g_j]; \mathcal{M}_j \uparrow P; S_j\ \mathbf{for}\ j = 1..i-1\ \sqcap \\
\quad\quad [g'_j]; \mathcal{T}_j \uparrow P; S'_j\ \mathbf{for}\ j = 1..i \\
\quad \mathbf{od}{\downarrow}P; \\
\quad (\mathbf{exit}\, l) {\downarrow}P \\
\sqsubseteq \{\ \mathbf{enter}\ \textit{and}\ \mathbf{exit}\ \textit{are conjunctive and indifferent to}\ P\textit{, thus} \\
\quad\ \textit{indifference rule, indifferent while rule}\ \} \\
\quad \mathbf{enter}\, l \mid p; \\
\quad \mathbf{while}\ g_1 \vee ... \vee g_{i-1} \vee g'_1 \vee ... \vee g'_i\ \mathbf{do} \\
\quad\quad ([g_j]; \mathcal{M}_j \uparrow P; S_j\ \mathbf{for}\ j = 1..i-1\ \sqcap \\
\quad\quad [g'_j]; \mathcal{T}_j \uparrow P; S'_j\ \mathbf{for}\ j = 1..i) {\downarrow}P \\
\quad \mathbf{od}; \\
\quad \mathbf{exit}\, l \\
\sqsubseteq \{ \sqcap\ \textit{rule},\ \ ;\ \textit{rule}\ \} \\
\quad \mathbf{enter}\, l \mid p; \\
\quad \mathbf{while}\ g_1 \vee ... \vee g_{i-1} \vee g'_1 \vee ... \vee g'_i\ \mathbf{do} \\
\quad\quad [g_j]{\downarrow}P; \mathcal{M}_j \uparrow P {\downarrow}P; S_j {\downarrow}P\ \mathbf{for}\ j = 1..i-1\ \sqcap \\
\quad\quad [g'_j]{\downarrow}P; \mathcal{T}_j \uparrow P {\downarrow}P; S'_j {\downarrow}P\ \mathbf{for}\ j = 1..i \\
\quad \mathbf{od}; \\
\quad \mathbf{exit}\, l
\end{array}
$$

$\sqsubseteq$ { $[g_j]$ *are indifferent to* P*, and* S_j *are conjunctive,*
thus indifference rule; wrapping rule }
enter $l \mid p$;
while $g_1 \vee ... \vee g_{i-1} \vee g'_1 \vee ... \vee g'_i$ **do**
$[g_j]; \mathcal{M}_j; S_j$ **for** $j = 1..i-1 \sqcap$
$[g'_j]; \mathcal{T}_j; S'_j$ **for** $j = 1..i$
od;
exit l

$=$ { *definition of block* }
begin var $l \mid p \cdot$
while $g_1 \vee ... \vee g_{i-1} \vee g'_1 \vee ... \vee g'_i$ **do**
$[g_j]; \mathcal{M}_j; S_j$ **for** $j = 1..i-1 \sqcap$
$[g'_j]; \mathcal{T}_j; S'_j$ **for** $j = 1..i$
od
end

□

Providing Orthogonal Persistence for Java™ Extended Abstract

Malcolm Atkinson[1] and Mick Jordan[2]

1 Introduction

A significant proportion of software requires persistent data, that is data that outlives the period of execution of individual programs. This is a simple consequence of the fact that most software is written to support human activities and many human activities continue for days, weeks, months or even tens of years. The design of an aircraft or the construction and maintenance of a large artefact, are typical examples. Over these longer periods it is common to find that a system must evolve to accommodate changing requirements, using additional programs and data, as well as (possibly transformed) earlier programs and data.

Two approaches dominate current provision of persistent data:

- File systems, and
- Database systems.

These have both proved effective for building and operating many applications. As we have argued elsewhere [ABC+83, AM95] these technologies have drawbacks which we believe can be overcome by developing and using orthogonal persistence. In short, orthogonal persistence delivers additional safety and consistency checks and is expected to reduce significantly the cost of building and maintaining sophisticated Persistent Application Systems (PASs) by automating data management tasks and using a consistent model encompassing both short-term execution and long-term data.

The basic strategy is to define and support *one* model for data and program that defines both structure and behaviour for program execution, data (and program) storage and system development. The goal is one computational model, which supports and describes all of the activities on and operations of a PAS. In contrast, the two conventional systems, identified above, have separate models for different parts of the system and for different time-scales. This dichotomy generates complex interactions between subsystems that have to be mastered by programmers. It may also result in unspecified or inefficient operational behaviour.

™ Java is a trademark or registered trademark of Sun Microsystems in the USA and other countries.

[1] University of Glasgow, Glasgow G12 8QQ, Scotland

[2] Sun Microsystems Laboratories, Palo Alto, California, USA

Nevertheless, these contemporary systems have strengths, which remain important. Consequently, we view orthogonal persistence as complementary to those systems; another technology capable of supporting the construction and maintenance of new PAS or the extension of an existing PAS. This requires that orthogonally persistent systems should be capable of inter-working with other contemporary technology.

We believe that there are some applications for which orthogonal persistence is the obvious choice of implementation technology, and that as it develops these will become a substantial proportion of all PAS. We are currently developing one such application, which is an integrated set of tools to support distributed collaborations of programmers building large Java applications[3].

Orthogonal Persistence was proposed twenty years ago [Atk78]. It has since received much research attention concerning both its definition and its implementation. This development is summarised in [AM95], which also provides an entry to the literature on orthogonal persistence research. One effect of that research has been to alert others to the benefits of orthogonality and persistence based on reachability. A prominent example is the latest definition of the ODMG model for orthogonal persistence [ODMG97].

Several strategies are possible for developing the common uniform model:

1. Attempting a design of the persistent computational model from scratch,
2. Evolving an existing database model to encompass computation,
3. Evolving an existing programming language model to accommodate persistence, and
4. Eliding two independently developed models.

The Napier88 research is an example of the first approach [MBC+90, MBC+94], the development of SQL3 is an example of the second, and the Java binding for the ODMG model [ODMG97] is an example of the fourth. In contrast, the development of the JDBC™ interface [HCF97], the standard binding to relational systems, though of much practical value, does not fit into any of these strategies since there is no attempt at developing a common model.

The advent of Java provided a "green field" development site for pursuing strategy 3. Java is particularly well suited to this because of its type safety and automated space management. It was also hoped that the fact that PASs built in Java were inevitably exploring new technology would free the architects of the new PAS to consider a new approach to persistence.

Our work developing PJama [ADJ+96, AJD+96] is just one example of the strategy 3 for Java. Several OODB vendors have developed persistence for Java, more or less

---

[3] See the paper by Michael Van Der Vanter in these proceedings.

™ JDBC is a trademark or registered trademark of Sun Microsystems in the USA and other countries.

compliant with the goals of persistence and with the ODMG binding. We will review their efforts below. Some vendors have also essayed automated mapping between Java and relational database systems, addressing some of the goals of orthogonal persistence.

Before taking a more detailed look at the PJama technology, it is useful to define the conceptual framework underpinning orthogonal persistence.

2 Persistence Defined

The term Persistent Programming Language (PPL) was coined to describe programming languages that complied with the three principles, which are restated below [ABC+83]. There is a tendency to use that term more loosely now, though we still consider these principles essential. But adhering to them completely is not easy.

2.1 Orthogonal Persistence

Persistence is the provision of arbitrary life times for data. They should continue to exist for as long as there are programs that can or will use them. On the other hand it is an almost essential engineering requirement that their space may be recycled soon after they are last needed.

Orthogonality requires that this range of life times is available for all types of data, irrespective of their type and other properties. We have found that whenever this orthogonality is not supported fully, programmers have to perform extra work translating between transitory and persistent forms of data. This increases program complexity (consequently increasing the frequency of errors) as well as execution costs.

Many systems are not orthogonally persistent because of the difficulty of implementing persistence for all types. For example, threads in general require the state of a thread be captured and stored outside its execution context so that it can be reconstructed in some other context on another occasion (see below).

2.2 Persistence by Reachability

Some mechanism is needed to determine which data are to be preserved. Generally a system provides some mechanism for identifying a data item, A, as persistent, e.g. by indicating that it is a persistent root. It is then required that all objects that are directly reachable from A (that is, referenced by pointers in A) should also be persistent. This rule applies recursively and guarantees the absence of dangling persistent pointers. It avoids programmers having to identify explicitly each persistent value (as happens in some systems) and is a natural extension to the retention rules that govern life times on a garbage collected heap. Overall, programmers find it easier to understand.

2.3 Persistence Independence

This principle requires that the semantics of programs be unchanged by the introduction of persistence, other than that some data may outlive a single program execution. It is a consequence of this rule that the strength of type checking is undiminished, all previously automated mechanisms are still automated and no explicit mechanism for transferring or locking data is used.

The primary goal of this rule is re-usability — code that has been written for other contexts can be used in the persistent context (on long-lived or transient data) and code developed in the persistent context can be re-used in 'conventional' execution contexts.

This principle cannot be obtained totally. Some code is needed to identify persistent roots for example, or to arrange intermediate atomic checkpoints. However, it can be a minimal proportion of the code. We find users of PJama writing less than ten lines of persistence specific code in applications with tens of thousands of lines of code and hundreds of classes. The rest of the code has the usual platform independence of all other Java code.

3 Matching Java and Persistence

There are several challenges to providing an orthogonally persistent platform for Java. Here we choose to split them between the semantic issues (discussed in this section) and implementation issues (discussed in the following section).

3.1 Orthogonality for PJama

The first decision is "How enthusiastically should orthogonality be pursued?" We decided for PJama that we sought total adherence to this principle (though we haven't achieved it yet—see section 6). This means that every instance of *every* class[4] should have the same rights to persistence. This is relatively straightforward for arrays and instances of user-defined classes and for all of the core classes that are written entirely in Java. However, many of the core classes, and some user-defined classes, have part of their implementation in some other language, typically C. This presents a technical difficulty; it becomes difficult, if not impossible, to keep track of the use of pointers. This will be overcome in the latest versions of Java by the near universal adoption for all native methods of the Java Native Interface (JNI), which allows such issues and automatic locking to be systematically implemented. We simply assert that we will not support any user-defined C code that isn't JNI compliant.

This still leaves a few core classes, such as `Thread`, those classes in the AWT packages, etc. which are so intimately inter-related with the Java Virtual Machine (JVM) that they require special treatment. Their code has to be manually modified by the PJama implementation team, to capture sufficient state when an instance is to be promoted to the persistent form and to restore that state when an instance is faulted back in.

---

[4] We assume readers are familiar with the standard Java language [GJS96].

3.2 Treatment of class `Class`

The target of complete orthogonality described above ineluctably leads to permitting instances of class `Class` to persist. They are one of the core classes that specialises the class `Object`, therefore they should be allowed to persist. However, there is a more important reason why they should persist. The instances of class `Class` contain all of the meta data describing objects and all methods describing their behaviour. To preserve objects without preserving this information, to enable their correct usage in the future, would be futile. The instances without this meta data would simply be a bag of bits with arbitrary interpretation and open to misuse. We therefore ensure that, whenever an instance of a class `C` or an array of instances of class `C` is preserved, we also preserve the `Class C`.

An alternative way of considering this is that we ensure that whenever we store data we also store all other data that is needed to enable consistent interpretation of that data. If we recognise that our computational model needs to be consistent, and that during a normal execution each instance of class `C` is bound to `C`, then we see that persistence independence requires that this precise binding continues unbroken. The requirement to preserve a class `C` in order to interpret its instances correctly extends to all of the classes used to define that class `C`.

The alternative semantics, in which only the class name is preserved with instances, we consider unsatisfactory for three reasons:

1. It enables the semantics of the language to be broken with long-term data, as during the next activation of the JVM that name may be bound to a totally different class (by accident or malevolence).
2. It fails to provide persistence for static variables, which, like all other data should be afforded the privileges of persistence.
3. It is inefficient and does not permit the mutual optimisation of program and data.

3.3 Static Initialisation and Static Variables

Java classes are permitted static variables and methods. Programs may exploit the values in static variables. If these variables are not allowed to persist, then data in this context is not treated orthogonally and the semantics of operations on static variables differ in the persistent context from that in the transient context. This would break two of the persistence principles, and so we chose to make static variables persistent if the class is persistent. For example, if a static variable holds the extent of a class (i.e. its current set of instances), this extent will persist.

This raises the issue of when static initialisation should occur. In standard Java initialisation occurs when a class is loaded, typically the first time it is required during a JVM execution that involves that class. In the persistent case, we choose to initialise the class the first time that the class is loaded into the persistent system. There after it retains its state as it receives successive values. This would yield a persistent extent in the above example.

Other systems choose to rebind to classes and to re-initialise them for each JVM execution. This excludes the persistent use of static variables.

3.4 Persistent Roots

In PJama we have chosen to introduce a set of persistent roots in a `Dictionary` structure which binds names, held as `Strings`, to values, held as `Objects`. Any data can then be reached via those `Objects`. Two simpler approaches might have been taken:

1. There could have been a single, pre-ordained root (c.f. PS-algol [ABC+83] and Napier 88 [MBC+94]) of the most general type, `Object`. Typically, programmers then agree to a convention that assigns an associative naming structure to the top value in this root. The advantages of simplicity and generality, which the single root implies, are outweighed by the unreliability of depending on a convention.
2. The static variables of classes that become persistent could act as persistent roots. The classes themselves would not become persistent initially because there would be no instances forcing them persistent in the absence of persistent classes. Therefore a bootstrap mechanism, e.g. explicitly stating that a class should persist, would be necessary. This then becomes equivalent to the named binding scheme, except that the naming scheme has been predefined.

We therefore chose explicit persistent roots. These are managed and a few other operations are made available via the interface `PJStore`. Our particular implementation of this interface is `PJStoreImpl`. This nomenclature has been chosen to encourage alternative implementations. To use persistence in its simplest form, with each persistent JVM execution behaving as a transaction, with atomic durable checkpoints provided by the method `stabilizeAll`, it is only necessary to use these two classes and our modified JVM, `opj`.

3.5 Transient Data

By default the PJama system will make *all* data structures that are reachable (directly and *indirectly*) from persistent roots persistent. All other data structures live their transient lives on the JVM's standard, garbage collected heap. There are two reasons why a programmer may wish to modify this:

1. It is known a priori that this data will never be re-used, and hence economies can be made by not saving it; and
2. The data is intrinsically transient, and must be replaced with equivalent but revised data during subsequent executions.

Standard Java provides the keyword `transient` to denote the former case. The effect of `transient` is to avoid capture of state onto long-term storage and to ensure that if this data is read in any subsequent (different) execution of the persistent

JVM, then that execution will encounter the items marked `transient` re-initialised to their standard default values. PJama honours this semantics[5].

The second case is more interesting, as it draws our attention to the fact that we are trying to define more carefully a computational model that describes long-term computation. In any long-term computation, we must recognise that the context of the computation may change, and that the computation may have to adapt to that change. A mechanism is therefore required to announce and identify the change, and to allow the computation to attempt to reconstruct an equivalent (external) binding. Examples are, connections to sockets, connections to databases, connections to files, and connections to windows. This recognition of an external world with which we interact and an attempt to accommodate its inherent autonomy is essential. However, it forces programmers to face this inevitable complexity.

We provide a set of major events (`PJActions`) e.g. `StartUp`, `Recovery`, `Stabilize` and `ShutDown`, and allow programmers to register `PJActionHandlers` to deal with these events, typically by attempting to reconstruct an external binding. Some standard handlers come with the system, so that programmers, dealing with standard connections to the external world, are provided with a standard rebinding and need not consider this issue.

3.6 Stable Hash Coding

Once we embark on developing a consistent computational model we encounter many deviations from consistency. Most of these are artefacts of the fact that the original design or implementation considered only a limited scope. The `hashCode` method of many classes in Java is a typical example. It has exhibited three problems:

- It is not stable. That is, the repeated application of `hashCode` method returns different hash code values on different occasions. For example, it is common to use the object's address in forming the hash code, but this changes when an object is saved by one Orthogonal Persistence for Java Virtual Machine (OPJVM) execution and re-instated by another.
- It is not sufficiently accurate or sufficiently uniform. The volumes of data that can accumulate in a persistent system are much larger than occur in a single execution of a JVM. Clustering of the values returned by `hashCode` means that it becomes a poorer approximation to equality than would be expected for the number of bits allocated and that long collision chains occur. The first of these flaws may mean data is brought from disk and read for the precise equality check unnecessarily and the second means that long chains have to be traversed on by faulting them, typically from different pages, on disk. Both have much more deleterious effects on a persistent computation than they have on conventional computations.

[5] At present we are forced to endure a work-around for **transient** instance fields because the keyword **transient** has been misused in the `Object Serialization` core class, to mean "this field has a special serialisation".

- The Java definition is ambiguous about whether `hashCode` relates to identity or content equality. Large-scale systems supported by persistence, involve many application programmers. They must interpret the data consistently, but such ambiguities militate against this.

3.7 General Requirement for Stable Definitions

Hash code calculation is just one example of the need to review computational definitions once a longer-term model is sought. We have made a start, but it seems that the scale, growth and complexity of the Java core classes, may mean that we have only scratched the surface of this issue. It is, in our opinion, one which should be of greater concern to those specifying languages such as Java. The requirements for definitions that are stable over many contexts leads to improved quality. It certainly is consistent with aspirations to "compile once and run anywhere" and to "serve the Enterprise".

3.8 Managing Evolution

Any long-lived system has to adapt to meet new requirements and to improve processes. This requires mechanisms that permit change. However, this change has to be managed in a consistent way and implemented efficiently. Our choice of keeping all of the class `Class` instances of relevance in the persistent store has both benefits and drawbacks.

On the one hand having both the class information (program and meta data) and the instances together means that there is enough information to make consistent changes and to ensure proposed changes are consistent. On the other hand, loading methods from the persistent store means that even the smallest program correction requires technology to replace corrected parts, which is avoided by those who load from class files every time.

4 Implementation Architecture

PJama has developed an architecture, which presents persistent data structures to the JVM so that they look to the interpreter identical with those that are found on the garbage collected heap. However, these are held in the object cache. Incremental algorithms fault in and evict these objects via the buffer-pool management system [DA97]. On a stabilisation (invoked by the program, at end of program or end of transaction) the updated data in the object cache is examined. Pointers to instances on the heap, indicate the roots of object graphs that must be promoted to the persistent object store. The mutated instances are then written back. This is implemented by building a special version of the JVM (OPJVM) and by modifying several core classes: `ClassLoader`, `Thread`, etc. Many optimisations of the simple scheme presented here are necessary to achieve acceptable performance. Some of these are described in [DA97].

We allow only one OPJVM to execute against a persistent store and use the concurrency and locking within Java to service concurrent loads. Multiple read-only use is also allowed. We also restrict the OPJVM to execute against only one persistent store at a time. These restrictions significantly simplify the requirements for persistent application programmers to understand new semantics and simplify our implementation. Only evaluation against serious applications will determine whether this is an appropriate trade-off.

5 Other Approaches

Several other approaches have been taken to providing persistence for Java[6]. The ODMG committee has defined a standard binding which respects both the principle of orthogonality and that of persistence by reachability. This leaves much flexibility over its implementation.

Several of the implementations have significantly restricted the use of core classes, even requiring that different `Hashtables` or proprietary collection classes be used. Such a lack of orthogonality and persistence independence militates against re-usability.

A variety of implementation architectures are in use; some implemented entirely in Java. This has the advantage of achieving acceptable platform independence at considerable cost to performance and (potential) orthogonality (it is difficult to see how to deal with a significant proportion of the core classes with this approach).

Some implementations re-use existing persistent object-store servers and allow multiple JVMs to interact with servers. Some implementations require a pre-processing pass over the Java source before using a standard compiler. Any implementation that requires access to source will reduce code re-use. To avoid this some implementations depend on post-processing the class files to produce new class files with modifications that provide persistence. Both these approaches suffer from two disadvantages:

- They perturb the Java program build process, and
- The output of diagnostics and debugging tools no longer corresponds to the source that the programmer is working with.

They both have the significant advantage that they should work with any compiler and with any implementation of the JVM. A variation that gives up on the second of these is to generate new byte codes and use an extended version of the JVM to interpret them to deliver persistence. PJama takes advantage of this technique, as we believe it gives a significant performance advantage. But we do not perturb the build process, as this transformation occurs when the class file is first loaded.

Our decision to include class `Class` in the orthogonal set does not appear to be replicated, though some products permit classes to be explicitly placed in the store.

[6] Specific products and papers are deliberately not identified here. To make explicit comparisons at this stage, when so many products and projects are evolving rapidly, would be injudicious and unfair.

There are also a group of products that map automatically between Java and relational (or object-oriented) databases. These appear to still be in an early state of development and consequently may have significant orthogonality failures or performance problems. However, they may work well for a carefully selected set of "Enterprise classes".

In a few cases, application programmers are being asked to achieve manually the effect of a write barrier; they have to write code to notify explicitly that an object has been updated. In some implementations they have to mark explicitly classes as constructing instances capable of being made persistent. They also have to mark methods (whole classes) as handling potentially persistent objects, presumably so that the read barrier for object faulting can be selectively inserted. Such requirements to adorn source code with annotations for persistence have pathological effects. It means that code sharing cannot take place at the class file level and that there is virtually no chance of code being re-usable in any other (persistent) context.

The total set of available implementations from both commerce and research indicates the importance attached to persistence for Java. It also presents consumers with a huge and confusing variety and with a potentially very difficult set of choices. It is certain that there are different kinds of application, and some approaches to persistence may be optimal for one kind, while other approaches match other applications. What is needed is a better categorisation of persistent applications and systematic evaluation against the criteria that that categorisation generates. We have begun such an evaluation, but it requires much broader input from the object-oriented research community.

6 Status and Future of PJama

Our close collaboration with Sun, and access to the developing versions of the JDK, have made it possible for us to release versions of PJama compatible with the JDK to run on Solaris SPARC, Solaris x86, Windows NT and Windows 95. These have typically been available on the web site,

`http://www.sunlabs.com/research/forest/`

within days of the corresponding JDK release. The tracking of Java development has taken, and continues to take, a significant amount of labour. However we consider it important, if we are to have our research properly evaluated.

We strongly encourage downloads of the system for evaluation and research purposes. For licensing reasons, each user organisation has to register with SunLabs. So far, there are about 100 registered user sites, as well as our own usage, and no one has been refused access to the system.

The system uses the standard Sun Java compiler, but a modified interpreter. Versions of this interpreter are available for the platforms mentioned above. We supply an off-line disk garbage collector and an off-line tool for substituting persistent classes. A recent achievement has been the provision of persistent RMI.

The facilities we deliver fall short of our goals at present, in the following respects:

- We have not yet achieved full orthogonality. The major limitation is the failure to deal fully with AWT peers, and with Threads. The reasons for this are, in the first case, the labour involved in dealing with so much C, which should become largely unnecessary when JNI is used universally. In the second case, it is currently hard to get at the complete state of a Thread. However, we currently support all of the Swing Set JFC.
- Our store is currently based on RVM [SMK+94]. This is limiting the maximum store size to 2 Gbytes and restricting us to a no-steal policy for buffer management. The largest store constructed so far had a population of 160 million objects.
- We do not yet have either concurrent or incremental disk garbage collection.
- The class substitution technology does not yet support reformatting existing class instances.

The plan that we are currently pursuing, includes:

- Development of our proposed concurrent and flexible transaction model [AJD96].
- Replacement of our existing store technology with store technology that is much more flexible and which is much less closely coupled to the particular interpreter technology [PAD+97], which allows a buffer steal policy and which will accommodate several orders of magnitude more data. This store will also support work on incremental and concurrent garbage collection.
- Development of co-ordinated store and class evolution techniques.
- Implementation of instrumentation, visualisation and diagnostic technology, appropriate for large persistent applications. This will be used to develop a better understanding of the factors that affect performance in large persistent object stores.
- Tracking the development of Java. For example, handling JDK 1.2 and HotSpot™. We believe that the move to HotSpot will put us in a position to achieve our goal of complete orthogonality.
- Developing further optimisations, both through code transformations and through better object cache and buffer management algorithms.
- Evaluating our technology via larger, more realistic test loads and by building extensive and long-running PAS. This will also continue to involve an element of comparison with other technologies, both with respect to execution costs and with respect to programming costs. We are concerned to develop an understanding of the total cost of running an application. Micro benchmarks that look at some particular aspect can be very misleading.

™ Java™ Foundation Classes (J.F.C.), JDK, Solaris and HotSpot are trademarks or registered trademarks of Sun Microsystems Inc. in the USA and other countries.

Our initial long-term research goals still remain:

- To develop an industrial strength persistent language and supporting system and exhibit its power,
- To develop a model of persistent computation that encompasses uniformly many more of the activities that occupy application programmers' working life.

7 Conclusions

PJama is a vehicle for research into how to design and build industrial strength persistent programming technology. It is also a useful tool that can be used now to experience the advantages of orthogonal persistence for a popular language.

Many research challenges remain. Perhaps the primary ones are:

- Developing a better understanding of the different nature of applications and a corresponding assessment of the technological choices available.
- Improving performance by combining the technologies of program optimisation with those of database optimisation.
- Extending the computational model to encompass coherently and consistently more of application programmers' total technical requirements.

Acknowledgements

This research is supported by a collaborative research grant from SunLabs, by grant GR/K87791 from the British Engineering and Physical Sciences Research Council, and by a scholarship from the University of Glasgow. The design and implementation of PJama has been achieved by a team: Laurent Daynès, Misha Dmitriev, Craig Hamilton, Gordon Haywood, Neal Gafter, Brian Lewis, Bernd Mathiske, Tony Printezis and Susan Spence. Useful feedback on the emerging system has been provided by: Huw Evans, Cathy Waite, Graham Kirby, Michael Van Der Vanter, Jos Marlow students at Glasgow and many others. Greg Czajkowski ported PJama to WINDOWS and Padmakar Vishnubhatt conducted many comparison studies.

Bibliography

ABC+83 Atkinson, M.P., Bailey, P.J., Chisholm, K.J., Cockshott, W.P. and Morrison, R., 1983. An Approach to Persistent Programming. *Computer Journal* 26, 4 pp 360-365.

ADJ+96 Atkinson, M.P., Daynès, L., Jordan, M.J., Printezis, T. and Spence, S. An Orthogonally Persistent Java, SIGMOD RECORD, 25, 4, December 1996.

AJD+96 Atkinson, M.P., Jordan, M.J., Daynès, L. and Spence, S. Design Issues for Persistent Java: a type-safe, object-oriented, orthogonally persistent system, May 1996, In Proceedings of the seventh international workshop on Persistent Object Systems (POS7).

AM95 Atkinson, M.P. and Morrison, M., Orthogonal Persistent Object Systems, VLDB Journal, 4, 3, 1995.

Atk78 Atkinson, M.P., 1978. Programming Languages and Databases. *In Proc. 4th IEEE International Conference on Very Large Databases* pp 408-419.

DA97 Daynès, L. and Atkinson, M.P., Main-Memory Management to support Orthogonal Persistence for Java, in [JA97] pp 37-60.

GJS96 Gosling, J., Joy, W.N. and Steele, G., The Java Language Specification, Addison-Wesley, 1996.

HCF97 Hamilton, G., Cattell, R. and Fisher, M. JDBC Database Access with Java, Adison-Wesley, 1997.

JA97 Jordan, M.J. and Atkinson, M.P., Proceedings of the second international workshop on Persistence and Java, Sun Microsystems, M/S MTV29-01, 901 San Antonio Road, Palo Alto, CA 94303-4900. Tech. Report SMLI-TR-97-63.

ODMG97 ODMG (Ed. Cattell, R.) The Object Database Standard: ODMG 2.0, Morgan Kaufmann, 1997.

MBC+90 Morrison, R., Brown, A.L., Carrick, R., Connor, R.C.H., Dearle, A. and Atkinson, M.P., 1990. The Napier Type System. In *Persistent Object Systems*, Rosenberg, J. and Koch, D.M. (ed.), Springer-Verlag, Proc. 3rd International Workshop on Persistent Object Systems, Newcastle, Australia pp 3-18.

MBC+94 Morrison, R., Brown, A.L., Connor, R.C.H., Cutts, Q.I., Dearle, A., Kirby, G.N.C. & Munro, D.S., 1994. The Napier88 Reference Manual (Release 2.0). University of St Andrews Technical Report CS/94/8.

PAD+97 Printezis, T., Atkinson, M.P., Daynès, L., Spence, S. and Bailey, P.J., The Design of a new Persistent Object Store for PJama, in [JA97], pp 61-74.

SMK+94 Satyanarayanan, M., Mashburn, H.H., Kumar, P., D.C. Steere and Kistler, J.J., Lightweight Recoverable Virtual Memory, ACM Trans. On Computing Systems, 12, 2 pp167-172, May 1994.

Wrappers to the Rescue

John Brant, Brian Foote, Ralph E. Johnson, and Donald Roberts

Department of Computer Science
University of Illinois at Urbana-Champaign
Urbana, IL 61801
{brant, foote, johnson, droberts}@cs.uiuc.edu

Abstract. Wrappers are mechanisms for introducing new behavior that is executed before and/or after, and perhaps even in lieu of, an existing method. This paper examines several ways to implement wrappers in Smalltalk, and compares their performance. Smalltalk programmers often use Smalltalk's lookup failure mechanism to customize method lookup. Our focus is different. Rather than changing the method lookup process, we modify the method objects that the lookup process returns. We call these objects *method wrappers*. We have used method wrappers to construct several program analysis tools: a coverage tool, a class collaboration tool, and an interaction diagramming tool. We also show how we used method wrappers to construct several extensions to Smalltalk: synchronized methods, assertions, and multimethods. Wrappers are relatively easy to build in Smalltalk because it was designed with reflective facilities that allow programmers to intervene in the lookup process. Other languages differ in the degree to which they can accommodate change. Our experience testifies to the value, power, and utility of openness.

1 Introduction

One benefit of building programming languages out of objects is that programmers are able to change the way a running program works. Languages like Smalltalk and CLOS, which represent program elements like Classes and Methods as objects that can be manipulated at runtime, to allow programmers to change the ways these objects work when the need arises.

This paper focuses on how to intercept and augment the behavior of existing methods in order to "wrap" new behavior around them. Several approaches are examined and contrasted and their relative performances are compared. These are:

1. Source Code Modifications
2. Byte Code Modifications
3. New Selectors
4. Dispatching Wrappers
5. Class Wrappers
6. Instance Wrappers
7. Method Wrappers

We then examine several tools and extensions we've built using wrappers:

1. Coverage Tool
2. Class Collaboration Diagram Tool
3. Interaction Diagram Tool
4. Synchronized Methods
5. Assertions
6. Multimethods

Taken one at a time, it might be easy to dismiss these as Smalltalk specific minutiae, or as language specific hacks. However, taken together, they illustrate the power and importance of the reflective facilities that support them.

Before and after methods as we now know them first appeared in Flavors [30] and Loops [5]. The Common Lisp Object System (CLOS) [4] provides a powerful method standard combination facility that includes `:before`, `:after`, and `:around` methods. In CLOS, a method with a `:before` qualifier that specializes a generic function, *g*, is executed before any of the primary methods on *g*. Thus, the before methods are called before the primary method is called, and the `:after` methods are called afterwards. An `:around` method can wrap all of these, and has the option of completing the rest of the computation. The method combination mechanism built into CLOS also lets programmers build their own method qualifiers and combination schemes, and is very powerful.

Unfortunately, misusing method combination can lead to programs that are complex and hard to understand. Application programmers use them to save a little code but end up with systems that are hard to understand and maintain. Using these facilities to solve application-level problems is often symptomatic of more serious design problems that should be addressed through refactoring instead. The result is that before and after methods have gained a bad reputation.

We use method wrappers mostly as a *reflective* facility, not a normal application programming technique. We think of them as a way to impose additional structure on the underlying reflective facilities. For example, we use them to dynamically determine who calls a method, and which methods are called. If methods wrappers are treated as a disciplined form of reflection, then they will be used more carefully and their complexity will be less of a problem.

Our experience with method wrappers has been with Smalltalk. Smalltalk has many reflective facilities. Indeed, Smalltalk-76 [17] was the first language to cast the elements of an object-oriented language itself, such as classes, as first-class objects. The ability to trap messages that are not understood has been used to implement encapsulators [26] and proxies in distributed systems [2, 23]. The ability to manipulate contexts has been used to implement debuggers, back-trackers [21], and exception handlers [15]. The ability to compile code dynamically is used by the standard programming environments and makes it easy to define new code management tools. Smalltalk programmers can change what the system does when it accesses a global variable [1] and can change the class of an object [16].

However, it is not possible to change every aspect of Smalltalk [10]. Smalltalk is built upon a virtual machine that defines how objects are laid out, how classes work, and how messages are handled. The virtual machine can only be changed by the

Smalltalk vendors, so changes have to be made using the reflective facilities that the virtual machine provides. Thus, you can't change how message lookup works, though you can specify what happens when it fails. You can't change how a method returns, though you can use `valueNowOrOnUnwindDo:` to trap returns out of a method. You can't change how a method is executed, though you can change the method itself.

We use method wrappers to change how a method is executed. The most common reason for changing how a method is executed is to do something at every execution, and method wrappers work well for that purpose.

2 Compiled Methods

Many of the method wrapper implementations discussed in this paper are based on CompiledMethods, so it is helpful to understand how methods work to understand the different implementations. While this discussion focuses on VisualWorks, we have also implemented wrappers in VisualAge Smalltalk. They can be implemented in most other dialects of Smalltalk. However, the method names and structure of the objects are somewhat different. A complete discussion of how to implement wrappers in these other dialects of Smalltalk is beyond the scope of this paper.

Smalltalk represents the methods of a class using instances of CompiledMethod or one of its subclasses. A CompiledMethod knows its Smalltalk source, but it also provides other information about the method, such as the set of messages that it sends and the bytecodes that define the execution of the method.

Interestingly, CompiledMethods do not know the selector with which they are associated. Hence, they are oblivious as to which name they are invoked by, as well as to the names of their arguments. They are similar to Lisp lambda-expressions in this respect. Indeed, a compiled method can be invoked even if it does not reside in any MethodDictionary. We will use this fact to construct MethodWrappers.

CompiledMethod has three instance variables and a literal frame that is stored in its variable part (accessible through the `at:` and `at:put:` methods). The instance variables are *bytes*, *mclass*, and *sourceCode*. The *sourceCode* variable holds an index that is used to retrieve the source code for the method and can be changed so different sources appear when the method is browsed. Changing this variable does not affect the execution of the method, though. The *mclass* instance variable contains the class that compiled the method. One of its uses is to extract the selector for the method.

The bytes and literal frame are the most important parts of CompiledMethods. The *bytes* instance variable contains the byte codes for the method. These byte codes are stored either as a small integer (if the method is small enough) or a byte array, and contain references to items in the literal frame. The items in the literal frame include standard Smalltalk literal objects such as numbers (integers and floats), strings, arrays, symbols, and blocks (BlockClosures and CompiledBlocks for copying and full blocks). Symbols are in the literal frame to specify messages being sent. Classes are in the literal frame whenever a method sends a message to a super-

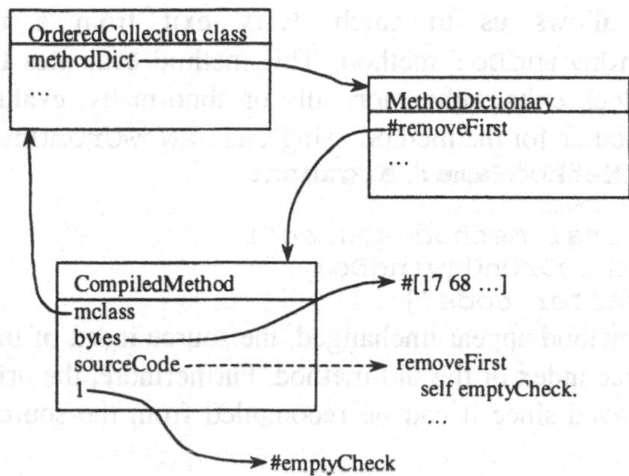

Fig. 1. `removeFirst` method in OrderedCollection

class. The class is placed into the literal frame so that the virtual machine knows where to begin method lookup. Associations are stored in the literal frame to represent global, class, and pool variables. Although the compiler will only store these types of objects in the literal frame, in principle any kind of object can be stored there.

Figure 1 shows the CompiledMethod for the `removeFirst` method in OrderedCollection. The method is stored under the #removeFirst key in OrderedCollection's method dictionary. Instead of showing the integer that is in the method's sourceCode variable, the dashed line indicates the source code that the integer points to.

3 Implementing Wrappers

There are many different ways to implement method wrappers in Smalltalk, ranging from simple source code modification to complex byte code modification. In the next few sections we discuss seven possible implementations and some of their properties. Although many of the implementation details that we use are Smalltalk-specific, other languages provide similar facilities to varying degrees.

3.1 Source code modification

A common way to wrap methods is to modify the method directly. The wrapper code is directly inserted into the original method's source and the resulting code is compiled. This requires parsing the original method to determine where the before code is placed and all possible locations for the after code. Although the locations of return statements can be found by parsing, these are not the only locations where the method can be exited. Other ways to leave a method are by exceptions, non-local block returns, and process termination.

VisualWorks allows us to catch every exit from a method with the `valueNowOrOnUnwindDo:` method. This method evaluates the receiver block, and when this block exits, either normally or abnormally, evaluates the argument block. The new source for the method using `valueNowOrOnUnwindDo:` is:

```
originalMethodName: argument
  "before code"
  ^["original method source"]
    valueNowOrOnUnwindDo:
      ["after code"]
```

To make the method appear unchanged, the source index of the new method can be set to the source index of the old method. Furthermore, the original method does not need to be saved since it can be recompiled from the source retrieved by the source index.

The biggest drawback of this approach is that it must compile each method that it changes. Moreover, it requires another compile to reinstall the original method. Not only is compiling slower than the other approaches listed here, it cannot be used in runtime images since they are not allowed to have the compiler.

3.2 Byte code modification

Another way to modify a method is to modify the CompiledMethod directly without recompiling [24]. This technique inserts the byte codes and literals for the before code directly into the CompiledMethod so that the method does not need to be recompiled. This makes installation faster. Unfortunately, this approach does not handle the after code well. To insert the after code, we must convert the byte codes for the original method into byte codes for a block that is executed by the `valueNowOrOnUnwindDo:` method. This conversion is non-trivial since the byte codes used by the method will be different than the byte codes used by the block. Furthermore, this type of transformation depends on knowledge of the byte code instructions used by the virtual machine. These codes are not standardized and can change without warning.

3.3 New selector

Another way to wrap methods is to move the original method to a new selector and create a new method that executes the before code, sends the new selector, and then executes the after code. With this approach the new method is:

```
originalMethodName: argument
  "before code"
  ^[self newMethodName: argument]
    valueNowOrOnUnwindDo:
      ["after code"]
```

This approach was used by Böcker and Herczeg to build their Tracers [3].

This implementation has a couple of desirable properties. One is that the original methods do not need to be recompiled when they are moved to their new selectors.

Since CompiledMethods contain no direct reference to their selectors, they can be moved to any selector that has the same number of arguments. The other property is that the new forwarding methods with the same before and after code can be copied from another forwarding method that has the same number of arguments. Cloning these CompiledMethods objects (i.e. using the Prototype pattern [11]) is much faster than compiling new ones. The main difference between the two forwarding methods is that they send different selectors for their original methods. The symbol that is sent is easily changed by replacing it in the method's literal frame. The only other changes between the two methods are the sourceCode and the mclass variables. The mclass is set to the class that will own the method, and the sourceCode is set to the original method's sourceCode so that the source code changes aren't noticed. Since byte codes are not modified, neither the original method nor the new forwarding method needs to be compiled, so the installation is faster than the source code modification approach.

One problem with this approach is that the new selectors are visible to the user. Böcker and Herczeg addressed this problem by modifying the browsers. The new selectors cannot conflict with other selectors in the super or subclasses and should not conflict with users adding new methods. Furthermore, it is more difficult to compose two different method wrappers since we must remember which of the selectors represent the original methods and which are the new selectors.

3.4 Dispatching Wrapper

One way to wrap new behavior around existing methods is to screen every message that is sent to an object as it is dispatched. In Smalltalk, the `doesNotUnderstand:` mechanism has long been used for this purpose [26, 2, 10, 12, 14] This approach works well when some action must be taken regardless of which method is being called, such as coordinating synchronization information. Given some extra data structures, it can be used to implement wrapping on a per-method basis. For example, Classtalk [8] used `doesNotUnderstand:` to implement a CLOS-style before- and after- method combination mechanism.

A common way to do this is to introduce a class with no superclass to intercept the dispatching mechanism to allow per-instance changes to behavior. However, the `doesNotUnderstand:` mechanism is slow, and screening every message sent to an object just to change the behavior of a few methods seems wasteful and inelegant. The following sections examine how Smalltalk's meta-architecture lets us more precisely target the facilities we need.

3.5 Class Wrapper

The standard approach for specializing behavior in object-oriented programming is subclassing. We can use subclassing to specialize methods to add before and after code. In this case, the specialized subclass essentially wraps the original class by creating a new method that executes the before code, calls the original method using `super` mechanism, and then executes the after code. Like the methods in the new selector approach, the methods for the specialized subclass can also be copied, so the compiler is not needed.

Once the subclass has been created, it can be installed into the system. To install the subclass, the new class has to be inserted into the hierarchy so that subclasses will also use the wrapped methods. It can be inserted by using the `superclass:` method to change the superclass of all of the subclasses of the class being wrapped to be the wrapper. Next, the reference to the original class in the system dictionary must be replaced with a reference to the subclass. Finally, all existing instances of the original class have to be converted to use the new subclass. This can be accomplished by getting `allInstances` of the original class and using the `changeClassToThatOf:` method to change their class to the new subclass.

Like the new selector approach this only requires one additional message send. However, these sorts of wrappers take longer to install. Each class requires a scan of object memory to look for all instances of the original class. Once the instances have been found, we have to iterate though them changing each of their classes.

3.6 Instance Wrapper

The class wrapper approach can also be used to wrap methods on a per instance basis, or a few at a time. Instead of replacing the class in the system dictionary, we can change only the objects that we want to wrap, by using the `changeClassToThatOf:` method on only those objects.

Instance wrappers can be used to change the way individual objects behave. This is the intent of the Decorator pattern [11]. However since these decorations are immediately visible though existing references to the original object, objects can be decorated dynamically.

3.7 Method Wrapper

A method wrapper is like a new selector in that the old method is replaced by a new one that invokes the old. However, a method wrapper does not add new entries to the method dictionary. Instead of invoking the old method by sending a message to the receiver, a method wrapper evaluates the original method directly. A method wrapper must know the original method, and must be able to execute it with the current arguments. Executing a CompiledMethod is easy, since a CompiledMethod responds to the `valueWithReceiver:arguments:` message by executing itself with the given a receiver and an array of arguments.

One way for a MethodWrapper to keep track of its original method is for MethodWrapper to be a subclass of CompiledMethod with one new instance variable, *clientMethod*, that stores the original method. MethodWrapper also defines `beforeMethod`, `afterMethod`, and `receiver:arguments:` methods as well as a few helper methods. The `beforeMethod` and `afterMethod` methods

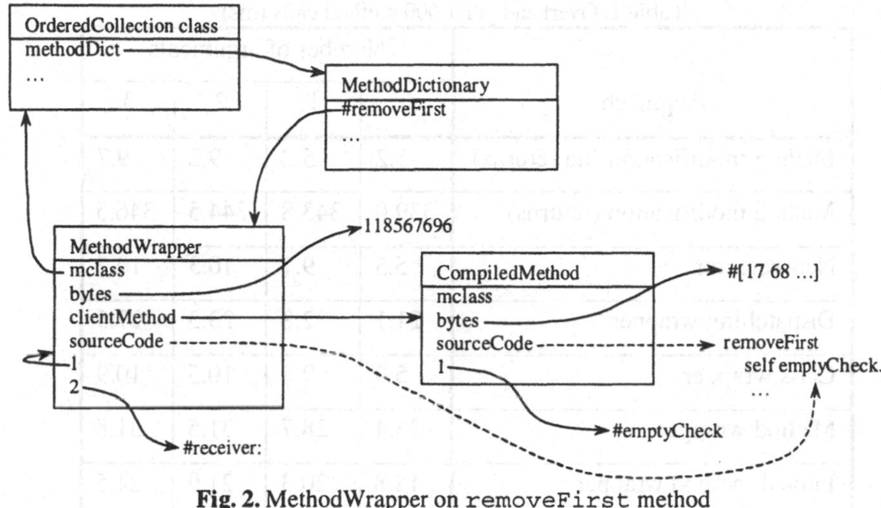

Fig. 2. MethodWrapper on `removeFirst` method

contain the before and after code. The `valueWithReceiver:arguments:` method executes the original method given the receiver and argument array.

```
valueWithReceiver: anObject arguments: args
  self beforeMethod.
  ^[clientMethod
       valueWithReceiver: anObject
       arguments: args]
     valueNowOrOnUnwindDo:
       [self afterMethod]
```

The only remaining problem is how to send the `valueWithReceiver:-arguments:` message to a MethodWrapper. The method must be able to refer to itself when it is executing, but Smalltalk does not provide a standard way to refer to the currently executing method. When a CompiledMethod is executing, the receiver of the message, and not the CompiledMethod, is the "self" of the current computation. In VisualWorks Smalltalk, the code "`thisContext method`" evaluates to the currently executing method, but it is inefficient. We need some kind of "static" variable that we could initialize with the method, but Smalltalk does not have that feature. Instead, we make use of the fact that each Smalltalk method keeps track of the literals (i.e. constants) that it uses. Each MethodWrapper is compiled with a marked literal (we use #(), which is an array of size 0). After it has been created, the system replaces the reference to the literal with a reference to the MethodWrapper. Using this trick the `receiver:value:` message can be sent to the MethodWrapper by compiling

```
originalMethodName: argument
  ^#() receiver: self value: argument
```

and replacing the empty array (in the first position of the literal frame) with the method. The `receiver:value:` method is one of the MethodWrapper's helper methods. It is responsible for converting its value argument into an array and sending them to the `valueWithReceiver:arguments:` method.

Table 1. Overhead per 1,000 method calls (ms)

Approach	Number of arguments			
	0	1	2	3
Method modification (no returns)	5.2	5.2	9.2	9.7
Method modification (returns)	339.0	343.8	344.5	346.5
New selector	5.5	9.7	10.3	10.7
Dispatching wrapper	21.1	22.8	23.5	27.5
Class wrapper	5.9	9.8	10.5	10.9
Method wrapper	23.4	28.7	31.5	31.8
Inlined method wrapper	18.8	20.3	21.9	24.5

Figure 2 shows a MethodWrapper wrapping the `removeFirst` method of OrderedCollection. The CompiledMethod has been replaced by the MethodWrapper in the method dictionary. The MethodWrapper references the original method through its clientMethod variable. Also, the empty array that was initially compiled into the method has been replaced with a reference to the wrapper.

Like the new selector approach, MethodWrappers do not need to be compiled for each method. Instead they just need a prototype (with the same number of arguments) that can be copied. Once copied, the method sets its method literal, source index, mclass, and clientMethod. Since the method wrapper can directly execute the original method, no new entries are needed in the method dictionary for the original method.

Smalltalk's CompiledMethod objects and byte code were designed primarily to make Smalltalk portable. As with `doesNotUnderstand:`, Smalltalk's historic openness continues to pay unexpected dividends.

Table 1 and Table 2 compare the different approaches for both runtime overhead and installation time. These tests were performed on an 486/66 with 16MB memory running Windows 95 and VisualWorks 2.0. The byte code modification approach was not implemented, thus it is not shown. The dispatching wrapper has been omitted from the installation times since it is only an instance based technique. Added to the listings is an inlined method wrapper. This new method wrapper inlines the before and after code into the wrapper without defining the additional methods. This saves four message sends over the default method wrapper. Although it helps runtime efficiency, it hurts installation times since the inlined wrappers are larger.

Table 1 shows the overhead of each approach. The method modification approach has the lowest overhead if the method does not contain a return, but when it contains a return, the overhead for method modification jumps to more than ten times greater than the other techniques. Whenever a return occurs in a block, a context object is

Table 2. Installation times for 3,159 methods in 226 classes (sec)

Approach	Time
Method modification	262.6
New selector	25.5
Class wrapper	44.2
Method wrapper	17.0
Inlined method wrapper	19.9

created at runtime. Normally these context objects are not created so execution is much faster. The new selector and class wrapper approaches have the best overall times. The two method wrapper approaches and the dispatching wrapper approaches have more than double the overhead as the new selector or class wrapper approaches since the method wrappers and dispatching wrappers must create arrays of their arguments.

Table 2 contains the installation times for installing the various approaches on all subclasses of Model and its metaclass (226 classes with 3,159 methods). The method wrapper techniques are the fastest since they only need to change one entry in the method dictionary. The new selector approach is slightly slower since it needs to change two entries in the method dictionary. Although the class wrapper only needs to add one entry, it must scan object memory for instances of each class to convert them to use the new subclass wrapper. Finally, the method modification approach is the slowest since it must compile every method.

Because wrappers are relatively fast, and because the overhead associated with them is predictable, they may be more suitable in time-critical applications than classical Smalltalk approaches based on `doesNotUnderstand:`.

4 Applications

Method wrappers can be used in many different areas. In this section we outline six different uses.

4.1 Coverage Tool (Image Stripper)

One application that can use method wrappers is an image stripper. Strippers remove unused objects (usually methods and classes) from the image to make it more memory efficient. The default stripper shipped with VisualWorks only removes the development environment (compilers, browsers, etc.) from the image.

A different approach to stripping is to see what methods are used while the program is running and remove the unused ones. Finding the used methods is a coverage problem and can be handled by method wrappers. Instead of counting how many times a method is called, the method wrapper only needs a flag to signify if its method has been called. Once the method has been called, the original method can be restored so that future calls occur at normal speeds.

We created a subclass of MethodWrapper that adds two new instance variables, *selector* and *called*. The *selector* variable contains the method's selector, and *called* is a flag that signifies if the method has been called. Since the method wrapper does not need to do anything after the method is executed, it only needs to redefine the `beforeMethod` method:

```
beforeMethod
 called ifFalse:
   [called := true.
   mclass addSelector: selector
     withMethod: clientMethod]
```

This method first sets its flag and then reinstalls its original method. The `ifFalse:` test avoids infinite recursion in case that the method is called while performing the `addSelector:withMethod:` operation. Execution of the application program is slow at first, but it rapidly increases once the base set of methods is reinstalled.

The method wrapper correctly reports whether it has been called. However, this stripping scheme requires 100% method coverage. Any method that is not used by the test suite will be removed, so if a test suite does not provide 100% method coverage (which they rarely do) then the stripper will remove a method that is needed later. Removing methods in this manner can introduce errors into an otherwise correct program. Therefore, all methods should be saved to a file before they are removed. If one of the removed methods is called, it must be loaded, installed, and executed. The best way to detect that a deleted method has been called is with the `doesNotUnderstand:` mechanism, though it is also possible to use method wrappers for this purpose.

4.2 Class Collaboration

Method wrappers can also be used to dynamically analyze collaborating objects. For example, we might create call graphs that can help developers better understand how the software works. Furthermore, such information can help the developer visualize the coupling between objects. This can help the developer more quickly analyze when inappropriate objects are interacting.

Method wrappers can capture this information by getting the current context, just like the debugger does. Whenever a method is called, its wrapper needs to record who called the method, where the call occurred (which method and statement inside the method), the starting and ending times for the method, and finally how the method terminated (either normally with a return, or abnormally by a signal). Meth-

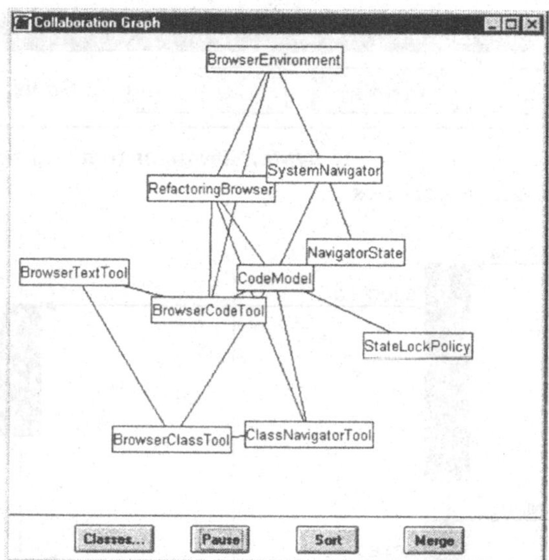

Fig. 3. Class collaboration graph of the Refactoring Browser

ods that return abnormally might be a problem since the programmers might not have programmed for such a case.

Using the information collected by the method wrappers, we can create a class collaboration graph such as the one shown in Figure 3. Whenever one object of a class sends a message to another object in another class, a line is drawn between them. Classes whose objects collaborate a lot are attracted to each other. The collaboration graph can help the programmer see which objects are collaborating as well as how much they are collaborating.

4.3 Interaction Diagrams

Interaction diagrams illustrate the dynamic sequence of the message traffic among several objects at runtime. The interaction diagram application allows users to select the set of methods that will be watched. These methods are wrapped, and the tool records traffic through them. When the wrappers are removed, the interactions among the objects that sent and received these messages are depicted, as in Figure 4.

The diagrams generated by the tool are similar to the interaction diagrams seen in many books, with one notable exception. Since we only select a few methods to observe, we miss some messages. As a result, there are times when a message is received, but the last method entered did not send the message. For example, suppose you have:

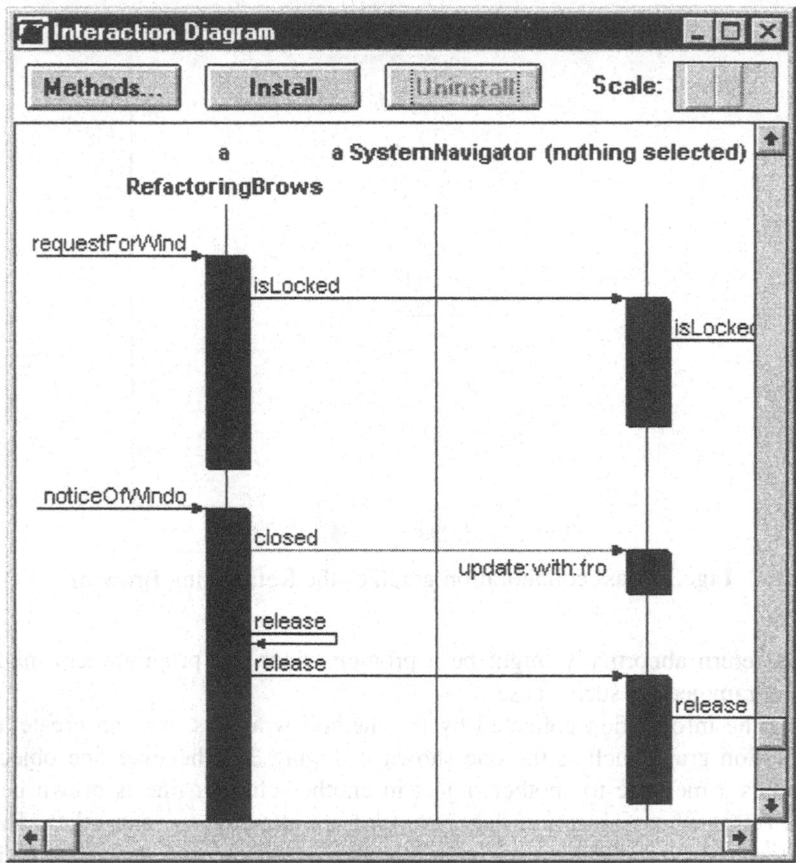

Fig. 4. Interaction Diagram on the Refactoring Browser

```
Foo>>createBar
   ^Bar new

Bar>>initialize
   "do some initialization"

Bar class>>new
   ^super new initialize
```

and that you only wrap `Foo>>createBar` and `Bar>>initialize`. If you send a `Foo` the `createBar` message, that event will be recorded. It will send the new message to `Bar` class, but since that method is not wrapped, it is not observed. When the new method sends the `initialize` method to a `Bar`, it is observed, but the last observed method did not send it. Such events are called indirect message sends and are displayed as yellow lines. In the figure, we can see that "a RefactoringBrowser" sent a `closed` message to some object that wasn't wrapped, which resulted in the `update:with:from:` method being called on "(nothing selected)" (a CodeModel).

Without a facility for wrapping the watched methods, tools would have to intervene at the source or binary code levels. For instance Lange and Nakamura [22] modify source code to instrument programs for tracing. The relative absence of such tools in languages without support for wrappers testifies to the difficulty of intervening at these levels.

Both Probe from Arbor Intelligent Systems and the Object Visualizer in IBM's VisualAge for Smalltalk generate interaction diagrams using method wrappers. Probe uses method wrappers that are very similar to those described in this paper except that the before and after code is been inlined into the wrapper.

The Object Visualizer uses a combination of lightweight classes and method wrappers to capture the runtime interaction information. However, their method wrappers do not directly reference the wrapped method. Instead they look up the method for every send. Instance wrappers would have been a better choice given this approach.

4.4 Synchronized Methods

Method wrappers are also useful for synchronizing methods. In a multithreaded environment, objects used concurrently by two different threads can become corrupt. A classic example in Smalltalk is the Transcript. The Transcript is a global variable that programs use to print output on. It is most often used to print debugging information. If two processes write to the Transcript at the same time, it can become corrupt and cause exceptions to be raised. To solve this problem we need to ensure that only one process accesses the Transcript at a time.

One solution would be to define a language construct for synchronization. For example, Java takes this approach by defining a method tag that is used to specify that a method is synchronized [13]. The system ensures that only one method that is tagged with the `synchronized` keyword is running at any time for an instance and only one static method that is tagged is running at any time for a single class.

The Smalltalk compiler does not need to directly support synchronized methods since Smalltalk exposes enough of its implementation to allow us to implement these features. For example, we can implement static synchronized methods by using method wrappers where each wrapper acquires its lock before executing the original method and releases it after the method executes. Similarly, the non-static synchronized methods can be implemented by using class wrappers where each instance would have its own class wrapper that would wrap each `super` message send with the lock. Method and class wrappers let us add this functionality in dynamically, whereas Java forces us to recompile to change the method's attribute.

4.5 Pre- and Post-conditions

Pre- and post-conditions help programmers produce quality software by describing a component and helping detect when it is being misused. The earlier an error is detected, the easier it is to fix. Eiffel supports pre- and post-conditions directly with the *require* and *ensure* keywords [25]. When conditions are enabled, invocations of the method are *required* to meet its conditions before executing and the method *ensures* its conditions after executing.

In systems like Smalltalk that do not directly support pre- and post-conditions, programmers sometimes write the checks directly into the code. For example, the `removeFirst` method in OrderedCollection checks that it is non-empty. Other times these conditions are written as comments in code, or not written down at all.

While it is useful to have these checks in the code when developing the software, they are not as useful after releasing the software. To the user, an unhandled empty collection signal raised by the empty check in `removeFirst` is the same as an unhandled index out of bounds signal that would be raised if the error check was eliminated. Both cause the product to fail. Therefore, to be useful to developer, a system that implements pre- and post-conditions should be able to add and remove them quickly and easily.

Pre- and post-conditions can be implemented by using method wrappers. For each method, a method wrapper would be created that would test the pre-condition, evaluate the wrapped method, and finally test the post-condition on exit.

Post-conditions can also have *old* values. Old values are useful in comparing values that occur before executing a method to the values after execution. To support old values, we added a special selector, `OLD`, that when sent to an expression will refer to the value of the expression before the execution of the method. Although this selector appears to be a message send, a preprocessing step replaces it with a temporary. The receiver of the message is then assigned to the temporary before the method is executed.

As an example, consider the `removeFirst` method of OrderedCollection. It might have a pre-condition such as "`self size > 0`" and a post-condition of "`self size OLD - 1 == self size`" (i.e., the size of the collection after execution is one less than the size before). The method wrapper for this example would be:

```
| old1 |
old1 := self size.
[self size > 0] value ifFalse:
   [self preconditionErrorSignal raise].
^["code to evaluate wrapped method"]
   valueNowOrOnUnwindDo:
      [[old1 - 1 == self size] value
        ifFalse: [self
         postconditionErrorSignal
          raise]]
```

Notice that the "`self size OLD`" from the post-condition has been replaced by a temporary and that the receiver, "`self size`", is assigned at the beginning of the wrapper.

Others have implemented pre- and post-conditions for Smalltalk [7, 27], but they modified the compiler to generate the conditions directly into the methods. Thus they require a complete recompile when (un)installing the conditions. [7] allowed conditions to be turned on and off, but they could only be completely eliminated by a complete recompile.

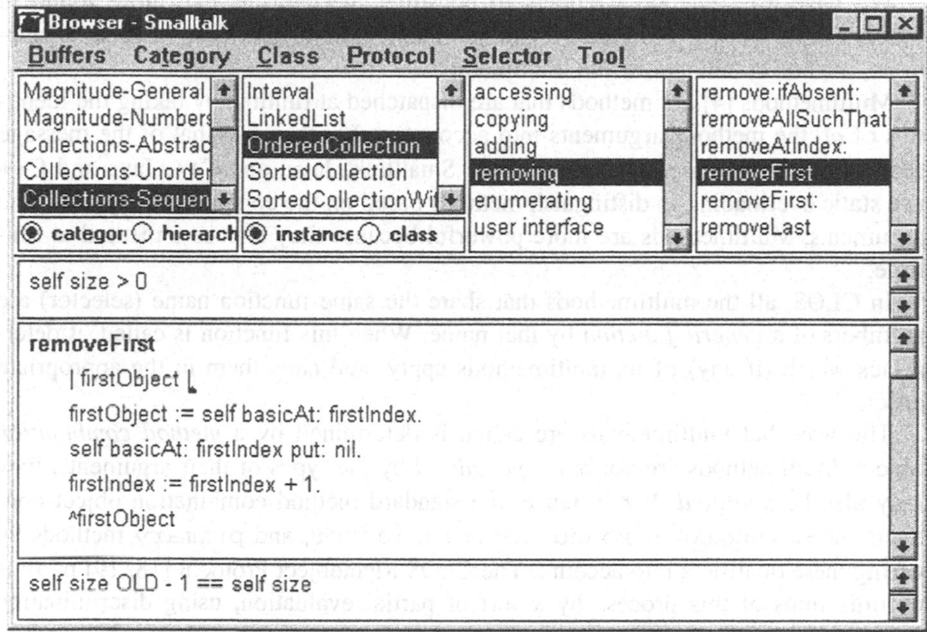

Fig. 5. Browser with pre and postconditions

Figure 5 shows a browser with pre- and post-conditions inspecting the `removeFirst` method. The three text panes at the bottom display the method's pre-condition, the source, and the post-condition. Both the pre-condition and the post-condition panes can be eliminated if the programmer does not wish to view them. Since the pre- and post-conditions are separated from the method, we don't need to augment the method definition with special keywords or special message sends as Eiffel and the other two Smalltalk implementations do.

4.6 Multimethods

The Common Lisp Object System and the CLOS Metaobject Protocol [18] provide elaborate facilities for method wrapping. The CLOS method combination mechanism provides programmers with a great deal of control over how different kinds of methods interact with the inheritance hierarchy to determine how and when methods are executed. The CLOS standard method combination mechanism executes the `:around` and `:before` methods in outermost to innermost order. Next, the primary methods are executed, followed by the `:after` methods in innermost to outermost order. Finally, the `:around` methods are resumed.

Our basic wrappers are much simpler. They execute the before code and primary code for each wrapper, before calling the wrapped method. If that method is wrapped, its before code and primary code is executed. Like CLOS `:around` methods, our wrappers may decide to not call their wrapped methods.

We have used method wrappers to construct mechanisms like those found in CLOS. Next, we will describe how to use them to build CLOS-style generic functions, method combination, and multimethods.

Multimethods [4] are methods that are dispatched at runtime by taking the identities of *all* the methods arguments into account, rather than just that of the message receiver, as is the case in languages like Smalltalk, Java, and C++. Java and C++ use static overloading to distinguish methods based on the compile-time types of the arguments. Multimethods are more powerful because they choose a method at runtime.

In CLOS, all the multimethods that share the same function name (selector) are members of a *generic function* by that name. When this function is called, it determines which (if any) of its multimethods apply, and calls them in the appropriate order.

The way that multimethods are called is determined by a *method combination* object. Multimethods are not only *specialized* by the types of their arguments, they may also be *qualified*. For instance, the standard method combination object conducts the execution of `:around`, `:before`, `:after`, and `primary` methods by taking these qualifiers into account. The CLOS Metaobject Protocol [18, 19] permits optimizations of this process by a sort of partial evaluation, using discriminating functions and effective methods.

Our Smalltalk multimethod implementation uses a dormant type syntax that is built into the VisualWorks Smalltalk compiler as its syntax for specializing multimethod arguments. This syntax lets us specify both ClassSpecializers, and EqualSpecializers for literal instances.

When the Smalltalk browser accepts a method with these specializations, it creates a MultiMethod object. MultiMethods are subclasses of CompiledMethod that are given selectors distinct from those of normal methods. MultiMethods also make sure there is an instance of GenericFunction for the selector for which they are being defined. GenericFunctions also keep track of one or more DiscriminatingMethods.

DiscriminatingMethods are subclasses of MethodWrapper that intercept calls that occupy the MethodDictionary slots where a normal method for their selector would go. When a DiscriminatingMethod gains control, it passes its receiver and arguments to its GenericFunction, which can then determine which MultiMethods to execute in what order. It does so by passing control to its MethodCombination object.

Subclasses of our MethodCombinations, besides implementing the standard before/after/primary –style combinations, can be constructed to collect the values of their primary methods, as in CLOS, or to call methods in innermost to outermost order, as in Beta [20].

Since a DiscriminatingMethod is called after a dispatch on its first argument has already been done, it can use that information to optimize its task.

To illustrate our syntax, as well as the power of multimethods, consider the impact of multimethods on the Visitor pattern [11]. First, consider a typical Smalltalk implementation of Visitor:

```
ParseNode>>acceptVistor: aVisitor
 ^self subclassResponsibility

VariableNode>>acceptVistor: aVisitor
 ^aVisitor visitWithVariableNode: self

ConstantNode>>acceptVistor: aVisitor
 ^aVisitor visitWithConstantNode: self

OptimizingVisitor>>visitWithConstantNode: aNode
 ^aNode value optimized

OptimizingVisitor>>visitWithVariableNode: aNode
 ^aNode lookupIn: self symbolTable
```

However, when MultiMethods are available, the double-dispatching methods in the ParseNodes disappear, since the type information does not need to be hand-encoded in the selectors of the calls to the Visitor objects. Instead, the Visitor correctly dispatches calls on the `visitWithNode:` GenericFunction to the correct MultiMethod. Thus, adding a Visitor no longer requires changing the ParseNode classes.

```
OptimizingVisitor>>visitWithNode: aNode <ParseNode>
        ^self value optimized

OptimizingVisitor>>
visitWithNode: aNode <VariableNode>
        ^aNode lookupIn: self symbolTable
```

The savings on the Visitor side may appear to be merely cosmetic. The `visitWithXxxNode:` methods are replaced by corresponding `visitWith-Node:` aNode <XxxNode> methods, which are specialized according to the sort of node they service. Even here, though, savings are possible when a particular node's implementation can be shared with that of its superclass. For instance, if many of `OptimizingVisitor's` multimethods would have sent the optimized message to their node's value, they can share the implementation of this method defined for `OptimizingVisitor` and `ParseNode`. The hand coded double-dispatched implementations usually provide a stub implementation of the subclass `Node's` version of the method so as to avoid a breach of encapsulation.

5 Other Approaches

Many systems provide ways for programs to augment or preempt the behavior of existing functions. If the language does not permit such modifications, programmers will often resort to low-level, implementation specific schemes to achieve their ends.

Wrapping strategies are not limited to languages. For instance, all the routines in the Macintosh Toolbox can be wrapped. The architects of the Toolbox designed it so that calls to the ROM-based built-in Toolbox functions were accessed indirectly through a table in RAM. This indirection allowed Apple to ship patched copies of

Toolbox entries to correct or supplement the existing routines. It also gave third-party software designers the opportunity to change the routines from which the system was built.

Over the years, Macintosh programmers have shown remarkable ingenuity in the ways that they've exploited these hooks into the system. For instance, applications like wide desktops and screen savers were built by wrapping the Toolbox. This shows the wisdom of designing systems with flexible foundations.

Programmers using Microsoft Windows have achieved similar results with the dynamic linking mechanism used to implement Dynamic Link Libraries (DLLs). A function can be wrapped by providing a wrapping implementation for it in a DLL that is referenced before the wrapped DLL.

C++ has no standard mechanisms for allowing programmers to intercept calls to C++ functions, virtual or otherwise. However, some programmers have exploited the most common implementation mechanism for dispatching C++ virtual functions, the "v-table" [9] to gain such access [29]. By falling back on unsafe C code, and treating v-table entries as simple C function pointers, programmers can dynamically alter the contents of the v-table entry for a class of objects. By substituting another function with the same signature for a given v-table entry, that entry can be wrapped with code that can add before and after actions before calling (or not calling) the original method.

Since the v-table mechanisms are not a part of the C++ standard, and since more complex features of C++ such as multiple inheritance and virtual bases often employ more elaborate implementations, programmers cannot write portable code that depends on "v-table surgery". Interestingly, C with Classes contained a mechanism [28] that allowed programmers to specify a function that would be called before every call to every member functions (except constructors) and another that would be called before every return from every member function. These `call` and `return` functions resemble dispatching wrappers.

In contrast to C++, the Microsoft Component Object Model (COM) [6] defines an explicit binary format that is similar to, and based upon, the customary implementation of simple C++ v-tables. Since any COM object must adhere to this format, it provides a potential basis for wrapping methods using v-table manipulation, since the rules by which v-tables must play are explicitly stated.

6 On the Importance of Being Open

Smalltalk's reflective facilities, together with our wrappers, allowed us to construct powerful program analysis tools and language extensions with relative ease. The ease with which we can add and remove wrappers at runtime makes tools like our interaction diagramming tool possible. In contrast, adding a feature like dynamic coverage analysis to an existing program is impossible for users of traditional systems, and difficult for the tool vendors.

While wrappers can, in principle, be used to solve problems at both the domain-level, or at the meta-, or language-level, the analysis tools and language extensions we present here are all reflective applications, in that they exploit our ability to manipulate program objects as pieces of the program itself, rather than as representations of application-level concerns.

In the case of *tools*, the fact that the program is built out of objects lets us inspect and alter these objects on-the-fly. Tools need an inside view of the program. For instance, when we wrap a CompiledMethod object using our interaction tool, we are exploiting its language level role as a program element and are indifferent to domain-specific behavior it engenders.

In the case of our *linguistic extensions*, the openness of the language's objects permitted us to construct these extensions, which were then used to write domain specific code. The use of raw reflective facilities to construct such extensions is a good way to harness the power of reflection.

None of the examples of method wrappers in this paper are domain specific. Domain specific uses of reflective facilities like before- and after- methods are frequently symptoms of problems with the application's structure that would be better addressed by refactoring its design. Reflective facilities are useful alternatives when a system becomes so overgrown that it can't be redesigned. Being able to change the language level gives programmers a big lever and can buy time until the resources to overhaul the system become available. However, metalevel tricks are no substitute for properly addressing a system's serious long-term structural problems.

A generation of Smalltalk programmers has turned to Smalltalk's lookup failure exception, `doesNotUnderstand:`, when the time came to extend the language. This paper has examined the strengths and weaknesses of several ways of intervening during the lookup process. Approaches based on `doesNotUnderstand:` have a brute force quality about them, since they must screen every message sent. Method wrappers let us intervene more precisely and selectively. When we needed a way to build power, efficient programming tools and language extensions, wrappers came to the rescue.

The original Smalltalk designers did a wonderful job of building a language out of objects that users can change. We rarely run into the "keep out" signs that so often frustrate users of other languages. This lets us add new tools to the programming environment, keep up with the latest database and network technology, and maintain and enhance our own systems as they evolve.

Acknowledgments

Ian Chai, Dragos Manolescu, Joe Yoder, and Yahya Mirza provided valuable comments and insights on an earlier version of this paper. James Noble suggested a useful simplification in our Visitor pattern example. The ECOOP '98 program committee reviewers also suggested a number of valuable improvements.

The interaction diagramming tool was originally a project done by David Wheeler, Jeff Will, and Jinghu Xu for Ralph Johnson's CS497 class. Their report on this project can be found at:

http://radon.ece.uiuc.edu/~dwheeler/interaction.html.

References

The code referenced in this article can be found at:

http://st-www.cs.uiuc.edu/~brant/Applications/MethodWrappers.html

1. Kent Beck. Using demand loading. *The Smalltalk Report*, 4(4):19-23, January 1995.
2. John K. Bennett. The design and implementation of distributed Smalltalk. In *Proceedings OOPSLA '87*, pages 318-330, December 1987. Published as ACM SIGPLAN Notices, volume 22, number 12.
3. Heinz-Dieter Böcker and Jürgen Herczeg, *What Tracers are Made Of*, ECOOP/OOPSLA '90 Conference Proceedings, SIGPLAN Notices, Volume 25, Number 10, October 1990
4. Dan G. Bobrow, Linda G. DeMichiel, Richard P. Gabriel, Sonya E. Keene, Gregor Kiczales, and David A. Moon. Common lisp object system specification. *SIGPLAN Notices*, 23, September 1988.
5. Daniel G. Bobrow and Mark Stefik. *The LOOPS Manual*. Xerox PARC, 1983.
6. Kraig Brockschmidt. *Inside OLE*, second edition, Microsoft Press, Redmond, Washington, 1995.
7. Manuela Carrillo-Castellon, Jesus Garcia-Molina, and Ernesto Pimentel. Eiffel-like assertions and private methods in Smalltalk. In *TOOLS 13*, pages 467-478, 1994.
8. Pierre Cointe, *The Classtalk System: a Laboratory to Study Reflection in Smalltalk*, OOPSLA/ECOOP '90 Workshop on Reflection and Metalevel Architectures in Object-Oriented Programming, Mamdouh Ibrahim, organizer.
9. Margaret A. Ellis and Bjarne Stroustrup. *The Annotated C++ Reference Manual*. Addison-Wesley, Reading, Massachusetts, 1990.
10. Brian Foote and Ralph E. Johnson. Reflective facilities in Smalltalk-80. In Proceedings *OOPSLA '89*, pages 327-336, October 1989. Published as ACM SIGPLAN Notices, volume 24, number 10.
11. Erich Gamma, Richard Helm, Ralph Johnson, and John Vlissides, *Design Patterns: Elements of Reusable Object-Oriented Software*, Addison-Wesley, 1995.
12. B. Garbinato, R. Guerraoui, and K. Mazoui. Implementation of the GARF Replicated Objects Platform. In *Distributed Systems Engineering Journal*, (2), 1995, 14–27.
13. James Gosling, Bill Joy, and Guy Steele, *The Java™ Language Specification*, Addison-Wesley, 1996.
14. R. Guerraoui, B. Garbinato, and K. Mazouni. The GARF System. In *IEEE Concurrency*, 5(4), 1997.
15. Bob Hinkle and Ralph E. Johnson. Taking exception to Smalltalk. *The Smalltalk Report*, 2(3), November 1992.
16. Bob Hinkle, Vicki Jones, and Ralph E. Johnson. Debugging objects. *The Smalltalk Report*, 2(9), July 1993.

17. Daniel H. H. Ingalls, The Evolution of the Smalltalk-80 Virtual Machine, in Smalltalk-80, Bits of History, Words of Advice, Glenn Krasner, editor, Addision-Wesley, Reading, MA, 1983
18. Gregor Kiczales, Jim des Rivieres, and Daniel G. Bobrow, *The Art of the Metaobject Protocol*, MIT Press, 1991.
19. Gregor Kiczales and John Lamping, *Issues in the Design and Implementation of Class Libraries*, OOPSLA '92, Vancouver, BC, SIGPLAN Notices Volume 27, Number 10, October 1992.
20. Bent Bruun Kristensen, Ole Lehrmann Madsen, Birger Moller-Pedersen, and Kristen Nygaard, *Object-Oriented Programming in the Beta Language*, 8 October, 1990.
21. Wilf R. LaLonde and Mark Van Gulik. Building a backtracking facility in Smalltalk without kernel support. In *Proceedings OOPSLA '88*, pages 105-122, November 1988. Published as ACM SIGPLAN Notices, volume 23, number 11.
22. Danny B. Lange and Yuichi Nakamura, Interactive Visualization of Design Patterns Can Help in Framework Understanding, In *Proceedings of OOPSLA '95*, pages 342-357, October 1995, Published as ACM SIGPLAN Notices, volume 30, number 10
23. Paul L. McCullough. Transparent forwarding: First steps. In *Proceedings OOPSLA '87*, pages 331-341, December 1987. Published as ACM SIGNPLAN Notices, volume 22, number 12.
24. Steven L. Messick and Kent L. Beck. Active variables in Smalltalk-80. Technical Report CR-85-09, Computer Research Lab, Tektronix, Inc., 1985.
25. Bertrand Meyer. *Eiffel: The Language*. Prentice-Hall, 1992.
26. Geoffrey A. Pascoe. Encapsulators: A new software paradigm in Smalltalk-80. In *Proceedings OOPSLA '86*, pages 341-346, November 1986. Published as ACM SIGPLAN Notices, volumc21, number 11.
27. Fred Rivard. Smalltalk: a reflective language. In *Proceedings Reflection '96*.
28. Bjarne Stroustrop. *The Design and Evolution of C++*. Addison-Wesley, Reading, MA 1994.
29. Michael D. Tiemann. Solving the RPC problem in GNU C++. In 1988 USENIX C++ Conference, pages 17-21, 1988.
30. D. Weinreb, and D. Moon. Lisp Machine Manual, Symbolics, 1981.

Design and Partial Evaluation of Meta-objects for a Concurrent Reflective Language

Hidehiko Masuhara[1] and Akinori Yonezawa[2]

[1] Department of Graphics and Computer Science, Graduate School of Arts and Sciences, University of Tokyo
masuhara@graco.c.u-tokyo.ac.jp
[2] Department of Information Science, University of Tokyo
yonezawa@is.s.u-tokyo.ac.jp

Abstract. Customizable meta-objects are a powerful abstraction for extending language features and implementation mechanisms, but interpretive execution suffers from severe performance penalty. Some of this penalty can be reduced by applying partial evaluation to meta-*interpreters,* but partial evaluation of meta-*objects* in existing concurrent object-oriented languages is ineffective. This paper proposes a new meta-object design for our reflective language ABCL/R3. It yields meta-objects that can be optimized effectively using partial evaluation. The crux of the design is the separation of state-related operations from other operations, and this separation is accomplished by using reader/writer methods in our concurrent object-oriented language called Schematic. Our benchmark trials show that non-trivial programs with partially evaluated meta-objects run more than six times faster than ones that are interpreted by meta-objects. In addition, a partially evaluated program that uses a *customized* meta-object runs as efficiently as a program that is manually rewritten so as to have the same functionality without using meta-objects.

1 Introduction

1.1 Reflection in Parallel/Distributed Programs

The structure of objects in parallel and distributed applications tends to be complex because they would otherwise not be efficient, reliable, portable and reusable. A number of language mechanisms—inheritance, transaction, object migration, etc.—reducing this complexity have therefore been proposed. Guarded method invocation, for example, which accepts invocation requests conditionally, is useful for describing objects like bounded buffers. In many languages, however, such mechanisms are not always implemented because (1) some are incompatible with each other, (2) supporting a new mechanism can degrade the language efficiency even when the mechanism is not used in a program, and (3) implementation of a new mechanism in the language requires a tremendous amount of effort.

A possibly better approach is to extend languages by using meta-objects. By installing a customized meta-object, the application programmer can use a new language mechanism as if it were built-in. Advanced programmers can even develop their own meta-objects to meet specific requirements. This approach is also beneficial to the language implementors; they can devote themselves to the implementation of *simple core* languages, leaving hard-to-be-implemented mechanisms to be dealt with as extensions.

We are consequently developing a reflective object-oriented concurrent language, ABCL/R3, in which we provide such extensibility by means of *computational reflection*[17, 24]. In ABCL/R3, a *meta-object* provides an abstraction with which the user can extend or modify crucial mechanisms of an object (e.g., method invocation request, method dispatch, state management, and mutual exclusion). In addition, a *meta-interpreter* provides an abstraction that can be used to customize the syntax and semantics of bodies of methods and functions. *Reflective annotations,* which can also be defined by means of meta-level programming, are used as programming directives in base-level programs.

The features of ABCL/R3 have been described in detail elsewhere[19, 21]. The present paper discusses the meta-object design of ABCL/R3 from the viewpoint of efficient implementation.

1.2 Techniques for Implementation of Meta-objects

Despite the extensibility they provide, customizable meta-objects have a problem with regard to efficiency. Assume that a meta-object implements a customized method dispatch algorithm. In a naive implementation, the method dispatch for the corresponding base-level object is achieved by a number of method invocations at the meta-level; i.e., by *interpretive execution.* Moreover, the customization hinders the application of important optimization techniques such as method inlining[4] because such techniques are defined under the assumption that the semantics (rules for method dispatch, in this case) of the language is stable. As a result, the existence of meta-objects easily slow the execution of the language by a factor of more than 10.

There have been several studies on this problem:

- Some parts of the meta-system are not subject to meta-level modification by means of reification. In the reflective language Open C++ version 1[6], for example, only message passing, object creation, and instance variable accesses can be reified. This not only restricts user programmability, but also makes the language model unclear because much of the meta-level functionalities are hidden inside 'black-boxes.' The programmer therefore cannot get a clear view of how his meta-level programming and the black boxes will interact.

  Another example is JDK 1.1, which offers "reflection" API[25]. It supports only introspective operations, which are obviously implemented efficiently. They give, however, few extensibility at the same time.

– The system embodies a set of ad-hoc optimizations transparent to the user. For example, our previous language ABCL/R2[20] assumes that most objects will not be customized, and thus compiles objects without meta-objects. When the user accesses a meta-object, the corresponding object is then switched to general interpreted execution. Its effectiveness, however, is limited to cases where optimization is possible. When optimization is not possible, the interpretation overhead greatly affects the overall performance.
– The compiler inspects behavior of a meta-level program with respect to a base-level program and removes interpretation by using techniques like partial evaluation[12]. This approach is more systematic than the above two approaches, but it requires intensive analysis of the meta-level program that may include user customization.

1.3 Optimization Using Partial Evaluation

A base-level program in a reflective language is executed by an interpreter. The interpreter, which is represented as an object at the meta-level of the language, can be customized by the programmer. Once the base-level program is given, however, most computation that depends only on the base-level program can be performed in advance to the program execution. By removing such computation, a specialized program that contains computation which depends on run-time data for the base-level program, can thus be extracted from the meta-level computation. This process is often referred as *partial evaluation*[12] of the meta-level program with respect to the base-level program, or as the first Futamura projection[7]. Our previous studies successfully apply partial evaluation to the meta-*interpreters* in reflective languages[2, 19].

Meta-*objects*, in theory, could also be optimized by partial evaluation, but they actually cannot because (1) the design of meta-objects in existing reflective languages is not suitable for partial evaluation, and (2) there are few partial evaluators that can deal with concurrent objects. We therefore redesigned meta-objects with consideration to the application of partial evaluation, and here we will show an optimization framework for the resulting meta-objects.

The rest of the paper is organized as follows: In Section 2 we discuss why reasoning about the meta-objects is difficult by reviewing an existing meta-object design. In Section 3 we describe our proposed meta-object design, and in Section 4 we describe its optimization technique by using partial evaluation. In Section 5 we show our performance evaluation of the optimized objects, and in Section 6 we discuss other techniques for the efficient implementation of meta-objects. In Section 7 we conclude by briefly summarizing the paper.

2 Problems of Existing Meta-object Design

Many concurrent object-oriented languages have mutual exclusion mechanisms to assure consistency. A conservative, commonly found, approach is to mutually exclude all method executions on an object. This approach alleviates the programmers' concern about interference with multiple read/write operations on an instance variable.

The mutual exclusion mechanism in a language drastically affects the meta-object design. This is because (1) the meta-objects explicitly implement the mechanism of base-level objects, and (2) the meta-objects, themselves, are implicitly controlled by a certain mutual exclusion mechanism, which is usually the same one as base-level objects.

In order to meet the above requirements, a meta-object is defined as a *state transition machine* in previous reflective languages. For example, Figure 1 is a simplified definition[1] of the default meta-object in the language ABCL/R[28]. Its state transition diagram can be illustrated as in Figure 2.

A method invocation on a base-level object is represented by an invocation of the method `receive!`[2] on its meta-object. In `receive!`, the message (an object that contains the method name and arguments) is immediately put into the message queue (`queue`), so that it will eventually be processed. If the object is not processing any methods (i.e., `mode` is `'dormant`), the meta-object changes `mode` to `'active` and calls the method `accept!`.

The method `accept!` gets one message from `queue` and lets the evaluator execute the matching method for the message. The evaluator interprets expressions of the method recursively, and when it reaches the end of the base-level method, it invokes the method `finish!` of the meta-object. The method `finish!` examines `queue` for any pending messages received during the evaluation. If `queue` is empty, the meta-object changes `mode` to `'dormant`. Otherwise, it invokes `accept!` again for further execution.

When we apply partial evaluation to this meta-object definition with respect to a certain base-level object, the result is far from satisfactory. The reasons are the following:

- Since the meta-object is defined as a state transition machine, its behavior cannot be determined without static information on some key instance variables such as `mode` and `queue`. For example, if the return value of `(get! queue)` in the method `accept!` were "unknown" (dynamic) at the specialization time, method dispatch (`(find methods m)`) and interpretation of the method body (`(eval evaluator exp env self)`) would be left unspecialized. This means that a large amount of interpretive computation cannot be eliminated by merely applying partial evaluation.
- Information that should be "known" (static) to the partial evaluator is transferred via instance variables between consecutive method invocations. Such information is not available on the receiver's side unless data structures are analyzed extensively. For example, the value of `(get! queue)` in `accept!`, which would be the value of `message` in `receive!`, is crucial for specializa-

[1] The syntax of the definition is that of in Schematic's[27] for the sake of uniformity.
[2] The exclamation mark in the method name conventionally indicates that the method may change the object's state.

```
;;; Class definition
(define-class metaobj ()
  mode queue state methods evaluator) ; instance variables

;;; Method definition for class metaobj
(define-method! metaobj (receive! self message)
  ;; Here, self is bound to the meta-object itself.
  (put! queue message)
  (if (eq? mode 'dormant)                  ; If it is dormant, the received
    (begin (set! mode 'active)             ; message is accepted immediately.
           (future (accept! self)))))

;;; method dispatch
(define-method! metaobj (accept! self)
  (let* ((mes (get! queue))                         ; Get a message from the queue.
         (m (find methods mes))                     ; method lookup
         (env (make-env self (formals m) mes)));  creation of an evaluation env.
    (future (eval evaluator (exps m) env self)))); evaluation

;;; end of method execution
(define-method! metaobj (finish! self)
  (if (empty? queue)                       ; Check the queue for pending messages.
      (set! mode 'dormant)                 ; If none, turn into the dormant mode.
      (future (accept! self))))            ; Otherwise, accept one of them.

;;; meta-interpreter
(define-method! metaobj (eval self exp env owner)
  It evaluates exp under env.  When finished, it invokes finish! of owner.  )
```

The expression (future (m r $e_1 \ldots e_n$)) *asynchronously* invokes method m of object r with parameters $e_1 \ldots e_n$. It is asynchronous in that the sender continues subsequent computation without waiting for the return value. The expression, (m r $e_1 \ldots e_n$), on the other hand, is *synchronous* invocation; the sender waits for the return value.

Fig. 1. Definition of an ABCL/R meta-object.

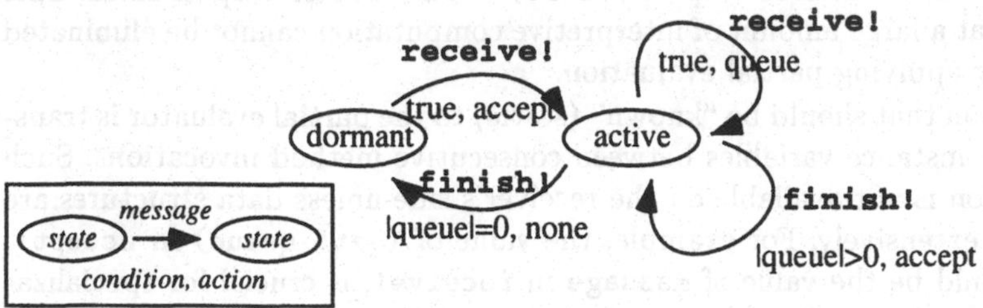

Fig. 2. State transition diagram of an ABCL/R meta-object.

tion, but obtaining it requires analysis of queue. This requirement sometimes become overwhelming because queue might be a user-defined object.

– The key instance variables are mutable; i.e., their values are changed during execution. The execution model of the meta-objects—ABCM[29] in this case—however, specifies that method invocations will be processed in FIFO order in each object. We thus have to anticipate that the execution of two consecutive methods may be interleaved; i.e., it is safe to assume that mutable instance variables may be changed between method invocations. For example, assume that the method `receive!` invokes the method `accept!`. The variable queue at the beginning of `accept!` may have a value different from the one in `receive!` because other methods can be executed before the execution of `accept!`. Though there are partial evaluators that can deal with mutable variables, they regard a mutable variable as unknown (dynamic) unless they can statically determine all update operations to the variable[1, 3].

For the above reasons, a partial evaluator conservatively regards most variables as "dynamic." Without much of "static" information, the partial evaluator yields a program that still performs almost all the computation as the program for the original meta-object does.

3 A New Meta-object Design

We propose, for a reflective concurrent object-oriented language ABCL/R3[19, 21], a meta-object design that can be effectively optimized by partial evaluation. The key idea is to separate, using the reader and writer methods of Schematic, state-related operations from the other operations.

3.1 Reader/Writer Methods

Schematic[23, 27] is a concurrent object-oriented language based on Scheme. It has concurrency primitives such as *future* and *touch* and has class-based objects, but we describe only the *reader/writer methods* because they play key roles in our meta-object design.

The construct `define-method!` defines a *writer method*, which can modify values of instance variables in an object. At the end of a writer method, there should be a form "(`become` *rexp* :v_1 e_1 :v_2 e_2 ...)". When this form is evaluated, expressions e_i are first evaluated in sequence. Then the results are set to the variables v_i all at once. Finally, the expression *rexp* is evaluated. The value of *rexp* is returned as the result of the `become` form. Multiple invocations of writer methods on an object are mutually excluded. (Precisely, the evaluation of *rexp* is not excluded; i.e., the *critical section* finishes immediately after updating instance variables.)

The construct `define-method` defines a *reader method*, which cannot modify instance variables. The reader methods are not governed by the mutual exclusion mechanism; a reader method on an object can even be executed concurrently with a writer method on the same object. During execution of a reader method, the instance variables are bound to the values extracted from the object's state at the beginning of the method. Even when a writer method executes `become` to modify some of the instance variables, reader methods that have started their execution before the `become` operation do not observe the effect of modification.

3.2 Proposed Meta-object Design

The outline of a new meta-object design solving the problems discussed in Section 2 is shown in Figure 3, in which we exploit the reader/writer methods of Schematic. Our design has the following characteristics:

- The behavior of the meta-object is principally defined in the reader methods. Operations that deal with mutable data are defined separately as writer methods or as method invocations on external objects. For example, values of instance variables that are mutable are packed in the mutable vector object `state-values`, and accesses to `state-values` are effected by using the writer methods `cell-set!` and `cell-ref`.
- The meta-object straightforwardly processes each method invocation request and provides mutual exclusion by using blocking operations (e.g., `acquire!` and `release!`). As a result, the meta-object is no longer a state-transition machine. The reader methods, which can be invoked without mutual exclusion, make it possible to define such a meta-object. If the meta-objects were defined with only writer methods, use of the blocking operations would easily lead to deadlock.
- For mutual exclusion, a meta-object has the instance variable `lock` in place of `mode` and `queue`. By default, `lock` is a simple semaphore that has the operations `acquire!` and `release!`. The user can replace `lock` with an arbitrary object, such as a FIFO queue and a priority queue, by means of the meta-level programming.

These characteristics solve the application problems of partial evaluation that were discussed in Section 2. (1) Under the execution model of Schematic[27], it is safe to assume that consecutive invocations of reader methods are not interrupted by other activities; we therefore can use most partial evaluation techniques for sequential languages by regarding the reader methods as functions. (2) Since the "known" (static) information is propagated through the arguments of the method invocations, the partial evaluators easily use such information for specialization. (3) The mutual exclusion mechanism, which is implemented by the blocking operations, gets rid of the dynamic branches (conditionals with dynamic predicates) that would cause a termination-detection problem during specialization.

How the methods in Figure 3 handle messages sent to the base-level object is explained as follows:

```
;;; Class definition
(define-class metaobj ()
  lock state-variables state-values methods evaluator)

;;; Reception of a message
(define-method metaobj (receive self message)
  (if (writer? (selector message))          ; check message type
      (accept-W self message)               ; for a writer method
      (accept self message 'dummy)))        ; for a reader method

;;; Processing for a writer method
(define-method metaobj (accept-W self message)
  (let ((c (make-channel)))                 ; channel for receiving updated state
    (acquire! lock)                         ; mutual exclusion begins
    (let ((result (accept self messages c)))
      (cell-set! state-values (touch c))    ; update instance variables
      (release! lock)                       ; end of mutual exclusion
      result)))

;;; Method lookup and invocation
(define-method metaobj (accept self message update-channel)
  (let* ((m (find methods message))        ; method lookup
         (env (make-env self (formals m) message)))
    (future (eval evaluator (method-body m) env update-channel))))

;;; Meta-interpreter
(define-method evaluator (eval self exp env update-channel)
  It evaluates exp under env. When a become form is evaluated, it creates a
  vector of new updated instance variables, and sends it to update-channel. )
```

The primitive `make-channel` creates an empty channel, which is a communication medium among concurrently running threads. A thread sends a value to a channel *c* by executing `(reply value c)`, and receives from *c* by `(touch c)`.

Fig. 3. Our new meta-object design.

receive: The method `receive` simply proceeds to invoke methods `accept-W` or `accept`, depending on the type of the base-level method that is to be invoked.

accept-W: The method `accept-W` wraps the method `accept` in the code for mutual exclusion and update of base-level instance variables. It first locks the object and then calls the method `accept` of the same object with a channel `c`. It then waits for a vector of updated instance variables—which is sent by the `become` form in the base-level method—on `c` by executing the `touch` form and updates `state-values` with the received value. Finally, it unlocks the object and returns the result of the method. Note that `accept-W` itself does not modify instance variables.

accept: The method `accept` merely looks up a method for a given message and lets the evaluator execute it. The method `make-env`, whose definition is omitted, creates an evaluation environment. It first extracts a vector of instance variable values by executing `(cell-ref state-values)` and then creates an association list that maps each of the instance variable names to the extracted value and maps each formal parameter name of the method to the parameter value in the `message`.

eval: The method `eval` of class `evaluator` and its auxiliary methods embody a meta-circular interpreter, which is similar to the traditional Lisp meta-circular interpreter. When it encounters a `become` form, it creates a vector of the updated instance variables and then sends the vector to `update-channel`.

Since the reader/writer methods are not supported in the previous meta-objects, the proposed meta-object design does not have the same semantics as the previous one.

4 Optimization Using Partial Evaluation

In our proposed meta-objects, most operations are defined in the reader methods, and a few invocations on external objects are used for mutual exclusion and state modification. As we stated earlier, the meta-objects can, from the viewpoint of partial evaluation, be regarded as functional programs with I/O-type side-effects. In this section we describe an optimization framework for our meta-objects by using partial evaluation.

The biggest problem we face in using partial evaluation is that there are no partial evaluators appropriate for our purpose because the meta-object is written in a *concurrent* object-oriented language. Although there are studies on partial evaluators for concurrent languages[8, 9, 18], they focus on concurrency and pay little attention to the support of features crucial to sequential languages, such as function closures and data structures.

Our solution is to translate meta-objects into a sequential program and use a partial evaluator for a sequential language. Partial evaluation is applied for each base-level method invocation; i.e., the specialization point is a base-level method invocation. Since the methods of meta-objects exhibit almost sequential

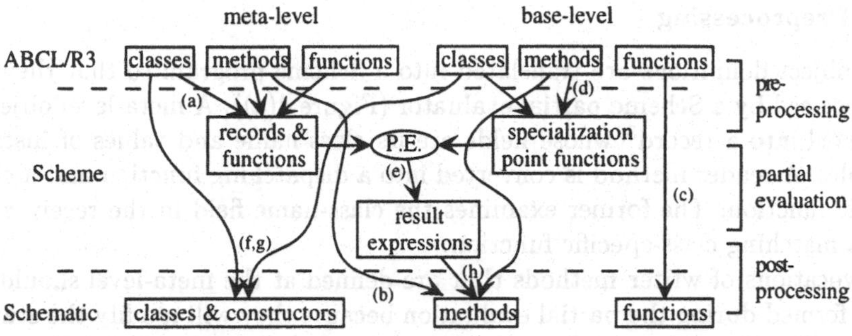

Fig. 4. Overview of our optimization framework.

```
;;; 2d-point
(define-class point () x y)

;;; returns the distance from the origin---a reader method
(define-method point (distance self)
  (sqrt (+ (square x) (square y))))

;;; moves a point---a writer method
(define-method! point (move! self dx dy)
  (become #t :x (+ x dx) :y (+ y dy)))
```

Fig. 5. Example base-level program.

behavior, the partial evaluator for a sequential language can effectively optimize the meta-objects. Concurrency in the meta-objects will be residualized as applications to primitives.

Another problem is compatibility with other objects. The optimized object should support meta-level operations that are defined in the original meta-object. At the same time, the object should behave like a base-level object so that it can be used with other base-level objects. To satisfy these two requirements, our framework generates an object that combines the base- and meta-level objects in a single level. The object has the same methods that are in the original base-level object, and the body of each method is a specialized code of the meta-object.

Figure 4 shows the overview of our optimization framework, in which there are three steps: (1) translation from ABCL/R3 to Scheme, (2) partial evaluation, and (3) translation from Scheme to Schematic. In the following subsections we explain each step in detail by using an example base-level program (Figure 5) and the default meta-object `metaobj` (Figure 3).

4.1 Preprocessing

Meta-object definitions are translated into a Scheme program so that they can be processed by a Scheme partial evaluator (Figure 4(a)). A meta-level object is converted into a record[3] whose fields are its class name and values of instance variables. A reader method is converted into a dispatching function and a class-specific function. The former examines the class-name field in the receiver and calls a matching class-specific function.

Invocations of writer methods that are defined at the meta-level should not be performed during the partial evaluation because they will modify the state of objects. Therefore, the writer methods are not passed to the partial evaluators but are instead simply copied into the resulting Schematic program (Figure 4(b)).

No translations are needed for the base-level definitions, since they are used as data for the meta-level program. Functions, however, are simply copied to the resulting Schematic program (Figure 4(c)).

4.2 Partial Evaluation

We partially evaluate the meta-level program for each *base-level method invocation.* For example, given the base-level program like that in Figure 5, the meta-level computation that will be processed is the one corresponding to the following base-level method invocation:

$$(\texttt{move!}\ p\ dx\ dy)$$
$$\text{where } p = \texttt{point\{x} = x,\ \texttt{y} = y\texttt{\}}.$$

The variables written in italic font (e.g., dx, dy, x, and y) are dynamic data. The data denoted by the variable p is a partially static; it is known as an object of class `point`, but values of instance variables `x` and `y` are dynamic (unknown).

The corresponding meta-level computation is the following expression:

$$(\texttt{receive}\ \mathit{mobj}\ \mathit{message})$$

where

$$\begin{aligned}
\mathit{mobj} &= \texttt{metaobj\{class} = \texttt{'point},\\
&\qquad \texttt{methods} = \texttt{'((distance (self) ...) ...)},\\
&\qquad \texttt{state-vars} = \texttt{'(x y)},\ \texttt{state-values} = s,\ \texttt{lock} = l,\\
&\qquad \texttt{evaluator} = \texttt{(make-evaluator)\}},\\
\mathit{message} &= \texttt{message\{selector} = \texttt{'move!},\ \texttt{arguments} = \texttt{(list}\ dx\ dy\texttt{)\}}.
\end{aligned}$$

To partially evaluate a meta-level computation like the above one, we generate a specialization point function for each base-level method (Figure 4(d)). The function takes as its arguments a vector of instance variables, lock, and parameters for the method. When called, it creates *mobj* and *message*, and it invokes the method `receive` on *mobj* (Figure 6). The function is specialized under the assumption that all the arguments are dynamic.

[3] Since our partial evaluator does not natively support records, we further translate the record into `cons`-cells.

```
(define (specalization-point-move!-point state-values lock dx dy)
  (let ((mobj (metaobject 'point '((distance (self) ...) ...)
                          '(x y) state-values lock
                          (make-evaluator)))
        (message (message 'move! (list dx dy))))
    (receive mobj message)))
```

Fig. 6. Specialization point function for method move! of class point.

An online partial evaluator for Scheme[3] (Figure 4(e)) specializes not only the methods of metaobj, but also those of evaluator[4]. The compilation techniques of the meta-interpreter are described elsewhere[19].

4.3 Postprocessing

The final step is to translate the results of partial evaluation (in Scheme) back into concurrent objects (in Schematic). This is done by generating class declarations, constructor functions, and methods as shown in Figure 7.

- For each combination of base- and meta-level classes, a specialized class is defined (Figure 4(f)). Since the class is a specialized version of the meta-level class, it has the same instance variables as the original meta-object. (E.g., the class metaobject**point in Figure 7.)
- A function that mimics the base-level constructor is defined for each specialized class (Figure 4(g)). For example, the function point in Figure 7 is a base-level constructor that creates an object belonging to class metaobject**point with proper initial values.
- Methods of the specialized classes are defined (Figure 4(h)). The name of each method is the same as that of the original base-level method. (The method distance and move! of class metaobject**point in Figure 7 are examples.) The specialized object therefore has the same interface as the original base-level program. The body of the method is the result of partial evaluation. Note that because the generated methods are specialized versions of receive of the meta-object, they should be defined as reader methods regardless of the type of the corresponding base-level method.

When a meta-object is specialized with respect to a reader method, the optimized method has the essentially same definition as the original base-level method, except for the indirect accesses to the instance variables (cf. the method distance in Figure 7). When it is specialized with respect to a writer method, on the other hand, the optimized method evidently contains extra operations. Although most of the operations in the optimized method are the same as the

[4] For convenience in executing the benchmark programs, instead of using a real meta-interpter we used a *fake evaluator* that directly executes the body of methods. This will be discussed in Section 5.

```
;;; a combined class of metaobject w.r.t. point
(define-class metaobject**point ()
  class methods state-vars state-values lock evaluator)

;;; constructor
(define (point x y)
  (metaobject**point
   (quote *metaobject*) (quote *methods*) (quote (x y))
   (make-cell (vector x y)) (make-lock) (quote *evaluator*)))

;;; reader method
(define-method metaobject**point (distance self)
  (begin (let* ((values0 (read-cell state-values))
                (x0 (vector-ref values0 0))
                (y0 (vector-ref values0 1))
                (g0 (square x0))
                (g1 (square y0)))
           (sqrt (+ g0 g1)))))

;;; writer method
(define-method metaobject**point (move! self dx dy)
  (begin (acquire! lock)
         (let* ((state-update-channel0 (make-channel))
                (values0 (read-cell state-values))
                (x0 (vector-ref values0 0))
                (y0 (vector-ref values0 1))
                (g0 (vector (+ x0 dx) (+ y0 dy))))
           (reply g0 state-update-channel0)
           (let ((new-state0 (touch state-update-channel0)))
             (update-cell! state-values new-state0)
             (release! lock)
             #t))))
```

Fig. 7. Result of optimization (the underlined expressions come from the base-level method).

operations performed in a writer method in Schematic, others are amenable to further optimization. For example, the newly created vector of instance variables g0 is handed over by means of `reply` and `touch` operations in the same thread because our current partial evaluator regards those operations as mere "unknown" functions. An optimized method less extra operations could be produced by using partial evaluators for concurrent languages or by applying static analysis for concurrent programs[10, 15, 16] to the resulting code.

5 Performance Evaluation

To evaluate the efficiency of our partially evaluated meta-objects, we executed benchmark programs in the following three ways:

PE(partially evaluated): The default meta-object was partially evaluated with respect to each benchmark program, and the generated code was further compiled by Schematic. This showed the performance of our optimization framework.

INT(interpreted): The default meta-object was directly compiled by Schematic, and then the compiled code interpreted the benchmark programs. This showed the performance of naively implemented meta-objects.

NR(nonreflective): The benchmark programs were directly compiled by Schematic[5]. This showed the performance of nonreflective languages.

All programs were executed on Sun UltraEnterprise 4000 that had 1.2GB memory, 14 UltraSparc processors,[6] each operating at 167MHz, and was running SunOS 5.5.1.

The differences between the PE and INT performances show the amount of speedup gained by partial evaluation, while the differences between the PE and NR performance show the *residual overheads*—the overheads that the partial evaluator fails to eliminate.

The overheads solely caused by the meta-objects, were evaluated by executing the body expressions in PE and INT without meta-interpreters. For example, when a base-level program has an expression "`(distance p)`," then a meta-object looks up `distance` in its method table and extracts instance variables from `p`. However, the method body "`(sqrt (+ (square x) (square y)))`" should be executed directly. To do this, we generate a *fake evaluator* for each base-level class (Figure 8). Without fake evaluators, interpretive execution of method bodies would make an overwhelmingly large contribution to the execution time in INT. The fake evaluators are also useful for skipping over the partial evaluation of meta-interpreters whenever a base-level object uses only the default meta-interpreter.

[5] Our Schematic compiler has some overheads for concurrent execution; a sequential program (Richards) compiled by a sequential Scheme compiler (DEC Scheme-to-C) was faster than the one compiled by Schematic by a factor of 5.4.

[6] Though we used a multi-processor machine, the programs are executed on a single processor execution.

```
;;; Class definition
(define-class evaluator**point ())

;;; The method called by the meta-object.
(define-method evaluator**point (eval-begin self method-name exp env)
  (cond ((eq? method-name 'distance) ; for method distance
         (let ((x (lookup 'x env)) (y (lookup 'y env)))
           (sqrt (+ (square x) (square y)))))
        ((eq? method-name 'move!)     ; for method move!
         (let ((x (lookup 'x env)) (y (lookup 'y env))
               (dx (lookup 'dx env)) (dy (lookup 'dy env)))
           (let ((new-values (vector (+ x dx) (+ y dy))))
             (update self new-values))))))
```

Each clause of the cond form in eval-begin corresponds to the method of the base-level class point. A clause is selected by the argument method-name. The body part of a clause has the code for extracting the base-level arguments and instance variables and for the method body. A become form in the original program is converted into an invocation of the update method of the meta-object, which takes a vector of the updated instance variables as an argument.

Fig. 8. "Fake" evaluator for point.

5.1 Base-level Applications

The following three kinds of programs were executed as the base-level applications:

Null Readers and Null Writers: Elapsed time for 1,000,000 method invocations was measured by repeatedly calling a null method on an object. We tested objects with different numbers of instance variables (i) and tested methods with different numbers of arguments (j). The average time over some parameter combinations ($i \in \{0, 5, 10\}, j \in \{1, 5, 10\}$) are shown as a representative result.

Become: Elapsed time for 1,000,000 invocations of writer methods which update instance variables was measured by repeatedly calling a method that immediately performs become. We tested objects with different numbers of updated variables (k), and the average time over the parameter combinations $i = 10, j = 1, k \in \{1, 5, 10\}$ is shown as the representative result[7].

Richards: The Richards benchmark is an operating system simulation that is used as a nontrivial program in evaluating several object-oriented languages[4].

RNA: RNA is a parallel search program for predicting RNA secondary structures[22, 26]. This program uses an object to maintain and to share information the found answers among concurrently running threads.

[7] The combination of the values of i and j yields the worst result in Null Writers.

Table 1. Performance improvement and residual overheads.

benchmark applications	elapsed time (sec.) PE	INT	NR	improvement INT/PE	residual overheads PE/NR
Null Readers	3.2	107.7	2.3	33.6	1.4
Null Writers	40.7	190.8	16.9	4.7	2.4
Become	46.6	272.8	15.7	5.9	3.0
(w/manual opt.)	(21.3)			(12.8)	(1.4)
Richards	20.7	140.7	9.4	6.8	2.1
RNA	1.7	53.3	1.6	30.8	1.1

Since Richards and RNA use both functions and methods, their executions show how the efficiency of the meta-objects affects overall execution speed in realistic applications.

The results are summarized in Table 1. As the "improvement" column shows, the programs in PE are more than four times faster than the ones in INT. This improvement is significant even in realistic applications such as Richards and RNA, whose speeds are increased by factors of 6.8 and 30.8, respectively.

As the "residual overheads" column shows, the programs in PE are slower than the ones in NR by factors of 1.1–3.0. These overheads are mainly due to the limitations of current partial evaluators, as we have pointed out in Section 4.3. In fact, when we further optimized the partially evaluated meta-objects for Become by hand—eliminating obvious channel communications, etc.—the average factor by which programs are slowed because of residual overheads was reduced to 1.4.

5.2 Performance of Customized Meta-objects

The above benchmark programs were executed under the default meta-objects, but of more practical interest is the efficiency of *customized* meta-objects. The next benchmark program was a bounded-buffer that uses the guarded method invocation mechanism, which is implemented by a customized meta-object. Since the guarded methods are not directly supported in Schematic, we simulated them by user-level programming, in which objects are programmed to check the guard conditions and to suspend/continue their invocation requests. The programs are described in Appendix A.

Table 2 shows the elapsed time for 1,000 read/write operations from/to a bounded buffer whose size is 10. The PE buffer shows almost the same efficiency as does the NR one. This result could be understood as that the the overheads caused by frequent method invocations in NR cancel out the residual overheads in the PE buffer. The NR buffer uses three methods in order to represent a guarded method. On the other hand, the PE buffer uses only one because the partial evaluator successfully inlines the methods of the meta-object that deal with the guarded methods.

Table 2. Performance of bounded buffer with guarded methods.

	elapsed time (sec.)			improvement	residual overheads
	PE	INT	NR	INT/PE	PE/NR
Bounded Buffer	3.94	4.46	3.96	1.13	0.99

The partially evaluated meta-objects are approximately 10 percent faster than the interpreted ones (INT). This improvement is less significant than that observed with the previous benchmarks. We conjecture that this is because each of these benchmark programs requires a large number of context switches, and context-switching is expensive in the current Schematic implementation. The time spent for context-switching is thus so great that the efficiency differences between the three programs are relatively small.

6 Related Work

In CLOS Meta-Object Protocols (MOP), meta-level methods are split into functional and procedural ones for caching (or *memoization*)[13, 14]. This splitting approach in principle similar to our meta-object design, but the memoization technique requires more careful protocol design because the unit of specialization is function. Thus the "functional" methods cannot include operations that touch dynamic data. On the other hand, such operations can be written in our reader methods, since the partial evaluator automatically residualizes them.

Another approach to efficient reflective systems is use compile-time MOP[5, 11], in which efficiency is guaranteed by allowing the meta-level computation to be performed only at the compile-time. This means that the changes in the run-time behavior of the base-level program should be made by writing translation rules that convert the program into one containing the expected behavior. This task could be burdensome if the modification involved run-time representation of an object, because no run-time meta-objects are available in compile-time MOPs.

7 Conclusion

We have described a method for designing meta-objects in the reflective language ABCL/R3 and presented a framework for their optimization using partial evaluation. In the meta-object's description, operations that are state-related are separated from operations that are not, and it is this separation that makes partial evaluation effective. The meta-objects and their reader methods are translated into records and functions in Scheme, and they are then optimized by using a Scheme partial evaluator. The optimized code is a combination of the base-level and meta-level programs, a combination from wihch most interpretive operations at the meta-level (such as the method dispatch and the manipulation of the environment) have been removed. Effectiveness of this optimization framework is shown by benchmark programs in which the partially evaluated objects run significantly faster than the interpretive meta-objects. Moreover, the partial evaluation lets a program with customized meta-objects run as efficiently as an equivalent nonreflective program.

Acknowledgments

The earlier version of ABCL/R3 was designed in collaboration with Satoshi Matsuoka, and we would like to express our thanks to him. We would also like to thank Kenjiro Taura, Kenichi Asai, and Ken Wakita for their valuable comments and for their technical help to run the Schematic compiler and the Scheme partial evaluator.

References

1. Andersen, L. O.: Program Analysis and Specialization for the C Programming Language. PhD thesis, DIKU, University of Copenhagen (1994). (DIKU Report 94/19)
2. Asai, K., Masuhara, H., Matsuoka, S., Yonezawa, A.: Partial Evaluation as a Compiler for Reflective Languages. Technical Report 95-10, Department of Information Science, University of Tokyo (1995)
3. Asai, K., Masuhara, H., Yonezawa, A.: Partial Evaluation of Call-by-value lambda-calculus with Side-effects. In Partial Evaluation and Semantics-Based Program Manipulation (PEPM'97), SIGPLAN Notices, Vol. 32, No. 12. ACM (1997) 12–21
4. Chambers, C., Ungar, D., Lee, E.: An Efficient Implementation of SELF, a Dynamically-Type Object-Oriented Language Based on Prototypes. In Object-Oriented Programming Systems, Languages, and Applications (OOPSLA'89), SIGPLAN Notices, Vol. 24, No. 10. ACM (1989) 49–70
5. Chiba, S.: A Metaobject Protocol for C++. In Object-Oriented Programming Systems, Languages, and Applications (OOPSLA'95), SIGPLAN Notices, Vol. 30, No. 10. ACM (1995) 285–299
6. Chiba, S. Masuda, T.: Designing an Extensible Distributed Language with a Meta-Level Architecture. In European Conference on Object-Oriented Programming (ECOOP'93), Lecture Notes in Computer Science, Vol. 707. Springer-Verlag (1993) 482-501.
7. Futamura, Y.: Partial Evaluation of Computation Process—an Approach to a Compiler-compiler. Systems, Computers, Controls, Vol. 2, No. 5 (1971) 45–50
8. Gengler, M. Martel, M.: Self-applicable partial evaluation for the pi-calculus. In Partial Evaluation and Semantics-Based Program Manipulation (PEPM'97), SIGPLAN Notices, Vol. 32, No. 12. ACM (1997)
9. Hosoya, H., Kobayashi, N., Yonezawa, A.: Partial Evaluation Scheme for Concurrent Languages and Its Correctness. Euro-Par'96 Parallel Processing, Lecture Notes in Computer Science, Vol. 1123. Springer-Verlag (1996) 625–632
10. Igarashi, A. Kobayashi, N.: Type-Based Analysis of Usage of Communication Channels for Concurrent Programming Languages. In International Static Analysis Symposium (SAS'97), Lecture Notes in Computer Science, Vol. 1302. Springer-Verlag, (1997) 187–201

11. Ishikawa, Y., Hori, A., Sato, M., Matsuda, M., Nolte, J., Tezuka, H., Konaka, H., Maeda, M., Kubota, K.: Design and Implementation of Metalevel Architecture in C++: MPC++ Approach. In Reflection Symposium'96 (1996) 153–166
12. Jones, N. D., Gomard, C. K., Sestoft, P.: Partial Evaluation and Automatic Program Generation. Prentice Hall (1993)
13. Kiczales, G., Rivières, J.des , Bobrow, D. G.: The Art of the Metaobject Protocol. MIT Press, Cambridge, MA (1991)
14. Kiczales, G. Rodriguez, L.: Efficient Method Dispatch in PCL. In LISP and Functional Programming (LFP'90), ACM (1990) 99–105
15. Kobayashi, N., Nakade, M., Yonezawa, A.: Static Analysis of Communication for Asynchronous Concurrent Programming Languages. In International Static Analysis Symposium (SAS'95), Lecture Notes in Computer Science, Vol. 983. Springer-Verlag (1995) 225–242
16. Kobayashi, N., Pierce, B. C., Turner, D. N.: Linearity and the Pi-Calculus. In Principles of Programming Languages (POPL'96) (1996) 358–371
17. Maes, P.: Concepts and Experiments in Computational Reflection. In Object-Oriented Programming Systems, Languages, and Applications (OOPSLA'87), SIGPLAN Notices Vol. 22, No. 12. ACM (1987) 147–155
18. Marinescu, M. Goldberg, B.: Partial Evaluation Techniques for Concurrent Programs. In Partial Evaluation and Semantics-Based Program Manipulation (PEPM'97), SIGPLAN Notices, Vol. 32, No. 12. ACM (1997) 47–62
19. Masuhara, H., Matsuoka, S., Asai, K., Yonezawa, A.: Compiling Away the Meta-Level in Object-Oriented Concurrent Reflective Languages Using Partial Evaluation. In Object-Oriented Programming Systems, Languages, and Applications (OOPSLA'95), SIGPLAN Notices, Vol. 30, No. 10. ACM (1995) 300–315
20. Masuhara, H., Matsuoka, S., Watanabe, T., Yonezawa, A.: Object-Oriented Concurrent Reflective Languages can be Implemented Efficiently. In Object-Oriented Programming Systems, Languages, and Applications (OOPSLA'92), SIGPLAN Notices, Vol. 27, No. 10. ACM (1992) 127–145
21. Masuhara, H., Matsuoka, S., Yonezawa, A.: Implementing Parallel Language Constructs Using a Reflective Object-Oriented Language. In Reflection Symposium'96, San Francisco, CA. (1996) 79–91
22. Nakaya, A., Yamamoto, K., Yonezawa, A.: RNA Secondary Structure Prediction Using Highly Parallel Computers. Compt. Appl. Biosci. **11** (1995) 685–692
23. Oyama, Y., Taura, K., Yonezawa, A.: An Efficient Compilation Framework for Languages Based on a Concurrent Process Calculus. In Euro-Par '97 Object-Oriented Programming, Lecture Notes in Computer Science, Vol. 1300. Springer-Verlag, (1997)
24. Smith, B. C.: Reflection and Semantics in Lisp. In Principles of Programming Languages (POPL'84), ACM (1984) 23–35
25. Sun Microsystems, : Java(TM) Core Reflection: API and Specification, (1997)
26. Taura, K.: Efficient and Reusable Implementation of Fine-Grain Multithreading and Garbage Collection on Distributed-Memory Parallel Computers. PhD thesis, Department of Information Science, University of Tokyo (1997).
27. Taura, K. Yonezawa, A.: Schematic: A Concurrent Object-Oriented Extension to Scheme. In Object-Based Parallel and Distributed Computation, Lecture Notes in Computer Science, Vol. 1107. Springer-Verlag, (1996) 59–82
28. Watanabe, T. Yonezawa, A.: Reflection in an Object-Oriented Concurrent Language. In Object-Oriented Programming Systems, Languages, and Applications (OOPSLA'88), SIGPLAN Notices, Vol. 23, No. 11. ACM (1988) 306–315.

29. Yonezawa, A. (ed.): ABCL: An Object-Oriented Concurrent System. MIT Press, Cambridge, MA (1990)

A Programs Using Guarded Methods

A.1 Base-level Program

A base-level object that uses the guarded method mechanism has an optional form "`(:metaclass ...)`" in the class declaration, and has an expression "`(:guard ...)`" in each guarded method. The following program is the definition of the bounded buffer used in Section 5.2:

```
(define-class bb () size elements
  (:metaclass guard-meta))

(define-method! bb (put! self item)
  (:guard (< (length elements) size)) ; guard expression
  (become self :elements (append elements (list item))))
```

A.2 Meta-level Program

We define the class **guard-meta**, as a subclass of metaobject, at the meta-level.

```
(define-class guard-meta (metaobject) ; a subclass of metaobject
  (guard (make-guard)))               ; scheduler
```

In the additional instance variable **guard**, each instance of **guard-meta** has a scheduler, which is a user-defined meta-level object. We also override the following two methods of **guard-meta**:

```
(define-method guard-meta (receive self mes &reply-to mresult)
  (let* ((selector (message-selector mes))
         (method (find-method methods selector))
         (guard-exp (cdr (method-find-option method ':guard))))
    (register guard
              (lambda ()
                (let* ((env (make-env self (formals method) mes))
                       (result (eval evaluator guard-exp env)))
                  (if result
                      (reply (accept-W self mes) mresult))
                  result))))) ; result of guard expression

(define-method guard-meta (accept-W self mes)
  (let ((r (make-channel)))
    (let ((result (accept self mes r)))
      (update self (touch r))
      (notify guard)
      result))) ; result of method body
```

The method **receive** registers a closure to **guard**. The closure, when activated by the scheduler, evaluates a guard expression and then invokes **accept-W** if the guard expression returns be true. The method **accept-W**, evaluates the method body, as **accept-W** of the class **metaobject** does, and also notifies **guard** at the end of the evaluation.

A.3 Optimized Program

From the base-level and the meta-level programs, our optimization framework generates the following combined program. The meta-level operations for guarded methods, which are defined in the methods **receive** and **accept-W** of **guard-meta**, are embedded in the method **put!** of the optimized class.

```
(define-class guard-meta**bb ()
  class methods state-vars state-values lock evaluator
  (guard (make-guard)))

(define-method guard-meta**bb (put! self item &reply-to mresult0)
  (let ((c0 (lambda ()
              ;; evaluation of guard expression
              (let* ((values0   (read-cell state-values))
                     (size0     (vector-ref values0 0))
                     (elements0 (vector-ref values0 1))
                     (result0   (< (length elements0) size0)))
               (if result0
                 ;; execution of method body
                 (let* ((state-update-ch0 (make-channel))
                        (values1   (read-cell state-values))
                        (size1     (vector-ref values1 0))
                        (elements1 (vector-ref values1 1)))
                   (reply (vector size1
                                  (append elements1 (list item)))
                          state-update-ch0)
                   (let ((new-state0 (touch state-update-ch0)))
                     (update-cell! state-values new-state0)
                     (notify guard)
                     (reply self mresult0))) ; result of method body
                 #f)
               result0)))) ; result of guard expression
    (register guard c0)))
```

A.4 Nonreflective Program

Instead of using customized meta-objects, we can manually rewrite programs that have the same functionality to the ones using guarded methods. One of the simplest approach is to split each guarded into three actual methods: an entry method, a guard method, and a body method. The following definitions are a manually rewritten bounded buffer:

```
(define-class bb ()     ; nonreflective version
  size elements (guard (make-guard))

(define-method bb (put! self item &reply-to r)
  (let ((c (lambda ()
             (let ((guard-result (put!-guard self item)))
               (if guard-result
                   (reply (put!-body self item) r))
               guard-result))))
    (register guard c)))

(define-method bb (put!-guard self item)
  (< (length elements) size))              ; guard expression

(define-method! bb (put!-body self item)
  (become (begin (notify guard)             ; notification
                 self)
          :elements (append elements (list item))))
```

The class definition has an additional instance variable **guard** for the scheduler. The method **put!** is an entry method that creates and registers a closure to the scheduler. The method **put!-guard** is the guard method, and **put!-body** is the body method. They are invoked from the closure created in **put!**.

Reflection for Statically Typed Languages

José de Oliveira Guimarães*

Departamento de Computação
UFSCar, São Carlos - SP, Brazil
jose@dc.ufscar.br

Abstract. An object-oriented language that permits changing the behavior of a class or of a single object is said to support computational reflection. Existing reflective facilities in object-oriented languages are either complex, type unsafe, or have a large performance penalty. We propose a simple, easy-to-understand, and statically typed model that captures much of the functionalities of other reflective facilities. It brings the power of reflection to the world of type safe and efficient languages.

1 Introduction

Computational reflection is the activity performed by a computational system when doing computation about its own computation [20]. Reflection has become an important issue in object-oriented programming and is usually realized through metaclasses and metaobjects which has the drawbacks of being difficult to learn [2] [7] [23] and/or causes reasonable performance penalty. This paper presents two new reflective constructs that have much of the functionalities of metaclasses and metaobjects. They can be introduced in many statically typed languages without damaging the type system. The performance is minimally affected and the constructs are easy to implement, learn and use.

This paper focuses on the ability of a program to change its computation. It does not discuss features that merely allow a program to examine its structure, such as features that allow a program to list all methods of a class, to discover the class of an object, to examine the types of the parameters of a method, and so on. These features are easy to implement efficiently and safely. Instead, this paper focuses on features that have not been implemented efficiently and safely before. This includes allowing an object to change its class and changing the implementation of an entire class of objects.

This paper is organized as follows. Section 2 describes existing reflective models of object-oriented languages and some problems with them. Section 3 proposes two new constructs for reflectivity. Some examples of problems that can be solved by these constructs are shown in Section 4. Section 5 describes the implementation of these constructs. Section 6 compares the proposed constructs with existing ones and presents related work.

* This work was partially supported by CNPq, the Brazilian financial agency for scientific projects under process number 200466-94.1

2 Existing Reflective Models

According to Ferber [9], reflective facilities of object-oriented languages can be divided in three categories:

1. the metaclass model;
2. the metaobject model;
3. the metacommunication model.

The Metaclass Model was introduced by Smalltalk [13]. In this language, each class is an instance of a metaclass that describes its structure (instance variables and methods it supports). A metaclass is automatically created by each program class and there is a one-to-one correspondence between classes and metaclasses. The programmer has no direct control in the creation of metaclasses.

The ObjVlisp model [7] removes the limitations of Smalltalk metaclasses. It allows the programmer to explicitly create metaclasses. A set of classes can share a single metaclass and the metalinks can be created indefinitely. A metalink is the linking between a class and its metaclass.

In Smalltalk and ObjVlisp, a message sent to an object is redirect to the object class. That is, the search for the appropriate method is made in the object class. Therefore, there is no way to change the methods of a single object or making a specific message interpreter to it.

The Metaobject Model was introduced by Maes [20] and allows specialized method look-up for a single object. Each object has an associated metaobject that holds the information about its implementation and interpretation. Since there is a one-to-one correspondence between objects and metaobjects, a metaobject can be modified to redirect the messages sent to the object, keep statistical information about this specific object, trace the messages sent to it and so on.

When a message is sent to an object with a metaobject, the normal method look-up is not performed. Instead, a message called `MethodCall` is sent to the metaobject taking as real parameter an object containing the original message data (selector and parameters). Then the metaobject can manipulate the selector and real parameters of the original message as data — the message is reified.

The Metacommunication Model permits reifying message sends. When a message is sent, the run-time system creates an object of class `MESSAGE` and initializes it with the message data (selector, receiver, parameters). Then, the message `SEND` is sent to this object that executes the appropriate method look-up algorithm. Subclasses of class `MESSAGE` can be defined and used with a special syntax thus modifying the original meaning of message send.

Problems with Metaclass/Metaobject Models

Metaclasses are the concept of Smalltalk most difficult to learn [23]. Borning and O'Shea [2] have even proposed that they should be eliminated from this language. It is difficult to understand the differences between the relationships created by instantiation, inheritance and metaclasses. It is difficult to realize the responsibilities of each of these relationships in complex inheritance/metaclass models like Smalltalk and ObjVlisp. For example, what will happen to an instance variable of class `A` if I modify the metaclass of an `A` superclass ? How can a class called `Class` inherit from class `Object` if `Object` is an instance of `Class` ? Should not a superclass be created before its subclasses and a class before its instances ? Metaclasses lead to the "infinite regression problem": a class should have a metaclass that should have a meta-metaclass and so on. In practice, this problem is solved by introducing nonstandard inheritance/metalink relationships (as the one between classes `Object` and `Class`) which damage the learnability of the language.

The three models described above are naturally type unsafe. They let a programmer remove methods from classes/objects, change inheritance links, modify method look-up, and so on. They can cause run-time type errors in most reflective languages with a few exceptions [4] [14] [22] [28] [29] [31]. It seems that there is no easy way to make reflective constructs type safe without removing some of their power. Just as there is no statically typed language that allows all the flexibility of untyped languages.

3 A Statically Typed Reflective Model

To present our proposal, we use a statically-typed language with single inheritance called Green [17]. Although Green separates subtyping from subclassing, in this paper we will consider Green has a type system similar to C++. That is, all subtypes are subclasses — an object of a class can be used whenever a superclass object is expected. Unlike C++, all instance variables are only accessed by message sends to public methods. The type of a variable can be a basic type (**integer**, **boolean**, ...) or a class. If the type is a class, the variable is a pointer to an object of that class, as in most object oriented language. All objects are dynamically allocated.

3.1 The Outline of a Model

Our objective is to create reflective features that can:

1. replace methods of a class and add instance variables to it at run time;
2. redirect messages sent to an object to another object.

1 and 2 play roles of metaclasses and metaobjects, respectively. These features should be statically-typed, simple, easy-to-understand and efficient. To achieve these goals, we eliminate the metalevel while still keeping most of its features. The model should use the language type system and method look-up algorithm. The absence of a metalevel implies that the familiar language mechanisms would be used to support reflectivity, although through the introduction of new constructs. The lack of a metalevel would make the model:

1. statically-typed and as simple as the language's type system;

2. easy-to-understand since the concepts would not be thoroughly new and;
3. efficient since the normal and fast method look-up algorithm would be used.

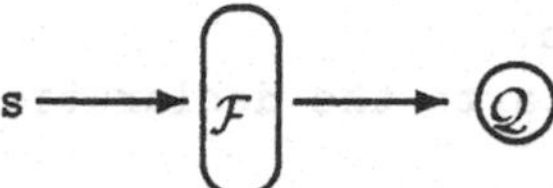

Fig. 1. A shell $\mathcal{F}$ attached to an object $\mathcal{Q}$

The following sections describe two reflective constructs that meet these conditions.

3.2 Dynamic Shell

The first construct is based on the concept of *shell*. A shell is a layer of method/instance variables that is placed between a variable and the object it refers to. Figure 1 shows a shell $\mathcal{F}$ that covers an object $\mathcal{Q}$. A message sent to $\mathcal{Q}$ through variable s will be searched for first in the shell $\mathcal{F}$ and then, if it is not found there, in $\mathcal{Q}$. If a message is sent to **self** inside $\mathcal{Q}$ methods, the search for a method begins at shell $\mathcal{F}$. So, shells allow a class-based language to have some characteristics of languages with delegation.

A shell can be put between an object and the variables that refer to it using *dynamic shell*. Any number of shell objects can be plugged into an object.

The shell object $\mathcal{F}$ of Fig. 1 must have a subset of $\mathcal{Q}$ methods. Since any messages sent through s are searched for in $\mathcal{F}$ and then in $\mathcal{Q}$, the composite object $\mathcal{F}$-$\mathcal{Q}$ has the same set of methods as $\mathcal{Q}$. Then, to attach a shell to $\mathcal{Q}$ does not introduce type errors because we are replacing an object by another one with the same set of methods.

Figure 2 defines a dynamic shell class called **BoundedPoint** whose shell objects can be attached to objects of **Point** and its subclasses. The set of methods of **BoundedPoint** must be a subset of the set of methods of **Point**. That means the shell objects created from **BoundedPoint** (as $\mathcal{F}$) have a subset of the set of methods of the objects they are attached to (as $\mathcal{Q}$). The syntactic and semantic rules for dynamic shell assures that each shell object is associated with exactly one object, although a sequence of shell objects may be plugged into an object.

Class-**BoundedPoint** methods can call class-**Point** methods by sending messages to "**object**", which is similar to "**super**" in Smalltalk. As an example, assume that the class of $\mathcal{F}$ of Fig. 1 is **BoundedPoint** and the class of $\mathcal{Q}$ is **Point**. A message send "**object.setX(newX)**" inside $\mathcal{F}$ (class **BoundedPoint**) methods causes the search for method **setX** begin in object $\mathcal{Q}$.

BoundedPoint shells can only be attached to objects of classes specified in advance through a compiler option. These classes must be subclasses of **Point**

```
shell class BoundedPoint(Point)
  private:
    ...
  public:

      { This is a comment.
        Keyword "proc" starts the declaration of methods. }

    proc setX(newX : integer) : boolean
      begin
      if newX >= 1 and newX <= 80
      then
        return object.setX(newX);
      else
        return false;
      endif
      end
endclass
```

Fig. 2. An example of dynamic shell class

and will be called "the allowed set" of `BoundedPoint`. By default, `Point` will always be in this set. It is not necessary to have the source code of the classes in the allowed set of `BoundedPoint`. It is only necessary to have the source code of `BoundedPoint`. We do not need to have the source code of a class in order to attach a dynamic shell to an object of that class.

Shells can be implemented without the specification of the "allowed set" but that would require the run-time creation of classes, which we want to avoid for performance reasons.

A dynamic shell object of class `BoundedPoint` is attached to an object `p` through the syntax

```
if Reflect.attachShell(p, BoundedPoint.new()) <> 0
then ...
```

`Reflect` is an object whose method `attachShell` attaches a shell to another object. This method returns `0` if there is no error, `1` if there is not enough memory to create the shell object, and `2` if the class of `p` does not belong to the "allowed set" of `BoundedPoint`. Since the class of the object `p` will be known only at run time, the compiler cannot guarantee the correctness of this statement.

A shell is removed from an object by calling method `removeShell`:

```
if Reflect.removeShell(p) <> 0
then ...
```

This method removes the last shell object that was attached to the object pointed to by `p`. It returns `0` if there is no error or `1` if `p` does not have a shell.

The **BoundedPoint** class can redefine the **new** method for creating objects. Then, we can redefine method **new** to take as parameter an object **ObjLimits** that will keep the allowed limits for the point. The shell would have a pointer to this object that could be shared by a set of points.

A class can be declared as reflective to shells using the syntax

```
reflective(shell) class Point
   ...
endclass
```

If a shell is attached to an object of this class, the access to shell instance variables will be faster than if class **Point** were declared as a normal class (without the "**reflective(shell)**" prefix). Details about the implementation of reflective(shell) and normal classes will be given in Sect. 5.

A New Feature for Dynamic Shells

When using metaobjects, each message sent to the object is packed in a message object containing the receiver, message name and real parameters. Then method **MethodCall** of the metaobject is called passing as parameter the message object. So, a single method (**MethodCall**) of the metaobject traces all messages sent to the object. In this way it is easy to send the message through a network or to gather statistic information using metaobjects. A single method of the metaobject must be modified to store data about all messages sent to the object.

To make shells support this functionality, one can declare a method

```
proc interceptAll(
      mi : Method;
      vetArg : array(Object)[]
      ) : Object
```

in the shell class. "**interceptAll**" is a language-Green reserved word and should only be used as method name in shell classes. Method **interceptAll** should always have the signature (interface) shown above. **Method** is a class of the introspective class library of the language. To each program method there is a **Method** object that describes it. The elements of the array **vetArg** are objects of class **Object** and its subclasses. Class **Object** is superclass of every other class or array in the program. **vetArg** stores the real parameters to method **mi**. If a parameter is a value of a basic type (e.g. **integer**) it is packed in an object of a wrapper class (e.g. **INTEGER**). An object of class **INTEGER** just stores an integer number.

When a message **m** is sent to an object Q with a shell, method **m** of the shell will be executed. If the shell does not have a method **m** but it does have a method **interceptAll**, the message parameters are packed in an array passed as a parameters in a call to shell method **interceptAll**. The first real parameter to this method call will be the object of class **Method** that describes the method **m** of object Q (the object the shell is attached to). Method **interceptAll** can call method **m** of Q using method **invoke** of class **Method**:

```
mi.invoke(self, vetArg)
```

Method **interceptAll** allows shells to have all the functionality of metaobjects although with the associate overhead. Class **Method** and method **invoke** were based in similar features of Java Core Reflection [32].

3.3 Dynamic Extension

Dynamic shells change individual objects. *Dynamic extension* does the same for classes. Dynamic extension allows a program to replace the methods of a class and its subclasses by the methods of another class at run time. The syntax for a dynamic extension class is similar to the one for dynamic shell. Like this construct, the keyword "**object**" in a dynamic extension class is used to call methods of the original class.

```
reflective(extension) class Window
  ...
  public:
    proc draw() ...
    ...
endclass

extension class BorderedWindow(Window)
    ...
  public:
    proc draw()
      begin
      self.drawBorder();
        { call Window method }
      object.draw();
      end
endclass
```

Fig. 3. An example of dynamic extension class declaration

An example of dynamic extension is class **BorderedWindow** of Fig. 3. This class can be attached to any class that:

1. is specified through a compiler option and;
2. is subclass of **Window** or **Window** itself.

The classes that obey these requirements compose the "allowed set" of **BorderedWindow**. By default, **Window** belongs to this set.

To attach an extension to class **A**, it must have been declared as

```
reflective(extension) class A
  ...
endclass
```

A class can be also declared as

```
reflective(shell, extension) class A
  ...
endclass
```

with the obvious meaning. If a class **A** is declared as

```
reflective(X) class A
```

then all subclasses must be declared in the same way. It does not mind whether **X** is **shell**, **extension** or both things.

The expression

```
Reflect.attachExtension(Window, BorderedWindow)
```

attaches **BorderedWindow** to **Window** at run time. It returns **0** if there is no error and **1** if there is not enough memory to create some auxiliary structures. If **Window** does not belong to the "allowed set" of **BorderedWindow**, there is a compile error. Any message "**draw**" sent to a **Window** object will now invoke **BorderedWindow** method **draw**. This method draw a border and then call method **draw** of **Window**.

An extension is removed from a class by calling method **removeExtension**:

```
if Reflect.removeExtension(Window) <> 0
then
  ...
endif
```

This method removes the last extension of class **Window**. It returns **0** if there is no error or **1** if no extension is attached to **Window**.

4 Some More Examples

An example of use of dynamic shell is to trace messages sent to an object. Figure 4 shows a dynamic shell class **TracePerson** whose shell objects print a message in the screen each time they receive the message "**set**". To trace object **p**, we should execute the code

```
if Reflect.attachShell(p, TracePerson.new()) <> 0
then
  ...
endif
```

Dynamic extension can be used to confirm pre- and post-conditions for methods of a class. As an example, Fig. 5 shows a class **String** that has a method **get** to return the ith character of the string. The dynamic extension class **SafeString** redefines method **get** to confirm the limits of the parameter **i**,

```
reflective(shell) class Person
  ...
  public:
    proc set( name : String; age : integer ) ...
    proc getName() : String ...
    ...
endclass

shell class TracePerson(Person)
  public:
    proc set( name : String; age : integer )
      begin
      printf("Message set sent to %s\n", object.getName());
      object.set( name, age );
      end
endclass
```

Fig. 4. Tracing using dynamic shell

which is a pre-condition for method **get** of class **String**. **SafeString** should be plugged into **String** during the test phase of the program and removed after that.

5 Implementation

The layout of an object in memory is shown in Fig. 6 and includes slots for its instance variables (IV) and a pointer **mt** to an array of pointers to the methods of the object class. If the object class is **A**, this array will be called the **class-A** method table. In fact, the first element of this array (**mt[0]**) does not point to a method but to an object that contains information about class **A**.

Objects of reflective(shell) classes have a pointer **sv** besides pointer **mt**, as shown in Fig. 7. **sv** points to a memory area that contains the shell instance variables.

We will explain the implementation of the shell constructs in detail now. To do that, it is necessary to understand how the algorithm for method look-up works.

All objects of the same class point to the same method table. Each method in a class is numbered, and a subclass reuses the numbers of its superclass. A method's number is used as an index in the method table. So, if object **p** belongs to class **Point** and the number of method **draw** is **3**, the address of **draw** is "**p.mt[3]**".[2]

[2] We consider that **p.mt[1]** means the second element of an array whose initial address is given by the pointer **p.mt**

```
reflective(extension) class String
  ...
  public:
       { number of characters }
    proc length() : integer    ...

       { get the i-th element }
    proc get( i : integer ) : char
      begin
      return s[i];
      end
    ...
endclass

extension class SafeString(String)
  public:
    proc get( i : integer ) : char
      begin
      if i >= 0 and i < object.length()
      then
        return object.get(i);
      else
        printf("Error ...");
        exit(1);
      endif
      end
endclass
```

Fig. 5. Conference of pre-conditions using dynamic extension

Message sends to **super** are usually resolved at compile time; i.e. they are statically bound. However if a class is declared as reflective(extension), message sends to **super** in its subclasses are made through the class method table. Dynamic extension makes methods of the dynamic extension class replace methods of a class. Therefore, static binding would cause errors. For example, suppose "**super.m()**" results in static binding to method m of class A. If a dynamic extension is attached to A replacing method m, "**super.m()**" continues to call the original class-A method m, when it is supposed to call method m of the dynamic extension. As will become clear later, to call methods through the method table solves this problem.

The implementation described next ignores the possibility that

1. a shell is attached to an object that already has a shell;
2. an extension is attached to a class that has an extension;

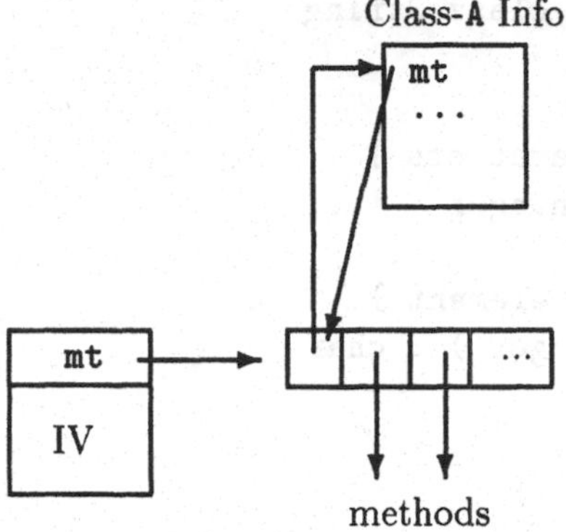

Fig. 6. The layout of a class-A object

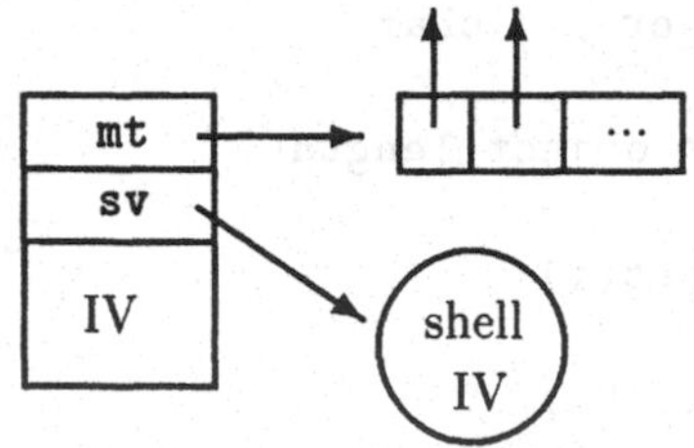

Fig. 7. Object of reflective(shell) class

To explain these cases is outside the scope of this paper.

Dynamic Shell Implementation

An "allowed set" of reflective(shell) classes is associated with a dynamic shell class `B`. A shell of class `B` can be attached to any object whose class belong to this set. For each class `A` belonging to the allowed set of a dynamic shell class `B`, the compiler

1. makes a copy of class `B`, renames it `B'`, and makes `B'` inherit from `A`. Each message send to "`object`" inside class-`B'` methods is changed to a call to the corresponding class-`A` method. This is made through class-`A` method table if `A` is a reflective(extension) class and through a static call to the class-`A` method otherwise. The compiler enforces that class `B` does not define any method not defined in class `A`. Class `B'` could be created at runtime but we chose to create it at compile time for performance reasons.
2. inserts in the beginning of each class-`B'` method:
    1. an assignment "`iv = self.sv`" if `A` is reflective(shell). That makes `iv`

point to the shell instance variables that are pointed to by **sv** in reflective(shell) classes. See Fig. 7.
2. code to retrieve the address of shell instance variables from a hash table using the object address as key if **A** is not reflective(shell). The address retrieved is also assigned to **iv**. Each class **B′** has its own hash table.

The access to a shell instance variable is made using **iv** through a single indirection. Even if the shell is removed by the shell method, **iv** will continue to point to the shell memory. It will be garbage collected as any other object.

A dynamic shell of class **B** is attached to an object of class **A** through an expression "**Reflect.attachShell(a, B.new())**". Method **attachShell**:

3. tests if **A** belongs to the allowed set of **B**. If it does not, the expression returns 2. Note that:
   1. the class of object **a** will only be known at run time;
   2. this test would be unnecessary if class **B′** were dynamically created.
4. allocates memory for the class-**B** instance variables. If there is not enough free memory, the expression returns **1**. If class **A** is reflective(shell), **attachShell** makes pointer **sv** of the object points to this memory. See Fig. 7 for the object layout. If class **A** is not reflective(shell), the pair (object, allocated memory address) is inserted into a hash table. The object address is used as key. In the shell methods this table is used to retrieve the address of the shell instance variables.
5. makes pointer **mt** of the object point to the class-**B′** method table created at compile time. Then the object will now use **B′** methods.

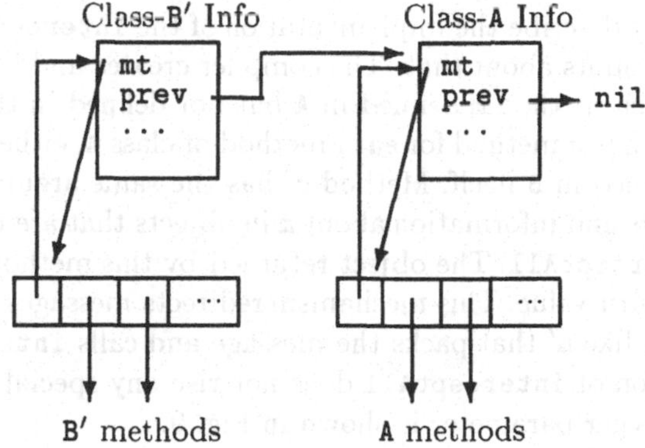

Fig. 8. Relationship between classes **B′** and **A**

Figure 8 shows the relationship between classes **B′** and **A**. The first pointer of class-**B′** method table points to an object with information about this class including a pointer **prev** to class **A** [3] and a pointer **mt** to **B′** method table.

To remove a **B′** shell from an object, method **removeShell** of **Reflect**:

1. makes pointer **mt** of the object points to class-**A** method table. This table is found following the links shown in Fig. 8.
2. assigns **nil** (**NULL** in C++) to instance variable **sv** of the object if class **A** is reflective(shell). Otherwise the shell memory is removed from the hash table in which it was inserted. In any case the shell memory will only be deallocated by the garbage collector.

```
proc m'( n : integer )
  var vetArg : array(Object)[];
begin
  { allocates memory for an array of one element }
vetArg = array(Object)[1].new();
  { creates a class-INTEGER object that wraps parameter n }
vetArg[0] = INTEGER.new(n);
  { method_A_m is a pointer to an object describing method m
    of class A }
self.interceptAll( method_A_m, vetArg );
end
```

Fig. 9. Method **m′** calling **interceptAll**

We will not describe the implementation of the **interceptAll** feature but we will give some hints about that. The compiler creates and inserts a method **m′** in class **B′** for each method **m** defined in **A** but not defined in the shell class **B**. This means class **B** has a method for each method of class **A**, either a method like **m′** or a method defined in **B** itself. Method **m′** has the same arguments as **m** and packs the parameters and information about **m** in objects that are used as arguments in a call to **interceptAll**. The object returned by this method is also returned by **m′** if it has return value. This mechanism redirects messages sent to the object to shell methods like **m′** that packs the message and calls **interceptAll**. Then the implementation of **interceptAll** does not rise any special problem. A method **m′** with an integer parameter is shown in Fig. 9.

Dynamic Extension Implementation

Suppose an extension class **B** is attached to a class **A**. By the definition of dynamic extension, the methods of **B** replace the corresponding methods of **A**.

[3] Object class before it was attached to the **B′** shell.

This is achieved by making all pointers that point to a class-A method[4] to point to the corresponding class-B method. There are pointers to class-A methods in method tables of this class and all of its subclasses (which includes classes B′ created by the implementation of dynamic shell). If a class C inherits from class A that defines a method m, class-C method table will point to class-A method m if C does not redefine this method.

If extension B defines instance variables, memory to these variables must be allocated to each object of class A and its subclasses. This is made in a lazy way. Only when a class-B shell method will use shell instance variables the run-time system allocates memory for them.

Let us see in details how dynamic extension is implemented. An extension can only be plugged into classes belonging to its "allowed set" which was specified through a compiler option. For each class A belonging to the allowed set of a dynamic extension B, the compiler

1. makes a copy of class B, renames it B′, and makes B′ inherit from A. Each message send to `object` inside class-B′ methods is changed to a static call to the corresponding class-A method. If dynamic extension implemented a message send to `object` as a call through class-A method table, there could be an infinite loop in a method m of class B if it had a statement like
   ```
   object.m();
   ```
   The entry in class-A method table corresponding to m would point to class-B method m after B is attached to A. Then the above statement would be a call to class-B method m, which is the method in which this statement is. This could result in an infinite loop and certainly does not obey the definition of dynamic extension.
2. inserts a hash table lookup in the beginning of each class-B′ method that uses instance variables.[5] The object that received the message (`self`) is given as key to retrieve the shell memory that is assigned to a variable sv. If the lookup fails, the run-time system allocates the shell memory and inserts its address in the hash table. It is worthy noting that each class B′ has its own hash table.

When the compiler finds an expression
```
Reflect.attachExtension(A, B)
```
which attaches a dynamic extension B to class A, it confirms if A belongs to the allowed set of B.

At run time, `attachExtension` makes all pointers that point to a class-A method[6] to point to the corresponding class-B method. That is, if a method table has a pointer to class-A method m, `attachExtension` makes this pointer point to class-B method m (if this method is defined in B). There are pointers to class-A methods in method tables of this class and all of its subclasses, which

[4] We consider a class-A method any method defined in class A or its superclasses.

[5] Of course, class-B instance variables since B′ is a copy of B.

[6] Methods of class A are those defined in A or inherited from superclasses.

includes classes B′ created by the implementation of dynamic shell.[7] The method table of a A subclass points to method m of class A if the subclass does not redefine this method.

When a superclass is declared as reflective(extension), message sends to **super** are made through the superclass method table. If an extension is attached to the superclass, its method table will be overwritten by the extension method addresses. Then a message send "**super.m()**" will call the extension method m if a method m is defined in the extension class.

Accesses to shell instance variables must be made through a pointer got from a hash table. To use a pointer **sv** in the object, as is made in the dynamic shell implementation, does not work. An object of a class C that inherits from a class A would need two pointers **sv** if an extension were attached to A and another to C. One pointer **sv** would point to a memory with the instance variables of the extension attached to A and the other pointer **sv** would point to a memory with the instance variables of the extension attached to C. When an extension is attached to a class A, all subclasses (as C) are affected because a subclass object is also considered a superclass object. Then to attach an extension to A affect class-C objects. This problem can be solved by putting several **sv** pointers in the object but that seems too expensive.

To remove an extension B′ from a class A, method **removeExtension** makes all pointers to class-B′ methods point to the corresponding class-A method. Class B′ hash table is deallocated and the memory for the shell instance variables will be garbage collected.

We have implemented a dynamic shell and dynamic extension using a compiler that translates our language code to C. In the current status of the compiler, a dynamic shell cannot be attached to an object that already has a shell object and an extension cannot be plugged into a class that already has another extension. The compiler, its source code, and some examples of dynamic shells and extensions are available at [16].

6 Discussion and Related Work

One can see the type correctness of dynamic shell considering a shell $\mathcal{F}$ plugged into an object $\mathcal{Q}$ as a composite object $\mathcal{Q}$-$\mathcal{F}$. The method signatures[8] of $\mathcal{Q}$-$\mathcal{F}$ are the union of those of $\mathcal{Q}$ and $\mathcal{F}$. Since the method signatures of $\mathcal{F}$ are a subset of those of $\mathcal{Q}$ (by definition), the set of method signatures of $\mathcal{Q}$-$\mathcal{F}$ and $\mathcal{Q}$ are equal. Then, to attach a shell to an object is to replace an object by another that can respond to the same set of messages, which of course does not introduce type errors.

Dynamic shell and dynamic extension have many of the non-introspective functionalities of metaobjects and metaclasses, respectively. Dynamic shell was

[7] Then dynamic extensions can be mixed with dynamic shells in any order without problems.

[8] The signature of a method is its name, types of formal parameters and type of the return value (if any).

not based in other language constructs although it is essentially the trap mechanism of KSL [18] and the metaobject construct of Foote and Johnson [10] introduced in Smalltalk. However, KSL and Smalltalk are untyped languages that allow run-time type errors. Dynamic shell and dynamic extension can be supported in a statically-typed language without damaging the language type system.

Predicate classes of Chambers [3] can make an object inherit from some classes dynamically if it satisfies some boolean expressions. The inheritance is removed whenever the boolean expression evaluates to false using the object. Then the methods of an object can be changed at run time by predicate classes which is related to dynamic shell. The main difference is that a dynamic shell is attached/removed by the programmer and the dynamic inheritance of predicate classes is automatically managed by the run-time system.

Related to predicate classes is the *metaCombiner* model [21]. A metaobject called metaCombiner combines *adjustments* that are roughly shells. *Adjustments* are activated (attached to an object) according to events that may depend on the object or program state. The metaCombiner coordinates the way the *adjustments* work together and with the object. The reflective architecture Guaraná for Java supports a similar feature. A metaobject may coordinate other metaobjects associated with the object.

Aksit et al. [1] defines *Composition Filters* to abstract communications among objects. Each message received or sent by an object can be intercepted by filters that have a metaobject-like behavior. By controlling the object communication with the external world, filters can enforce the cooperative behavior of a set of objects. Ours shells filter messages sent to an object intercepting some of them and there is no way to intercept the messages sent by an object.

A mixin class [8] can refer to its superclass even though it does not inherit from anyone. This class is not intended to create objects but to be composed with other class that plays the role of its superclass. In the composition of a mixin with a class `A`, the references to a superclass in the mixin methods are rebound to class `A`. This is similar to have a subclass that can be plugged to several superclasses. That is why mixin classes are called "abstract subclasses".

The language Agora [27] supports dynamic application of mixins. A class can be dynamically created by combining an existing class with a mixin. This is very similar to dynamic extension. A class `B` defined as a dynamic extension class can send messages (through the keyword "`object`") to the class it will be attached to. If `B` is attached to `A`, any messages sent through "`object`" in `B` methods will invoke class-`A` methods.

In fact, dynamic extension was based in the statically-typed mixin extension to Modula-3 proposed by Bracha and Cook [8].

Feature-oriented programming [25] is much like a compile-time version of dynamic extension. A feature is like a class that can be combined with other feature through a class-like construction called *lifter*. This is similar to attach an extension `B` into a class `A` using a class `C` to define how `B` methods will call `A` methods. We believe that to create a compile-time version of dynamic extension emulating feature-oriented programming would require minor modifications in the language syntax and in the compiler.

Gil and Lorenz [12] proposed *environmental acquisition* to allow an object to behave accordingly to the composite object in which it is connected. So, a **Door** object could acquire the **getColor()** method from the **Car** object that contains it. Environmental acquisition resembles dynamic shells since methods of individual objects can be replaced by others. The difference is that, in environmental acquisition, the object methods are automatically changed according to the surrounding object whereas one must explicitly attach a shell to an object in order to change its methods.

Contexts [26] are similar to shells. When a context is attached to an object, some methods of the context can replace the object methods. Although shells and contexts have some similarities, we believe shells have more functionalities of metaobjects than contexts:

1. by our knowledge, a context method can only replace a method of a specific class, preventing it to be used with subclasses;
2. the attachment of several contexts to an object is not addressed;
3. no feature similar to method **interceptAll** is defined.

No performance evaluation of contexts is discussed in [26]. Then, we cannot compare the performance of shells and contexts.

The old version of Open C++ [4] [5] is a reflective C++ that supports metaobjects. Its goal is to allow programmers extend Open C++ with facilities that cannot be easily added to C++ as support to distributed and parallel programming. In Open C++, a message sent to an object of a reflective class causes the execution of method **Meta_MethodCall** of the object metaobject, whichever is the message selector. A message send using a metaobject is 10 times slower than a normal one if no optimization is done.

A new version of Open C++ [6] uses metaobjects to control the compilation of classes. The metaobjects exist only at compile time and are not directly related to our proposals.

There are some Java extensions that support metaobjects [14] [22] [31] and a feature similar to dynamic extension. In all these meta architectures a single method (like **Meta_MethodCall** of Open C++) traces all message sends to an object with an attached metaobject, which results in poor performance.

In the old version of Open C++ the call to a reflective method is ten times slower than a call to a normal method if no optimization is done. In MetaJava a call to a method of an object with a metaobject takes 170 μs according to tests made by Golm [14]. A normal call takes 6.1 μs, which gives a ratio of 28 between the two options. Golm used a method without parameters and a metaobject that implemented the default behavior (to call the object method). In our implementation of dynamic shell there is no overhead in the call to a shell method or to any method of an object attached to a shell.

By defining method **interceptAll**, to shells are given the full functionality of metaobjects. Then, it is worthwhile to compare the performance of metaobjects

Fig. 10. Shell performance in a Pentium

	Optimiz.	Non-optimiz.
`a.m()`	2.7	4.2
`b = a.get()`	2.5	3.4
`a.put(b)`	2.7	9.2

Fig. 11. Shell performance in a Sparc 10

	Optimiz.	Non-optimiz.
`a.m()`	3.3	4.6
`b = a.get()`	2.4	3.5
`a.put(b)`	3.0	11.6

with that of shells with **interceptAll**, which is made in Figures 10 and 11. We use a class **Store** that stores a class-**B** object with methods to store (**put**) and retrieve (**get**) the object. There is also an empty method **m** without parameters. Figures 10 and 11 give the ratio **tshell/tnormal** where **tshell** and **tnormal** are the execution time of a message send using a shell with **interceptAll** and normal message send, respectively. Method **interceptAll** simply delegates the message send to the object, which is the default behavior. Figures 10 and 11 show the results of the measurements made in a Pentium and a Sparc 10.

In Fig. 10, a call "**a.m()**" through a shell with **interceptAll** takes 4.2 times the execution time of the normal call. See column "Non-optimiz.". A simple optimization in method **interceptAll** (column "Optimiz.") reduces this overhead to 2.7. This optimization is to allocate array **vetArg** (**interceptAll** real parameter) statically and replace the call "**mi.invoke(self, vetArg)**" by a switch statement with a case label for each method that can be called.

Performance measurements of metaobject is not available for most languages. Albeit that, we can say shells with **interceptAll** are faster than the implementation of metaobjects with available performance data.

Templ [28] introduced reflection in the Oberon-2 language. Each procedure has an associated metaprocedure that knows how to call the procedure. By acting on the metaprocedure, the program can change the procedure behavior. For example, the metaprocedure can call other procedure instead of the one it is associated with. If a metaprocedure could be associated to a method, Oberon-2 would have a feature similar to dynamic extension. The metaprocedure would control a class method in the same way dynamic extension does.

7 Conclusion

The reflective model described in this paper does not really have a "meta level" — it uses the method look-up algorithm and type system of the language. As a result, dynamic shell and dynamic extension are statically typed and easy to understand. They use a syntax very similar to normal classes, do not suffer the "infinite regression problem", and the performance penalty caused by them is minimal.

The reflective features described here do not require any modification in objects of non-reflective (normal) classes. Objects of reflective(shell) classes need one more pointer per object.

Message sends to objects or shell objects are not slowed down by dynamic shell or dynamic extension. In particular, message sends to shells are as fast as message sends to objects. Performance degradation only occurs in two cases:

1. an assignment "**iv = self.sv**" or a hash table lookup is inserted at the beginning of each shell/extension method;
2. when the superclass is reflective(extension) message sends to **super** are implemented by indexing the method table of the superclass. So, the overhead corresponds to an array indirection plus a function call through a pointer.

However, that is not too bad. In most cases shells will be plugged into objects of reflective(shell) classes since their use will be *planned*. In this case just an assignment will be inserted in each shell method that uses shell instance variables. If the object class is not reflective(shell), there will be an extra hash table lookup in each shell method. This lookup always exist when an extension method accesses an extension instance variable.

This hash table lookup is expensive for a statically-typed language but difficult to avoid since shell and extension instance variables must be added to some structure that cannot be the object itself. This inefficience is due to the problem itself and not to the definition of shells and extensions. However, if we prohibit dynamic shells and dynamic extensions to act on the same classes, the shell instance variables can be allocated in the method table the object points to. Each object attached to a shell would have its own method table. If few shell objects are created, this scheme may be more space efficient than to add an instance variable **sv** in each object of reflective(shell) classes. An optimized compiler could analyze the source code and use this implementation instead of the one described in this paper if dynamic extensions were not used with the same classes as dynamic shells.

Message sends to **super** by indexing the method table is 24% slower than a static call.[9] This is less expensive than a normal message send although slower than the normal implementation, which calls the method directly. However only a few percent of all classes are reflective(extension) thus making the overhead of calling **super** using a table very small.

[9] It was used a empty method without parameters in a Sparc 10.

In the reflective architecture Guaraná [22] for Java and languages as Reflective Java [31], MetaJava [14], and the old version of Open C++ [4] [5], the method **Meta_MethodCall** of the metaobject is called whenever the corresponding object receives a message. The message is packed as an object passed as a parameter to **Meta_MethodCall** that then may call methods of the original receiver. There are special constructs to handle the parameters of a message, which are not necessary in order to use dynamic shell and dynamic extension.[10] When a message is sent to an object and intercepted by a metaobject, the most common case is that the metaobject delegates the message to the object without doing any computation. Then the message is packed when passed to the metaobject and again unpacked when delegated to the object, resulting in two wasteful operations. With dynamic shells, the object method is called directly in this case at the speed of a normal message send.

Although dynamic shells and extensions were implemented in Green [17] they do not need any particular feature of this language. In fact, we are adding shells to Java [30] with a implementation different from the one described in this paper.

Dynamic shell and dynamic extensions are among the five constructs proposed by Guimarães in [15]. The others are *class view*, *adapters* and *class extension*. All of these constructs share the idea of *shell*. A shell can be attached to a single object using dynamic shell and to a whole class using dynamic extension.

Adapters change the type of an object through a shell and are used to glue otherwise type-incompatible classes. They play a role similar to the Adapter pattern [11]. *Class extension* is a kind of mixin that can be applied to classes without editing the classes themselves. It is based on mixins and extensions of Ossher and Harrison [24]. *Class view* solves the problem of the misinterpretation of a class semantics in the code of other classes. Shells are used to correct the semantic of the objects. Using *class view*, the programmer can restrict the use of shells to specific regions[11] of the program. This is similar to use metaobjects to specific parts of the code.

The dynamic extension construct defined in this paper is simpler than the one proposed in [15]. This one allows a kind of parameterized dynamic extension. The dynamic extension class can use as type for variables and method parameters the name of the class in which the dynamic extension will be attached to.

Acknowledgments. We thank Ralph Johnson for many helpful comments, Brian Foote for suggesting some bibliography to this article and Mamdouh Ibrahim by responding some questions about the KSL language and sending us some papers.

[10] We are not considering method `interceptAll`.

[11] Code composed by methods, procedures, and functions.

References

1. Aksit, Mehmetl Wakita, Ken; Bosch, Jan; Bergmans, Lodewijk, and Yonezawa, Akinori. Abstracting Object Interactions Using Composition Filters. *Proceedings of ECOOP'93. Workshop on Object-Based Distributed Programming.* Lecture Notes in Computer Science No. 791, 1993.
2. Borning A. and O'Shea, T. DeltaTalk: An Empirically and Aesthetical Motivated Simplification of the Smalltalk-80 Language. *Proceedings of ECOOP 88. Lecture Notes in Computer Science* No. 322.
3. Chambers, Craig. Predicate Classes. *Proceedings of ECOOP'93. Lecture Notes in Computer Science* No. 707.
4. Chiba, Shigeru and Masuda, Takashi. Designing an Extensible Distributed Language with a Meta-Level Architecture. *Proceeding of ECOOP'93. Lecture Notes in Computer Science* No. 707, 1993.
5. Chiba, S. Open C++ Programmer's Guide. Technical Report 93-3, Department of Information Science, University of Tokyo, Tokyo, Japan, 1993.
6. Chiba, S. A Metaobject Protocol for C++. *SIGPLAN Notices*, Vol. 30, No. 10, October 1995, pg. 285-299, OOPSLA'95.
7. Cointe, Pierre. Metaclasses are First Class : the ObjVlisp Model. *SIGPLAN Notices*, Vol. 22, No. 12, December 1987. OOPSLA 87.
8. Cook, W. and Bracha, G. Mixin-based Inheritance. *SIGPLAN Notices*, Vol. 25, No. 10, October 1990, OOPSLA 90.
9. Ferber, Jacques. Computational Reflection in Class Based Object Oriented Languages. *SIGPLAN Notices*, Vol. 24, No. 10, October 1989. OOPSLA 89.
10. Foote, Brian and Johnson, Ralph. Reflective Facilities in Smalltalk-80. *SIGPLAN Notices*, Vol. 24, No. 10, October 1989. OOPSLA 89.
11. Gamma, Erich; Helm, Richard; Johnson, Ralph; Vlissides, John. *Design Patterns: Elements of Reusable Object-Oriented Software.* Professional Computing Series, Addison-Wesley, Reading, MA, 1994.
12. Gil, Joseph and Lorenz, David. Environmental Acquisition: A new Inheritance-Like Abstraction Mechanism. *SIGPLAN Notices*, Vol. 31, No. 10, October 1996, OOPSLA'96.
13. Goldberg, Adele and Robson, D. *Smalltalk-80: The Language and its Implementation.* Addison-Wesley, 1983.
14. Golm, M. Design and Implementation of a Meta Architecture for Java. Diplomarbeit im Fach Informatik, Friedrich-Alexander Uniersität, Erlangen-Nürnberg, Jan 1997.
15. Guimarães, José de Oliveira. *Filtros para Objetos.* PhD thesis, 1996. An English version of the thesis is also available with the title *Shells to Objects.*
16. Guimarães, José de Oliveira. Shells: The Green Metaobjects. http://www.dc.ufscar.br/~jose/shell.html.
17. Guimarães, José de Oliveira. The Green Language. http://www.dc.ufscar.br/~jose/green.html.
18. Ibrahim, Mamdouh and Bejcek, W. and Cummins, F. Instance Specialization without Delegation. *Journal of Object-Oriented Programming*, June 1991.
19. Ibrahim, Mamdouh. Reflection in Object-Oriented Programming. *International Journal on Artificial Intelligence Tools*, Vol. 1, No. 1, 1992.

20. Maes, Pattie. Concepts and Experiments in Computational Reflection. *SIGPLAN Notices*, Vol. 22, No. 12, December 1987. OOPSLA 87.
21. Mezini, Mira. Dynamic Object Evolution without Name Collisions. *Proceedings of ECOOP'97. Lecture Notes in Computer Science* No. 1241, 1997.
22. Oliva, Alexandre. The Reflexive Architecture of Guaraná. http://www.dcc.unicamp.br/~oliva/guarana.ps.gz.
23. O'Shea, Tim. Panel: The Learnability of Object-Oriented Programming Systems. *SIGPLAN Notices*, Vol. 21, No. 11, November 1986, OOPSLA 86.
24. Ossher, Harold and Harrison, Willian. Combination of Inheritance Hierarchies. *SIGPLAN Notices*, Vol. 27, No. 10, October 1992, OOPSLA'92.
25. Prehofer, Christian. Feature-Oriented Programming: A Fresh Look at Objects. *Proceedings of ECOOP'97. Lecture Notes in Computer Science* No. 1241, 1997.
26. Seiter, Linda; Palsberg, Jens, and Lieberherr, Karl. Evolution of Object Behavior using Context Relations. Accepted to publication in *IEEE Transactions on Software Engineering*. Available at http://www.ccs.neu.edu/research/demeter/biblio/context.html.
27. Steyaert, Patrick at al. Nested Mixin-Methods in Agora. *Proceedings of ECOOP'93. Lecture Notes in Computer Science* No. 707, 1993.
28. Templ, Joseph. Reflection in Oberon. In *ECOOP'92 Workshop on Object-Oriented Reflection and Metalevel Architectures.*
29. Templ, Joseph. Metaprogramming in Oberon. Swiss Federal Institute of Technology, Zurich, 1994.
30. Tomioka, Elisa; Guimarães, José de Oliveira; Prado, Antônio Francisco do. R-Java: uma Extensão de Java com Metaobjetos. *In English: R-Java, a Java Extension with Metaobjects.* Federal University of São Carlos, SP, Brazil. Unpublished report, 1998.
31. Wu, Z. and Schwiderski, S. Reflective Java: Making Java Even More Flexible. FTP: Architecture Projects Management Limited (apm@ansa.co.uk), Cambridge, UK, 1997.
32. Java Core Reflection: API and Specification. Java Soft, Mountain View, CA, USA, October 1996.

An Imperative, First-Order Calculus with Object Extension

Viviana Bono[1] and Kathleen Fisher[2]

[1] Dipartimento di Informatica
dell'Università di Torino
C.so Svizzera 185,
10149 Torino, Italy
bono@di.unito.it

[2] AT&T Labs—Research,
180 Park Ave.,
Florham Park, NJ 07932
+1 973 360-8675
kfisher@research.att.com
http://www.research.att.com/info/kfisher

Abstract. This paper presents an imperative object calculus designed to support class-based programming via a combination of extensible objects and encapsulation. This calculus simplifies the language presented in [17] in that, like C++ and Java, it chooses to support an imperative semantics instead of method specialization. We show how Java-style classes and "mixins" may be coded in this calculus, prove a type soundness theorem (via a subject reduction property), and give a sound and complete typing algorithm.

1 Introduction

Many theoretical studies have addressed the problem of modeling object-oriented languages via primitive operations [2, 18, 17, 6, 28, 30]. Most of these approaches have centered on object-based calculi, where objects, not classes, are seen as the primitive building blocks. However, statically-typed, class-based languages like Simula [5], Eiffel [26], C++ [16, 31], and Java [4] are the most common form of object-oriented language. Hence it is important to evaluate object-based calculi with respect to how well they support class-based programming. The main contribution of this paper is the formal study of a calculus of encapsulated extensible objects, which we use to model class hierarchies. This language simplifies the type system described in Fisher's dissertation [17], presents an imperative operational semantics, and gives a sound and complete typing algorithm. No such algorithm is known for the type system described in Fisher's dissertation.

To motivate our study, we begin with a comparison between our approach to modeling classes and the well-known *record-of-premethods* approach. This comparison, which summarizes [21], reveals why extensible calculi are relevant to class-based programming. Interested readers are referred to that paper for more details.

1.1 Premethod Model

In the context of object calculi, it seems natural to define inheritance using *premethods*, functions that are written with the intent of becoming object methods, but which are not yet installed in any object. Premethods are functions that explicitly depend on the "object itself," typically assumed to be the first parameter to the function. Following this idea, Abadi and Cardelli encoded classes in a pure object system using records of premethods [3]; these ideas are also used by Reppy and Riecke [29]. In this approach, a class is an object that contains a record of premethods and a constructor function used to package these premethods into objects.

The primary advantage of the record-of-premethods encoding is that it does not require a complicated form of object. All that is needed is a way of forming an object from a list of component definitions. However, this approach has some serious drawbacks. We discuss these drawbacks using a list of criteria [21] that characterizes the role of classes in class-based languages.

Does the class construct provide a coherent, extensible collection? The combination of a record of premethods and a constructor function may be thought of as a coherent, extensible collection. Because premethods are simply fields in a record, nothing requires that they be coherent until a constructor function is supplied. Since the constructor function installs the premethods into an object, however, the fact that a given constructor is typable implies that the premethods it uses are coherent. Notice, however, that nothing requires a given constructor to mention all of the premethods in a given premethod record.

Does the class construct guarantee initialization? In more elaborate record-of-premethod models, the code to initialize private instance variables is guaranteed to run if any of the associated premethods is installed into an object. However, constructor functions cannot be reused usefully in derived classes. A consequence is that if a class designer puts initialization code into a class constructor, that code will not be executed for derived classes. There are several program-development scenarios where this weakness would be a serious problem. For example, class designers may wish to perform some kind of bookkeeping whenever objects are instantiated from a class or its descendants. To achieve it, programmers need a place to put code that will execute whenever an object is instantiated. With the record-of-premethods approach, however, there is no appropriate place: no base class constructor function will be called for derived classes, and a premethod function may be called without creating an object.

Does the class construct provide an explicit type hierarchy? In many existing class-based languages, it is possible to restrict the subtypes of an "implementation" object type (*i.e.*, a class) to classes that inherit all or part of the object's implementation. This restriction may be useful for optimizing operations on objects, allowing access to argument objects in binary methods, and guaranteeing semantic consistency beyond type considerations [24]. A special case of this capability is the ability to define *final* classes, as recognized in work on Rapide [24] and incorporated (presumably independently) as a language feature in Java. This ability is lacking in the record-of-premethods approach since any object whose type is a structural subtype of another type τ can be used as an object of type τ.

Does the class mechanism automatically propagate base class changes? Because derived class constructors must explicitly name the methods that they wish to inherit, the record-of-premethods approach does not automatically propagate base class method changes. In particular, if a derived class `D` is defined from a base class `B` in Java or related languages, then adding a method to `B` will result in an additional method of `D`, and similarly for every other class derived from `B` (and there may be many). With the record-of-premethods approach, derived class constructors must be explicitly rewritten each time base classes change. Since object-oriented programs are typically quite large and maintenance may be distributed across many people, the person who maintains a base class may fail to inform those maintaining its derived classes of its change, causing unpredictable errors. There is no mechanism in this approach to detect such errors automatically.

1.2 Extensible Object Model

While we readily admit that its simplicity is a virtue, the above discussion reveals that several important and desirable features of class-based programming are lost in the record-of-premethods model. Extensible objects provide a rich alternative. A principled way to think about class-based object-oriented languages is as the combination of two orthogonal components [21, 17]: (*i*), an object system that supports inheritance and message sending and (*ii*), an encapsulation mechanism that provides hiding. We call this model of classes the "Classes = Extensible Objects + Encapsulation" approach. Referring to the class-evaluation checklist we used to evaluate the pre-methods model, we can see that this approach successfully addresses each of the points listed there: it provides an extensible coherent collection, guarantees initialization, supports an explicit type hierarchy, and automatically propagates base class changes.

Extensible, Coherent Collection. Extensible objects obviate the need for premethods, since collections of methods that are already installed in objects may be extended. Because of this fact, we may impose static constraints on the ways in which one method may be combined with others. For example, if an object contains two mutually recursive methods, then we cannot replace one with another of a different type. In contrast, in the record-of-premethods approach, it is possible to form a record of premethods without a "covering" constructor that checks to be sure that all of the premethods are coherent.

Guaranteed Initialization. A second advantage of extensible objects is that class constructors and initialization code can be inherited, *i.e.*, reused in derived classes. For example, to create `ColorPoint` objects, we may invoke a `Point` class constructor and add color methods to the resulting extensible object. This process guarantees that the `Point` class has the opportunity to initialize any inherited components properly. It also guarantees that the designers of the `Point` class have the opportunity to update any bookkeeping information they may be keeping about instantiations of `Point` objects.

Explicit Type Hierarchy. A further advantage is the rich subtyping structure of this approach. In particular, it provides "implementation" types that subtype along the inheritance hierarchy, "interface" types that subtype via structural subtyping rules, and a hybrid subtyping relation that allows implementation types to be subtypes of interface types. With this subtyping structure, programmers can use implementation types where the extra information is useful and interface types where more generality is required.

Automatic Propagation of Changes. Another advantage arises with private (or protected) methods. In the extensible-object formulation, methods always remain within an object, even when it is extended. These hidden methods exist in all future extensions, but they can only be accessed by methods that were defined before the method became hidden. Furthermore, these private methods need not be manipulated explicitly by derived class constructors to insure that they are treated properly.

These advantages may be seen in our encoding of the traditional `Point` and `ColorPoint` hierarchy, presented in pseudo-type-theory in the next section to develop intuitions for our model. In Section 3, we present our formal language and its type system. In Section 4, we revisit the `Point` hierarchy, this time in full formality. We also illustrate how our model can accommodate *mixins*, functions that return extensions of their argument objects. We introduce our imperative operational semantics in Section 5, and in Section 6 we sketch the soundness proof for the calculus with respect to the operational semantics (via a subject reduction theorem in the style of Abadi and Cardelli [1]). Section 7 presents a typing algorithm for our system. We conclude with a discussion of related work and some thoughts on future directions. A preliminary version of this paper (without type soundness and without the typing algorithm) appeared in the FOOL'98 workshop proceedings [8].

2 Pseudo-Type-Theoretic `Point`, `ColorPoint` Hierarchy

In the "Classes = Extensible Objects + Encapsulation" model of classes [17], extensible objects support the inheritance aspects of classes, while an encapsulation mechanism provides the hiding. We illustrate the ideas behind this model by encoding the familiar `Point`, `ColorPoint` hierarchy in pseudo-type theory. The code, which appears in Figure 2, contains two class declarations followed by "*Client Code.*"

To explain the model, we focus on the **Class** encapsulation construct, which provides the outer wrapping for each of the class declarations. In it, the **Class** clause names the abstraction-as-class, `Point` in the first case, `ColorPoint` in the second. The **implements** clause gives the public and protected interfaces supported by the class, *"Point_public_interface"* and *"Point_protected_interface,"* respectively, in the `Point` case. A public interface lists the methods available from instances of its class. Such a list for a simple `Point` class might be of the form ⟪`getX` : *int*, `setX` : *int* → *unit*⟫, revealing that objects of the class contain `getX` and `setX` methods of the indicated types. At the discretion of the

Class Declarations

Class `Point` **implements** *"Point_public_interface"*, *"Point_protected_interface"*
exports `newP` : *int* → *"extensible object type from* `Point` *class"*
is
⦃ *"Point_private_interface"*; *"code to implement* `newP`*"* ⦄
end;

Class `ColorPoint` **implements** *"CP_public_interface"*, *"CP_protected_interface"*
exports `newCP` : *color* → *int* → *"non-extensible object type from* `ColorPoint` *class"*
is
⦃ *"CP_private_interface"*; *"code to implement* `newCP`*"* ⦄
end;

in
"If desired, restrict return types of non-final constructors;"
"Client Code"
end

Fig. 1. Pseudo-type-theoretic version of a `Point`, `ColorPoint` hierarchy.

class designer, a class's public interface may explicitly name its parent class, if one exists. For example, the `ColorPoint` public interface might be of the form ⟨`Point` | `getC` : *color*, `setC` : *color* → *unit*⟩. The `Point` portion of this interface indicates that objects created from the `ColorPoint` class were formed via inheritance from the `Point` class; hence, they have the `Point` class methods. In addition, by thus indicating the parent class, the `ColorPoint` class designer declares that the "implementation type" associated with the `ColorPoint` class is a subtype of the `Point` class's "implementation type." Through this declaration mechanism, the model supports an explicit type hierarchy. The second half of the `ColorPoint` public interface indicates that the `ColorPoint` class added `getC` and `setC` methods.

The protected interface augments the public one with information for deriving classes. In our model, this information consists of method and field names that may not be used in derived classes without introducing name clashes.

The **exports** clause of our encapsulation mechanism reveals the names and types of the non-dynamically dispatched operations defined by the class. In general, this clause lists constructor and "friend" functions. In our example, the `Point` class designer chose to export a single constructor function, `newP` of type *int* → "*extensible object type from* `Point` *class.*" By making the return type an extensible object type, the class designer enabled inheritance from this class: a derived class calls `newP` to get the implementation of the `Point` class and then adds and redefines components as necessary. Since the `ColorPoint` class designer made `newCP` return a non-extensible object, the `ColorPoint` class is "final," in the sense that no other class can be formed by extending its implementation. The

`Point` class designer opted to make the return type of `newP` flag its defining class (via the "*from* `Point` *class*" annotation). Because this information is present in the constructor type, the `ColorPoint` class designer can export its parent's identity. Without it, the derived class could reuse its parent's implementation but could not reveal this fact nor make the `ColorPoint` implementation type a subtype of the `Point` implementation type.

The **is** clause of the encapsulation mechanism has two pieces. The first part, the private interface, lists all the methods defined within the class. For a simple `Point` class, this interface might be of the form $\langle\!\langle$`x` : *int*, `getX` : *int*, `setX` : *int* → *unit*$\rangle\!\rangle$, where `x` is a private field.

The second piece of a class implementation is the code to implement the constructor and friend functions listed in the **exports** clause. In the `Point` class case, this code simply defines an extensible object with field `x` and methods `getX` and `setX`. For the `ColorPoint` class, the constructor implementation first calls `newP` to inherit the `Point` class behavior and then adds color-related fields and methods. Such code appears in Section 3.1. If the `ColorPoint` class advertises the fact that it inherits from `Point` in its public interface, then the type system insures that the `ColorPoint` constructor function calls `newP` and returns an extension of the resulting object. Thus the type system guarantees that the `Point` class has a chance to initialize its private variables and set up its desired invariants for any object instantiated from it, either directly or via a derived class.

Because the **Class** construct is an encapsulation mechanism, only the aspects of the **is** code specifically mentioned in the **implements** and **exports** clauses can be used in the rest of the program. Hence in the encoding, this mechanism ensures the privacy of private methods and fields.

After we process all the class declarations in the pseudo-code, we are almost ready to execute the "*Client Code.*" Without any further adjustment, however, non-final classes have constructor functions that return extensible objects, which enable run-time inheritance. If we wish to disable this feature, we may restrict the return types of these constructor functions to return "non-extensible" objects instead. This type restriction does not involve changing the values in any way; it simply adjusts the types. The restriction is safe because every extensible object type in our system is a subtype of the corresponding non-extensible version.

Now that we have examined the overall structure of a simple class hierarchy in our model, we move to formalizing our language.

3 Our Extensible Calculus

Fisher's dissertation [17] formally presents a functional object calculus that includes extensible objects and encapsulation. This calculus realizes the benefits described in the previous sections. In addition, it includes "mytype" type variables to support method specialization. Unfortunately, these variables greatly complicate analysis. Consequently, to understand the "Classes = Extensible Objects + Encapsulation" idea in its simplest form, Fisher and Mitchell [21] use a simpler language without a "mytype" mechanism, but they do not study the formal properties of that simpler language. The formal study of such a language is the subject of this paper.

Our calculus, like the one in Fisher's dissertation, includes extensible objects and encapsulation; however, it differs in several key aspects. In particular, to compensate for the lack of a "mytype" mechanism, we have adopted an imperative semantics. Hence instead of cascading messages:

$$((\mathtt{ob} \Leftarrow \mathtt{m_1}(\mathtt{arg_1})\ldots) \Leftarrow \mathtt{m_n}(\mathtt{arg_n})$$

a programmer can send a sequence of messages to the same object:

$$\mathtt{ob} \Leftarrow \mathtt{m_1}(\mathtt{arg_1}); \quad \cdots; \quad \mathtt{ob} \Leftarrow \mathtt{m_n}(\mathtt{arg_n});$$

Moreover, the more complex type system insures the soundness of the object extension operator by tracking method *absences*. Tracking absences requires recording the list of all methods which might be added to the object in the future. This practice has the unfortunate consequence of requiring parent classes to guess what methods their descendants will want to add. In contrast, in the calculus described in this paper, we adjust the type system to track potential method *presences* instead, relieving super objects (*i.e.*, parent classes) of the need for clairvoyance.

To facilitate the type soundness proof, we have added bounded universal types to our language. In the process, we have gained the ability to write "mixins," functions that take an object as an argument and return an extension of that object as a result. For example, a `color` mixin might add a `color` method to any extensible object that does not already contain `color`.

Finally, our calculus differs from that in [17] in that there is no known typing algorithm for the language with "mytype".

3.1 The Syntax

The calculus extends an untyped lambda calculus with (*i*) object primitives to build extensible (and updateable) objects, (*ii*) existential types to provide encapsulation, and (*iii*) universal types to write polymorphic method bodies. Classes as primitive expressions do not appear in our calculus. Instead, (hierarchies of) classes may be modeled within our language features: inheritance and information hiding are rendered in an orthogonal way, respectively by extensible objects and encapsulation.

Intuitively, an object is a collection of *methods* and *fields*, each of which has a name and a body. We syntactically distinguish between methods and fields because they have different semantic and typing properties. Briefly, a method is a function which takes as an (implicit) argument its host object, whereas a field can be seen as part of its host object's state.

An expression of the untyped calculus can be any of the following:

$$
\begin{aligned}
e ::= \; & x \mid c \mid \lambda x.e \mid e_1 e_2 \mid \textbf{let } x = e_1 \textbf{ in } e_2 \mid \\
& \langle\rangle \mid \\
& e \Leftarrow m \mid \langle e_1 \leftarrow m = e_2 \rangle \mid \langle e_1 \leftarrow\!\!+\; m = e_2 \rangle \mid \\
& e.f \mid \langle e_1.f := e_2 \rangle \mid \langle e_1 \leftarrow\!\!+ : f = e_2 \rangle \mid \\
& \{\!| r <:_w R :: L = R_1,\, e |\!\} \mid \\
& \textbf{Abstype } r <:_w R :: L \textbf{ with } x : \tau \textbf{ is } e_1 \textbf{ in } e_2 \mid \\
& \Lambda().e \mid e * ()
\end{aligned}
$$

where x is a term variable, c is a constant, $\lambda x.e$ is function abstraction, $e_1 e_2$ is function application, and **let** $x = e_1$ **in** e_2 is let abstraction. In the object-related forms, we use m to denote method names and f for field names. These object forms may be interpreted as follows:

- $\langle\rangle$ is the empty object.
- $e \Leftarrow m$ and $e.f$ are respectively method and field invocation on object e.
- $\langle e_1 \leftarrow m = e_2 \rangle$ and $\langle e_1.f := e_2 \rangle$ respectively override an existing method or field in e_1 with a new body e_2.
- $\langle e_1 \leftarrow\!\!+\; m = e_2 \rangle$ and $\langle e_1 \leftarrow\!\!+ : f = e_2 \rangle$ extend e_1 with a new method or a new field, respectively. In either case, expression e_2 provides the body of the new component.

We defer a discussion about the remaining syntactic forms to Section 3.2, as they are closely related to types.

To illustrate our language, we show how the `newP` and `newCP` constructor functions from Section 2 may be written.

$$
\begin{aligned}
\texttt{newP} \stackrel{def}{=} \lambda\texttt{ix}.\langle\langle\langle\, \langle\rangle \leftarrow\!\!+ : \; & \texttt{x} = \texttt{ix}\,\rangle \\
\leftarrow\!\!+\; & \texttt{getX} = \Lambda().\,\lambda\texttt{self}.(\texttt{self.x})\rangle \\
\leftarrow\!\!+\; & \texttt{setX} = \Lambda().\,\lambda\texttt{self}.\,\lambda\texttt{newX}.\ \texttt{self.x} := \texttt{newX}\rangle
\end{aligned}
$$

The Λ symbols in the method bodies serve to flag the polymorphic nature of the methods. To define `newCP`, we add the appropriate color-related fields and methods to the result of invoking `newP` with parameter `ix`:

$$
\begin{aligned}
\texttt{newCP} \stackrel{def}{=} \; & \lambda\texttt{ic}.\,\lambda\texttt{ix}. \\
& \langle\langle\langle \texttt{newP ix} \leftarrow\!\!+ : \; \texttt{c} = \texttt{ic}\rangle \\
& \leftarrow\!\!+\; \texttt{getC} = \Lambda().\,\lambda\texttt{self}.(\texttt{self.c})\rangle \\
& \leftarrow\!\!+\; \texttt{setC} = \Lambda().\,\lambda\texttt{self}.\,\lambda\texttt{newC}. \\
& \qquad \texttt{self.c} := \texttt{newC}\rangle
\end{aligned}
$$

3.2 The Type System

Our type system is centered around object types. Informally, an object type is a list of *label:type* pairs, each representing a method or field name with its type. Our calculus supports two sorts of object [19]: *prototypes*, typed with **pro**-types, and "proper" objects, typed with **obj**-types. A prototype can be extended with new methods and fields and its components can be overridden, but it supports only trivial subtyping. A prototype can be "sealed" to reach the status of proper object (see Section 3.4), to which subtyping applies, but then it is no longer extensible or overrideable. This restriction is to avoid the well-known unsoundness that arises when combining object operations with subsumption (*c.f.* [20]).

The type syntax is as follows:

Types:

$$\tau ::= unit \mid \iota \mid \tau_1 \rightarrow \tau_2 \mid \mathbf{pro}.R \mid \mathbf{obj}.R \mid$$
$$\forall (r <:_w R :: L)\tau \mid \exists (r <:_w R :: L)\tau$$

Rows:

$$R ::= r \mid \langle\!\langle\rangle\!\rangle \mid \langle\!\langle R \mid l : \tau \rangle\!\rangle$$

Kinds:

$$\gamma ::= \mathtt{T} \mid L$$

All ::= A countable set of method and field labels.

$$L ::= \mathrm{L} \subseteq All$$

Types include the *unit* type, constant types, function types, object types of the two sorts, and universally and existentially quantified types. We will use the syntax $\mathbf{probj}.R$ as shorthand for either $\mathbf{pro}.R$ or $\mathbf{obj}.R$.

Rows, which are intuitively lists of typed method and field names, include row variables r, the empty row $\langle\!\langle\rangle\!\rangle$, and rows formed by extending other rows with a *label:type* pair, $\langle\!\langle R \mid l : \tau \rangle\!\rangle$. Well-formed types have kind T, while rows have kinds that are subsets of All, the set of all labels that can occur in any row. Intuitively, if row R has kind L, then at least all the labels listed in R appear in L. For notational convenience, we write closed rows (*i.e.*, rows without row variables) using the notations $\langle\!\langle m_i : \tau_i, f_j : \tau'_j \rangle\!\rangle^{i \in I, j \in J}$ and $\langle\!\langle l_1 : \tau_1, \ldots, l_n : \tau_n \rangle\!\rangle$.

Introduced by Wand [32], rows are the tool we use to incorporate polymorphism into our system. We need polymorphism to type extensible objects. Because each method takes its host object as an argument, each method body must be polymorphic to work properly in extensions of its original host. Technical considerations require that method body types be closed to prove our subject reduction theorem. Consequently, we have introduced universal quantifiers on row variables to provide closed, polymorphic types. Fortuitously, this type construct makes our system more expressive for it allows us to type *mixins*, functions that take objects as parameters and return extensions of those objects as results. Finally, existential quantifiers on row variables produce abstract "object" types. Intuitively, such types reveal an object's interface (*i.e.*, the list of methods and fields to which the object will respond) and abstract away implementation details in a fashion similar to abstract data types.

Because of their roles, we find it useful to have partial information about the row variables quantified in $\forall$ and $\exists$ types. To that end, each row variable is declared with a width-supertyping bound R and a kind L: $(r <:_w R ::$

L). Intuitively, R provides a lower bound on the amount of information that instances of r must contain: every such instance must have at least the methods mentioned in R. The kind L records an upper bound on the labels present in any instance of r. A new label can be added to a row only if it is not already present in L.

3.3 Judgment Forms

We use *row* and *term contexts* in our calculus, defined respectively as follows:

$$\rho ::= \epsilon \mid \rho, (r <:_w R :: L)$$
$$\Gamma ::= \emptyset \mid \Gamma, x : \tau$$

Intuitively, row contexts record assumptions about row variables, while term contexts associate types with term variables. Functions $dom(\rho)$ and $dom(\Gamma)$ return the variables listed in the domains of ρ and Γ, respectively. Judgments are as follows:

$\rho \vdash *$	well-formed row context ρ
$\rho \vdash \tau : \mathrm{T}$	well-formed type τ in context ρ
$\rho \vdash R :: L$	row R has kind L in context ρ
$\rho \vdash \tau_1 <: \tau_2$	type τ_1 is a subtype of τ_2 in context ρ
$\rho \vdash R_1 <:_B R_2$	row R_1 is a B-subtype of R_2 in context ρ
$\rho ; \Gamma \vdash *$	well-formed contexts ρ and Γ
$\rho ; \Gamma \vdash e : \tau$	term e has type τ in contexts ρ and Γ

where the B in the fifth judgment form is a ***subtyping annotation*** that denotes which subtyping relation has been applied between the two rows R_1 and R_2 (width, or width and depth). Intuitively, width subtyping "forgets" the presence of methods and fields, while depth subtyping "forgets" details about particular method types.

3.4 Subtyping

Our subtyping system includes the standard rules for reflexivity, transitivity, and the contravariant rule for function subtyping. It also makes type *unit* the top type with respect to the subtyping order. In addition, we have a rule for subtyping between object types:

$$(<: obj) \qquad \frac{\rho \vdash R_1 <:_B R_2}{\rho \vdash \mathbf{probj}.R_1 <: \mathbf{obj}.R_2}$$

This rule is used both to "seal" objects, *i.e.*, promote them from an extensible form to a nonextensible one, and to infer subtyping relations between **obj**-types. Subtyping between objects occurs at the level of their component lists, *i.e.*, the rows. For example, we have the following rules to compute the standard width and depth subtyping, respectively:

$$(<:w)\quad \frac{\rho \vdash R_1 <:_B R_2 \qquad \rho \vdash \langle\!\langle R_1 \,|\, l : \tau \rangle\!\rangle :: L_1}{\rho \vdash \langle\!\langle R_1 \,|\, l : \tau \rangle\!\rangle <:_B R_2}$$

$$(<:d)\quad \frac{\rho \vdash R_1 <:_B R_2 \qquad \rho \vdash \tau_1 <: \tau_2 \qquad \rho \vdash \langle\!\langle R_i \,|\, m : \tau_i \rangle\!\rangle :: L_i \quad i \in \{1,2\}}{\rho \vdash \langle\!\langle R_1 \,|\, m : \tau_1 \rangle\!\rangle <:_{B+d} \langle\!\langle R_2 \,|\, m : \tau_2 \rangle\!\rangle}$$

Note that the depth subtyping rule applies only to methods. Because fields are updatable, we prevent depth subtyping from applying to fields to preserve type soundness. As this point illustrates, width and depth subtyping have different properties. It is therefore crucial that we control where depth subtyping can occur. For example, when we substitute a row R for an existentially or universally bound row variable r, we need to know that R is a width-only subtype of r's bound. To that end, we annotate the "$<:$" symbol with B:

$$B ::= w \mid w,d \mid B_1 + B_2$$

Here, w stands for "width-only" and w,d stands for "depth-allowed." Annotation w is less than w,d, and $+$ denotes the least upper bound of B_1 and B_2 with respect to this ordering. Our subtyping rules on rows are designed to track where depth subtyping occurs with these annotations.

The complete set of subtyping rules appears in Appendix A.

3.5 Type-Related Expressions

With this background, we may now discuss the term expressions that involve quantified row variables. The universal quantifier forms are $\Lambda().\,e$ for row abstraction and $e * ()$ for row application. These forms, which signal where row polymorphism occurs, can be considered as place-holders for the universal quantifier introduction and elimination typing rules.

We use the existential quantifier forms to provide a data abstraction mechanism. In general, data abstraction is a well-known technique for building a complex data structure with an internal representation not directly accessible by its clients (the *implementation*) and a set of (public) operations which provide controlled access to the structure. Our **Abstype** construct, which has the form:

$$\textbf{Abstype } r <:_w R :: L \textbf{ with } x : \tau \textbf{ is } e_1 \textbf{ in } e_2$$

declares a data abstraction named r with an available operation x. The construct binds r, which is technically a row variable, to a concrete row defined in e_1, the implementation of the abstraction. When we use this construct to model classes, r serves as the name of a class and is bound to the class's private interface. Similarly, the construct binds x, technically a term variable, to an implementation defined within e_1. In the class model, x names the class constructor function. The public interface of this abstraction is mediated by the bounds R and L on r and the type τ declared for x. Typically, τ will be written in terms of r. Intuitively, R describes the components guaranteed to be in r; it is the class's *"public_interface."* L describes the component names that *may* be used in r. Data structure r can only be extended with components whose names are not listed in L. Hence L may be viewed as the class's *"protected_interface."* Expression e_2 represents the code in which this data structure may be used; it is the *"Client Code."*

An implementation ($\{\!|r <:_w R :: L = R', e|\!\}$) of an abstract type is characterized by R' and e. Row R' is the actual set of components used to implement the data structure. The components listed in both R and R' may be regarded as public, while those appearing only in R' are private. In the class model, R' serves as the *"private_interface."* Expression e is the (hidden) implementation code; it provides the constructor implementation in the class model.

3.6 Typing Rules

In this section, we discuss two of the key typing rules of the system. For reference, all typing rules appear in Appendix A, together with the standard rules for inferring the well-formedness of contexts, rows, and types.

We examine the (*meth ext*) rule in detail to illustrate how we use row-polymorphism:

$$(meth\ ext)\quad \frac{\begin{array}{c}\rho\,;\,\Gamma \vdash e_1 : \mathbf{pro}.R \\ \rho \vdash R :: L \qquad\qquad m \notin L \\ \rho\,;\,\Gamma \vdash e_2 : \forall (r <:_w \langle\!\langle R \,|\, m : \tau\rangle\!\rangle :: All)\mathbf{pro}.r \rightarrow \tau\end{array}}{\rho\,;\,\Gamma \vdash \langle e_1 \longleftrightarrow\!\!+\, m = e_2\rangle : \mathbf{pro}.\langle\!\langle R \,|\, m : \tau\rangle\!\rangle}$$

Judgment $\rho\,;\,\Gamma \vdash e_1 : \mathbf{pro}.R$ asserts that expression e_1 is a prototype with methods listed in row R. The next judgment insures that row R has at most the labels in L; the side-condition assures us that m is not one of these labels. The final judgment guarantees that method body e_2 is appropriately polymorphic: it will map any possible extension of its current host object, (*i.e.*, its first parameter, which we call *self*), to an expression of type τ, the type of method m. Type $\mathbf{pro}.r$ is an appropriate choice to represent the type of *self* since r may be instantiated with any row that has *at least* the methods in $\langle\!\langle R \,|\, m : \tau\rangle\!\rangle$ and may have *any* other methods, reflected in its maximal kind *All*. Internal extensions (*i.e.*, extensions on *self*) are unsound, so they must be forbidden. The kind *All* in the (*meth ext*) typing rule asserts that *self* may already contain "all" possible methods, so it cannot be extended with any more.

The existential quantifier introduction rule matches the semantics of data type implementations:

$$(\exists\ intro)\quad \frac{\rho \vdash R' <:_w R \qquad \rho \vdash R' :: L \qquad \rho\,;\Gamma \vdash e : [R'/r]\tau}{\rho\,;\Gamma \vdash \{\!|(r <:_w R :: L) = R',\ e|\!\} : \exists(r <:_w R :: L)\tau}$$

In this rule, row R' is the private interface of the data structure. It must be consistent with the public bound R and kind L, as required by the first two hypotheses. The final hypothesis requires expression e, the implementation of the abstraction, to have the appropriate type when r is replaced by R'.

4 Examples

4.1 Class Hierarchy

Using the extensible objects and abstract datatype mechanism from the previous section, we may formalize Section 2's simple class hierarchy of `Points` and `ColorPoints` as shown in Figure 2. As in Section 2, the two abstract type declarations in the figure define `Point` and `ColorPoint` classes, in that order. The first **Abstype** expression introduces row variable *Point*, which serves as the "name" of the formal `Point` class. (The **Abstype** keyword replaces the keyword **Class** from the pseudo-code of Section 2.) Row *Point* is width-bounded by row P_{pub}, `Point`'s *"public_interface."* This row, defined in Figure 2, lists the methods and fields available to clients and descendants of the `Point` class, namely **getX** and **setX**. The kind L_p, defined in Figure 2 to be label set {x, **getX**, **setX**}, indicates that descendant classes may add any methods except ones with these names; it serves as `Point`'s *"protected_interface."*

The **with** clause of the declaration, replacing the earlier **exports** clause, specifies that the constructor for the `Point` class, named **newP**, returns expressions with type **pro**.*Point*, an *"extensible object type from* `Point` *class."* The constructor returns a prototype so that descendant classes may define their objects via extension from the `Point` class constructor. The row variable *Point* in the return type signals that objects returned by the constructor are defined in the `Point` class. We call such types ***partially abstract*** after [13] because a portion of their structure is hidden. The constructor for the `ColorPoint` class returns expressions with type **obj**.*CPoint*, a *"non-extensible object type from* `ColorPoint` *class."* The fact that **obj** types do not support inheritance primitives insures that the `ColorPoint` class is final.

The **is** clause of the abstraction describes the implementation of the `Point` class. Within this implementation, the row P_{priv} describes the full representation of `Point` class objects by listing all of the components defined in the class and giving their associated types; it is the *"private_interface."* The expression $\mathtt{Imp}_p$, defined towards the bottom of Figure 2, gives the implementation of the

$$
\begin{array}{l}
\textbf{Abstype } \mathit{Point} <:_w P_{pub} :: L_p \\
\quad \textbf{with } \mathtt{newP} : \mathit{int} \rightarrow \textbf{pro}.\mathit{Point} \\
\qquad \textbf{is } \{\!\!\{ \mathit{Point} <:_w P_{pub} :: L_p = P_{priv},\ \mathtt{Imp}_p \}\!\!\} \\
\qquad \textbf{in} \\
\qquad\quad \textbf{Abstype } \mathit{CPoint} <:_w CP_{pub} :: L_{cp} \\
\qquad\qquad \textbf{with } \mathtt{newCP} : \mathit{color} \rightarrow \mathit{int} \rightarrow \textbf{obj}.\mathit{CPoint} \\
\qquad\qquad\quad \textbf{is } \{\!\!\{ \mathit{CPoint} <:_w CP_{pub} :: L_{cp} = CP_{priv},\ \mathtt{Imp}_{cp} \}\!\!\} \\
\qquad\qquad\quad \textbf{in} \\
\qquad\qquad\qquad \textbf{let } \mathtt{newP} : \mathit{int} \rightarrow \textbf{obj}.\mathit{Point} = \mathtt{newP} \\
\qquad\qquad\qquad \textbf{in } \ \langle \mathtt{Client\ Code} \rangle
\end{array}
$$

where

$$
\begin{array}{ll}
P_{pub} & \stackrel{def}{=} \langle\!\langle \mathtt{getX} : \mathit{int},\ \mathtt{setX} : \mathit{int} \rightarrow \mathit{unit} \rangle\!\rangle \\
P_{priv} & \stackrel{def}{=} \langle\!\langle \mathtt{x} : \mathit{int},\ \mathtt{getX} : \mathit{int},\ \mathtt{setX} : \mathit{int} \rightarrow \mathit{unit} \rangle\!\rangle \\
CP_{pub} & \stackrel{def}{=} \langle\!\langle \mathit{Point} \,|\, \mathtt{getC} : \mathit{color},\ \mathtt{setC} : \mathit{color} \rightarrow \mathit{unit} \rangle\!\rangle \\
CP_{priv} & \stackrel{def}{=} \langle\!\langle \mathit{Point} \,|\, \mathtt{c} : \mathit{color},\ \mathtt{getC} : \mathit{color},\ \mathtt{setC} : \mathit{color} \rightarrow \mathit{unit} \rangle\!\rangle \\
L_p & \stackrel{def}{=} \{\mathtt{x}, \mathtt{getX}, \mathtt{setX}\} \\
L_{cp} & \stackrel{def}{=} \{\mathtt{x}, \mathtt{getX}, \mathtt{setX}, \mathtt{c}, \mathtt{getC}, \mathtt{setC}\}
\end{array}
$$

and

$$
\begin{array}{l}
\mathtt{Imp}_p \stackrel{def}{=} \lambda \mathtt{ix}.\langle\langle\langle\ \langle\rangle \leftarrow\!\!\!+ :\ \ \mathtt{x} = \mathtt{ix}\ \rangle \\
\qquad\qquad\qquad\qquad \leftarrow\!\!\!+\ \mathtt{getX} = \Lambda().\ \lambda\mathtt{self}.(\mathtt{self.x})\rangle \\
\qquad\qquad\qquad\qquad \leftarrow\!\!\!+\ \mathtt{setX} = \Lambda().\ \lambda\mathtt{self}.\ \lambda\mathtt{newX}.\ \mathtt{self.x} \coloneqq \mathtt{newX}\rangle
\end{array}
$$

$$
\begin{array}{l}
\mathtt{Imp}_{cp} \stackrel{def}{=} \lambda\mathtt{ic}.\ \lambda\mathtt{ix}. \\
\qquad\qquad \langle\langle\langle\, \mathtt{newP\ ix} \leftarrow\!\!\!+ :\ \ \mathtt{c} = \mathtt{ic}\rangle \\
\qquad\qquad\qquad\qquad \leftarrow\!\!\!+\ \mathtt{getC} = \Lambda().\ \lambda\mathtt{self}.(\mathtt{self.c})\rangle \\
\qquad\qquad\qquad\qquad \leftarrow\!\!\!+\ \mathtt{setC} = \Lambda().\ \lambda\mathtt{self}.\ \lambda\mathtt{newC}. \\
\qquad\qquad\qquad\qquad\qquad\qquad \mathtt{self.c} \coloneqq \mathtt{newC}\rangle
\end{array}
$$

Fig. 2. Nested abstract datatypes for `Point` and `ColorPoint` classes.

constructor `newP`. The type system insures that $\texttt{Imp}_p$'s type is **pro.**Point with *Point* replaced by `Point`'s private interface, P_{priv}. The **Abstype** construct binds row variable *Point* to P_{priv} and variable `newP` to $\texttt{Imp}_p$ within the scope of its **in** clause.

The structure of the `ColorPoint` **Abstype** declaration is similar. There are several aspects of this declaration that are worth mentioning however. In particular, notice that the `ColorPoint` constructor, implemented via the $\texttt{Imp}_{cp}$ function defined at the bottom of Figure 2, invokes `newP` to inherit `Point`'s implementation and initialization code. Notice also that the `ColorPoint` class publicly names the `Point` class as its parent by listing *Point* in its public interface CP_{pub}. Without thus naming its parent, the `ColorPoint` object type (**obj.**CPoint) would not be a subtype of `Point`'s object type (**obj.**Point) because the only way to be a subtype of a partially abstract type is to extend that type. The row variable *Point* in CP_{pub} signals that `ColorPoint` objects were formed via extension from `Point` prototypes, and hence their partially abstract types may be related via subtyping. This fact is the theoretical counterpart to the observation we made in the introduction: a portion of the subtyping hierarchy is determined by inheritance relationships.

Finally, the **let** declaration in Figure 2 restricts the type of the extensible constructor function `newP` to its non-extensible variant. Technically, this shadowing is type correct because **pro** types are subtypes of **obj** types [19].

4.2 Mixins

The bounded universal quantifiers in our calculus allow us to type *mixins*, functions that take extensible objects as parameters and return extensions of those objects as results. For example, we may write a mixin that adds a `move` method to any object that already has *int* `getX` and $\mathit{int} \rightarrow \mathit{unit}$ `setX` methods:

$$\begin{array}{l}
\textbf{let}\ \texttt{addMove}\ =\ \Lambda().\,\lambda\texttt{ob}.\langle \texttt{ob} \leftarrow\!\!+\ \texttt{move} = \Lambda().\,\lambda\texttt{s}.\,\lambda\texttt{dx}.\,\texttt{s} \Leftarrow \texttt{setX}(\texttt{dx} + \texttt{s} \Leftarrow \texttt{getX})\rangle \\
\quad \textbf{in let}\ \texttt{y}\ = \langle\ \langle\rangle \leftarrow\!\!+ :\quad \texttt{x} = 3, \\
\qquad\qquad\qquad \leftarrow\!\!+\ \texttt{getX} = \Lambda().\,\lambda\texttt{s}.\,\texttt{s.x}, \\
\qquad\qquad\qquad \leftarrow\!\!+\ \texttt{setX} = \Lambda().\,\lambda\texttt{s}.\,\lambda\texttt{nx}.\langle \texttt{s.x} := \texttt{nx}\rangle\rangle \\
\qquad \textbf{in}\ \texttt{addMove} * ()\,\texttt{y}
\end{array}$$

We may give the various program fragments the following types:

$$\begin{array}{c}
\texttt{addMove} : \forall (r <:_w \langle\!\langle \texttt{getX} : \mathit{int}, \texttt{setX} : \mathit{int} \rightarrow \mathit{unit} \rangle\!\rangle :: L) \\
\qquad \textbf{pro.}r \rightarrow \textbf{pro.}\langle\!\langle r \mid \texttt{move} : \mathit{int} \rightarrow \mathit{unit} \rangle\!\rangle \\[1ex]
\texttt{y} : \textbf{pro.}\langle\!\langle \texttt{x} : \mathit{int}, \texttt{getX} : \mathit{int}, \texttt{setX} : \mathit{int} \rightarrow \mathit{unit} \rangle\!\rangle \\[1ex]
\texttt{addMove} * ()\,\texttt{y} : \textbf{pro.}\langle\!\langle \texttt{x} : \mathit{int}, \texttt{getX} : \mathit{int}, \texttt{setX} : \mathit{int} \rightarrow \mathit{unit}, \texttt{move} : \mathit{int} \rightarrow \mathit{unit} \rangle\!\rangle
\end{array}$$

In this example, L can be any kind not containing the label `move`, as we are tracking components that may have already been added. (If we were tracking method absences, then the kind should *include* `move`.)

5 Operational Semantics

The operational semantics, presented in full in Appendix B, is inspired by the semantics for the imperative first-order calculus of [1]. It is based solely on reduction relations, without any equational theory. The semantics relates expressions of the calculus to addresses of a global store in which the results of the evaluation are recorded. The Abadi-Cardelli calculus has only object terms and hence only one sort of result, which consists of sequences of store locations, one for each component of the object. Since our calculus is an extension of lambda calculus, we have values that are not objects (for instance, lambda abstractions and polymorphic functions). For the sake of uniformity, we have chosen to evaluate all terms to store addresses. These addresses then contain results. In particular, the evaluation of an object term does not return a sequence of store locations but the address in which such a sequence of locations is stored. In the sequel, we will use the terms "location" and "address" synonymously. As in [1], we avoid using formal substitution during reduction, keeping to standard implementation techniques for imperative languages.

In more detail, the semantics is based on *environments* and *stores*. An environment E associates term variables to addresses. A store S associates addresses to values. Values are the results to which expressions of the calculus evaluate (for instance, a lambda abstraction evaluates to a closure, an object to a sequence of labeled addresses, and so on). The operational semantics is expressed via reduction judgments of the form $\{\!|S; E|\!\} \models e \longrightarrow a \bullet S'$, indicating that expression e evaluates to address a starting from store S and environment E. In the process, store S is modified to produce store S'. The value associated with expression e is stored in location a of store S'.

For the most part, the reduction rules are intuitive. In rule ($\leftarrow\!\!\circ$), we describe how to evaluate method and field extensions and method override. We use the symbol $\leftarrow\!\!\circ$ as a meta-notation standing for any of $\leftarrow\!\!+$, $\leftarrow$, or $\leftarrow\!\!+\!:$. Symbol η denotes a finite map from addresses to values; we use η to denote object values. The notation $\eta[l = a]$ denotes the finite map just like η except that $\eta[l = a]$ maps l to a. With this notation, we may now consider the rule:

$$(\leftarrow\!\!\circ)\quad \frac{\{\!|S; E|\!\} \models e_1 \longrightarrow a_1 \bullet S_1 \qquad \{\!|S_1; E|\!\} \models e_2 \longrightarrow a_2 \bullet S_2 \qquad S_2(a_1) = \eta \qquad a_3 \notin dom(S_2)}{\{\!|S; E|\!\} \models \langle e_1 \leftarrow\!\!\circ\, l = e_2 \rangle \longrightarrow a_3 \bullet (S_2, a_3 \mapsto \eta[l = a_2])}$$

Intuitively, we require e_1 to evaluate to an address containing an object (condition $S_2(a_1) = \eta$). Expression e_2 need only evaluate to an address. The type system will insure that $l \notin dom(\eta)$ if $\leftarrow\!\!\circ$ is either $\leftarrow\!\!+$ or $\leftarrow\!\!+\!:$ and that $l \in dom(\eta)$ if $\leftarrow\!\!\circ$ is $\leftarrow$. It will also insure that $S_2(a_1)$ is an object value, not a closure. The result of the evaluation is then a modification of a "clone" of the targeted object, allocated in a fresh address (a_3). This cloning is necessary for type soundness of the extension operations. It is worth remarking that the field override operation (for which we have a different rule (:=)) changes the value of the field of the object to which it is applied instead of creating and modifying a clone. Hence field override is inherently imperative.

The rule for method invocation is slightly more complicated:

$$(\Leftarrow)\quad \frac{\begin{array}{c}\{\!|S;\, E|\!\} \models e \longrightarrow a_1 \bullet S_1 \\ S_1(a_1) = \eta \qquad\qquad \eta(m) = a_1' \\ S_1(a_1') = \langle \Lambda().\, e_1,\, E_1\rangle \\ \{\!|S_1;\, E_1|\!\} \models e_1 \longrightarrow a_2 \bullet S_2 \\ S_2(a_2) = \langle \lambda x.\, e_2,\, E_2\rangle \qquad x \notin dom(E_2) \\ \{\!|S_2;\, E_2, x \mapsto a_1|\!\} \models e_2 \longrightarrow a_3 \bullet S_3\end{array}}{\{\!|S;\, E|\!\} \models e \Leftarrow m \longrightarrow a_3 \bullet S_3}$$

First, we evaluate the receiver object to its address a_1 to obtain η, the list of methods and fields associated with object e. We then look up the row closure associated with method m in η and evaluate its body e_1 to find the term closure that stores the method body $\lambda x.\, e_2$. We then evaluate e_2 with x bound to the address of the receiver object. This binding is where the first term parameter to a method body is bound to its host object, modeling *self*. The field selection evaluation rule (*field selection*) is simpler because fields are not polymorphic.

6 Soundness Proof

To show that the operational semantics is consistent with the type system, we must give types to results, *i.e.*, give a type to each store location. As noted in Chapter 11 of [2], it is impossible to determine the type of a result simply by recursively examining its subcomponents because stores may contain cycles. To address this problem, we follow Abadi and Cardelli in introducing *store typings* to allow us to type results independently of a particular store. This approach is reasonable because type-safe computations always store results of different types in different locations. Intuitively, all store locations are typed "globally" with respect to the whole store. Store types and the machinery to prove subject reduction are complicated in our case by the presence of types with free row variables. Since it only makes sense to give store locations closed types, we need a *row environment substitution*, denoted by $[E_\rho \rightarrow]$, to enable comparisons between static types that contain free row variables and run-time store types (Appendix C.2) that do not. This technique was inspired by the substitution operation in Chapter 17 of [2] for their imperative calculus with *Self* type.

Using these tools, we may show that our system enjoys a subject reduction property. Informally, we may state this property as follows:

> If we may statically give expression e type τ and e evaluates in store S with store type Σ to a result stored in address a of the modified store S', then there exists a type τ' and a store type Σ' such that τ' subtypes

(a closed version of) type τ and Σ' extends Σ, correctly types S', and gives address a type τ' (*i.e.*, $\Sigma(a) = \tau'$).

The formal statement of subject reduction is Theorem 4 in Appendix D.

Using the subject reduction property, we can prove that our system is type sound, in the sense that if a closed expression is typable, its evaluation will not reach a *stuck* state. More formally, given a store S, an environment E, and an expression e, there are three possibilities:

- $\{\!\!\{S; E\}\!\!\} \models e \longrightarrow a \bullet S'$ for some location a and store S';
- the proof tree generated by the reduction rules is infinite, *i.e.*, the program runs for ever;
- the proof tree is finite, but it does not produce a conclusion for S, E, and c, *i.e.*, the program gets stuck. This can happen, for example, if a method is invoked on an object that does not contain such a method.

We have formally defined the concept of *partial* evaluation by means of the *depth* of a deduction in the operational semantics. If the depth is finite, then the evaluation converges to a location or gets stuck. For lack of space, we state the soundness theorem without further formal details. These details appear in [7].

Theorem 1 (Type Soundness). *If judgment* $\varepsilon\,;\emptyset \vdash e : \tau$ *is derivable and the evaluation of* e *does not diverge, then* $\{\!\!\{\emptyset; \emptyset\}\!\!\} \models e \longrightarrow a \bullet S$ *for some location* a *and some store* S *well typed with respect to a store type* Σ *such that* $\Sigma(a) <: \tau$.

7 The Typing Algorithm

In this section, we sketch a typing algorithm for our system. Formal details can be found in the full version of our paper [7]. Our system results from the composition of seven interleaved subsystems: well-formedness of row and term contexts, kinding of rows, well-formedness of types, row subtyping, type subtyping, and typing expressions. Consequently, we must give a sound and complete algorithm for each of these subsystems. Our work was inspired by Compagnoni [14] and Hofmann and Pierce [23]. Although their type systems are quite different from ours, they demonstrated a useful structure for developing typing algorithms.

The first step is to define an *algorithmic* version of our type system S, *i.e.*, a type system S' in which the last rule applied is unequivocally determined by the syntax of the expression in question. For example, in the subtyping subsystem, producing a syntax-directed system requires eliminating transitivity and restricting reflexivity to atomic types. In the row-kinding subsystem, we must develop a system that calculates *minimal* kinds. For expressions, we must produce *minimal* types, *etc.* In addition to modifying the typing rules to produce equivalent algorithmic versions, we must add type annotations to some of our expressions in S'. For example, in S' λ-abstraction is expressed as $\lambda x{:}\tau.e$. An inspection of the *Type* algorithm below reveals where the other annotations must be added. These annotations are needed to insure that the minimal typing property holds for expressions. Although we omit the details here, we have proven that S and S' are appropriately related.

The second step is represented by the algorithms given in Definitions 1 to 4, one for each subsystem. In the algorithms, we use the following notation:

- $WFR(\rho; R)\downarrow$ stands for $WFR(\rho; R) = L$, for some L. ($WFR(\rho; R)$ is defined in Definition 1).
- $label(r, \rho)$ is L whenever $(r <:_w R :: L) \in \rho$.
- $bound(r, \rho)$ is R whenever $(r <:_w R :: L) \in \rho$.
- $B \leq B'$ means that the subtyping annotation B is less than or equal to the the subtyping annotation B', according to the order given in Section 3.4.
- $\Gamma(x)$ stands for the type of x in Γ.
- $WB_l(\rho, R)$ returns the type of l in R.

Definition 1 (Well-Formedness Algorithms). *Well-formedness algorithm for row contexts ($WFRC(\rho)$: `bool`) and types ($WFT(\rho;\tau)$: `bool`), and minimal kind algorithm for rows ($WFR(\rho; R) = L$, for some kind L, or `error`):*

$$
\begin{aligned}
&WFRC(\epsilon) &&= \mathtt{true}\\
&WFRC(\rho, (r <:_w R :: L)) &&= WFRC(\rho) \wedge WFR(\rho, R) \subseteq L \wedge r \notin dom(\rho)\\
&WFT(\rho; unit) &&= WFRC(\rho)\\
&WFT(\rho; \tau_1 \to \tau_2) &&= WFT(\rho; \tau_1) \wedge WFT(\rho; \tau_2)\\
&WFT(\rho; \mathbf{probj}.R) &&= WFR(\rho, R)\downarrow\\
&WFT(\rho; \forall(r <:_w R :: L)\tau) &&= WFT(\rho, (r <:_w R :: L); \tau)\\
&WFT(\rho; \exists(r <:_w R :: L)\tau) &&= WFT(\rho, (r <:_w R :: L); \tau)
\end{aligned}
$$

$$
\begin{aligned}
&WFR(\rho; r) &&= \mathtt{if}\ WFRC(\rho) \wedge r \in dom(\rho)\ \mathtt{then}\ label(r, \rho)\ \mathtt{else\ error}\\
&WFR(\rho; \langle\!\langle\rangle\!\rangle) &&= \mathtt{if}\ WFRC(\rho)\ \mathtt{then}\ \emptyset\ \mathtt{else\ error}\\
&WFR(\rho; \langle\!\langle R \mid l : \tau\rangle\!\rangle) &&= \mathtt{if}\ WFT(\rho; \tau) \wedge l \notin WFR(\rho; R)\ \mathtt{then}\ \{l\} \cup WFR(\rho; R)\\
& && \quad \mathtt{else\ error};
\end{aligned}
$$

Definition 2 (Subtyping Algorithms). *Algorithm for type subtyping ($ST(\tau_1, \tau_2)$: `bool`) and row subtyping ($SR(\rho, R_1, R_2, B)$: `bool`):*

$$
\begin{aligned}
&ST(\rho, \tau, unit) &&= WFT(\rho, \tau)\\
&ST(\rho, \tau_1 \to \tau_2, \tau_1' \to \tau_2') &&= ST(\rho, \tau_1', \tau_1)\ \wedge\ ST(\tau_2, \tau_2')\\
&ST(\rho, \mathbf{probj}.R_1, \mathbf{obj}.R_2) &&= SR(\rho, R_1, R_2, B)\ \textit{for some } B\\
&ST(\rho, \forall(r <:_w R :: L)\tau, \forall(r <:_w R :: L)\tau) &&= WFT(\rho, \forall(r <:_w R :: L)\tau)\\
&ST(\rho, \exists(r <:_w R :: L)\tau, \exists(r <:_w R :: L)\tau) &&= WFT(\rho, \exists(r <:_w R :: L)\tau)
\end{aligned}
$$

$$
\begin{aligned}
&SR(\rho, \langle\!\langle\rangle\!\rangle, R, B) &&= \mathtt{if}\ R = \langle\!\langle\rangle\!\rangle\ \wedge\ WFRC(\rho)\ \mathtt{then\ true}\\
& && \quad \mathtt{else\ false}\\
&SR(\rho, r, R, B) &&= \mathtt{if}\ R \neq r\ \wedge\ WFR(\rho, r)\downarrow\ \mathtt{then}\\
& && \quad SR(\rho, bound(r, \rho), R, B)\ \mathtt{else\ false}\\
&SR(\rho, r, r, B) &&= WFR(\rho; r)\downarrow\\
&SR(\rho, \langle\!\langle R_1 \mid l : \tau\rangle\!\rangle, && \\
&\quad \langle\!\langle R_2 \mid l : \tau\rangle\!\rangle, B) &&= SR(R_1, R_2, B)\ \wedge\ WFR(\rho, \langle\!\langle R_1 \mid l : \tau\rangle\!\rangle)\downarrow\\
& && \quad \wedge\ WFR(\rho, \langle\!\langle R_2 \mid l : \tau\rangle\!\rangle)\downarrow
\end{aligned}
$$

$$SR(\rho, \langle\!\langle R_1 \mid l:\tau_1 \rangle\!\rangle, \langle\!\langle R_2 \mid l:\tau_2 \rangle\!\rangle, B') = \tau_1 \neq \tau_2 \wedge SR(\rho, R_1, R_2, B) \wedge ST(\rho, \tau_1, \tau_2) \wedge WFR(\rho, \langle\!\langle R_1 \mid l:\tau_1 \rangle\!\rangle)\downarrow \wedge WFR(\rho, \langle\!\langle R_2 \mid l:\tau_2 \rangle\!\rangle)\downarrow \wedge B' = B + d$$

$$SR(\rho, \langle\!\langle R_1 \mid l:\tau_1 \rangle\!\rangle, R_2, B) = \texttt{if } R_2 \neq \langle\!\langle R_1' \mid l:\tau_1' \rangle\!\rangle \texttt{ for any } R_1' \texttt{ and } \tau_1' \texttt{ then } SR(\rho, R_1, R_2, B) \wedge WFR(\rho, \langle\!\langle R_1 \mid l:\tau_1 \rangle\!\rangle)\downarrow \texttt{ else false;}$$

Definition 3 (Well-formed Term Contexts). *Algorithm for well-formed term contexts:* $WFEC(\rho;\Gamma)$: bool;

$$WFEC(\rho;\varepsilon) = WFRC(\rho)$$
$$WFEC(\rho;\Gamma, x:\tau) = WFEC(\rho;\Gamma) \wedge WFT(\rho;\tau) \wedge x \notin dom(\Gamma);$$

Definition 4 (Minimal Typing Algorithm). Minimal *type algorithm for terms:* $Type(\rho;\Gamma;e) = \tau$*, for minimal type* τ *with respect to subtyping, or* error;

$Type(\rho;\Gamma;x) =$
  if $WFEC(\rho;\Gamma) \wedge x \in dom(\Gamma)$ then $\Gamma(x)$ else error

$Type(\rho;\Gamma;\langle\rangle) =$
  if $WFEC(\rho;\Gamma)$ then **pro**.$\langle\!\langle\rangle\!\rangle$ else error

$Type(\rho;\Gamma;\lambda x{:}\tau.e) =$
  if $Type(\rho;\ \Gamma, x{:}\tau;\ e) = \tau_2$ then $\tau \rightarrow \tau_2$ else error

$Type(\rho;\Gamma;e_1 e_2) =$
  if $Type(\rho;\Gamma;e_1) = \tau_1 \rightarrow \tau_2 \ \wedge\ Type(\rho;\Gamma;e_2) = \tau_1' \ \wedge\ ST(\rho;\tau_1',\tau_1)$
  then τ_2 else error

$Type(\rho;\Gamma;\textbf{let } x{:}\tau = e_1 \textbf{ in } e_2) =$
  if $Type(\rho;\Gamma;e_1) = \tau_1' \ \wedge\ ST(\rho,\tau_1',\tau) \ \wedge\ Type(\rho;\Gamma, x:\tau;e_2) = \tau_2'$
  then τ_2' else error

$Type(\rho;\Gamma;\langle e_1 \leftarrow\!\!+ m = e_2\rangle) =$
  if $Type(\rho;\Gamma;e_1) = \textbf{pro}.R \ \wedge\ WFR(\rho,R) = L \ \wedge\ m \notin L \ \wedge$
    $Type(\rho;\Gamma;e_2) = \forall(r <:_w \langle\!\langle R \mid m{:}\tau \rangle\!\rangle :: All)\textbf{pro}.r \rightarrow \tau$
  then **pro**.$\langle\!\langle R \mid m{:}\tau \rangle\!\rangle$ else error

$Type(\rho;\Gamma;\langle e_1 \leftarrow\!\!+ : f{:}\tau = e_2\rangle) =$
  if $Type(\rho;\Gamma;e_1) = \textbf{pro}.R \wedge WFR(\rho,R) = L \wedge f \notin L \wedge$
    $Type(\rho;\Gamma;e_2) = \tau' \ \wedge\ ST(\rho,\tau',\tau)$
  then **pro**.$\langle\!\langle R \mid f{:}\tau \rangle\!\rangle$ else error

$Type(\rho;\Gamma;\langle e_1 \leftarrow m = e_2\rangle) =$
  if $Type(\rho;\Gamma;e_1) = \textbf{pro}.R \ \wedge\ WB_m(\rho,R) = \tau \ \wedge$
   $Type(\rho;\Gamma;e_2) = \forall(r <:_w R :: All)\textbf{pro}.r \rightarrow \tau$
  then **pro**.R else error

$Type(\rho;\Gamma;\langle e_1 := f = e_2\rangle) =$
  if $Type(\rho;\Gamma;e_1) = \textbf{probj}.R \ \wedge\ WB_f(\rho,R) = \tau \ \wedge$
   $Type(\rho;\Gamma;e_2) = \tau_2 \ \wedge\ ST(\rho,\tau_2,\tau)$
  then **probj**.R else error

$Type(\rho; \Gamma; e \Leftarrow m) \quad =$
$\quad$ **if** $Type(\rho; \Gamma; e) = \mathbf{probj}.R \ \wedge \ WB_m(\rho, R) = \tau$ **then** τ **else error**

$Type(\rho; \Gamma; e.f) \quad =$
$\quad$ **if** $Type(\rho; \Gamma; e) = \mathbf{probj}.R \ \wedge \ WB_f(\rho, R) = \tau$ **then** τ **else error**

$Type(\rho; \Gamma; \Lambda(r <:_w R :: L).e{:}\tau) \quad =$
$\quad$ **if** $Type(\rho, (r <:_w R :: L); \Gamma; e) = \tau' \ \wedge$
$\quad\quad ST(\rho, (r <:_w R :: L); \Gamma; \tau'; \tau) \ \wedge \ r \notin FV(\Gamma)$
$\quad$ **then** $\forall(r <:_w R :: L)\tau$ **else error**

$Type(\rho; \Gamma; e * R') \quad =$
$\quad$ **if** $Type(\rho; \Gamma; e) = \forall(r <:_w R :: L)\tau \ \wedge \ SR(\rho, R', R, w) \ \wedge$
$\quad\quad WFR(\rho, R') = L' \ \wedge \ L' \subseteq L$
$\quad$ **then** $[R'/r]\tau$ **else error**

$Type(\rho; \Gamma; \{\!|r <:_w R :: L = R', \ e{:}\tau|\!\})) \quad =$
$\quad$ **if** $SR(\rho, R', R) \ \wedge \ WFR(\rho, R') = L' \ \wedge \ L' \subseteq L \ \wedge$
$\quad\quad Type(\rho; \Gamma; e) = \tau' \wedge ST(\rho; \tau'; [R'/r]\tau)$
$\quad$ **then** $\exists(r <:_w R :: L)\tau$ **else error**

$Type(\rho; \Gamma; \mathbf{Abstype}\ r <:_w R :: L\ \mathbf{with}\ x : \tau\ \mathbf{is}\ e_1\ \mathbf{in}\ e_2) \quad =$
$\quad$ **if** $Type(\rho; \Gamma; e_1) = \exists(r <:_w R :: L)\tau \ \wedge$
$\quad\quad Type(\rho, (r <:_w R :: L); \Gamma, x : \tau; e_2) = \tau_2' \ \wedge \ WFT(\rho, \tau_2')$
$\quad$ **then** τ_2' **else error**

We prove the correctness and completeness of these algorithms in the following theorem.

Theorem 2 (Soundness and Completeness).

- *For all row contexts* ρ, $WFRC(\rho) = \mathtt{true}$ *if and only if* $\rho \vdash *$;
- *For all row contexts* ρ *and all types* τ, $WFRC(\rho; \tau) = \mathtt{true}$ *if and only if* $\rho \vdash \tau : \mathrm{T}$;
- *For all row contexts* ρ *and all rows* R, $WFR(\rho) = L$ *if and only if* $\rho \vdash R :: L$ *and for all* L' *such that* $\rho \vdash R :: L'$ *is derivable,* $L \subseteq L'$;
- *For all row contexts* ρ *and all term contexts* Γ, $WFEC(\rho; \Gamma) = \mathtt{true}$ *if and only if* $\rho; \Gamma \vdash *$;
- *For all row contexts* ρ, *all rows* R_1, R_2, *and all subtyping labels* B, *predicate* $SR(\rho, R_1, R_2, B)$ *is* $\mathtt{true}$ *if and only if* $\rho \vdash R_1 <:_{B'} R_2$ *where* $B' \leq B$;
- *For all row contexts* ρ *and all types* τ_1, τ_2, $ST(\rho, \tau_1, \tau_2) = \mathtt{true}$ *if and only if* $\rho \vdash \tau_1 <: \tau_2$;
- *For all row contexts* ρ, *all term contexts* Γ, *and all terms* e, $Type(\rho; \Gamma; e) = \tau$ *if and only if* $\rho; \Gamma \vdash e : \tau$ *and for all types* τ' *such that* $\rho; \Gamma \vdash e : \tau'$ *is derivable, we have* $\rho \vdash \tau <: \tau'$.

Finally, we prove that each algorithm given in Definitions 1 to 4 terminates with the correct answer if one exists or with `error` otherwise. To prove this theorem, we define appropriate measures on each sort of expression and then proceed by induction on these measures.

Theorem 3 (Termination). *For all* ρ, τ, τ_1, τ_2, R, R_1, R_2, Γ, B, *and* e, *the functions* $WFRC(\rho)$, $WFT(\rho; \tau)$, $WFR(\rho; R)$, $WFEC(\rho; \Gamma)$, $SR(\rho, R_1, R_2, B)$, $ST(\rho, \tau_1, \tau_2)$, *and* $Type(\rho; \Gamma; e)$ *all converge.*

8 Related Work

In the literature, there are various approaches to modeling classes other than ours and the record-of-premethods approach that we discussed in Section 1.1:

- *Existential Model*: In [28], Pierce and Turner interpret classes as object-generating functions. In their interpretation, inheritance is interpreted as modifications to the object-generating functions that model classes. This encoding is somewhat cumbersome, since it requires programmers to explicitly manipulate **get** and **put** functions, which intuitively convert between the hidden state of parent class objects and derived class objects. Also, because this model provides protection at the object-level, as opposed to the class-level, binary methods require extra machinery. One such solution appears in [27]. Another solution is proposed in [23]; Hofmann and Pierce introduce a refined version of $F_{<:}$ that permits only positive subtyping. With this restriction, **get** and **put** functions are both guaranteed to exist and hence may be handled in a more automatic fashion in class encodings.
- *Direct Models*: Bruce has developed a family of type-safe formal languages that model classes directly instead of via an interpretation as the combination of more basic primitives. In [10], Bruce describes TOOPL, a functional object-oriented language. PolyTOIL, presented in [11], incorporates imperative features and introduces the notion of *matching*, a relationship between object types that holds whenever the first is an extension of the second, regardless of the variance of the "mytype" type variable. In these languages, the type of an object reflects only its public interface; it cannot convey implementation information. Smith and the Hopkins Object Group have designed a type-safe class-based object-oriented language with a rich feature set called I-LOOP, [15]. Their type system is based on polymorphic recursively constrained types, for which they have a sound type inferencing algorithm. The main advantage of this approach is the extreme flexibility afforded by recursively constrained types. Currently, the main problem is that it returns large, difficult-to-read types. Some form of simplification may be required. Work in this area is in progress.

Our system falls in the category of prototype calculi with subtyping. We briefly mention here three other approaches to extensible objects compatible with some form of subtyping.

- In [9] a type system is presented for the functional Lambda Calculus of Objects [18], in which a limited form of width subtyping compatible with object extension is introduced. Only methods that are not invoked by other methods in the object can be "forgotten" by subtyping. The machinery to track information about used methods is somewhat heavy, but it avoids constraints on the variance of the *self*-type, which is instead one of the weak points of [19].
- The type system of [2] is extended in [25] to allow a form of extension in the presence of a limited form of width subtyping. This approach combines

a variant of [9] with that of [19]: an object may be in one of two states, one allowing extensions and limited width subtyping, the other forbidding extensions but supporting unrestricted width subtyping.

- PolyTOIL combines a form of (match-bounded) universal quantification and extensible structures. It uses the matching relation on types to type check inheritance of extensible classes and uses match-bound quantification to type check polymorphic functions.

9 Conclusion

We have presented a formal study of a calculus to support the "Classes = Extensible Objects + Encapsulation" interpretation of classes. Despite its apparent complexity (although this impression may be caused more by the number of rules than by the complexity of the rules themselves), the calculus is rather intuitive, since:

- it uses well-established concepts such as universal and existential quantifiers,
- it enables straightforward translations of Java-like classes and mixins, and
- it has a clear imperative semantics and a well-developed formal meta-theory, including a soundness theorem and a typing algorithm.

We have not completed our study of the system. Future work includes:

- adopting a module construct and a dot notation as in [12, 22] to replace the present nested structure of class hierarchies, and
- introducing a form of alpha-conversion to allow us to hide the private names that are currently exposed by our positive kinds, as in [30].

References

1. M. Abadi and L. Cardelli. An imperative object calculus. *Theory and Practice of Object Systems*, 1(3):151–166, 1996. Earlier version appeared in TAPSOFT '95 proceedings.
2. M. Abadi and L. Cardelli. *A Theory of Objects*. Springer, 1996.
3. M. Abadi and L. Cardelli. A theory of primitive objects: Untyped and first-order systems. *Information and Computation*, 125(2):78–102, 1996. Earlier version appeared in TACS '94 proceedings, LNCS 789.
4. K. Arnold and J. Gosling. *The Java Programming Language*. Addison Wesley, 1996.
5. G.M. Birtwistle, O.-J. Dahl, B. Myhrhaug, and K. Nygaard. *Simula Begin*. Studentlitteratur, Box 1717, S-222 01 Lund, Sweden; Auerbach, Philadelphia, 1973.
6. V. Bono, M. Bugliesi, and L. Liquori. A lambda calculus of incomplete objects. In *Proc. MFCS '96*, pages 218–229. Springer LNCS 1113, 1996.
7. V. Bono and K. Fisher. A first-order, extensible-object calculus with support for classes. Unpublished manuscript; work-in-progress, 1998.
8. V. Bono and K. Fisher. An imperative, first-order calculus with object extension. In *Proc. 5th Annual FOOL Workshop*, pages 8.1–8.13, January 1998.

9. V. Bono and L. Liquori. A subtyping for the Fisher-Honsell-Mitchell lambda calculus of objects. In L. Pacholsky and J. Tiuryn, editors, *Proc. of Int'l Conf. of Computer Science Logic*, pages 16–30, Berlin, June 1995. Springer LNCS 933.
10. K. Bruce. Safe type checking in a statically-typed object-oriented programming language. In *Proc. 20th ACM Symp. Principles of Programming Languages*, pages 285–298, 1993.
11. K. Bruce, A. Schuett, and R. van Gent. PolyTOIL: A type-safe polymorphic object-oriented language. In *Proc. 9th European Conference on Object-Oriented Programming*, pages 26–51, Aarhus, Denmark, 1995. Springer LNCS 952.
12. L. Cardelli and X. Leroy. *Abstract types and the dot notation*, pages 479–504. IFIP State of the Art Reports. North Holland, March 1990. Also appeared as SRC Research Report 56.
13. L. Cardelli and P. Wegner. On understanding types, data abstraction, and polymorphism. *Computing Surveys*, 17(4):471–522, 1985.
14. A.B. Compagnoni. *Higher-Order Subtyping with Intersection Types*. PhD thesis, Katholieke Universiteit Nijmegen, 1994.
15. J. Eifrig, S. Smith, and V. Trifonov. Sound polymorphic type inference for objects. In *ACM Conf. Object-Oriented Programming: Systems, Languages and Applications*, pages 169–184, October 1995.
16. M. Ellis and B. Stroustrup. *The Annotated C^{++} Reference Manual.* Addison-Wesley, 1990.
17. K. Fisher. *Type Systems for object-oriented programming languages.* PhD thesis, Stanford University, 1996. Available as Stanford Computer Science Technical Report number STAN-CS-TR-98-1602.
18. K. Fisher, F. Honsell, and J.C. Mitchell. A lambda calculus of objects and method specialization. *Nordic J. Computing (*formerly *BIT)*, 1:3–37, 1994. Preliminary version appeared in *Proc. IEEE Symp. on Logic in Computer Science*, 1993, 26–38.
19. K. Fisher and J.C. Mitchell. A delegation-based object calculus with subtyping. In *Proc. 10th Int'l Conf. Fundamentals of Computation Theory (FCT'95)*, pages 42–61. Springer LNCS 965, 1995.
20. K. Fisher and J.C. Mitchell. The development of type systems for object-oriented languages. *Theory and Practice of Object Systems*, 1(3):189–220, 1995. Preliminary version appeared in TACS '94 proceedings.
21. K. Fisher and J.C. Mitchell. On the relationship between classes, objects, and data abstraction. *Theory and Practice of Object Systems*, 4(1):3–25, 1998. Special Issue on Third Workshop on Foundations of Object-Oriented Languages (FOOL 3). Preliminary version appeared in Marktoberdorf '97 proceedings.
22. R. Harper and M. Lillibridge. A type-theoretic approach to higher-order modules with sharing. In *Proc. 21st ACM Symp. on Principles of Programming Languages*, 1994.
23. M. Hofmann and B.C. Pierce. Positive subtyping. *Information and Computation*, 126(1):11–33, 1996. Preliminary version appeared in *Proc. 22nd ACM Symp. on Principles of Programming Languages*, 1995.
24. D. Katiyar, D. Luckham, and J.C. Mitchell. A type system for prototyping languages. In *Proc. 21st ACM Symp. on Principles of Programming Languages*, 1994.
25. L. Liquori. An extended theory of primitive objects: First and second order systems. Technical Report CS-23-96, Dipartimento di Informatica, Universitá di Torino, 1996. A portion of this work appears in ECOOP '97 Proceedings, LNCS 1241.
26. B. Meyer. *Eiffel: The Language.* Prentice-Hall, 1992.

27. B.C. Pierce and D.N. Turner. Statically typed friendly functions via partially abstract types. Technical Report ECS-LFCS-93-256, University of Edinburgh, LFCS, April 1993. Also available as INRIA-Rocquencourt Rapport de Recherche No. 1899.

28. B.C. Pierce and D.N. Turner. Simple type-theoretic foundations for object-oriented programming. *Journal of Functional Programming*, 4(2):207–248, 1994. Preliminary version appeared in *Proc. 20th ACM Symp. on Principles of Programming Languages*, 1993, under the title "Object-oriented programming without recursive types".

29. J.H. Reppy and J.G. Riecke. Classes in Object ML via modules, 1996. Presented at FOOL3 workshop.

30. J.G. Riecke and C. Stone. Privacy via subsumption. In *Proc. 5th Annual FOOL Workshop*, pages 9.1–9.10, January 1998.

31. B. Stroustrup. *The Design and Evolution of* C^{++}. Addison-Wesley, 1994. Chapter 3: The birth of C^{++}.

32. M. Wand. Complete type inference for simple objects. In *Proc. IEEE Symp. on Logic in Computer Science*, pages 37–44, 1987. Corrigendum in *Proc. IEEE Symp. on Logic in Computer Science*, page 132, 1988.

A Typing rules

We will use the meta-judgment $H \vdash A$ to range over all judgment forms. In addition, we use the meta-variable U to range over types τ and rows R. The meta-judgment $\rho \vdash U : -\gamma$ represents judgments of the form $\rho \vdash \tau : \mathtt{T}$ and $\rho \vdash R :: L$. Similarly, meta-judgment $\rho \vdash U_1 <:_{(B)} U_2$ represents the judgments $\rho \vdash \tau_1 <: \tau_2$ and $\rho \vdash R_1 <:_B R_2$.

A.1 Context Rules

$$(start)\ \frac{}{\epsilon \vdash *}$$

$$(exp\ var)\ \frac{\rho\,;\,\Gamma \vdash * \quad \rho \vdash \tau : \mathtt{T} \quad x \notin dom(\Gamma)}{\rho\,;\,\Gamma,\, x : \tau \vdash *}$$

$$(row\ var)\ \frac{\rho \vdash * \quad r \notin dom(\rho) \quad \rho \vdash R :: L_1 \quad L_1 \subseteq L_0}{\rho,\, (r <:_w R :: L_0) \vdash *}$$

$$(empty)\ \frac{\rho \vdash *}{\rho\,;\,\epsilon \vdash *}$$

A.2 Rules for Row Expressions

$$(row\ proj)\ \frac{\rho \vdash * \quad r <:_w R :: L \in \rho}{\rho \vdash r :: L}$$

$$(label)\ \frac{\rho \vdash R :: L_1 \quad L_1 \subseteq L_2}{\rho \vdash R :: L_2}$$

$$(empty\ row)\ \frac{\rho \vdash *}{\rho \vdash \langle\!\langle\rangle\!\rangle :: \emptyset}$$

$$(row\ ext)\ \frac{\rho \vdash R :: L \quad l \notin L \quad \rho \vdash \tau : \mathtt{T}}{\rho \vdash \langle\!\langle R \,|\, l : \tau \rangle\!\rangle :: L \cup \{l\}}$$

A.3 Rules for Type Expressions

$$(unit)\ \frac{\rho \vdash *}{\rho \vdash unit : \mathtt{T}}$$

$$(\forall)\ \frac{\rho,\ (r <:_w R :: L) \vdash \tau : \mathtt{T}}{\rho \vdash \forall (r <:_w R :: L)\tau : \mathtt{T}}$$

$$(arrow)\ \frac{\rho \vdash \tau_1 : \mathtt{T} \quad \rho \vdash \tau_2 : \mathtt{T}}{\rho \vdash \tau_1 \rightarrow \tau_2 : \mathtt{T}}$$

$$(\exists)\ \frac{\rho,\ (r <:_w R :: L) \vdash \tau : \mathtt{T}}{\rho \vdash \exists (r <:_w R :: L)\tau : \mathtt{T}}$$

$$(probj)\ \frac{\rho \vdash R :: L}{\rho \vdash \mathbf{probj}.R : \mathtt{T}}$$

A.4 Subtyping Rules for Types

$$(<:\rightarrow)\ \frac{\rho \vdash \tau_1' <: \tau_1 \quad \rho \vdash \tau_2 <: \tau_2'}{\rho \vdash \tau_1 \rightarrow \tau_2 <: \tau_1' \rightarrow \tau_2'}$$

$$(<: unit)\ \frac{\rho \vdash \tau : \mathtt{T}}{\rho \vdash \tau <: unit}$$

$$(<: obj)\ \frac{\rho \vdash R_1 <:_B R_2}{\rho \vdash \mathbf{probj}.R_1 <: \mathbf{obj}.R_2}$$

$$(<: proj)\ \frac{\rho \vdash * \quad \iota_1 <: \iota_2 \in \rho}{\rho \vdash \iota_1 <: \iota_2}$$

A.5 Subtyping Rules for Rows

(*row proj bound*)
$$\frac{\rho \vdash * \qquad r <:_w R :: L \in \rho}{\rho \vdash r <:_w R}$$

($<:$ *cong*)
$$\frac{\rho \vdash R_1 <:_B R_2 \qquad \rho \vdash \langle\!\langle R_i \,|\, l : \tau \rangle\!\rangle :: L_i \quad i \in \{1,2\}}{\rho \vdash \langle\!\langle R_1 \,|\, l : \tau \rangle\!\rangle <:_B \langle\!\langle R_2 \,|\, l : \tau \rangle\!\rangle}$$

($<: d$)
$$\frac{\rho \vdash R_1 <:_B R_2 \qquad \rho \vdash \tau_1 <: \tau_2 \qquad \rho \vdash \langle\!\langle R_i \,|\, m : \tau_i \rangle\!\rangle :: L_i \quad i \in \{1,2\}}{\rho \vdash \langle\!\langle R_1 \,|\, m : \tau_1 \rangle\!\rangle <:_{B+d} \langle\!\langle R_2 \,|\, m : \tau_2 \rangle\!\rangle}$$

($<: w$)
$$\frac{\rho \vdash R_1 <:_B R_2 \qquad \rho \vdash \langle\!\langle R_1 \,|\, l : \tau \rangle\!\rangle :: L_1}{\rho \vdash \langle\!\langle R_1 \,|\, l : \tau \rangle\!\rangle <:_B R_2}$$

A.6 Subtyping Rules for Rows and Types

($<:$ *refl*)
$$\frac{\rho \vdash U : -\gamma}{\rho \vdash U <:_{(B)} U}$$

($<:$ *trans*)
$$\frac{\rho \vdash U_1 <:_{(B)} U_2 \qquad \rho \vdash U_2 <:_{(B')} U_3}{\rho \vdash U_1 <:_{(B+B')} U_3}$$

A.7 Rules for Assigning Types to Terms

(*exp proj*)
$$\frac{\rho\,;\,\Gamma \vdash * \qquad x : \tau \in \Gamma}{\rho\,;\,\Gamma \vdash x : \tau}$$

(*empty*)
$$\frac{\rho\,;\,\Gamma \vdash *}{\rho\,;\,\Gamma \vdash \langle\rangle : \mathbf{pro}.\langle\!\langle\rangle\!\rangle}$$

(*exp abs*)
$$\frac{\rho\,;\,\Gamma,\ x : \tau_1 \vdash e : \tau_2}{\rho\,;\,\Gamma \vdash \lambda x.\, e : \tau_1 \to \tau_2}$$

(*exp app*)
$$\frac{\rho\,;\,\Gamma \vdash e_1 : \tau_1 \to \tau_2 \qquad \rho\,;\,\Gamma \vdash e_2 : \tau_1}{\rho\,;\,\Gamma \vdash e_1\, e_2 : \tau_2}$$

(*sub*)
$$\frac{\rho\,;\,\Gamma \vdash e : \tau_1 \quad \rho \vdash \tau_1 <: \tau_2}{\rho\,;\,\Gamma \vdash e : \tau_2}$$

(*let*)
$$\frac{\rho\,;\,\Gamma \vdash e_1 : \tau_1 \qquad \rho\,;\,\Gamma,\ x : \tau_1 \vdash e_2 : \tau_2}{\rho\,;\,\Gamma \vdash \mathbf{let}\ x = e_1\ \mathbf{in}\ e_2 : \tau_2}$$

(*meth ext*)
$$\frac{\begin{array}{l}\rho\,;\,\Gamma \vdash e_1 : \mathbf{pro}.R \\ \rho \vdash R :: L \qquad\qquad m \notin L \\ \rho\,;\,\Gamma \vdash e_2 : \forall(r <:_w \langle\!\langle R \mid m : \tau\rangle\!\rangle :: \mathit{All})\mathbf{pro}.r \to \tau\end{array}}{\rho\,;\,\Gamma \vdash \langle e_1 \longleftrightarrow\!\!+\ m = e_2\rangle : \mathbf{pro}.\langle\!\langle R \mid m : \tau\rangle\!\rangle}$$

(*meth over*)
$$\frac{\begin{array}{l}\rho\,;\,\Gamma \vdash e_1 : \mathbf{pro}.R \\ \rho \vdash R <:_w \langle\!\langle m : \tau\rangle\!\rangle \\ \rho\,;\,\Gamma \vdash e_2 : \forall(r <:_w R :: \mathit{All})\mathbf{pro}.r \to \tau\end{array}}{\rho\,;\,\Gamma \vdash \langle e_1 \leftarrow m = e_2\rangle : \mathbf{pro}.R}$$

($\Leftarrow$ *select*)
$$\frac{\begin{array}{l}\rho\,;\,\Gamma \vdash e : \mathbf{probj}.R \\ \rho \vdash R <:_w \langle\!\langle m : \tau\rangle\!\rangle\end{array}}{\rho\,;\,\Gamma \vdash e \Leftarrow m : \tau}$$

(*field ext*)
$$\frac{\begin{array}{l}\rho\,;\,\Gamma \vdash e_1 : \mathbf{pro}.R \\ \rho \vdash R :: L \qquad\qquad f \notin L \\ \rho\,;\,\Gamma \vdash e_2 : \tau\end{array}}{\rho\,;\,\Gamma \vdash \langle e_1 \longleftrightarrow\!\!+ : f = e_2\rangle : \mathbf{pro}.\langle\!\langle R \mid f : \tau\rangle\!\rangle}$$

(*field over*)
$$\frac{\rho\,;\Gamma \vdash e_1 : \mathbf{probj}.R \quad \rho \vdash R <:_w \langle\!\langle f : \tau \rangle\!\rangle \quad \rho\,;\Gamma \vdash e_2 : \tau}{\rho\,;\Gamma \vdash \langle e_1.f := e_2\rangle : \mathbf{probj}.R}$$

(*field select*)
$$\frac{\rho\,;\Gamma \vdash e : \mathbf{probj}.R \quad \rho \vdash R <:_w \langle\!\langle f : \tau \rangle\!\rangle}{\rho\,;\Gamma \vdash e.f : \tau}$$

($\forall$ *elim*)
$$\frac{\rho\,;\Gamma \vdash e : \forall(r <:_w R :: L)\tau \quad \rho \vdash R' <:_w R \quad \rho \vdash R' :: L}{\rho\,;\Gamma \vdash e * () : [R'/r]\tau}$$

($\forall$ *intro*)
$$\frac{\rho, (r <:_w R :: L)\,;\Gamma \vdash e : \tau \quad r \notin FV(\Gamma)}{\rho\,;\Gamma \vdash \Lambda().\,e : \forall(r <:_w R :: L)\tau}$$

($\exists$ *intro*)
$$\frac{\rho \vdash R' <:_w R \quad \rho \vdash R' :: L \quad \rho\,;\Gamma \vdash e : [R'/r]\tau}{\rho\,;\Gamma \vdash \{\!|(r <:_w R :: L) = R',\ e|\!\} : \exists(r <:_w R :: L)\tau}$$

($\exists$ *elim*)
$$\frac{\rho\,;\Gamma \vdash e_1 : \exists(r <:_w R :: L)\tau \quad \rho, (r <:_w R :: L)\,;\Gamma, x : \tau \vdash e_2 : \tau_2 \quad \rho \vdash \tau_2 : \mathbf{T}}{\rho\,;\Gamma \vdash \mathbf{Abstype}\ (r <:_w R :: L)\ \mathbf{with}\ x : \tau\ \mathbf{is}\ e_1\ \mathbf{in}\ e_2 : \tau_2}$$

B Operational Semantics

Addresses

a ::= an integer, selected from one of four disjoint sets: S_{OBJ}, S_{RCL}, S_{CL}, or S_{EXIS}

Storeable Values

$sv ::= \eta \,|\, c \,|\, rc \,|\, a$

Object Value

$\eta ::= [l_i = a_i]^{i \in I}$

Closure Value

$c ::= \langle \lambda x.\, e,\, E \rangle$

Row Closure Value

$rc ::= \langle \Lambda().\, e,\, E \rangle$

Environment

$E ::= x_i \mapsto a_i,\ i \in 1, \ldots, n$

Store

$S ::= a_i \mapsto sv_i,\ i \in 1, \ldots, n$

Contexts

$\{\!\!\{S;\, E\}\!\!\}$ ::= store/environment pair.

B.1 Semantic Judgments

$S \models *$	well-formed store
$\{\!\!\{S;\, E\}\!\!\} \models *$	well-formed store/env pair.
$\{\!\!\{S;\, E\}\!\!\} \models c \longrightarrow a \bullet S'$	expression e evaluates to address a and produces store S'.

B.2 Context Judgments

(empty store)

$$\frac{}{\emptyset \models *}$$

(insert exist)

$$\frac{S \models * \quad a \notin dom(S) \qquad a' \in dom(S)}{S,\, a \mapsto a' \models *}$$

(insert closure)

$$\frac{\{\!\!\{S;\, E\}\!\!\} \models * \quad a \notin dom(S)}{S,\, a \mapsto \langle \lambda x.\, e,\, E \rangle \models *}$$

(empty environment)

$$\frac{S \models *}{\{\!\!\{S;\, \emptyset\}\!\!\} \models *}$$

(*insert Λ−closure*)

$$\frac{\{\!\!\{S;\ E\}\!\!\} \models * \quad a \notin dom(S)}{S,\ a \mapsto \langle \Lambda().\, e,\ E\rangle \models *}$$

(*insert var*)

$$\frac{\{\!\!\{S;\ E\}\!\!\} \models * \qquad x \notin dom(E) \qquad a \in dom(S)}{\{\!\!\{S;\ E, x \mapsto a\}\!\!\} \models *}$$

(*insert object*)

$$\frac{S \models * \qquad a \notin dom(S) \qquad a_i \in dom(S) \text{ for all } i \in I}{S,\ a \mapsto [l_i = a_i]^{i \in I} \models *}$$

B.3 Reduction Rules

(*var*)

$$\frac{\{\!\!\{S;\ E\}\!\!\} \models * \qquad E(x) = a}{\{\!\!\{S;\ E\}\!\!\} \models x \longrightarrow a \bullet S}$$

(*lambda*)

$$\frac{\{\!\!\{S;\ E\}\!\!\} \models * \qquad a \notin dom(S)}{\{\!\!\{S;\ E\}\!\!\} \models \lambda x.\, e \longrightarrow a \bullet (S, a \mapsto \langle \lambda x.\, e,\ E\rangle)}$$

(*app*)

$$\frac{\{\!\!\{S;\ E\}\!\!\} \models e_1 \longrightarrow a_1 \bullet S_1 \qquad \{\!\!\{S_1;\ E\}\!\!\} \models e_2 \longrightarrow a_2 \bullet S_2 \qquad S_2(a_1) = \langle \lambda x.\, e,\ E'\rangle \quad x \notin dom(E') \qquad \{\!\!\{S_2;\ E',\ x \mapsto a_2\}\!\!\} \models e \longrightarrow a_3 \bullet S_3}{\{\!\!\{S;\ E\}\!\!\} \models e_1\, e_2 \longrightarrow a_3 \bullet S_3}$$

(*empty object*)

$$\frac{\{\!\!\{S;\ E\}\!\!\} \models * \qquad a \notin dom(S)}{\{\!\!\{S;\ E\}\!\!\} \models \langle\rangle \longrightarrow a \bullet (S, a \mapsto [])}$$

In the following rule, we use symbol $\leftarrow\!\!\circ$ as a meta-notation standing for any of $\longleftrightarrow\!\!+$, $\longleftarrow$, or $\longleftrightarrow\!\!+ :$. The notation $\eta[l = a]$ denotes the finite map just like η except that $\eta[l = a]$ maps l to a.

($\leftarrow\!\!\circ$)

$$\frac{\{\!\!\{S;\ E\}\!\!\} \models e_1 \longrightarrow a_1 \bullet S_1 \qquad \{\!\!\{S_1;\ E\}\!\!\} \models e_2 \longrightarrow a_2 \bullet S_2 \qquad S_2(a_1) = \eta \qquad a_3 \notin dom(S_2)}{\{\!\!\{S;\ E\}\!\!\} \models \langle e_1 \leftarrow\!\!\circ\ l = e_2\rangle \longrightarrow a_3 \bullet (S_2, a_3 \mapsto \eta[l = a_2])}$$

In the following rule, the notation $S_2[a_1 \mapsto \eta[f = a_2]]$ denotes the finite map just like S_2 except that a_1 is mapped now to $\eta[f = a_2]$.

$$(:=) \quad \frac{\{\!\!\{S;\, E\}\!\!\} \models e_1 \longrightarrow a_1 \bullet S_1 \qquad \{\!\!\{S_1;\, E\}\!\!\} \models e_2 \longrightarrow a_2 \bullet S_2 \qquad S_2(a_1) = \eta}{\{\!\!\{S;\, E\}\!\!\} \models \langle e_1.f := e_2\rangle \longrightarrow a_1 \bullet S_2[a_1 \mapsto \eta[f = a_2]]}$$

$$(\Leftarrow) \quad \frac{\begin{array}{c}\{\!\!\{S;\, E\}\!\!\} \models e \longrightarrow a_1 \bullet S_1 \\ S_1(a_1) = \eta \qquad \eta(m) = a_1' \\ S_1(a_1') = \langle \Lambda().\, e_1,\, E_1\rangle \\ \{\!\!\{S_1;\, E_1\}\!\!\} \models e_1 \longrightarrow a_2 \bullet S_2 \\ S_2(a_2) = \langle \lambda x.\, e_2,\, E_2\rangle \qquad x \notin dom(E_2) \\ \{\!\!\{S_2;\, E_2, x \mapsto a_1\}\!\!\} \models e_2 \longrightarrow a_3 \bullet S_3\end{array}}{\{\!\!\{S;\, E\}\!\!\} \models e \Leftarrow m \longrightarrow a_3 \bullet S_3}$$

$$(\mathit{field\ selection}) \quad \frac{\{\!\!\{S;\, E\}\!\!\} \models e \longrightarrow a_1 \bullet S_1 \qquad S_1(a_1) = \eta \qquad \eta(f) = a_2}{\{\!\!\{S;\, E\}\!\!\} \models e.f \longrightarrow a_2 \bullet S_1}$$

$$(\mathit{let}) \quad \frac{\{\!\!\{S;\, E\}\!\!\} \models e_1 \longrightarrow a_1 \bullet S_1 \qquad \{\!\!\{S;\, E,\, x \mapsto a_1\}\!\!\} \models e_2 \longrightarrow a_2 \bullet S_2 \qquad x \notin dom(E)}{\{\!\!\{S;\, E\}\!\!\} \models \textbf{let}\ x = e_1\ \textbf{in}\ e_2 \longrightarrow a_2 \bullet S_2}$$

$$(\forall\ \mathit{intro}) \quad \frac{\{\!\!\{S;\, E\}\!\!\} \models * \qquad a \notin dom(S)}{\{\!\!\{S;\, E\}\!\!\} \models \Lambda().\, e \longrightarrow a \bullet (S, a \mapsto \langle \Lambda().\, e,\, E\rangle)}$$

$$(\forall\ \mathit{elim}) \quad \frac{\{\!\!\{S;\, E\}\!\!\} \models e_1 \longrightarrow a_1 \bullet S_1 \qquad S_1(a_1) = \langle \Lambda().\, e,\, E'\rangle \qquad \{\!\!\{S_1;\, E'\}\!\!\} \models e \longrightarrow a_2 \bullet S_2}{\{\!\!\{S;\, E\}\!\!\} \models e_1 * () \longrightarrow a_2 \bullet S_2}$$

$$(\exists\ intro)\quad \frac{\{\!|S;\ E|\!\} \models e \longrightarrow a_1 \bullet S_1 \qquad a_2 \notin dom(S_1)}{\{\!|S;\ E|\!\} \models \{\!|(r <:_w R :: L) = R',\ e|\!\} \longrightarrow a_2 \bullet (S_1, a_2 \mapsto a_1)}$$

$$(\exists\ elim)\quad \frac{\{\!|S;\ E|\!\} \models e_1 \longrightarrow a_1 \bullet S_1 \qquad S_1(a_1) = a_1' \qquad x \notin dom(E) \qquad \{\!|S_1;\ (E, x \mapsto a_1')|\!\} \models e_2 \longrightarrow a_2 \bullet S_2}{\{\!|S;\ E|\!\} \models \textbf{Abstype}\ (r <:_w R :: L)\ \textbf{with}\ x : \tau\ \textbf{is}\ e_1\ \textbf{in}\ e_2 \longrightarrow a_2 \bullet S_2}$$

C Semantic Typing

Store Types

$\Sigma ::= a_i \mapsto \tau_i,\ i \in 1,\dots,n \quad \tau_i$ closed.
Furthermore, if τ_i is of the form $\exists(r <:_w R :: L)\tau$, then there is a subsidiary map $\Sigma_\exists$:

$\Sigma_\exists ::= a_i \mapsto R_i \quad R_i$ closed.
Intuitively, R_i is the hidden implementation row associated with existential type $\exists(r <:_w R :: L)\tau$.

Row Environment

$E_\rho ::= r_i \mapsto R_i,\ i \in 1,\dots,m \quad R_i$ closed

C.1 Semantic Typing Judgments

$\Sigma \models *$ — if $\forall a \in dom(\Sigma)$, $\epsilon \vdash \Sigma(a) : \mathtt{T}$, and if $\Sigma(a) = \exists(r <:_w R :: L)\tau$, then $\epsilon \vdash \Sigma_\exists(a) <:_w R$ and $\epsilon \vdash \Sigma_\exists(a) :: L$.

$\Sigma' \succeq \Sigma$ — if $dom(\Sigma) \subseteq dom(\Sigma')$ and $\forall a \in dom(\Sigma)$, $\Sigma(a) = \Sigma'(a)$, and $\forall a \in dom(\Sigma_\exists)$, $\Sigma_\exists(a) = \Sigma'_\exists(a)$.

$\Sigma \models E_\rho \bullet E : \rho \bullet \Gamma$ — Row environment E_ρ and value environment E consistent with row context ρ and expression context Γ.

$\Sigma \models_{ob} S$ — object portion of S well-typed wrt store type Σ

$\Sigma \models_{cl} S$ — closure portion of S well-typed wrt store type Σ.

$\Sigma \models_{rcl} S$ — row closure portion of S well-typed wrt store type Σ.

$\Sigma \models_\exists S$ — existential portion of S well-typed wrt store type Σ.

$\Sigma \models S$ — S well-typed wrt store type Σ.

C.2 Row Environment Substitution

$$[E_\rho \to]* \stackrel{def}{=} *$$

$$[E_\rho \to]\tau \stackrel{def}{=} [R_i/r_i]^{i\in 1\ldots n}\tau \quad \text{for } E_\rho \equiv r_i \mapsto R_i, i \in 1\ldots n$$

$$[E_\rho \to]R \stackrel{def}{=} [R_i/r_i]^{i\in 1\ldots n}R \quad \text{for } E_\rho \equiv r_i \mapsto R_i, i \in 1\ldots n$$

$$[E_\rho \to]e \stackrel{def}{=} [R_i/r_i]^{i\in 1\ldots n}e \quad \text{for } E_\rho \equiv r_i \mapsto R_i, i \in 1\ldots n$$

$$[E_\rho \to](\tau_1 <: \tau_2) \stackrel{def}{=} [E_\rho \to]\tau_1 <: [E_\rho \to]\tau_2$$

$$[E_\rho \to](R_1 <:_B R_2) \stackrel{def}{=} [E_\rho \to]R_1 <:_B [E_\rho \to]R_2$$

$$[E_\rho \to](e : \tau) \stackrel{def}{=} [E_\rho \to]e : [E_\rho \to]\tau$$

$[E_\rho \to]\Gamma$ is defined by:

$$[E_\rho \to]\epsilon \stackrel{def}{=} \epsilon$$
$$[E_\rho \to](\Gamma, x : \tau) \stackrel{def}{=} [E_\rho \to]\Gamma, x : [E_\rho \to]\tau$$

$[E_\rho \to]\rho$ is defined by:

$$[E_\rho \to]\epsilon \stackrel{def}{=} \epsilon$$
$$[E_\rho \to](\rho, (r <:_w R :: L)) \stackrel{def}{=} [E_\rho \to]\rho \quad \text{if } r \in dom(E_\rho)$$
$$[E_\rho \to](\rho, (r <:_w R :: L)) \stackrel{def}{=} [E_\rho \to]\rho, (r <:_w [E_\rho \to]R :: L) \quad \text{if } r \notin dom(E_\rho)$$

$$[E_\rho \to](\rho; \Gamma) \stackrel{def}{=} [E_\rho \to]\rho; [E_\rho \to]\Gamma$$

C.3 Semantic Consistency Judgments

(*Empty*)

$$\frac{\Sigma \models *}{\Sigma \models \emptyset \bullet \emptyset : \epsilon \bullet \epsilon}$$

(*Exp Var*)

$$\frac{\Sigma \models E_\rho \bullet E : \rho \bullet \Gamma \qquad \epsilon \vdash \Sigma(a) <: [E_\rho \to]\tau \qquad x \notin dom(\Gamma)}{\Sigma \models E_\rho \bullet (E, x \mapsto a) : \rho \bullet (\Gamma, x : \tau)}$$

(*Row Var*)

$$\frac{\Sigma \models E_\rho \bullet E : \rho \bullet \Gamma \qquad \epsilon \vdash R_1 <:_w [E_\rho \to]R_2 \qquad \epsilon \vdash R_1 :: L \qquad r \notin dom(\rho)}{\Sigma \models (E_\rho, r \mapsto R_1) \bullet E : (\rho, (r <:_w R_2 :: L)) \bullet \Gamma}$$

C.4 Store Typing Judgments

$$(\models_{ob})\quad \frac{\begin{array}{c}\Sigma \models * \\ \Sigma(a_j) = \mathbf{pro.}\langle\!\langle m_i : \tau_i,\ f_k : \tau'_k \rangle\!\rangle^{i\in I,\, k\in K} \\ j \in 1..|S_{OBJ}| \\ \Sigma(a_i) = \forall(r_i <:_w R_i :: All)\mathbf{pro.}r_i \to \tau_i \qquad i \in I \\ \epsilon \vdash \Sigma(a_k) <: \tau'_k \qquad k \in K \\ \epsilon \vdash \langle\!\langle m_i : \tau_i,\ f_k : \tau'_k \rangle\!\rangle^{i\in I,\, k\in K} <:_w R_i \end{array}}{\begin{array}{c}\Sigma \models_{ob} a_j \mapsto [m_i = a_i,\ f_k = a_k]^{i\in I,\, k\in K} \\ j \in 1..|S_{OBJ}|\end{array}}$$

$$(\models_{cl})\quad \frac{\begin{array}{c}\Sigma \models * \\ \Sigma(a_j) = \tau_j \to \tau'_j \qquad j \in 1..|S_{CL}| \\ \Sigma \models \emptyset \bullet E_j : \epsilon \bullet \Gamma_j \\ \epsilon\,;\, \Gamma_j,\, x_j : \tau_j \vdash e_j : \tau'_j \end{array}}{\begin{array}{c}\Sigma \models_{cl} a_j \mapsto \langle \lambda x_j . e_j,\, E_j \rangle \\ j \in 1..|S_{CL}|\end{array}}$$

$$(\models_{rcl})\quad \frac{\begin{array}{c}\Sigma \models * \\ \Sigma(a_j) = \forall(r_j <:_w R_j :: L_j)\tau_j \qquad j \in 1..|S_{RCL}| \\ \Sigma \models \emptyset \bullet E_j : \epsilon \bullet \Gamma_j \\ (r_j <:_w R_j :: L_j)\,;\, \Gamma_j \vdash e_j : \tau_j \end{array}}{\begin{array}{c}\Sigma \models_{rcl} a_j \mapsto \langle \Lambda().\, e_j,\, E_j \rangle \\ j \in 1..|S_{RCL}|\end{array}}$$

$$(\models_{\exists})\quad \frac{\begin{array}{c}\Sigma \models * \\ \Sigma(a_j) = \exists(r_j <:_w R_j :: L_j)\tau_j \qquad j \in 1..|S_{EXIS}| \\ \Sigma_{\exists}(a_j) = R'_j \\ \epsilon \vdash \Sigma(a'_j) <: [R'_j/r_j]\tau_j \end{array}}{\begin{array}{c}\Sigma \models_{\exists} a_j \mapsto a'_j \\ j \in 1..|S_{EXIS}|\end{array}}$$

$$(\models)\quad \frac{\begin{array}{cc}\Sigma \models_{ob} S & \Sigma \models_{cl} S \\ \Sigma \models_{rcl} S & \Sigma \models_{\exists} S\end{array}}{\Sigma \models S}$$

D Meta-theory

In this appendix, we briefly list some of the key lemmas needed to prove subject reduction.

Lemma 1 (Bound Transformation). *If the judgments* $\rho, (r <:_w R :: L), \rho'; \Gamma \vdash A$, $\rho \vdash R_1 <:_w R$, *and* $\rho \vdash R_1 :: L_1$ *are all derivable, where* $L_1 \subseteq L$, *then the judgment* $\rho, (r <:_w R_1 :: L), \rho'; \Gamma \vdash A$ *is derivable as well.*

Lemma 2 (Row Substitution). *If the judgments* $\rho, (r <:_w R :: L), \rho'; \Gamma \vdash A$, $\rho \vdash R_1 <:_w R$, *and* $\rho \vdash R_1 :: L_1$ *are all derivable, then so is the judgment* $\rho, [R_1/r]\rho'; [R_1/r]\Gamma \vdash [R_1/r]A$.

Lemma 3 (Strengthening). *If the judgments* $\rho; \Gamma, x : \tau, \Gamma' \vdash A$ *and* $\rho \vdash \tau' <: \tau$ *are derivable, then so is* $\rho; \Gamma, x : \tau', \Gamma' \vdash A$

Lemma 4 (Properties of Consistency Judgments). *If* $\Sigma \models E_\rho \bullet E : \rho \bullet \Gamma$ *is derivable, then*

1. $r \in dom(E_\rho)$ *iff* $r \in dom(\rho)$,
2. $\Sigma \models \emptyset \bullet E : \epsilon \bullet [E_\rho \rightarrow]\Gamma$ *is derivable as well,*
3. *if* $\rho \vdash A$ *is derivable, then so is* $[E_\rho \rightarrow](\rho) \vdash [E_\rho \rightarrow]A$, *and*
4. *if* $\rho ; \Gamma \vdash A$ *is derivable, then so is* $[E_\rho \rightarrow](\rho) ; [E_\rho \rightarrow](\Gamma) \vdash [E_\rho \rightarrow]A$.

Lemma 5 (Store Type Weakening).

If $\Sigma \models E_\rho \bullet E : \rho \bullet \Gamma$,
$\Sigma' \models *$, *and*
$\Sigma' \succeq \Sigma$ *all hold, then*
$\Sigma' \models E_\rho \bullet E : \rho \bullet \Gamma$ *holds as well.*

Theorem 4 (Subject Reduction). *If*

$$\rho ; \Gamma \vdash e : \tau,$$
$$\{\!|S; E|\!\} \models e \longrightarrow a \bullet S',$$
$$\Sigma \models S,$$
$$dom(\Sigma) = dom(S), \text{ and}$$
$$\Sigma \models E_\rho \bullet E : \rho \bullet \Gamma,$$

there exists a closed type τ' *and a store type* Σ' *such that*

$$\Sigma' \succeq \Sigma,$$
$$\Sigma' \models S',$$
$$dom(\Sigma') = dom(S'),$$
$$\Sigma'(a) = \tau', \text{ and}$$
$$\epsilon \vdash \tau' <: [E_\rho \rightarrow]\tau.$$

Proof. The proof is by induction on the derivation of $\{\!|S; E|\!\} \models e \longrightarrow a \bullet S'$.

On Object Extension

Luigi Liquori

DIMI, Dip. Matematica ed Informatica, Università di Udine,
Via delle Scienze 206, I-33100 Udine, Italy
e-mail: liquori@dimi.uniud.it

Abstract. The last few years have seen the development of statically typed object based (also called prototype-based) programming languages. Two proposals, namely the *Lambda Calculus of Objects* of Fisher, Honsell, and Mitchell [15], and the *Object Calculus* of Abadi and Cardelli [2], have focused the attention of the scientific community on object calculi, as a foundation for the more traditional class-based calculi and as an original and safe style of programming. In this paper, we apply four type systems to the functional Lambda Calculus of Objects: (a) the Original type system [15]; (b) the Fisher's Ph.D type system [14]; (c) the Bruce's *Matching-based* type systems of Bono and Bugliesi [4], and (d) of Liquori [20]. We then compare these type systems with respect to the following points:

- small-step versus big-step semantics;
- implicit versus explicit polymorphism;
- Curry style versus Church style;
- static type checking versus run-time type checking;
- object extension and/or binary methods versus object subsumption (short account).

Categories. Type Systems of object-oriented languages (panorama).

1 Introduction

In this paper we present the functional Lambda Calculus of Objects of [15]. In its simplest version à la Curry[1], it is essentially an untyped lambda calculus enriched with three primitive operations on objects: *method addition* to define new methods, *method override* to redefine existing methods, and *method call* to send a message to (i.e. invoke a method on) an object. The calculus is simple and powerful enough to capture the class-based paradigm, since classes can be easily codified by appropriate objects, following the "classes-as-objects" analogy of Smalltalk-80 [18].

In the calculus of [15], objects can be seen as sequences (i.e. lists) of pairs *(method names, method bodies)* where the method body is (or reduces to) a lambda abstraction whose first formal parameter is always *self*. This calculus can be given an operational semantics which, in the case of a message send

[1] By *à la Curry*, we mean that the terms of the calculus are not annotated with types. This does not signify that a type system does not exist.

(written as $e \Leftarrow m$), produces the so-called *dynamic method lookup* in order to inspect the structure of objects and perform method extraction. This semantics can be given in terms of a transition (i.e. *small-step*) semantics, or in terms of an evaluation (i.e. *big-step*) semantics. To this calculus four static and sound type systems are applied, which enable us to prevent the unfortunate *message-not-found* run time error:

- the original type system of [15];
- the Fisher's Ph.D type system [14];
- the Bruce's *Matching-based* type system of Bono and Bugliesi [4];
- the Bruce's *Matching-based* type system of Liquori [20].

All of these solutions reinterpret the type of the *self* (or *this* in C^{++}), occurring inside a method body, in the type of the object which inherits that method; this capability is usually referred to as *mytype method specialization*.

For each of these solutions, we analyze how method specialization takes place and we show how the different object extension rules enable us to build polymorphic methods that work (hopefully) for all future extensions of the prototype (here the word *prototype* means the object we are extending or overriding).

The presentation is intentionally kept informal, with few definitions, no full type systems in appendix and no theorems. Quite simply, the main aim of this paper is to explain and compare existing systems concerning object extension.

We then take the step of enriching the above calculi with *explicit polymorphism*, in order to make our method bodies first-class values.

As a final step, we try to build a corresponding calculus à la Church[2], to which apply the four type systems described. As we will see, the progression from a totally untyped calculus to a fully decorated one is a not trivial task; in fact, one may need to resort to a *type-driven*[3] operational semantics, in the style of [13,11].

We finally build a calculus based on the Object Calculus of [2], where ordinary (i.e. fixed size) objects are extendible. This calculus considers the dynamic method lookup phase as an *implicit* phase that can be performed in just one step; in fact it eliminates all the rules concerning the method search from the operational semantics and the type systems (that are made explicit in [15]). Moreover, it includes as part of its syntax the lambda calculus (that was, instead, simulated by suitable objects in [2]).

We also compare this "hybrid" calculus with the Lambda Calculus of Objects: this comparison is interesting since objects in [2] are sets consisting of pairs *(method name, method body)* and, as it is customary in programming, sets can usually be implemented with lists.

The paper is organized as follows. In Section 2, we present the Lambda Calculus of Objects in Curry style together with a small-step and a big-step operational semantics. In Section 3 we present, quite informally, four type systems

[2] By *à la Church*, we mean that the terms of the calculus are annotated with types.

[3] By type-driven, we mean that some evaluation steps are constrained by suitable typing derivations.

with their *golden* rules of object extension. A comparison between these systems is given in Subsection 3.6. In Section 4, we try to build a corresponding calculus in Church style: we choose to study the type system of [14], since it is much more "plug-and-play" than other ones. Section 5 defines the calculus based on the Object Calculus of [2] and compares it with the Lambda Calculus of Object. Finally, Section 6 deals (concisely) with issues concerning the cohabitation of object extension and/or binary methods with object subsumption.

2 The Lambda Calculus of Objects à la Curry

In this section, we present the syntax and the dynamic semantics of the Lambda Calculus of Objects. The expressions are defined by the following grammar:

$$\begin{array}{llr} e ::= & c \mid x \mid \lambda x.e \mid e_1\, e_2 \mid & \text{(untyped } \lambda\text{-calculus)} \\ & \langle\,\rangle \mid e \Leftarrow m \mid \langle e_1 \longleftarrow m = e_2 \rangle \mid \langle e_1 \longleftarrow\!\!\!+\; m = e_2 \rangle \mid & \text{(object expressions)} \\ & e \hookleftarrow m, & \text{(auxiliary expression)} \end{array}$$

where c is a constant, x is a variable, and m is a method name. The object expressions have the following intuitive meaning:

- $\langle\,\rangle$ is the empty object;
- $e \Leftarrow m$ send message m to object e;
- $\langle e_1 \longleftarrow\!\!\!+\; m = e_2 \rangle$ extend e_1 with a new method m;
- $\langle e_1 \longleftarrow m = e_2 \rangle$ replace the existing body of m in e_1 with body e_2.

Observe that the notation for methods and fields is unified. The auxiliary expression $e \hookleftarrow m$ searches the body of the m method within the object e; this form is mainly used to define the operational semantics and, in practice, is not available to the programmer[4]. The employment of the "search" expression is peculiar to the use of a different reduction semantics for the calculus; this semantics, inspired by [24,3,6], provides a more direct *dynamic method lookup* than the *bookkeeping* reductions originally introduced in [15].

The body of a method is (or reduces to) a lambda abstraction whose first parameter is always *self* (i.e. $\lambda self \ldots$); in fact, the operational semantics will reduce a message send to the application of the body of the method to the recipient of the message. Note that argument passing can be modeled via lambda application (i.e. $(e \Leftarrow m)\ arg_1 \ldots arg_n$, with $n \geq 0$).

2.1 Operational Semantics

In this subsection we present a small-step reduction semantics and a big-step operational semantics.

[4] If a program is allowed to use such operator, then it breaks object encapsulation since the state of the object and the methods implementation are usually hidden from the outside.

Small-step Reduction Semantics. The core of the small-step reduction semantics is given by the following reduction rules. Let $\hookleftarrow\!\!\!*$ denote either $\hookleftarrow\!\!+$ or $\longleftarrow$.

$$(Beta)\quad (\lambda x.e_1)\, e_2 \quad \overset{ev}{\to} [e_2/x]e_1$$

$$(Select)\; e \Leftarrow m \quad \overset{ev}{\to} (e \hookleftarrow m)\, e$$

$$(Succ)\quad \langle e_1 \longleftarrow\!\!* \; m = e_2\rangle \hookleftarrow m \overset{ev}{\to} e_2$$

$$(Next)\quad \langle e_1 \longleftarrow\!\!* \; n = e_2\rangle \hookleftarrow m \overset{ev}{\to} e_1 \hookleftarrow m \qquad m \neq n.$$

In addition to the standard (*Beta*) rule for lambda calculus expressions, the main operation on objects is method invocation, whose reduction is defined by the (*Select*) rule: the result of sending a message m to an object e containing an m method is the result of self-applying the body of m to the object e itself. To account for this behavior, the (*Succ*) and (*Next*) reduction rules recursively inspect the structure of the object (implemented as a list) and perform method extraction; by looking at these last two rules, it follows that the $\hookleftarrow$ operator is *destructive*, i.e. it goes "through" the object until it finds the searched method. This will also be semantically enforced in the (*search*) type rules (see Section 3). We could then define the relation $\overset{ev}{\twoheadrightarrow}$ as the symmetric, reflexive, transitive and contextual closure of $\overset{ev}{\to}$. As it is customary, the reduction semantics does not specify an evaluation strategy which is forced, instead, in a big-step operational semantics.

Big-step Operational Semantics. We define an operational semantics via a natural proof deduction system à la Plotkin [27]. The purpose of the reduction is to map every closed expression into a normal form, i.e. an irreducible term. The strategy is "lazy" since it does not work under lambda binders and inside object expressions. We define the set of results (i.e. values) as follows:

$$obj ::= \langle e_1 \longleftarrow\!\!* \; m = e_2\rangle \mid \langle\rangle$$
$$v ::= c \mid obj \mid \lambda x.e.$$

The deduction rules are presented as follows:

$$\frac{}{v \Downarrow v}\;(Red\!-\!Val) \qquad \frac{e_1 \Downarrow \lambda x.e_1' \qquad [e_2/x]e_1' \Downarrow v}{e_1\, e_2 \Downarrow v}\;(Red\!-\!Beta)$$

$$\frac{e \Downarrow obj \qquad obj \hookleftarrow m \Downarrow \lambda x.e' \qquad [obj/x]e' \Downarrow v}{e \Leftarrow m \Downarrow v}\;(Red\!-\!Select)$$

$$\frac{e_2 \Downarrow v}{\langle e_1 \longleftarrow\!\!* \; m = e_2\rangle \hookleftarrow m \Downarrow v}\;(Red\!-\!Succ)$$

$$\frac{e_1 \Downarrow obj \qquad obj \hookleftarrow m \Downarrow v \qquad m \neq n}{\langle e_1 \longleftarrow\!\!* \; n = e_2\rangle \hookleftarrow m \Downarrow v}\;(Red\!-\!Next)$$

Big-step operational semantics is deterministic, and immediately suggests how to build an interpreter for the calculus. Moreover, big-step semantics is sound with respect to the reduction $\stackrel{ev}{\twoheadrightarrow}$, since it holds:

Proposition 1 (Soundness of $\Downarrow$). *If $e \Downarrow v$, then $e \stackrel{ev}{\twoheadrightarrow} v$.*

Definition 2. Given a closed expression e, we say that e *converges*, and we write it as $e \Downarrow$, if there exist a v such that $e \Downarrow v$.

Given the above definition, we also conjecture the completeness, which shows that every terminating program also terminates in our interpreter.

Conjecture 3 (Completeness of $\Downarrow$). *If $e \stackrel{ev}{\twoheadrightarrow} v$, then e converges, i.e. $e \Downarrow$.*

2.2 Some Intuitive Examples

Let $\langle m_1{=}e_1 \ldots m_k{=}e_k \rangle$ be as shorthand for $\langle \ldots \langle \langle \rangle \longleftrightarrow\!\!+\ m_1 = e_1 \rangle \ldots \longleftrightarrow\!\!+\ m_k = e_k \rangle$ for $k \geq 1$.

Example 4 (Method Dependencies). This very simple example will follow us through the presentation of the type systems: it will help us to highlight how method dependencies are carried out in the systems. The object

$$e \triangleq \langle m = \lambda self.1, n = \lambda self.self \Leftarrow m \rangle,$$

represents a point with two methods m and n, where n gives the same result as m. Moreover, we find it useful to consider the following objects:

$$\begin{aligned} e' &\triangleq \langle e \longleftrightarrow\!\!+\ p = \lambda self.self \Leftarrow n \rangle \\ e'' &\triangleq \langle e \longleftrightarrow\!\!+\ q = \lambda self.self \Leftarrow n \rangle \\ e''' &\triangleq \langle l = \lambda self.1, n = \lambda self.self \Leftarrow l, q = \lambda self.self \Leftarrow n \rangle. \end{aligned}$$

Example 5 (A "funny" object). Let the object *funny* be defined as follows:

$$funny \triangleq \langle m = \lambda self.\langle self \longleftarrow m = \lambda self'.self' \Leftarrow m \rangle \rangle.$$

This is an object whose evaluation may be infinite. If we send the message m to *funny*, then we have the following computation:

$$\begin{aligned} funny \Leftarrow m &\stackrel{ev}{\to} (funny \hookleftarrow m)\, funny \\ &\stackrel{ev}{\to} (\lambda self.\langle self \longleftarrow m = \lambda self'.self' \Leftarrow m \rangle) funny \\ &\stackrel{ev}{\to} \langle funny \longleftarrow m = \lambda self'.self' \Leftarrow m \rangle. \end{aligned}$$

Conversely, if we send the message m to *funny* twice, then the computation becomes infinite:

$$\begin{aligned} (funny \Leftarrow m) \Leftarrow m &\stackrel{ev}{\twoheadrightarrow} \langle funny \longleftarrow m = \lambda self'.self' \Leftarrow m \rangle \Leftarrow m \\ &\stackrel{ev}{\to} (\lambda self'.self' \Leftarrow m)\langle funny \longleftarrow m = \lambda self'.self' \Leftarrow m \rangle \\ &\stackrel{ev}{\to} \langle funny \longleftarrow m = \lambda self'.self' \Leftarrow m \rangle \Leftarrow m \\ &\stackrel{ev}{\twoheadrightarrow} \langle funny \longleftarrow m = \lambda self'.self' \Leftarrow m \rangle \Leftarrow m \\ &\stackrel{ev}{\twoheadrightarrow} \ldots \end{aligned}$$

Since *funny* is typable in all the type systems to be presented, it illustrates the failure of strong normalization for typable object expressions.

3 The Four Type Systems

In this section we present the four type systems applied to the Lambda Calculus of Objects. In particular we show the syntax of types and contexts, the various judgments, and the main typing rules: for the purpose of the comparison between systems, we only are interested in discussing the rules of method extension, method override, message send and method search.

Typing the Examples The objects presented in Examples 4, and 5 can be typed *in all the four type systems* as follows:

$$\begin{aligned}
&\varepsilon \vdash e : \texttt{obj}\, t.\langle\!\langle m : int, n : int\rangle\!\rangle\\
&\varepsilon \vdash e' : \texttt{obj}\, t.\langle\!\langle m : int, n : int, p : int\rangle\!\rangle\\
&\varepsilon \vdash e'' : \texttt{obj}\, t.\langle\!\langle m : int, n : int, q : int\rangle\!\rangle\\
&\varepsilon \vdash e''' : \texttt{obj}\, t.\langle\!\langle l : int, n : int, q : int\rangle\!\rangle\\
&\varepsilon \vdash \mathit{funny} : \texttt{obj}\, t.\langle\!\langle m : t\rangle\!\rangle.
\end{aligned}$$

Note that, in the judgment for *funny*, the method m has a type t which refers to the type of the object *funny* itself.

Remark 6. All the considered type systems do not have a *subsumption* rule of the shape:

$$\frac{\Gamma \vdash e : \sigma \qquad \Gamma \vdash \sigma \; ord \; \tau}{\Gamma \vdash e : \tau} \; (subsume)$$

where *ord* is any partial order on types. The issue of object subsumption in presence of object extension has been widely studied [6,17,2,14,5,21,20,28]. A detailed comparison of calculi with object extension in presence of object subsumption is under development (see also Section 6).

3.1 The Original Type System of [15]

Definition 7 (Type Syntax). The set of types, rows and kinds are mutually defined by the following grammar:

$$\begin{aligned}
&\text{Types } \tau ::= t \mid \tau{\to}\tau \mid \texttt{obj}\, t.R\\
&\text{Rows } R ::= r \mid \langle\!\langle\rangle\!\rangle \mid \langle\!\langle R \mid m : \tau\rangle\!\rangle \mid \lambda t.R \mid R\,\tau\\
&\text{Kinds } \kappa ::= T \mid T^p{\to}[m_1, \ldots, m_k] \; (p \geq 0, k \geq 1).
\end{aligned}$$

The binder `obj` is a sort of fixed-point operator that scopes over the row-part: the bound type-variable t may occur freely within the scope of the binder, with every free occurrence referring to the object itself, i.e. *self*. Thus, object-types are a form of recursively-defined types. A *row* R is an unordered collection of pairs *(method label, method type)*; we consider α-conversion of type-variables bound by obj. Additional equations between types and rows arise as a result of β-reduction. Intuitively, if an object-type $\mathtt{obj}\, t.\langle\!\langle m_1 : \tau_1 \ldots m_k : \tau_k \rangle\!\rangle$ with $k \geq 0$ is assigned to an object e, then e can receive $m_1 \ldots m_k$ messages, and the final result types are $\tau_1 \ldots \tau_k$. We write $\overline{m} : \overline{\tau}$ to abbreviate $m_1 : \tau_1, \ldots, m_k : \tau_k$, for some unimportant k.

Contexts and Type Judgments. Contexts are ordered lists (not sets) of the following shape:

$$\Gamma ::= \varepsilon \mid \Gamma, x : \tau \mid \Gamma, t : T \mid \Gamma, r : \kappa,$$

and judgments have the following form:

$$\Gamma \vdash *, \text{ or } \Gamma \vdash R : \kappa, \text{ or } \Gamma \vdash \tau : T, \text{ or } \Gamma \vdash e \, : \, \tau.$$

The judgment $\Gamma \vdash *$ can be read as "Γ is a well-formed context". Intuitively, the meaning of the judgment $\Gamma \vdash R : [m_1, \ldots, m_k]$ assures that the row R does *not* include method names $m_1, \ldots, m_k$. For example:

$$\varepsilon \vdash \langle\!\langle m : int, n : int \rangle\!\rangle : [p],$$

being that $m \neq n \neq p$. We need this *negative* information to guarantee statically that methods are not multiply defined. When $\Gamma \vdash R : T \rightarrow [\overline{m}]$, then it follows that R must be a row-abstraction, e.g.:

$$\varepsilon \vdash \lambda t.\langle\!\langle \overline{n} : \overline{\tau} \rangle\!\rangle : T \rightarrow [\overline{m}],$$

being that $\overline{n} \neq \overline{m}$. The meaning of the other judgments is the standard one (i.e. τ is a "well-formed context" in Γ, and τ is assigned to e in the context Γ).

Main Typing Rules. The empty object $\langle\rangle$ has the object-type $\mathtt{obj}\, t.\langle\!\langle\rangle\!\rangle$: this object cannot respond to any message, but can be extended with other methods. The typing rule is:

$$\frac{\Gamma \vdash *}{\Gamma \vdash \langle\rangle : \mathtt{obj}\, t.\langle\!\langle\rangle\!\rangle} \quad (empty\!-\!obj)$$

The rule to give a type to a message send is simple:

$$\frac{\Gamma \vdash e : \mathtt{obj}\, t.\langle\!\langle R \mid n : \tau \rangle\!\rangle}{\Gamma \vdash e \Leftarrow n : [\mathtt{obj}\, t.\langle\!\langle R \mid n : \tau \rangle\!\rangle / t]\tau} \quad (send)$$

This rule says that we can give a type to a message send provided that the receiver has the method we require in its object-type. Since the order of methods in rows is irrelevant, we can write n as the last method listed in the object-type. The result of a message send will have a type in which every occurrence of the type-variable t has to be substituted by the full type of the object itself, thus reflecting the recursive nature of the object-type.

The most subtle and intriguing rule is the one that enable us to build another object by extending an existing prototype.

$$\frac{\begin{array}{ll}\Gamma \vdash e_1 \ : \ \mathtt{obj}\, t.\langle\!\langle R \mid \overline{m} : \overline{\sigma} \rangle\!\rangle & \Gamma, t : T \vdash R \ : \ [\overline{m}, n] \\ \Gamma, r : T \to [\overline{m}, n] \vdash e_2 \ : \ [\mathtt{obj}\, t.\langle\!\langle r\, t \mid \overline{m} : \overline{\sigma}, n : \tau \rangle\!\rangle / t](t \to \tau) & r \text{ not in } \tau\end{array}}{\Gamma \vdash \langle e_1 \longleftrightarrow n = e_2 \rangle \ : \ \mathtt{obj}\, t.\langle\!\langle R \mid \overline{m} : \overline{\sigma}, n : \tau \rangle\!\rangle} \ (obj\!-\!ext)$$

In this rule, we assume the type of the object e_1 does not contain the method n we want to add. This condition is guaranteed by the first two premises. The meaning of the explicitly listed methods $\overline{m}$ in the types of e_1 and e_2 is crucial:

- in the typing of e_2 they represent the methods which are *useful* to type n's body: i.e. (at least) the messages that are sent to *self* or the methods overridden to *self* inside the body of n[5].
- in the typing of e_1 they guarantee that the methods $\overline{m}$, which are useful to type the body of n, are *already* present in the prototype to be extended.

The side condition "r not in τ" is an "hygiene condition" that avoids to introduce unsound free occurrences of r. As an example, if the body e_2 of method n is:

$$body_n = \lambda self.\langle self \longleftarrow m_1 = \lambda self'.self' \Leftarrow m_2 \rangle,$$

then the addition of n to an object e_1 (not containing n) requires the following judgment to be derivable:

$$r : T \to [m_1, m_2, n] \vdash body_n : [\mathtt{obj}\, t.\langle\!\langle r\, t \mid m_1 : {}_{-1}, m_2 : {}_{-2}, n : t \rangle\!\rangle / t](t \to t),$$

for some unknown types ${}_{-1}$, and ${}_{-2}$, such that ${}_{-1} = {}_{-2}$[6].

Self-Application. Note that the typing of e_2 is an arrow-type of the shape $(t \to \tau)$ with t substituted by an object-type. Since t is hidden in the final typing of $\langle e_1 \longleftrightarrow n = e_2 \rangle$, it is necessary in the typing of e_2, because the semantics of sending messages would result in the application of the body of the method to the host object itself.

Higher-Order. Note also that the typing for e_2 contains occurrences of the "open" object-type $\mathtt{obj}\, t.\langle\!\langle r\, t \mid \overline{m} : \overline{\sigma}, n : \tau \rangle\!\rangle$. Inside that object-type there occurs an application of the row-variable r (which is implicitly quantified in the context) to the type t (representing the type of *self*). Because of this implicit

[5] Cardelli [10] defines the capability of a method of operating directly on its own self as a *self-inflicted* operation.

[6] In UNIX jargon, in order to type an object extension, we need to be able to **grep** all the $\overline{m}$ methods that are essential to the typing of the body of n (plus n itself, to guarantee recursive method definition).

quantification, for every substitution of r with a row R' of the same kind of r, e_2 will have the indicated type in which r will be substituted by R'. This guarantees that for all future extensions of the object $\langle e_1 \longleftarrow\!\!\!+ n = e_2 \rangle$[7], the body e_2 of n will specialize its functionality. The "very high mutability" of the type of a method will be very useful when we introduce *explicit quantification* for method bodies (see Subsection 3.7).

The rule that allows to build another object by overriding a method which already belongs to the prototype is as follows:

$$\frac{\begin{array}{l}\Gamma \vdash e_1 \;:\; \mathtt{obj}\,t.\langle\!\langle R \mid \overline{m}:\overline{\sigma}, n:\tau \rangle\!\rangle \\ \Gamma, r : T \to [\overline{m}, n] \vdash e_2 \;:\; [\mathtt{obj}\,t.\langle\!\langle r\,t \mid \overline{m}:\overline{\sigma}, n:\tau \rangle\!\rangle / t](t \to \tau)\end{array}}{\Gamma \vdash \langle e_1 \longleftarrow n = e_2 \rangle \;:\; \mathtt{obj}\,t.\langle\!\langle R \mid \overline{m}:\overline{\sigma}, n:\tau \rangle\!\rangle} \quad (obj{-}over)$$

The first premise says that the method $n : \tau$ we are overriding and the methods $\overline{m} : \overline{\sigma}$ which are useful to type the e_2 body are present in the type of e_1. The second premise is as in the $(obj{-}ext)$ rule. Note that the type of the overridden method is left unchanged, and that the type of the new object is the same as the one of the prototype.

Finally the rule of method search is as follows (this rule does not pertain to the type system of [15], since a different operational semantics is adopted that uses the "bookkeeping" reduction rules to extract the appropriate method out of an object):

$$\frac{\Gamma \vdash e \;:\; \mathtt{obj}\,t.\langle\!\langle R \mid n:\tau \rangle\!\rangle \qquad \Gamma, t : T \vdash \langle\!\langle R \mid \overline{m}:\overline{\sigma} \rangle\!\rangle : [n]}{\Gamma \vdash e \hookleftarrow n \;:\; [\mathtt{obj}\,t.\langle\!\langle R \mid \overline{m}:\overline{\sigma}, n:\tau \rangle\!\rangle / t](t \to \tau)} \quad (search)$$

The first premise of this rule says that that the object e contains n in its interface, while the second premise "attaches" to object e all the methods which where skipped during the right-to-left traversing of object e' (built using e as a prototype), which received the message n in question. Hence, the final type for $e \hookleftarrow n$ will have the same functionality of the body of n, i.e. an arrow-type whose first parameter has the type of e' i.e. $\mathtt{obj}\,t.\langle\!\langle R \mid \overline{m}:\overline{\sigma}, n:\tau \rangle\!\rangle$.

As an important remark, we note that there is no way of finding the $\overline{m} : \overline{\sigma}$ methods; in fact, the search operator is "destructive" and does not keep track of the already skipped method. This rule only guarantees that the body of n will specialize its functionality for all future extensions of e.

Example 8 (Typing Example 4 in [15]). In order to build the object e', using e as a prototype, we need (i) to know that p does not belongs to e, (ii) to assure that $n : int$ is present in the the type of e, and (iii) to derive for the body of p the judgment

$$r : T \to [n, p] \vdash \lambda self.self \Leftarrow n : [\mathtt{obj}\,t.\langle\!\langle r\,t \mid n : int, p : int \rangle\!\rangle / t](t \to int). \qquad (*)$$

[7] Much more precisely: all prototypes containing the $\overline{m} : \overline{\sigma}$ methods, and not containing the n method, can be extended with $n = e_2$, since the type of n specializes its functionality.

It follows that, to type the body of p, we need to know only the types of methods n (the method directly used inside p), and p (i.e. the method to be added); there is no need to extract the indirect dependencies of n (i.e. m). Of course one can also add indirect dependencies, but these are not essential to the method specialization of p. This form of polymorphism is quite powerful for two reasons:

- the body of the added method has a very high "degree of polymorphism", since a very small amount of information is needed in order to give a correct type for the body of p. Method specialization of p will follow for all future extensions of e'.
- the body of p should also be used to extend other objects such as the e'' or e''', using the same judgment $(*)$.

For the sake of curiosity, the object *funny* can be typed using the following judgment:

$$r : T{\rightarrow}[m] \vdash \lambda self.\langle self \longleftarrow m = \lambda self'.self' \Leftarrow m\rangle : [\mathtt{obj}\, t.\langle\!\langle r\, t \mid m : t\rangle\!\rangle/t](t{\rightarrow}t).$$

3.2 Fisher's Type System [14]

The set of types, rows and kinds are defined exactly as in Definition 7.

Contexts and Type Judgments. Contexts have the following shape:

$$\Gamma ::= \varepsilon \mid \Gamma, x : \tau \mid \Gamma, t : T \mid \Gamma, r <\!: R : \kappa,$$

and judgments have the following form:

$$\Gamma \vdash *, \text{ or } \Gamma \vdash R : \kappa, \text{ or } \Gamma \vdash \tau : T, \text{ or } \Gamma \vdash e \ : \ \tau, \text{ or } \Gamma \vdash R <\!: R'.$$

With respect to contexts and judgments of [15], there are some differences:

- the judgment $\Gamma \vdash R <\!: R'$ formalizes *with subrowing*, i.e. row R has *more* methods than row R', and common methods have the same type.
- the declaration $r <\!: R : \kappa$ occurring in a context gives us some kind of *positive* information about the possible shape of the rows to be substituted with r inside an object-type. More precisely, the row-variable r must be a *subrow* of the explicitly listed row R. The kind κ still continues to have the same meaning as in [15].

The meaning of the other judgments is the same as in [15].

Main Typing Rules. The type rule to build an empty object is the same as in [15].

The rule to give a type to a message send is as follows:

$$\frac{\Gamma \vdash e : \mathtt{obj}\, t.R \qquad \Gamma, t : T \vdash R <\!: \langle\!\langle n : \tau\rangle\!\rangle}{\Gamma \vdash e \Leftarrow n : [\mathtt{obj}\, t.R/t]\tau} \ (send)$$

This rule is rather different from the one of [15]; in fact, it requires that the row R occurring in the type of e contains (this is the "positive" information given by the subrowing judgment) the message n to be received. The object-type $\mathtt{obj}\, t.R$ could be also "open" i.e. of the shape $\mathtt{obj}\, t.r\, t$, or $\mathtt{obj}\, t.\langle\!\langle r\, t \mid \ldots\rangle\!\rangle$ (and so on), in order to type a message send to objects whose types may be partially abstract.

The rule to extend an object is as follows:

$$\frac{\Gamma \vdash e_1 : \mathtt{obj}\, t.R \qquad \Gamma, t : T \vdash R : [n] \qquad \Gamma, r <: \lambda t.\langle\!\langle R \mid n : \tau\rangle\!\rangle : T \to [\,] \vdash e_2 : [\mathtt{obj}\, t.r\, t/t](t \to \tau) \quad r \text{ not in } \tau}{\Gamma \vdash \langle e_1 \longleftrightarrow\!\!+\, n = e_2\rangle : \mathtt{obj}\, t.\langle\!\langle R \mid n : \tau\rangle\!\rangle} \; (obj\!-\!ext)$$

In this rule we require that the prototype e_1 does not contain the method n to be added (this is the "negative" information given by the "well kindness" judgment), and we require that the type of e_2 is an arrow-type of the shape $(t \to \tau)$ with t substituted by an open (i.e. still unknown) object-type of the shape $\mathtt{obj}\, t.r\, t$, being that $r <: \lambda t.\langle\!\langle R \mid n : \tau\rangle\!\rangle$. The constraint on the shape of r together with its kinding (i.e. $T \to [\,]$) are crucial in order to understand this rule:

- the positive information of the subrowing judgment gives us the information that for all future extensions of the object $\langle e_1 \longleftrightarrow\!\!+\, n = e_2\rangle$, the body e_2 of n will specialize its functionality.
- the negative information $T \to [\,]$ force that the body of n cannot self-inflict an object extension to the host object.

The rule for object override is simpler:

$$\frac{\Gamma \vdash e_1 : \mathtt{obj}\, t.R \qquad \Gamma, t : T \vdash R <: \langle\!\langle n : \tau\rangle\!\rangle \qquad \Gamma, r <: \lambda t.R : T \to [\,] \vdash e_2 : [\mathtt{obj}\, t.r\, t/t](t \to \tau)}{\Gamma \vdash \langle e_1 \longleftarrow n = e_2\rangle : \mathtt{obj}\, t.R} \; (obj\!-\!over)$$

The only remark about this rule is that the subrowing judgment forces the method n in the row R.

Finally, the rule of method search is as follows (also in [14] the "bookkeeping" reduction rules are adopted):

$$\frac{\Gamma \vdash e : \mathtt{obj}\, t.R \qquad \Gamma, t : T \vdash R <: \langle\!\langle n : \tau\rangle\!\rangle \qquad \Gamma, t : T \vdash R' <: R}{\Gamma \vdash e \hookleftarrow n : [\mathtt{obj}\, t.R'/t](t \to \tau)} \; (search)$$

The first two premises assure that n is a method of e, while the last premise finds a row R' that extends R. The final type for the host object will be $\mathtt{obj}\, t.R'$. This type represents the receiver of message n in question.

As in the $(search)$ rule for [15], and due to the nature of the "search" operator, there is no way of finding a precise R' which extends R.

Example 9 (Typing Example 4 in [14]). In order to build the object e', using e as a prototype, we need (i) to know that p does not belongs to e, and (ii) to derive for the body of p the judgment:

$$r <: \lambda t.\langle\!\langle m : int, n : int, p : int\rangle\!\rangle : T \to [\,] \vdash \lambda self.self \Leftarrow n : [\mathtt{obj}\, t.r\, t/t](t \to int). \; (*)$$

It follows that, in order to type the body of p, we need to know the types of methods m, n (i.e. *all methods of the prototype* e) and p itself.

This "degree of polymorphism" (lower with respect to [15]) is exactly what we need in order to capture method specialization of p for all future extensions of e'. Note that the judgment $(*)$ can be used to extend e'' but not e''', since, of course, e''' is not an extension of e.

3.3 Bruce's Matching-based Type System of Bono and Bugliesi [4]

This solution is well known to perform a substantial simplification of the original type system of [15].

Type Syntax. Types and rows have the following shape:

$$\begin{array}{l} \text{Types } \tau \;::= t \mid \tau \to \tau \mid \mathtt{obj}\, t.R \\ \text{Rows } \; R ::= \langle\!\langle\rangle\!\rangle \mid \langle\!\langle R \mid m : \tau\rangle\!\rangle. \end{array}$$

Contexts and Type Judgments. Contexts have the following shape:

$$\Gamma ::= \varepsilon \mid \Gamma, x : \tau \mid \Gamma, u <\!\# \sigma,$$

and the judgments have the following form:

$$\Gamma \vdash *, \text{ or } \Gamma \vdash \tau : T, \text{ or } \Gamma \vdash e : \tau, \text{ or } \Gamma \vdash \sigma <\!\# \tau.$$

The relation of *Matching* [8], formalized by the judgment $\Gamma \vdash \sigma <\!\# \tau$, captures the capability of an object to inherit the behavior and to specialize the types of the methods of the prototype.

The main rule underlining this relation is the following one:

$$\frac{\Gamma \vdash \mathtt{obj}\, t.\langle\!\langle \overline{m} : \overline{\sigma}, \overline{n} : \overline{\tau}\rangle\!\rangle}{\Gamma \vdash \mathtt{obj}\, t.\langle\!\langle \overline{m} : \overline{\sigma}, \overline{n} : \overline{\tau}\rangle\!\rangle <\!\# \,\mathtt{obj}\, t.\langle\!\langle \overline{m} : \overline{\sigma}\rangle\!\rangle} \; (<\!\#)$$

Hence, an object-type matches an other if and only if the former has more methods than the latter. Note that the type-variable u "match-bounded" in a context Γ always refers to the type of *self*. This condition is enforced in the typing rules.

Main Typing Rules. Again, the type rule for building an empty object is the same as in [15] and [14].

The rule to give a type to a message send behaves as follows:

$$\frac{\Gamma \vdash e : \sigma \qquad \Gamma \vdash \sigma \mathrel{<\!\!\#} \mathtt{obj}\, t.\langle\!\langle n : \tau \rangle\!\rangle}{\Gamma \vdash e \Leftarrow n : [\sigma/t]\tau} \quad (send)$$

In this rule we require that the type σ has the method n in its protocol; this can be achieved when σ is an object-type containing n, but also when the type σ of e is partially abstract (e.g. when σ is a type-variable match-bounded in the context Γ).

The type rule to extend an object is as follows:

$$\frac{\begin{array}{l}\Gamma \vdash e_1 \ : \ \mathtt{obj}\, t.R \\ \Gamma, u \mathrel{<\!\!\#} \mathtt{obj}\, t.\langle\!\langle R \mid n : \tau \rangle\!\rangle \vdash e_2 \ : \ [u/t](t \to \tau) \quad n \text{ not in } R\end{array}}{\Gamma \vdash \langle e_1 \longleftrightarrow\!\!\!+ \; n = e_2 \rangle \ : \ \mathtt{obj}\, t.\langle\!\langle R \mid n : \tau \rangle\!\rangle} \quad (obj\!-\!ext)$$

In this rule, as in all the rules for object extension we have previously seen, we require that e_1 does not contain the method n to be added (enforced by the side condition n not in R), and that the type of e_2 is an arrow type $(t \to \tau)$ with t substituted for a unknown type u, match-bounded by the object-type $\mathtt{obj}\, t.\langle\!\langle R \mid n : \tau \rangle\!\rangle$. The implicit match-bound of the type-variable u (referring to the type of *self*) assures that e_2 specializes its functionality for all future extensions of $\langle e_1 \longleftrightarrow\!\!\!+ \; n = e_2 \rangle$.

The rule for object override is simpler:

$$\frac{\begin{array}{l}\Gamma \vdash e_1 \ : \ \sigma \qquad \Gamma \vdash \sigma \mathrel{<\!\!\#} \mathtt{obj}\, t.\langle\!\langle \overline{m} : \overline{\sigma}, n : \tau \rangle\!\rangle \\ \Gamma, u \mathrel{<\!\!\#} \mathtt{obj}\, t.\langle\!\langle \overline{m} : \overline{\sigma}, n : \tau \rangle\!\rangle \vdash e_2 \ : \ [u/t](t \to \tau)\end{array}}{\Gamma \vdash \langle e_1 \longleftarrow n = e_2 \rangle \ : \ \sigma} \quad (obj\!-\!over)$$

The only interesting remark is that σ could be a type-variable match-bounded in the context Γ: it follows that a self-inflicted object override is allowed (as well as in all other type systems) inside method bodies.

As a side remark, we conjecture the soundness of the type system by substituting the (*obj−over*) with the following rule which better captures the "philosophy" of the matching as a protocol extension.

$$\frac{\begin{array}{l}\Gamma \vdash e_1 \ : \ \sigma \quad \Gamma \vdash \sigma \mathrel{<\!\!\#} \mathtt{obj}\, t.\langle\!\langle n : \tau \rangle\!\rangle \\ \Gamma, u \mathrel{<\!\!\#} \sigma \vdash e_2 \ : \ [u/t](t \to \tau)\end{array}}{\Gamma \vdash \langle e_1 \longleftarrow n = e_2 \rangle \ : \ \sigma} \quad (obj\!-\!over')$$

Finally the rule of method search is as follows:

$$\frac{\Gamma \vdash e \ : \ \sigma \qquad \Gamma \vdash \sigma \mathrel{<\!\!\#} \mathtt{obj}\, t.\langle\!\langle n : \tau \rangle\!\rangle \qquad \Gamma \vdash \rho \mathrel{<\!\!\#} \sigma}{\Gamma \vdash e \hookleftarrow n \ : \ [\rho/t](t \to \tau)} \quad (search)$$

The first and the second premises assure that e is typable with a type σ that has $n : \tau$ in its protocol, while the last judgment finds a type ρ which represents exactly the type of the *self* object (whose e represents a sub-object), to which the message n was sent, and to which the body of n will be applied. Again, as in the previous (*search*) rule, there is no way of finding a type ρ matching with σ.

Expressivity. By looking at this type system and at the one of [14], we can see that there are similarities: in particular the use of the match-bound variable $u \mathrel{<\!\#} \mathtt{obj}\, t.\langle\!\langle R \mid n : \tau\rangle\!\rangle$ in [4] plays the same role as the open object-type $\mathtt{obj}\, t.r\, t$ of [14], since $r <: \lambda t.\langle\!\langle R \mid n : \tau\rangle\!\rangle$. Although this is not formally proved, we could conjecture that the expressive powers of the two systems are the same, since, by [9,1], the matching relation can be fruitfully interpreted using a higher order polymorphism.

Example 10 (Typing Example 4 in [4]). As in the type system of [14], if we want to build e' using e as a prototype, then we need to insure that p does not belong to e, and derive for the body of p the judgment:

$$u \mathrel{<\!\#} \mathtt{obj}\, t.\langle\!\langle m : int, n : int, p : int\rangle\!\rangle \vdash \lambda self.self \Leftarrow n : [u/t](t \rightarrow int). \qquad (*)$$

Observe that the same amount of polymorphism of [14] captures the method specialization of p for all future extensions of e'. Note that the judgment $(*)$ can be used to extend e'' but not e''', since, again, e''' is not an extension of e.

3.4 Bruce's Matching-based Type System of Liquori [20]

This solution was originally adopted to add an extension operator to the Object Calculus (à la Church) of Abadi and Cardelli (cf. [20], Section 3), but can be similarly adopted to the Lambda Calculus of Objects. As in [4], this type system appeals to the notion of Matching of [8], by avoiding object subsumption over extendible objects. However, as we will show, this solution exploits a higher "degree of polymorphism" than either [14] and [4], and comparable with [15]. This will become useful when we add an explicit polymorphism in Subsection 3.7. The set of types, contexts, and judgments are exactly as in [4].

Main Typing Rules. The typing rules to build an empty object are routine; the rule to override a method, send a message to an object and search a method, instead, are the same as in [4].

The type rule to extend an object is as follows:

$$\frac{\begin{array}{l}\Gamma \vdash e_1 \;:\; \mathtt{obj}\, t.\langle\!\langle R \mid \overline{m} : \overline{\sigma}\rangle\!\rangle \\ \Gamma, u \mathrel{<\!\#} \mathtt{obj}\, t.\langle\!\langle \overline{m} : \overline{\sigma}, n : \tau\rangle\!\rangle \vdash e_2 \;:\; [u/t](t \rightarrow \tau) \quad n \text{ not in } \langle\!\langle R \mid \overline{m} : \overline{\sigma}\rangle\!\rangle\end{array}}{\Gamma \vdash \langle e_1 \leftarrow\!\!+\, n = e_2\rangle \;:\; \mathtt{obj}\, t.\langle\!\langle R \mid \overline{m} : \overline{\sigma}, n : \tau\rangle\!\rangle} \; (obj\!-\!ext)$$

Even if this rule looks similar to [4], the bound for u (playing the role of the type of *self*) in the judgment for e_2 has a different meaning: in fact, the $\overline{m} : \overline{\sigma}$ methods explicitly listed in the bound (and also present in the type of e_1) represent the methods that are *essential* to the typing of the body of e_2, and nothing more ([14,4] use the *entire* type of e_1 plus the method n). A consequence of this less restrictive bound is that all prototypes containing the $\overline{m} : \overline{\sigma}$ methods, and not containing the n method, can be extended with $n = e_2$, since that the type of n specializes its functionality.

Example 11 (Typing Example 4 in [20]). As in [15], in order to build the object e', using e as a prototype, we need (i) to know that p does not belongs to e, (ii) to insure that $n : int$ is present in the the type of e, and (iii) to derive for the body of p the judgment:

$$u \mathrel{<\!\!\#} \mathbf{obj}\, t.\langle\!\langle n : int, p : int \rangle\!\rangle \vdash \lambda self.self \Leftarrow n : [u/t](t \to int). \qquad (*)$$

Therefore, to type the body of p, we need to know only the types of methods n (the method directly used inside p), and p (i.e. the method to be added); there is no need to extract the indirect dependencies of n (i.e. m); this is sound, since the body of p, i.e. $\lambda self.self \Leftarrow n$ only self-inflicts a message send of n to *self*. Method specialization of p will follow for all future extensions of e'. Finally, as in [15], the body of p should also be used to extend other objects such as the e'' or e''', using the same judgment $(*)$.

3.5 Binary Methods

One of the best features of the Lambda Calculus of Objects is its ability to define the so-called *binary methods* smoothly. In short, a binary method receives as input an argument of the same type of *self*. A prototypical example of such methods is the (omnipresent) *equal* method that has the following shape:

$$equal \triangleq \lambda self.\lambda p.(self \Leftarrow x) == (p \Leftarrow x) \&\& (self \Leftarrow y) == (p \Leftarrow y),$$

where == is the equality test among real, && is a boolean operator, and both *self* and p are points of type

$$\mathbf{obj}\, t.\langle\!\langle R \mid x : real, y : real, equal : t \to bool \rangle\!\rangle,$$

for some suitable R. Hence, in binary methods, the type-variable denoting the type of *self* (i.e. t) occurs in *contravariant* position with respect to the arrow-type constructor. As clearly stated in [7], the addition of (unrestricted) object subsumption in presence of binary methods makes the type system unsound (see also Section 6).

3.6 Comparison Between the Four Type Systems

The following table summarizes the systems with respect to the methods which are useful to build the object e' (using e as a prototype, as in Example 4) and with respect to the foundational type models.

Type System	Example 4	Type Model
[15]	$\{n,p\}$	Higher Order Rows
[14]	$\{n,m,p\}$	Higher Order Rows & Row Subtyping
[4]	$\{n,m,p\}$	Bruce's Matching
[20]	$\{n,p\}$	Bruce's Matching

The following table summarizes the typing of the $(obj\!-\!ext)$ rules for the body of n in all the four systems:

Type System	Judgments for e_2
[15]	$\Gamma, r : T \to [\overline{m}, n] \vdash e_2 \; : \; [\mathtt{obj}\, t.\langle\!\langle r\, t \mid \overline{m} : \overline{\sigma}, n : \tau\rangle\!\rangle/t](t \to \tau)$
[14]	$\Gamma, r <\!\#\, \lambda t.\langle\!\langle R \mid n : \tau\rangle\!\rangle : T \to [\,] \vdash e_2 \; : \; [\mathtt{obj}\, t.r\, t/t](t \to \tau)$
[4]	$\Gamma, u <\!\#\, \mathtt{obj}\, t.\langle\!\langle R \mid n : \tau\rangle\!\rangle \vdash e_2 \; : \; [u/t](t \to \tau)$
[20]	$\Gamma, u <\!\#\, \mathtt{obj}\, t.\langle\!\langle \overline{m} : \overline{\sigma}, n : \tau\rangle\!\rangle \vdash e_2 \; : \; [u/t](t \to \tau)$

Finally, we would like to mention that the expressive power of the systems is the same: *all partial recursive functions* are typable. We leave open the issue of decidability of the type inference problem for the four systems, and we refer to [25,26] for all related issues.

3.7 Adding Explicit Polymorphism

In our "pilgrimage" toward a Church version of the Lambda Calculus of Objects, we must pass through the addition of explicit polymorphism. To the author's knowledge, the only Church version of the Lambda Calculus of Object is the one presented in [22], based on the type system of [15]. For pedagogical reason, we prefer to introduce explicit polymorphism in a Curry setting.

In all the presented type systems, an *implicit*[8] form of polymorphism is sufficient to capture method specialization of the inherited methods. However, if we want methods to be first-class entities, then we need to add *explicit* quantification. Having explicit quantification increases the expressivity of the calculus, since it enables us to write "portable methods", i.e. methods whose bodies may not be defined at the time but provided later, i.e. resolved at run-time. We sometime refer to these functions as *mixins*. When a mixin is applied to a (pre-compiled) polymorphic method, it installs this method into the object, in a *plug-and-play* fashion. The next example clarifies the point. Consider the following function:

$$f \triangleq \lambda p.\lambda c.\langle p \longleftarrow\!\!+\; col = c\rangle.$$

This simple mixin cannot be typed in any of the type systems presented in this paper; the key point is that it is impossible to give a type to the object $\langle p \longleftarrow\!\!+\; col = c\rangle$ since the body c of col as a type *selftype*$\to$*colors* where *selftype* denotes the type of the host object that could be an open object-type (i.e.

[8] By implicit polymorphism we mean that the universal type quantifier $\forall$ is not part of the syntax of types, but the quantified type (or row) variable is bounded (i.e. declared) in the context.

with the row-variable r occurring free) or a simple type-variable u bound in the context. Now, since c is a simple expression-variable, it should be declared *after* r [15,14] or u [4,20] and not *before*, otherwise we break the well-formation rules of contexts in all systems.

Therefore[9], if we want to type f then we must extend the set of types as follows:

[15] Types $\tau ::= \ldots\text{as before}\ldots \mid \forall r:\kappa.\sigma$
[14] Types $\tau ::= \ldots\text{as before}\ldots \mid \forall r <: R:\kappa.\tau$
[4] Types $\tau ::= \ldots\text{as before}\ldots \mid \forall u <\!\# \sigma.\tau$
[20] Types $\tau ::= \ldots\text{as before}\ldots \mid \forall u <\!\# \sigma.\tau.$

The rules for polymorphic introduction/elimination and object extension becomes as follows, taking into account that, since the calculus is untyped, the operational semantics and the polymorphic abstraction and application are implicit (for related issues see also [19,30]).

In the type system of Fisher, Honsell, and Mitchell [15]

$$\frac{\Gamma, r:\kappa \vdash e:\tau}{\Gamma \vdash e:\forall r:\kappa.\tau}\ (\forall{-}I) \qquad \frac{\Gamma \vdash e:\forall r:\kappa.\tau \quad \Gamma \vdash R:\kappa}{\Gamma \vdash e:[R/r]\tau}\ (\forall{-}E)$$

$$\frac{\begin{array}{l}\Gamma \vdash e_1 : \mathtt{obj}\,t.\langle\!\langle R \mid \overline{m}:\overline{\sigma}\rangle\!\rangle \quad \Gamma, t:T \vdash R : [\overline{m}, n] \qquad r \text{ not in } \tau \\ \Gamma \vdash e_2 : \forall r : T \rightarrow [\overline{m}, n].[\mathtt{obj}\,t.\langle\!\langle r\,t \mid \overline{m}:\overline{\sigma}, n:\tau\rangle\!\rangle/t](t \rightarrow \tau)\end{array}}{\Gamma \vdash \langle e_1 \longleftarrow\!\!\!+\ n = e_2\rangle : \mathtt{obj}\,t.\langle\!\langle R \mid \overline{m}:\overline{\sigma}, n:\tau\rangle\!\rangle}\ (obj{-}ext)$$

In the type system of Fisher [14]

$$\frac{\Gamma, r <: R:\kappa \vdash e:\tau}{\Gamma \vdash e:\forall r <: R:\kappa.\tau}\ (\forall{-}I) \qquad \frac{\Gamma \vdash e:\forall r <: R:\kappa.\tau \quad \Gamma \vdash R' <: R}{\Gamma \vdash e:[R'/r]\tau}\ (\forall{-}E)$$

$$\frac{\begin{array}{l}\Gamma \vdash e_1 : \mathtt{obj}\,t.R \qquad \Gamma, t:T \vdash R : [n] \qquad r \text{ not in } \tau \\ \Gamma \vdash e_2 : \forall r <: \lambda t.\langle\!\langle R \mid n:\tau\rangle\!\rangle : T \rightarrow [\,].[\mathtt{obj}\,t.r\,t/t](t \rightarrow \tau)\end{array}}{\Gamma \vdash \langle e_1 \longleftarrow\!\!\!+\ n = e_2\rangle : \mathtt{obj}\,t.\langle\!\langle R \mid n:\tau\rangle\!\rangle}\ (obj{-}ext)$$

In the type system of Bono and Bugliesi [4]

$$\frac{\Gamma, u <\!\# \sigma \vdash e:\tau}{\Gamma \vdash e:\forall u <\!\# \sigma.\tau}\ (\forall{-}I) \qquad \frac{\Gamma \vdash e:\forall u <\!\# \sigma.\tau \quad \Gamma \vdash \rho <\!\# \sigma}{\Gamma \vdash e:[\rho/u]\tau}\ (\forall{-}E)$$

$$\frac{\begin{array}{l}\Gamma \vdash e_1 : \mathtt{obj}\,t.R \qquad n \text{ not in } R \\ \Gamma \vdash e_2 : \forall u <\!\# \mathtt{obj}\,t.\langle\!\langle R \mid n:\tau\rangle\!\rangle.[u/t](t \rightarrow \tau)\end{array}}{\Gamma \vdash \langle e_1 \longleftarrow\!\!\!+\ n = e_2\rangle : \mathtt{obj}\,t.\langle\!\langle R \mid n:\tau\rangle\!\rangle}\ (obj{-}ext)$$

[9] **Disclaimer.** These extensions are not proved to be "type safe". However, in our modest opinion, at least the [15] one (based on a previous work [22]) should be safe.

In the type system of Liquori [20]

$$\frac{\Gamma, u <\!\!\# \sigma \vdash e : \tau}{\Gamma \vdash e : \forall u <\!\!\# \sigma.\tau}\ (\forall\text{–}I) \qquad \frac{\Gamma \vdash e : \forall u <\!\!\# \sigma.\tau \quad \Gamma \vdash \rho <\!\!\# \sigma}{\Gamma \vdash e : [\rho/u]\tau}\ (\forall\text{–}E)$$

$$\frac{\begin{array}{l}\Gamma \vdash e_1 \ :\ \mathtt{obj}\,t.\langle\!\langle R \mid \overline{m} : \overline{\sigma}\rangle\!\rangle \qquad n \text{ not in } \langle\!\langle R \mid \overline{m} : \overline{\sigma}\rangle\!\rangle \\ \Gamma \vdash e_2 \ :\ \forall u <\!\!\# \mathtt{obj}\,t.\langle\!\langle \overline{m} : \overline{\sigma}, n : \tau\rangle\!\rangle.[u/t](t \to \tau)\end{array}}{\Gamma \vdash \langle e_1 \longleftarrow\!\!\!+\, n = e_2\rangle \ :\ \mathtt{obj}\,t.\langle\!\langle R \mid \overline{m} : \overline{\sigma}, n : \tau\rangle\!\rangle}\ (obj\text{–}ext)$$

Remark. We have omitted the rule for method search, since these rules are the same as in the corresponding calculi with implicit polymorphism; this is not surprising, since the polymorphic row/type instantiation is performed before the self-application step.

Example 12 (Typing Example 4 revisited). Let us suppose to have some a method library $\mathcal{L}$, containing a set of polymorphic method bodies to be "plugged-and-played" into e, i.e. $\mathcal{L} = \{b_p = body_p : \sigma_p, b_q = body_q : \sigma_q, \ldots\}$, with $k \geq 0$. Besides e, we want such bodies to be as polymorphic as possible, i.e. to be applicable to the biggest number of objects. We then compile $\mathcal{L}$ in the four systems. Borrowing from Example 4 the objects e', e'', and e''', we could build the following programs:

$$p \triangleq (\lambda x.\langle e \longleftarrow\!\!\!+\, p = x\rangle)\, b_p \qquad p' \triangleq (\lambda x.\langle e' \longleftarrow p = x\rangle)\, b_p$$
$$p'' \triangleq (\lambda x.\langle e'' \longleftarrow\!\!\!+\, p = x\rangle)\, b_p \qquad p''' \triangleq (\lambda x.\langle e''' \longleftarrow\!\!\!+\, p = x\rangle)\, b_p.$$

It is not difficult to verify that, while p, p' and p'' can be type-checked in all the systems including the (already compiled) $\mathcal{L}$, p''' can be compiled only with the library compiled within the type systems of [15,20].

The following table summarizes the typing for the body of p in all systems with explicit polymorphism:

Type System	Judgments for e_2
[15]	$\Gamma \vdash e_2 \ :\ \forall r : T \to [\overline{m}, n].[\mathtt{obj}\,t.\langle\!\langle r\, t \mid \overline{m} : \overline{\sigma}, n : \tau\rangle\!\rangle/t](t \to \tau)$
[14]	$\Gamma \vdash e_2 \ :\ \forall r <: \lambda t.\langle\!\langle R \mid n : \tau\rangle\!\rangle : T \to [\ ].[\mathtt{obj}\,t.r\,t/t](t \to \tau)$
[4]	$\Gamma \vdash e_2 \ :\ \forall u <\!\!\# \mathtt{obj}\,t.\langle\!\langle R \mid n : \tau\rangle\!\rangle.[u/t](t \to \tau)$
[20]	$\Gamma \vdash e_2 \ :\ \forall u <\!\!\# \mathtt{obj}\,t.\langle\!\langle \overline{m} : \overline{\sigma}, n : \tau\rangle\!\rangle.[u/t](t \to \tau)$

4 Curry versus Church

In this section we try to transform the Lambda Calculus of Objects à la Curry into a corresponding calculus à la Church. To do this, we decorate it with types. The goals we want to achieve in this transformation are as follows:

- *uniqueness of typing* (mandatory); intuitively, this property says that we could transform a type system into an equivalent one where for all expressions of our calculus, there is *at most* one type rule to apply (those systems are usually called *algorithmic*). Since we do not deal with object subsumption, it follows that every expression has an unique type.

- *explicit polymorphism and first-class method bodies* (mandatory); in short, without explicit polymorphism the language cannot be "fully typed" in its total sense, since there will be expressions whose polymorphism is not explicitly annotated in the expressions itself. As we have seen in Subsection 3.7, adding explicit polymorphism enable us to build mixins.
- *binary methods and/or static typing*; these two requirements are strictly related, since very often the possibility to have binary methods leads to a type-driven semantics (mandatory if you need *multiple dispatching*). For this and related issues, see the seminal paper of [11], and also [7,12,22]. As we will see, by avoiding subtyping, we will keep binary methods and static type checking.

For obvious lack of space, we therefore cannot apply all systems to the Lambda Calculus of Objects à la Church. We choose to adopt the type system of [14], even if it is "less polymorphic" than the one of [15,20], since it allows a nice and smooth extension into a calculus à la Church.

4.1 The Lambda Calculus of Objects à la Church

The set of types is defined as in Subsection 3.7. The expressions of the fully decorated calculus are defined by the following grammar:

$$\begin{array}{lr} e ::= c \mid x \mid \lambda x:\sigma.e \mid e_1\, e_2 \mid & \text{(typed } \lambda\text{-calc.)} \\ \quad e\,R \mid \lambda r <: R : \kappa.e \mid & \text{(polymorphic expr.)} \\ \quad \langle\rangle \mid e \Leftarrow m \mid \langle e_1 \longleftarrow m = e_2 \rangle \mid \langle e_1 \longleftarrow\!\!+\, m = e_2 \rangle \mid & \text{(object expr.)} \\ \quad e \hookleftarrow m, & \text{(auxiliary expr.)} \end{array}$$

where the last two forms represent the polymorphic lambda abstraction and application.

Small-step Reduction Semantics. The small-step operational semantics is type-driven: its core is given by the following reduction rules:

$$\begin{array}{llll} (Beta) & (\lambda x:\sigma.e_1)\, e_2 & \overset{ev}{\to} [e_2/x]e_1 & \\ (Select) & e \Leftarrow m & \overset{ev}{\to} (e \hookleftarrow m)\, (\lambda t.R)\, e & \text{if } \Gamma \vdash_{\mathcal{A}} e : \mathbf{obj}\, t.R^{10} \\ (Succ) & \langle e_1 \longleftarrow\!\!*\, m = e_2 \rangle \hookleftarrow m \overset{ev}{\to} e_2 & & \\ (Next) & \langle e_1 \longleftarrow\!\!*\, n = e_2 \rangle \hookleftarrow m \overset{ev}{\to} e_1 \hookleftarrow m. & & \end{array}$$

As for the calculus à la Curry with explicit polymorphism, the body of a method is a (explicitly annotated) polymorphic lambda abstraction; it follows that before

[10] To be precise, $\lambda t.R$ becomes $\lambda t : T.R$. We could also add the stronger condition $m \in R$ (i.e. $R \equiv \langle\!\langle R' \mid m : \tau \rangle\!\rangle$, for some R' and τ), but this constraint is guaranteed when $(e \hookleftarrow m)$ is well-typed.

applying the body of the method to *self*, we need to instantiate the polymorphic lambda abstraction correctly with an adequate row-abstraction. To deduce this row, we use an algorithmic type system, denoted by $\vdash_{\mathcal{A}}$, equivalent to the one of [14], obtained by using standard techniques[11].

Big-step Operational Semantics. We extend the set of results as follows:

$$v ::= \ldots \text{as before} \ldots \mid \lambda r <: R : \kappa . e.$$

The big step semantics is equally type-driven, but the only point where a type derivation is needed is the (*Red–Select*) rule:

$$\frac{\begin{array}{l}\varepsilon \vdash_{\mathcal{A}} e : \mathtt{obj}\, t.R^{12} \\ e \Downarrow obj \qquad obj \hookleftarrow m \Downarrow \lambda r <: R' : \kappa . e' \qquad ([(\lambda t.R)/r]e')\, e \Downarrow v\end{array}}{e \Leftarrow m \Downarrow v} \; (\mathit{Red\text{-}Select})$$

In this rule, before the self-application, we need to instantiate correctly the polymorphic body of n with a suitable row-abstraction (i.e. R) obtained invocating the algorithmic type system $\vdash_{\mathcal{A}}$ on e.

4.2 The Type System à la Church Inspired to [14]

We will not present the full set of rules in detail: the rules of explicit introduction of polymorphism are similar to those presented in Subsection 3.7, taking into account that here term decoration is explicit:

$$\frac{\Gamma, r <: R : \kappa \vdash_{\mathcal{A}} e : \tau}{\Gamma \vdash_{\mathcal{A}} \lambda r <: R : \kappa . e : \forall r <: R : \kappa . \tau} \; (\forall\text{-}I) \qquad \frac{\Gamma \vdash_{\mathcal{A}} e : \forall r <: R : \kappa . \tau \quad \Gamma \vdash_{\mathcal{A}} R' <: R}{\Gamma \vdash_{\mathcal{A}} e\, R' : [R'/r]\tau} \; (\forall\text{-}E)$$

The only rule that merits to be mentioned is the one concerning method search in the algorithmic type system. It behaves as follows:

$$\frac{\Gamma \vdash_{\mathcal{A}} e \;:\; \mathtt{obj}\, t.\langle\!\langle R \mid n : \tau \rangle\!\rangle}{\Gamma \vdash_{\mathcal{A}} e \hookleftarrow n \;:\; \forall r <: (\lambda t.\langle\!\langle R \mid n : \tau \rangle\!\rangle) : T \to [\;].[\mathtt{obj}\, t.r\, t/t](t \to \tau)} \; (\mathit{search})$$

This rule simply says that a body of a method is a polymorphic lambda abstraction, bounded by $\lambda t.\langle\!\langle R \mid n : \tau \rangle\!\rangle$, since $\mathtt{obj}\, t.\langle\!\langle R \mid n : \tau \rangle\!\rangle$ is the type of the object e in which we are performing the recursive (right-to-left) traversing in order to reach the right-most definition of n.

---

[11] Intuitively, we usually remove all the subrowing rules concerning transitivity and reflexivity, and we rearrange the rules for expressions to take these modifications into account (see [12]).

[12] In this case, we could also add the judgment $t : T \vdash_{\mathcal{A}} R <: R'$, but the subrowing condition is enforced by the well-typedness of $obj \hookleftarrow m$.

Exercise. If you'd like to play with explicit polymorphism and Church calculi, then you should first try to adapt the operational semantics (small and big-step) to the remaining type systems, and then write the most interesting type rules concerning polymorphism and method extraction.

4.3 Binary Methods

Also in the Lambda Calculus of Object à la Church, binary methods are allowed. The *equal* method of Section 3.5 is rewritten à la Church with [14] types as:

$$\begin{aligned} equal \triangleq\ & \lambda r <: (\lambda t.\langle\!\langle R \mid equal : t \to bool \rangle\!\rangle : T \to [\,]).\lambda self : \mathtt{obj}\, t.r\, t. \\ & \lambda p : \mathtt{obj}\, t.r\, t.(self \Leftarrow x) == (p \Leftarrow x) \&\& (self \Leftarrow y) == (p \Leftarrow y), \end{aligned}$$

of type $\forall r <: (\lambda t.\langle\!\langle R \mid equal : t \to bool \rangle\!\rangle : T \to [\,]).\ [\mathtt{obj}\, t.r\, t/t](t \to t \to bool)$, for some suitable R representing the methods of the prototype e extended with the *equal* method.

4.4 Switching to an Untyped Operational Semantics

All type systems presented here were conceived to work without the subsumption rule (*subsume*) presented at the very beginning of Section 3. The rest of this section is devoted to explain how a type-driven operational semantics can be switched into an untyped one in a calculus without subsumption.

Following [22], we could build an *erasing* function $\mathcal{E}$ from typed to untyped expressions, so that every expression derivable à la Curry (with explicit polymorphic types) can be derivable as the erasure of some typed expression à la Church. The erasing function $\mathcal{E}$ simply erases the type annotations on the abstracted variables, and eliminates the expression-row applications:

$$\begin{aligned} \mathcal{E}(e\, R) &= \mathcal{E}(e) & \mathcal{E}(\lambda x : \tau.e) &= \lambda x.\mathcal{E}(e) \\ \mathcal{E}(\lambda r <: R : \kappa.e) &= \mathcal{E}(e) & \mathcal{E}(e \hookleftarrow n) &= \mathcal{E}(e) \hookleftarrow n \\ \mathcal{E}(\forall r <: R : \kappa.\tau) &= \mathcal{E}(\tau) & \mathcal{E}(\langle\!\langle R \mid n{:}\tau \rangle\!\rangle) &= \langle\!\langle \mathcal{E}(R) \mid n{:}\mathcal{E}(\tau) \rangle\!\rangle \\ \mathcal{E}(\lambda t : T.R) &= \lambda t.\mathcal{E}(R) \end{aligned}$$

In all the other expressions, $\mathcal{E}$ is compositional or the identity.

It is not difficult to see that the type-driven reduction semantics becomes the untyped one of Section 2.

The following lemma ensures that, after type checking, the computation of an expression of the typed calculus can be performed on its erasure, since the result will be the same (modulo erasure).

Lemma 13. *Let $\Gamma \vdash e : \tau$ in the Lambda Calculus of Objects à la Church. If $\mathcal{E}(e) \overset{ev}{\twoheadrightarrow}_u e'$, then there exists e'' such that $e' \equiv \mathcal{E}(e'')$ and $e \overset{ev}{\twoheadrightarrow}_t e''$, where $\overset{ev}{\twoheadrightarrow}_u$ and $\overset{ev}{\twoheadrightarrow}_t$ denotes the untyped and the type-driven small-step operational semantics, respectively.*

5 A Calculus based on [2]

As we said in Section 2, in our Lambda Calculus of Objects, the objects are considered as lists of pairs *(method names-method bodies)*, and method lookup is performed via a right-to-left traversing of the object until the searched method is found.

In the Object Calculus of [2], instead, objects are considered as *sets* of pairs *(method names-method bodies)*. Although it is well-known that a set can be implemented with a list, this view of objects has some interesting properties:

- it enables us to build an operational semantics where object override (and from [21] also object extension) could be axiomatized via a simple rewriting step that reduces a more complex object, usually an object where some methods are redefined, into a simpler one, where the older methods are substituted with the newly redefined ones.
- it enables us to perform method lookup *in one single step*, since the lookup is reduced to a *simple set membership test*, thus avoiding all matters of typability of explicit method lookup.

For reason of simplicity, in this section we deal only with calculi à la Curry. We introduce a calculus inspired to the Object Calculus, where objects are sets, as follows:

$$e ::= x \mid \lambda x.e \mid e_1 e_2 \mid \langle \overline{m} = \overline{e} \rangle \mid e \leftarrow\!\!+\, m = e' \mid e \longleftarrow m = e' \mid e \Leftarrow m.$$

The $\leftarrow\!\!+$, and $\longleftarrow$ (shortly $\leftarrow\!\!*$) operators have the following (informal) signature: $\leftarrow\!\!*$ :: (Sets × Method Names × Method Bodies) ⇒ Sets. Observe that, in the object expressions, the order of methods is unimportant.

There are some differences between this calculus and the Object Calculus:

- the Object Calculus does *not* include all the expressions related to the lambda calculus that are, instead, codified into suitable objects;
- in the Object Calculus, the body of methods always has the shape $\varsigma(self)e$, where ς is a binder (as λ) that occurs only *inside* objects, and e is an object expression. Here, instead, a body of a method can be any expression which can reduce to a lambda abstraction.

In this section, we do not deal with types, since all four type systems presented in this paper could be easily adapted with minor changes.

5.1 Operational Semantics

Small-step Operational Semantics. The small-step operational semantics is directly inspired to [2] and it is axiomatized by the following rewriting steps:

$$\begin{array}{lll} (Select) & \langle \overline{m} = \overline{e}, n = e \rangle \Leftarrow n & \stackrel{ev}{\to} e\ \langle \overline{m} = \overline{e}, n = e \rangle \\ (Override) & \langle \overline{m} = \overline{e}, n = e' \rangle \longleftarrow n = e & \stackrel{ev}{\to} \langle \overline{m} = \overline{e}, n = e \rangle \\ (Extension) & \langle \overline{m} = \overline{e} \rangle \leftarrow\!\!+\, n = e & \stackrel{ev}{\to} \langle \overline{m} = \overline{e}, n = e \rangle \qquad n \notin \overline{m} \\ (Beta) & (\lambda x.e_1)e_2 & \stackrel{ev}{\to} [e_2/x]e_1. \end{array}$$

Note that in [2] the (*Beta*) axiom can be simulated with the help of the rules (*Select*) and (*Override*) rules.

Big Step Operational Semantics. Building a big-step semantics is quite simple. It is essentially what we have shown in Section 2, except that now the dynamic method lookup is implicit; this means that we need to reconsider the (*Red–Select*) rule, and add two rules for overriding and extending objects. The semantics uses the (*Red–Val*) and (*Red–Beta*) deduction rules of Section 2, plus the following rules:

$$\frac{e \Downarrow \langle \overline{m} = \overline{e}, n = e' \rangle \qquad e' \Downarrow \lambda x.e'' \qquad [\langle \overline{m} = \overline{e}, n = e' \rangle / x]e'' \Downarrow v}{e \Leftarrow n \Downarrow v} \quad (Red\text{–}Select)$$

$$\frac{e \Downarrow \langle \overline{m} = \overline{e}, n = e'' \rangle}{e \longleftarrow n = e' \Downarrow \langle \overline{m} = \overline{e}, n = e' \rangle} \quad (Red\text{–}Over)$$

$$\frac{e \Downarrow \langle \overline{m} = \overline{e} \rangle \qquad n \notin \overline{m}}{e \longleftarrow\!\!+\, n = e' \Downarrow \langle \overline{m} = \overline{e}, n = e' \rangle} \quad (Red\text{–}Ext)$$

Also in this case, the (*Red–Beta*) deduction rule can be simulated with the help of the remaining deduction rules.

One can easily see that the (*Red–Select*) rule of Section 2 and the above (*Red–Select*) rule are very similar. This is not surprising: in fact, in the former rule the method lookup phase is explicit with the help of the (*Red–Next*) and (*Red–Succ*) rules, while in the latter the method lookup phase is hidden in the set notation. This approach greatly simplify all the proofs; in particular, the one of subject reduction.

Moreover, as we can observe in the above (*Red–Select*) rule, the body e' of the method n reduces to a lambda abstraction $\lambda x.e''$. This abstraction will be applied directly (as in the (*Red–Beta*) rule) by substituting for every occurrences of x in the body of e' the object itself: this, very informally, means to *open* first the encapsulated method n and then to *evaluate* the body of e' of n.

6 About Object Subsumption

Object subsumption has been fundamental in the object-oriented paradigm, since it allows a significant reuse of code. Unfortunately, (see [16,2]), extension in presence of subtyping makes the type system unsound. In this final section, we try to point out the solutions (without criticism) proposed in the literature which add object subsumption to object calculi with an extension operator.

- one may permit unrestricted subsumption in absence of binary methods, maintaining static type checking, by allowing occurrences of the type of *self* only in covariant position (cf, among others, [2,17,20,28]). We can also use the *variance annotations* of [2]

- one may decide to keep binary methods in presence of subsumption, and use a type-driven operational semantics in the style of Castagna *et alt* [13,11,12];
- one may restrict subtyping by "hiding" only the methods that are not referred to any other method [6,5];
- one may not forget the type of the "hidden methods" in order to guarantee that any future addition of those methods will have a type consistent with the hidden one [21,20];
- one may use method dictionaries inside object-types [29], and permitting to re-add an "hidden" method with two different types.

A detailed comparison of calculi with object extension in presence of object subsumption is under development.

7 Conclusions

We hope to have contributed to the understanding of some basic concepts of object calculi and other related type systems which have been presented in the literature. Object-based calculi are not as well-know as the class-based ones, but their importance will increase especially when mixed with class-based features, such as in the *Beta* [23], or *O2* of [2].

Acknowledgments. I would like to thank the *Logics of Programs* group of the Department of Computer Science of Turin, for the time spent to teach me the fundamentals of Theoretical Computer Science, to Furio Honsell for his fruitful discussions and suggestions, Stefania Garlatti-Costa for the careful reading of the paper and one anonymous referee for the insightful comments which helped me to improve the paper greatly.

References

1. M. Abadi and L. Cardelli. On Subtyping and Matching. In *Proc. of ECOOP*, volume 952 of *Lecture Notes in Computer Science*, pages 145–167. Springer–Verlag, 1995.
2. M. Abadi and L. Cardelli. *A Theory of Objects*. Springer-Verlag, 1996.
3. G. Bellè. Some Remarks on Lambda Calculus of Objects. Technical report, Dipartimento di Matematica ed Informatica, Università di Udine, 1994.
4. V. Bono and M. Bugliesi. Matching Constraints for the Lambda Calculus of Objects. In *Proc. of TLCA*, volume 1210 of *Lecture Notes in Computer Science*, pages 46–62. Springer-Verlag, 1997.
5. V. Bono, M. Bugliesi, M. Dezani-Ciancaglini, and L. Liquori. Subtyping Constraint for Incomplete Objects. In *Proc. of TAPSOFT/CAAP*, volume 1214 of *Lecture Notes in Computer Science*, pages 465–477. Springer-Verlag, 1997.
6. V. Bono and L. Liquori. A Subtyping for the Fisher-Honsell-Mitchell Lambda Calculus of Objects. In *Proc. of CSL*, volume 933 of *Lecture Notes in Computer Science*, pages 16–30. Springer-Verlag, 1995.
7. K. Bruce, L. Cardelli, G. Castagna, The Hopkins Object Group, G. Leavens, and B. Pierce. On Binary Methods. *Theory and Practice of Object Systems*, 1(3), 1996.
8. K.B. Bruce. A Paradigmatic Object–Oriented Programming Language: Design, Static Typing and Semantics. *Journal of Functional Programming*, 4(2):127–206, 1994.

9. K.B. Bruce, A. Shuett, and R. van Gent. Polytoil: a Type-safe Polymorphic Object Oriented Language. In *Proc. of ECOOP*, volume 952 of *Lecture Notes in Computer Science*, pages 16–30, 1995.
10. L. Cardelli. A Language with Distributed Scope. *Computing System*, 8(1):27–59, 1995.
11. G. Castagna. Covariance and contravariance: conflict without a cause. *ACM Transactions on Programming Languages and Systems*, 17(3):431–447, 1995.
12. G. Castagna. *Object-Oriented Programming: A Unified Foundation.* Progress in Theoretical Computer Science. Birkäuser, Boston, 1996.
13. G. Castagna, G. Ghelli, and G. Longo. A Calculus for Overloaded Functions with Subtyping. *Information and Computation*, 117(1):115–135, 1995.
14. K. Fisher. *Type System for Object-Oriented Programming Languages.* PhD thesis, University of Stanford, August 1996.
15. K. Fisher, F. Honsell, and J. C. Mitchell. A Lambda Calculus of Objects and Method Specialization. *Nordic Journal of Computing*, 1(1):3–37, 1994.
16. K. Fisher and J. C. Michell. Notes on Typed Object-Oriented Programming. In *Proc. of TACS*, volume 789 of *Lecture Notes in Computer Science*, pages 844–885. Springer-Verlag, 1994.
17. K. Fisher and J. C. Mitchell. A Delegation-based Object Calculus with Subtyping. In *Proc. of FCT*, volume 965 of *Lecture Notes in Computer Science*, pages 42–61. Springer-Verlag, 1995.
18. A. Goldberg and D. Robson. *Smalltalk-80: the Language and its Implementation.* Addison-Wesley, 1983.
19. D. Leivant. Polymorphic Type Inference. In *Proc. of the 10th ACM Symposium on Principles of Programming Languages*, pages 88–98. The ACM Press, 1983.
20. L. Liquori. Bounded Polymorphism for Extensible Objects. Technical Report CS-24-96, Computer Science Department, University of Turin, Italy, 1996.
21. L. Liquori. An Extended Theory of Primitive Objects: First Order System. In *Proc. of ECOOP*, volume 1241 of *Lecture Notes in Computer Science*, pages 146–169. Springer-Verlag, 1997.
22. L. Liquori and G. Castagna. A Typed Lambda Calculus of Objects. In *Proc. of Asian*, volume 1179 of *Lecture Notes in Computer Science*, pages 129–141. Springer-Verlag, 1996.
23. O.L. Madsen, Moller-Pedersen, and K. B. Nygaard. *Object-Oriented programming in the Beta programming language.* Addison-Wesley, 1993.
24. P. Paladin. Teoremi di Congruenza per Lambda-Calcoli Orientati agli Oggetti. Master's thesis, Dipartimento di Matematica ed Informatica, Università di Udine, 1993. In Italian.
25. J. Palsberg. Efficient Inference of Object Types. In *Proc. of LICS*, pages 186–195, 1993.
26. J. Palsberg and T. Jim. Type Inference for Simple Object Types is NP-Complete. *Nordic Journal of Computing*, 1997.
27. Gordon Plotkin. A structural approach to operational semantics. Technical Report DAIMI FN-19, Computer Science Department, Aarhus University, Denmark, 1981.
28. D. Rémy. From Classes to Objects via Subtyping. In *Proc. of ESOP*, 1998.
29. J.G. Riecke and C. Stone. Privacy via Subsumption. In *Electronic proceedings of FOOL-98*, 1998.
30. S. van Bakel, L. Liquori, S. Ronchi della Rocca, and P. Urzyczyn. Comparing Cubes of Typed and Type Assignment System. *Annals of Pure and Applied Logics*, 86(3):267–303, 1997.

A Statically Safe Alternative to Virtual Types

Kim B. Bruce*[1], Martin Odersky[2], and Philip Wadler[3]

[1] Williams College, Williamstown, MA, USA,
kim@cs.williams.edu, http://www.cs.williams.edu/~kim/
[2] University of South Australia,
odersky@cis.unisa.edu.au, http://www.cis.unisa.edu.au/~cismxo/
[3] Bell Labs, Lucent Technologies,
wadler@research.bell-labs.com, http://www.cs.bell-labs.com/~wadler/

Abstract. Parametric types and virtual types have recently been proposed as extensions to Java to support genericity. In this paper we investigate the strengths and weaknesses of each. We suggest a variant of virtual types which has similar expressiveness, but supports safe static type checking. This results in a language in which both parametric types and virtual types are well-integrated, and which is statically type-safe.
Keywords: Language design, virtual types, parametric polymorphism, static type checking

1 Introduction

The first step to a good answer is a good question. This note raises (and suggests an answer to) the question: Can the best features of parametric types and virtual types be integrated?

Parametric types and virtual types have both been proposed as extensions to Java, and address roughly similar issues. Parametric types date back to arrays in Fortran, with key contributions to their theory coming from Strachey [Str67] and Reynolds [Rey74,Rey83], and examples of practice appearing in languages as diverse as Ada (generics), C++ (templates), and Standard ML (parametric polymorphism). Parametric types for Java have been proposed by Myers, Bank, and Liskov [MBL97], by Agesen, Freund, and Mitchell [AFM97], by Bruce [Bru97], and by Odersky and Wadler as part of Pizza [OW97,OW98]. Virtual types first appeared in Beta [KMMN83,MM89,MMN93] and have been proposed for Java by Thorup [Tho97].

Parametric types and virtual types have complementary strengths. Parametric types are especially useful for collection types, such as lists or sets. (Users of C++ templates and collection classes will know many examples [KM96].) Virtual types are especially useful for families of types, such as the Subject/Observer family. (Users of design patterns will know many examples [GRJV94].)

The first step to a good question is a good example. This note presents two paradigmatic examples. The first, zip, demonstrates the strengths of parametric

* Kim Bruce's research was partially supported by NSF grant CCR-9424123.

types. The second, lists with lengths, demonstrates the strengths of virtual types; we illustrate the important case of mutual recursion by extending this example to alternating lists. In each case, the program structure made easy by one approach can be mimicked by the other, but with difficulty.

In an attempt to bring together the strengths of each of these techniques, we present a variant of the virtual types notation that is statically type-safe. The new notation generalizes the `MyType` notation of Bruce and others to apply to mutually recursive types. This notation can be considered as a variant of the proposal for handling inheritance in the presence of mutual recursion put forward by Palsberg and Schwartzbach [PS94].

The ideas reported here gestated in the deliberations of a mailing list organized by Ole Agesen to discuss extensions of Java that support generic types. Gilad Bracha, Corky Cartwright, Guy Steele, Kresten Thorup, and Mads Torgersen made particularly significant contributions.

The rest of the paper is organized as follows. Section 2 reviews parametric types and virtual types. Section 3 presents examples which are easy to express with parametric types, but are hard to express with virtual types. Section 4 presents an example that is easy to express with virtual types, but hard to express with parametric types. To highlight comparisons we write each example using both notations.

Section 5 proposes a notation that is similar to virtual types, but which can be statically type checked. Section 6 shows how this notation combines with parametric types in a smooth way. Section 7 concludes.

Appendix A reworks an example of Thorup's based on the Observer pattern.

2 Parametric and virtual types

We briefly review the extension of Java to include parametric types as in Odersky and Wadler's Pizza [OW97,OW98], and virtual types as in Thorup's proposal [Tho97]. Both extensions are defined by their translation into ordinary Java.

2.1 Parametric types

Here is a simple program using parametric types.

```
public class Cell<A> {
  protected A value;
  public Cell (A v) { value = v; }
  public void set (A v) { value = v; }
  public A get () { return value; }
}
public class Test {
  public static void main (String[] args) {
    Cell<String> c = new Cell("even");
    c.set("s"+c.get());
    Cell<Object> d = c;  // compile-time error
```

```
    d.set(new Integer(7));
  }
}
```

An object of class `Cell<A>` has a protected `value` field containing an object of type `A`, which is updated by the `set` method and retrieved by the `get` method. The test code shows a trivial use of this class: creating a cell with a string value, then updating the cell to append a string to the front of its contents.

The test code also shows a trivially wrong use: trying to put an integer in a cell that should contain a string. Since type parameters are not maintained at run-time, this error must be detected at compile time. To allow this, the type system must be quite strict, prohibiting a `Cell<String>` from being assigned to a `Cell<Object>`. (Compare this will Java arrays, where it is possible to assign a `String[]` to an `Object[]`, but this requires that each array carries its type with it at run-time, and that a run-time type check is performed each time an array element is updated.)

If we omit the last two statements of the `main` method, then the code above is type-safe. It is equivalent to the following code in Java without parametric types. (Odersky and Wadler [OW97] describe two different translations of parametric types into Java, homogeneous and heterogeneous. We use the former here.)

```
public class Cell {
  protected Object value;
  public Cell (Object v) { value = v; }
  public void set (Object v) { value = v; }
  public Object get () { return value; }
}
public class Test {
  public static void main (String[] args) {
    Cell c = new Cell("even");
    c.set("s"+(String)c.get());
  }
}
```

All type parameters have been erased, and all occurrences of the parameter `A` within `Cell` have been replaced by `Object`. An appropriate cast has been added to the call to `get`, and one can guarantee at compile-time the added cast will never fail at run-time.

The final code closely resembles an idiom often used by Java programmers to mimic the effect of parametric types. For instance, this idiom is used extensively in the collection class library in Java JDK 1.2. The latest revision of Pizza is designed to exploit this confluence [OW98]. For instance, the user can write code that refers to a class `Collection<A>` and compile this to code that refers to the library class `Collection`. So one can combine the benefits of parametric types with reuse of existing code; this is especially attractive when one realizes that the collection library will be part of all JDK 1.2 compliant browsers, eliminating the need to transmit collection code over the web.

2.2 Virtual types

Here is a roughly equivalent program using virtual types.

```
public class Cell {
  public typedef A as Object;
  protected A value;
  public Cell (A v) { value = v; }
  public void set (A v) { value = v; }
  public A get () { return value; }
}

public class StringCell extends Cell {
  public typedef A as String;
}

public class Test {
  public static void main (String[] args) {
    StringCell c = new StringCell("even");
    c.set("s"+c.get());
    Cell d = c;
    d.set(new Integer(7));  // run-time error
  }
}
```

Here `A` is not a parameter to the class, but instead is treated as a virtual field of the class. Instead of instantiating the parameter to refer to a class `Cell<String>`, one defines a new subclass `StringCell` of `Cell`.

Whereas with parametric types it was a compile-time error to assign a `Cell<String>` to a `Cell<Object>`, with virtual types it is permitted to assign a `StringCell` to a `Cell`. It is still not permitted to place an integer in a string cell, but this is now detected at run-time when the assignment occurs. (This is possible because the new class `StringCell` in effect maintains type information at run-time, and results in behavior that is similar to Java arrays.)

The code above is equivalent to the following code in Java without virtual types.

```
public class Cell {
  public Object cast$A (Object x) { return (Object)x; }
  protected Object value;
  public Cell (Object v) { value = v; }
  public void set (Object v) { value = v; }
  public A get () { return value; }
}

public class StringCell extends Cell {
  public String cast$A (Object x) { return (String)x; }
}

public class Test {
```

```
  public static void main (String[] args) {
    StringCell c = new StringCell("even");
    c.set("s"+(String)c.get());
    Cell d = c;
    d.set(d.cast$A(new Integer(7)));
  }
}
```

Each virtual type declaration for the type variable `A` is now replaced by code for a method `cast$A` that accepts an object and casts it to the class corresponding to `A`. As before, method calls are translated to add casts where appropriate. But now sometimes calls are required to the `cast$A` methods, and these casts may fail at run-time. In this case, the call to `cast$A` in the last line will fail, since the call dynamically selects the method in `StringCell` but passes it an `Integer` argument.

It does not appear possible to layer virtual types over existing libraries in the same way as with parametric types. For instance, the user could not write code that refers to a class `Collection` with a virtual type and compile this to code that refers to the library class `Collection`.

In summary, parametric types provide more checking at compile-time, while virtual types are more flexible. Parametric types resemble the idiom used in Java to represent polymorphism in a class (such as the collection class library), while virtual types resemble the mechanism used in Java to implement polymorphism over arrays.

3 Strengths of parametric types

Here is something that is easy to do with parametric types, but hard to do with virtual types. The example is given in Pizza, with type parameters written between angle brackets `<...>`.

```
public class Pair<Fst, Snd> {
  public Fst fst;
  public Snd snd;
}

public class List<A> {
  ...
  public <B> List<Pair<A,B>> zip(List<B> yl) { ... }
}
```

So `zip` is a method where the receiver is a list with elements of type `A` and the argument is a list with elements of type `B` and that returns a list of pairs with components of types `A` and `B`. The types here are so expressive that it is easy to guess what `zip` does: it pairs corresponding elements of two lists. Thus if `xl` is the list of integers `[1,2,3]` and `yl` is the list of strings `["a", "b", "c"]`, then `xl.zip(yl)` returns the list of pairs of integers and strings `[(1,"a"),(2,"b"),(3,"c")]`.

This example is especially compact because both the class **List** and the method **zip** are parameterized (by **<A>** and **<B>** respectively). Some proposals for parametric types (such as Myer, Bank, and Liskov [MBL97] and Agesen, Freund, and Mitchell [AFM97]) allow classes but not methods to be parametric. In this case, the method **zip** can be defined via an inner class with the appropriate type parameters.

```
public class Pair<Fst, Snd> {
  public Fst fst;
  public Snd snd;
}

public class List<A> {
  ...
  public class Zipper<B> {
    public List<Pair<A,B>> zip(List<B> yl) { ... }
  }
}
```

Whereas before one wrote **xl.zip(yl)**, now one would write **xl.new Zipper().zip(yl)**. (Some proposals require explicit types in expressions that create objects, so this would become **xl.new Zipper<B>().zip(yl)** when **yl** has type **List<B>**.) This is more awkward and performs an extra allocation, but permits essentially the same program structure.

It's a frustrating exercise to attempt to express the same information with virtual types. Here is an attempt to do so.

```
public class Pair {
  public typedef Fst as Object;
  public typedef Snd as Object;
  public Fst fst;
  public Snd snd;
}

public class List {
  public typedef A as Object;
  public class Zipper {
    public typedef B as Object;
    public class PairAB extends Pair {
      public typedef Fst as A;
      public typedef Snd as B;
    }
    public class ListB extends List {
      public typedef Elt as B;
    }
    public class ListPairAB extends List {
      public typedef Elt as PairAB;
    }
    public ListPairAB zip (ListB yl) { ... }
  }
    }
```

The proliferation of class definitions is bad enough, but there is a more serious problem: each argument to `zip` must explicitly extend the class `List.Zipper.ListB`. So this solution is awkward and of restricted applicability.

3.1 Collections and subtyping

The following observation is due to Gilad Bracha.

Often one wants one collection class to inherit from another. For instance, the class for lists may inherit from a more general class for collections.

This is easy to arrange with parametric types. Here is the code outline in Pizza.

```
public class Collection<A> { ... }

public class List<A> extends Collection<A> { ... }
```

Now one can pass, say, an argument of type `List<String>` where one of type `Collection<String>` is expected.

Again, this is more problematic with virtual types. The obvious approach does not work.

```
public class Collection {
  public typedef A as Object;
  ...
}

public class List extends Collection { ... }

public class StringCollection extends Collection {
  public typedef A as String;
}

public class StringList extends List {
  public typedef A as String;
}
```

The problem here is that `StringList` does not extend `StringCollection`, so the former cannot be passed where the latter is expected.

One can do a little better by exploiting inner classes.

```
public class Collection {
  public typedef A as Object;
  ...
  public class List extends Collection { ... }
}
```

Here it is essential that `List` be an inner class of `Collection`, so that it inherits use of the virtual type `A`. Now one can declare, say, collections of strings.

```
public class StringCollection extends Collection {
  public typedef A as String
}
```

And now StringCollection.List is a subtype of StringCollection, as desired. However, this approach requires that the designer of collections has the foresight to include lists. A crucial flexibility of object-oriented languages, that one may define lists long after collections, has been lost.

3.2 Discussion

The difficulties with virtual types appear to arise from two sources. One is sheer length. The other is that virtual types relate solely via subtyping, which in Java must be explicitly declared by the user, whereas the relationship between parametric types is structural. Thus virtual types require one to carefully set up relations between types in advance, whereas with parametric types these relations fall out naturally. Hence, parametric types support program structures that are difficult or impossible to support with virtual types.

4 Strengths of virtual types

The previous examples focussed attention on strengths of parametric types and weaknesses of virtual types. Here is another example, aimed to focus attention on weaknesses of parametric types and strengths of virtual types: families of classes.

Palsberg and Schwartzbach [PS94] tell a compelling story about a common situation where families of classes arise. We will repeat that story here, and then abstract from it to give two examples, 'lists with lengths' and 'alternating lists with lengths'. (The examples are closely related to the 'lists with lengths' and XY-grammar examples of Palsberg and Schwartzbach.)

Consider a processor for a programming language. An early phase of the processor uses abstract syntax trees. These are represented by a family of classes: one class for each non-terminal of the grammar. (Each of these classes might in turn have subclasses to represent each alternative production for the non-terminal.) A later phase of the processor uses annotated abstract syntax trees (they might be annotated with types, flow analysis information, or the like). These are represented by a second family of classes, each original class being subclassed to add the annotation. There might be multiple families, one for each phase.

The simplest possible abstraction of this idea is based on the grammar:

```
X ::= char X | empty
```

which corresponds to lists of characters. The inherited class is augmented with a simple annotation, the length of the list.

The next simplest abstraction is based on the grammar

```
X ::= char Y | empty
Y ::= float X | empty
```

which corresponds to lists that consist alternately of characters and floats. Again, the inherited classes augment each list with its length.

Although these examples are simple, the analogy with grammars and annotations should make it clear that they correspond to a range of examples of interest.

Here is the second example, rendered with virtual types.

```
public class XList {
  public typedef YThis as YList;
  protected char h;
  protected YThis t;
  public XList (char h, YThis t) {
    super(); setHead(h); setTail(t);
  }
  public char head () { return h; }
  public YThis tail () { return t; }
  public void setHead (char h) { this.h = h; }
  public void setTail (YThis t) { this.t = t; }
}

public class YList {
  public typedef XThis as XList;
  protected  float h;
  protected XThis t;
  public YList (float h, XThis t) {
    super(); setHead(h); setTail(t);
  }
  public float head () { return h; }
  public XThis tail () { return t; }
  public void setHead (float h) { this.h = h; }
  public void setTail (XThis t) { this.t = t; }
}

public class LenXList extend XList {
  public typedef YThis as LenYList;
  protected int l;
  public LenXList (char h, YThis t) {
    super(h,t);
  }
  public void setTail (YThis t) {
    super.setTail(t);
    if (t == null) l = 1; else l = 1+t.length();
  }
  public int length () { return l; }
}

public class LenYList extend YList {
```

```
    public typedef XThis as LenXList;
    protected int l;
    public LenYList (float h, XThis t) {
      super(h,t);
    }
    public void setTail (XThis t) {
      super.setTail(t);
      if (t == null) l = 1; else l = 1+t.length();
    }
    public int length () { return l; }
  }

  public class Breakit {
    public void breakit () {
      XList xl = new LenXList('a', null);
      YList yl = new YList(3.142f, null);
      xl.setTail(yl);  // run-time error
    }
  }
```

Observe that `XThis` and `YThis`, rather than `XList` and `YList`, are used for the types of the list tails. Thus, within `XList` it is guaranteed is that the tail is a `YList` (and vice versa), while within `LenXList` it is guaranteed that the tail is a `LenYList` (and vice versa). Hence in the `setTail` method in `LenXList`, the new tail of type `YThis` may safely be called with the `length` method (and ditto for `LenYList` with a tail of type `XThis`).

To demonstrate why covariance (and so-called *binary methods*) are difficult, a `breakit` method has been included. In the absence of suitable run-time or compile-time checks, the `breakit` code would violate the invariant that the tail of a list with length is itself a list with length. In Thorup's version of virtual types, the call labeled above signals a run-time error.

It's a frustrating exercise to express the same information with parametric types. Here is an attempt to do so. The translation is presented mainly because it offers some interesting insights, as it is too complex to use in practice.

Each class is paired with a 'functor' class (indicated by the suffix `F`), which takes one parameter for each virtual type. The actual class is derived by instantiating the parameters appropriately.

This translation gives `extends` an (arguably counterintuitive) meaning, in that the extended class is a subclass of the generator, not the named class. This sad complication does carry with it a happy benefit, as it causes the `breakit` method to fail at compile-time rather than run-time: one cannot assign a `LenXList` to an `XList`, since the former no longer extends the latter.

In the following the bodies are omitted since they are identical to the initial example (save that constructor names are changed as appropriate, so that the constructor `XList` becomes `XListF` in that class, and so on). The class `XList` is a fixpoint of the functor `XListF`, and so on. The fixpoint classes only contain constructor definitions, which are required since they cannot be inherited.

```
public class XListF
  <XThis extends XListF<XThis,YThis>,
   YThis extends YListF<YThis,XThis>>
  { ... }

  public class YListF
    <YThis extends YListF<YThis,XThis>,
     XThis extends XListF<XThis,YThis>>
  { ... }

  public class XList extends XListF<XList,YList> {
    public XList (char h, YList t) { super(h, t); }
  }

  public class YList extends YListF<YList,XList> {
    public YList (char h, YList t) { super(h, t); }
  }

  public class LenXListF
    <XThis extends LenXListF<XThis,YThis>,
     YThis extends LenYListF<YThis,XThis>>
    extends XListF<XThis,YThis>
  { ... }

  public class LenYListF
    <YThis extends LenYListF<YThis,XThis>,
     XThis extends LenXListF<XThis,YThis>>
    extends YListF<YThis,XThis>
  { ... }

  public class LenXList
      extends LenXListF<LenXList,LenYList> {
    public LenXList (char h, LenYList t) { super(h, t); }
  }

  public class LenYList
      extends LenYListF<LenYList,LenXList> {
    public LenYList (char h, LenXList t) { super(h, t); }
  }

  public class Breakit {
    public void breakit () {
      XList xl = new LenXList('a', null); // compile-time error
      YList yl = new YList(3.142, null);
      xl.setTail(yl);
    }
  }
```

Now the **breakit** method fails at compile time rather than run time. The marked line is a type error because **LenXList** is no longer a subtype of **XList**.

If the above code referred to `this`, an additional trick would be required to give `this` the appropriate type (namely, `XThis` within `XList`, and `YThis` within `YList`). Replace `this` by calls to a method `this.asXThis()`, and add to `XListF` the abstract method declaration

```
abstract XThis asXThis();
```

and then add to `XList` the method body

```
public XList asXThis() { return this; }
```

and similarly for `LenXList`. The types work out because `XThis` is instantiated to `XList` in `XList`.

This translation of virtual types into parameterized types closely resembles the usual semantics of object-oriented features in terms of F-bounded polymorphism [CCHOM89,Bru94].

4.1 Discussion

Mutually recursive families of classes are common in programming. Hierarchically related classes are common in object oriented programming. The combination of the two, hierarchies of mutually recursive classes, is less common but occasionally of central importance. Palsberg and Schwartzbach give one compelling example of this sort, a grammar (one mutually recursive family) and an annotated grammar (a second mutually recursive family, hierarchically related to the first). Here we have given a simplified example to capture the essence of the problem, alternating lists (one family) and alternating lists with lengths (a second family, hierarchically related to the first). Parameterized types offer no special support for hierarchical recursive families, but virtual types cater to them neatly.

The `MyType` or `ThisType` construct evolved to deal with the special case of hierarchical families where each family member only needs to refer recursively to itself. Lists are a classic example of a recursive class, and adding lists with lengths gives a classic example for which `ThisType` is perfectly suited. Generalizing to alternating lists with lengths would take one beyond the scope to which `ThisType` applies, but where virtual classes do well. On the other hand, `ThisType` is subject to static checking, while virtual types traditionally require dynamic checking. In the next section, we suggest a generalization to `ThisType` as a way to resolve this conflict.

5 Providing virtual types statically

In this section of the paper we present a proposal for extending Java (or indeed any statically typed object-oriented language) with a construct which is similar to virtual types, but which can be statically type-checked with rules which can be easily understood by programmers. In particular we show that if $I_1, \ldots, I_n$ is a system of interfaces whose definitions are mutually referential (i.e., each may refer to any of the others), then it is possible to define (in a type-safe way) a system of subinterfaces, $J_1, \ldots, J_n$ of the I_i such that all inherited references to the I_i's behave as references to J_i's in the subinterfaces. Moreover classes implementing these interfaces will also have the signatures of methods and fields change appropriately in subclasses implementing the subinterfaces. An important feature of this construction is that classes defined in this way can be statically type-checked to ensure that no type errors can occur at run-time.

5.1 The simple case: Understanding ThisType

In earlier work [BSvG95] the authors solved a similar problem with *self*-referential interfaces and classes using a MyType or ThisType construct. In an interface or class definition, ThisType stands for an interface of this, the object being declared or defined. In the most recent languages designed in this research project [BFP97,Bru97], "exact" types were added in order to simplify dealing with binary methods.

The prefix @ associated with a type indicates an "exact" type. That is, if a variable aExact is declared to have type @A, then values stored in aExact must be of exactly that type, not from an extension. If B extends A, variable a is declared to have type A, and b has (static) type B, then the assignment a = b is legal because a variable of type A can hold values from any type extending it. However if aExact is declared to have type @A, then the assignment aExact = b will be determined to be illegal by the static type checker since only values of exactly type A can be held in aExact. In fact, even aExact = a is considered illegal since a could hold a value of type B. Of course one can always insert an explicit cast aExact = (@A)a to generate a run-time check and let it pass the type checker.

The ability to specify exact types is helpful in defining homogeneous data structures, but a very important use of exact types is in supporting the use of *binary methods* [BCCHLP95], *i.e.*, methods with a parameter of type ThisType, as we shall see below. See below and either [Bru97] or [BFP97] for more detailed explanations of the use of exact types with *binary methods*.

The following example illustrates the use of exact types and ThisType in the context of a list whose head is a character and whose tail is a List.

```
interface ListIfc {
  public char head ();
  public @ThisType tail ();
  public void setHead (char h);
  public void setTail (@ThisType t);
}
```

Uses of ThisType in method signatures denote an interface which is the same as that being defined. Thus it supports recursive references to the interface. We discuss below how the use of ThisType differs from the use of the explicit interface name being defined.

```
public class List implements @ListIfc {
  protected char h;
  protected @ThisType t;
  public List (char h, @ThisType t) {
    super(); setHead(h); setTail(t);
  }
  public char head () { return h; }
  public @ThisType tail () { return t; }
  public void setHead (char h) { this.h=h; }
  public void setTail (@ThisType t) { this.t=t; }
}
```

Uses of **ThisType** in a method of a class refer to the interface formed by the public methods of the object executing that method. Alternatively, we can say that **ThisType** is exactly the public interface of **this**.

As a first approximation, one might think of **ThisType** as another name for **ListIfc**. However its meaning is a bit more subtle. Just as the meaning of **this** changes when methods are inherited in subclasses, the meaning of **ThisType**, which represents its interface, changes in tandem. Because the meanings of both **this** and **ThisType** change in extensions, all methods in **List** are type-checked under the assumption that **this** has interface **@ThisType** and that **ThisType** extends **ListIfc**.

List implements **@ListIfc** because the public methods of **List** are exactly those specified by **ListIfc**. The instance variable **t** of **List** is declared to be exactly **ThisType** in order to assure that the tail of the list has exactly the same interface as the whole list. We shall see below that this is useful in maintaining the consistency of objects defined in extensions. As might be expected, the use of **@ThisType** for the instance variable type leads to the use of the same type as the parameter of **setTail** and the return type of **tail**.

The real advantage in using **ThisType** comes when we define extensions of a class. We can define an extension of **List** which keeps track of the length of the list.

```
public interface LenListIfc extends ListIfc {
  public int length();
}

public class LenList extends List implements @LenListIfc {
  protected int l;
  public LenList (char h, ThisType t) {
    super(h, t);
  }
  public void setTail (@ThisType t) {
    super.setTail(t);
    if (t == null) l = 1; else l = 1+t.length();
  }
  public int length() { return l; }
}
```

Because the instance variable `t` is declared to have type `@ThisType` (rather than `List` or `ListIfc`), when it is inherited its meaning changes along with the meaning of `this`. Thus an object generated by `List` will have a protected instance variable `t` holding a value with interface `@ListIfc`, while the corresponding `t` in an object generated by `LenList` will hold a value with interface `@LenListIfc`. Similarly, the value returned by sending the `tail()` message to a `List` object will be of type `@ListIfc`, while the result returned will be of type `@LenListIfc` if the same message is sent to a value generated from `LenList`. In particular, note that the expression `t.length()` in the body of the `setTail` method of `LenList` type checks correctly only because the type of parameter `t` was declared to be `ThisType`. A type error would have been generated if its type had instead been declared to be `ListIfc`. Thus the use of `ThisType` provides greater flexibility when defining classes with fields or methods whose signatures should be the same as the object.

There is one restriction when using methods with parameters whose type involves `ThisType` (the so-called binary methods), like `setTail`. It is that the corresponding messages can only be sent to objects for which we know the exact types. Thus if `list` has type `@ListIfc` (or `@List`), then `list.setTail(otherList)` will be well-typed only if `otherList` has type `@ListIfc`.

Suppose instead that all we know about `list` is that it has type `ListIfc`. Then `list` could have been generated by `List` or `LenList` (or indeed any other classes which implement the interface). But now if we consider `list.setTail(otherList)` we cannot determine statically what the type of `otherList` should be. If at run-time the value of `list` really comes from `List`, then `otherList` should be of type `@ListIfc`. But if the value of `list` comes from `LenList`, then `otherList` must be of type `@ListIfc`. Note that a run-time error will result in the latter case if `otherList` is from `List`, as it does not have a method corresponding to the `length` message called in the body of `LenList`'s `setTail` method.

There are two cases for type-checking message sends depending on whether or not we know the exact interface of the receiver. If the interface of the receiver is `@T` then all occurrences of `ThisType` in the method signature are replaced by `T`. If we are not provided with the exact interface, but only know the interface of the receiver is `T` then only non-binary messages can be sent and for those messages all occurrences of `ThisType` and `@ThisType` in the signature are replaced by `T`.

Aside from this rule, type checking of most other constructs is straightforward. The only subtlety is that when type checking a class, we presume that `this` has an anonymous class which is an extension of the class being defined, and which implements exactly `ThisType`. For example, an occurrence of `this` in class `List` is type-checked under the assumption that it is from an anonymous class which extends `List` and implements `@ThisType`. `ThisType` is also assumed to be an extension of `ListIfc`.

Type checking is done this way in order to ensure that methods remain type safe in all possible extensions of the class being defined. In particular, `this` has access to all of the instance variables and methods of the class being defined, but may not be restricted to only represent an object of the class being defined. (See [BFP97] or [Bru97] for details.) With these type-checking rules, the language with exact types and ThisType supports a static type discipline that guarantees that type errors will not occur at run-time.

The reader may wonder why we have chosen to have ThisType denote an interface rather than a class. Suppose instead that we had included a ThisClass construct. Here is a reworking of the previous example using ThisClass.

```
public interface ListClassIfc {
  public char head ();
  public @ThisClass tail ();
  public void setHead (char h);
  public void setTail (@ThisClass t);
}

public class ListClass implements ListClassIfc {
  protected char h;
  protected @ThisClass t;
  public List (char h, @ThisClass t) {
    super(); setHead(h); setTail(t);
  }
  public char head () { return h; }
  public @ThisClass tail () { return t; }
  public void setHead (char h) { this.h=h; }
  public void setTail (@ThisClass t) { this.t=t; }
}
```

The use of ThisClass greatly reduces flexibility, since we can no longer utilize a variable with the interface type ListClassIfc with methods whose signatures mention ThisClass. Indeed, suppose xl has type ListClassIfc, and consider the expression xl.setTail(yl). What type should the parameter yl have? Intuitively it should be generated by the same class as xl, but we cannot determine statically what class generated xl. Hence we cannot statically type check this construct. Because of these problems and our desire to encourage the use of interfaces, we choose for ThisType to range over interfaces rather than classes.

5.2 Generalizing ThisType to mutually recursive interfaces and classes

We wish to provide a type-safe statically checkable language construct to define mutually referential classes, in which the classes (and their interfaces) are expected to change in parallel in extensions. Since they refer to each other, we need some way of grouping them together and providing the same sort of flexible names as ThisType. In particular, we need a way of associating these flexible names with the appropriate classes.

We explicitly associate a ThisType-style name to an interface by including it in parentheses immediately after the interface name.

```
interface AnInterface (TType) { ... }
```

Here **AnInterface** is the name of the interface, while **TType** is a type variable used analogously to the **ThisType** interface, which automatically changes in extensions of the interface. We will designate the name following the keyword "**interface**" as the *specific* name of the interface and the parenthesized name as its *variable* name.

We can rewrite interface **ListIfc** and class **List** above using this new notation:

```
public interface ListIfc (TType) {
  public char head ();
  public @TType tail ();
  public void setHead (char h);
  public void setTail (@TType t);
}

public class List (TType) implements @ListIfc {
  protected char h;
  protected @TType t;
  public List (char h, @TType t) {
    super(); setHead(h); setTail(t);
  }
  public char head () { return h; }
  public @TType tail () { return t; }
  public void setHead (char h) { this.h=h; }
  public void setTail (@TType t) { this.t=t; }
}
```

The parenthesized expression which introduces the variable name **TType** in the declaration of the interface **ListIfc** indicates that the variable name **TType** is to be used as the interface of **this** in classes which implement that interface. Thus the only changes made to the class **List** were to explicitly include the *variable* name of the interface in parentheses and to replace all occurrences of **ThisType** with the variable name **TType**.

Mutually referential interfaces and classes which need to refer to each other's **ThisType** will be grouped together so as to delimit the scope of the definitions. Fortunately, Java 1.1 now includes "inner" or nested interfaces and classes which provide the framework for this grouping. (Thanks to Kresten Thorup for suggesting this use of inner classes.)

The following is a reworking of the alternating list example in the new notation.

```
public interface AltListGrpIfc {
  public interface XListIfc (XThis) {
    char head ();
    @YThis tail ();
    void setHead (char h);
    void setTail (@YThis t);
```

```
  }

  public interface YListIfc (YThis) {
    float head ();
    @XThis tail ();
    void setHead (float h);
    void setTail (@XThis t);
  }
}
```

The intention is that any implementation of the "outer" interface, **AltListGrpIfc** must provide implementations of the "inner" interfaces, **XListIfc** and **YListIfc**. The scope of the variable names of the inner interfaces, **XThis** and **YThis**, includes the entire body of the outer interface, **AltListGrpIfc**.

```
public class AltListGrp implements AltListGrpIfc {
  public static class XList (XThis) implements @XListIfc
  {
    protected char h;
    protected @YThis t;
    public XList (char h, @YThis t) {
      super(); setHead(h); setTail(t); }
    public char head () { return h; }
    public @YThis tail () { return t; }
    public void setHead (char h) { this.h=h; }
    public void setTail (@YThis t) { this.t=t; }
  }

  public static class YList (YThis) implements @YListIfc
  {
    protected float h;
    protected @XThis t;
    public YList (float h, @XThis t) {
      super(); setHead(h); setTail(t);
    }
    public float head () { return h; }
    public @XThis tail () { return t; }
    public void setHead (float h) { this.h=h; }
    public void setTail (@XThis t) { this.t=t; }
  }
}
```

We also make a minor extension to Java, in that we assume that since **AltListGrp** implements **AltListGrpIfc**, the names **XListIfc** and **YListIfc** can be used without qualification inside **AltListGrp**. (Java proper requires one to write **AltListGrp.XListIfc** and **AltListGrp.YListIfc** instead.)

Type checking of the classes is performed similarly to that of the simpler case discussed in the previous section. Inside **XList**, **this** is presumed to have an anonymous class which is an extension of **XList** and which implements **@XThis**, while inside **YList**, similar assumptions are made of **this** and **@YThis**. Because each class and interface may be replaced by extensions in a subclass of **AltListGrp**, we only assume that **XThis** extends **XListIfc** and **YThis** extends **YListIfc** when type-checking the classes. We emphasize that the constraints on both **XThis** and **YThis** are available when type-checking each of **XList** and **YList**.

The notion of binary methods must be extended for this notation. A method of an inner interface is considered "binary" if any of its parameters have a type which is a variable name of any other inner interface of the same outer interface. Thus the methods named **setTail** in **XListIfc** and **YListIfc** are binary because they have parameters of type **YThis** or **XThis**. For the same reasons as in section 5.1, binary messages may only be sent to objects for which we know the exact types.

We can now define the subinterfaces and subclasses.

```
public interface LenAltListGrpIfc extends AltListGrpIfc
{
  public interface LenXListIfc (XThis) extends XListIfc
  {
    public int length();
  }

  public interface LenYListIfc (YThis) extends YListIfc
  {
    public int length();
  }
}

public class LenAltListGrp extends AltListGp
{
  public static class LenXList (XThis)
            extends XList implements @LenXListIfc
  {
    protected int l;
    public LenXList (char h, @YThis t) {
      super(h, t);
    }
    public void setTail (@YThis t){
      super.setTail(t);
      if (t == null) l = 1; else l = 1+t.length();
    }
    public int length () { return l; }
  }

  public static class LenYList (YThis)
            extends YList implements @LenYListIfc
  {
    protected int l;
```

```
    public LenYList (float h, @XThis t) {
      super(h,t);
    }
    public void setTail (@XThis t) {
      super.setTail(t);
      if (t == null) l = 1; else l = 1+t.length();
    }
    public int length () { return l; }
  }
}
```

The subinterface **LenAltListGrpIfc** contains extensions of the interfaces **XListIfc** and **YListIfc**, while the subclass **LenAltListGrp** contains extensions of the classes **XList** and **YList** from **AltListGrp**. This time both classes are type checked assuming that **XThis** extends **LenXListIfc** and **YThis** extends **LenYListIfc**. If a new interface redefining a variable interface name is not provided in an extension of the outer class, the old one is inherited unchanged. For example, if an interface with **XThis** as its variable name were not included in **LenAltListGrpIfc**, then uses of **XThis** inside the "outer interface" would be interpreted as being tied to **XListIfc**.

We access the inner classes and interfaces by qualifying their names with the enclosing class.

```
public class Useit {
  public void useit () {
    @AltListGrpIfc.XThis xl
      = new AltListGrp.XList('a',null);
    @AltListGrpIfc.YThis yl
      = new AltListGrp.YList('b',null);
    xl.setTail(yl);
  }
}
```

When using qualified names, we can choose to use either the specific or variable name of the interface. For maximum flexibility (and in anticipation of the next section) we have chosen to use the latter (*e.g.*, **XThis** rather than **XListIfc**) in this example.

We expect it will be more useful to use variable names (like **YThis**) for interfaces, rather than the specific names (like **YListIfc**). However, specific names of classes must be used in **new** expressions, since classes must be used to create new instances. There may also be circumstances in which the specific names of interfaces are used because the programmer does not wish an interface specification to change in extensions. Thus if we wished the method **setTail** to take a parameter of type **YListIfc** in all subclasses (rather than having it change with the subclass) then we could write **YListIfc** rather that **YThis** in its declaration.

The example in Appendix A also includes a "**use** clause" which can be used to bring externally-defined interfaces and classes into a collection so that extensions can also depend on extensions of those declarations. While this will likely not be used regularly, there are times when it is very helpful to bring in externally defined interfaces or classes.

6 Parametric polymorphism with mutually recursive groups

These new constructs interact smoothly with parametric polymorphism, both in defining polymorphic inner classes, and in using the "outer" interface as a constraint for type variables. As an example of the first sort we could change our implementation of **AltListGrp** to hold values of a type specified by a type parameter.

```
public interface PolyAltListGrpIfc
  <XType extends Object, YType extends Object>
{
  public interface XListIfc (XThis) {
    public XType head ();
    public @YThis tail ();
    public void setHead (XType h);
    public void setTail (@YThis t);
  }

  public interface YListIfc (YThis) {
    public YType head ();
    public @XThis tail ();
    public void setHead (YType h);
    public void setTail (@XThis t);
  }
}

public class PolyAltListGrp <XType extends Object, YType extends Object>
  implements PolyAltListGrpIfc<XType,YType>
{
  public static class XList (XThis) implements XListIfc
  {
    protected XType h;
    protected YThis t;
    ...
  }

  public static class YList (YThis) implements YListIfc
  {
    protected YType h;
    protected XThis t;
    ...
  }
}
```

The class **AltListGrp.XList** defined earlier is equivalent to **PolyAltListGrp<char,float>.XList**, and similarly for **YList**.

A different use of polymorphism arises when we use an "outer" interface as a type constraint.

```
public class Useit<T extends AltListGrpIfc> {
   ... T.XThis ... T.YThis ...
}
```

Because the type variable T extends `AltListGrpIfc`, it must support inner interfaces with variable names `XThis` and `YThis`. These inner interfaces are mutually referential and extend `AltListGrpIfc.XThis` and `AltListGrpIfc.YThis`, respectively. For example, an expression with type `@T.XThis` can be sent a `setTail` message with a parameter of type `@T.YThis`. As a result, groups of interfaces (packaged as inner interfaces) can be passed around and used polymorphically. This extension would be simple to accommodate in proposals where parametric types are implemented by expansion into specialized instances, as in the proposal of Agesen *et.al.* [AFM97] or in the heterogeneous translation of Pizza [OW97]. It is not clear how to implement the extension in a homogeneous translation where type parameters are erased.

7 Conclusion

Parametric types and virtual types each do things well that the other does poorly. Both parametric types and virtual types have been given semantics expressed as translations from extensions to Java into Java as it stands (see [Tho97,OW97,OW98]), and these translations look remarkably similar.

One way forward is to tack features that mimic parametric types onto virtual types (as proposed by Cartwright and Steele [CS97] and Thorup and Torgersen [TT98]), or to tack features that mimic virtual types onto parametric types as proposed here.

Our proposal supports parametric types directly, and supports virtual types by using inner interfaces and classes to group together mutually recursive declarations that may be changed simultaneously. An important advantage of this language design is that all type checking can be done statically — it does not require extra dynamic type checking, and the resulting type system guarantees type safety.

A statically safe method to model virtual types was proposed by Torgersen [Tor98]. His work is similar to, but independent from ours. Where we write `interface I (IThis)`, Torgersen would write:

```
public interface I{
   IThis <= I;
```

Instead of relying on exact types, Torgersen requires that a class containing a virtual type is `final bound` (so it cannot be redeclared in subclasses) before it can be used as an ordinary type:

```
public interface IFinal extends I{
   IThis = IFinal;
```

The meaning of `IThis` is thus fixed in all extensions of `IFinal`. Only those classes in which all virtual types are final bound can have instances. If the only type known for an object in a context contains non-final bound virtual types then no binary messages can be sent to it.

Torgersen's scheme has the advantage of needing less machinery, but some inheritance hierarchies cannot be expressed using his technique. Moreover, one must often create new extensions of classes and interfaces just to finalize a virtual type.

Thorup and Torgersen have suggested that virtual types can take on more of the benefits of parametric types if structural subtyping is used rather than declared subtyping, but the details of their proposal remain to be worked out [TT98].

It is interesting to note that many of the difficulties encountered here have to do with providing explicit types for code which clearly will execute without errors. Languages with type inference shift this work from the programmer to the inference system. Thus in Objective ML [RV98] one can write the code in a way similar to that given here and have the system deduce safe typings. The trade-off is that in such systems it is harder to see what changes will be allowable in extensions since the type information is not explicit .

Our notation can be considered as a variant of the proposal for handling inheritance in the presence of mutual recursion put forward by Palsberg and Schwartzbach [PS94]. It differs from their proposal by requiring the interaction of inheritance with recursion to be explicitly declared, which is interesting because they claimed such an option was not possible.

We have presented this proposal as an extension of Java (in particular an extension of the earlier proposal [Bru97]), but it could relatively easily be adapted to other statically-typed object-oriented languages.

Does our proposal constitute the ultimate solution to integrating parametric and virtual types? We think we've made a useful step, but further study is required.

References

[AFM97] Ole Agesen, Stephen Freund, and John C. Mitchell. Adding parameterized types to Java. In *Symposium on Object-Oriented Programming: Systems, Languages, and Applications*, ACM, 1997.

[BCCHLP95] Kim B. Bruce, Luca Cardelli, Giuseppe Castagna, The Hopkins Objects Group, Gary T. Leavens, and Benjamin Pierce. On binary methods. *Theory and Practice of Object-Oriented Systems*, 1(3): 221–242,1995.

[BFP97] Kim B. Bruce, Adrian Fiech, and Leaf Petersen. Subtyping is not a good "match" for object-oriented languages. In *ECOOP '97*, pages 104–127. LNCS 1241, Springer-Verlag, 1997.

[Bru94] Kim B.Bruce. A paradigmatic object-oriented programming language: design, static typing and semantics. *Journal of Functional Programming*, 4(2):127–206, 1994.

[Bru97] Kim B. Bruce. Increasing Java's expressiveness with ThisType and match-bounded polymorphism. Technical report, Williams College, 1997. Available via `<http://www.cs.williams.edu/~kim/README.html>`.

[Bru97b] Kim B. Bruce. Safe static type checking with systems of mutually recursive classes and inheritance. Technical report, Williams College, 1997.

[BSvG95] Kim B. Bruce, Angela Schuett, and Robert van Gent. PolyTOIL: A type-safe polymorphic object-oriented language, extended abstract. In *European Conference on Object-Oriented Programming*, pages 27–51, LNCS 952, Springer-Verlag, 1995.

[CCHOM89] Peter Canning, William Cook, Walter Hill, Walter Olthoff, and John C. Mitchell, F-bounded polymorphism for object-oriented programming. In *Conference on Functional Programming Languages and Computer Architecture*, pages 273–280, ACM, 1989.

[CS97] Corky Cartwright and Guy Steele. Yet another parametric types proposal. Message to Java genericity mailing list, August, 1997.

[GRJV94] Erich Gamma, Richard Helm, Ralph Johnson, and John Vlissides. *Design Patterns.* Addison-Wesley, 1995.

[KM96] Andrew Koenig and Barbara Moo. *Ruminations on C++.* Addison-Wesley, 1996.

[KMMN83] B. B. Kristensen, O. L. Madsen, B. Møller-Pedersen, and K. Nygaard. Abstraction mechanisms in the Beta programming language. In *Symposium on Principles of Programming Languages*, ACM, 1983.

[MBL97] Andrew C. Myers, Joseph A. Bank, and Barbara Liskov. Parameterized types for Java. In *Symposium on Principles of Programming Languages*, pages 132–145, ACM, 1997.

[MM89] O. L. Madsen and B. Møller-Pedersen. Virtual classes: A powerful mechanism for object-oriented programming. In *Object-Oriented Programming: Systems, Languages, and Applications*, ACM, 1989.

[MMN93] O. L. Madsen, B. Møller-Pedersen, and K. Nygaard. *Object-Oriented Programming in the Beta Programming Language.* Addison-Wesley, 1993.

[OW97] Martin Odersky and Philip Wadler. Pizza into Java: Translating theory into practice. In *Symposium on Principles of Programming Languages*, pages 146–159, ACM, 1997.

[OW98] Martin Odersky and Philip Wadler. Leftover Curry and reheated Pizza: How functional programming nourishes software reuse. In *IEEE Fifth International Conference on Software Reuse*, Vancouver, BC, June 1998.

[PS94] Jens Palsberg and Michael I. Schwartzbach. *Object-Oriented Type Systems.* Wiley, 1994.

[RV98] Didier Rémy and Jérôme Vouillon. Objective ML: An effective object-oriented extension to ML. *Theory and Practice of Object-Oriented Systems*, 4(1): 27–50, 1998.

[Rey74] J. C. Reynolds, Towards a theory of type structure. In B. Robinet, editor, *Proc. Colloque sur la Programmation*, LNCS 19, Springer-Verlag.

[Rey83] J. C. Reynolds, Types, abstraction, and parametric polymorphism. In R. E. A. Mason, editor, *Information Processing 83*, pp. 513–523. North-Holland, Amsterdam.

[Str67] C. Strachey, Fundamental concepts in programming languages. Lecture notes for International Summer School in Computer Programming, Copenhagen, August 1967.

[Tho97] Kresten Krab Thorup. Genericity in Java with virtual types. In *European Conference on Object-Oriented Programming*, pages 444–471, LNCS 1241, Springer-Verlag, 1997.

[Tor98] Mads Torgersen. Virtual types are statically safe. *5th Workshop on Foundations of Object-Oriented Languages*, January 1998.

[TT98] Kresten Krab Thorup and Mads Torgersen. Structural virtual types. Informal session on types for Java, *5th Workshop on Foundations of Object-Oriented Languages*, January 1998.

A The subject-observer example

In this section we examine another example of the use of virtual types and demonstrate how this would be written in the Java extension suggested in the paper. Thorup's paper [Tho97] used the following example based on the Observer pattern from [GRJV94].

```
public class Observer {
  public typedef SType as Subject
  public typedef EventType as Object;
  public void notify (SType s, EventType e) { ... }
}

public class Subject {
  public typedef OType as Observer;
  public typedef EventType as Object;
  protected OType observers[];
  ...
  public void notifyObservers(EventType e) {
    int n = observers.length;
    for (int i = 0; i < n; i++)
      observers[i].notify(this,e);
    }
  }

public class WindowObserver extends Observer {
  public typedef SType as WindowSubject;
  public typedef EventType as WindowEvent;
}

public class WindowSubject extends Subject {
  public typedef OType as WindowObserver;
  public typedef EventType as WindowEvent;
  ...
}
```

The following is a reworking of Thorup's example in our notation.

```
public interface SubObsGrpIfc{
  public interface ObserverIfc (OType) {
```

```
    void notify (SType s, EventType e);
  }

  public interface SubjectIfc (SType) {
    ...
    void notifyObservers (EventType e);
  }
  public use Object (EventType);
}

public class SubObsGrp implements SubObsGrpIfc {
  public static class Observer (OType) implements @ObserverIfc
  {
    public void notify (SType s, EventType e) { ... }
  }

  public static class Subject (SType) implements @SubjectIfc
  {
    protected @ThisObserver observers[];
    ...
    public void notifyObservers(EventType e){
      int n = observers.length;
      for (int i = 0; i < n; i++)
        observers[i].notify(this,e);
    }
  }
}
```

The only feature not previously introduced is the "use" clause in the definition of `SubObsGrpIfc`. This indicates that the variable type `EventType` will be allowed to vary in extensions of `SubObsGrpIfc`, and hence that methods of `SubObsGrp` should be type checked under only the assumption that `EventType` extends `Object`.

By our earlier remarks, the occurrence of `this` in the body of `notifyObservers` is type-checked as having an anonymous class which extends `Subject` and which implements `@ThisSubject`.

```
public interface WindowSubObsGrpIfc extends SubObsGrpIfc
{
  public interface WindowObserverIfc (OType) extends ObserverIfc
  { ... }

  public interface WindowSubjectIfc (SType) extends SubjectIfc
  { ... }

  public use WindowEvent (EventType);
}

public class WindowSubObsGrp extends SubObsGrp
  implements WindowSubObsGrpIfc
```

```
{
  public static class WindowObserver (OType)
    extends Observer implements WindowObserverIfc
  { ... }

  public static class WindowSubject (SType)
    extends Subject implements WindowSubjectIfc
  { ... }
}
```

The "use" clause in `WindowSubObsGrpIfc` introduces `WindowEvent` as the new interpretation for `EventType`. Type-checking rules require that the new interpretation of `EventType` be an extension of the meaning in the super-interface, in this case `Object`. As with the inner interfaces, if no replacement is provided for a variable name specified in a "use" clause, the old one is inherited.

Implementing Layered Designs with Mixin Layers[1]

Yannis Smaragdakis and Don Batory
Department of Computer Sciences
The University of Texas at Austin
Austin, Texas 78712
{smaragd, dsb}@cs.utexas.edu

Abstract. *Mixin layers* are a technique for implementing layered object-oriented designs (e.g., collaboration-based designs). Mixin layers are similar to abstract subclasses (mixin classes) but scaled to a multiple-class granularity. We describe mixin layers from a programming language viewpoint, discuss checking the consistency of a mixin layer composition, and analyze the language support issues involved.

1 Introduction

The complexity of software has driven both researchers and practitioners toward design methodologies that decompose design problems into intellectually manageable pieces and that assemble partial products into complete software artifacts. The principle of separating logically distinct and (largely independent) facets of an application is behind many good software design practices. A key objective in designing reusable software modules is to encapsulate within each module a single (and largely orthogonal) aspect of application design. Many design methods in the object-oriented world build on this principle of design modularity (e.g., *design patterns* [12] and *collaboration-based* designs [7][14][15][28][37]). The central issue is to provide implementation (i.e., programming language) support for expressing modular designs concisely.

Our work addresses this problem in the context of collaboration-based (or *role-based*) designs. Such designs decompose an object-oriented application into a set of classes *and* a set of *collaborations*. Each application class encapsulates several *roles*, where each role embodies a separate aspect of the class's behavior. A cooperating suite of roles is called a *collaboration*. In collaboration-based designs, collaborations express distinct (and largely independent) aspects of an application. This property makes collaborations an interesting way to express software designs in a modular way. Collaboration-based design is an example of a *layered* design methodology: collaborations are components and layered compositions of these components define an application.

While collaboration-based designs cleanly capture different aspects of application behavior, their implementations often do not preserve this modularity. *Application frameworks* [17] are a standard implementation technique. As shown in [37], frameworks not only do not preserve the design structure but also may result in inefficient implementations, requiring excessive use of dynamic binding. VanHilst and Notkin

[1] We gratefully acknowledge the sponsorship of Microsoft Research, the Defense Advanced Research Projects Agency (Cooperative Agreement F30602-96-2-0226), and the University of Texas at Austin Applied Research Laboratories.

proposed an alternative technique [37][38][39] using *mixin classes* [8] in C++. Their approach mapped design-level entities (roles) directly into implementation components (mixin classes). It suffered, however, from highly complex parameterizations in the presence of multiple classes, and the inability to contain intra-collaboration design changes. This caused them to question its scalability [37], and seek a way to explicitly capture collaborations as distinct implementation entities.

Our work shows how to remove the difficulties of the VanHilst and Notkin method by scaling the concept of a mixin to multiple classes. We call these scaled entities *mixin layers*. A mixin layer can be viewed as a mixin class encapsulating other mixins with the restriction that the parameter (superclass) of an outer mixin must encapsulate all parameters of inner mixins. We will use C++ templatized nested classes as our primary means of expressing mixin layers, but the ideas are not specific to C++. We will discuss in detail the language support issues involved, mainly relative to C++, CLOS, and Java. There are several examples of designs that can be expressed using mixin layers (e.g., see the enumeration in [2], as well as [4], [15], [31]). We will illustrate a simple example in this paper.

The primary emphasis of this paper is on mixin layers from a programming language standpoint. In a previous paper [33] we studied the applications of a particular implementation of mixin layers. Here, we will consider how the mechanism depends on specific language features and how it addresses fundamental problems associated with layered object-oriented implementations. Such problems include verifying the consistency of a composition of layers and handling the propagation of type information from a subclass to a superclass.

2 Background

2.1 Layered Designs

In an object-oriented design, objects are encapsulated entities but are rarely self-sufficient. Although an object is fully responsible for maintaining the data it encapsulates, it needs to cooperate with other objects to complete a task. An interesting way to encode object interdependencies is through collaborations. A *collaboration* is a set of objects and a protocol (i.e., a set of allowed behaviors) that determines how these objects interact. The part of an object enforcing the protocol that a collaboration prescribes is called the object's *role* in the collaboration. Objects of an application generally participate in multiple collaborations simultaneously and, thus, may encode several distinct roles. Each collaboration, in turn, is a collection of roles, and represents relationships across the corresponding objects. Essentially, a role isolates the part of an object that is relevant to a collaboration from the rest of the object. Different objects can participate in a collaboration, as long as they support the required roles.

In collaboration-based design, we try to express an application as a composition of largely independently-definable collaborations. ***Viewed in terms of design modularity, collaboration-based design acknowledges that a unit of functionality (module) is neither a whole object nor a part of it, but can cross-cut several different objects.*** If a collaboration is reasonably independent of other collaborations (i.e., a good approximation of an ideal module) the benefits are great. First, the collaboration can be

Object Classes

Collaborations (Layers)	*Object OA*	*Object OB*	*Object OC*
Collaboration c1	Role A1	Role B1	Role C1
Collaboration c2	Role A2	Role B2	
Collaboration c3		Role B3	Role C3
Collaboration c4	Role A4	Role B4	Role C4

Figure 1: Example collaboration decomposition. Ovals represent collaborations, rectangles represent objects, their intersections represent roles.

reused in a variety of circumstances where the same functionality is needed, by just mapping its roles to the right objects. Second, any changes in the encapsulated functionality will only affect the collaboration and will not propagate throughout the whole application.

Figure 1 depicts the overlay of objects and collaborations in a design. The figure contains three different objects (*OA*, *OB*, *OC*), each supporting multiple roles. Object *OB*, for example, encapsulates four distinct roles: `B1`, `B2`, `B3`, and `B4`. Four different collaborations (*c1*, *c2*, *c3*, *c4*) capture distinct aspects of the application's functionality. To do this, collaborations have to prescribe certain roles for objects. For example, collaboration *c2* contains two distinct roles, `A2` and `B2`, which are assumed by distinct objects (namely *OA* and *OB*). An object does not need to play a role in every collaboration — *c2* does not affect object *OC*.

Collaboration-based designs are an example of layered designs. In this paper we will concentrate on collaboration-based designs, but a more general classification of layered designs can be found in [2] and [33]. Additionally, the designs we will examine (as well as those examined by VanHilst and Notkin) are *static*: the roles played by an object are uniquely determined by its class. For instance, in Figure 1, all three objects must belong in different classes (since they all support different sets of roles).

2.2 Mixin Classes

The term "mixin class" (or just "mixin") has been overloaded to mean several specific programming techniques and a general mechanism that they all approximate. Here we will use "mixin" in the general sense of [8]. Common alternative meanings include CLOS classes whose superclasses are determined by linearization of multiple inheritance, as well as C++ classes used in a specific multiple inheritance pattern (as superclasses of a single class that themselves have a common "virtual base class").

The main idea implemented by mixins is quite simple: in object-oriented languages, a superclass can be defined without specifying its subclasses. This is not, however, symmetric: when a subclass is defined, it must have a specific superclass. Mixins (also commonly known as *abstract subclasses* [8]) represent a mechanism for specifying classes that will eventually inherit from a superclass. This superclass, however, is not specified at the site of the mixin's definition. Thus a single mixin can be instantiated with different superclasses yielding widely varying classes. This property of mixins makes them appropriate for defining uniform incremental extensions for a multitude of classes. When the mixin is instantiated with one of these classes as a superclass, it produces a class incremented with the additional behavior.

Mixins can easily be implemented using parameterized inheritance. In this case, a mixin is a parameterized class with the parameter becoming its superclass. Using C++ syntax we can write a mixin as:

```
template <class Super>
class Mixin : public Super { ... /* mixin body */ };
```

This was the primary implementation technique used by VanHilst and Notkin in their approach to mapping collaboration-based designs into programs. *Their mixin classes represented roles* and were also parameterized by any other classes that interacted with the given role in its collaboration. For instance, role B4 in Figure 1 would be expressed as:

```
template <class RoleSuper, class OA, class OC>
class B4 : public RoleSuper {
   ... /* role implementation, using OA, OC */
};                                                        (1)
```

Consider that the actual values for parameters OA, OC would themselves be the result of template instantiations, and their parameters also, and so on (up to a depth equal to the number of collaborations). This makes the VanHilst and Notkin method complicated even for relatively small examples. The programmer has to explicitly keep track of the mapping between roles and classes. Additionally, the programmer has to make explicit the collaborations in which a class participates. For instance, the mixin for role A4 in Figure 1 has to be parameterized with the mixin for role A2 — the programmer cannot ignore the fact that collaboration *c3* does not specify a role for object *OA*. These limitations make the approach unscalable. As we show in [33], the length of parameterization expressions increases exponentially with the number of different roles for a class. This is illustrated in Appendix A by showing the parameterization code from an example in [37].

Conceptually, the scalability problems of the VanHilst and Notkin approach are due to the small granularity of the entities they represent. In their methodology, each mixin class represents a role. Roles, however, have many external dependencies (for instance, they often depend on many other roles in the same collaboration). To avoid hard-coding such dependencies, we have to express them as extra parameters to the mixin class, as in (1). VanHilst and Notkin acknowledged this limitation [37]. They suggested trying to map entire collaborations to implementation entities as future work. This is accomplished with the concept of a mixin layer.

3 Mixin Layers

We solve the scalability problems identified by VanHilst and Notkin by implementing collaborations as *mixins that encapsulate other mixins*. We will call the encapsulated mixin classes *inner mixins*, and the mixin that encapsulates them the *outer mixin*. Inner mixins can be inherited, just like any member variables or methods of a class. An outer mixin is called a *mixin layer* when *the parameter (superclass) of the outer mixin encapsulates all parameters (superclasses) of inner mixins*[2]. This is illustrated in Figure 2. `ThisMixinLayer` is a mixin that refines (through inheritance) `SuperMixinLayer`. `SuperMixinLayer` encapsulates three classes: `FirstClass`, `SecondClass`, and `ThirdClass`. `ThisMixinLayer` also encapsulates three inner classes that are themselves mixins and refine the corresponding classes of `SuperMixinLayer`.

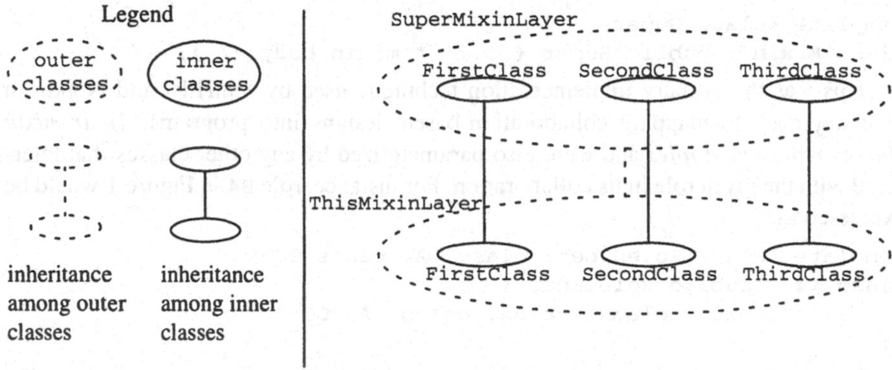

Figure 2: Mixin layers schematically.

We can conceptually see how some of the problems of the VanHilst and Notkin method are addressed if collaborations are expressed as mixin layers: classes that do not participate in a certain collaboration are inherited from collaborations above (we will subsequently use the term "collaboration" for the mixin layer representing a collaboration when no confusion can result). This way every collaboration can be expressed in terms of its superclass collaboration only (since the superclass defines roles for all objects, either explicitly or by inheritance). Parameters like `OA` and `OC` in example (1) are not needed — a role can directly refer to other roles in the same collaboration.

We would like to support mixin layers using the same language mechanisms as those used for mixin classes. To do this, we can standardize the names used for role implementations (make them the same as the name of the class that plays them). This yields an elegant form of mixin layers that can be expressed using common programming language features. For instance, using C++ parameterized inheritance and nested classes, we can express a mixin layer (see again Figure 2) implementing a collaboration as:

---

[2] Inner mixins can actually themselves be mixin layers.

```
template <class CollabSuper>
class CollabThis : public CollabSuper {
public:
   class FirstRole  : public CollabSuper::FirstRole  { ... };
   class SecondRole : public CollabSuper::SecondRole { ... };
   class ThirdRole  : public CollabSuper::ThirdRole  { ... };
   ...          // more roles
};                                                          (2)
```

The code fragment in (2) represents the form of mixin layers that we will use in this paper. Note that specifying a parameter for the outermost mixin automatically determines the parameters of all inner mixins.

In (2) we mapped the main elements of the mixin layer definition to specific implementation techniques: we used nested classes to implement class encapsulation. We also used parameterized inheritance to implement mixins. *None of these implementation choices is part of the mixin layer definition.* There are very different ways of encoding the same design. For example, we can encode mixin layers in CLOS with different implementation dependencies. Class encapsulation is implemented by defining member methods that return CLOS class-metaobjects. No lexical nesting of any kind (as in (2)) is necessary. This combines nicely with the method-based character of CLOS mixins and the reflective capabilities of the language. (To keep the discussion short, we put the CLOS counterpart of code fragment (2) in Appendix B). Note the importance of the above discussion: mixin layers are not a linguistic idiom. Many flavors of the mixin layer concept, however, can be expressed via specific programming language idioms: as stand-alone language constructs, as a combination of C++ nested classes and parameterized inheritance, as a combination of CLOS class-metaobjects and mixins, etc. We will use a C++ idiom in our examples, in the belief that concrete syntax will clarify, rather than obscure, our ideas.

Back to (2), composing mixin layers to form concrete classes is now as simple as composing mixin classes. If, like in Figure 1, we have four mixin layers (`Collab1`, `Collab2`, `Collab3`, `Collab4`) implementing four different collaborations, we can compose them as `Collab4 < Collab3 < Collab2 < Collab1 > > >`[3]. Note that even though some collaborations (like *c2*, *c3* in Figure 1) do not specify roles for all classes, they inherit such roles from their superclasses. This results in linear length expressions for collaboration-based designs and, hence, solves the scalability problems of the VanHilst and Notkin approach (see Appendix A).

4 A Concrete Example

In this section, we will show the benefits of mixin layers through an example. More complex examples are presented in [6] and [33].

4.1 A Data Structure

We examine a data structure design that was used in both the P2 lightweight

---

[3] `Collab1` will then have to be a concrete class (i.e., not a mixin). Alternatively we can have a collaboration of empty roles that we use as the root of all compositions.

DBMS generator [3][4], as well as in the DiSTiL library for data structures [32]. In this example we add functionality to a data structure by assigning more roles to the classes that participate in the design. There are two such classes: a *node* class, of which all data nodes are instances, and a *container* class, which has one instance per data structure. A third class for data structure cursors (iterators) is generally needed but to keep the example simple we will equate cursors with pointers to node objects. This model for data structure construction is, in fact, quite general. Composite data structures, run-time bound checks, garbage collection, a lock and transaction manager, etc., can all be specified as new roles for the node and container classes (see [4]). This can be achieved using mixin layers, as we will show with extensions to a binary tree data structure.

Our target data structure consists of four different collaborations: *bintree*, *alloc*, *timestamp*, and *sizeof*. *Bintree* captures the functionality of a binary tree. *Alloc* captures the functionality of memory allocation. *Timestamp* is responsible for maintaining timestamps for data structure and element updates. *Sizeof* simply keeps track of the data structure size. The design is simple and we will not concern ourselves with its schematic representation (in the form of Figure 1) or the way we obtained it. For a good reference on how to obtain collaboration-based designs from use-case scenarios [29] see VanHilst's Ph.D. dissertation [40].

A mixin layer implementing a binary tree collaboration has the form[4]:

```
template <class Super> class BINTREE : public Super {
public:
   class Node : public Super::Node {
      Node* parent_link,
         left_link, right_link ;    // Node data members
   public:
      ...                           // Node interface
   };

   class Container : public Super::Container {
      Node* header;                 // Container data members
   public:
      void insert ( EleType el ) { ... }
                           // Definition of EleType inherited
      void erase ( Node* node ) { ... }
      bool find ( EleType* el ) { ... }
      ...                           // Other methods
   };
};
```

Note that the `Container` class is aware of the `Node` class (e.g., it declares a member variable of type `Node*`). The two classes must be designed together and, hence, it makes sense to encapsulate both in a single unit.

---

[4] We will present simplified code fragments, ignoring implementation details that are not directly relevant to our discussion. We will highlight class definitions for readability and use ellipses (. . .) for omitted code.

Now consider the implementation of the *timestamp* collaboration: the data structure maintains the time of its last update, as well as the creation and update time of each node. The set of exported operations on the data structure can be enriched (e.g., by defining an operation that returns the data structure update time, as well as a variant of `find`: `find_newer`). This enrichment can be viewed as a collaboration prescribing roles for both the `Node` and the `Container` class. Its implementation using mixin layers has the form:

```
template <class Super> class TIMESTAMP : public Super {
public:
   class Node : public Super::Node {
      time_t creation_time, update_time; // Node data members
   public:
      bool more_recent (time_t t) { ... }
      ...                      // Other time-related methods
   };

   class Container : public Super::Container {
      time_t update_time;            // Container data members
   public:
      bool find_newer ( EleType* el, time_t t ) { ... }
      void insert ( EleType el ) { ... }
      ...                         // Other time-related methods
   };
};
```

Not all collaborations need to specify roles for all classes in a design. The *sizeof* collaboration, for instance, only needs to maintain a counter of elements associated with a container and only prescribes a role for the `Container` class. It can be implemented as a mixin layer that is a trivial wrapper around a mixin class:

```
template <class Super> class SIZEOF : public Super {
public:
   class Container : public Super::Container {
      int count;                  // Container data members
   public:
      Container() : count(0), Super::Container() {};
                                  // Constructor
      void insert ( EleType el ) {
         Super::Container::insert(el); count++; }
      void erase ( Node* node ) {
         Super::Container::erase(el); count--; }
      int size () { return count; }
   };
};
```

Again, classes generated by instantiating the `SIZEOF` mixin layer do have a `Node` nested class — this class is inherited from mixin layers above `SIZEOF` in the inheritance chain.

To put everything together we need a concrete (i.e., non-mixin) class to be the root of our inheritance hierarchy. This could be a "dummy" class, containing only empty roles. In most applications, however, it is easy to identify a collaboration, which has to be the basis upon all other functionality is built. In this particular example, the *alloc* collaboration serves this purpose. *Alloc* is responsible for the actual memory allocation for the data structure. Note that the implementation of this collaboration (as well as any of the other mixin layers) can have parameters other than the one we used to designate the superclass. These extra parameters can be used to specify polymorphic behavior. In our example, it makes sense to parameterize the layer representing *alloc* by the type of the elements stored in the data structure. Then we have:

```
template <class EleType> class ALLOC {
public:
   class Node {
      EleType element;   // The actual stored data
   public:
      ...                // Any methods pertaining to stored data
   };

   class Container {
   protected:
      typedef Super::EleType EleType;
                         // The actual type of stored data
      void* node_alloc();
      ...                // Other allocation methods
   };
};
```

We form our target data structure by composing mixin layers. A binary tree storing integers and maintaining time information and size is defined as:

```
typedef SIZEOF < TIMESTAMP < BINTREE < ALLOC < int > > > >
 Tree1;
```
(3)

The `Node` and `Container` classes are accessible[5] as `Tree1::Node` and `Tree1::Container`. An outline of the composition of (3) is shown in Figure 3. We have annotated the design with some of the inherited member variables and methods. Note how both the `SIZEOF` and the `TIMESTAMP` mixin layers depend on layers above them to insert and erase elements from the data structure. We will return to this later.

4.2 Discussion

Our example illustrates the benefits of mixin layers:

- *Mixin layers preserve the structure of the design.* This enhances the maintainability of an application. If changes are introduced in the design (e.g., in our data structure example, if we want to use a different form of a binary tree, if we want to maintain time information for retrievals as well, etc.) it is easy to isolate them. A single mixin layer encapsulates changes to multiple classes. Additionally, the specification of the inheritance hierarchy is separate from the definition of class

---

[5] There is no reason why the `Node` class should be user accessible. What really needs to be user accessible is an iterator class, which for this example is the same as a pointer to a `Node` object.

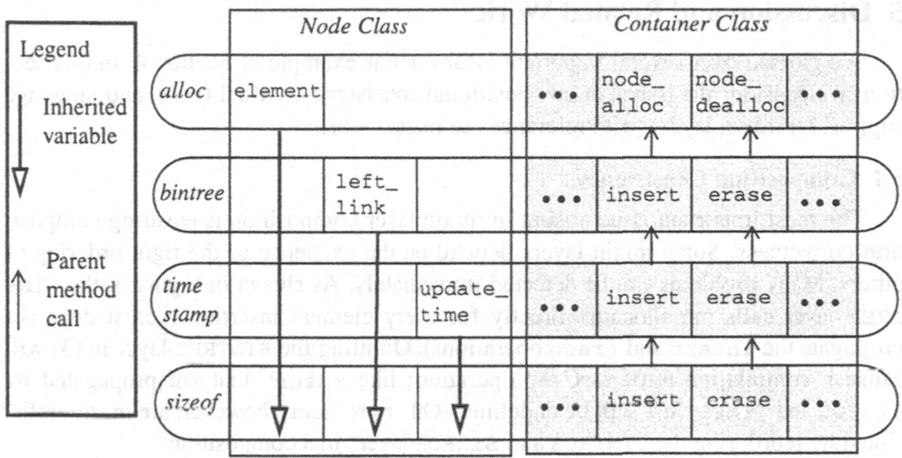

Figure 3: A composite data structure. Shaded areas represent roles.

functionality. Hence, changing the inheritance chain is as simple as editing a composition like (3), above.

- *Mixin layers are reusable and interchangeable.* A single layer can be used in several different compositions and is, to an extent, isolated from other layers. In our data structure example, the `SIZEOF`, `ALLOC`, and `TIMESTAMP` layers are not specific to binary trees. They could just as well be used with a doubly-linked list or many other data structures. The change is minimal: we only have to swap the `BINTREE` layer with a different layer.
- *Mixin layer compositions are scalable.* In our example, if we have more than one variation of a data structure in the same application, very little hand editing is involved. For instance, we could have a second binary tree that maintains no time information in the same program. The definition would be:
  ```
  typedef SIZEOF < BINTREE < ALLOC < int > > > Tree2;
  ```
  Consider what would happen if application frameworks were used to implement our design. (Frameworks specify superclasses and implementations are defined via subclassing). To express the second data structure, we would have to explicitly subclass from the binary tree abstract class and reintroduce by hand the changes dictated by the `SIZEOF` class. In general, application frameworks cannot express more than one feature variation without code replication. Mixin layers, on the other hand, can be composed in an exponential number of ways to express a large variety of implementations (see also [3]).

Such benefits have usually been claimed for techniques that group many objects into large-scale components (e.g., [2], [13], [19], [31]). In these approaches, grouping objects into components was not done with existing object-oriented mechanisms. Mixin layers can be used to express similar functionality using a novel combination of object-oriented constructs.

5 Discussion and Related Work

We glossed over several important issues in our example of Section 4. In this section, we consider the issues of compositional consistency, virtual types, and language support for mixin layers, with references to related work.

5.1 Composition Consistency

The most important issue arising in mixin layer composition is ensuring composition correctness. Some mixin layers depend on the existence or the right ordering of others. Many problems can be detected immediately. As shown in Figure 3, the BINTREE layer calls the allocator directly for every element insertion (i.e., it does not propagate the `insert` and `erase` operations). Omitting the BINTREE layer in (3) will cause a compilation error in C++: operations like `insert` that are propagated by SIZEOF and TIMESTAMP will be undefined. Other problems, however, are more subtle. Consider reordering the BINTREE and SIZEOF layers in a composition:

```
typedef BINTREE < SIZEOF < ALLOC < int > > >  Tree3;
```

This will cause the `insert` and `erase` methods of SIZEOF to be shadowed (overridden) by those of BINTREE. Hence, the implementation is wrong: the count of elements in the data structure will never be updated (since this is only done in the `insert` and `erase` methods of SIZEOF and these methods are not called by BINTREE). The `size` operation will be visible, however, and will always return 0, although the data structure may contain elements.

Such mistakes may not actually cause a compilation error. This can be true even for statically typed languages — in C++, for instance, no error will be signalled even though `SIZEOF::Container` has an explicit call to the `insert` method of its superclass and no such method is defined. This has to do with the treatment of methods in parameterized classes as function templates, as we will discuss in Section 5.3. In essence, the `insert` method for `SIZEOF::Container` is never compiled since it is not needed, thus the error is never discovered.

In general, mixin layers may have subtle semantic dependencies that are not reflected in their interfaces. In large libraries there may be a variety of layers supporting identical interfaces but implementing different semantics. Many combinations of layers may be illegal but there may not be a way to detect this from the interfaces alone.

This problem has been studied in the context of layered systems. The *design rule checking* approach of [5] offers a solution using propositional properties and requirements that are propagated both up and down a layer hierarchy. The *nested mixin-methods* of [34] resulted in a powerful constraint system. Nesting of mixins was used as a way to restrict their scope. A mixin class of [34] can define other mixins that can be composed with it, inherit some mixins when composed, and cancel inherited mixins. The *feature-oriented* programming approach of [27] uses the `assumes` keyword to express the property that the correctness of one feature (layered component) assumes the existence of another.

Interestingly enough there is a simple way to express basic dependencies within the mixin layers framework. Every mixin layer can export propositional properties describing its behavior (essentially encoding semantic knowledge in its interface). Recall that when mixin layers are composed, they are linked in an inheritance chain. Properties are propagated in the same direction as inherited methods and variables: from superclasses to subclasses. Layers can explicitly make inherited properties unavailable to their subclasses. Finally, a layer can check (require) whether it has inherited a property or not. A composition is correct if none of these requirements fails. This technique is similar to the `assumes` functionality of [27] and the design rule checking of [5]. Consider the example of Section 4. There are four requirements that we need to express:

- A `BINTREE` mixin layer cannot have a `SIZEOF` layer as an ancestor in its inheritance chain (because otherwise the `insert` method of `SIZEOF` will be shadowed).
- A `BINTREE` mixin layer cannot have a `TIMESTAMP` layer as an ancestor (same reason as above).
- A `SIZEOF` mixin layer needs to ensure that some sort of a data structure is present in the composition. In our example the only data structure is a binary tree but we can easily imagine the same mixin layer being composed, for instance, with a doubly linked list layer.
- A `TIMESTAMP` mixin layer also needs to ensure that a data structure is present.

These can be specified as requirements on the existence of three properties (inherited from ancestors in the inheritance chain):

- No `SIZEOF` layer is present (call this property `P_NoSizeof`).
- No `TIMESTAMP` layer is present (call this property `P_NoTimestamp`).
- A data structure layer is present (call this property `P_DataStructure`).

The implementation is simple. All properties can be expressed as empty classes encapsulated in a mixin layer. Properties are inherited but can be negated by using access control (that is, "hiding" of class members — e.g., by making them "private" members in C++). If the class representing the property is made visible to subclasses (either by declaration or by inheritance without "hiding"), then the property is asserted. Otherwise the property is negated. The requirement that a certain property be satisfied is then enforced by declaring an instance of this class.

In our example, `BINTREE` exports property `P_DataStructure` and requires properties `P_NoSizeof` and `P_NoTimestamp`.

```
template <class Super> class BINTREE : public Super {
protected:
   class P_DataStructure { };
        // Assert this property for subclasses
private:
   P_NoSizeof dummy1;
   P_NoTimestamp dummy2;
        // Require P_NoSizeof and P_NoTimestamp from ancestors
public:
   ...  // nested mixins (same as before)
};
```

The other three mixin layers are modified accordingly:

```
template <class Super> class SIZEOF : public Super {
private:
```

```
   class P_NoSizeof { };         // Negate property for subclasses
   P_DataStructure dummy1;       // Require P_DataStructure
public:
   ...                           // nested mixins (same as before)
};

template <class Super> class TIMESTAMP : public Super {
private:
   class P_NoTimestamp { };      // Negate property for subclasses
   P_DataStructure dummy1;       // Require P_DataStructure
public:
   ...                           // nested mixins (same as before)
};

template <class EleType> class ALLOC {
protected:
   class P_NoSizeof { };         // Assert property for subclasses
   class P_NoTimestamp { };      // Assert property for subclasses
public:
   ...                           // nested classes (same as before)
};
```

Note how the constraint is enforced: the `ALLOC` mixin layer asserts properties `P_NoSizeof` and `P_NoTimestamp`. The `BINTREE` layer requires that they not be negated by some layer between `BINTREE` and `ALLOC` in the inheritance hierarchy. `SIZEOF` and `TIMESTAMP` negate `P_NoSizeof` and `P_NoTimestamp`, respectively. Also they require that they have some ancestor asserting property `P_Datastructure`. This accurately describes the constraints we want to impose on the compositions of these four mixin layers: a `BINTREE` has to be present and if a `TIMESTAMP` or `SIZEOF` are present they must be descendants of `BINTREE` in the inheritance chain.

The method described above only makes use of access control (such as commonly found in C++ or Java and easily emulated in CLOS) and the same general language mechanisms used for mixin layers. The method's clarity could be improved using some form of syntactic sugar. In the absence of static typing (e.g., if we were to implement this technique in CLOS) the checking would have to be performed at run-time by calling an appropriate method. We have developed other constraint techniques for C++ but they are language-specific (or even compiler-specific as is the case with many compile-time techniques that rely on constant-folding).

There is a more important restriction of the technique we presented, however. Even though an erroneous composition will be detected, the error message will be far from informative. In essence, we express relatively deep errors (e.g., semantic incompatibilities among large scale components) as the absence of an inherited class. The compiler will still complain about an undefined type, but the cause of the error (not to mention a possible fix) is not immediately apparent. The problem is intensified in the case of mixin layers developed and used independently by different programmers. A casual user will expect much more expressive error reporting from a black-box component than our technique can offer. Reference [5] presents a general technique for automatically detecting (and suggesting repairs to) errors in layered implementations.

5.2 Virtual Types

An interesting issue arises in various layered implementations that use inheritance together with static typing (not necessarily in *fully* statically typed languages). This is essentially a symmetric problem to the one that originally motivated mixins. Recall that mixins were introduced to remove the restriction that the definition of a subclass in an inheritance relation needs to reference its superclass. This restriction, however, means that superclasses are generally known when a subclass is defined (and references to them may exist in subclass code) while the converse is not true. This is not a problem when a superclass only needs to transfer control to a subclass (i.e., when a superclass needs to call a subclass method). The usual dynamic binding (or *late binding*) of methods (the hallmark of object-oriented programming) deals with exactly this. When, however, superclass code depends on type information that is specific to the current subclass, the problem is harder — type sub-languages usually do not have late binding capabilities.

Recall the `ALLOC` layer from our data structure example. `ALLOC` is the root of the inheritance hierarchy for all compositions of mixin layers in Section 4. One of the compositions we examined is replicated here:

```
typedef SIZEOF < TIMESTAMP < BINTREE < ALLOC < int > > > >
 Tree1;
```
(4)

The `node_alloc` method in the `Container` nested class of `ALLOC` is responsible for allocating storage for a data structure element. One would think that the implementation of this method would be as simple as:

```
{ return new Node; }
```

Unfortunately, this is not true. The actual allocated object should not be of type `Node`, as defined in the `ALLOC` layer (that is, `ALLOC<int>::Node` in (4)). Instead it should be of class `Node` as defined in the most refined layer (i.e., the final subclass in the hierarchy — `Tree1::Node` in (4)). In this way, the allocated node will have enough room for the stored data as well as fields added by every one of the mixin layers of composition `Tree1` (e.g., the `parent_link`, `left_link`, and `right_link` pointers added by `BINTREE`). We can circumvent this problem by weakening our type constraints and obtaining the necessary information at run-time through dynamic binding. In this particular example we need to set the return value of the `node_alloc` method to a universal pointer type (`void*`) and get the size of the allocated node through a C++ `virtual` call (not shown). This solution is general but inconvenient, error-prone (type information is lost), and possibly inefficient (depending on the overhead of dynamic binding). Although there appear to be no generally available alternatives, the problem has been studied extensively and it is interesting to cite some language mechanisms that address it.

A complete and elegant solution to the problem is offered by *virtual types* language mechanisms. Virtual types can be refined by subclasses in an inheritance chain and the most refined version is the one used by superclass code. In our data structure example, by declaring `Node` as a virtual type we express precisely our intention. Any references to `Node` (for instance, in "`new Node`") are taken relative to the most refined class in the inheritance chain (`Tree1::Node` in (4)).

Virtual types first appeared as *virtual class patterns* in the Beta programming language (see [21], ch.9). Recently they have been employed in a variety of programming language mechanisms implementing parameterization and layered frameworks similar to mixin layers. The work of [36], proposes an approach for genericity in Java using virtual types. We recognize the "`assumes inner`" primitive of feature-oriented programming [27] as a virtual type declaration specifier. The `forward` construct in the P++ language [31] serves exactly the same purpose, declaring that a certain type will be refined by subsequent layers in a composition. Our language extensions to Java that add support for mixin layers (currently under implementation — see Section 5.3) include virtual types.

5.3 Language Support

Mixin layers are mixins that encapsulate other mixins. Therefore, *the actual semantics of mixin layers depends directly on the class manipulation and inheritance semantics of the host language*. Mixin layers in CLOS or Smalltalk are semantically different than mixin layers in C++, but they can all be viewed as different implementation flavors of the same concept. For example, CLOS classes (and, therefore, mixins) have no default *class encapsulation* (class encapsulation can be emulated by defining an appropriate metaclass, however). This means that class *slots* (i.e., member variables) are not proprietary to the class that defines them. Thus, in an inheritance hierarchy, slots with the same name are merged. This prevents reusing a mixin in a single composition.

Keeping such differences in mind, we would like to examine the support for mixin layers provided by different languages. The language techniques used for encapsulation of mixins vary from reflection (i.e., methods that return class meta-objects) to lexical nesting of classes. In all the examined languages, supporting mixin layers seems to be as simple as supporting mixin classes.

CLOS. The original use of mixins was a CLOS idiom so it makes sense to ask how well our ideas are supported in CLOS. As we show in Appendix B, encapsulation of mixins can be expressed using methods that return mixins. Combined with the CLOS mixin functionality, this provides a flavor of mixin layers, adapted to the CLOS inheritance and class manipulation capabilities. In all, CLOS offers a very powerful extensibility platform for object systems, so it is no surprise that mixin layers are expressible in this context. We are, however, satisfied that the CLOS mixin layer idiom described in Appendix B is a natural one and directly relates the concept to CLOS mixins. The syntactic transformation machinery of Common Lisp (macros) can be used to add syntactic sugar to this implementation.

Smalltalk. Although we have not experimented with the Smalltalk language, we expect that the ideas explored in CLOS will be largely applicable. Smalltalk has been a traditional test bed for mixins, both for researchers (e.g., [9], [22], [34]) and for practitioners [24]. Like CLOS, the language has powerful reflective capabilities. These can be used to emulate encapsulated classes by methods that return classes. We believe (but have yet to verify) that this technique can be used in conjunction with existing mixin mechanisms to implement mixin layers.

C++. As we have seen, C++ offers direct support for most of the mixin layers ideas. Nevertheless, there are interesting issues that arise in statically typed languages (like C++ and Java). Programming with C++ inheritance and templates can be cumbersome due to the lack of type-checking for templates. C++ templates are not types in the language (in the terminology of [10], they are *type operators*). Hence, their consistency is not checked until composition time. Furthermore, methods of templatized classes are themselves considered function templates. This means that, even after mixin layers are composed, not all of their methods will be type-checked. Only the methods actually referenced in the object code will be instantiated and, hence, type-checked (see [35] p.330-331). The result is an "interpretive" behavior of template programming. Type errors (including type mismatches and references to undeclared methods) can only be detected with the right template instantiations and method calls. This makes it hard to develop C++ mixin layers independently of the application that will use them.

Java. The Java language is an obvious next candidate for mixin layers. Java has no support for mixins, but this is the topic of active research [1][11]. The work of [11] presented a semantics for mixins in Java. This is particularly interesting from a theoretical standpoint as it addresses issues of mixin integration in a type-safe framework. Also, the latest additions to the language [16] support nested classes and interfaces (actually both "nested" classes as in C++ and *member* classes — where nesting has access control implications). Nested classes can be inherited just like any other members of a class. Thus, mixin layers will be straightforwardly supported by any extension adding mixin functionality to Java.

As we saw, mixins can be expressed in C++ using parameterized inheritance. There have been several recent proposals for adding parameterization/genericity to Java [1][25][26][36]. All of them have relatively clean semantics and address most of the problems we identified with C++ templates. Only the first [1] supports parameterized inheritance and, hence, can express mixin layers. Additionally, we are already working on our own Java language extensions to support mixins and mixin layers. In this effort we are using our JTS set of tools [6] for creating pre-compilers for domain-specific languages. The system currently supports a form of parameterized inheritance (and, therefore, mixin layers, when combined with nested classes). We are in the process of implementing language extensions that capture mixins and mixin layers explicitly. The extensions include a form of virtual types to address the problems identified in Section 5.2. Additionally, the fundamental building blocks of the JTS system itself were expressed as mixin layers, resulting in an elegant bootstrapped implementation.

It is interesting to examine the technical issues involved in supporting mixins in Java parameterization mechanisms. Two of these mechanisms [26][36] are based on a *homogeneous* model of parameterization: the same code is used for different instantiations of generics. This is not applicable in the case of parameterized inheritance — the superclass needs to actually change (see [1] for more details). Additionally, there may be conceptual difficulties in adding parameterized inheritance capabilities: The parameterization approach of [36] is based on virtual types. Parameterized inheritance can be approximated with virtual types by employing *virtual superclasses* [20], but this is not part of the design of [36]. The conceptual problems in the case of Pizza [26] are different. Pizza employs *type inference* (a characteristic of Hindley/Milner [23] type systems): it infers the type of parameters directly from the code (instead of requiring that the programmer declare the type explicitly and then checking that the type is indeed valid). There seem to be difficulties in combining parameterized inheritance with type inference. The difficulties are not insurmountable but an implementation may be quite complex and may require significant changes to the existing Pizza semantics.

The approaches of Myers et al. [25] and Agesen et al. [1] are conceptually similar from a language design standpoint. Even though parameterized implementations are not types in the language, their parameters can be explicitly constrained. Instantiation is explicit with constraint checking but no type inference involved. This makes these techniques easily amenable to adding parameterized inheritance capabilities, as was demonstrated in [1].

5.4 Other Related Work

There is a wealth of related research in the area of adding new responsibilities to objects — we will selectively mention a few examples. Subject-oriented programming [13] supports defining new roles for multiple objects dynamically. Aspect-oriented programming [19] also emphasizes changing the semantics of multiple objects, although in a more abstract way (aspects may encapsulate changes in the semantics of components or in implementation policies). Mezini's approach [22] emphasizes dynamic (single-)object evolution with mixin components. The context relations of [30] concentrate on dynamic modifications to a group of classes. Feature-oriented programming [27] focuses on role (or *feature*) interaction, through explicit entities (called *lifters*) that determine how two features interact. The nested mixin-methods of Agora [34] offer a powerful mechanism to control the addition of new roles.

None of the above has been associated with object-oriented design techniques and all of them require special-purpose programming language support. Nevertheless, it will be interesting to examine the main elements of these approaches (e.g., dynamic extensions, support for role interaction, and extension control through member mixins) in the context of mixin layers. We expect this to be part of our future work.

6 Conclusions

Software design methodologies that identify reusable building blocks of application construction are important. Collaboration-based design is one such methodology. It asserts that an application building block, called a *collaboration*, is neither a whole object nor a part of it, but rather cooperating parts of many different objects (called *roles*). A collaboration encapsulates one aspect of an application that is largely independent of other aspects. When this modularity is preserved in an implementation, we end up with components suitable for application synthesis through modular composition. There is a substantial track record in building applications through modular composition in this manner. This approach corresponds to layered implementation paradigms (see [2], [3], [31]). Nevertheless, the connection between this work and object-oriented design and implementation techniques has not been recognized in the above cited references.

The contribution of our work is in bridging the gap between layered design ideas and their implementations in object-oriented languages. The main point of this paper is that encapsulation of mixins within mixins is a central concept in scalable implementations of layered designs. We named this concept "mixin layers" and showed how it can be expressed in a variety of ways using object-oriented language constructs. We believe this work is important: it directly maps a design methodology to an implementation methodology. It emphasizes object-oriented programming at the level of multiple-object components in a novel way. It shows a direction of programming language research that holds promise for realistic component-based application development.

Our work has immediate consequences: a form of mixin layers is already well supported by widely-used programming languages and can concisely express collaboration-based designs. In particular, using mixin layers in C++, we can eliminate the scalability problems of the VanHilst and Notkin implementation method. The result is a practical layered implementation approach in C++.

There remain several issues to be explored. One of the primary concerns of layered designs is that of compositional correctness: given a composition we need to ensure that it is consistent. We indicated how compositional constraints could be captured within the mixin layer framework. We also indicated the limitations of such an approach (w.r.t. unintelligible error messages). Work on composition validation raises interesting questions on how type systems can accommodate such checking. We expect this to remain a fruitful area of research for some time to come.

Appendix A — Problems with the VanHilst/Notkin Model

The length of a parameterization expression in the VanHilst/Notkin method depends on the actual roles composed and their interdependencies. In the worst case, as we show in [33], it is equal to m^n for n collaborations, each with m roles. Usually, however, not all roles need to be parameterized by all classes. Instead of devising an example, we show the one presented by VanHilst and Notkin in Figure 6 of [37]. The parameterization expression for a design with seven collaborations and three classes is:

```
class Empty {};
class WS        : public WorkspaceNumber                  {};
class WS2       : public WorkspaceCycle                   {};
class VGraph    : public VertexAdj<Empty>                 {};
class VWork     : public VertexDefaultWork<WS,VGraph>     {};
class VNumber   : public VertexNumber<WS,VWork>           {};
class V         : public VertexDFT<WS,VNumber>            {};
class VWork2    : public VertexDefaultWork<WS2,V>         {};
class VCycle    : public VertexCycle<WS2,VWork2>          {};
class V2        : public VertexDFT<WS2,VCycle>            {};
class GGraph    : public GraphUndirected<V2>              {};
class GWork     : public GraphDefaultWork<V,WS,GGraph>    {};
class Graph     : public GraphDFT<V,WS,GWork>             {};
class GWork2    : public GraphDefaultWork<V2,WS2,Graph>   {};
class GCycle    : public GraphCycle<WS2,GWork2>           {};
class Graph2    : public GraphDFT<V2,WS2,GCycle>          {};
```

Note the introduction of many intermediate types that encode common sub-expressions (so as to avoid making the expression even lengthier). Considering that we have encountered designs with several collaborations and more than 30 roles in some of them, this approach is clearly unrealistic.

In contrast, the same composition using mixin layers was as simple as:

```
class NumberC : public DFT < NUMBER < DEFAULTW < UGRAPH > > > {};
class CycleC  : public DFT < CYCLE < DEFAULTW < NumberC > > > {};
```

The actual application classes are nested inside `NumberC` and `CycleC`.

Appendix B — Mixin Layers in CLOS

Mixin layers can be easily expressed in CLOS by combining CLOS mixins with its powerful reflective capabilities. Keep in mind that the semantics of every incarnation of mixin layers depends on the semantics of the host language. Thus, although CLOS mixin layers are not semantically equivalent to C++ mixin layers (e.g., there is no default class encapsulation), they are just a different flavor of the same idea.

The main mixin layer template, illustrated in code fragment (2), is written as:

```
(defclass first-dummy() (...))  ; Definition of 1st inner mixin
(defclass second-dummy () (..)) ; Definition of 2nd inner mixin
(defclass third-dummy () (...)) ; Definition of 3rd inner mixin
...
(defclass collab-this () ())
(defmethod first-role ((self collab-this))
  (cons (find-class 'first-dummy) (call-next-method)))
                                ; Encapsulate class as method
(defmethod second-role ((self collab-this))
  (cons (find-class 'second-dummy) (call-next-method)))
(defmethod third-role ((self collab-this))
  (cons (find-class 'third-dummy) (call-next-method)))
```
(5)

Note that, just like in the C++ example, the root of the outer inheritance hierarchy must be concrete (i.e., not parameterized). In the above, this means that its role-defining methods should not use `call-next-method`. Composition of mixin layers is a simple matter of using CLOS multiple inheritance (same as with regular mixins). For instance, if we have mixin layers `first-collab`, `second-collab`, `third-collab`, their composition is defined as:

```
(defclass composition
  (first-collab second-collab third-collab) (...))
(setq composite-obj (make-instance 'composition))
```

Note that role-defining methods (like `first-role`, `second-role`, etc. in (5)) return a list of all inner mixins. Constructing the inner classes is then a simple matter of creating classes programmatically using this list. This is a standard CLOS technique (e.g., see function `find-programmatic-class` in [18], p.68). For instance, creating the first of the inner classes could be expressed as:

```
(setq first-inner-class (find-programmatic-class
                            (first-role composite-obj)))
```

The above idiom should be taken as a proof-of-concept, rather than an optimal implementation of mixin layers in CLOS.

References

[1] O. Agesen, S. Freund, and J. Mitchell, "Adding Type Parameterization to the Java Language", *OOPSLA 1997*, 49-65.

[2] D. Batory and S. O'Malley, "The Design and Implementation of Hierarchical Software Systems with Reusable Components", *ACM TOSEM*, October 1992.

[3] D. Batory, V. Singhal, M. Sirkin, and J. Thomas, "Scalable Software Libraries", *ACM SIGSOFT* 1993.

[4] D. Batory and J. Thomas, "P2: A Lightweight DBMS Generator", *Journal of Intelligent Information Systems*, 9, 107-123 (1997).

[5] D. Batory and B.J. Geraci, "Component Validation and Subjectivity in GenVoca Generators", *IEEE Transactions on Software Engineering*, February 1997, 67-82.

[6] D. Batory, B. Lofaso, and Y. Smaragdakis, "JTS: Tools for Implementing Domain-Specific Languages", to appear at the *5th International Conference on Software Reuse (ICSR '98)*. See `ftp://ftp.cs.utexas.edu/pub/predator/jts.ps`.

[7] K. Beck and W. Cunningham, "A Laboratory for Teaching Object-Oriented Thinking", *OOPSLA 1989*, 1-6.

[8] G. Bracha and W. Cook, "Mixin-Based Inheritance", *ECOOP/OOPSLA 90*, 303-311.

[9] G. Bracha and D. Griswold, "Extending Smalltalk with Mixins", *Workshop on Extending Smalltalk* at OOPSLA 96. See `http://java.sun.com/people/gbracha/mwp.html`.

[10] L. Cardelli and P.Wegner, On Understanding Types, Data Abstraction, and Polymorphism, *Computing Surveys*, 17(4): Dec 1985, 471-522.

[11] M. Flatt, S. Krishnamurthi, M. Felleisen, "Classes and Mixins". ACM *Symposium on Principles of Programming Languages*, 1998 (PoPL 98).

[12] E. Gamma, R. Helm, R. Johnson, and J. Vlissides, *Design Patterns: Elements of Reusable Object-Oriented Software*. Addison-Wesley, 1994.

[13] W. Harrison and H. Ossher, "Subject-Oriented Programming (A Critique of Pure Objects)". *OOPSLA 1993*, 411-428.

[14] R. Helm, I. Holland, and D. Gangopadhyay, "Contracts: Specifying Behavioral Compositions in Object-Oriented Systems". *OOPSLA 1990*, 169-180.

[15] I. Holland, "Specifying Reusable Components Using Contracts", *ECOOP 92*, 287-308.

[16] JavaSoft, "Inner Classes Specification", from `http://java.sun.com/products/jdk/1.1/docs/`.

[17] R. Johnson and B. Foote, "Designing Reusable Classes", *Journal of Object-Oriented Programming*, 1(2): June/July 1988, 22-35.

[18] G. Kiczales, J. des Rivieres, and D. G. Bobrow, *The Art of the Metaobject Protocol*. MIT Press, 1991.

[19] G. Kiczales, J. Lamping, A. Mendhekar, C. Maeda, C. Lopes, J. Loingtier, and J. Irwin, "Aspect-Oriented Programming", *ECOOP 97*, 220-242.

[20] O. L. Madsen and B. Møller-Pedersen, "Virtual classes: A powerful mechanism in object-oriented programming", *OOPSLA 1989*, 397-406.

[21] O. L. Madsen, B. Møller-Pedersen, and K. Nygaard, *Object-Oriented Programming in the BETA Programming Language*. Addison-Wesley, 1993.

[22] M. Mezini, "Dynamic Object Evolution without Name Collisions", *ECOOP 97*, 190-219.

[23] R. Milner, "A Theory of Type Polymorphism in Programming", *Journal of Computer and System Sciences*, 17:Dec 1978, 348-375.

[24] T. Montlick, "Implementing Mixins in Smalltalk", *The Smalltalk Report*, July 1996.

[25] A. Myers, J. Bank and B. Liskov, "Parameterized Types for Java", ACM *Symposium on Principles of Programming Languages*, 1997 (PoPL 97).

[26] M. Odersky and P. Wadler, "Pizza into Java: Translating theory into practice", ACM *Symposium on Principles of Programming Languages*, 1997 (PoPL 97).

[27] C. Prehofer, "Feature-Oriented Programming: A Fresh Look at Objects", *ECOOP* 97, 419-443.

[28] T. Reenskaug, E. Anderson, A. Berre, A. Hurlen, A. Landmark, O. Lehne, E. Nordhagen, E. Ness-Ulseth, G. Oftedal, A. Skaar, and P. Stenslet, "OORASS: Seamless Support for the Creation and Maintenance of Object-Oriented Systems", *Journal of Object-Oriented Programming*, 5(6): October 1992, 27-41.

[29] J. Rumbaugh, "Getting Started: Using use cases to capture requirements", *Journal of Object-Oriented Programming*, 7(5): Sep 1994, 8-23.

[30] L. Seiter, J. Palsberg, and K. Lieberherr, "Evolution of Object Behavior using Context Relations", *ACM SIGSOFT* 1996.

[31] V. Singhal, "A Programming Language for Writing Domain-Specific Software System Generators", Ph.D. Dissertation, Department of Computer Sciences, University of Texas at Austin, August 1996.

[32] Y. Smaragdakis and D. Batory, "DiSTiL: a Transformation Library for Data Structures", *USENIX Conference on Domain-Specific Languages (DSL 97)*.

[33] Y. Smaragdakis and D. Batory, "Implementing Reusable Object-Oriented Components", to appear at the *5th International Conference on Software Reuse (ICSR '98)*. See `ftp://ftp.cs.utexas.edu/pub/predator/icsrtemp.ps`.

[34] P. Steyaert, W. Codenie, T. D'Hondt, K. De Hondt, C. Lucas, and M. Van Limberghen, "Nested Mixin-Methods in Agora", *ECOOP 93*, 197-219.

[35] B. Stroustrup, *The C++ Programming Language, 3rd Ed.*, Addison-Wesley, 1997.

[36] K. Thorup, "Genericity in Java with Virtual Types", *ECOOP 97*, 444-471.

[37] M. VanHilst and D. Notkin, "Using C++ Templates to Implement Role-Based Designs", *JSSST International Symposium on Object Technologies for Advanced Software*, Springer-Verlag, 1996, 22-37.

[38] M. VanHilst and D. Notkin, "Using Role Components to Implement Collaboration-Based Designs". *OOPSLA 1996*.

[39] M. VanHilst and D. Notkin, "Decoupling Change From Design", *ACM SIGSOFT* 1996.

[40] M. VanHilst, "Role-Oriented Programming for Software Evolution", Ph.D. Dissertation, University of Washington, Computer Science and Engineering, 1997.

Classifying Inheritance Mechanisms in Concurrent Object-Oriented Programming

Lobel Crnogorac[1], Anand S. Rao[2], and Kotagiri Ramamohanarao[1]

[1] Department of Computer Science, The University of Melbourne, Parkville, Victoria 3052, Australia, {lobel,rao}@cs.mu.oz.au
[2] Mitchell Madison Group, Level 49, 120 Collins Street, Melbourne, Victoria 3000, Australia, anand_rao@mmg.net.au

Abstract. Inheritance is one of the key concepts in object-oriented programming. However, the usefulness of inheritance in concurrent object-oriented programming is greatly reduced by the problem of inheritance anomaly. Inheritance anomaly is manifested by undesirable re-definitions of inherited code. The problem is aggravated by the lack of a formal analysis, with a multitude of differing proposals and conflicting opinions causing the current state of research, and further directions, to be unclear. In this paper we present a formal analysis of inheritance anomaly in concurrent object-oriented programming. Starting from a formal definition of the problem we develop a taxonomy of the anomaly, and use it to classify the various proposals. As a result, the major ideas, trends and limitations of the various proposals are clearly exposed. Formal analysis of the anomaly and a thorough exposition of its causes and implications are the pre-requisites for a successful integration of inheritance and concurrency.

1 Introduction

Inheritance is one of the key concepts in object-oriented programming (OOP). It is a widely used methodology for code re-use in sequential object-oriented programming. In recent years, the concepts from OOP have been applied in a concurrent setting, leading to the emergence of concurrent object-oriented programming (COOP) [2]. In its full generality the COOP paradigm allows inter-object concurrency (multiple objects existing concurrently) and intra-object concurrency (multiple threads inside an object). It was found that most OOP concepts (*e.g.*, encapsulation) could be naturally integrated into COOP. However, the integration of inheritance and COOP has not been smooth. One of the main problems with inheritance in COOP is the *inheritance anomaly* [22–25]. Inheritance anomaly arises when additional methods of a subclass cause undesirable re-definitions of the methods in the superclass. Instead of being able to incrementally add code in a subclass the programmer may be required to re-define some inherited code, thus the benefits of inheritance are lost.

Inheritance anomalies have been researched extensively, but they are still only vaguely defined and often misunderstood. There is a wealth of language proposals in the literature trying to solve the problem, but almost no formal work has been done. For comparison purposes the proposals were usually evaluated on a set of standard examples introduced by Matsuoka and Yonezawa [23]. Such informal approach cannot guarantee that some examples of anomaly are not omitted from consideration. Many proposals claim to have solved the anomaly, however there is a serious lack of agreement due to a large variety of informal definitions used by different researchers, and to the lack of a formal framework. Consequently, there is no satisfactory method of comparing the various language proposals.

Inheritance anomaly is most commonly believed to be caused by the interference between inheritance and concurrency. In this paper we adopt a much more precise view of the cause of the problem, building upon our previous work [11] which presents the formal definition of the inheritance anomaly. As a result it becomes clear that concurrency is not the real cause of inheritance anomaly, implying that the problem may also arise in other paradigms.

Starting from an intuitive explanation of the issues involved (Section 2) we present our formal framework (Section 3). Inheritance anomaly is defined in this framework as a relationship between (behavioural) subtyping and inheritance. This general definition is then specialised to a particular version of the anomaly which has been the focus of most research in COOP literature. The main contribution of this paper is the development of a formal taxonomy for this particular version of inheritance anomaly (Section 4), thus enabling us to classify many of the languages proposed in literature (Section 6). Inheritance anomaly is highly language dependent. However, by using our framework we are able to avoid most of the language dependent issues in the different proposals. As a result, our comparison yields a clear, uniform view of the current state of research showing that the main progress has been made in the area of languages that do not allow intra-object concurrency. The version of inheritance anomaly analysed in this paper has motivated a large number of proposed solutions. However, we prove that an ideal solution does not exist. We also present some examples of the anomalies which have not been considered in literature before, and discuss the major ideas used to minimise the effects of the anomaly (Section 5).

Finally, our framework is general and can be easily used to investigate other versions of the anomaly in COOP, as well as to investigate inheritance anomaly in paradigms other than COOP [3,10].

2 Inheritance anomaly

In this section we present an intuitive explanation of the inheritance anomaly problem. We do not consider any particular language, relying only on the most basic notions of object-oriented programming such as methods, classes, class-based inheritance and subtyping.

2.1 Incremental inheritance hierarchies in OOP

Inheritance is one of the major components of the OOP paradigm. It is a syntactic mechanism for code re-use (or code sharing). The main benefits of inheritance

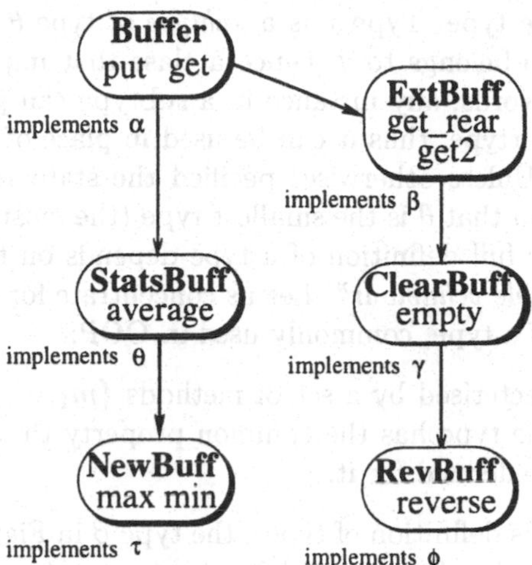

Fig. 1. An incremental inheritance hierarchy. The arrows represent inheritance and point from the superclass to the subclass.

are the reduction of the implementational effort, since new classes can be developed by starting from already written and tested classes, as well as the improved flexibility of the software system, since changes to one class are automatically reflected in its subclasses.

Consider the inheritance hierarchy in Figure 1. Class *Buffer* is a *superclass* of class *ExtBuff*. Class *ExtBuff* is a *subclass* of class *Buffer*, and a superclass of class *ClearBuff*. The interesting property of this inheritance hierarchy is that all subclasses are derived from their superclasses only by adding new methods. None of the subclasses re-define any of their inherited methods. For example, class *ExtBuff* defines new methods *get_rear* and *get2*, and inherits the methods *put* and *get*. In our terminology we refer to this type of inheritance hierarchy as an *incremental inheritance hierarchy*. Incremental inheritance hierarchies exhibit maximum code re-use. A superclass in such a hierarchy is completely re-used by its subclass, since none of its methods are re-defined in the subclass.

The inheritance relationship between classes also suggests another relationship. If class B inherits from class A, it will necessarily have at least all the variables and methods that class A has. Therefore, whenever we require an instance of class A, an instance of class B would do equally well. Note that in this case we are concerned with the relationship between the external behaviour of instances, rather than with the internal structure of a class (as in the case of inheritance). A *type* is a set of instances that have some "*externally observable behaviour*" in common [4]. Hence, any instance belonging to the type can produce the common behaviour. A class implements a type if each instance of the class belongs to the type. Type τ is a ***subtype*** of type θ if $\tau \subseteq \theta$. An instance belonging to τ also belongs to θ, hence a class that implements τ also implements θ. In other words, any instance in a subtype can produce the behaviour common to its supertype, thus it can be used in place of an instance belonging to the supertype. Unless otherwise specified the statement "*A implements θ*" will be used to mean that θ is the smallest type (the most specialised type) that A implements. The full definition of a type depends on the precise meaning of "*externally observable behaviour*". Let us concentrate for the moment on a very simple definition of a type, commonly used in OOP:

> A type is characterised by a set of methods $\{m_1, \ldots, m_n\}$. Every instance belonging to the type has the common property that at least the methods $m_1, \ldots, m_n$ are defined for it.

According to this definition of types, the type β in Figure 1, characterised by the methods {*put*, *get*, *get_rear*, *get2*} is a subtype of type α since each instance in β (*e.g.*, an instance of *ExtBuff*), is also an instance in α. That is, *ExtBuff* implements β and α, but β is the smallest type that it implements. In order to keep the definition of a type simple we ignore the issue of method parameters - this can be easily extended.

Definition 1. A *chain* is a finite sequence of types $\alpha \supseteq \beta \supseteq \gamma \ldots$ ∎

A chain is a set of types in which there are no unrelated types, all types are related by the subtyping relation. The set $\{\beta, \theta\}$ in Figure 1 is not a chain since each type requires a method that the other type does not have. When a system is designed as a chain of subtypes this generally means that re-usable abstractions have been discovered, by factoring out the common properties into re-usable components. Missing abstractions, overly specialised components, or deficient object modelling may prevent the system from being designed as a chain of subtypes, thus seriously impairing the re-usability of that collection of classes. Also, subtype chains are usually much easier to understand than more complicated relationships that exist in other subtype hierarchies. A chain of subtypes can be understood through a single conceptual relationship - *specialisation*. Every subtype corresponds to a specialisation of its supertype.

Observation 1 *Every path in an incremental inheritance hierarchy implements a chain of subtypes.*

In Figure 1 *ExtBuff* implements β which is a subtype of α, *ClearBuff* implements γ which is a subtype of β etc. Whenever a subclass adds new methods, then the type implemented by the subclass is necessarily a subtype of the type implemented by its superclass.[1]

Observation 2 *Every chain of subtypes can be implemented by an incremental inheritance hierarchy.*

[1] Actually, for this definition of a type, every path in any inheritance hierarchy (as long as the deletion of methods is disallowed) defines a chain of subtypes.

The second observation is the converse of the first one. Given a chain of subtypes $\alpha \supseteq \beta \supseteq \gamma \ldots$, it is always possible to construct an incremental inheritance hierarchy with the root superclass implementing the type α, its subclass implementing the type β etc.

Observations 1 and 2 together imply that the notions of incremental inheritance and subtyping are interchangeable. The two observations trivially hold for our simple definition of a type. However, with slightly different definitions of a type the two observations do not necessarily hold. With a more restrictive definition (in which the subclass needs to satisfy more conditions in order to implement a subtype) Observation 1 is less likely to hold. For example, Observation 1 was found not to hold in the context of recursive types [8] (with contravariant, *i.e.*, argument occurrences of *self*), which uses a more restrictive definition. Adopting a less restrictive definition of a type (*e.g.*, a definition that includes contravariance/covariance rules) may invalidate Observation 2, since there are many more subtype chains, and some of them may not be implementable by incremental inheritance hierarchies. The work on behavioural subtyping [4, 19] examines the different notions of a type in OOP.

2.2 Inheritance anomaly in COOP

Concurrent object-oriented programming (COOP) paradigm introduces the concept of an *active* object. Most commonly an active object has its own thread of control, unlike objects in OOP which are *passive*. The model of an active object in COOP is most commonly based on the *actor* model [1], in which each object maintains a *mail queue* for receiving messages. Concurrency implies the need for synchronisation, without which the state of an active object may become inconsistent. Therefore, COOP introduces the notion of *interface control*, an entity (possibly a separate thread of execution, or a locking mechanism) that controls which methods are allowed to proceed and execute, and which methods are suspended. Messages initially enter the mail queue of an object, and are suspended there until the interface control allows them to proceed. Interface control is said to enforce concurrency (or synchronisation) constraints.

Example 1. Consider the class *Buffer* from Figure 1 in the context of COOP. Method *put* stores an element, while *get* removes an element. In order to maintain consistency the interface control of *Buffer* needs to constrain *put* to be acceptable only when the object is not full. Similarly, *get* is constrained to be acceptable only when the object is not empty. The notation $\langle m_1, \ldots, m_n \rangle$ is used to denote a sequence of accepted messages $m_1, \ldots, m_n$. Assuming an instance of *Buffer* starts off being empty, the sequence $\langle put, put, get \rangle$ is a valid sequence of the object while $\langle put, get, get, put, get \rangle$ is not. ■

Suppose that we characterise a type by a set of message sequences $\{u_1, \ldots, u_k\}$. Every instance belonging to this type has the property that at least each u_i is a valid sequence of the instance. If $\tau \subseteq \theta$ then each instance in τ is also an element of θ, and therefore is capable of accepting the set of message sequences common to θ. Hence, any instance from τ can be used in place of an instance from θ, without any observable change in the resulting behaviour.

Clearly, the two observations from Section 2.1 hold without change in COOP, if a type is simply characterised by a set of methods. However, in the context of COOP Observation 1 holds for a different, more restrictive notion of a type, in which a type is characterised by a set of message sequences. Consider the class *ExtBuff* (Figure 1) in the context of COOP. *ExtBuff* incrementally adds new methods *get_rear* and *get2* to class *Buffer*. Immediately we observe that any valid sequence of an instance of *Buffer* is also a valid sequence of an instance of *ExtBuff*. This holds because if we only send messages *put* and *get* to an instance of *ExtBuff* then this instance is indistinguishable from an instance of *Buffer*. Therefore, *ExtBuff* implements a subtype of the type implemented by *Buffer*. Naturally, an instance of *ExtBuff* may also have many more additional valid sequences involving all four of its methods, thus extending the behaviour defined by class *Buffer*. Therefore, in COOP a subclass in an incremental inheritance hierarchy is related to its superclass by an even stronger relationship (based on the sequences of message acceptances) than the simple relationship based on sets of methods.

The problem of *inheritance anomaly* arises in COOP because for many COOP languages Observation 2 does not hold with the stronger notion of a type. We proceed with an example.

2.3 An example of inheritance anomaly

Consider Figure 2, which illustrates an implementation of the concurrent *Buffer* class. This implementation uses the concept of *method guards*, which are Boolean conditions of the form "`method` *method_name* `when` *guard*" [12,23]. A message is acceptable only if the guard of the corresponding method evaluates to *true*. The *Buffer* class shown in Figure 2 implements the synchronisation constraints discussed in Example 1. Suppose that we wish to implement a new type λ characterised by the following property:

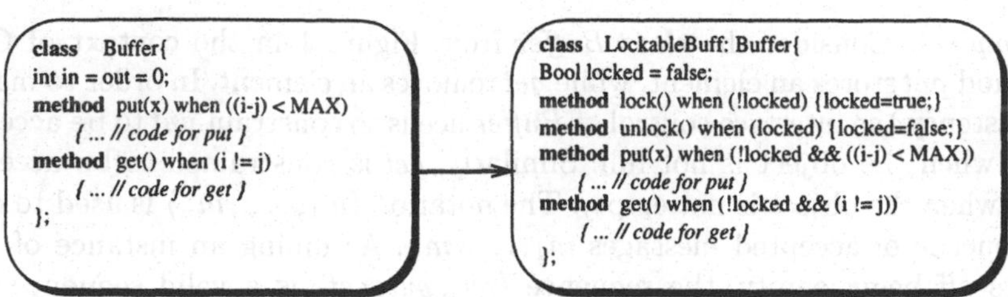

Fig. 2. An example of inheritance anomaly

Any instance belonging to λ is capable of accepting any message sequence in the set that characterises α (the type of *Buffer*). Furthermore, at any moment an instance belonging to λ is capable of accepting a message *lock*, which must be followed by an acceptance of *unlock*, unless it is the final message of the sequence.

Informally, an instance belonging to λ behaves like an instance of *Buffer*, but it can also be locked, thus becoming incapable of accepting any message except *unlock*. After being unlocked the instance again behaves like an instance of *Buffer*. We have $\lambda \subseteq \alpha$ since any instance in λ satisfies the characteristic property of α. Ideally, we would like to implement the chain $\alpha \supseteq \lambda$ as an incremental inheritance hierarchy, by constructing *LockableBuff* as another subclass of *Buffer* which inherits the complete specification of *Buffer* without any re-definitions. Simply adding the methods *lock* and *unlock* does not implement the desired subtype (*e.g.*, *put* could still be accepted after the message *lock*), leading to a complete re-write of the inherited methods. This is an example of inheritance anomaly since the two-class hierarchy shown in Figure 2 is not an incremental hierarchy. The benefits of inheritance are lost since all the inherited methods must be re-written. This example (introduced originally in [23]) shows the difficulties encountered when a simple, natural approach of method guards is chosen. The problems arising from inheritance anomalies are numerous.

Firstly, the total amount of code required to implement the desired subtype is much larger than necessary.

Secondly, if the methods of *Buffer* need to be re-implemented (*e.g.*, in order to improve efficiency), then this change is not reflected in *LockableBuff* unless the methods *put* and *get* are re-implemented in *LockableBuff* as well. Hence, re-implementation is not localised. Changes that should be local thus become spread all through the hierarchy in presence of an anomaly.[2]

Thirdly, inheritance anomaly increases the effort of making functionality changes to a system. It is well known that user needs are rarely stable. Additional functionality has to be constantly integrated into existing applications, and the existing functionality needs to be constantly improved. Suppose that we wish to add a new method *numElems* (returns the current number of elements) to each class of the hierarchy in Figure 1. This can be achieved by simply adding *numElems* to the definition of *Buffer*. This change is reflected in the whole hierarchy. However, suppose that we wish to add the *lock*/*unlock* capabilities to each class in Figure 1. This cannot be achieved by simply re-writing *Buffer* into *LockableBuff*. Rather, it is necessary to re-write every class of the hierarchy. Figure 3a shows one such re-implementation. Again, instead of just making local changes we are forced to spread the changes all through the hierarchy.

Fourthly, inheritance anomaly reduces the re-usability of classes. In principle, instead of re-writing the class *Buffer* into *LockableBuff* it is possible to achieve the same effect by letting the class *Buffer* inherit from a new root class *Lock*

[2] Languages that do not enforce encapsulation with respect to subclasses (including the simple illustrative language in Figure 2) have even more problems since subclass methods may depend on the implementational details of the superclass [28].

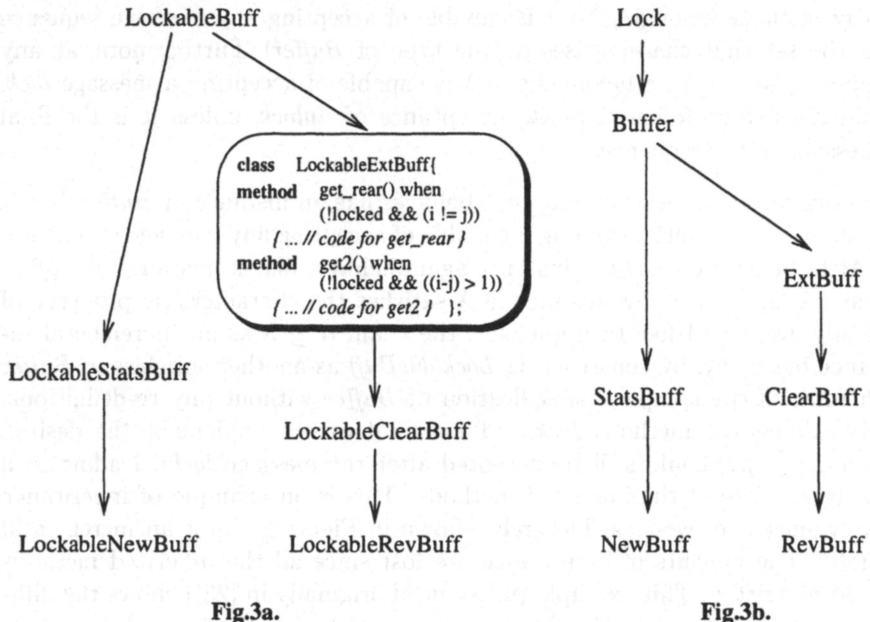

Fig. 3. The effects of the anomaly on inheritance hierarchies

(Figure 3b). The class *Lock* is a re-usable component which can be used in exactly the same way in numerous other hierarchies.[3] However, due to the occurrence of inheritance anomaly, in many languages we are forced to re-write every class of the hierarchy after adding *Lock* as the new root class. Thus, the smooth evolution of the hierarchy is prevented. The burden on the programmer increases, since the programmer is forced to check whether re-definitions are required, even when the anomaly does not occur. The problems become even more serious in the context of compiled libraries, where the programmer may have no access to the code, and is therefore unable to implement the re-definitions.

Inheritance anomaly is a serious problem which has a large impact on the implementation and evolution of a software system. It is crucial that a thorough, formal analysis of the problem is undertaken, before attempting to propose a solution. In the next section we formalise the notions of incremental inheritance, behavioural subtyping and inheritance anomaly.

3 Formal framework

In this section we present a formal framework of inheritance and behavioural subtyping, developed initially in [11]. Inheritance anomaly is defined as a relation-

[3] The problems may arise if the inheritance hierarchy already contains methods *lock* or *unlock*. Thus, the orthogonality of functionalities is required.

ship (informally expressed by Observation 2) between incremental inheritance hierarchies and behavioural subtyping.

3.1 Modelling inheritance as a transition relation

An inheritance mechanism defines the way a new class can be obtained by reusing code from an existing class. A general inheritance mechanism allows new methods to be added, the inherited methods to be re-defined or omitted. An inheritance mechanism of a language is usually given by defining the semantics of its inheritance operator [9]. We take a different approach. We formalise the inheritance mechanism of an arbitrary language as a transition relation on the set of classes. A pair of classes forms a transition if the second class can be derived from the first by employing the inheritance mechanism. Expressing all inheritance mechanisms in terms of transition relations allows us to separate the issues of inheritance from other, language specific issues. Thus, we obtain a general, uniform view of inheritance in different COOP languages.

Method System Domains			Method System Operations		
Instances	p, q, r	$\in$ **Instance**	*class*	:	**Instance** $\rightarrow$ **Class**
Classes	P, Q, R	$\in$ **Class**	*instances*	:	**Class** $\rightarrow \mathcal{P}$(**Instance**)
Message Keys	m	$\in$ **Key**	*methods*	:	**Class** $\rightarrow$ **Key** $\rightarrow$ $\mathbf{Exp}_\perp$
Method Expressions	e, f	$\in$ **Exp**	$\mathcal{M}$	:	**Class** $\rightarrow \mathcal{P}$(**Key**)
			$\mathcal{M}(P)$	=	$\{m : methods(P)m \neq \perp\}$

Fig. 4. Method System domains and operations

We employ a variation of the method system formalism of Cook and Palsberg [9], shown in Figure 4. Method systems are a simple formalisation of object-oriented programming encompassing instances, classes, and method descriptions, which are mappings from message keys to method expressions. The operation *class* gives the class of an instance, while *instances* returns the set of all possible instances of a class. For a given class the operation *methods* maps message keys to either the corresponding expression (the method code), or to the undefined element $\perp$. The operation $\mathcal{M}$ returns the set of all defined methods for a class. The set $Exp_\perp$ is a partial order under the "*less defined than or equal to*" ordering defined as follows.

Definition 2. A *preordering* on a set is a binary relation that is reflexive and transitive. A *partial ordering* is an antisymmetric preordering. Let $e, f \in Exp_\perp$. Then, e is "*less defined than or equal to*" f, written $e \preceq f$, if either $e = \perp$ or $e = f$. We extend $\preceq$ to functions. ■

The main difference from the Cook and Palsberg's framework is that we do not allow a class to inherit from another class. That is, inheritance is not a part of our method system formalism. Rather, we capture a language with inheritance as a set of classes that can be defined in the language without using inheritance, and a transition relation between them.

Definition 3. An *inheritance mechanism* is a pair $(\mathit{Class}, \dashrightarrow)$ where $\dashrightarrow \subseteq \mathit{Class} \times \Delta \times \mathit{Class}$. An element of $\dashrightarrow$, (P, δ, Q) is called a *transition* where $P, Q \in \mathit{Class}$ and $\delta \in \Delta$. Δ is the set of syntactic entities specifying the differences between P and Q. We write $P \overset{\delta}{\dashrightarrow} Q$ for $(P, \delta, Q) \in \dashrightarrow$. Furthermore, $P \overset{\delta \in \Delta^*}{\dashrightarrow} Q$ is used to denote the reflexive and transitive closure of $\dashrightarrow$ *i.e.*, a sequence of individual transitions. Remark that overloading of the notion $P \overset{\delta}{\dashrightarrow} Q$ is harmless. ■

The transition relation $\dashrightarrow$ is a set of triples (P, δ, Q). Transitions specify how inheritance can be used to derive a new class Q from class P by specifying the differences (*e.g.*, new methods) in δ.[4] Transitions may simulate re-definitions, additions or deletions of components of classes. Hence, very general inheritance mechanisms can be modelled, including the use of *self* and *super* [9]. The sets *Class* and Δ are determined by the language being analysed. Since $Q \in \mathit{Class}$ (Q is defined without inheritance) Definition 3 assumes that everything that can be defined by means of inheritance can also be defined without it.

Example 2. The hierarchy in Figure 1 illustrates several transitions of some inheritance mechanism. We have $\mathit{Buffer} \in \mathit{Class}$. Since *ExtBuff* is defined by inheriting from *Buffer*, in our framework $\mathit{ExtBuff} \notin \mathit{Class}$. However, it is simple to construct *ExtBuff'*, a class which explicitly defines *put,get,get2* and *get_rear*. *ExtBuff'* is an element of *Class*, and it corresponds to the *fully expanded* version of *ExtBuff*. The transition is $\mathit{Buffer} \overset{get2,get\_rear}{\dashrightarrow} \mathit{ExtBuff}'$. In practice, a class specifies the transition by giving the modification δ from the superclass. ■

We now formalise the notion of an incremental inheritance hierarchy. Intuitively, every transition used in such a hierarchy must be an *incremental* transition, that is, it must only define new methods without re-defining any of the inherited methods.

Definition 4. Transition $P \overset{\delta}{\dashrightarrow} Q$ is *incremental* iff $\mathit{methods}(P) \preceq \mathit{methods}(Q)$. The subset of all incremental transitions is denoted $\dashrightarrow_I \subseteq \dashrightarrow$. ■

If $P \overset{\delta}{\dashrightarrow}_I Q$ then whenever $\mathit{methods}(P)$ maps a message key to the corresponding method expression, $\mathit{methods}(Q)$ maps the same key to the same expression also (Definition 2). Alternatively, if $\mathit{methods}(P)$ maps a key to $\perp$, then $\mathit{methods}(Q)$ maps the same key to $\perp$ or to a defined expression (thereby adding new methods).

[4] The definition of the transition relation can be extended to model multiple inheritance. We focus on single inheritance in this paper.

Example 3. All the transitions in Figure 1 are incremental. The transition from *Buffer* to *LockableBuff'* (the class constructed by expanding *LockableBuff* in Figure 2) is not incremental since the method expressions of *put* and *get* differ in the two classes (the guards are modified). Note that the definition of *LockableBuff'* is almost identical to the *LockableBuff* in Figure 2, except that *LockableBuff'* does not inherit from *Buffer*. ■

3.2 The definition of inheritance anomaly

This section presents the formal definition of inheritance anomaly. We firstly define the notion of *imp*(P), a function which returns the most specialised type that P implements. This function is firstly used to formalise Observation 1 by defining the concept of *behaviour preservation*. The definition of inheritance anomaly is then obtained by formalising Observation 2.

Definition 5. Let $(X, \leq)$ be a partially ordered set and let Y be a subset of X. An element $x \in X$ is a *lower bound* for Y iff $x \leq y$ for all $y \in Y$. A lower bound x for Y is the *greatest lower bound* for Y iff, for every lower bound x' for Y, $x' \leq x$. When it exists, we denote the greatest lower bound for Y by $\sqcap Y$. We use the following two well known results [21] in the paper: If x is a lower bound for Y and $x \in Y$, then $\sqcap Y = x$. If $\sqcap Y$ exists then it is unique. ■

Suppose that the notion of a type has been defined, and that *Types* is the set of all possible types. We now consider the smallest type implemented by a class.

Definition 6. Consider $\theta \in \textit{Types}$. Class P implements θ iff $\forall p \in \textit{instances}(P)$, $p \in \theta$. Furthermore, $\textit{imp}(P) = \sqcap\{\theta : P \text{ implements } \theta\}$. An inheritance mechanism $(\textit{Class}, \dashrightarrow)$ is *behaviour preserving* with respect to *Types* iff $P \overset{\delta}{\dashrightarrow}_I Q \implies \textit{imp}(Q) \subseteq \textit{imp}(P)$. ■

For any notion of types, *Types*, we require the existence of *imp*(P) for any class P. *imp*(P) denotes the smallest type that P implements, and it is a function since the greatest lower bound is unique. The function *imp* is not injective in general, since there are usually many different implementations of the same type. An inheritance mechanism is behaviour preserving if along any path in an incremental hierarchy the subclass is related to its superclass by the subtype relation.

Definition 7. Consider an inheritance mechanism $(\textit{Class}, \dashrightarrow)$ and $P, Q \in \textit{Class}$. Define $G_P = \{Q : P \overset{\delta \in \Delta^*}{\dashrightarrow} Q\}$. Let $I_P = \{Q : P \overset{\delta \in \Delta^*}{\dashrightarrow}_I Q\}$, $B_P = \{Q : \textit{imp}(Q) \subseteq \textit{imp}(P)\}$. Finally, let $S_P = \{\tau \in \textit{Types} : \tau \subseteq \textit{imp}(P)\}$. ■

Consider Figure 5. For each class P we define sets G_P, I_P, B_P and S_P. The set G_P is the set of all classes that can be obtained from P by repeated applications of the inheritance mechanism. Note that $G_P \subseteq \textit{Class}$, but commonly, $G_P = \textit{Class}$ since in many inheritance mechanisms we can obtain any given class from P by repeated re-definitions, deletions and additions. The set I_P is a subset of

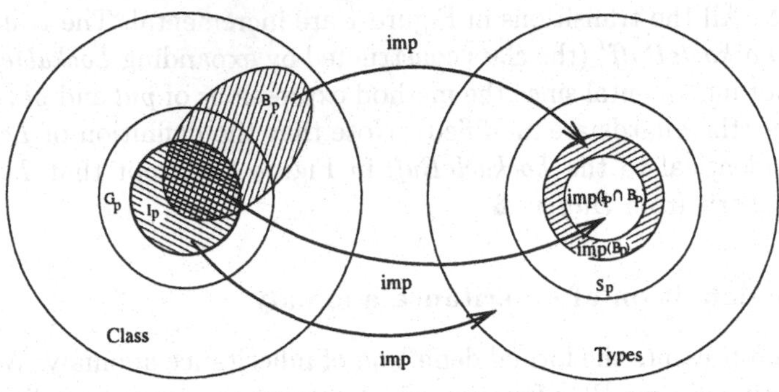

Fig. 5. The definition of inheritance anomaly

G_P which allows only incremental transitions from P. Let $imp(P) = \theta$. The set of all classes which implement subtypes of θ is denoted by B_P. In general, I_P is not a subset of B_P unless the inheritance mechanism is behaviour preserving. The intersection $(I_P \cap B_P)$ is the set of all classes which implement the subtypes of θ, and which can be incrementally obtained from P. The image of B_P under *imp* is denoted $imp(B_P)$ and it is a subset of S_P, the set of all possible subtypes of θ. In most cases we have $S_P = imp(B_P)$.

Definition 8. An inheritance mechanism $(Class, \dashrightarrow)$ is *anomaly-free* with respect to *Types* iff $\forall P \in Class, imp(I_P \cap B_P) = imp(B_P)$. ■

Consider the scenario from Figure 2, Section 2.3: The programmer has defined class *Buffer* which implements type α. The programmer envisions a (non-empty) subtype of α (type λ), containing instances that preserve and extend the behaviour of instances of *Buffer*. The programmer should be able to incrementally obtain *LockableBuff* (which implements the subtype λ) from *Buffer*. Proposition 1 shows that this scenario is a consequence of Definition 8. Of course, if the programmer does not require a subtype of α (*i.e.*, a modification of the behaviour is required) then some inherited methods may need to be re-defined.

Proposition 1. Let $P \in Class$. Inheritance mechanism $(Class, \dashrightarrow)$ is anomaly-free with respect to the given definition of *Types* iff $\forall Q \in Class$, if $imp(Q) \subseteq imp(P)$ then $\exists \delta \in \Delta^*, R \in Class$ such that $P \overset{\delta}{\dashrightarrow}_I R$ and $imp(R) = imp(Q)$.
Proof: Assume the inheritance mechanism is anomaly-free. Clearly, $Q \in B_P$. By Definition 8 $\exists R \in (I_P \cap B_P)$ such that $imp(R) = imp(Q)$. Hence, $P \overset{\delta}{\dashrightarrow}_I R$ for some $\delta \in \Delta^*$. The converse statement can be proven similarly. ■

Definition 8 is the general definition of inheritance anomaly in COOP. A particular version of this definition is obtained by providing a particular notion of *Types*. An inheritance mechanism may be anomaly-free with respect to one such version of the anomaly, while it may have anomalies with respect to another. This observation leads to an explanation of the inconsistency in the current literature. Until now, the notion of a type that causes inheritance anomaly was only given informally by researchers, through examples. Hence, the difference in these notions (*e.g.*, between [25] and [23]) leads to the different conclusions about the occurrences and the implications of inheritance anomalies.

Inheritance anomaly is most commonly believed to be caused by the interference between inheritance and concurrency. However, this view does not generalise well. For example, inheritance anomalies have been discovered in *sequential* real-time specification languages [3]. Our formal framework allows the analysis of inheritance anomaly in different paradigms (*e.g.*, [10] presents an application in the area of agent-oriented programming).

4 Taxonomy

This section presents a formal taxonomy of the inheritance anomaly which arises when the COOP notion of a type (as discussed in Section 2.2) is used in Definition 8. The taxonomy is then developed by considering two additional notions of a type, which are shown to define subsets of the set of all anomalies. We prove that even for a subset of all anomalies, an ideal solution does not exist in COOP, thus strengthening our previous result [11].

The main goal in this section is to ensure that all inheritance anomalies that have been considered in literature are encompassed by the taxonomy. The formal approach leads to examples of anomalies that have not been discussed in literature before, thus illustrating the disadvantages of the informal approach. Note that it is possible to develop an arbitrarily fine-grained taxonomy of the anomaly. However, this would unnecessarily complicate our effort to formally present the major trends amongst the various language proposals. We also relate our taxonomy to the three different types of anomalies identified in [23].

Trace Semantics	Derived State Semantics
$beh \quad : \ \mathbf{Instance} \to \mathcal{P}(\mathbf{Key}^*)$	$state \quad : \ \mathcal{P}(\mathbf{Key}^*) \to \mathbf{Key}^* \to \mathcal{P}(\mathbf{Key}^*)$
$bec \quad : \ \mathbf{Class} \to \mathcal{P}(\mathbf{Key}^*)$	$state(\xi)u = \begin{cases} \{z \ : \ u\hat{\ }z \in \xi\} & \text{if } u \in \xi \\ \bot & \text{otherwise} \end{cases}$
$bec(P) = \sqcap\{beh(p) \ : \ p \in instances(P)\}$	
	$States \quad : \ \mathcal{P}(\mathbf{Key}^*) \to \mathcal{P}(\mathcal{P}(\mathbf{Key}^*))$
	$States(\xi) = \{state(\xi)u \ : \ u \in \xi\}$

Fig. 6. Semantic domains and operations

For each of the three different notions of a type we require a precise statement of the behavioural property common to all instances belonging to a type. The semantic domains and operations (Figure 6) are used to formalise the behaviour of an instance. The notion of behaviour used in this paper considers an object to be a "*black box*" which either accepts, or does not accept a given message, while an external observer notes down all the message acceptances. Hence, the behaviour of an instance is a set of message sequences. Consider the trace semantics in Figure 6. Function *beh* gives the set of all possible message sequences that an instance can accept[5], while *bec* returns the behaviour of a class. The behaviour of a class is defined as the common behaviour of all of its instances. If θ is a set of instances then the notation $\sqcap_{beh}\theta$ denotes the greatest lower bound of the behaviours of instances in θ, *i.e.*, $\sqcap\{beh(p) : p \in \theta\}$. We use the formalism of *traces* [16] to manipulate message sequences. A trace $u \in Key^*$ is a finite sequence of messages. *Concatenation* constructs a trace from a pair of traces u and v by putting them together in that order. The result is denoted $u\hat{\ }v$. *Head* of a trace u is the first symbol in u, and is denoted u_0.

Definition 9. Let $\xi, \zeta \in \mathcal{P}(Key^*)$. Then, $\xi \sqsubseteq_T \zeta$ iff $\xi \subseteq \zeta$ and $\forall u \in \zeta, u = v\hat{\ }z$ for some $v \in \xi$ and for some z (possibly empty) such that the symbol z_0 (if it exists) never occurs in ξ. Non-empty set of instances θ is an element of $Types_T$ iff $\forall p \in \theta, \sqcap_{beh}\theta \sqsubseteq_T beh(p)$. Furthermore, if $q \in Instance$ such that $\sqcap_{beh}\theta \sqsubseteq_T beh(q)$ then $q \in \theta$. ∎

Definition 9 states that a set of instances θ is a type, characterised by $\sqcap_{beh}\theta$, if and only if every instance in θ can accept at least all the message sequences in $\sqcap_{beh}\theta$. An instance in θ may also accept some additional sequences. However, such an additional trace of the instance must start with a trace v from $\sqcap_{beh}\theta$ until a new message z_0 (that never occurs in $\sqcap_{beh}\theta$) is accepted by the instance. Thus, an instance belonging to θ behaves identically to $\sqcap_{beh}\theta$ until it accepts a new message, after which it produces some additional functionality. Furthermore, θ is the set of *all* instances satisfying the characteristic property of θ.

Example 4. *bec*(*Buffer*) $\sqsubseteq_T$ *bec*(*LockableBuff'*) since *bec*(*LockableBuff'*) contains the same traces as *bec*(*Buffer*) (if the observer is not sending *lock*/*unlock* messages), but it also contains additional traces involving *lock*/*unlock*, all of which start with some trace from *bec*(*Buffer*). For instance, the trace $\langle put, put, lock, unlock, get\rangle$ is such an additional trace which starts with the trace $\langle put, put\rangle$ from *bec*(*Buffer*). Similarly, the trace $\langle lock, unlock, put\rangle$, which starts with the empty trace from *bec*(*Buffer*), is a trace in *bec*(*LockableBuff'*). ∎

One limitation of the $Types_T$ definition of a type is that it does not satisfactorily capture the case when instances of the same class have different behaviour. For example, consider a class *Buffer*(n) which given an argument n, can be used to instantiate an instance that can store n elements. Under $Types_T$, the only type that this class implements is the type characterised by $\{\langle\rangle\}$ - the type which contains all instances of all classes (consider the case $n = 0$, *bec* must return $\{\langle\rangle\}$). As a consequence, the information about the common behaviour of instances of *Buffer*(n) is lost. This limitation can be avoided by refining the definition of

[5] It is assumed that this set is prefix-closed. That is, if $\langle put, put, get\rangle$ is a valid sequence, then $\langle\rangle$, $\langle put\rangle$, $\langle put, put\rangle$ are also valid sequences.

$Types_T$ (outlined in Section 7). In this section we use the simpler definition in order to focus on the taxonomy issues. Therefore, we assume that all instances of a class have the same behaviour, that is, $\forall p \in instances(P)$, $beh(p) = bec(P)$.

Proposition 2. Suppose some relation $\sqsubseteq$ captures the common property of all instances that belong to a certain type. If $\sqsubseteq$ is a preordering then $\sqcap_{beh}\theta \sqsubseteq \sqcap_{beh}\tau$ iff $\tau \subseteq \theta$. Furthermore, for any class P, $imp(P) = \theta$ exists and $\sqcap_{beh}\theta = bec(P)$.
Proof: Suppose $\sqcap_{beh}\theta \sqsubseteq \sqcap_{beh}\tau$ and consider $p \in \tau$. We have $\sqcap_{beh}\tau \sqsubseteq beh(p)$. By transitivity of $\sqsubseteq$ we obtain $\sqcap_{beh}\theta \sqsubseteq beh(p)$, and therefore $p \in \theta$. Now suppose $\tau \subseteq \theta$. Consider an instance p such that $beh(p) = \sqcap_{beh}\tau$. By reflexivity of $\sqsubseteq$ we have $p \in \tau$. Hence, $p \in \theta$ also, and $\sqcap_{beh}\theta \sqsubseteq beh(p)$. Since $beh(p) = \sqcap_{beh}\tau$ we obtain $\sqcap_{beh}\theta \sqsubseteq \sqcap_{beh}\tau$. Consider a class P and a type θ such that $\sqcap_{beh}\theta = bec(P)$. Let p be an instance of P. By reflexivity of $\sqsubseteq$ and by the assumption $bec(P) = beh(p)$, we have $\sqcap_{beh}\theta \sqsubseteq beh(p)$. Hence for any instance of P, $p \in \theta$ and therefore P implements θ. Suppose P also implements τ. Hence, $\sqcap_{beh}\tau \sqsubseteq bec(P)$ and since $\sqcap_{beh}\theta = bec(P)$ we obtain $\sqcap_{beh}\tau \sqsubseteq \sqcap_{beh}\theta$. By the previous result $\theta \subseteq \tau$. Hence, θ is a lower bound of the set $\{\tau : P \text{ implements } \tau\}$, and since it is also an element of this set, $\theta = imp(P)$. ■

Proposition 3. $\sqsubseteq_T$ is a preordering.
Proof: Suppose $\xi \sqsubseteq_T \zeta$ and $\zeta \sqsubseteq_T \omega$, where $\xi, \zeta, \omega \in \mathcal{P}(Key^*)$. Then, $\xi \subseteq \zeta$ and $\forall u \in \zeta, u = v\hat{\ }z$ for some $v \in \xi$ and for some z (possibly empty) such that the symbol z_0 (if it exists) never occurs in ξ. Clearly, $\xi \subseteq \omega$. Consider $u \in \omega$. $u = v\hat{\ }z$ for some $v \in \zeta$ and since $\xi \sqsubseteq_T \zeta$ we have $v = v_1\hat{\ }v_2$ for some $v_1 \in \xi$. Hence, $u = v_1\hat{\ }(v_2\hat{\ }z)$ and by construction the first symbol of $v_2\hat{\ }z$ never occurs in ξ. Hence, $\xi \sqsubseteq_T \omega$. Also, by the definition of $\sqsubseteq_T$ it is clearly reflexive. ■

Propositions 2 and 3 imply that for every class there exists a unique smallest type that it implements. Such a type, denoted $imp_T(P)$ is characterised by the behaviour of class P. We can now consider practical examples of inheritance anomaly with respect to $Types_T$. Consider two classes P and Q. If the most specific type implemented by Q ($imp_T(Q) \in Types_T$) is a subtype of the most specific type implemented by P then by Proposition 1 there should exist a class R that can be incrementally derived from P and which implements $imp_T(Q)$. Otherwise, an inheritance anomaly arises. It is important to examine whether our definition corresponds to the informal examples given in literature.

Example 5. In Example 4 it was noted that $bec(Buffer) \sqsubseteq_T bec(LockableBuff')$. By Proposition 2 we obtain $imp_T(LockableBuff') \subseteq imp_T(Buffer)$. Hence, in an anomaly-free inheritance mechanism there must exist a class, incrementally derivable from *Buffer*, which implements $imp_T(LockableBuff')$. However, in the language shown in Figure 2 such incremental transition cannot be written. Therefore, this is an example of inheritance anomaly. The other examples of anomalies given in literature also satisfy our definition [11]. ■

Inheritance anomaly induced by $Types_T$ is only one version of the general problem of inheritance anomaly in COOP. There are many other useful notions of a type that could be analysed, for example, a subtype may be defined to restrict the possible message sequences of the supertype. The reason inheritance anomaly induced by $Types_T$ has been the main focus of research to date is that Observation 1 holds for this notion. It was then often incorrectly assumed that Observation 2 should also hold for $Types_T$.

We now consider two subsets of the set of anomalies induced by $Types_T$. In order to formally define these two subsets we use a stronger notion of a type. We consider an object to be a "*state machine*" which evolves from its current state to a new state by accepting a message and executing the corresponding method expression. The first subset of the anomalies is obtained by requiring all instances in the same type to evolve through the same number of strongly related core states (Definition 10). Thus, all instances in the type can be considered to be implemented by very similar state machines. The second subset of the anomalies is obtained by allowing instances in the same type to evolve to additional states, but only if those states are restricted versions of core states (Definition 11).

Intuitively, the state of an object is determined by the values of its instance variables. However, this is not externally observable. Therefore, we consider a state to be the set of currently acceptable message sequences. Consider an instance p of *Buffer*. Initially, p can accept any sequence in $beh(p)$. Hence, the initial state of p is simply $beh(p)$. After accepting a message *put*, the set of acceptable message sequences changes, *e.g.*, the sequence $\langle get, put\rangle$ which was not acceptable from the initial state is now acceptable.[6] We say that p has evolved from the initial state to a new state. Note that accepting different message sequences may lead to the same state. For example, the message sequences $\langle put\rangle$, $\langle put, put, get\rangle$ and $\langle put, get, put\rangle$ all lead to the same state of p. Consider the derived state semantics in Figure 6. Function *state* takes the initial state of an instance and returns the state of the instance after it has accepted the message sequence u. The function *States*, given the initial state of an instance, returns the (possibly infinite) set of all states of the instance.

Proposition 4. Suppose $\xi, \zeta \in \mathcal{P}(Key^*)$ and $\xi \sqsubseteq_T \zeta$. Then, $\forall u \in \xi, state(\xi)u \sqsubseteq_T state(\zeta)u$.
Proof: Consider $u \in \xi$. Since $\xi \subseteq \zeta, u \in \zeta$ and $state(\zeta)u \neq \bot$. Let $t \in state(\xi)u$. Then $u\hat{}t \in \xi$ and $u\hat{}t \in \zeta$. Hence, $t \in state(\zeta)u$ and we have $state(\xi)u \subseteq state(\zeta)u$. Let $z \in state(\zeta)u$. It follows that $u\hat{}z \in \zeta$ and since $\xi \sqsubseteq_T \zeta$, $u\hat{}z = (u\hat{}z_1)\hat{}z_2$ for some $u\hat{}z_1 \in \xi$ and the first symbol of z_2 never appears in ξ. Hence, $z_1 \in state(\xi)u$. ∎

Example 6. Consider an instance p of *Buffer*. After accepting a message sequence u, p is in some state ξ. An instance q of *ExtBuff*, after accepting u is in some state ζ. Intuitively, we expect a strong relationship between the states ξ and ζ. Proposition 4 states that any message sequence acceptable from ξ is also acceptable from ζ. This must hold since *ExtBuff* implements a subtype of the type implemented by *Buffer*, and therefore must be capable of behaving like *Buffer*. However, ζ may allow some additional message sequences involving the

[6] Note that the sequence $\langle put, get, put\rangle$ is the corresponding trace which is acceptable from the initial state.

new messages *get2* and *get_rear*. In general, after accepting such an additional sequence, q may evolve to a completely new state not related to any state of p. In this example however, q never evolves to a state unrelated to p. An instance of *LockableBuff* does evolve to a new, unrelated state by accepting a message *lock*. In the resulting state messages *put* and *get* are both rejected, which is never the case for an instance of *Buffer*. ■

The first subset of the set of inheritance anomalies induced by $Types_T$ is defined by considering the restricted notion of a type in which an instance belonging to a subtype never evolves to a new, unrelated state.

Definition 10. Let $\xi, \zeta \in \mathcal{P}(Key^*)$. Then, $\xi \sqsubseteq_f \zeta$ iff $\xi \sqsubseteq_T \zeta$ and $\exists f : States(\xi) \rightarrow States(\zeta)$ such that f is a bijection. Non-empty set of instances θ is an element of $Types_f$ iff $\forall p \in \theta$, $\sqcap_{beh}\theta \sqsubseteq_f beh(p)$. Furthermore, if $q \in Instance$ and $\sqcap_{beh}\theta \sqsubseteq_f beh(q)$ then $q \in \theta$. ■

Definition 10 states that a set of instances θ is a type, characterised by $\sqcap_{beh}\theta$, if and only if θ is a type under Definition 9, and each instance in θ has the same number of states. By Proposition 4, every state of $\sqcap_{beh}\theta$ is related to a state of an instance in θ. Since the number of states is the same, it follows that every state of an instance is related to a state of $\sqcap_{beh}\theta$ as well. Hence, all instances belonging to θ behave as very similar state machines.

Proposition 5. $\sqsubseteq_f$ is a preordering. The proof is straightforward. ■

Proposition 6. The set of anomalies with respect to $Types_f$ is a subset of the set of anomalies with respect to $Types_T$.
Proof: Consider an occurrence of inheritance anomaly for classes P and Q, with respect to $Types_f$. Hence, $imp_f(Q) \subseteq imp_f(P)$ and $\nexists \delta \in \Delta^*, R \in Class$ such that $P \overset{\delta}{\dashrightarrow}_I R$ and $imp_f(R) = imp_f(Q)$. By Proposition 2 $bec(P) \sqsubseteq_f bec(Q)$. Hence, $bec(P) \sqsubseteq_T bec(Q)$ and $imp_T(Q) \subseteq imp_T(P)$. Suppose $\exists \delta' \in \Delta^*, R' \in Class$ such that $P \overset{\delta'}{\dashrightarrow}_I R'$ and $imp_T(R') = imp_T(Q)$. By Proposition 2 we have $bec(R') \sqsubseteq_T bec(Q)$ and $bec(Q) \sqsubseteq_T bec(R')$. From Definition 9 it follows that $bec(R') = bec(Q)$, and therefore $imp_f(R') = imp_f(Q)$. Hence, R' cannot exist since it would solve the anomaly with respect to $Types_f$. ■

The notion of types $Types_f$ induces a subset of the problem. It is the smallest subset that we consider in this paper, hence it is the easiest to solve. Examples of COOP languages that are not anomaly-free with respect to $Types_f$ are the languages with *centralised* interface control, and languages that use *accept sets*. Languages employing centralised interface control (*e.g.*, Eiffel// [7],POOL-I [4], [14] etc.) adopt bodies that explicitly regulate the acceptance of messages. These languages are not anomaly-free with respect to Definition 10 because centralised interface control groups all synchronisation constraints into a single body. An addition of a new method in a subclass always requires the re-definition of the body, otherwise the new method could never be executed.

Some languages that employ decentralised interface control are also not anomaly-free with respect to $Types_f$. Most of these languages have synchronisation control based on the concept of accept sets, that is, at each moment the synchronisation code specifies the set of currently acceptable methods. The set of acceptable methods changes as the object evolves, and this is typically achieved by each method explicitly specifying the next accept set.

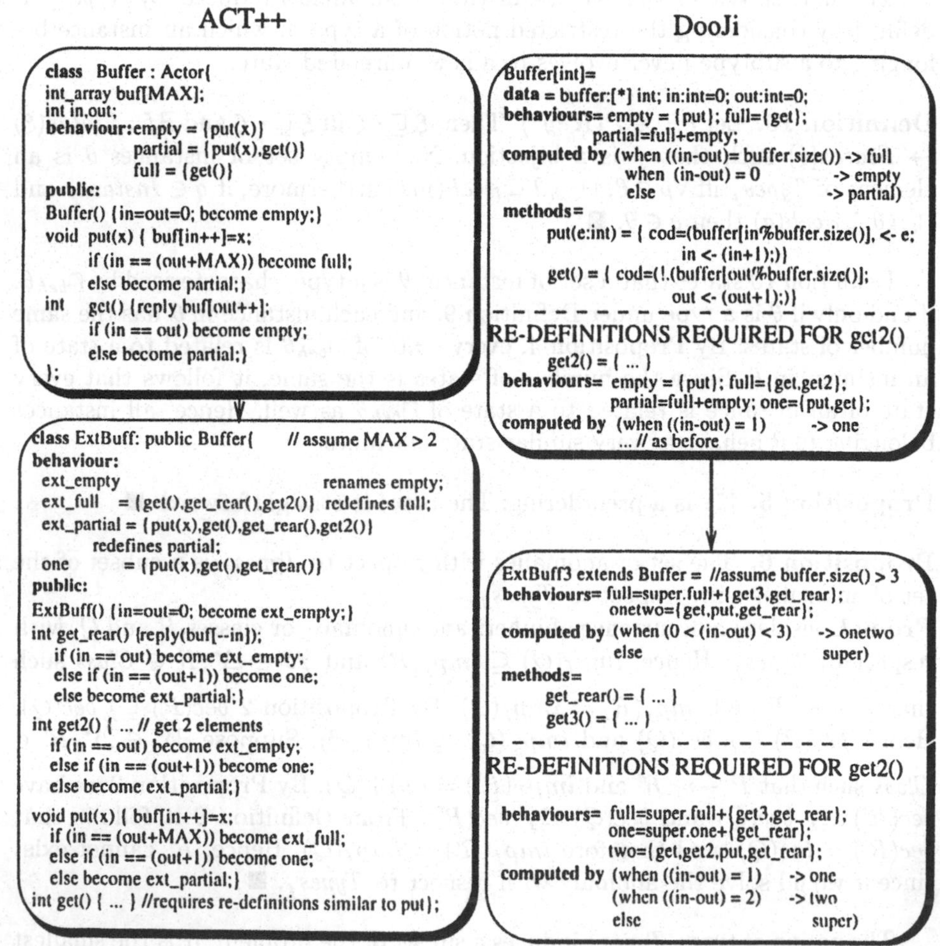

ACT++
class Buffer : Actor{
int_array buf[MAX];
int in,out;
behaviour:empty = {put(x)}
partial = {put(x),get()}
full = {get()}
public:
Buffer() {in=out=0; become empty;}
void put(x) { buf[in++]=x;
if (in == (out+MAX)) become full;
else become partial;}
int get() {reply buf[out++];
if (in == out) become empty;
else become partial;}
};
class ExtBuff: public Buffer{ // assume MAX > 2
behaviour:
ext_empty renames empty;
ext_full = {get(),get_rear(),get2()} redefines full;
ext_partial = {put(x),get(),get_rear(),get2()}
redefines partial;
one = {put(x),get(),get_rear()}
public:
ExtBuff() {in=out=0; become ext_empty;}
int get_rear() {reply(buf[--in]);
if (in == out) become ext_empty;
else if (in == (out+1)) become one;
else become ext_partial;}
int get2() { ... // get 2 elements
if (in == out) become ext_empty;
else if (in == (out+1)) become one;
else become ext_partial;}
void put(x) { buf[in++]=x;
if (in == (out+MAX)) become ext_full;
else if (in == (out+1)) become one;
else become ext_partial;}
int get() { ... } //requires re-definitions similar to put};
DooJi
Buffer[int]=
data = buffer:[*] int; in:int=0; out:int=0;
behaviours= empty = {put}; full={get};
partial=full+empty;
computed by (when ((in-out)= buffer.size()) -> full
when (in-out) = 0 -> empty
else -> partial)
methods=
put(e:int) = { cod=(buffer[in%buffer.size()], <- e;
in <- (in+1);)}
get() = { cod=(!.(buffer[out%buffer.size()];
out <- (out+1);)}
RE-DEFINITIONS REQUIRED FOR get2()
get2() = { ... }
behaviours= empty = {put}; full={get,get2};
partial=full+empty; one={put,get};
computed by (when ((in-out) = 1) -> one
... // as before
ExtBuff3 extends Buffer = //assume buffer.size() > 3
behaviours= full=super.full+{get3,get_rear};
onetwo={get,put,get_rear};
computed by (when (0 < (in-out) < 3) -> onetwo
else super)
methods=
get_rear() = { ... }
get3() = { ... }
RE-DEFINITIONS REQUIRED FOR get2()
behaviours= full=super.full+{get3,get_rear};
one=super.one+{get_rear};
two={get,get2,put,get_rear};
computed by (when ((in-out) = 1) -> one
(when ((in-out) = 2) -> two
else super)

Fig. 7. Inheritance anomalies induced by $Types_f$

Example 7. Figure 7 illustrates an example of inheritance anomaly with respect to $Types_f$ in ACT++ [17]. *ExtBuff* inherits from *Buffer* and adds new methods *get_rear* (acceptable unless the object is empty) and *get2* (which removes two elements and hence is acceptable if there are at least two elements). Each method specifies the next accept set by a `become` statement. In order to define *ExtBuff* in `ACT++` extensive re-definitions of the inherited methods *put* and *get* are required. Note that, even if *ExtBuff* only defined the new method *get_rear*, this would still be an occurrence of inheritance anomaly. The inherited methods would not require re-definitions. However, the `behaviour` block would still need to be rewritten, thus reducing the flexibility of the hierarchy (*e.g.*, a new method could not be added to *Buffer* without re-defining *ExtBuff*). The problems are reduced in `DooJi` [29] (*e.g.*, *ExtBuff* can be solved) which instead of explicit `become` statements has a `computed by` block which computes the current accept set. Suppose that instead of implementing *ExtBuff*, we define class *ExtBuff3* with a new method *get3* which removes three elements. `DooJi` succeeds in localising re-implementation and localising some changes to the hierarchy (*e.g.*, a method *numElems* could be easily added). This is achieved by the use of the "+" operator to re-define the `behaviours` block, thus preserving flexibility. However, the definition of *ExtBuff3* is not re-usable. Furthermore, suppose that we add the method *get2* to *Buffer*. Naturally, some re-definitions are required in class *Buffer*, but inheritance anomaly also causes undesirable re-definitions in *ExtBuff3*. ■

The `ACT++` example shown in Figure 7 was initially introduced by Matsuoka and Yonezawa [23], where this type of anomaly was termed the ***state-partitioning*** anomaly. It can be checked that every state-partitioning anomaly satisfies Definition 10. Hence, state-partitioning anomalies are examples of anomalies with respect to $Types_f$. It was formally proven [22] that the languages employing accept sets always suffer from the state-partitioning anomaly. It follows that all such languages are not anomaly-free with respect to $Types_f$. The anomaly induced by $Types_f$ is avoided in proposals which use *method guards*.

Proposition 7. A COOP language that employs method guards is anomaly-free with respect to $Types_f$. The proof is given in the Appendix. ■

We now define the second subset of inheritance anomalies.

Definition 11. Let $\xi, \zeta \in \mathcal{P}(Key^*)$. Then, $\xi \sqsubseteq_R \zeta$ iff $\xi \sqsubseteq_T \zeta$ and $\forall s \in States(\zeta)\ \exists s' \in States(\xi)$ such that, $\forall u \in s$ either u contains a symbol m which never appears in ξ, or $u \in s'$. Non-empty set of instances θ is an element of $Types_R$ iff $\forall p \in \theta, \sqcap_{beh}\theta \sqsubseteq_R beh(p)$. Furthermore, if $q \in Instance$ such that $\sqcap_{beh}\theta \sqsubseteq_R beh(q)$ then $q \in \theta$. ■

Definition 11 states that a set of instances θ is a type, characterised by $\sqcap_{beh}\theta$ if and only if θ is a type under Definition 9 and every state of an instance in θ is a restriction of some state of $\sqcap_{beh}\theta$. That is, an instance from θ may have more states than $\sqcap_{beh}\theta$ (reached when the newly defined messages are accepted). Each such additional state must contain traces from some state of $\sqcap_{beh}\theta$ or traces that involve the new methods.

Example 8. The example of *LockableBuff* satisfies Definition 11. The state obtained after accepting *lock* is a restriction of the corresponding state of an instance of *Buffer*, since it contains the trace $\langle\rangle$ (any state of an instance of *Buffer* contains this trace), and all the other traces involve the new message *unlock*. Another example of inheritance anomaly induced by $Types_R$ arises when a class *HistoryBuff* is derived from *Buffer*. *HistoryBuff* adds a new method *gget*, which behaves exactly like *get*, except that it cannot be executed immediately after an execution of *put*. The sequences $\langle put, put, get\rangle$ and $\langle put, get, put\rangle$ now lead to two different states, unlike in the case of *Buffer*. The state obtained by accepting the first trace is a restriction of the corresponding state of an instance of *Buffer* (it contains additional traces that involve *gget*), while the state obtained by accepting the second trace is also a restriction of the original state. Many proposals succeed in localising re-implementation for this example, but none succeed in localising changes to the hierarchy and preserving re-usability. Furthermore, many proposals deteriorate considerably when handling more complicated cases involving constraints that depend on the history of invocations (*e.g.*, [27]). The example of *HistoryBuff* was introduced in [23] as a separate type of anomaly - ***the history sensitive*** anomaly, while *LockableBuff* was named ***state-modification*** anomaly. In this paper both, *LockableBuff* and *HistoryBuff* are captured by Definition 11. Intuitively, these two examples can be seen as being related, since no methods are acceptable *after* an execution of *lock*, while *gget* is not acceptable *after* an execution of *put*. It is possible to refine our taxonomy in order to separate these two examples. ■

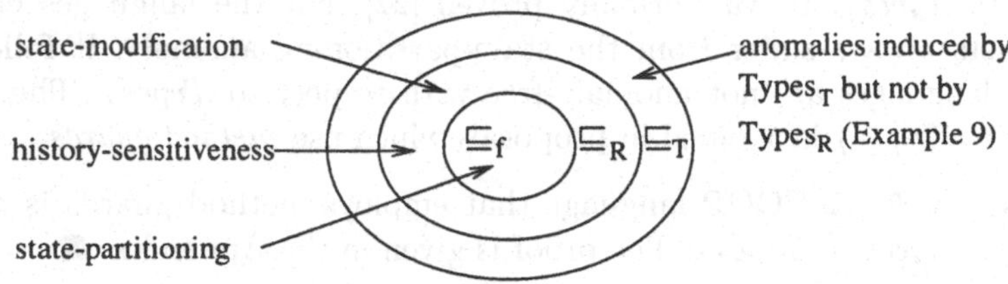

Fig. 8. The anomalies induced by the three definitions of a type

Proposition 8. $\sqsubseteq_R$ is a preordering. The proof is straightforward. ■

Similarly to Proposition 6 it can be shown that the set of anomalies induced by $Types_R$ is a subset of the set of anomalies induced by $Types_T$, leading to the hierarchy in Figure 8.

Theorem 1. Consider an inheritance mechanism $(Class, \dashrightarrow)$. If $(Class, \dashrightarrow)$ is behaviour preserving with respect to $Types_T$ then it is not anomaly-free with respect to $Types_R$. The proof is given in the Appendix. ■

Theorem 1 states that even for a subset of the anomalies (induced by $Types_R$), an anomaly-free, behaviour preserving COOP language cannot be designed. Most

COOP languages are naturally behaviour preserving with respect to $Types_T$. The problems with non-behaviour preserving languages are discussed in Section 5. It follows that an ideal solution to the version of inheritance anomaly induced by $Types_R$ (and $Types_T$) does not exist.

The third subset of the inheritance anomalies considered in this paper contains the anomalies that do not satisfy the conditions of Definition 10 or Definition 11. This type of anomaly has not been discussed in literature, but it naturally arises from our taxonomy. We present an example for illustration.

```
class ResourceManager{
int granted_A = granted_B = 0;
guards:
    guard gA   ( granted_A < max_A )
    guard gB   ( granted_B < max_B )
    guard fA   ( granted_A > 0 )
    guard fB   ( granted_B > 0 )
synchronizers:
    gA  enables  access_A;
    gB  enables  access_B;
    fA  enables  free_A;
    fB  enables  free_B;
methods:
  int access_A(request) { ... granted_A++; ... }
  int access_B(request) { ... granted_B++; ... }
  int free_A(request) { ... granted_A--; ... }
  int free_B(request) { ... granted_B--; ... }};
```

```
class PriorityAccess{
int priority = 0;
method_sets:  mset  P_OFF  #{priority_off}
              mset  P_ON   #{priority_on}
synchronizers:
  initially         enables  all-except(P_OFF);
  (priority==1)  enables  all-except(P_ON);
  (priority==0)  enables  all-except(P_OFF);
methods:  void priority_on() { ... priority=1; ... }
          void priority_off() { ... priority=0; ... }  };

class ResourceManager: PriorityAccess{
guards:  guard  gA   priority || (granted_A < max_A)
         guard  gB   priority || (granted_B < max_B)  };
  // note that if method sets were used in
  // the original definition of
  // ResourceManager, then even more
  // re-definitions would be required
```

Fig. 9. An example of the third type of anomaly

Example 9. Consider a hierarchy of resource managers which is derived from the class *ResourceManager* shown in Figure 9. This class, implemented in ABCL [23], is used to control access to a pool of two types of resources, A and B. At most *max_A* resources of type A, and at most *max_B* resources of type B can be granted at any time. Suppose that a new class *PriorityAccess* is written. This class is intended to be a re-usable class which adds two new methods: *priority_on* and *priority_off*. If we let *PriorityAccess* class be the superclass of all classes in the *ResourceManager* hierarchy then we expect the following behaviour: A client of an instance of the new *ResourceManager* class is allowed to use *priority_on*, after which all *access_A* requests disregard the *max_A* limit. The method *priority_off* resets the object to use the limit again. None of the current proposals are capable of avoiding re-definitions of the hierarchy. Figure 9 shows the re-definitions required for *ResourceManager* in ABCL. ■

Finally, we look at the problem of inheritance anomalies in the presence of internal concurrency (intra-object concurrency). Many languages allow multiple threads within an object. However, we only consider the languages that allow the programmer to specify the constraints under which methods are allowed to run concurrently. Internal concurrency is introduced by refining the definition of *Key*, the set of message keys. For each key $m \in Key$ the refined set Key_{intra} contains keys m_s (denoting the start of an invocation), and m_e (denoting the end of an invocation). Function $beh_{intra} : Instance \rightarrow \mathcal{P}(Key^*_{intra})$ returns the set of all acceptable sequences of message starts and completions.[7]

```
Type Concurrent{
Integer meth_A();
Integer meth_B();
CC:
    Bool Allow();
    Delay meth_A Until Allow();
    Delay meth_B Until Allow(); };

Class Conc_AB Implements Concurrent{
Mix   AB, CC_AB; };

Class CC_AB Controls AB
Data  Bool(CBool) allow;
CC_AB() { allow=true; ... }
Bool Allow() { return allow; }
Wrapper meth_A
  { allow := false; }
    Inner
  { allow := true; }
Wrapper meth_B
  { allow := false; }
    Inner
  { allow := true; } };
```

```
Type Concurrent2 SubtypeOf Concurrent{
Integer meth_C();
CC:
    Bool Allow_C();
    Delay meth_B Until (Allow() &&
                        Allow_C());
    Delay meth_C Until Allow_C(); };
Class Conc_ABC Implements Concurrent2{
Mix  ABC, CC_ABC; };

Class CC_ABC Controls ABC
Inherits CC_AB
Data Bool(CBool) allow_C;
CC_ABC() { allow_C=true; ... }
Bool Allow_C() { return allow_C; }
Wrapper meth_B
  { allow_C := false; }
    Inner
  { allow_C := true; }
Wrapper meth_C
  { allow_C := false; }
    Inner
  { allow_C := true; } };
```

Fig. 10. Inheritance anomaly in presence of internal concurrency - BALLOON [5]

Example 10. Consider a class *Conc_AB* which defines two mutually exclusive methods, *meth_A* and *meth_B*. Furthermore, at most one invocation of either method can be active at a time. Hence, $beh_{intra}(Conc\_AB)$ contains $\langle meth\_A_s, meth\_A_e, meth\_B_s, meth\_B_e\rangle$, but it does not contain traces $\langle meth\_A_s, meth\_B_s, meth\_B_e, meth\_A_e\rangle$ or $\langle meth\_A_s, meth\_A_s, meth\_A_e, meth\_A_e\rangle$. Consider a class *Conc_ABC* which defines a new method *meth_C*. This method can be executed concurrently with *meth_A*, but not with *meth_B*. As before, at most one invocation of *meth_C* can be active at a time. We have, $beh_{intra}(Conc\_AB) \sqsubseteq_T beh_{intra}(Conc\_ABC)$. Some additional traces are $\langle meth\_A_s, meth\_C_s, meth\_A_e, meth\_A_s, meth\_C_e, meth\_A_e\rangle$ and $\langle meth\_C_s, meth\_C_e, meth\_B_s, meth\_B_e\rangle$. ■

The definition of inheritance anomaly and the taxonomy of the anomaly developed in this section are easily generalised to include internal concurrency by simply using the new semantic operations beh_{intra}, bec_{intra}, $state_{intra}$ and $States_{intra}$. Clearly, every anomaly described until now is a special case of this

[7] Some assumptions are relevant. For example, each completion must occur after the corresponding start.

generalised notion of inheritance anomaly. Hence, internal concurrency possibly causes even more inheritance anomalies.

Example 11. Figure 10 illustrates an implementation of classes *Conc_AB* and *Conc_ABC* in BALLOON [5]. BALLOON supports a complete separation of subtyping from inheritance. Hence, types *Concurrent* and *Concurrent2* specify the concurrency control (CC block), classes *AB* and *ABC* (which are not shown) implement the sequential methods *meth_A, meth_B* and *meth_C*. Classes *CC_AB* and *CC_ABC* implement the concurrency control of the methods using synchronisation variables *allow* and *allow_C*. Finally, the classes *Conc_AB* and *Conc_ABC* are obtained by mixing the sequential methods and their concurrency control. Since $beh_{intra}(Conc\_AB) \sqsubseteq_T beh_{intra}(Conc\_ABC)$ an anomaly-free language should allow an incremental inheritance transition from *Conc_AB* to *Conc_ABC*. However, re-definitions (*Concurrent2* and *CC_ABC* cannot be derived incrementally) are required in BALLOON. Consider Figure 11, which illustrates an approach proposed in [6]. Synchronisation class *Sync_DE* allows concurrent execution of methods *D* and *E*. At most one invocation of each method can be active at a time, but the two methods may be active concurrently. Consider a subtype of the type implemented by *Sync_DE*. Instances belonging to this subtype (implemented by *Flexible_DE*) behave like instances of *Sync_DE*, but they also allow disabling and enabling of internal concurrency. This subtype cannot be implemented by incremental inheritance from *Sync_DE*, because the **allow_start** condition of all methods needs to be re-written. ■

The example of inheritance anomaly in BALLOON (Figure 10) is induced by the internal concurrency version of the notion $Types_f$. It occurs in most languages that support internal concurrency. This shows that the research into the inheritance anomaly in the context of internal concurrency is still in the initial stages, mainly due to the additional complexity which makes an informal analysis impractical.

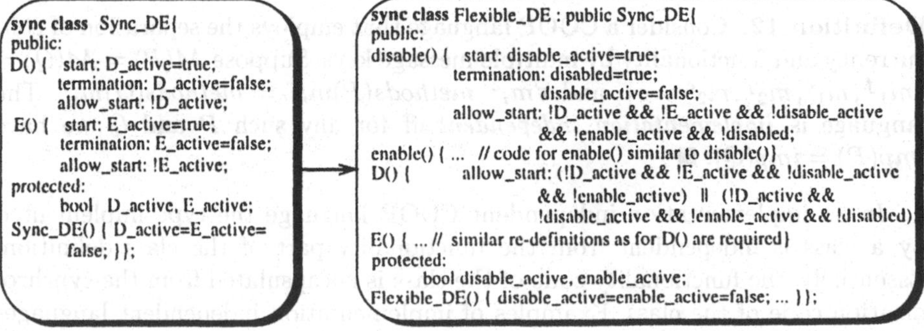

Fig. 11. The anomaly in presence of internal concurrency - synchronisation classes [6]

5 Minimising the anomaly

This section examines three major ideas that can be used to minimise the effects of inheritance anomaly. The three ideas that we consider are ***separation of concerns***, ***non-behaviour preserving inheritance***, and ***generic policies***. One of the major aims of COOP is to separate the concerns of concurrency from the functionality concerns. Then, the concurrency part of a class can be re-used separately from the functionality part of the class. Since the separation of concerns in COOP increases the possibility of re-use, it needs to be investigated whether this may lead to a reduction of the effects of the inheritance anomaly.

Example 12. Recall the implementation of ***LockableBuff*** in Figure 2. The code for ***put*** and ***get*** had to be re-written even though only the guards of the two methods required modifications. If each method is separated into a ***guard*** part, and a ***functionality*** part, then the amount of re-definition can be reduced. For instance, in the case of ***put*** the statement "**guard** ***put(x)*** `when` (***!locked ...***)" would be the only re-definition required. In the method system framework this separation of concerns is modelled by using multiple message keys for each method. Hence, $\mathcal{M}(\mathit{Buffer}) = \{\mathit{put}^c, \mathit{put}^f, \mathit{get}^c, \mathit{get}^f\}$ where $\mathit{methods}(\mathit{Buffer})\mathit{put}^c$ maps to the guard expression, while $\mathit{methods}(\mathit{Buffer})\mathit{put}^f$ maps to the functionality code. ■

Example 12 illustrates how separation of concurrency from functionality can reduce the effects of the anomaly. Note however that nothing prevents the programmer from mixing the functionality code with the concurrency code. Since guards have access to instance variables they in general depend on the implementational details of methods. Hence, re-implementing a method may lead to re-implementation of the concurrency code as well. Similarly, if concurrency issues are mixed in with the functionality code then an occurrence of inheritance anomaly may lead to unnecessary changes in the functionality code, as well as to the changes in the concurrency code. Clearly, the mixing of concurrency and functionality reduces the possibility of re-use, and it should be prevented by enforcing a complete separation of the two concerns.

Definition 12. Consider a COOP language that employs the separation of concurrency and functionality by multiple message keys. Suppose $\mathcal{M}(P) = \mathcal{M}(Q) = \{{m_1}^f, {m_1}^c, {m_2}^f, {m_2}^c, \dots\}$, and $\forall {m_i}^c\ \mathit{methods}(P){m_i}^c = \mathit{methods}(Q){m_i}^c$. The language is ***implementation independent*** iff for any such P and Q we have $\mathit{imp}(P) = \mathit{imp}(Q)$. ■

In an implementation independent COOP language the type implemented by a class is independent from the functionality part of the class definition. Essentially, the functionality code of the class is encapsulated from the synchronisation code of the class. Examples of implementation independent languages are [6, 14, 24, 26]. Some of these proposals encapsulate the concurrency issues into a separate class in order to facilitate re-use of the concurrency part. Naturally, a language may be implementation independent with respect to one notion of types, while not being implementation independent with respect to a different notion. We now show that if a language is implementation independent with respect to $Types_T$ then re-definition of the functionality code is never required.

Proposition 9. Consider a COOP language that is implementation independent with respect to $Types_T$. An inheritance anomaly in this language never requires the re-definition of the functionality part of any method.
Proof: Consider classes P, Q and suppose $imp_T(Q) \subseteq imp_T(P)$. Since we have an occurrence of inheritance anomaly it follows that $\nexists \delta \in \Delta^*, R \in Class$ such that $P \overset{\delta}{\dashrightarrow}_I R$ and $imp_T(R) = imp_T(Q)$. Let $\mathcal{M}(P) = \{m_1{}^f, m_1{}^c, \ldots, m_n{}^f, m_n{}^c\}$ and $\mathcal{M}(Q) = \{m_1{}^f, m_1{}^c, \ldots, m_n{}^f, m_n{}^c, \ldots\}$. Construct R which is identical to Q except that $methods(R)m_i{}^f = methods(P)m_i{}^f$ for $1 \leq i \leq n$. By Definition 12, $imp_T(R) = imp_T(Q)$, and by the construction of R it does not re-define any functionality code of P. ■

Hence, any language which enforces a complete separation of concurrency from functionality always avoids any re-definitions of the functionality code in presence of inheritance anomalies. This reduces the total amount of code required, and maintains the flexibility of the hierarchy under re-implementation (it does not help with localising functionality changes and with re-usability). The effects of the anomaly are reduced, but the anomaly still occurs since re-definitions of the concurrency code are still required.[8] Many proposals that claim to have solved the inheritance anomaly actually only succeed in re-using the functionality code. Solving the inheritance anomaly in our framework means re-using the whole specification of the superclass - including the synchronisation code.

The second approach we consider is a consequence of Theorem 1 which states that if an anomaly-free inheritance mechanism exists then it must be non-behaviour preserving. In such a mechanism addition of new methods does not necessarily lead to a subtype of the original type. In practice, this means that the mechanism has access to, and is capable of changing meta-level information.

Example 13. Recall the example of class *HistoryBuff* from Example 8. Suppose that in some language it is possible to write a re-usable class *History.* Any subclass of *History* will have all the invocations of all of its methods logged. Then, *HistoryBuff* can be incrementally defined from *Buffer* (which now is a subclass of *History*) by defining the new method *gget.* The guard of *gget* would use some constructs introduced by *History, e.g.,* `int` *gget()* `when` (*last_invocation()* != *put*). Such a language would solve this particular inheritance anomaly, but the implementation of *History* would most likely add a non-practical overhead. ■

Non-behaviour preserving inheritance mechanisms are more expressive than behaviour preserving inheritance mechanisms, and therefore they are likely to handle more inheritance anomalies. However, there are very few proposals which employ non-behaviour preserving concepts. This is a consequence of very serious

[8] It is still possible to mix in the functionality code into the concurrency code, but this can be prevented by restricting the expressiveness of the concurrency component, or by using different languages for the different components [14].

problems that arise from such mechanisms. Firstly, non-behaviour preserving mechanisms do not guarantee the subtype relationship. Hence, for each case it must be manually checked (undecidable in general) whether the subclass implements a subtype. Secondly, the efficiency issues are likely to make such proposals prohibitively expensive. However, more research into static analysis techniques and into optimisation techniques is needed before a definite answer can be given concerning non-behaviour preserving inheritance mechanisms.

The third approach towards reducing the effects of the anomaly is to build libraries of generic synchronisation/concurrency policies [20, 24]. Then, instead of attempting to inherit the concurrency part of its superclass, a subclass may simply instantiate a different policy. Generic policies are especially useful in the context of internal concurrency, where there is a small number of frequently used policies (*e.g.*, ReadersWriter, ReadersPriority etc.).

6 Classification

In this section we present the results of classifying the various proposals from literature. Firstly, the languages are compared with respect to their inheritance mechanism (centralised, decentralised with accept sets, or decentralised with method guards[9]), whether they are behaviour preserving, and whether they are implementation independent. We use "-" to denote that some feature is not supported. We use KEYS to denote that a language employs the separation of keys, but is not implementation independent. Secondly, the inheritance mechanisms are compared with respect to inheritance anomalies. LOC-R signifies that a language achieves the localisation of re-implementation.

language	inheritance mechanism	behaviour preserving	implementation independent	inheritance anomaly			
				$Types_f$	$Types_R$	$Types_T$	internal
CUBL [27]	GUARDS	Yes	KEYS	Yes	No	No	-
ACT++ [17]	ACCEPT SETS	Yes	No	No	No	No	$Types_f$
ROSETTE [30]	ACCEPT SETS	Yes	No	No	No	No	$Types_f$
DEMETER [20]	GUARDS	Yes	KEYS	Yes	LOC-R	LOC-R	$Types_f$
MAUDE [25]	PATTERNS	Yes	No	Yes	No	No	$Types_f$
MAUDE [18]	PATTERNS	Yes	No	Yes	LOC-R	LOC-R	$Types_f$
[26]	GUARDS/SETS	Yes	Yes	Yes	LOC-R	LOC-R	$Types_f$
[6]	GUARDS	Yes	Yes	Yes	LOC-R	LOC-R	$Types_f$
BALLOON [5]	GUARDS	Yes	KEYS	Yes	LOC-R	LOC-R	$Types_f$
GUIDE [12]	GUARDS	Yes	KEYS	Yes	No	No	$Types_f$
[13]	GUARDS	Yes	No	Yes	LOC-R	No	-
DOOJI [29]	GUARDS/SETS	Yes	KEYS	LOC-R	No	No	$Types_f$
[15]	GUARDS	No	No	Yes	No	No	-
[14]	CENTRALISED	No	Yes	LOC-R	LOC-R	LOC-R	$Types_f$
DESP [24]	GUARDS	Yes	Yes	Yes	LOC-R	LOC-R	$Types_f$
ABCL [23]	GUARDS/SETS	No	No	Yes	LOC-R	LOC-R	-

[9] Two proposals employ pattern matching with some similarity to the mechanism of method guards.

Our comparison shows that none of the proposals solve the anomaly. Most proposals only succeed in localising re-implementation of some subset of the anomalies. Furthermore, none of the three types of anomalies has been solved in the context of internal concurrency - all of the proposals suffer from anomalies with respect to the internal concurrency definition of $Types_f$. Three proposals [14,15,23] implement limited forms of non-behaviour preservation. This enables a successful solution to the *LockableBuff* example. Because of the limited nature of their non-behaviour preserving constructs these proposals avoid most of the problems associated with non-behaviour preservation, in particular they do not sacrifice efficiency. There are other issues, not considered in this paper, that are important in comparing the different proposals. For instance, on the conceptual level it is interesting to examine which proposals succeed in presenting a single concept of inheritance that is used uniformly to inherit the concurrency and the functionality code. The proposals should also be compared with respect to efficiency.

7 Conclusion and further work

This paper investigated the problem of the inheritance anomaly. Starting from a formal definition of the anomaly we developed a taxonomy used to compare the various inheritance mechanisms proposed in literature. We presented a theoretical limitation of inheritance mechanisms, showing that an ideal solution for the version of the anomaly that has been investigated in the COOP literature does not exist. As a result it becomes clear that the problem of inheritance anomaly has not been solved, with most proposals merely reducing its harmful effects.

There are many other notions of types in COOP that could be examined. For example, the code that specifies internal concurrency is commonly added to a class as an attempt to increase efficiency. Therefore, the natural notion of a type would encompass all versions of the same class with different degrees of concurrency ($Types_T$ separates different degrees of concurrency into different types). Also, it may be desirable to separate inter-object and internal concurrency in order to be able to re-use them separately [29].

Inheritance anomalies may arise in many other paradigms, *e.g.*, agent-oriented programming [10], coordination languages, real-time specification languages [3] etc. It is important to note that discovering an anomaly in a paradigm does not necessarily imply that the anomaly will cause problems in practice. For example, inheritance anomaly exists in the context of sequential OOP. As noted in Section 2.1, if the notion of a type includes contravariance/covariance rules then Observation 2 does not hold, and inheritance anomaly arises. The reason this anomaly does not create problems in OOP is that most OOP inheritance mechanisms never incrementally produce subclasses with parameter types that are different from the parameter types of methods in the superclass.[10] Therefore, this notion of a type is not interesting with respect to inheritance anomaly.

[10] There are some exceptions. For instance, the use of *self* does change the parameter types in the subclass. Such a mechanism actually turns out to be anomaly-free.

Another possible extension of our framework is to refine $Types_T$ in order to capture the case when the behaviour of a class is different from the behaviour of its instances (Section 4). This can be achieved by characterising each type by a set of behaviours, rather than by a single behaviour as in Definition 9. Such generalisation of $Types_T$ is required in the analysis of more expressive mechanisms, which make use of message arguments and various other control information (*e.g.*, a message may be accepted based on the identity of the sender, the sender's location, the time it was sent etc.).

References

1. G. Agha. *Actors: A Model of Concurrent Computation in Distributed Systems.* MIT Press, 1986.
2. G. Agha, P. Wegner, and A. Yonezawa. Proceedings of the ACM SIGPLAN workshop on object-based concurrent programming. *SIGPLAN Notices*, 24(4), 1989.
3. M. Aksit, J. Bosch, W. van der Sterren, and L. Bergmans. Real-time specification inheritance anomalies and real-time filters. In *Proceedings of ECOOP'94*, LNCS 821, pages 386–407, Bologna,Italy, July 1994. Springer-Verlag.
4. P. America. Designing an object-oriented programming language with behavioural subtyping. In *Foundations of Object-Oriented Languages*, LNCS 489, pages 60–90, Noordwijkerhout, The Netherlands, June 1990. Springer-Verlag.
5. C. Baquero, R. Oliveira, and F. Moura. Integration of concurrency control in a language with subtyping and subclassing. In *USENIX Conference on Object-Oriented Technologies (COOTS'95)*, Monterey, California, USA, June 1995.
6. M.Y. Ben-Gershon and S.J. Goldsack. Using inheritance to build extendable synchronisation policies for concurrent and distributed systems. In *TOOLs Pacific '95*, pages 109–121, Melbourne,Australia, November 1995. Prentice-Hall.
7. D. Caromel. Toward a method of object-oriented concurrent programming. *Communications of the ACM*, 36(9):90–101, September 1993.
8. W. Cook, W. Hill, and P. Canning. Inheritance is not subtyping. In *Proceedings of POPL'90*, pages 125–135, San Francisco, California, January 1990.
9. W. Cook and J. Palsberg. A denotational semantics of inheritance and its correctness. In *OOPSLA'89*, pages 433–443, New Orleans, 1989. ACM Press.
10. L. Crnogorac, A. Rao, and K. Ramamohanarao. Analysis of inheritance mechanisms in agent-oriented programming. In *Proceedings of IJCAI'97*, pages 647–652, Nagoya, Japan, August 1997. Morgan Kaufmann Publishers.
11. L. Crnogorac, A. Rao, and K. Ramamohanarao. Inheritance anomaly - a formal treatment. In *FMOODS'97*, pages 319–334, England, July 1997. Chapman & Hall.
12. D. Decouchant et. al. A synchronization mechanism for typed objects in a distributed system. *SIGPLAN Notices*, 24(4):105–107, April 1989.
13. S. Ferenczi. Guarded methods vs. inheritance anomaly - inheritance anomaly solved by nested guarded method calls. *SIGPLAN Notices*, 30(2):49–58, February 1995.
14. G. Florijn. Object protocols as functional parsers. In *Proceedings of ECOOP'95*, LNCS 952, pages 351–373, Aarhus, Denmark, August 1995. Springer-Verlag.
15. S. Frølund. Inheritance of synchronization constraints in concurrent object-oriented programming languages. In *Proceedings of ECOOP'92*, LNCS 615, pages 185–196, Utrecht, The Netherlands, June 1992. Springer-Verlag.
16. C.A.R. Hoare. *Communicating Sequential Processes.* Prentice-Hall International Series in Computer Science. Prentice-Hall, 1985.

17. D. G. Kafura and K. H. Lee. Inheritance in Actor based concurrent object-oriented languages. In *ECOOP'89*, pages 131–145, UK, 1989. Cambridge University Press.
18. U. Lechner, C. Lengauer, F. Nickl, and M. Wirsing. How to overcome the inheritance anomaly. In *ECOOP'96*, LNCS 1098, Linz, Austria, 1996. Springer-Verlag.
19. B. Liskov and J. M. Wing. A behavioral notion of subtyping. *TOPLAS*, 16(6):1811–1841, 1994.
20. C. Lopes and K. Lieberherr. Abstracting process-to-function relations in concurrent object-oriented applications. In *Proceedings of ECOOP'94*, LNCS 821, pages 81–99, Bologna, Italy, July 1994. Springer-Verlag.
21. Z. Manna. *Mathematical Theory of Computation*. McGraw-Hill, 1974.
22. S. Matsuoka, K. Wakita, and A. Yonezawa. Synchronization constraints with inheritance: What is not possible - so what is? Technical Report 10, University of Tokyo, 1990.
23. S. Matsuoka and A. Yonezawa. Analysis of inheritance anomaly in object-oriented concurrent programming languages. In *Research Directions in COOP*, chapter 1, pages 107–150. MIT Press, 1993.
24. C. McHale. *Synchronisation in COO Languages: Expressive Power, Genericity and Inheritance*. PhD dissertation, Trinity College, 1994.
25. J. Meseguer. Solving the inheritance anomaly in concurrent object-oriented programming. In *Proceedings of ECOOP'93*, LNCS 707, pages 220–246, Kaiserlautern, Germany, July 1993. Springer-Verlag.
26. C. Neusius. Synchronising actions. In *Proceedings of ECOOP'91*, LNCS 512, pages 118–132, Geneva, Switzerland, July 1991. Springer-Verlag.
27. A. Poggi. Interface methods: a means for the integration of inheritance in a concurrent OOP language. *Informatica*, 20:125–134, 1996.
28. A. Snyder. Encapsulation and inheritance in object-oriented programming languages. In *Proceedings of OOPSLA'86*, pages 38–45. ACM Press, September 1986.
29. L. Thomas. Inheritance anomaly in true concurrent object oriented languages: A proposal. In *IEEE TENCON'94*, pages 541–545, August 1994.
30. C. Tomlinson and V. Singh. Inheritance and synchronization with enabled-sets. In *Proceedings of OOPSLA '89*, pages 103–112, New Orleans, 1989. ACM Press.

Appendix

Proof of Proposition 7 (sketch): The complete proof requires a formalisation of the semantics of guards. Consider Proposition 1 and classes P, Q such that $imp_f(Q) \subseteq imp_f(P)$. Suppose that $\mathcal{M}(P) = \{m_1, \ldots, m_n\}$ and $\mathcal{M}(Q) = \{m_1, \ldots, m_k\}$ where $n \leq k$. Without loss of generality we assume that $k = n + 1$. Suppose that both P and Q use method guards. We incrementally construct R from P such that $imp_f(R) = imp_f(Q)$. Since $bec(P) \sqsubseteq_f bec(Q)$ it is sufficient to construct a guard for m_{n+1} in R which accepts m_{n+1} iff Q's guard accepts it. We would like to use Q's guard in the construction of R, but this cannot be done directly since Q's guard makes use of instance variables of Q which are different from R. Therefore, we construct the guard for m_{n+1} as follows: The guard has a local pool of instances of P and Q. Upon reception of m_{n+1} the guard needs to determine which sequence of messages led to the current state of the object. This is achieved by trying all possible message sequences of length $1, 2, \ldots$ Clearly, this process will eventually find either the message sequence which led to the current state, or another sequence which also leads to the current state. The first such sequence is then applied to an instance of Q, followed by the message m_{n+1}. The guard of R then accepts the original message m_{n+1} iff the guard of Q accepts m_{n+1}. Note that the guard of R is side-effect free with respect to instance variables of R. Hence, R satisfies Proposition 1. ■

Proof of Theorem 1: Firstly note that we will only consider the languages that are at least as expressive as finite state machines (otherwise, some useful synchronisation constraints cannot be defined). That is, let $Reg \subset \mathcal{P}(Key^*)$ be the set of all regular languages over *Key*. We assume that $Reg \subseteq bec(Class)$. Hence, every regular language can be accepted by (is the behaviour of) instances of some class. Assume the mechanism is anomaly-free with respect to $Types_R$, and behaviour preserving with respect to $Types_T$. Consider $P \in Class$ such that $bec(P) = \{m_1, m_2\}^*$ for some $m_1, m_2 \in Key$. Let $u \in bec(P)$ and $m \in Key$ such that m does not occur in $bec(P)$. Then, $v = u\hat{~}\langle m \rangle \notin bec(P)$. Consider the type $\theta \in Types_R$, where $\sqcap_{beh}\theta = bec(P) \cup \{v, v\hat{~}\langle m_1 \rangle\}$. We have $bec(P) \sqsubseteq_R \sqcap_{beh}\theta$, hence $\theta \subseteq imp_R(P)$. To check this note that v starts with $u \in bec(P)$. Also, every state of $\sqcap_{beh}\theta$ contains traces that involve either m, m_1 or m_2, and every trace that involves m_1 and/or m_2 is a trace in the (only) state of $bec(P)$. By closure $\sqcap_{beh}\theta \in Reg$. Hence, $\exists Q \in Class$ such that $bec(Q) = \sqcap_{beh}\theta$, hence $imp_R(Q) \subseteq imp_R(P)$. **A:** By Proposition 1, $\exists \delta \in \Delta^*, R \in Class$ such that $P \overset{\delta}{\dashrightarrow}_I R$ and $imp_R(R) = imp_R(Q) = \theta$.

The second assumption is that whenever $P \dashrightarrow_I Q$ and $z \in bec(Q)$ then it is possible to construct P', Q' such that $P' \dashrightarrow_I Q'$, $bec(Q') = state(bec(Q))z$ and $bec(P') = state(bec(P))w$ for some $w \in bec(P)$.[11] Q' and P' differ from Q and P only in their initial states. The state of an instance is determined by the values of its instance variables. Hence, Q' is obtained from Q by changing the initial values of some variables. Depending on the language this may invalidate the incremental transition between P to Q'. Hence, we require that it is always possible to change the initial values of variables in P (obtaining P') so that $P' \dashrightarrow_I Q'$. This assumption holds for all COOP languages we are aware of.[12]

Returning to point **A**, consider $v = u\hat{~}\langle m \rangle \in bec(R)$ and construct R' such that $bec(R') = state(bec(R))v$. By assumption we have $P' \overset{\delta'}{\dashrightarrow}_I R'$ and $bec(P') = state(bec(P))w$ for some $w \in bec(P)$. However, $bec(R') = \{\langle\rangle, \langle m_1 \rangle\}$, while $bec(P') = \{m_1, m_2\}^*$ (P has only one state). Hence, $bec(P') \not\sqsubseteq_T bec(R')$ and $imp_T(R') \not\subseteq imp_T(P')$. Therefore, the inheritance mechanism is not behaviour preserving. ■

[11] This assumption is neeeded because at the moment the inheritance mechanism is unrestricted allowing quite "*unnatural*" mechanisms.

[12] If P and Q use constructors to specify the initial values of variables, then P' and Q' are simply constructed by modifying the two constructors without affecting the incremental relationship between them. If the initial state is specified by the initial values of variables (as in Figure 2), then any variable changed to obtain Q' is changed to the same initial value in P' (if the variable exists in P).

The Complexity of Type Analysis of Object Oriented Programs

Joseph (Yossi) Gil *

IBM T.J. Watson Research Center
(*on Sabbatical leave from the Technion*)
P.O. Box 704
Yorktown Heights, NY 10598
USA
yogi@cs.technion.ac.il

Alon Itai

Department of Computer Science
Technion---Israel Institute of Technology
Haifa 32000
Israel
itai@cs.technion.ac.il

Abstract. One of the price tags attached to the blessings that OO brings about is a drop in efficiency due to dynamic method dispatch. Much research effort is being spent on the problem of eliminating it, by applying static analysis to predict the set of dynamic types which a variable might store at any given program location. It was previously shown that the problem is NP-hard even if the program under analysis has no multi-level pointers. In this work, we show that under similar conditions, the problem is P-SPACE complete, provided that the program is not recursive. In the presence of recursion, the problem becomes EXP-TIME complete. (These two results also give an exponential time algorithm for a family of type analysis problems.) If multi-level pointers are allowed then the problem becomes EXP-SPACE complete without recursion and DEXP-TIME with it. Further, if the program under analysis may use recursive data structures then the problem becomes undedicable. Despite these, somewhat discouraging, results, we can prove that the type analysis becomes tractable, as evident from past practical experience, if the program under analysis obeys some few simple software engineering rules, while the analysis algorithm makes a corresponding simplifying assumption.

1 Introduction

1.1 Background and Motivation

At the very basis of object-oriented (OO) programming stands the notion of *dynamic binding* of a method name to a method body. Since variables in OO programs may be *polymorphic*, it is necessary to determine, based on the receiver's run-time (dynamic) class, the actual method to execute in response to a message send, or to use a SIMULA [ND81] jargon, to execute a *virtual function call.* Almost by definition, dynamic binding incurs both space and time penalties. In order to distinguish between receivers

---

* contact author

of different classes it is necessary to store some encoding of an object's class in memory. This memory overhead is rather minimal and is considered at worst a necessary evil. However, the cost in time due to the need to retrieve this encoding and to branch to the appropriate method body can be significant. It has been reported that the cost in time of a virtual function call can be two to three times higher than that of a global function or non-virtual method call [HLS97]. A higher penalty in performance is due to a secondary effect, which is that the code optimizer is deprived of the opportunity to use simple inlining of routines in the presence of dynamic binding. This effect is only aggravated by the fact that OO programming style effects many small routines.

A large body of research has been dedicated to the study of cost in time of dynamic binding and in efforts to minimize it. See [HCU91, DGC95, DMM96, PBF96, ZCC97] for some examples of the many works on the various aspects of the topic. It has been widely observed that a large portion of virtual function calls, if not most of them, are in fact *monomorphic*, i.e., that the class of the receiver in a particular call site was always the same at program run time. Empirical numbers in the range of 50% to 95% for some program according to some studies were observed for the ratio of monomorphic calls, both statically, as a fraction of the number of call sites, and dynamically, as a fraction of the number of actual calls (See, e.g., Fig. 2-5 in [BS96] and Fig. 13 in [DMM96]).

One of the most important research problems today in the area of implementation of OO languages is the efficient identification of monomorphic call sites. The computational complexity of this problem is the subject of this work. More specifically, we study a slightly more general variant known as the *object oriented type analysis problem* (OOTA) which is to determine the set of types (classes) that a polymorphic variable may assume at a certain program location. A call site is monomorphic if and only if the receiver's set is singleton.

The OOTA problem is difficult compared to many static analyses problems since it tangles intra- and inter-procedural analysis which is known to be difficult [SP82]. Moreover, it inherently involves dealing with something very similar to function pointers, which are usually ignored by traditional data flow algorithms: The type (class) of a variable determines the method called and the method called may in turn determine the type a variable may have. We are not aware of any actual experiments of trying to run a full-blown analysis except [G97] and [GP97], which were limited to a toy language. Despite many experiments of using various approximation algorithms and heuristics, the OOTA problem remains open. These algorithms usually leave a certain gray area of call sites, which are observed monomorphic in some experimental runs, but aren't shown by the algorithm to be as such in all runs. It is not clear whether these are a result of a shortcoming of an algorithm, or due to insufficient runs. Eliminating that gap and the cost of doing so is still open. The results of this paper give a fundamental reason to believe that the cost of doing so might be too high in the general case, but within reach for well-written programs.

Aside from optimization, it should be noted that OOTA has also applications to type checking in co-variant languages such as EIFFEL [M92]. In order to type-check the arguments to a method call, it is necessary to determine the set of classes the receiver might assume. This is done for example in Meyer's "polymorphic catcalls" algorithm [M95].

1.2 Results

Before stating our results, a brief overview of complexity classes may be in place. For more information, the reader may consult a textbook, such as Hopcroft and Ullman [HU79] or David Johnson's survey paper [J90]. The most familiar complexity class is NP---the class of all sets (sometimes called languages) whose membership can be decided in non-deterministic polynomial time. Informally, one may say that NP is the class of problems that can be non-deterministically solved in polynomial time. By the same token, P, EXP-TIME, and DEXP-TIME are the classes of all problems which can be solved in polynomial ($n^{O(1)}$), exponential ($2^{n^{O(1)}}$), and doubly exponential ($2^{2^{n^{O(1)}}}$) time, respectively. Similarly, P-SPACE and EXP-SPACE, are the classes of problems that can be solved in polynomial and exponential space respectively. It is not too difficult to establish that

$$P \subseteq NP \subseteq \text{P-SPACE} \subseteq \text{EXP-TIME} \subseteq \text{EXP-SPACE} \subseteq \text{DEXP-TIME}.$$

However, although there is strong evidence that all these classes are different, and despite tremendous work geared towards this, very few (and mostly trivial) such separation were proved.

For a complexity class X, we say that a problem L is X*-hard* (with respect to polynomial time-reductions) if any other problem $L' \in X$ can be reduced to L in polynomial time. A hardness result is in effect a lower bound on the complexity of a problem. Asserting that it is in a certain complexity class provides an upper bound to the complexity of this problem. We say that problem L is X*-complete* if in addition to being X*-hard* we also have $L \in X$, and hence in a sense captures the heart of the complexity of class X.

Informally stated, our main results are:

In its simplest incarnation, i.e., no recursion and no muli-level pointers, the OOTA problem is P-SPACE complete. This means that the problem is exactly as hard as the hardest problem that can be solved in polynomial space. It is believed that P-SPACE complete problems are not tractable (i.e., cannot be solved in polynomial time), but no proof for this is known yet.

1. If the program under analysis is recursive, then OOTA becomes EXP-TIME complete. In other words, the problem becomes provably intractable.
2. If, however, the program under analysis uses multi-level pointers, but no recursive data structures, then OOTA is EXP-SPACE complete.
3. If the both recursion and multi-level pointers are allowed, then OOTA becomes DEXP-TIME complete.
4. If the program has recursive data-types, then the problem becomes undecidable, regardless of the setting of the other parameters.

These results are also summarized in Table 1.

Recursion	Multi-level pointers	Recursive Data Types	Complexity
No	No	No	P-SPACE complete
Yes	No	No	EXP-TIME complete
No	Yes	No	EXP-SPACE complete
Yes	Yes	No	DEXP-TIME complete
—	—	Yes	Undecidable

Table 1 The complexity of the object oriented type analysis problem

It should be said that all of these results are subject to the standard hypothesis of static analysis, namely, that all paths in the program flow graph are possible [B78, MJ81]. In the absence of this, the problem is trivially undecidable. In addition, our results can only characterize algorithms that give an *exact* answer relative to some simplifying assumptions. Heuristics that give some conservative approximation are much more difficult to deal with rigorously.

Even with the all-paths-possible assumption, an easy consequence of our result is that in *general*, OOTA of dynamically typed languages is undecidable, since a priori a program written in such a language may contain recursive data types.

On the positive side, we prove that if the total number of variables that can be simultaneously reached from any single routine is at most logarithmic in the size of the program, then OOTA can be solved in sub-exponential time. Indeed, we may expect this to be the case in all well-written programs! The number of local variables and parameters of a routine should be bounded by a small constant. Global variables should rarely occur; in the worst case, at most one global variable should be introduced for a constant factor increase in the program size. Further, in a good object oriented program, the inheritance tree should be reasonably balanced, and the number of instance variables that each class introduces should not depend on its location in the inheritance hierarchy, but rather bounded by a small constant. Thus, the total (inherited and introduced) number of instance variables in each class should be logarithmic.

To show that the problem can be solved in polynomial time, it is required in addition that the degree of polymorphism of each variable, i.e., the number of different classes it may have, is not too large. More precisely, we define a new metric called chameleonicity, which should be useful in assessing the relative difficulty of the

OOTA problem of a given program. If chameleonicity is logarithmic, then OOTA can be done in polynomial time.

1.3 Related Work

There are not too many results characterizing the complexity of static-analysis problem. Landi [L92] showed that a general static analysis problem is undecidable. A more recent result is due to Horwitz [H97] to the effect that "may-alias" analysis is NP-hard. Closer to our field, Pande and Ryder [PR94] assert a theorem that OOTA is NP-hard in the presence of single level pointers and give some indications on the ideas behind their proof. To our knowledge, this is the only previous result to deal with the complexity of OOTA. In this work, we show that OOTA is in fact P-SPACE complete provided it contains no recursive calls. Our result extends Pande and Ryder's in several other respects. First, we deal the variants of multi-level pointers, recursive data structures, and recursive programs. Second, we give an exact characterization of input programs in which the OOTA problem is tractable. Third, by showing completeness in a complexity class, we provide algorithms, albeit quite inefficient for most cases, but with sound asymptotic time bounds. This is to be compared with much of the practical research in the field in which only empirical run-times are reported. See for example [CGDD97] for a comparison of various algorithms and heuristics for many sorts of inputs in different languages. Asymptotic results using the O-notation are rare: Golubski [G97] claims a doubly-exponential bound on the run time of his type-analyzer. (We believe there is a flaw in his estimate, and that sometimes his algorithm might not halt.) For some cases Pande and Ryder [Pr97] claim a bound which is polynomial in the program's input size (and linear in the output size), but they have no claims regarding the worst or average case. Another polynomial algorithm is that of Palsberg and Schwartzbach's algorithm, which is limited to the intra-procedural version of the problem.

1.4 Outline

The remainder of this paper is organized as follows. In the following Section 2 we provide a more precise definition of the OOTA problem, which makes it possible to state our results in a precise manner. Section 3 presents the proof that OOTA, in the absence of recursion, multi-level pointers, and recursive data types is P-SPACE complete. Section 4 shows that the introduction of recursion makes the problem EXP-TIME complete. This section also shows that if the number of accessible variables is logarithmically bounded, then the problem becomes polynomial. Sections 5 shows that the problem is EXP-SPACE (without recursion) or DEXP-TIME (in its presence) when multi-level pointers allow access to up to an exponential number of variables, while Section 6 shows that it is undecidable when recursive data types allow access to an unbounded number of variables. Finally, the conclusions are drawn in Section 7.

2 Problem Definition and Exact Statement of Results

Type analysis algorithms usually make simplifying assumptions of many sorts and take various shortcuts in order to make the problem tractable. For example, an algorithm may not distinguish between array entries, and apply a shortcut of breaking out of one of its internal loops if it iterates more than a pre-set number of times. Shortcuts like this resist the traditional methods of complexity analysis. Not much can be said about an algorithm that stops with the best (conservative) result it has after at most one second, regardless of the program's input size and complexity.

Simplifying assumptions, on the other hand, can be studied by expressing them as restrictions on the programming model, while requiring the algorithm to produce the exact result in this restricted model. The impact of the unification of array elements on complexity can be understood by considering a variation of the type analysis problem in which the input program is forbidden from using any arrays. Thus, in order to investigate algorithms that unify all array elements we will use an OO *language* that does not admit arrays.

More generally, the object-oriented type analysis problem is parameterized by the language of the input program. Of course, it is only important to consider the abstract properties of the language, since the exact syntax, and many of the semantic variations play no role. When concrete programs need to be written, we will sometimes use an appropriate subset of C++ [S97].

Note that for the purpose of studying complexity, the ease of writing programs in a language is of no relevance. In fact, some of the languages we will use are so weak that it is impossible to write any useful programs in them. The sole purpose is the study of the impact of the various simplifying assumptions type-analysis algorithms can make. Conversely, by studying the OOTA problem in these various languages we can gain a better understanding of the challenge different input programs pose to type analysis algorithms.

Let L be an OO language. Then, by $p \in L$ we mean that program p is written in L. We use the following notations: $|p|$ is the length of the source code of p (measured e.g., in characters, or in tokens), $C(p)$ is the set of all classes defined in p, $G(p)$ is the set of all of global variables of p. For $v \in G(p)$, $S(v) \subseteq C(p)$ is the set of all classes c such that there is a legal run of p which upon termination set variable v to c.

Definition 1 *The* Object-Oriented Type-Analysis *of a language L, or for short* OOTA(*L*), *is: given a program* $p \in L$ *determine* $S(v)$ *for each* $v \in G(p)$.

2.1 Comments

Global vs. local variables. We intentionally restrict our attention to global variables. Examining local variables brings about a new, but rather inessential, dimension of context-sensitivity. There are potenitally many different contexts in which a procedure may be called, and the set of dynamic types of a certain local variable in each of those might be different. If there is a need to analyze the type of a local variable of a procedure in the union of *all* calling contexts to that procedure, then our assumption does not lead to any loss of generality. This is since the program under analysis can be modified to include a non-deterministic assignment of that local to a global variable at the end of the procedure. Alternatively, the procedure can be made into a main program, while all calling contexts of that procedure are transformed into different legal runs of this program.

This issue becomes more delicate if it is required to do a type analysis of a local variable in each calling context, where a calling context is defined as a certain configuration of functions in the call stack. The number of such calling contexts can be exponential (e.g., in the case the program comprises of procedures $p_1,\ldots,p_n,q_1,\ldots,q_n$, such that both p_i and q_i may call either p_{i+1} or q_{i+1} for $i=1,\ldots,n-1$). The situation becomes even worse in the presence of recursion, in which case the number of different contexts is infinite. Thus, it makes more sense to investigate the complexity of determining the kind of type transformation that a routine does. In other words, the routine is thought of as an operator operating in type space. This operator takes as parameters the vector of assignment of types to the routine input arguments. Its output is the set of all type vector assignment to the routine arguments that may be generated as a result of the a run of the routine with this type assignment to its arguments. Global variables that are accessed by the routine are treated here as input, output, or input-output arguments, as appropriate. An interesting research question might be to explore the complexity of determining what this operator is, and finding out a compact representation for it. However, this lies beyond the scope of this paper.

On the other hand, the problem of type analysis of a (potentially recursive) routine r in a particular calling context $R=r_1,\ldots,r_n$, $r_n=r$ can be modeled as an instance of OOTA as follows: for each occurrence of a routine p as r_i in context R, create an auxiliary version p'_i of p. This auxiliary version would be different than p in that if q is a routine that p calls, and q is r_{i+1}, then instead of calling q, routine p'_i calls its auxiliary version q'_{i+1}. This transformation does not increase the program size by more than the context size. If, as before, upon termination, r'_n assigns its local variables to global variables, then the type analysis of the transformed program yields that of the routine in its calling context.

Inter-procedural vs. intra-procedural. In this paper we are only interested in the inter-procedural variant of the problem. In other words, the analysis of the main program is allowed to inductively examine the routines of that the program may invoke, and it must take into account the effect of each such routine. The intra-procedural variant of the problem, in which each routine is analyzed separately, while making only conservative assumptions on the invoked routines based on what can be inferred from their header is much simpler, and as shown by Palsberg and

Scwarztbach [PS91] is polynomial. The tendency toward small routines in modern OO programming casts some doubt on the utility of intra-procedural analysis.

Number of global variables. As might be expected, all of our lower bounds results make use of only one global variable. In fact, an algorithm *A* which can only deal with a single global variable, can be readily adapted to work with programs with several global variables: Let p be a program with several global variables. Then, for each $v \in G(p)$, create a program p_v, $G(p_v) = \{v'\}$ such that $S(v')$ in p_v is the same as $S(v)$ in p. Program p_v calls p as a procedure (thus making all its global variables into locals) that prior to its return assigns v to v'. We do not assume nested scopes, and hence, in this transformation, global variables are passed as additional parameters to all procedures of p. Now, *A* can be run on each p_v, $v \in G(p)$. Thus, we are free to assume that $|G(p)| = 1$.

Set of types. Although for practicality, it may be necessary to compute the whole set $S(v)$ together, it would become convenient to rephrase the problem as a decision problem, i.e., checking whether a variable may assume a single type in the run of the program. Repeatedly solving this variant for each of the types that may be assigned to v will yield $S(v)$, and the number of such repetitions is at most linear. Thus, we may assume the following alternative and polynomial-time equivalent definition of the OOTA problem:

> **Definition 2** *The* Object-Oriented Type-Analysis *of a language L, or for short OOTA(L), is: given a program* $p \in L$, *a variable* $v \in p$ *and a class* $c \in p$ *determine whether* $c \in S(v)$.

Point of type examination. Similarly, we have restricted our attention to the type of a variable on termination. Type analysis of a variable v at program location ℓ can be simulated by introducing a new global variable v_ℓ, and adding an assignment of v to v_ℓ immediately after location ℓ.

Arrays. A closer look at the issue of array elements reveals that, at least for our purpose, the unification of array elements is not a matter of choice. References to array elements with constant indexes (e.g., `a[4]`) can be thought of as references to scalar variables. The number of such references is upper bounded by the input program size, and they do not interfere with one another. On the other hand, variable array references (such as `a[i]`) bring about issues such as constant propagation and range-analysis, which are not only known to be difficult [WZ91, CH95, VCH96] but lie outside of our domain of investigation. Consequently, none of the languages we will consider contain arrays.

In the literature one sees various different approaches to the issue of arrays. This is because practical algorithm must cater for actual programs written in specific languages while making different simplifying assumptions. In [CGDD97], for example, all arrays of elements of any kind are unified together into one, highly polymorphic variable, for the purpose of the analysis. Diwan et. al [DMM96] treat them the same as linked lists, etc. We maintain that it is still in many ways orthogonal to the OOTA analysis problem. More complicated polymorphic data structures such as linked lists are still part of our study.

2.2 Base OO Language

Let us start the analysis with the abstract grammar BASE of Figure 1 for our OO programs with the almost obvious semantics.

Program → (VarDeclaration | Routine | Class) * Statement*
VarDeclaration → VarName TypeName
Routine → RoutineName FormalArgument* Body
FormalArgument → VarDeclaration
Body → VarDeclaration* Statement*
TypeName → ClassName | **integer** | **boolean** | **any**
Class →ClassName (BaseName) VarDeclaration* Method*
Method → MethodName TypeName FormalArgument* (**abstract** | Body)
Statement → Control I Atomic
Control → If | While | **return** Expression | **abort**
If → Expression Statement* Statement*
While →Expression Statement*
Atomic → **new** VarName | **read** VarName | Assignment
Assignment → Reference Expression
Reference → VarName FieldName*
MethodCall → VarName MethodName Actual*
Actual → VarName
ClassName | BaseName | VarName→ Id
MethodName | FieldName → Id
Expression → MethodCall | VarName | Constant
Expression → Expression Op Expression
Op → + | - | * | / | = | <> | **nand**
Constant → **true** | **false** | Number

Figure 1. Abstract grammar of language BASE

In the figure, a program is a sequence of statements to be executed in the context defined by the preceding routines, class definitions and global variable declarations. A single inheritance model is used in which the type **any**— the implicit root of the hierarchy— is also used for as the return type of procedural methods. Types **boolean** and **integer** do not take part in the inheritance hierarchy. All variables and methods are **public**. Method overriding is disallowed, except for making an **abstract** method concrete. As usual, a variable of class C might be assigned to a variable of class C', if and only if $C = C'$ or C inherits directly or indirectly from C'. No downcasting is allowed. The programming model is statically typed, i.e., all method calls are statically checked. The **read** instruction is similar to an assignment, except that the actual class of the read variable is unknown. The input is assumed to be legal, i.e., not leading to type errors.

These assumptions are not crucial to the results, but they do make it possible to concentrate on the more essential aspects of the OOTA problem.

Theorem 1 OOTA(BASE) *is undecidable.*

Proof. By reduction to the halting problem. Type analysis of the program of Figure 2 will yield that $S(v)$ is not empty if and only if procedure p halts. QED

```
routine any p() {
...
}
class Stop {}
any a;
a := p();
a := new Stop;
```

Figure 2 Reduction of Halting to OOTA(BASE)

2.3 Languages All-Paths and No-Flow

Theorem 1 is not very surprising. In fact, it follows immediately from a deep theorem due to Rice [HU79] which rather informally states that any prediction on the runtime of a program is undecidable. To circumvent this for the purpose making static analysis feasible, one makes the standard assumption of all-paths-probable. This can be described as a language mode with the abstract syntax of language ALL-PATHS specified in Figure 3 expressed as changes to Figure 1.

```
...
If → Maybe Statement* Statement*
While → Maybe Statement*
Maybe → maybe
...
Expression → MethodCall* | VarName | Constant
...
```

// The other derivation rules are the same as language Base of Figure 1.

Figure 3 Abstract grammar of language **ALL-PATHS**

The semantics of maybe is to return non-deterministically either **true** or **false**. In other words, conditionals may choose non-deterministically between the two branches and loops may execute a non-deterministic number of times including none. Expressions are simplified in ALL-PATHS and operators are eliminated.

Despite these simplifications, the OOTA problem remains undecidable. In fact, we can even assert that:

Theorem 2 OOTA(NO-FLOW) *is undecidable.*

Where NO-FLOW is an even weaker language than ALL-PATHS defined in Figure 4 below, in which control flow statements are all but eliminated. Language NO-FLOW is designed to emulate a flow insensitive analysis.

```
...
Body → VarDeclaration* ( Simple* | Control )
Control → mix Simple*
...
```

The other derivation rules are the same as language ALL-PATHS of Figure 3

Figure 4 Abstract grammar of language NO-FLOW

In this language, there are two kinds of procedures and methods. If there is a control flow statement in Body then all simple statements in the routine may be executed in any non-deterministic order. If however, there are no control flow statements in the routine body, then all such statements are executed in sequence. One motivation for assuming that sequential execution order is that an expression which is usually executed in order, may include a sequence of method calls, thus imposing order. The extreme and more pure flow-insensitive execution model, in which the method calls in an expression may execute in any order and in which even a routine with a single statement may execute that statement any number of times, seems to be rather recalcitrant. We are unable to provide any analytic results for the complexity of OOTA under this model.

2.4 Variants on No-Flow and All-Paths

2.4.1 DEFINITION DEPTH

The undecidability result of Theorem 2 is due to the fact that our programming model allows recursive data types such as linked lists and trees. Their presence makes it possible to define aggregates of unbounded capacity. It is not too surprising that an algorithms that sets to analyze separately all members of a linked list may run indefinitely. Indeed, in the literature we find that algorithms actually make various simplifying assumptions as to the contents of complex data structures even to the types of non primitive instance variables (see e.g., [DMM96] for their "aggregate analysis" phase). We explicate these assumptions as restrictions on the language model. To be able to do so, we need the following definition:

Definition 3 (Definition depth) *For a class c, let $d(c)$, the definition depth of c is defined recursively as the minimal function that satisfies the following. If the instance variables of c are all of primitive types then $d(c)=1$, otherwise*

$$d(c) = \min(\infty, \max_v d(t(v)))$$

where v ranges over all instance variables of c, and $t(v)$ is the class of v. For a program p, let

$$d(p) = \max_{c \in C(p)} d(c).$$

Thus, $d(c)$ is ∞ for any directly or indirectly recursively defined class. Otherwise, it is the maximal depth of data member definitions in a class.

Definition 4 *For a language L and a function $f(n)$ let $L(f(n))$ be the language of all $p \in L$, $|p| = n$, such that the at most $d(p) = O(f(n))$ nested class definitions are used in P.*

We have already seen that OOTA(NO-FLOW(∞)) is undecidable. The other extreme case occurs if $d(p) = O(1)$, in which we can the time for solving the OOTA problem is provably exponential.

Theorem 3 OOTA(NO-FLOW(1)) *is* EXP-TIME *complete.*

This language model corresponds to an algorithmic simplifying assumption which, in the interest of avoiding the undecidability predicament of Theorem 3, avoids, in one way or another, analyzing the content of instance variables, and limits its interest to simple variables.

The next theorem answers the question of what happens should an algorithm just avoid recursive data structures, while still delving into the analysis of field definitions?

Theorem 4 OOTA(NO-FLOW (n)) *is* DEXP-TIME *complete.*

2.4.2 NON RECURSIVE COMPUTATION

The proofs of both Theorem 3 and Theorem 4 rely on the fact that the algorithm may need to do distinct type analysis for each incarnation of a recursive routine. To see if the problem becomes any easier in the presence of a common simplifying assumption in which all incarnations of a routine are treated alike, we need the following definition:

Definition 5 *For a language L let L' be the language of all $p \in L$, p has no recursive routines or methods.*

As it turns out, the elimination of recursion does not help much:

Theorem 5 OOTA(NO-FLOW $(1)'$) *is* P-SPACE *complete.*

In other words, the problem becomes only "probably" intractable.

Similarly, the case of making the non-recursive assumption in the case of multi-level pointers, reduces the complexity just a bit:

Theorem 6 OOTA(NO-FLOW $(n)'$) *is* EXP-SPACE *complete.*

2.4.3 POLYMORPHIC SCOPE AND CHAMELEONICITY

Despite these gloomy results, it is evident from practical research that in many cases it is possible to do exact OOTA in less than exponential time. In this sub-section we try to define some cases in which the OOTA is likely to be easier than the general case.

Definition 6 (Polymorphic Scope) *The* polymorphic scope *of a routine* r, *denoted by* $\mathrm{pscope}(r)$ *is the set of all memory locations that* r *may assign values of different types to. Also, let* $\mathrm{ps}(r) \equiv |\mathrm{pscope}(r)|$. *For a program* p *let* $\mathrm{ps}(p) \equiv \max_{r \in p} \mathrm{ps}(r)$. *For a language* L, *and a function* $\omega(n)$ *let* $L(ps \leq \omega(\cdot))$, *be the set of all* $p \in L$, $|p| = n$, *such that* $\mathrm{ps}(p) \leq \omega(n)$.

Thus, the set $\mathrm{pscope}(r)$ includes all polymorphic program global variables, the polymorphic local variables of r, polymorphic parameters to r and any memory location that can be accessed through these variables. Further, if r is a method, then its polymorphic scope spans also all polymorphic instance variables that are either defined in r's class, or in any super class thereof.

We may argue rather informally that for a well-written program p, of size $|p| = n$, it is reasonable to expect that $\mathrm{ps}(p) = O(\lg n)$: The number of local variables and parameters should be a small constant in the order of 3 or 4. This constant should not increase too much even if multi-level pointers are allowed (we assume that there are no recursive data types, and if there are, the algorithm makes some suitable simplifying assumption to become oblivious of their existence.) Similarly, the number of instance variables introduced in each class should be upper bounded by another small constant (say in the order of 10-15). Further, a good use of inheritance will avoid very long inheritance chains, and will make the inheritance tree of height $O(\lg n)$. Thus, if there are n classes, then the total number of instance variables accessible from each class should be also $O(\lg n)$. This situation should not change much also in the presence of multiple inheritance; one may expect that the number of direct and indirect parents a class may have should be logarithmic. Finally, although global variables are universally condemned, they are sometimes a necessary evil. Their number however should not increase by more than a constant for any constant factor increase in the program size. If this is indeed the case, then the time for solving OOTA is less than exponential.

Theorem 7 *The time for computing* OOTA(ALL-FLOW($\mathrm{ps} \leq \lg n$)) is $n^{O(\lg n)}$.

Although less than exponential, this time is still super polynomial (sometimes called quasi-polynomial in the literature). Nevertheless, such a high run time is required only if most of the polymorphic variables may each store many different dynamic types. To characterize the cases in which OOTA can be done in polynomial time, we define the notion of *chameleonicity* which is basically the number of bits required to represent an instantaneous assignment of dynamic types to polymorphic variables.

Definition 7 (Chameleonicity) *The* chameleonicity of a variable v, *denoted by* $\mathrm{chm}(v)$ *is* $\lceil \lg u \rceil$ *where* u *is the number of concrete classes in the transitive reflexive inheritance relation with the class of* v. *The* chameleonicity of a routine r *is defined by*

$$\mathrm{chm}(r) \equiv \sum_{v \in \mathrm{pscope}(r)} \mathrm{chm}(v).$$

The chameleonicity of a program p *is defined by*

$$\mathrm{chm}(p) \equiv \max_{r \in p} \mathrm{chm}(r).$$

For a language L, *and a function* $\omega(n)$ *let* $L(chm \le \omega(n))$, *be the set of all* $p \in L, |p| = n$, *such that*

$$\mathrm{chm}(p) \le \omega(n).$$

With this definition, we can more accurately characterize a set of input programs for which the OOTA is polynomial.

Theorem 8 OOTA(ALL-FLOW $(\mathrm{chm} \le \lg n)) \in P$.

3 Proof of Theorem 5

This section shows that the OOTA problem in the absence of multi-level pointers and recursion is P-SPACE complete. There are two parts to the proof. Hardness is shown in Section 3.1, while membership in P-SPACE is shown in Section 3.2. These two proofs provide the skeleton of several other proofs in the sequel.

3.1 P-SPACE Hard

The proof is by reduction of the halting problem of a *linear bounded automaton* [HU79] (page 225) which is complete in P-SPACE. Such an automaton is just a different name for a Turing machine with a tape of length linear in the input size. For simplicity, we assume that the alphabet on which the machine operates is just the set $\{0,1\}$. No generality is lost since any finitely sized alphabet, which may include special symbols such as blank or end-of-input, can be encoded with $\{0,1\}^k$, for some finite k. We denote the tape length by n and assume that the input has the same length. (If the input has length εn, we can pad the end of the input thus increasing the input size. Such a change only affects the constants of the construction, but not the complexity classes.) The more precise definition given below is pertinent for the reduction. A *linear-space Turing machine* M over the alphabet $\{0,1\}$ consists of a *finite state control*, a *tape* T of n *cells* numbered $0,1,\ldots,n-1$, each of which is either 0 or 1, and a *read-write head* that points to the *current* tape cell. The finite state control of M is defined by a quadruple $\langle Q,q_0,F,\delta\rangle$ where

- Q is a set of *internal states*,
- $q_0 \in Q$ is the *initial state*,
- $F \subseteq Q$ is the set of *accepting states*, and
- $\delta: Q\times\{0,1\}\rightarrow Q\times\{0,1\}\times\{-1,0,1\}$ is the *transition function*, specifying the next state, the symbol to be written to the current tape cell, and the head movement.

The machine receives its input on the tape T, which is also used for temporary storage throughout the computation. Initially, M is at state q_0 and the head is at position 0. In each computation step, the following is performed. Let $s\in\{0,1\}$ be the value of the current cell, $q\in Q$ be the current internal state, and $0\le i<n$ be the current cell number. Then, if $\delta(q,s)=(q',s',m)$, where $q'\in Q$, $s'\in\{0,1\}$ and $m\in\{-1,0,1\}$, then s' is written to the current cell, the machine changes its internal state to q' and the head moves to cell $i+m$. The machine is not permitted to move beyond the tape boundaries; any computation that leads to such a move is excluded from our considerations. When the machine enters an accepting state, no further changes in its state may occur. Thus, for all $q\in F$ and $s=0,1$ we have $\delta(q,s)=(q,s,0)$.

Definition 8. *Given a specification* $\langle Q,q_0,F,\delta\rangle$ *of a machine* M, *and an assignment* $\tau\in\{0,1\}^n$ *of initial values to the tape* T, *then* the halting problem of M over τ *is to determine whether starting with a tape initialized to* τ, *machine* M *ever reaches any state* $q\in F$.

Given M and τ we construct a C++ program P_M of length $O(n)$ such that a type analysis of P_M also solves the halting problem of M over τ. This construction is possible since the description of M and τ are both finite. We will show that the size of τ is linear in the size of these.

The basic idea of the construction is to define abstract classes corresponding to the set of states, the head position and the tape. Concrete classes will reflect the contents of the tape, and the head position. Virtual function calls will model the function δ. More specifically, we distinguish three main techniques that are employed in the construction:

- **Values as types.** A *configuration* of M consists of the internal state, the head position, and the contents of the tape cells. These are all entities, which assume different *values* at different times throughout the course of the computation of M.

Each of these entities is modeled in the C++ program as a pointer variable to an abstract class. A value that might be stored in such a variable is modeled as a C++ concrete class inheriting from the abstract class. A change in the configuration is modeled by storing in the corresponding C++ pointer the address of an instance of the appropriate concrete class.

- **Conditionals as virtual function call.** Modeling configurations as variables is not enough; it is also necessary to model value-dependent behavior. At each computation step, M takes different actions depending on the value of its "variables". This is modeled in P_M by constructing a class with two derived classes (corresponding to true and false), a pure virtual function for the action itself, and having an appropriate different override for that function in each derived class. Thus, for example, if `f()` is a virtual function, and `x` a pointer that can point to classes `true` and `false`, then the call `x->f()` will invoke one of two concrete functions, depending on the dynamic type of `*x`.
- **Multi-parameter functions as nested calls.** Virtual function call can model dependence on one variable (i.e., in the previous example, only the parameter `x` can affect which concrete `f()` is invoked. To model the fact that the δ function takes more than one parameter, we apply a technique similar to currying: the dependence on the first parameter is modeled as a call to a first virtual function which in turn calls a second virtual function that models the dependence on the second variable, etc.

The construction of P_M is next described. We start by modeling the set of states of M and the δ function, as in Figure 5.

```
class Q {
   public:
      virtual void delta0() = 0;
      virtual void delta1() = 0;
};

class q0: public Q {
   public:
      void delta0();
      void delta1();
};
class q1: public Q {
   public:
      void delta0();
      void delta1();
};
...
```

Figure 5 Modeling Turing machine states as C++ classes

Note that there are two delta functions: `delta0()` is called if the value at the current tape cell is 0; otherwise, `delta1()` is called. As explained above, there is a concrete class for each of the states in Q.

For brevity only, we can write the above (and some of the subsequent code) in C++ using templates, as outlined in Figure 6. Note however that there is nothing in the construction that requires this language feature.

```
class Q {
   public:
      virtual void delta0() = 0;
      virtual void delta1() = 0;
};

template <unsigned m>
   class q: public Q {
      public:
         void delta0() {}
         void delta1() {}
   };
Q *state = new q<0>;
```

Figure 6 Alternate modeling of Turing machine states as C++ classes using templates

Then, the template is instantiated for each $m = i$, $q_i \in Q$. The body of `delta0()` and `delta1()` will in general depend on $\delta(0,q)$ and $\delta(1,q)$. However, for all $q \in F$, these two functions are empty. We therefore provided an empty default for these two functions. For $q \in Q \setminus F$ specific specialization will be provided as outlined later. To model the current internal state of M, we introduce a global variable `state` initialized appropriately.

We now turn to modeling the tape cells. The three classes of Figure 7 model the two values that might be assigned to any of the cells in the tape. The convention of defining variables with names identical to these of the corresponding class will prove handy.

```
class Tape {
   public:
      virtual void delta() = 0;
};

class Tape0: public Tape {
   public:
      void delta() { state->delta0() }
} Tape0;

class Tape1: public Tape {
   public:
      void delta() { state->delta1(); }
} Tape1;
```

Figure 7 Modeling tape cell values as C++ classes

The n cells of the tape are modeled using n pointers to class `Tape`. It is easier to define these using as **`static`** variables of a class template as done in Figure 8, but a slightly longer (but still $O(n)$) definition is possible without using this feature.

```
template<unsigned i>
   class Cell {
      public: static Tape *t;
   };

Tape *Cell<0>::t = &Tape0;
Tape *Cell<1>::t = &Tape1;
Tape *Cell<2>::t = &Tape0;
Tape *Cell<3>::t = &Tape1;

...
```

Figure 8 Modeling tape cells as C++ classes with initialization $\tau = 0,1,0,1,...$

We initialize these pointers according to the input assignment τ. Figure 8 gives the initialization of these for τ which is an alternating sequence of zeroes and ones.

The current position of the read-write head is realized as a global pointer to an abstract class, which might assume values of n concrete classes deriving from it, as depicted in Figure 9. For brevity, the n concrete classes are defined using a template, but could be defined manually without increasing the program size beyond $O(n)$. Take note that if the head is at position i, i.e., `head` points to an instance of `position<i>`, then the virtual function call `head->set0()` would assign the dynamic type 0 to the ith tape cell, and similarly for `head->set1()`. Also, the virtual calls `head->inc()`, and `head->dec()`, would move the tape head appropriately, by changing the dynamic type of `*head`. These positioning functions must be specialized for the boundary cases, to prevent infinite expansion of the template, and to cater for movements beyond tape boundaries. These specializations are done at the last two lines of Figure 9, where it is assumed that `N` is an appropriately defined `#defined` constant.

```
class Position {
   public:
      virtual void set0() = 0;
      virtual void set1() = 0;
      virtual void inc() = 0;
      virtual void dec() = 0;
      virtual void delta() = 0;
} *head;

template <unsigned i>
   class position: public Position {
      public:
         void set0() { Cell::t<i> = &Tape0; }
         void set1() { Cell::t<i> = &Tape1; }

         void inc() { head = new position<i+1>; †}
         void dec() { head = new position<i-1>; }

         void delta() { Cell::t<i> -> delta(); }
};

void position<0>::dec() { exit(1); }
void position<N-1>::inc() { exit(1); }
```

Figure 9 Modeling head position using C++ classes.

The function `delta()` in Figure 10 demonstrates our third modeling technique of function nesting. The virtual call `head->delta()` invokes either `Tape0::delta()` or `Tape1::delta()`, depending on the value at the current input cell. If `Tape0::delta()` is called, then `state->delta0()` is called, and similarly for `Tape1::delta1()`.

We are now in a good position to elaborate the definitions of the `delta` functions in the template classes `q<i>`. This is best done with an example: suppose that the value of $\delta(q_4,0)$, $q_4 \in Q \setminus F$ is $(q_7,1,-1)$, then, we specialize the template definition of `q<4>::delta0()` as in Figure 10.

```
void q<4>::delta0() {
   state = new q<7>;
   head->set1();
   head->dec();
}
```

Figure 10 Realizing $\delta(q_4,0) = (q_7,1,-1)$ as a C++ function

All that remains now is to write the main program, which is given in Figure 11. It should be obvious that at the termination of function `main`, $S(\texttt{state}) \cap Q \setminus F \neq \varnothing$ if and only if machine M has a halting run. Without loss of generality it may be assumed that $|F| = 1$, and thus the question can be also formulated as the decision variant of the OOTA problem.

---

† Although the program effects a huge memory leak, it is still acceptable as a "legitimate" C++ program since its sole purpose is to exercise an optimizer compiler.

```
state = new q<0>;
head = new head<0>;

main() // Program P_M
{
    for (;;) {
        head -> delta();
    }
}
```

Figure 11 Main function for realizing a Turing Machine as a C++ function.

Note. Program P_M was quite simple according to many traditional software engineering complexity measures: the call stack was $O(1)$, the number of instance variables was minimal. No multi-level pointers were used at all. Further, the depth of the inheritance hierarchy was $O(1)$, and although as a result of this the number of children classes was large, it is easy to see that almost any given inheritance hierarchy could have been used in the reduction. P_M basically uses $n+O(1)$ global variables and $n+O(1)$ classes. No complicated parameter passing is used, the vast majority of functions have exactly one statement, and the maximal number of statements in any function is three. This indicates that intuition might be misleading in understanding the complexity of sample programs and the extent by which they are typical.

3.2 In P-SPACE

To complete the proof of Theorem 5 it remains to show that OOTA(NO-FLOW (1)') is in P-SPACE. We do so by demonstrating a polynomial time reduction of the slightly more general problem OOTA(ALL-PATHS (1)') to the following P-SPACE problem.

Definition 9. *The* S-T Connectivity problem *is, given a graph G whose vertices are bit vectors of length $n^{O(1)}$ and two vertices $s,t \in G$, determine if there is a path in G leading from s to t.*

It is assumed that the graph is given in an efficient representation, i.e., that the query $\langle x, y\rangle \in G$ can be evaluated in polynomial time.

In order to solve an instance $\langle p,v,c\rangle$ of OOTA(ALL-PATHS (1)') of length n, we first reduce it to an instance $\langle n,G,s,t\rangle$ of S-T connectivity, then apply a P-SPACE algorithm to solve $\langle n,G,s,t\rangle$. For the reduction we define a *configuration* of program *p*, which represents a potential instantaneous point during its run time, to include the following components:

1. The current dynamic type of all global variables;
2. A list of all active methods and procedures (call stack);
3. The program counter in all active methods and procedures;

4. The current dynamic type of all active local and parameter variables;
5. The current dynamic type of all memory locations reachable from global variables and local variables.

Each such configuration is represented as a vertex in G. Two crucial factors makes it possible to represent a configuration using only a polynomial number of bits. Since p contains no recursion, the call stack has depth $\leq n$. Also, if the definitions depth is $O(1)$, then the total number of accessible memory locations is $O(n)$. The rest is trivially polynomial, since the number of different classes and routines is necessarily linear. In fact, a careful accounting would show that only $O(n \lg n)$ bits are actually required to encode a configuration as a bit vector.

The edges of graph G are defined as follows: vertex x is connected to vertex y if executing the instruction indicated by the program counter of x *might* change the configuration to y. This dimension of non-determinism arises from the fact that we assume the ALL-PATHS programming model. Let s be the vertex representing the initial configuration of p. Finally, we add a new vertex t to the graph G which does not correspond to any specific configuration, with an edge from any configuration vertex x to t if the call stack and the program counter of x are those of a program termination, and if global variable v of p has the dynamic type c in x. Clearly, there is a path in G from s to t if and only if $c \in S(v)$ in p.

Note. To the best of our knowledge, the above reduction also gives the best algorithm with a closed asymptotic time bound (which happens to be $2^{O(n \lg n)}$) to the inter-procedural object-oriented type analysis problem. Although several algorithms described in the literature were demonstrated to be efficient for some sample inputs, their asymptotic complexity was never established. This seems to be also the case for Pande and Ryder result [PR94], which is claimed to be polynomial, but only for the "*typical*" case.

4 The Impact of Recursion

In this section we address the issue of the impact of recursion in the input program on the complexity of the OOTA problem (proof of Theorem 3 as well as Theorem 7 and Theorem 8). With the presence of recursion, the reduction to S-T connectivity is no longer valid, since the number of different configuration is unbounded. The main difficulty is that the program may include an unbounded number of live variables on the call stack, all of which may take part in the type analysis. The stack regime that controls the access to these variables makes it still possible to control the complexity of the problem. Section 4.1 provides the upper bound results, while Section 4.2 gives the lower bound result.

4.1 Cook's Theorem

The results shown in this section are all based on a fairly old and deep theorem of Stephen Cook [C71] characterizing the computational power of a Turing machine equipped with a stack. Following Cook we define an auxiliary pushdown machine (aux-PDM) as a single-tape Turing machine which has an extra tape called the *pushdown tape*, which operates in a special fashion. Throughout the computation, all tape positions of the pushdown tape, which are right of its head, contain the blank symbol. Initially, the pushdown head is at the leftmost position of its tape that contains a special "bottom-of-stack" symbol, and all other positions are blank. The storage requirements of an aux-PDM are the size of the working tape, ignoring the pushdown tape. Cook showed that

Theorem 9 (Cook). *Let $\omega(n) \geq \lg m$. Then the following three conditions are equivalent:*

1. *A is accepted by some deterministic aux-PDM within storage $\omega(n)$.*
2. *A is accepted by some non-deterministic aux-PDM within storage $\omega(n)$.*
3. *A is accepted by some time-bounded computer within time $2^{c\omega(n)}$, for some constant $c > 0$.*

(In fact, Cook's result related to multi-tape aux-PDMs, but it is not hard to see that they carry equally well to single-tapes aux-PDMS.)

We reduce OOTA(NO-FLOW (1)) to the acceptance problem of a non-deterministic aux-PDM M, which takes as input a copy of the program source code. An instance $\rangle p,v,c\langle$ of OOTA(NO-FLOW(1)) of length n is fed to M which uses $\omega(n) = O(n \lg n)$ work tape and accepts if and only if $c \in S(v)$. The reduction technique is similar in principle to that of Section 3.2, but this time instead of reducing to a graph theoretic problem, we make the reduction directly to the Turing machine variant. A run of M is in fact a simulation of an abstract interpretation of program p, where all values are abstracted out and only type information is stored. We use the same notion of configuration as in Section 3.2. At any given point during the execution of M, the current configuration in the simulation of p is stored on M's tapes as follows: The types of all active local variables and parameters, as well as memory locations reachable from these are stored in the pushdown tape. This tape also stores the program counter of routines in the call stack of p. The types of all global variables and memory locations reachable from them are stored on the working tape. Further, the working tape stores a copy of the topmost stack frame, i.e., that of the currently executing routine. For simplicity we may assume that the working tape has dedicated locations for all local variables of all local routines. Whenever a procedure `P(v1,v2,...,vm)` is called with actual parameters $a_1,\ldots,a_m$, the values of `v1,v2,...,vm` are saved on the pushdown tape, and the tape locations that held `v1,v2,...,vm` are given the values $a_1,\ldots,a_m$. Thus the working tapes require $O(n\lg n)$ space, while we have no a priori bound on the size of the pushdown tape.

The finite state control of M is a universal interpreter machine, devised to examine the current configuration, check the program text to determine the set of permissible subsequent configurations and non-deterministically change the current configuration to one of these. Aux-PDM M will have an accepting computation if and only if a variable v is of dynamic type c at the end of the run. By Cook's Theorem, we can solve the acceptance problem for such aux-PDM within time $2^{c\omega(n)} = 2^{cn\lg n}$, i.e., within exponential time.

Note that since M is non-deterministic it is not very useful in solving the more interesting complementary problem namely if a variable v cannot assume type c. However, by Cook's Theorem we can find an equivalent deterministic AUX-PDM M', so the complementary problem can also be solved by changing the accepting state of M'. We can now use Cook's Theorem to obtain a (deterministic) algorithm to solve OOTA(NO-FLOW(1)).

The same simulation with exactly the same finite control together with Cook's theorem proves Theorem 8. To see this, observe that the simulation can be carried out by using $O(\text{chm}(p))$ bits in the work tape to store the types of active variables. The simulation can thus be computed in time $2^{c\,\text{chm}(p)}$ and if $\text{chm}(p)$ is $O(\lg n)$ we have that OOTA can be done in polynomial time. The proof of Theorem 7 trivially follows from the observation that $\text{chm}(p) \leq \text{ps}(p)\lceil \lg n \rceil$.

4.2 EXP-TIME Completeness

We now proceed to show that problem NO-FLOW (1) is EXP-TIME complete. It follows from Cook's theorem that this can be done by a reduction of the halting problem of a given deterministic aux-PDA M with memory $\omega(n) = n$ to a C++ function which is an instance of NO-FLOW (1).

The reduction is quite similar to that of Section 3.1. Hence, while providing most of the code, we will only stop to highlight the differences. The first of these is the fact that the transition function δ of M depends on four variables, which are the current internal state, and the values under the heads of the input tape, the work tape and the pushdown tape. Thus, if we assume a binary alphabet, then in the C++ classes that model the state, there should be eight different `delta` functions, and a three-way dispatch before the right one is selected. However, in the case $\omega(n) = n$ we may assume, without loss of generality, that the input tape is also used as a work tape, thus reducing the number of tapes to two. The dispatch code is given in Figure 12. The extension to multi-tapes when necessary is straightforward.

```
class Loop;

class Q {
   public:
      virtual Loop *delta00() = 0;
      virtual Loop *delta01() = 0;
      virtual Loop *delta10() = 0;
      virtual Loop *delta11() = 0;
};

template <unsigned m>
   class q: public Q {
      public:
         Loop *delta00(); Loop *delta01();
         Loop *delta10(); Loop *delta11();
   };

Q *state= new q<0>;

class Tape {
   public:
      virtual Loop *delta0() = 0;
      virtual Loop *delta1() = 0;
};

class Tape0: public Tape {
   public:
      Loop *delta0() { return state->delta00(); }
      Loop *delta1() { return state->delta10(); }
} Tape0;

class Tape1: public Tape {
   public:
      Loop *delta0() { return state->delta01(); }
      Loop *delta1() { return state->delta11(); }

} Tape1;
```

Figure 12 Multi-dispatch for modeling an aux-PDM.

Note that instead of type **void** as before, all `delta` functions are now of type `Loop *`, where the body of class `Loop` is yet to be defined. The reason for this will become clear in the sequel.

The modeling of the n tape input/work cells is identical to the code in Figure 8. To model the head position we use the code of Figure 9, except for the changes required to make the `delta` functions to be of type `Loop *`.

```
class Position {
   public: // ...
      virtual Loop *delta0() = 0;
       virtual Loop *delta1() = 0;
} *head;
template <unsigned i>
   class position: public Position {
      public: // ...
         Loop *delta0() {
            return Cell::t<i> -> delta0();
         }
         Loop *delta1() {
            return Cell::t<i> -> delta1();
         }
};
```

Figure 13 Modeling head position C++.

The types for the values in the pushdown tape are defined in Figure 14, which also details the first step of the multi-dispatch required for selecting the correct delta function in a class representing an internal state.

```
class Stack {
   public:
      virtual Loop *delta() = 0;
};
class Stack0: public Stack {
   public:
      virtual Loop *delta() {
          return head->delta0();
      }
} Stack0;
class Stack1: public Stack {
   public:
      virtual Loop *delta () {
          return head->delta1(); }
      }
} Stack1;
```

Figure 14 Types for values on the pushdown stack.

The emulation of the pushdown tape is done, as might be expected, using local variables of types `Stack0` or `Stack1`. Note that in addition to a state change, a tape write and a head move, each transition of M consists a pushdown tape operation which might be one of the following three: move back of the head of the pushdown tape (stack pop), or a write of a value, which might be either 0 or 1, plus a forward move of the head(stack push). The body of each `deltaij` function in each class corresponding to a state $q \in Q \setminus F$ is similar to that depicted in Figure 10, except that for the purpose of modeling these operations, each such function includes at its end one of the following three additional instructions:

1. **return** `pop();`
2. **return** `push(&Stack0);`
3. **return** `push(&Stack1);`

The crucial and most challenging aspect of the simulation is in the definition of `pop` and `push` so as to correctly model the operations on the pushdown tape. The difficulty is that at each point during the run of M, although the machine might potentially do either a push or a pop to the stack, exactly one of these operations is done. This conflicts with the all-flows-probable standard assumption of static analysis, in which at any point during the execution, all potential operations are permissible even though only one of them is legal. It is tempting to overcome this hurdle by modeling a non-deterministic aux-PDM, which would have sufficed for the result according to Cook's theorem. However, this would have only obscured the problem without actually solving it: even in non-deterministic machines, both push and pop are not permitted in *all* computation steps,

The approach we use is to define a new type, `Error`, which is assigned to the variable `state` in any illegal execution path. The necessary definitions for this type are in Figure 15. Function ERROR makes `state` to be of type `Error`, after which, it never changes its type again. Since our queries to the static type analyzer would only check if `state` might become of type corresponding to $q \in Q \setminus F$, such an assignment effectively excludes the execution path that follows it.

```
class Error: public Q {
   public:
      virtual void delta00() {}  void delta01() {}
      virtual void delta10() {}  void delta11() {}
} Error;

void ERROR() { state = &Error; }
void OK() {}
```

Figure 15 C++ code for invalidating illegal execution paths

We next define in Figure 16 a set of three classes that are used to force loop breaks and continuations under the all-paths-probable assumption.

```
class Loop {
   virtual void break_permitted() = 0;
   virtual void continue_permitted = 0;
};

class Break: public Loop {
   public:
      break_permitted() { OK(); }
      continue_permitted() { ERROR(); }
} Break;

class Continue: public Loop {
      break_permitted() { ERROR(); }
      continue_permitted() { OK(); }
} Continue;
```

Figure 16 Classes for loop control

Suppose that variable x is declared of type `Loop *`, and that x is determined to store a value of type `Break`, then the call, `x->continue_permitted()` would make a static analyzer conclude that `state` would be forever of type `Error`. On the other hand, tracing the polymorphic call `x->continue_permitted()` would not change the static analyzer state. The exact opposite happens if x is of dynamic type `Continue`.

With these classes, we can now describe the modeling of the pushdown tape and functions `push()` and `pop()` as illustrated in Figure 17.

```
Loop *stack_loop(Stack *s, Loop &*l)
{
   for (;;) {
      l->continue_permitted();
      l = s->delta();
   }
}

Loop *pop() {
   return &Break;
}

Loop *push(Stack *s) {
   Loop *l = &Continue;
   l = stack_loop(s, l);
   l->break_permitted();
   return &Continue;
}
```

Figure 17 Functions `stack_loop`, `pop` and `push`..

At each point during the computation of the C++ program, all values of the pushdown tape are stored as the s parameter to the recursive function `stack_loop`. This function repeatedly calls, using the multi-level dispatch mechanism starting from parameter s, the appropriate `delta` function of the appropriate internal state class of M . If the transition function δ of M is such that for the current values under the

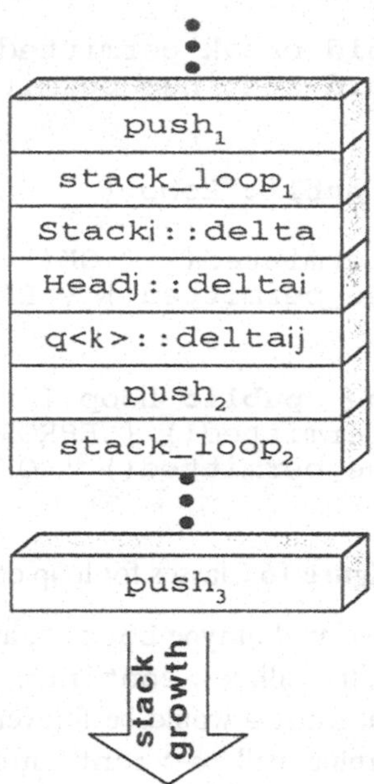

Figure 18. Call stack for pushdown tape value i, work tape value j and internal state k.

pushdown and work/input tape and the current internal state, a stack pop is to be done, then this `delta` function will terminate with instruction **`return`** `pop();`. This will assign a value of type `Break` to variable `l` in function `stack_loop`. The only execution path not leading to an assignment of a value of type `Error` to `state` would be the one in which the loop terminates after this call to the `delta` function.

The situation becomes more complicated if δ prescribes a write to the pushdown tape. In this case, the invoked `delta` function in `stack_loop` would terminate in a statement such as **`return`** `push(Stack0);` which might make yet another recursive call to `stack_loop`.

To understand this better, consider Figure 18, depicting a typical such situation. We use the convention of distinguishing between different invocations of the same function by subscripts. Consider invocation $\texttt{stack\_loop}_1$ (which was called by $\texttt{push}_1$). Then, if after the multi-level dispatch it was determined that the transition includes a stack push, then another copy of push, denoted $\texttt{push}_2$, is invoked, which would in turn invoke $\texttt{stack\_loop}_2$.

Let us study for a moment $\texttt{stack\_loop}_2$. This function should continue its **`for`** loop, until it invokes (indirectly) the function `pop`, at which case $\texttt{stack\_loop}_2$ should return control to $\texttt{stack\_loop}_1$. We have already seen how a call to pop "enforces" a break of the **`for`** loop, and a return of $\texttt{stack\_loop}_2$. The danger is that even after a call to a `push` the static type analyzer would consider an execution path in which the **`for`** is broken. To eliminate these paths from consideration, `push` always returns a value of type `Continue`. Thus, after an indirect invocation of $\texttt{push}_3$, variable `l` of $\texttt{stack\_loop}_2$ would be of type `Continue` as well. Thus, in the execution path in which at this point $\texttt{stack\_loop}_2$ breaks the loop and returns to $\texttt{push}_2$, the statement `l->break_permitted();` leads to an erroneous execution path.

Thus, $\texttt{stack\_loop}_1$ is suspended until $\texttt{stack\_loop}_2$ executes a `pop`. When this happens, $\texttt{stack\_loop}_1$ resumes its iterations calling recursively other copies of `push` (and then `stack_loop`) until a stack `pop` transition is made, breaking out of the loop and returning to $\texttt{push}_1$.

5 Multi-Level Pointers

Multi-level pointers allow a program of size n to address c^n memory location, for some constant c. This is exemplified in Figure 19. While there are only N classes, there are in potential 2^N distinct memory locations, all of type `Tape *` organized in balanced binary tree of height N, which are reachable from variable `h`. (Again, the C++ template mechanism was used as a shorthand for writing the N classes.)

```
template <unsigned i>
    class T { public:
            T<i+1> *left, *right;
    };
    class T<N> { public:
        Tape *cell;
    };
T<1> *h;
```

Figure 19 Modeling exponential tape size using C++ using multi-level pointers.

It is not difficult, in principle, to extend the definitions of Figure 19 to simulate a Turing machine work tape of length 2^n. To do so, we need to store in each node of the binary tree a pointer to a selected child. This defines a chain of selected children from the root to a specific cell located in a leaf of the tree, which corresponds to the current location of the head. Tape read and writes are simulated by a chain of function calls along the path to that leaf. A head forward (and backward) movement is done by a nested function call along that path which flips as necessary the selected child. These are implemented with appropriate types and virtual function calls employing techniques similar to what we have used so far. For lack of space we omit the details in this version of the paper.

We can therefore reduce the halting problem of a Turing-Machine with an exponential work space to OOTA(NO-FLOW $(n)'$), thereby showing that the problem is EXP-SPACE hard. Furthermore, it is easy to construct a non-deterministic Turing machine that uses exponential space to solve OOTA(ALL-PATHS $(n)'$), where the exponential space is used for storing the type of each accessible memory location of the input program. Since in the space complexity classes, non-deterministic and deterministic computations are polynomially equivalent, we have completed the proof of Theorem 6.

The proof of Theorem 4 is carried out similarly to what was done in Section 4 and using Cook's theorem. The main difference to that proof is that the aux-PDM uses both an input tape, which is modeled similarly to Figure 7, Figure 8, and Figure 9, and an exponentially large work tape, modeled according to the principles outlined above in this section. The dispatch according to the three values under the heads is done as a generalization of Figure 12.

6 Undecidability Result in Case of Recursive Data Types

In this section we prove Theorem 2, i.e., we show that in the presence of recursive data structures, the OOTA problem is undedicable. We do so by reduction of the halting problem of an unbounded Turing machine M, which is similar to this defined in Section 3.1, except that it may use a tape of unbounded length. All cells which do not contain the input to M are assumed to be zero.

We assume the same class structure for Figure 20 gives the C++ code for modeling an unbounded tape. This is done by creating a finite doubly linked list of elements of abstract class `Tape`, with a variable `head` that emulates the read/write head of M, pointing into the list. At both ends of the list there are special marks of class `EOT`, the remaining elements are either of class `Tape0` or of class `Tape1`. The head is moved by means of a non-virtual function call: `head->inc()` for a forward move or `head->dec()` for a backward move. At each such move the `next` and `prev` pointers of the linked list are set to their correct values (see body of functions `inc`, `dec` and `init` in class `Tape`). However, if `inc` (respectively `dec`) is called on the last (respectively first) non-`EOT` linked list item, then the virtual function `init` in class `EOT` creates a new list item of type `Tape0`. This item is appended (prepended) to the list by the code of function `inc` (`dec`).

```
class Tape *head;
class Tape { public:
      Tape *next, *prev;
      virtual void delta() = 0;
      virtual Tape *init() { return this; }
      void inc() {
         head = next->init();
         next = head;
         next->prev = this;
      }
      void dec() {
         head = prev->init();
         prev = head;
         prev->next = this;
      }
} *head;
class Tape0: public Tape { public:
      void delta() { state->delta0(); }
};
class Tape1: public Tape { public:
      void delta() { state->delta1(); }
};
class EOT: public Tape { public:
      Tape *init() {
         Tape *new_cell = new Tape0;
         new_cell->prev = new_cell->next = new EOT;
         return new_cell;
      }
} EOT;
```

Figure 20 Modeling an unbounded tape using a C++ linked-list class.

Two functions, `set0` and `set1` are used for writing a value to the cell under the tape head. The code for these functions is given in Figure 21. The write operation is realized by creating a new value of the appropriate type and inserting it into the list to replace the previous cell that head pointed to.

```
void set0() {
   Tape *new_head = new Tape0;
   new_head->next = head->next;
   new_head->prev = head->prev;
   head->next->prev = new_head;
   head->prev->next = new_head;
   head = new_head;
}
void set1() {
   Tape *new_head = new Tape0;
   new_head->next = head->next;
   new_head->prev = head->prev;
   head->next->prev = new_head;
   head->prev->next = new_head;
   head = new_head;
}
```

Figure 21 Writing a value to a linked list modeling an unbounded tape.

Finally, we show in Figure 22 how the code for initializing the linked list and then setting it to the right input values for M might be written. In order to make sure that the head is at the first input cell, we do the initialization from the last value backwards.

```
void initialize() {
   head = new Tape0;
   head->prev = new EOT;
   head->next = new EOT;
}
void set_inputs() {
   head->set0();
   head->dec();
   head->set1();
   head->dec();
   head->set1();
   ...
}
void run() {
   for (;;) {
      head->delta();
   }

main() {
   initializa();
   set_inputs();
   run();
}
```

Figure 22 Initializing the linked list with input values.

The remaining parts of the reduction, i.e., abstract class Q and the body of the concrete classes derived from it, are as in Figure 6 and Figure 10. This completes the proof of Theorem 2.

Note. The language features used in the reduction, other than the recursive data types, were minimal: no parameters were passed, all functions contained very few simple instructions and the depth of the call stack was very small. Undecidability was a direct consequence of the fact that the static analyzer is required to deal with an unbounded number of polymorphic variables.

7 Conclusions

The results presented in this paper give a precise characterization of the abstract computational complexity of the object-oriented type analysis problem. Experimental research is still required to assess the validity of the theoretical predictions of the relationship between the chameleonicity. It is not clear from Cook's theorem what is the complexity of OOTA in the case the chameleonicity is sub-logarithmic. It is also interesting to identify other well-defined quantities and qualities of the program under analysis, which would provably effect tractability of the OOTA problem. As mentioned in the paper, yet another direction for a future research might be the analysis of the OOTA of a routine in each calling context, and the study of the pure and extreme flow insensitive programming model.

Acknowledgments. We are indebted to Oscar Ibarra for referring us to Cook's theorem. Inspiring discussions with Bertrand Meyer helped shape this paper.

8 References

[B78] Barth J. A Practical Interprocedural Data Flow Analysis Algorithm, CACM 21(9):724-736, 1978.

[BS96] Bacon, D. F., and P. F. Sweeney, *Fast Static Analysis of Virtual Function Calls in C++*, OOPSLA'96, pp. 324-341.

[C71] Cook S. A., *Characterizations of Pushdown Machines in Terms of Time-Bounded Computers*, JACM 18(1):4-18, Jan. 1971.

[CH95] Carini P. R. and M. Hind, *Flow-sensitive interprocedural constant propagation*, PLDI'95, pp. 23-31.

[CGDD97] Chambers C., Grove D., DeFouw G., and J. Dean, *Call Graph Construction in Object-Oriented Languages*, OOPSLA'97, pp. 108-124.

[DGC95] Dean J., Grove D. and C. Chambers, *Optimization of Object-Oriented Programs Using Static Class Hierachy Analysis*, ECOOP'95, pp. 77-101.

[DMM96] Diwan, A., Moss J. E. B. and K. S. McKinley, *Simple and Effective Analysis of Statically-Typed Object-Oriented Programmes.*, OOPSLA'96, pp. 292-305.

[J90] Johnson, D.S., *A Catalog of Complexity Classes,* in Handbook of Theoretical Computer Science, ed. J.van Leuuwen , MIT Press 1990.

[G97] Golubski W., *Data-Flow Analysis in Object-Oriented Programs*, TOOLS USA'97.

[GP97] Golubski W. and B. Pohlers, *SOLAT - A Simple Object-Oriented Language Analysing Tool*, TOOLS USA'97.

[HLS97] Harrison, T. H., Levine D. L., and D. C. Schimdt., *The Design and Performance of a Real-Time COBRA Event Service*, OOPSLA'97, pp. 184-200.

[H97] Horwitz S., *Precise Flow-Insensitive May-Alias Analysis is NP-Hard*, TOPLAS Jan. 1997.

[HCU91] Holzle U., Chambers C. and D. Ungar., *Optimizing Dynamically-Typed Object-Oriented Languages with Polymorphic Inline Caches.* ECOOP'91.

[HU79] Hopcroft, J.E., and J. D. Ullman, *Introduction to Automata Theory, Languages and Computation*, Addison-Wesley 1979.

[L92] Landi W., *Undecidability of Static Analysis*, LOPLAS 1(4):323-337, Dec. 1992.

[M92] Meyer B., *Eiffel- The Language*, Prentice-Hall, 1992.

[M95] Meyer B., *Beware of Polymorphic Catcalls*, White paper, Interactive Software Engineering, 1995. In

http://www.eiffel.com/doc/manuals/technology/typing/cat.html

[MJ81] Muchnick S. S., and N. D. Jones eds., *Program Flow Analysis: Theory and Applications*, Prentice Hall 1981.

[ND81] Nygaard K. and O-J Dahl, *Simula 1967*, In History of Prog. Lang., ed. R. W. Wexelblat, 1981.

[PBF96] Porat S., Bernstein D., Fedrov Y., and J. Rodrigue, *Compiler Optimization of C++ Virtual Function Call*, COOTS'96, pp. 3-14.

[PR94] Pande H. D. and B. G. Ryder, *Static Type Determination for C++*, Usenix C++ Conf. 1994, pp. 85-97.

[PS91] Palsberg J. and M. Schwartzbach, *Object-Oriented Type Inference*, OOSPLA'91, pp. 146-161.

[S97] Stroustrup B., *The C++ Programming Language.* 3rd ed. Addison Wesley, 1997.

[SP82] Sharir M. and A. Pnueli, *Two Approaches to Interprocedural Data Flow Analysis*, in [MJ81].

[VCH96] Verbrugge, C., Phong C., and L. Hendren. *Generalized Constant Propagation—A Study in C.* In Proc. of the 6th International Conference on Compiler Construction (CC'96), pages 74-90, Link• ping, Sweden, Springer LNCS 1060, 1996.

[WZ91] Wegman, M. N. and F. K. Zadek, *Constant Propagation with Conditional Branches*, ACM TOPLAS 13(2):181-210, Apr. 1991.

[ZCC97] Zendra O., Colnet C., and S. Collin, *Efficient Dynamic Dispatch without Virtual Function Tables: The Small Eiffel Compiler*, OOPSLA'97, pp. 125-141.

Author Index

Lecture Notes in Computer Science

For information about Vols. 1–1361

please contact your bookseller or Springer-Verlag

Vol. 1362: D.K. Panda, C.B. Stunkel (Eds.), Network-Based Parallel Computing. Proceedings, 1998. X, 247 pages. 1998.

Vol. 1363: J.-K. Hao, E. Lutton, E. Ronald, M. Schoenauer, D. Snyers (Eds.), Artificial Evolution. XI, 349 pages. 1998.

Vol. 1364: W. Conen, G. Neumann (Eds.), Coordination Technology for Collaborative Applications. VIII, 282 pages. 1998.

Vol. 1365: M.P. Singh, A. Rao, M.J. Wooldridge (Eds.), Intelligent Agents IV. Proceedings, 1997. XII, 351 pages. 1998. (Subseries LNAI).

Vol. 1366: Z. Li, P.-C. Yew, S. Chatterjee, C.-H. Huang, P. Sadayappan, D. Sehr (Eds.), Languages and Compilers for Parallel Computing. Proceedings, 1997. XII, 428 pages. 1998.

Vol. 1367: E.W. Mayr, H.J. Prömel, A. Steger (Eds.), Lectures on Proof Verification and Approximation Algorithms. XII, 344 pages. 1998.

Vol. 1368: Y. Masunaga, T. Katayama, M. Tsukamoto (Eds.), Worldwide Computing and Its Applications — WWCA'98. Proceedings, 1998. XIV, 473 pages. 1998.

Vol. 1370: N.A. Streitz, S. Konomi, H.-J. Burkhardt (Eds.), Cooperative Buildings. Proceedings, 1998. XI, 267 pages. 1998.

Vol. 1371: I. Wachsmuth, M. Fröhlich (Eds.), Gesture and Sign Language in Human-Computer Interaction. Proceedings, 1997. XI, 309 pages. 1998. (Subseries LNAI).

Vol. 1372: S. Vaudenay (Ed.), Fast Software Encryption. Proceedings, 1998. VIII, 297 pages. 1998.

Vol. 1373: M. Morvan, C. Meinel, D. Krob (Eds.), STACS 98. Proceedings, 1998. XV, 630 pages. 1998.

Vol. 1374: H. Bunt, R.-J. Beun, T. Borghuis (Eds.), Multimodal Human-Computer Communication. VIII, 345 pages. 1998. (Subseries LNAI).

Vol. 1375: R. D. Hersch, J. André, H. Brown (Eds.), Electronic Publishing, Artistic Imaging, and Digital Typography. Proceedings, 1998. XIII, 575 pages. 1998.

Vol. 1376: F. Parisi Presicce (Ed.), Recent Trends in Algebraic Development Techniques. Proceedings, 1997. VIII, 435 pages. 1998.

Vol. 1377: H.-J. Schek, F. Saltor, I. Ramos, G. Alonso (Eds.), Advances in Database Technology - EDBT'98. Proceedings, 1998. XII, 515 pages. 1998.

Vol. 1378: M. Nivat (Ed.), Foundations of Software Science and Computation Structures. Proceedings, 1998. X, 289 pages. 1998.

Vol. 1379: T. Nipkow (Ed.), Rewriting Techniques and Applications. Proceedings, 1998. X, 343 pages. 1998.

Vol. 1380: C.L. Lucchesi, A.V. Moura (Eds.), LATIN'98: Theoretical Informatics. Proceedings, 1998. XI, 391 pages. 1998.

Vol. 1381: C. Hankin (Ed.), Programming Languages and Systems. Proceedings, 1998. X, 283 pages. 1998.

Vol. 1382: E. Astesiano (Ed.), Fundamental Approaches to Software Engineering. Proceedings, 1998. XII, 331 pages. 1998.

Vol. 1383: K. Koskimies (Ed.), Compiler Construction. Proceedings, 1998. X, 309 pages. 1998.

Vol. 1384: B. Steffen (Ed.), Tools and Algorithms for the Construction and Analysis of Systems. Proceedings, 1998. XIII, 457 pages. 1998.

Vol. 1385: T. Margaria, B. Steffen, R. Rückert, J. Posegga (Eds.), Services and Visualization. Proceedings, 1997/1998. XII, 323 pages. 1998.

Vol. 1386: T.A. Henzinger, S. Sastry (Eds.), Hybrid Systems: Computation and Control. Proceedings, 1998. VIII, 417 pages. 1998.

Vol. 1387: C. Lee Giles, M. Gori (Eds.), Adaptive Processing of Sequences and Data Structures. Proceedings, 1997. XII, 434 pages. 1998. (Subseries LNAI).

Vol. 1388: J. Rolim (Ed.), Parallel and Distributed Processing. Proceedings, 1998. XVII, 1168 pages. 1998.

Vol. 1389: K. Tombre, A.K. Chhabra (Eds.), Graphics Recognition. Proceedings, 1997. XII, 421 pages. 1998.

Vol. 1390: C. Scheideler, Universal Routing Strategies for Interconnection Networks. XVII, 234 pages. 1998.

Vol. 1391: W. Banzhaf, R. Poli, M. Schoenauer, T.C. Fogarty (Eds.), Genetic Programming. Proceedings, 1998. X, 232 pages. 1998.

Vol. 1392: A. Barth, M. Breu, A. Endres, A. de Kemp (Eds.), Digital Libraries in Computer Science: The MeDoc Approach. VIII, 239 pages. 1998.

Vol. 1393: D. Bert (Ed.), B'98: Recent Advances in the Development and Use of the B Method. Proceedings, 1998. VIII, 313 pages. 1998.

Vol. 1394: X. Wu. R. Kotagiri, K.B. Korb (Eds.), Research and Development in Knowledge Discovery and Data Mining. Proceedings, 1998. XVI, 424 pages. 1998. (Subseries LNAI).

Vol. 1395: H. Kitano (Ed.), RoboCup-97: Robot Soccer World Cup I. XIV, 520 pages. 1998. (Subseries LNAI).

Vol. 1396: E. Okamoto, G. Davida, M. Mambo (Eds.), Information Security. Proceedings, 1997. XII, 357 pages. 1998.

Vol. 1397: H. de Swart (Ed.), Automated Reasoning with Analytic Tableaux and Related Methods. Proceedings, 1998. X, 325 pages. 1998. (Subseries LNAI).

Vol. 1398: C. Nédellec, C. Rouveirol (Eds.), Machine Learning: ECML-98. Proceedings, 1998. XII, 420 pages. 1998. (Subseries LNAI).

Vol. 1399: O. Etzion, S. Jajodia, S. Sripada (Eds.), Temporal Databases: Research and Practice. X, 429 pages. 1998.